The Papers of
George Washington

The Papers of
George Washington

W. W. Abbot and Dorothy Twohig, *Editors*

Philander D. Chase, *Senior Associate Editor*
Beverly H. Runge, *Associate Editor*

Mark A. Mastromarino, Frank E. Grizzard, Jr.,
Beverly S. Kirsch, Debra B. Kessler, and Elizabeth B. Mercer
Assistant Editors

Confederation Series
4

April 1786–January 1787

W. W. Abbot, *Editor*

UNIVERSITY PRESS OF VIRGINIA

CHARLOTTESVILLE AND LONDON

This edition has been prepared by the staff of
The Papers of George Washington
sponsored by
The Mount Vernon Ladies' Association of the Union
and the University of Virginia
with the support of
the National Endowment for the Humanities,
the National Historical Publications and Records Commission,
and the Packard Humanities Institute.
The publication of this volume
has been supported by a grant from
the National Historical Publications
and Records Commission.

THE UNIVERSITY PRESS OF VIRGINIA

First published 1995

Library of Congress Cataloging-in-Publication Data
Washington, George, 1732–1799.
    The papers of George Washington. Confederation
series.
    Includes bibliographical references and indexes.
    Contents: 1. January–July 1784—[etc.]—4. April
1786–January 1787.
    1. Washington, George, 1732–1799—Archives.   2.
Presidents—United States—Archives.   3. United
States—History—Confederation, 1783–1789.   I.
Abbot, W. W. (William Wright), 1922–   II.
Twohig, Dorothy.   III. Confederation series.   IV.
Title.
E312.7   1992   973.4′1′092   91-3171
ISBN 0-8139-1348-9 (v. 1)
ISBN 0-8139-1560-0 (v.4)

Printed in the United States of America

For Edmund S. Morgan,
Friend of Washington and his *Papers*

Contents

NOTE: Volume numbers refer to the *Confederation Series*.

Editorial Apparatus   xix
  Symbols Designating Documents   xx
  Repository Symbols   xx
  Short Title List   xxii

1786

To Timothy Dwight, 1 April   *see* 3:332
From Daniel Morgan, 3 April   1
To Charles Carroll, 5 April   *see* 4:5
To Thomas Cushing, 5 April   2
To Henry Lee, Jr., 5 April   3
To Robert Morris, 5 April   *see* 4:5
To Samuel Powel, 5 April   5
To David Ramsay, 5 April   5
From William Moultrie, 7 April   6
From William Gordon, 9 April   7
To Thomas Newton, Jr., 9 April   9
From Alexander Doyle, 10 April   10
From Jean Le Mayeur, 10 April   11
To Benjamin Lincoln, 10 April   12
To Jonathan Trumbull, Jr., 10 April   12
To William Washington, 10 April   13
From John Sedwick, 11 April   14
From Thomas Brereton, 12 April   14
To Robert Morris, 12 April   15
To Bushrod Washington, 13 April   18
From Leonard Henley, 14 April   18
From William Gordon, 15 April   *see* 4:8
From John Rumney, Jr., 16 April   19
To John Armistead, 17 April   19
To Noah Webster, 17 April   20
To William Hartshorne, 19 April   21
To Thomas Brereton, 20 April   22
From Joseph Eckley, 20 April   23
To William Gordon, 20 April   23
To Benjamin Lincoln, 20 April   24
From Henry Lee, Jr., 21 April   25

From Thomas Ringgold Tilghman, 22 April 27
From Francis Asbury, 24 April 27
From Benjamin Grymes, 24 April 28
To George Augustine Washington, 24 April 28
From Robert Morris, 26 April 29
From Doilliamson, 28 April 30
From Alexander White, 29 April 31
From John Hopkins, 1 May 31
To Martin Cockburn, 3 May 32
From Benjamin Lincoln, 3 May 32
From John Langdon, 5 May   *see* 4:34
From Samuel Haven, 6 May   *see* 4:34–35
From Battaile Muse, 6 May 33
From Tobias Lear, 7 May 34
To Thomas Cresap, 8 May 35
To Thomas Freeman, 8 May 36
To Thomas Smith, 8 May 36
From d'Estaing, 9 May   *see* 4:164
From Benjamin Lincoln, 9 May 37
To Joseph Eckley, 10 May 39
To Adrienne, Marquise de Lafayette, 10 May 39
To Lafayette, 10 May 41
From Benjamin Lincoln, 10 May   *see* 4:38
From Samuel Powel, 10 May 45
To Saint Simon-Montbléru, 10 May 46
To Thomas Ringgold Tilghman, 10 May 47
From John Dandridge, 12 May 47
To Battaile Muse, 12 May 48
From Samuel Purviance, 12 May 49
From Joseph Jones, 14 May 50
To William Fitzhugh, Jr., 15 May 52
To John Rumney, Jr., 15 May 53
From Joseph Willard, 15 May   *see* 4:35
To Clement Biddle, 18 May 53
To John Jay, 18 May 55
To Robert Lewis & Sons, 18 May 56
From Alexander Steel, 18 May 57
To George Taylor, Jr., 18 May 61
From Thomas Marshall, 19 May 61
From Robert Sanderson, 19 May 62
To Henry L. Charton, 20 May 63
To Neil Jamieson, 20 May 66
To John Marsden Pintard, 20 May 67

To Thomas Ridout, 20 May   68
From David Humphreys, 23 May   68
From Josiah Parker, 23 May   69
From Daniel of St. Thomas Jenifer, 24 May   70
From Lafayette, 24 May   71
To Joseph Jones, 25 May   *see* 4:51
To William Moultrie, 25 May   73
To Samuel Powel, 25 May   75
To Alexander Steel, 25 May   76
From William Fitzhugh, Jr., 26 May   77
To Thomas Newton, Jr., 26 May   77
From James Tilghman, 26 May   78
From Thomas Ringgold Tilghman, 26 May   *see* 4:80
From William Grayson, 27 May   81
From Colt MacGregor, 29 May   83
To Joseph Brown, 30 May   84
Articles of Agreement with James Bloxham, 31 May   86
To Alexander Spotswood, May   88
To Henry Knox, 1 June   89
From Richard Sprigg, 1 June   90
To Mary Bristow, 2 June   91
To Daniel of St. Thomas Jenifer, 4 June   *see* 4:71
From Battaile Muse, 4 June   92
To Thomas Ringgold Tilghman, 4 June   *see* 4:80
To John Fitzgerald, 5 June   93
To William Fitzhugh, Jr., 5 June   94
From Charles MacIver, 5 June   94
To John Rumney, Jr., 5 June   96
To James Tilghman, 5 June   96
From John Fitzgerald, 6 June   99
From David Stuart, 6 June   100
From Thornton Washington, 6 June   100
To Thomas Bedwell, 7 June   102
To Benjamin Lincoln, 7 June   103
To Charles MacIver, 7 June   104
To Lafayette, 8 June   104
To Edward Newenham, 10 June   105
From Gardoqui, 12 June   106
From John Fitzgerald, 13 June   108
From Henry Knox, 13 June   108
To William Moultrie, 14 June   111
From William Fitzhugh, Jr., 15 June   112

From Charles MacIver, 17 June   113
To Sarah McCarty Johnston Darrell, 18 June   115
To Henry Lee, Jr., 18 June   116
To Pierre François Cozette, 19 June   *see* 3:559
To Count de Grouchet, 19 June   *see* 3:313
From Peter Dow, 20 June   118
To David Humphreys, 20 June   119
From André Michaux, 20 June   120
To Nicholas Pike, 20 June   120
To Clement Biddle, 21 June   121
To Joseph Dashiell, 21 June   122
To Thornton Washington, 22 June   122
From William Foster, 23 June   124
From George Fisher, 24 June   124
From Clement Biddle, 25 June   125
To George William Fairfax, 25 June   126
From Alexander McCabe, 26 June   129
From John Jay, 27 June   130
From Thomas West, 27 June   132
From Rochambeau, 28 June   133
To Richard Sprigg, 28 June   134
To William Brown, 30 June   135
To George William Fairfax, 30 June   135
From Thomas Fairfax, 30 June   141
From William Fitzhugh, Sr., c.1 July   142
To Battaile Muse, 1 July   144
To Wakelin Welch, c.1 July   144
To William Fitzhugh, Sr., 2 July   146
From Henry Lee, Jr., 3 July   147
From Timothy Dwight, 5 July   149
From James Tilghman, 7 July   150
To Thomas Johnson, 8 July   152
From Peregrine Fitzhugh, 10 July   152
From Richard Harrison, 10 July   154
From Henry Lee, Jr., 11 July   154
From Battaile Muse, 11 July   154
From Benjamin Ogle, 12 July   156
To Edmund Randolph, 12 July   157
From William Gordon, 13 July   157
To Samuel Athawes, 15 July   *see* 4:129
From Macarty de Marteigne, 18 July   160
From Edward Peyton, 18 July   161
From Joseph Dashiell, 20 July   162
From Mauduit du Plessis, 20 July   163

To James Tilghman, 20 July 165
To Henry L. Charton, 22 July 167
From Gardoqui, 22 July *see* 4:107
To Battaile Muse, 25 July 167
From Richard Thomas, 25 July 168
To William Grayson, 26 July 169
To Henry Lee, Jr., 26 July 170
From James Moyler, 27 July *see* 4:207
To Mauduit du Plessis, 28 July *see* 4:165
To Thomas Smith, 28 July 172
From William Moultrie, 30 July 174
To Clement Biddle, 31 July 177
To Baron de Holtzendorff, 31 July *see* 3:37
To Lauzun, 31 July 178
From Battaile Muse, 31 July 179
To Rochambeau, 31 July 179
To Antoine-Felix Wuibert, 31 July 181
Articles of Agreement with Thomas Mahony, 1 August 182
To John Jay, 1 August *see* 4:213
To Thomas Jefferson, 1 August 183
To La Luzerne, 1 August 185
To Battaile Muse, 1 August 187
To John Marsden Pintard, 2 August 188
From John Sullivan, 2 August 189
From James Tilghman, 2 August 190
To Henry Hill, 3 August 190
To Lamar, Hill, Bisset, & Co., 3 August 191
To Wakelin Welch, 4 August 191
To William Peacey, 5 August 192
    Enclosure: James Bloxham to William Peacey, 23 July 193
To Wakelin Welch, 5 August 195
To Wakelin Welch, 5 August *see* 4:199
To Arthur Young, 6 August 196
From Henry Lee, Jr., 7 August 200
From William Moultrie, 7 August 201
Potomac Company Annual Report, 7 August 202
From John Rutledge, 7 August *see* 4:177
To Armand, 10 August 203
From Matthew Whiting, 10 August 204
From John Ariss, 12 August 205
From Henry Lee, Jr., 12 August 205
To John Francis Mercer, 12 August 206
From Edward Newenham, 12 August 207
From Clement Biddle, 13 August 208

From John Witherspoon, 14 August   209
To Theodorick Bland, 15 August   210
To John Jay, 15 August   212
To Lafayette, 15 August   214
From a Committee of the Potomac Company,
    15 August   *see* 4:235
To David Stuart, 15 August   217
From John Peck, 16 August   217
To Clement Biddle, 18 August   218
To Chastellux, 18 August   218
To Metcalf Bowler, 19 August   220
To Thomas Newton, Jr., 19 August   221
To William Hunter, Jr., 20 August   221
To Thomas Hutchins, 20 August   222
From William Jackson, 20 August   223
From James Monroe, 20 August   223
To George Morgan, 20 August   *see* 4:222
To Henry Knox, 21 August   225
From Samuel Powel, 21 August   226
From Elizabeth Powel, 21 August   *see* 4:226–27
To Desdevens, 22 August   *see* 4:226
To Jonathan Loring Austin, 23 August   227
To John Witherspoon, 23 August   227
From George Lewis, 25 August   228
From John Augustine Washington, 25 August   *see* 4:229
To Thornton Washington, 25 August   229
From Jean Le Mayeur, 28 August   231
To James Hill, 29 August   231
To Gardoqui, 30 August   232
From Battaile Muse, 31 August   233
From Floridablanca, 1 September   *see* 4:380
To George Gilpin and John Fitzgerald, 1 September   234
To William Hartshorne, 1 September   *see* 4:236
From William Hartshorne, 1 September   *see* 4:236
To David Humphreys, 1 September   236
To James Tilghman, 2 September   237
From Horatio Clagett, 4 September   *see* 4:218
From John Peck, 4 September   238
From James Rumsey, 5 September   238
From Henry Lee, Jr., 8 September   240
To John Fitzgerald, 9 September   241
From Henry Hill, 9 September   242
To John Francis Mercer, 9 September   243

From Josiah Parker, 9 September 244
From Thomas Ridout, 10 September 245
From David Hoar, 12 September *see* 3:599
From Leven Powell, 12 September 246
To Samuel Vaughan, 12 September 247
From Charles Lee, 13 September 247
To James Brindley, 16 September *see* 4:202
From Comtesse d'Anterroche, 18 September 249
From James Rumsey, 19 September 253
To Charles Simms, 22 September 254
To Thomas Smith, 22 September 259
To Clement Biddle, 23 September 262
From James Tilghman, 23 September 262
From James Hill, 24 September 263
From David Humphreys, 24 September 264
From Benjamin Lincoln, Jr., 24 September 267
To William Triplett, 25 September 268
From Bushrod Washington, 27 September 274
From William Gordon, 28 September 275
To William Jackson, 28 September *see* 4:223
To John Sullivan, 28 September *see* 4:189
To Leven Powell, 30 September 277
To Bushrod Washington, 30 September 278
To George Augustine Washington, 30 September 279
From Henry Hill, Jr., 1 October 280
From Henry Lee, Jr., 1 October 281
From Jeremiah Wadsworth, 1 October 282
To John Augustine Washington, 1 October 285
From William Hickman, 5 October 286
To Thomas Snowden, 7 October 288
From Lafayette, 8 October 288
From Catharine Sawbridge Macaulay Graham, 10 October 289
From Henry Lee, Jr., 11 October 290
From Fielding Lewis, Jr., 11 October 293
From James Manning, 11 October 293
To Edmund Randolph, c.12 October 294
From Clement Biddle, 15 October 294
From Henry Lee, Jr., 17 October 295
From John Jay, 20 October *see* 3:524
To David Humphreys, 22 October 296
To Jeremiah Wadsworth, 22 October 298
From Henry Knox, 23 October 299
From Joseph Mandrillon, 24 October 302

From John Henry, 25 October 304
From William Hull, 25 October 305
To George Augustine Washington, 25 October 307
From George Augustine Washington, 25 October 310
From Lafayette, 26 October 311
From John Leigh, 30 October 313
From George McCarmick, c.30 October 314
To the Society of the Cincinnati, 31 October 316
To Henry Lee, Jr., 31 October 318
From George McCarmick, 31 October 320
To William Moultrie, 31 October 321
From Bushrod Washington, 31 October 322
From John Brown, 1 November 323
From David Humphreys, 1 November 324
From James Madison, 1 November 326
To Benjamin Franklin, 3 November 327
From Lamar, Hill, Bisset, & Co., 4 November 328
From Clement Biddle, 5 November 329
To George Clinton, 5 November 330
From James McHenry, 5 November 330
To James Madison, 5 November 331
To David Stuart, 5 November 333
To Elias Dayton, 6 November 335
To John Francis Mercer, 6 November 336
To Thomas West, 6 November 338
To Benjamin Lincoln, 7 November 339
From Thomas Smith, 7 November 339
To Horatio Gates, 8 November   *see* 4:318
To William Heth, 8 November   *see* 4:318
From Thomas Hutchins, 8 November 343
From James Madison, 8 November 344
From David Stuart, 8 November 346
From Peter Trenor, 8 November 348
From William Deakins, Jr., 9 November 350
From David Humphreys, 9 November 350
To Benjamin Lincoln, Jr., 9 November 352
From Ezra Stiles, 9 November 352
From Rawleigh Colston, 10 November 353
From James McHenry, 10 November   *see* 4:356
From Nathaniel Smith, 10 November 354
From Henry Lee, Jr., 11 November 357
To James McHenry, 11 November 358
To Thomas Johnson, 12 November 359

From Samuel Purviance, 12 November   *see* 4:356
From James McHenry, 13 November   360
From David Stuart, 13 November   361
To Robert Alexander, 14 November   363
From Thomas Jefferson, 14 November   363
From James Tilghman, 14 November   366
To Anne Ennis, 15 November   366
To Bushrod Washington, 15 November   368
To Wakelin Welch, 15 November   370
To Arthur Young, 15 November   371
From Comtesse d'Anterroche, 16 November   *see* 4:252
From David Humphreys, 16 November   373
To William Peacey, 16 November   375
From George Weedon, 17 November   376
To Theodorick Bland, 18 November   377
From Gardoqui, 18 November   379
From James McHenry, 18 November   380
To James Madison, 18 November   382
From Thomas Peters, 18 November   383
To Samuel Vaughan, 18 November   384
To d'Estaing, 19 November   *see* 4:164–65
To Lafayette, 19 November   385
To James Mercer, 19 November   385
To Edmund Randolph, 19 November   387
To David Stuart, 19 November   387
To Samuel Branden, 20 November   388
To William Drayton, 20 November   389
From William Hansbrough, 20 November   390
To Richard Harrison, 20 November   391
To William Hull, 20 November   *see* 4:307
To Samuel Purviance, 20 November   *see* 4:356
To Nathaniel Smith, 20 November   *see* 4:356
To William Hansbrough, 22 November   *see* 4:391
From Benjamin Tupper, 23 November   391
To John Francis Mercer, 24 November   393
From Edmund Randolph, 24 November   395
To David Stuart, 24 November   396
From Battaile Muse, 26 November   397
To Richard Butler, 27 November   398
To Robert Townsend Hooe, 27 November   400
To George McCarmick, 27 November   401
To Philip Marsteller, 27 November   402
From Philip Marsteller, 27 November   403

To Presley Neville, 27 November   404
To John Cannon, 28 November   405
To Thomas Freeman, 28 November   407
To John Stephenson, 28 November   408
To James McHenry, 29 November   408
To Tobias Lear, 30 November   410
To Gardoqui, 1 December   413
From L'Enfant, 1 December   *see* 4:445
From James Maury, 3 December   415
To Rawleigh Colston, 4 December   415
To Fielding Lewis, Jr., 4 December   416
From Benjamin Lincoln, 4 December 1786–4 March 1787   417
To Battaile Muse, 4 December   436
To Thomas Peters, 4 December   438
From Francisco Rendón, 4 December   439
To James Tilghman, 4 December   440
To Clement Biddle, 5 December   440
To John Francis Mercer, 5 December   442
From L'Enfant, 6 December   443
From Edmund Randolph, 6 December   445
To David Stuart, 6 December   446
From Thomas Johnson, 7 December   447
From James Madison, 7 December   448
From George William Fairfax, 12 December   450
To Edmund Randolph, 12 December   452
From Charles Little, 15 December   452
To Philip Marstellar, 15 December   453
To Josiah Watson, 15 December   455
To James Madison, 16 December   457
From Henry Knox, 17 December   460
From Thomas Freeman, 18 December   463
From Philip Marstellar, 18 December   *see* 4:455
To John Francis Mercer, 19 December   465
From David Stuart, 19 December   467
From Henry Knox, 21 December   470
To Leven Powell, 21 December   471
To Edmund Randolph, 21 December   471
To Gilles de Lavallée, 23 December   472
From William Roberts, 23 December   473
From James Madison, 24 December   474
To Edmund Randolph, 25 December   *see* 4:473
From David Stuart, 25 December   476
To David Humphreys, 26 December   477

To Henry Knox, 26 December   481
To Theodorick Bland, 28 December   484
To George Digges, 28 December   485
To Thomas Johnson, 28 December   486
To John Armistead, 29 December   487
To William Hull, 29 December   488
From Lachlan McIntosh, 29 December   490
To George Weedon, 29 December   491
From Charles Willson Peale, 31 December   492

1787

To Pierre L'Enfant, 1 January   493
Mount Vernon Store Book, 1–31 January   494
To Unknown, 1 January   497
From Clement Biddle, 2 January   497
From Henry Emanuel Lutterloh, 3 January   498
To Battaile Muse, 3 January   499
From Battaile Muse, 3 January   500
From Edmund Randolph, 4 January   500
From George Digges, 5 January   501
From John Jay, 7 January   502
To Jabez Bowen, 9 January   504
To Daniel Carroll, 9 January   505
To John Leigh, 9 January   *see* 4:314
To Charles Willson Peale, 9 January   506
To Thomas Seddon & Co., 9 January   507
To Charles Carter, 10 January   507
From William Deakins, Jr., 10 January   508
From William Drayton, 10 January   509
To Bushrod Washington, 10 January   509
To James Hill, 12 January   510
To John Price Posey, 12 January   512
From Robinson, Sanderson, & Rumney, 12 January   513
From Lafayette, 13 January   514
From Alexander Spotswood, 13 January   517
From Henry Knox, 14 January   518
From R., c.15 January   523
From John Hoomes, 16 January   *see* 4:488
From Horatio Gates, 19 January   523
From William Gordon, 20 January   524
From David Humphreys, 20 January   526
From Battaile Muse, 20 January   531
To Thomas Peters, 20 January   532

From Samuel Blachley Webb, 20 January   532
From Henry Knox, 21 January   534
To John Henry, 23 January   *see* 4:305
To David Humphreys, 23 January   535
To John Nicholson, 23 January   536
To Alexander Spotswood, 23 January   536
To George Gilpin, 24 January   537
From Benjamin Lincoln, Jr., 24 January   538
From Mandrillon, 24 January   539
To Battaile Muse, 24 January   542
From William Deakins, Jr., 25 January   542
From Robert Townsend Hooe, 25 January   543
From Henry Knox, 25 January   543
From Baron von Steuben, 26 January   *see* 4:534
From Samuel Hanson, 27 January   544
From John Price Posey, 27 January   545
From James Swan, 27 January   548
From Henry Knox, 29 January   549
From Henry Knox, 30 January   549
From Thomas Stone, 30 January   550
From William Deakins, Jr., 31 January   550
From Henry Knox, 31 January   551

Index   553

Editorial Apparatus

Transcription of the documents in the volumes of *The Papers of George Washington* has remained as close to a literal reproduction of the manuscript as possible. Punctuation, capitalization, paragraphing, and spelling of all words are retained as they appear in the original document. Dashes used as punctuation have been retained except when a dash and another mark of punctuation appear together. The appropriate marks of punctuation have always been added at the end of a paragraph. When a tilde is used in the manuscript to indicate a double letter, the letter has been doubled. Washington and some of his correspondents occasionally used a tilde above an incorrectly spelled word to indicate an error in orthography. When this device is used the editors have corrected the word. In cases where a tilde has been inserted above an abbreviation or contraction, usually in letter-book copies, the word has been expanded. Otherwise, contractions and abbreviations have been retained as written except that a period has been inserted after an abbreviation when needed. Superscripts have been lowered. Editorial insertions or corrections in the text appear in square brackets. Angle brackets ⟨ ⟩ are used to indicate illegible or mutilated material. A space left blank in a manuscript by the writer is indicated by a square-bracketed gap in the text [   ]. Deletion of material by the author in a manuscript is ignored unless it contains substantive material, and then it appears in a footnote. If the intended location of marginal notations is clear from the text, they are inserted without comment; otherwise they are recorded in the notes. The ampersand has been retained and the thorn transcribed as "th." The symbol for per (℔) is used when it appears in the manuscript. The dateline has been placed at the head of a document regardless of where it occurs in the manuscript.

Since GW read no language other than English, incoming letters written to him in foreign languages generally were translated for his information. Where this contemporary translation has survived, it has been used as the text of the document and the original version has been included either in the notes or in the CD-ROM edition of the Papers. If there is no contemporary translation, the document in its original language has been used as the text. All of the documents printed in this volume, as well as other ancillary material (usually cited in the notes), may be found in the CD-ROM edition of Washington's Papers (CD-ROM:GW).

Individuals usually are identified only at the first appearance of their names. The index to each volume of the Confederation Series indicates where an identification may be found in earlier volumes.

A number of letters to and from Washington have been printed, in whole or in part, out of their chronological sequence, usually in footnotes. All of these letters are listed in the table of contents with an indication where they may be found in this or another volume.

Symbols Designating Documents

AD   Autograph Document
ADS   Autograph Document Signed
ADf   Autograph Draft
ADfS   Autograph Draft Signed
AL   Autograph Letter
ALS   Autograph Letter Signed
D   Document
DS   Document Signed
Df   Draft
DfS   Draft Signed
LS   Letter Signed
LB   Letter-Book Copy
[S]   Signature clipped (used with other symbols: e.g., AL[S], Df[S]

Repository Symbols

CD-ROM:GW   See "Editorial Apparatus"
CSfBo   Bohemian Club Library, San Francisco
CSmH   Henry E. Huntington Library, San Marino, Calif.
CStbKML   The Karpeles Manuscript Library, Santa Barbara, Calif.
CtHWa   Wadsworth Athenaeum, North Hartford, Conn.
CtY   Yale University, New Haven
DLC   Library of Congress
DLC:GW   George Washington Papers, Library of Congress
DNA   National Archives
DNA:PCC   Papers of the Continental Congress, National Archives
DSoCi   Society of the Cincinnati, Washington, D.C.
ICU   University of Chicago
InHi   Indiana Historical Society, Indianapolis
LNHT   Tulane University, New Orleans
MdBJ   Johns Hopkins University, Baltimore
MH   Harvard University, Cambridge, Mass.
MHi   Massachusetts Historical Society, Boston

MiDbGr	Greenfield Village and the Henry Ford Museum, Dearborn, Mich.
MiU-C	William L. Clements Library, University of Michigan, Ann Arbor
MnHi	Minnesota Historical Society, St. Paul
MnSM	Macalester College, Weyerhaeuser Library, St. Paul
MoSW	Washington University, St. Louis, Mo.
MWeHM	Wenhem Historical Association and Museum, Iric-Wenhem, Mass.
MWiW	Williams College Library, Williamstown, Mass.
NcD	Duke University, Durham, N.C.
NhD	Dartmouth College, Hanover, N.H.
NHi	New-York Historical Society, New York
NhHi	New Hampshire Historical Society, Concord
NIC	Cornell University, Ithaca, N.Y.
NjMoNP	Washington Headquarters Library, Morristown, N.J.
NjP	Princeton University, Princeton, N.J.
NN	New York Public Library, New York
NNC	Columbia University, New York
NNGL	The Gilder Lehrman Library, New York
OCCtH	Clement County Courthouse, Ohio
PEL	Lafayette College, Easton, Pa.
PHi	Historical Society of Pennsylvania, Philadelphia
PP	Philadelphia Free Library
PPAmP	American Philosophical Society, Philadelphia
PPRF	Rosenbach Foundation, Philadelphia
PVF	Freedoms Foundation at Valley Forge, Pa.
PVFHi	Valley Forge Historical Society, Valley Forge, Pa.
PWacD	David Library of the American Revolution, Washington Crossing, Pa.
RHi	Rhode Island Historical Society, Providence
Vi	Virginia State Library and Archives, Richmond
ViFaCt	Fairfax County Courthouse, Fairfax, Va.
ViHi	Virginia Historical Society, Richmond
ViMtV	Mount Vernon Ladies' Association of the Union
ViStCH	Augusta County Courthouse, Staunton, Va.
ViU	University of Virginia, Charlottesville

Short Title List

Bacon-Foster, *Development of Patomac Route*.   Corra Bacon-Foster. *Early Chapters in the Development of the Patomac Route to the West*. Washington, D.C., 1912.

Boyd, *Jefferson Papers*.   Julian P. Boyd et al., eds. *The Papers of Thomas Jefferson*. 24 vols. to date. Princeton, N.J., 1950—.

Brown, *Annals of Clarke County*.   Stuart E. Brown, Jr., ed. *Annals of Clarke County*. Berryville, Va., 1983.

Burnett, *Letters*.   Edmund C. Burnett, ed. *Letters of Members of the Continental Congress*. 8 vols. 1921–36. Reprint. Gloucester, Mass., 1963.

Calendar of Virginia State Papers.   William Pitt Palmer et al., eds. *Calendar of Virginia State Papers and Other Manuscripts . . . Preserved in the Capitol at Richmond*. 11 vols. Richmond, 1875–93.

Chappelear, "Early Landowners."   Curtis Chappelear. "Early Landowners in the Benjamin Harrison and Robert Carter Nicholas Tracts." *Proceedings of the Clarke County Historical Association*, 7 (1947), 33–48.

Chastellux, *Travels in North America*.   Howard C. Rice, Jr., ed. *Travels in North America in the Years 1780, 1781, and 1782 by the Marquis de Chastellux*. 2 vols. Chapel Hill, N.C., 1963.

Cutler, *Life of Cutler*.   William Parker Cutler and Julia Perkins Cutler. *Life Journals and Correspondence of Rev. Manasseh Cutler*. 2 vols. Cincinnati, 1888.

Detweiler, *Washington's Chinaware*.   Susan Gray Detweiler. *George Washington's Chinaware*. New York, 1982.

Diaries.   Donald Jackson and Dorothy Twohig, eds. *The Diaries of George Washington*. 6 vols. Charlottesville, Va., 1976–79.

Dickinson, *The Fairfax Proprietary*.   Josiah Look Dickinson. *The Fairfax Proprietary: The Northern Neck, the Fairfax Manors and Beginnings of Warren County in Virginia*. Front Royal, 1959.

Eisen, *Portraits of Washington*.   Gustavus A. Eisen. *Portraits of Washington*. 3 vols. New York, 1932.

Feer, *Shays's Rebellion*.   Robert A. Feer. *Shays's Rebellion*. New York and London, 1988.

Fitzpatrick, *Writings*.   John C. Fitzpatrick, ed. *The Writings of George Washington from the Original Manuscript Sources, 1745–1799*. 39 vols. Washington, D.C., 1931–44.

Ga. Historical Quarterly.   *Georgia Historical Quarterly*.

Gerlach, "Firmness and Prudence."   Larry R. Gerlach. "Firmness and Prudence: Connecticut, the Continental Congress, and the National Domain, 1776–1786." *Connecticut Historical Society Bulletin*, 31 (July 1966), 65–75.

Goodwin, *Colonial Church in Virginia*.　Edward Lewis Goodwin. *The Colonial Church in Virginia*. Milwaukee, 1927.

Griffin, *Boston Athenæum Collection*.　Appleton P. C. Griffin, comp. *A Catalogue of the Washington Collection in the Boston Athanæum*. Cambridge, Mass., 1897.

Hamilton, *Writings of Monroe*.　Stanislaus Murray Hamilton, ed. *The Writings of James Monroe*. 7 vols. New York and London, 1898.

Harris, *Old New Kent*.　Malcolm Hart Harris. *Old New Kent County: Some Account of the Planters, Plantations, and Places in New Kent County*. 2 vols. West Point, Va., 1977.

Hening.　William Waller Hening, ed. *The Statutes at Large: Being a Collection of All the Laws of Virginia from the First Session of the Legislature, in the Year 1619*. 13 vols. 1819–23. Reprint. Charlottesville, Va., 1969.

House of Delegates Journal, 1786–1790.　*Journal of the House of Delegates of the Commonwealth of Virginia; Begun and Holden in the City of Richmond, in the County of Henrico, on Monday the Sixteenth Day of October, in the Year of Our Lord One Thousand Seven Hundred and Eighty-Six*. Richmond, 1828.

Hume, *Society of the Cincinnati*.　Edgar Erskine Hume, ed. *General Washington's Correspondence concerning the Society of the Cincinnati*. Baltimore, 1941.

Jackson, *Chronicles of Georgetown*.　Richard Plummer Jackson. *The Chronicles of Georgetown, D.C., from 1751 to 1878*. Washington, D.C., 1878.

JCC.　Worthington C. Ford et al., eds. *Journals of the Continental Congress*. 34 vols. Washington, D.C., 1904–37.

Johnson and Cullen, *Marshall Papers*.　Herbert A. Johnson, Charles T. Cullen, et al., eds. *The Papers of John Marshall*. 5 vols. to date. Chapel Hill, N.C., 1974—.

Johnston, *Jay Papers*.　Henry Phelps Johnston. *The Correspondence and Public Papers of John Jay*. 4 vols. New York and London, 1890.

Journal of Virginia Council.　H. R. McIlwaine et al., eds. *Journals of the Council of the State of Virginia*. 5 vols. Richmond, 1931–82.

Ledger A.　Manuscript Ledger in George Washington Papers, Library of Congress.

Ledger B.　Manuscript Ledger in George Washington Papers, Library of Congress.

Lewis, *Walpole Correspondence*.　W. S. Lewis, ed. *Horace Walpole's Correspondence with Sir Horace Mann*. Vol. 7. New Haven, Conn., 1967.

Mattern, "Benjamin Lincoln."　David B. Mattern. "A Moderate

Revolutionary: The Life of Major General Benjamin Lincoln." Ph.D. dissertation, Columbia University, 1990.

Mayer, *Tah-Gah-Jute*.   Brantz Mayer. *Tah-Gah-Jute; or, Logan and Cresap, an Historical Essay.* Albany, N.Y., 1867.

Md. House of Delegates Proceedings.   *Votes and Proceedings of the House of Delegates of the State of Maryland. November Session, 1784. Being the First Session of This Assembly.*

Memoir of Richard Henry Lee.   Richard H. Lee. *Memoir of Richard Henry Lee.* 2 vols. Philadelphia, 1825.

Miller, *Peale Papers*.   Lillian B. Miller, ed. *The Selected Papers of Charles Willson Peale and His Family.* 3 vols. New Haven, Conn., 1983–88.

Minot, *History of the Mass. Insurrections.*   George Richards Minot. *The History of the Insurrections, in Massachusetts, in the Year 1786, and the Rebellion Consequent Thereon.* Worcester, Mass., 1788.

Miscellaneous Works.   *The Miscellaneous Works of David Humphreys.* 1804. Reprint. Gainesville, Fla., 1968.

N.C. State Records.   Walter Clark, ed. *The State Records of North Carolina.* 26 vols. Raleigh and various places, 1886–1907.

Papers, Colonial Series.   W. W. Abbot et al., eds. *The Papers of George Washington. Colonial Series.*   Charlottesville, Va., 1983—.

Pickell, *A New Chapter.*   John Pickell. *A New Chapter in the Early Life of Washington, in Connection with the Narrative History of the Potomac Company.* New York, 1856.

Publications of Col. Soc. of Mass.   *Publications of the Colonial Society of Massachusetts.* Vol. 11, 1906–7. Boston, 1910.

Rutland, *Mason Papers*.   Robert A. Rutland, ed. *The Papers of George Mason, 1725–1792.* 3 vols. Chapel Hill, N.C., 1970.

Rutland and Rachal, *Madison Papers*, vol. 9.   William T. Hutchinson, Robert A. Rutland, William M. E. Rachal, J. C. A. Stagg, et al., eds. *The Papers of James Madison.* [1st series]. 17 vols. Chicago and Charlottesville, Va., 1962–91.

S.C. State Records.   *The State Records of South Carolina: Journals of the House of Representatives, 1785–1786.* Ed. Lark Emerson Adams. Columbia, 1979.

Secret Journals of Congress.   *Secret Journals of the Acts and Proceedings of Congress, from the First Meeting Thereof to the Dissolution of the Confederation, by the Adoption of the Constitution of the United States.* 4 vols. Boston, 1821.

Slaughter, *Truro Parish*.   Philip Slaughter. *The History of Truro Parish in Virginia.* Philadelphia, 1907.

Sparks, *Writings*.   Jared Sparks, ed. *The Writings of George Washington: Being His Correspondence, Addresses, Messages, and Other Papers, Of-*

ficial and Private, Selected and Published from the Original Manuscripts. 12 vols. Boston, 1833–37.

Spotsylvania County Records. William Armstrong Crozier, ed. *Virginia County Records: Spotsylvania County, 1721–1800*. Vol. 1. New York, 1905.

Stegeman and Stegeman, *Caty*. John F. Stegeman and Janet A. Stegeman. *Caty: A Biography of Catharine Littlefield Greene*. Athens, Ga., 1977.

Syrett, *Hamilton Papers*. Harold C. Syrett et al., eds. *The Papers of Alexander Hamilton*. 27 vols. New York, 1961–87.

Wick, *Graphic Portraits of Washington*. Wendy C. Wick. *George Washington: An American Icon. The Eighteenth-Century Graphic Portraits*. Washington, D.C., 1982.

The Papers of George Washington
Confederation Series
Volume 4
April 1786–January 1787

Letter not found: to Leonard Henley, 2 April 1786. On 14 April Henley acknowledges to GW the receipt of "Your letter of the 2d of Apl."

From Daniel Morgan

Dear sir   Frederick county 3d april 1786
   Before I recd your accompt against Colo. Kennedy I had paid him all that I was to give him for the house lotts &c. that I bought of him and chiefly in orders accepted—I was desirous to get the money for you It being the first time I ever had it in my power to serve you in a domestick line—his circumstances (I knew) did enable him to pay without a suite of them by the time the suite was determin'd—I therefore thought it most advisable to try to get so much in my hand and detain it—for which reason I did not show him the acompg nor let him or any other person know I had it—but a bad woman which he kept for a house keeper made such a Deep stroke at him that frustrated all my designs & left the old man poor indeed, he has an estate in scotland worth about £500 Sterling which he has been offering for sail which was my reason for not returning you the accompt as thinking the accompt could be of no service to you without the money—I recd a line from Mr Muse the other day respecting the Matter and shall give him the accompt and order at our court—but will still keep a look out, and if I can see a chance of securing the money I will give Mr Muse Notice as I understand he dose your business in this quarter[1]—I am happy to understand that an easy passage is discovered for the water to [be] taken round the G. fall of patomack, I wish you great success in that Interprize, Never the less I had great faith in you judgment I do candidly tell you, I was fearfull of its not being effected Never the less if my expences in building had Not exceeded my Resources I would have taken two or three shares I wish you success in every undertaking and shall ⟨be⟩ allways happy to serve you in every thing in my power. I have the Honor to be your most obedt Hble servt
                                            Danl Morgan

2 *April* 1786

ALS, NjMoNP.

1. For the attempts to collect David Kennedy's debt to GW, see GW to Battaile Muse, 8 Mar. 1786, n.3.

To Thomas Cushing

Dr Sir,   Mount Vernon 5th April 1786.

I have now the honor to acknowledge the receipt of your several favors of the 6th 9th & 16th of Novr & 22d of Feby.[1] I purposely delayed my acknowledgments of the first three, 'till I should receive the one promised therein, that I might give you no more trouble with my concerns than was unavoidable.

I feel myself under great obligation to you for your obliging & disinterested attention to my Jack; & for your kindness to the person who was sent to conduct him home: he, the Spaniard, & the Jack Ass all arrived safely, & in as short a time as could well have been expected from the great distance, & manner of their traveling.[2]

Your draft on me in favor of Messrs Isaac & William Smith, was paid the moment it was presented; & I have since paid Captn Pearce's Accot, but not to the amount of his order in favor of Mr Hartshorne Mercht in Alexandria: for I believe Captn Pearce was ashamed himself of his charges after they were made, as he requested the above Gentleman, in a second letter, to receive whatever should be thought right. Mr Hartshorne therefore, adding for the full passage of the Jack, made the ⟨Acc.⟩ of Mr Ashton, in other respects, his government for the residue, & instead of demanding £63.5.6. was content to receive £33.3.6. & thought it enough.[3] You have, I am persuaded, hit upon the true & only reason why Captn Pearce withheld his Accot from your examination; preferring to send it hither, exorbitant as it appeared from the face of it, rather than have entered into any dispute concerning it, I should have paid it had I not waited a while to learn the result of your application to him.

Mrs Washington joins me in respectful compliments to your self & Lady, & with sentiments of great esteem & regard I am Dr Sir Yrs &c.

G: Washington

LB, DLC:GW.

1. Cushing's letter of 22 Feb. 1786 has not been found.

2. John Fairfax and Pedro Tellez walked the jackass, the gift of the king of Spain, from Boston to Mount Vernon in twenty-five days. See Cushing to GW, 6 Nov. 1785, n.2.

3. See William Hartshorne to GW, 26 Nov., n.1, and its references, particularly Hartshorne to GW, 25 Mar. 1786.

To Henry Lee, Jr.

Dear Sir,   Mount Vernon April 5th 1786.

Ascribe my silence to any cause rather than the want of friendship, or to a disinclination to keep up a friendly intercourse with you by letter. Absences from home, hurry of business, company, &ca, however justly they might be offered, are too stale & commonplace, to be admitted. I therefore discard them. Throwing myself upon your lenity, and depending more upon your goodness than on any apology I could make, as an excuse for not having acknowledged the receipt of your favors of the 16th of Feb. and 2d of march, before this time.

The first came to hand just after I had made one trip to our Works at the great Falls of this River, and when I was upon the eve of a second to the same place; where the board of Directors met, by appointment, the 1st day of last month. I can therefore, from my own observation, inform you, that this business is progressing in a manner that exceeds our most sanguine expectations. Difficulties vanish as we proceed. The time & expence which it was supposed we shd have to encounter at this place, will both, be considerably reduced. After a thorough investigation of the ground there, we have departed from Ballendines rout for the Canal—marked a fresh one—(which in our judgments will save ⅘ths of the labour, time, & expence; and in the opinion of Mr Brindley, who has just been to view them ⁹⁄₁₀ths)—and be equally good when effected. To sum up the whole in one word—if there are any doubts remaining of the success of this undertaking, they must be confined to three classes of people—1 those who have not opportunities of investigation—2, those who, having it in their power will not be at the trouble of doing it—and 3, those whose interests being opposed, do not wish to be convinced. The great Falls, is the only place where, under our present view of the river, we conceive it necessary to establish Locks. The ground favors them. and there can be no doubt (this being the case) of their succeeding as well in this, as in other Countries, as the materials for erecting them are abundant & cheap. What difficulties may hereafter be found, where none was apprehended, I will not take upon me to determine; but where they were thought wholly to lie, we are free from apprehension.[1]

My sentiments with respect to the Fœderal government are very well known—publickly, & privately, have they been communicated without reserve. but my *opinion* is, that there is more wickedness than ignorance in the conduct of the States, or in other words, in the conduct of those who have too much influence in the fabrication of our Laws; and that, till the curtain is withdrawn, and the private views, & selfish principles upon which these men act, are exposed to public notice & resentment, I have little hopes of amendment; without another convulsion. The picture of our affairs as drawn by the Committee, approved by Congress, and handed to the public, did not at all surprize me. before that report appeared, though I could not go into the minutiæ of matters, I was more certain of the agregate of our distresses than I am now of the remedy which will be applied. And without the latter, I do not see upon what ground your Agent at the Court of Morocco, and the other at Algeirs are to treat, unless—having to do with new hands—they mean to touch the old string again, and make them dance a while, to the tune of promises.[2]

I thank you for the Pamphlet which contains the corrispondence between Mr Jay & Mr Littlepage; and shall be obliged to you for a Gazette containing the publication of the latter, which appears to have given rise to it.[3] With sentiments of great esteem & regard I am—Dear Sir Yr Obedt & Affec. Servt

Go: Washington

ALS, PP; LB, DLC:GW.

1. GW gives an account of the meeting of the officers of the Potomac River Company, of which he was president, in snowy weather at the Great Falls of the Potomac, 1–4 Mar., in *Diaries*, 4:288–89.

2. GW is referring to Thomas Barclay and John Lamb. See David Humphreys to GW, 1 Nov. 1785, n.1.

3. For the controversy between John Jay and his former protégé Lewis Littlepage, see Lafayette to GW, 6 Feb. 1786, n.10.

To Samuel Powel

Dear Sir,   Mount Vernon Aprl 5th 1786.

The Revd Mr Griffith, who will present this letter to you, is possessed of much property in the Town of Alexandria, the value of which he is desirous of encreasing by buildings.[1] To enable him to do this, he wishes to borrow, on interest, about Two thousand five hundred pounds. As security for such a loan, he is willing to mortgage his interest in the above place; and proposes as a further security, to offer other means. The nature of all, he will explain to you. They are, in my opinion, amply sufficient, such as I should not hesitate to take, if I had the money to lend; but you will be able to judge more fully of the matter when they are laid before you. From a long & intimate acquaintance with Mr Griffith, I have a high opinion of his worth, and entire dependence on his representations, which (as he may, in some degree, be a stranger to you) I have thought it a piece of justice to mention. With great estm I am—Dear Sir Yr most Obedt Hble Servt

Go: Washington

ALS, ViMtV; LB, DLC:GW. The clerk indicates in the letter book that the same letter was sent to both Charles Carroll and Robert Morris.

1. David Griffith was rector of Fairfax Parish. At the general meeting of the Episcopal church in Philadelphia in June 1786, he was designated bishop of Virginia. See Powel's response of 21 August.

To David Ramsay

Sir,   Mount Vernon 5th April 1786.

I pray you to accept my best acknowledgments of your letter of the 22d of Feby, & thanks for the history of the revolution of South Carolina, with which you have been so good as to present me. From what I have heard of its merits, I anticipate much pleasure in the perusal of the work.

It is to be regretted that your local situation did not allow you, with convenience, to take a more comprehensive view of the war.

My gratitude for the favourable sentiments you have been pleased to express for me is due, and with esteem & respect I have the honor to be &c.

G: Washington

LB, DLC:GW.

From William Moultrie

Dear Sir,   Charleston South Carolina 7th April 1786

I have been highly honoured and particularly obliged by you, in introducing the Count De Castiglioni to me; I have found him a most agreeable & accomplished Gentleman; & as such, he has received every mark of polite attention from our Citizens; he expresses great satisfaction on his Visit to this State. The Count left this City a few days ago for Georgia & intends to take his rout through the interior Country, down to Mount Vernon, by which he will be able to add greatly to the information he is desirous of obtaining respecting the different States.[1]

Convinced of your wish & desire to promote every public benefit that may possibly present itself to you, in which any part of the United States may be concerned: I presume to take the liberty of addressing you in a matter relative to this State, & without further apology for the freedom I now use, shall proceed to the point.

A number of Gentlemen of this State have entered into an association which is sanctioned by the legislature to open an Inland Navigation, by a communication from the Santee to the Cooper River, the distance across being about twenty miles; we intend it to be done by Locks & Canals, & will be a means of shortening the present Navigation at least 150 Miles.[2]

Many of the Gentlemen who compose the Board of Directors for carrying the plan into execution, having the honor of being personally acquainted with you were induced to recommend that, endeavour be made to obtain Mr Brinley to superintend it, if in your Opinion, you judged him capable of the undertaking—it is said Mr Brinley was constantly with his Brother, while carrying on the Duke of Bridgewater's Works, & possessed great knowledge and abilities—To begin right, is all in all with us—

the practicability of bringing it to perfection cannot admit of a doubt.

However, the engagements that Mr Brinley may now have of the same kind, may possibly prevent him entering into a New One, yet if he could be spared only to inspect into the situation, & to give his opinion and directions how to proceed, it may at least prevent us from begining wrong, & we may be going on untill he or some other as equal can be procured; the Board of Directors will chearfully pay every expence that Mr Brinley may be at, by coming here, exclusive of a compensation.[3]

Mrs Moultrie request her best respects to be tendered to Mrs Washington & yourself[4]—and I most sincerely wish you both health & happiness. I am with perfect Esteem, Dear Sir Your most Obedient Humble Servant

Willm Moultrie

LS, ICU.

1. GW's letter of 27 Dec. 1785 to Moultrie is printed in Tench Tilghman's first letter to GW, 13 Dec. 1785.

2. The Santee Canal was chartered in 1786, but work was not begun until 1793, under the direction of Christian Senf. The 22-mile canal, 35 feet wide and 5½ feet deep, was completed in 1800. Among the other directors known to GW were John and Edward Rutledge, Gen. Thomas Sumter, and Gen. Francis Marion.

3. See James Rumsey to GW, 29 Mar., n.1.

4. Moultrie's second wife was Hannah Motte Lynch Moultrie, daughter of Jacob Motte (1700–1770) and widow of Thomas Lynch (1727–1776).

Letter not found: from Thomas Cresap, 8 April 1786. GW wrote Cresap on 8 May: "Your letter of the 8th of last month came to my hands."

From William Gordon

My Dear Sir   Boston Apr. 9. 1786

This will probably be the last letter, you will receive from me till I have crossed the Atlantic. Should I get safe to London, through the kind orderings of Providence, shall take the first opportunity of writing to you. Expect to sail next wednesday wind & weather permitting. Shall take your present with me, to remind me of your friendship.[1] The honour your Excellency has done me in confiding in my prudence not to abuse the information received from your papers, binds me to yourself & will oblige me to answer your expectations. The abuse with which I have been loaded by the public prints shall only make me the more cautious in answering the character of a faithful Historian.[2] If I can, will contrive that you may have the Chronicle as usual.[3] Mrs Gordon joins in most affectionate regards to Your Excellency, Your Lady, & the rest of your worthy family. Your Excellencys sincere friend & humble servant

William Gordon

ALS, DLC:GW.

1. As a matter of fact Gordon wrote one more letter from Boston, on 15 April, to report: "The ship not sailing so soon as expected, gives me the opportunity of forwarding another paper. I have engaged the Revd Mr [Joseph] Eckley of this place to send you it from week to week. He will have pleasure in doing it; & it will be no expence to him as he takes it in weekly. We are now waiting only for a wind" (DLC:GW). See Joseph Eckley to GW, 20 April. GW had sent Gordon flowering trees (see GW to Gordon, 6 Dec. 1785).

2. After Gordon published his prospectus, dated 1 Dec. 1785, announcing the intended publication of his history of the American Revolution and inviting subscribers to remit one-half the price of the work (see GW to James Mercer, 20 Jan. 1786), he was attacked in the Boston press, for being British, for his plans to have his work printed in Britain, and for demanding immediate payment by subscribers. One correspondent to the *Massachusetts Centinel* (Boston) suggested that before paying, subscribers should inquire "whether their MONEY, together with the MANUSCRIPT, are to be carried by the AUTHOR to Britain, for the sole benefit and advantage of the typical gentry of LONDON" (8 Feb. 1786). Another correspondent returned Gordon's prospectus "without one subscriber, our people in this quarter say that they hear he is going to England to print it, and observe that our country must be in a dangerous situation, for . . . when a Ship is to be cast away, the Rats leave her before she sails" (18 Feb. 1786). A third complained of Gordon's pompous advertisement and of his failure to show his manuscript "even to his most intimate friends" (22 Feb. 1786). On 1 Mar. the *Centinel* printed under the headline "Anti-American HISTORY!!" an attack on the proposed "History of the American Revolution, by WILLIAM WHACKUM, D.D.," which ends: "Whose expectation can be so high raised by the *proposals* of a certain Compiler, as to expect any other than a *dirty* performance, as all the merit this *mealy-mouthed* writer lays claim to, is his having been permitted to view the *secrets* of Congress, and look into the *privies* of the American Generals."

3. See note 1.

To Thomas Newton, Jr.

Sir,　　　　　　　　　　　Mount Vernon 9th April 1786.

I have been favored with your letters of the 20th of Jany—24th of Feby & 13th of March—the last of which speaks of a letter written by you to me of the same date—this letter has never got to hand: but I have received in Alexandria the £60—which Messrs Pennock & Skipwith promised to remit me on your accot—as also the Wine from Captn Earle, in very good order.[1]

My situation, since my retreat from public life, has been such as to put it out of my power to go into an examination & settlement of Accots with that precision which is requisite; & among others, the transactions between the deceased Colo. Lewis & myself stand open. I do not know (from any thing my memory affords) on what account he could draw an order in favor of Henry Mitchell, as I recollect no dealings with that Gentn—but presume it must be right. Nevertheless, if there is an accot annexed to the order, or if the order is expressive of the purpose for which it was drawn, you would do me a favor in transmitting a copy of it.[2]

I have made several ineffectual applications for my Accot with Mr Hill; but as Dr Stuart is again going into that part of the country in which he lives, I will make one effort more to obtain it—'till this happens I can say nothing with respect to his credits, but will advise you as soon as it is in my power.[3]

In one of your former letters you intimated that my superfine Flour would sell well in Norfolk, & it was my intention to have consigned you some 'ere this; but as the quantity I make is small, the demand for it in Alexandria has generally kept pace with my manufactory. However I believe it would now be in my power to send you from 50 to 100 barrels, if you thought the present prices in your Town would answer; and that you may be enabled to judge I shall inform you that I have not sold one barrel this year which has not netted at my Mill 38/ —cash paid on delivery; & some at 40/ —Would it nett the former at Norfolk, free of freight commission & storage?[4] Your answer would determine my conduct, & I shall be glad to receive it by the return of the Post. I am Sir &c.

　　　　　　　　　　　　　　　　　Geo: Washington

LB, DLC:GW.

1. None of these letters from Newton has been found. On 3 Sept. 1785 GW resumed his correspondence with Newton, who before the Revolution had been GW's agent to sell his flour in Norfolk and in the West Indies. GW wrote in response to Newton's missing letter of 27 April 1785 in which Newton enclosed his account with GW. GW notes in his account with Newton having received on 25 Feb. 1786 £60 "of Wm Hunter Junr" (Ledger B, 85).

2. In the 1770s GW's brother-in-law Fielding Lewis, who died in 1782, often handled business matters for him in Williamsburg.

3. See GW to James Hill, 29 Aug. 1786, and Hill to GW, 24 Sept. 1786.

4. See GW to Newton, 26 May, and note 1 of that document.

From Alexander Doyle

Sir   George Town [Md.] April 10th 1786

From a Sense of your Excellency's Universal Benevolence and Willingness to Countenance and Incourage any design of Public Utility, I have taken the Liberty to entreat your Excellency to give the Paper you will Receive herewith the Sanctions of your Name.[1] In Conjunction with Several well disposed persons of this Town, who Consider Religion and Virtue as the best Basis of the Happiness, Security and Permanency of States, I have purchased a Lot of Ground and Materials for building a Chapel. we have with concern observed some vices and disorders Introduced by an Influx of Foreigners of the Lowest Class who are Settling here May in a great measure be Attributed to a want of Attention to Religious Duties. Men are generally Strongly attached to that Religion in which they are Educated, and as this Town the Populous and daily encreasing has but one place of Worship, we have determined to Build another[2] as our motive whether viewed in a Religous or Political Light (we hope) is good, we beg Leave to solicit your Excellency's concurence, Satisfied your Example will Influence the gentry of the Neighbouring parts of Virginia and Maryland. I am with the greatest respect your Excellency's most Obt Servt

Alexr Doyle

ALS, DLC:GW.

1. Neither the enclosure nor GW's response has been found.

2. At this time the only church building in town was that of the Presbyterians, recently built under the supervision of their pastor, Stephen Bloomer

Balch. Alexander Doyle is credited with having erected in the 1790s Trinity Church for Roman Catholics, partly at his own expense, on land acquired earlier by Bishop John Carroll. It served as the chapel for Georgetown College, which repaid Doyle in part by contracting to educate Doyle's sons (Jackson, *Chronicles of Georgetown*, 140–41).

Letter not found: to Leonard Henley, 10 April 1786. On 14 April Henley acknowledged receipt of GW's letter "of the 10th."

From Jean Le Mayeur

Sir   Richmond 10th april 1786
    i have this day only—had the honour of your Excellency's favour of the 28th march owing i supose to the neglect of the Post office in not forwarding it to me before now[1] i can not sufficiently Express the high sence i have of your Excellencys polite and frindly attention to the care of my Cavallry i am at a loss for words to Express my Gratitude for the new offer of the services of yr horse magnolio. i think him and Elegant horse and would prefer my mares Going to him rather than any one i have seen in America but the choice is more agreable to me being recommended by yr Excellancy to whose favour i am not ashamed to be further indebted.[2]
    this come by my servant who will relive you from the trouble of my Black horse and about the second week in may i hope the honour of paying my respects in person to mrs washington and your Excellancy at mount vernon.[3] i have the honour to be with Every sentiment of regard and veneration your Excellancy's most most Respectfull and very humble servant
                                        j. Le Mayeur

ALS, DLC:GW.
    1. Letter not found.
    2. Magnolio (Magnolia), an Arabian horse that GW acquired from the estate of John Parke Custis, was chestnut colored, nearly sixteen hands high, and "thought by all who have seen him to be perfect" (*Virginia Journal and Alexandria Advertiser*, 24 Mar. 1785).
    3. GW wrote in his diary for 14 April: "Doctr. La Moyeur sent for his Black horse & Chaise which his Servant carried away to day." Le Mayeur himself arrived at Mount Vernon on 15 June "with a Servant, Chaise, & 3 Horses" (*Diaries*, 4:310, 348).

To Benjamin Lincoln

My dear Sir,   ♪   Mount Vernon Aprl 10th 1786
The violent rains, and consequent freshes, have given such
interruption to the Stages in this part of the world, as to prevent
your favor of the 15th Ulto getting to my hands till Saturday last.
I accede to the sum of Two hundred Dollars in addition to the
stipulations mentioned in my last, as compensation for Mr
Lear's Services a year; and shall be glad to receive him into my
family as soon as he can make it convenient to repair to it. At
any rate I shall be glad to know, as nearly as may be, when to
expect him, that I may arrange matters accordingly.
There can be little doubt of Mr Lear's obtaining, by method &
arrangement, more time than he speaks of for study—to facilitate, rather than retard wch, as far as it can be made to comport
with the purposes for which he is employed, would give me
pleasure. With the greatest esteem & regard, I am, Dr Sir Yr
Most Obedt and Affecte Servant

Go: Washington

ALS, MH; LB, DLC:GW.

To Jonathan Trumbull, Jr.

My dear Sir,   Mount Vernon 10th Apl 1786
Your favor of the 20th of Feby came safely, tho' tedeously; as
it is not more than a few days since I received it, and the inclosure, for which I thank you. The author at the sametime that
he pays a just tribute to the deceased does no discredit to his
own talents.
I hope nothing will intervene to prevent the tour you have in
contemplation to the Southward; and I persuade myself you will
believe me very sincere, when I assure you of the pleasure I shall
feel at seeing you under my roof; in wch every inhabitant of the
mansion (acquainted with you) will participate. Your acquaintance G.A. Washington has taken unto himself a wife (Fanny
Bassett the Niece of Mrs Washington) both of whom live with us.
The inclosed for Mr Dwight, I take the liberty of committing
to your care, because the letter which I received from him (and
of which this is an acknowledgment) having neither date nor

place to it, I am at a loss where to direct it. If my address is wrong (for your Parsons sometimes turn Lawyers) I pray you to correct it.[1]

Mrs Washington & George, join me in every good wish for your self, Mrs Trumbull & family, and with sentiments of sincere esteem and perfect friendship I am, Dear Sir Yr Affecte & Obt Hble Ser⟨vt⟩

Go: Washington

ALS, ViMtV.

1. For GW's letter to Timothy Dwight, see Dwight to GW, October 1785, n.2.

To William Washington

Dr Sir, Mt Vernon 10th April 1786.

Three days ago *only*, I had the pleasure to receive your favor of the 18th of December, under cover of one from Mr Hammond of Baltimore. This gentleman writes me that the boxes which you had the goodness to send me, were then shipped on board the Baltimore packet for Alexandria. I every moment look for them, & feel myself much indebted for your kind attention to my request in this instance. I shall plant the acorns, & nurture the young trees, when they arrive, with great care: those brought last year by my Nephew (chiefly of the Laurel) stood the passage, the summer, & the winter, with very little covering, very well. I am now transplanting them from the box in which they were brought.[1]

At the proper season if you could make it convenient, I should be obliged to you for saving for me some seed of the Palmetto, & of any other trees or shrubs that are curious, in Carolina, & not natives of this Country.

Mrs Washington, & my Nephew Geo: A. Washington who has taken unto himself a wife, join me in every good wish for your Lady & Self, & with sincere esteem & regard, I am Dr Sir, &c. &c.

G: Washington

LB, DLC:GW.

1. See notes 1–3 in William Washington to GW, 18 Dec. 1785. William Hammond's letter has not been found.

From John Sedwick

Sir   Leesburgh April the 11th 1786
    The Suit that I mentioned to you at Shannan-Doah Falls that was Isued in your Name, hath been tryed & Mr Snickers was cast. There was a Suit commenced in the General Court in the same affair in your Name which hath cost me considerable I have no otherways of recovering the Cost but by taking an Execution against you beg you will not be displeasd, as I am only acting as an Executor.[1] I am Sir Yr Most Obdt Hble Srt
                                        John Sedwick

N.B. Mr Snickers with drew the Suit in the General Court. J.S.

ALS, DLC:GW.
    1. See Sedwick to GW, 8 Aug. 1785, and note 2 of that document. By "Snickers was cast" is meant that Snickers was defeated, that he lost in court.

From Thomas Brereton

                                Baltimo[re] 12th April 1786
    I had the Honor to Address your Excelency the 30th of July last on an affair you were formerly concernd with Brian Fairfax Esqr. as a Trustee and laterally with him and others as a Legatee in the Will of the late Mrs Margrt Savage who Died in Dublin in the year 1781 Wife of Doctor Willm Savage of Dumfrise & Pce William County Virginia.[1] I then acquainted your Excelcy that said Will regularly proved and Probrt of Administation granted to Richard and Ann Ennis Executors and residuary Legatees with their Letter of Attorney to Francis & Hannah Moore to Act, had just come to my hands Fras & Hanh being dead the Power ceased. as it recited a great part of the Will I then inclosd for your Excelcys further information, but have never receivd a line in return.
    This day I receivd letters from Dublin. Mrs Ennis Surviving Exctr is very desirous of hearing from Us to know how to Act or be advisd she supposes the property Mrs Savage bequeathd rests in your Execlys and Bryan Fairfaxs hands as Trustees, Prior to the Mariage with Savage he with Mr Thompson Mason passd a joint Bond for £5000. about 1st Janry 1767 Penalty conditiond to pay into your hands £100 Annualy for the use of Mrs Green

afterward Savage during her life. said Savage with his Wife some time after saild for Ireland where he left her destitute and re-turnd to Virginia to Enjoy her fortune the good woman dis-tress'd in Ireland was there for years supportd by the Charitable donations of a few acquaintances she had made amongst whom was this Mr & Mrs Ennis and a Mrs Bumford to whom she be-queathd £200., should you[r] Excelcy incline to write Mrs Ennis may direct to Mr Jas Templeton No. 56 Henry street Dublin. I am with respect Your Excelcys most Obedt Hhble Servt

Tho. Brereton

ALS, DLC:GW.

1. Letter not found. In his response to this letter on 20 April, GW summa-rizes his involvement in the problems of Margaret Savage with her husband Dr. William Savage, from the time of their marriage in 1767 until the death of Doctor Savage in 1784 after his wife had died. For a full account of GW's involvement, see Henry Lee and Daniel Payne to GW and George William Fairfax, 24 April 1767, n.1. See also Edmund Randolph to GW, 19 Feb. 1784, n.3. Thomas Brereton (d. 1787) advertised himself in the *Maryland Journal, and Baltimore Advertiser* on 28 Nov. 1786 as a "*Scrivener, Conveyancer*, and *Com-mission-Broker*, at his *Insurance-Office*, next Door to the Sign of the *Angel*, in *Gay-Street*."

To Robert Morris

Dr Sir,   Mt Vernon 12th April 1786

I give you the trouble of this letter at the instance of Mr Dalby of Alexandria; who is called to Philadelphia to attend what he conceives to be a vexatious law-suit respecting a slave of his, which a Society of Quakers in the City (formed for such pur-poses) have attempted to liberate. The merits of this case will no doubt appear upon trial; but from Mr Dalby's state of the matter, it should seem that this Society is not only acting repugnant to justice so far as its conduct concerns strangers, but, in my opin-ion extremely impolitickly with respect to the State—the City in particular; & without being able (but by Acts of tyranny & oppression) to accomplish their own ends. He says the conduct of this society is not sanctioned by Law: had the case been other-wise, whatever my opinion of the Law might have been, my re-spect for the policy of the State would on this occasion have appeared in my silence; because against the penalties of promulgated Laws one may guard; but there is no avoiding the snares of individuals, or of private societies—and if the practice of this Society of which Mr Dalby speaks, is not discountenanced, none of those whose *misfortune* it is to have slaves as attendants will visit the City if they can possibly avoid it; because by so doing they hazard their property—or they must be at the expence (& this will not always succeed) of providing servants of another description for the trip.[1]

I hope it will not be conceived from these observations, that it is my wish to hold the unhappy people who are the subject of this letter, in slavery. I can only say that there is not a man living who wishes more sincerely than I do, to see a plan adopted for the abolition of it—but there is only one proper and effectual mode by which it can be accomplished, & that is by Legislative authority: and this, as far as my suffrage will go, shall never be wanting.

But when slaves who are happy & content to remain with their present masters, are tampered with & seduced to leave them; when masters are taken at unawar[e]s by these practices; when a conduct of this sort begets discontent on one side and resentment on the other, & when it happens to fall on a man whose purse will not measure with that of the Society, & he looses his property for want of means to defend it—it is oppression in the latter case, & not humanity in any; because it introduces more evils than it can cure.

I will make no apology for writing to you on this subject; for if Mr Dalby has not misconceived the matter, an evil exists which requires a remedy; if he has, my intentions have been good though I may have been too precipitate in this address. Mrs Washington joins me in every good & kind wish for Mrs Morris & your family, and I am &c.

G: Washington

LB, DLC:GW.

1. Philip Dalby, who opened a store in Alexandria in May 1785, placed a notice in the *Virginia Journal and Alexandria Advertiser* on 30 Mar. 1786, which GW probably had read. Dalby's "A CAUTION to all TRAVELLERS to PHILADELPHIA from the Southern STATES" runs to more than three full columns in the newspaper and includes this account of how it all began: ". . . there is a society established in Pennsylvania, for the purpose of aiding and assisting all those unhappy persons who are cruelly and unjustly detained in bondage, in

obtaining their freedom. The society have a committee of their members who reside in Philadelphia, and whose business it is, to inquire after, and assist all who come within the line laid down by the society at their institution. This committee has council retained, and agents employed, to give them information of all such; and of the arrival of every gentleman, who has with him a slave for a waiting-man, who is immediately tampered with. If he proves to be well disposed, and satisfied with his station, arguments are used, and every measure taken, to disgust him with it, and to spur him on to prosecute his master for his freedom. Having given you the outlines of this committee, and their business, I am to inform you, that in the month of February, 1785, business called me to Philadelphia, I took with me as a waiter, a Mulatto boy, a slave for life, purchased for my use the January before, by Mr. John Nicholson, of Doctor Belt of Leesburg. The boy was soon after my arrival, accosted by some of the agents employed by the committee, and informed that a fair opportunity now presented him of procuring his liberty, if he would avail himself of it, which he for some time declined: but having been guilty of a small theft, he was apprehended, and previous to his examination brought before me. I ordered him a corporal punishment in presence of the person he had plundered. who thereupon discharged him from further prosecution. The chastisement seemed to inflame him, and he then applied to the committee for their assistance to procure his freedom. Upon hearing his relation, they very candidly informed him, that they could not render him that service, which from his complexion, they were induced to think they could. Thus matters rested, until I had finished my business and was preparing to set off, on my return home, when the day preceding my departure the boy was again brought before the committee, who carried him to their council, who undertaking his case that evening, served me with an *habeas corpus*, commanding my attendance at Judge Bryan's chambers the next morning." Dalby goes on to describe the court proceedings, and while declaring himself "as much disposed to lament the hard fate of any set of men, who are doomed to groan under the galling yoke of slavery, as any of the worthy" members of the Society of Friends, he explains at great length how he perceives the actions of the Society as subversive of property rights and the rule of law as well as raising disturbing questions about interstate relations within the American union. Morris wrote GW on 26 April that the Pennsylvania court had decided for Dalby and that he had recovered his slave.

Nearly a year later Dalby ran an advertisement dated 12 Feb. 1787 in the Alexandria and Baltimore newspapers, offering a $20 reward for the recovery of a slave who "RAN AWAY, from the subscriber, on the 10th inst. a light Mulatto SLAVE, named FRANK, 18 years of age, about 5 feet 4 inches high, one tooth out before, bushy brown hair, which he sometimes ties, is very artful, and will endeavour to pass for a freeman. He formerly belonged to Dr. Belt, of Leesburg. He had on when he went away, a brown cloth jacket, (with a green collar) and trousers, new shoes, with yellow buckles, but I expect he will change his clothes. He is well known on the road to Philadelphia, as he is the boy on whose account a suit was brought against me there" (*Maryland Journal, and Baltimore Advertiser*, 16 Feb. 1787).

To Bushrod Washington

Dear Bushrod,　　　　　　　　　Mount Vernon April 13th 1786

If royal gift will administer, he shall be at the Service of your Mares, but at present he seems too full of royalty, to have any thing to do with a plebean race. perhaps his stomach may come to him—if not, I shall wish he had never come from his most Catholic Majesty's Stables.

Your Papa has not been here, yet. I am just come in from a ride—the Dinner bell rings—and your Man says he must go off after it[1]—so offer me affectionately to all—and believe me to be sincerly Yrs

　　　　　　　　　　　　　　　　　　　Go: Washington

ALS, DLC: John Davis Batchelder Autograph Collection.

1. GW "Rid to Muddy hole and river Plantations" (*Diaries*, 4:310). John Augustine Washington arrived at Mount Vernon from Berkeley County on 9 May for a two-day visit (ibid., 327–28).

From Leonard Henley

Sir　　　　　　　　　　　　　　　　New Kent 14th Apl 1786

Your letter of the 2d of Apl Sent by Colo. Bassetts Boy, also that of the 10th Sent by Majr Washington's Servant came safe to hand,[1] & the information you have given me respecting the Corn that I Sent to you from the Esta. of the late Mr Custis gives me much Concern, but hope the Skipper to whom it was deliver'd did me the Justice to Say that the Corn was in good order when he recd it. that it was perfectly Sound & dry, beaten out on a plank'd Floor, & cleanly winnowed from the Chaff. but if he has fail'd to do me that Justice I can assure you that it was the Case. I am Sorry that it is not in my power to Send you the Peas you have wrote for having disposed of all that I had, & can hear of no person that has any to part with—I have Sent a few Pumkin Seed which was all I Could procure.[2]

I expect the price of the Corn you have had from Mr Custis's Esta. will be fixed at 18/ ℔ Barl as I have been Offer'd that price in ready money for all the Corn I had to Spare, & I believe that 25/ ℔ Barrl might be had on giving Some Credit. I am Sir Your mo: Obdt Servt

　　　　　　　　　　　　　　　　　　　Leonard Henley

ALS, DLC:GW.
    1. Neither letter has been found.
    2. See Henley to GW, 27 Feb., and GW to George Savage, 8 Feb., n.2.

From John Rumney, Jr.

Sir   W[hi]tehaven [England] 16th April 1786
    I have to acknowledge rect of your much esteem'd Favor of the 18th Novr last inclosing your Dft on Wakelyn Welsh Esqr. for £50 which is honor'd & rather overpays your Acct for the Flags sent, which Ballce our Store in Alexandria will pay you. The Person who procured those Flags would not prepare another Parcell at the same rate, having been a loosing Bargain to him, indeed no other Person would have undertaken them without 1½[d.] per Flag more. I hope they will fully answer your Purpose, which wd give me great Pleasure to hear.[1] I hope to have the Pleasure of seeing you in Virginia this Summer, as Mr Sanderson is coming Home.[2] I have the Honor to be with the Greatest respect, Sir Yr mo. obdt & hble Servt
                                        John Rumney

ALS, DLC:GW.
    1. GW wrote Rumney on 15 May before receiving this letter but wrote again on 5 June in response to it. The flagstones were for the floor of the piazza at Mount Vernon. See GW to Rumney, 22 June, 18 Nov. 1785, and Rumney to GW, 3 July, 5 Sept. 1785.
    2. Rumney was back in Virginia no later than 8 Oct. when he had dinner at Mount Vernon. Robert Sanderson left Virginia in July.

To John Armistead

Sir,   Mount Vernon 17th April 1786.
    It has been my hope since my return, that it would be unnecessary for me to remind you of the debt due to me from the Estate of your deceased Father; the speedy payment of which, at different times I have received assurances of from your self. Besides standing much in need of the money (which alone will, I persuade myself, be a stimulus to the discharge of my claim) it may be well for you to consider the nature of it, and with what rapidity a protested Bill encreases the original sum.[1] This is no

inducement however for me to let it lie; for, as I have just hinted, I can with truth declare to you that my want of the money is more essential to me, than the interest arising therefrom. I am Sir &c.

G: Washington

LB, DLC:GW.

John Armistead, the son of William Armistead (d. 1755) of Gloucester County, became before the Revolution a large planter in Caroline County where he served on the county court, in 1775 became captain of one of the new militia companies, and served as sheriff in 1780.

1. In the final settlement of the estate of Daniel Parke Custis in November 1761, a debt of £132.1.8 sterling at 5 percent interest owed to the Custis estate by the estate of William Armistead was assigned to Martha Washington. Despite two payments totaling £260.12.2, the debt stood at £104.3.3 at the end of 1772. See doc. III-B, n.14, in Settlement of the Daniel Parke Custis Estate, 20 April 1759–5 November 1761. Receiving no response to this letter, GW wrote Armistead again on 29 Dec. 1786, declaring that he would have to resort to the courts if he did not receive what was owed him "without more delay." More than two years later, on 17 Mar. 1789, GW wrote his attorney John Marshall about the Armistead debt and enclosed "a protested bill of Exchange drawn in 1765 by the Exts. of William Armsted Esqr. in my favor," which Marshall was "to take the necessary steps to recover." (For reference to a protested bill drawn by the Armistead executors, see *Papers, Colonial Series*, 6:259, n.14). Marshall's reply of 8 April 1789 has not been found, but apparently he reported that the executors claimed the debt had been transferred from William Armistead's estate to John Armistead. GW responded to Marshall on 11 April 1789 that he had "been lately informed that Mrs Armsteads sons are dead and have left their families in not very good circumstances. If this is the case—and the payment of the debt due to me would distress them," Marshall was not to "proceed any further in the matter." No earlier letters to or from John Armistead have been found.

To Noah Webster

Sir,   Mount Vernon Apri 17th 1786

Mr Lee, yesterday evening, gave me the pleasure of receiving your letter of the 31st Ulto, and the book with wch it was accompanied—for both, I pray you to accept my thanks. The author, some time ago, had the goodness to send me two copies of the poem.[1]

I am equally obliged to you, Sir, for your kind assurance of looking out for an Instructor for the little folks of this family;

but believe I have no occasion to trouble you in this business, now. Sometime in the course of last summer, when Gen. Lincoln was here, I made particular enquiry of him on this head; and though he could not, at that time, point out a character which he thought would answer my purposes in all respects, yet he has lately named a Gentlemn of whom he speaks in high terms; and has given the conditions on which he wd come; which being acceded to on my part, and a letter written to that effect, I conceive the matter is closed. If it should be otherwise, I will again give you the trouble of hearing from me on this subject.

My best wishes will attend you in your lectures, and in the prosecution of your design of refining the language and improving the system of education, so as to reduce it to perfect regularity. I am, Sir Yr Most Obedt Hble Servt

Go: Washington

ALS, NN: Washington Collection; LB, DLC:GW.

1. The "book" was Timothy Dwight's *The Conquest of Canaan*. In his diary GW records Arthur Lee's arrival on Saturday, 15 April, and his departure on Sunday, 16 April, "after breakfast" (*Diaries*, 4:311, 312).

To William Hartshorne

Sir,   Mount Vernon 19th April 1786.

I am sorry that I have been so troublesome & teasing to you on accot of the seeds you were so obliging as to endeavour to procure for me; but as my Boat is sent to Town, I am induced to ask if they are arrived, that they may in that case embrace the present conveyance.[1] If they are not already at hand, I shall be obliged to you for countermanding the order for the Buck wheat, as it is now totally useless for the experimental purposes for which I wanted it. This is nearly the case with respect to the Flax seed; but I will try late sowing, rather than let the season pass over altogether—consequently will wait a few days longer for this, in which time if it does not arrive, I pray it may be countermanded also. I am &c.

G: Washington

LB, DLC:GW.

1. GW asked Hartshorne in January or earlier to secure buckwheat and flax seeds for him. See Hartshorne to GW, 10 February.

To Thomas Brereton

Sir,   Mt Vernon 20th Apl 1786

Within these few days I have received your letter of the 12th, & some time ago, I recollect to have been favored with another letter from you, which in the hurry of business got over-looked.[1]

It is now more than two years, since indirectly I obtained a sight of the deceas'd Mrs Savage's will[2]—I then thought, & still do think it strange that the Executors of this will, should never have made any official communication thereof to the Trustees of that Lady in this country; nor have made any direct enquiry concerning the situation of her affairs here. These may be summed up in a few words; & will be found to be as follows.

When matters came to extremity between Doctr Savage & his wife—& Mr Fairfax & myself were obliged to put the trust Bond in suit to recover her annuity; the Doctor made use of all the chicanery of Law & Lawyers, to procrastinate the Suit; which the tardiness of our Courts (& during one period of the revolution the suspension of justice) but too well enabled him to effect. It was therefore long before a judgment at common Law could be obtained; & this was no sooner done, than he threw the matter into Chancery, where I am told, for I have had no share in the management of this business for the last ten years, (that is since I took the command of the American forces) it has lain ever since. I believe Mr Fairfax has done every thing in his power to bring the matter to issue; & I have heard, I think from himself, that there is now a probability of its happening soon. With great truth I can assure you that not one farthing of Mrs Savage's annuity was ever paid to the Trustees; whilst we have been obliged to advance money out of our own pockets to carry on the prosecution—& whilst, moreover, from a representation of the distress that Lady was involved in, I gave her a Bill to the amot of £53—on Jas Gildart Esqr. of Liverpool—which is still due to me.

This is the best Accot I am able to give you of the Trust, & you are at liberty to communicate the purport of it to Mrs Innis. I am &c.

G: Washington

LB, DLC:GW; LS, sold by Robert F. Batchelder, item 258, catalog 77, September 1990.

1. Brereton's earlier letter has not been found.

2. GW had his indirect "sight" of Margaret Savage's will in December 1783. See Hanna Moore to GW, 20 Jan. 1785, n.2.

From Joseph Eckley

Sir,   Boston 20 April 1786

It was the desire of the Revd Dr Gordon who, a few days ago, embarked for Europe, that according to his own practice I would weekly send to you the Independent Chronicle printed in this Town. I have the honor of enclosing one of the Papers for your Excellency at this time; requesting you to permit me to assure you that it will afford me very great satisfaction to continue so to do in a regular manner, agreably to the Doctors wish, & my promise to him.[1] With great Respect I am Your Excellency's Most Obedient & Obliged Humble Servant

Joseph Eckley

ALS, DLC:GW.

Joseph Eckley (1750–1811), who came from London to New Jersey in 1767 and received his bachelor and masters degrees from Princeton in 1775, had been pastor of Old South Church in Boston since 1779.

1. See William Gordon to GW, 9 April, n.1, and GW to Eckley, 10 May.

To William Gordon

Dr Sir,   M[ount] Vernon 20th Aprl 1786.

Mr Lund Washington having expressed a wish to quit business & live in retirement & ease, I could not oppose his inclination; & his having carried these desires into effect, that kind of business which he usually transacted for me, is now thrown on my shoulders in addition to what they bore before, & has left me less time than ever for my numerous correspondences & other avocations. I mention this by way of apology for not having acknowledged the receipt of your several late favors, at an earlier date.[1]

As soon as your subscription papers came to my hands, I offered one in Alexandria & sent another to Fredericksburgh: from the first, a specific return has been made of the subscribers & is now enclosed; from the other, eleven pounds have been sent me without the paper; the Gentleman (the Hon[orabl]e James Mercer Esqr. one of the Judges of our General Court) having informed me that he would take it with him to Richmond, and endeavor to encrease the number of subscribers there.[2] This sum of eleven pounds added to the amount of the paper inclosed, makes £42 with which I have bought a Bill on Rhode Island. I endeavoured to get one on Boston, but could not without waiting; which I thought might be more inconvenient, than the negotiation at the former place.[3]

Your Cypher came safely to hand—I have not had leisure to examine it, but presuming no difficulty will arise in the use, I have laid it by 'till occasion may call it forth.[4] From the purport of your letters, you must be on the eve of your departure for Europe. My best wishes, in wch Mrs Washington & the family join me, are offered for a prosperous voyage, & the accomplishment of your plans. I am Dr Sir &c.

G: Washington

Note—the Bill referred to in the above is drawn by Josiah Watson & Co., on Messrs Cromel & Caleb Child, Merchants, Warren, Rhode Island for £42 at three days sight with or without advice; & is dated the 19th April 1786.[5]

LB, DLC:GW.
    1. See the editorial note, Farm Reports, 26 Nov. 1785–16 April 1786.
    2. See GW to James Mercer, 20 Jan., n.3.
    3. See GW to Benjamin Lincoln, 20 April, 7 June, and Benjamin Lincoln, Jr., to GW, 24 Sept., as well as note 1 of the latter document.
    4. See Gordon to GW, 4 February.
    5. See note 3.

To Benjamin Lincoln

Dear Sir,   Mount Vernon Aprl 20th 1786
    As Doctr Gordons departure for England is an event that was to have taken place about this time & may have happened I take the liberty, in that case, of requesting the favor of you to do what shall appear right with the inclosed Subscription Paper & Bill.[1]

I will make no apology for the trouble this request may give you as I persuade myself your inclination to serve the Doctr will keep pace with mine, and neither can have any other motive in the business than to serve & oblige him. With every sentiment of esteem & regard, I am—Dear Sir Yr most Obedt & Affecte Sert

Go: Washington

ALS, MH: Autograph File; LB, DLC:GW.
  1. See GW to William Gordon, this date.

From Henry Lee, Jr.

My dear Genl   New York 21st April 86
    Your very polite reply to my two letters reached me a few days past.[1]
    It is impossible for my mind so thoroughly impressed with testimonials of your friendship, when that friendship operated both to my honor and happiness to ascribe any act of yours in which I am interested to disregard or neglect. My cheif object in my correspondence with you, was to manifest the unabated respect which continues to govern my feelings, when change of situation and circumstances, forbid the derivati[o]n of my attachment from any principles, but those bottomed on the purest and warmest respect. Then my dear Sir, let me hope that you will not consider it as due or expected that you should be regular in your replys, but rather be governed by inclination and leisure, otherwise I shall be forced from the same feelings which induced me to commence a correspondence so truely agreable, to decline the continuance of it. Your communications with respect to the process of our internal navigation has given to me and our countrymen here, the highest satisfaction, for certainly no event comprehends more fully the strength and future consequence of our particular country than the cementing to the interest of Virginia by the strong ties of commerce the western world. This I beleive will take place effectually if the potomac & James river companys succeed in their exertions before the navigation of the Missisippi becomes free to the western emigrants. I have my doubts whether good policy does not dictate forcibly every measure which tends to delay to distant time the free use

of that river—It is very certain that the spanish court are in no temper for admitting it at present, in any degree, nor will they ever consent to it as long as they retain in subjection their American colonys—I have taken the liberty to shew in some private circles your observations with respect to the present prospect of our fœderal affairs, and I flatter myself the justice and decision of your remarks will aid the friends to the Union in this city in their exertions to incline the Assembly of this state to adopt the revenue system asked for by Congress, and at this period essential to the existence of the Union.

The lower house have passed the impost fettered with conditions which render it inadmissible by Congress. I hope the senate will amend it, and that at length we shall be possessed of some permanent and adequate fund for the discharge of our foreign debt.

We have no accounts by the packet of the progress of our negotiators with the barbary powers, nor have we much reason to hope for a tolerable termination of their mission—The british cabinent evidence whenever they can their zeal to destroy our commerce, and they certainly will succeed in their favorite plan, unless the states give adequate powers to Congress to counteract by commercial regulations the injurys imposed on our trade.

I enclose the late gazzettes a letr from England for you, and the papers you require.[2]

Please to present me to your Lady and accept my best wishes for your health and happiness. With the most respectful attachment I am dear General, your ob. sert

Henry Lee Junr

I enclose a plan for the government of militia, which does great honor to its author.[3]

ALS, DLC:GW.

1. GW wrote on 5 April.

2. The only thing GW requested in his letter of 5 April was a copy of the newspaper in which Lewis Littlepage's attack on John Jay appeared. The letter was from Arthur Young (see GW to Lee, 18 June).

3. On 18 Mar. Henry Knox transmitted to Congress *A Plan for the General Arrangement of the Militia of the United States* (New York, 1786).

From Thomas Ringgold Tilghman

Sir   Baltimore 22d April. 1786
I have the most melancholy Task to perform, that was ever yet imposed upon me; that of making you acquainted with the Death of my poor Brother Tench. Painful however as it is, I thought a duty not to be dispensed with towards one for whom he had so high a Reverence & so warm an Attachment as for yourself. Not above three days before his death every symptom bade fair for a speedy Recovery, when an unexpected Change took place, which in a short time destroyed every hope. He retained his senses perfectly till within a few hours of the time that he expired, which was in the Evening of the 18th, when he went off without the least pain & even without a struggle: As it is our Wish to settle his Affairs as speedily as possible, I enclose your account, the Bale of which £54.10.4 you will be pleased to pay into the hands of Messrs Josiah Watson & Co. of Alexanda which mode of settling it, is agreable to his Intentions.[1] I am, Sir with the highest Respect Yr most obt servt

Thos R. Tilghman

ALS, DLC:GW.
Thomas Ringgold Tilghman (1765–1789) was one of James and Ann Francis Tilghman's twelve children and the youngest of six brothers.
1. See GW to Tilghman, 10 May.

From Francis Asbury

Honoured Sir   Alexandria April 24th 1786
Give me leave to prensent you, with one of our Prayer Books, and another to your Lady. Please to accept the Sermons also to your candid perusal.[1] Receive them as a small token of my great respect and veneration for your Person who am your most obedient friend & Servant

Francis Asbury

ALS, PHi: Dreer Collection—American Clergy.
1. *An Address to the Annual Subscribers for the Support of Cokesbury-College, and to the Members of the Methodist Society,* by Thomas Coke and Asbury, a pamphlet printed in New York in 1787, was in GW's library at the time of his death. Francis Asbury (1745–1816) was the leader of the Methodist Episcopal Church in America.

From Benjamin Grymes

Dr Sr   Eagles Nest Apl 24th &Ca
    I received your favour a few days past, and have now the plea-
sure of sending you the two Does from this place, and a third
which I received to day from Chatham, I have pd the Man 18/
for their passage, and think it proper to mention it for he might
otherwise charge you for taking of them up.¹ I am very sorry it
is not in my power to spare you any peaze. I believe I can get
you a few bushels at Pt royal if I can, I will send them to you by
the middle of May if not sooner—Our best respects to you and
yr Lady I am with the greatt respt yr Most Ob. H. St
                                                    B. Grymes

ALS, DLC:GW.
    1. See William Fitzhugh to GW, 17 January.

To George Augustine Washington

Dear George,   Stafford Court Ho[use] 24th Apl 1786
    The extreme heaviness of the roads occasioned by the late
rains, and gullied situation, prevented my getting further than
this place yesterday. and now I am waiting a while for a cessation
of rain, rather than to take Joe out in it.¹
    It did not occur to me when I was making out my Memoran-
dum for you, that the cause which prevented Morris from proceeding in his field for experiments, might not be unfavourable
for scratching over with the harrow (which was then idle) the
grd in which the clover Seed failed last; and which I would wish
to put in Timothy. Should this letter therefore reach you in
time—it is to desire, in case the harrow is not otherwise employed, that you will have it run over the ground last mentioned
just to loosen a little of the Soil on the top, then sow the Timothy
Seed, and cross harrow it—this I presume, will enable the Seed
to take root. I request this on the supposition that the harrow
and Oxen are idle, for if they are otherwise engaged, I do not
desire it.²
    As the Season is fast advancing when Corn should be in the
ground, no plow work should be lost that can be avoided—

therefore, if they cannot go on with the experiment, they may be listing, or doing something to facilitate this business.[3]

Let the farmer get forks and poles and support the drilled Wheat behind the stables; without which I fear it will Col-l[ap]se, & I shall miss saving seed from it. If there is any thing else he can be employed usefully about, and he is inclined to do, it will be better than idleness—Let him also ride round all the plantations with you, and hear his observations, if he points out any thing that appears preferable in the mode of working, it might be tried—Give my love to all at home—the weather seems inclined to moderate, & I am preparing to proceed. Sincerely & affectionately I am, Yrs

Go: Washington

ALS, MiU-C: Schoff Collection.

1. In his diary entry for Sunday, 23 April, GW wrote: "Set off after breakfast, on a journey to Richmond—to acknowledge in the General Court some Deeds for Land sold by me as Attorney for Colo. George Mercer which, it seems, could not be executed without" (*Diaries*, 4:316). For the sale of George Mercer's Virginia property in November 1774, which GW conducted, see GW to John Tayloe, 30 Nov. 1774, n.2. Joe was GW's postilion.

2. It was at this point that George Augustine Washington, as the new estate manager at Mount Vernon, took over from GW the task of assembling and writing the weekly farm reports. See the editorial note in Farm Reports, 26 Nov. 1785–16 April 1786. For George Augustine Washington's Mount Vernon farm reports, see CD-ROM:GW.

3. Listing was preparing land for a crop of cotton or Indian corn by making ridges and furrows with the plow or beds and alleys with the hoe.

From Robert Morris

Dear Sir   Philad[elphi]a April 26th 1786

I am happy to confirm what Mr Dalby will have informed you off, the Successfull Issue of his Suit respecting his Slave, could any interference on my part have been usefull, your letter would have commanded it, indeed I had done him before what little service I could when his Petition was before the Assembly from a perfect Conviction both of the Injustice and impolicy of the treatment he had met with. The Society which attacked him tread on popular ground, and as their Views are disinterested as to themselves, and *sometimes* very laudable as to the objects of their Compassion, it is not a very pleasant thing to Attack them & this consideration deters Mr Dalby from seeking redress at Law for the Expense & trouble they have occasioned, altho I think he would meet a just determination in our Courts of Law.[1] We are happy to hear that Mrs Washington & you are well, Mrs Morris is at present occupied in carefull attention to our youngest Son in the Small pox which is now out, & very fircely. She joins me in praying Mrs Washington & you to accept our best wishes for the long Continuance of your Health & happiness. Poor Tilghman, you my Dear Sir have lost in him a most faithfull and Valuable Friend, He was to me the same I esteemed him, very, very, much, and I lament the loss of him exceedingly. I am with sincere attachment Dear Sir Your most Obedient humble Servant

Robt Morris

ALS, DLC:GW.
   1. GW wrote Morris on 12 April about the attempt by the Society of Friends in Philadelphia to free Philip Dalby's slave.

From Doilliamson

Sir,   Versailles 28th Aprl 1786
   I am exceeding happy that the Marquis de la Fayette, gave me an opportunity of doing something agreeable to you.
   I was overjoyed at receiving the letter which you did me the honor to write, it never came to my hands 'till the other day on acct of a journey which I had taken.[1]
   Madam Doilliamson has charged me to do myself the honor of telling you, that she felt very sensibly the acknowledgements which you made her, & is delighted that her favorite gave you as much pleasure as she experienced in offering it to the greatest man of the Age, the Friend of Mankind & Liberty—that he may long enjoy that happiness which he has procured to Millions is the prayer of us both—I am, with respect Sir Yr most Obedt & most Hble Servt

Doilliamson

Translation, DLC:GW; ALS, in French, DLC:GW. The ALS is transcribed in CD-ROM:GW.

1. GW wrote the comte Doilliamson (d'Oilliamson) on 1 Sept. 1785 to thank him and his wife for the seven hounds that they had sent him (GW to Lafayette, 1 Sept. 1785, n.2).

From Alexander White

Sir   Woodville 29th April 1786

I have at length so far settled the affairs of General Lees Estate as to be enabled to pay his American debts. it will give me pleasure to discharge the account due to your Excellency—I am sorry you did not take a Bond to secure the interest, but do not think myself authorised to supply the defect.[1] With Sentiments of the highest respect I am Your Excellencys most Obt Servt

Alexr White

ALS, DLC:GW.

1. For Alexander White's acting as attorney for the settlement of Gen. Charles Lee's American estate, see especially Sidney Lee to GW, 23 May 1784, and notes. GW sent Tobias Lear in December 1786 to collect what was due him (GW to Lear, 30 Nov. 1786).

From John Hopkins

Sir   Richmond May 1st 1786.

Enclosd I have the honor to transmit you the Treasurer's receipt for the sum of fifteen pounds lodged by you with me, for the purpose of making the first payment on your five shares in the James River Company.[1] I have spoken to Mr Brown respating the expences of recording your deed &c.—but the business not yet being done, he cannot ascertain the amount—As soon, as the Account can be procured, the Money shall be paid, and his rect transmitted to you.[2] With the most perfect respect I am Sir Your most obt & very Humble Servant

Jno. Hopkins

ALS, DLC:GW.

John Hopkins (c.1757–1827) was commissioner of Continental loans for Virginia and a Richmond businessman. James Buchanan was treasurer of the James River Company.

1. GW records in his Cash Accounts in April paying out £15 as "my Adva. for Five Shares in the Jas River Coy" (Ledger B, 223). GW was in Richmond from 26 to 28 April. See also Edmund Randolph to GW, 2 Mar., and notes 1 and 2.

2. GW went to Richmond to attend to business regarding the sale of George Mercer's Virginia property in November 1774. See GW to George Augustine Washington, 24 April, n.1. On 27 April, in Richmond, GW "Acknowledged in the General Court a Deed to James Mercer Esqr. for the Lotts he and I bought at the Sale of his deceased Brother Colo. George Mercer and received a reconveyance from him of my part thereof" (*Diaries*, 4:318). Presumably it was to this deed that Hopkins was referring. When writing "respating," perhaps Hopkins meant to write "respecting." John Brown was the clerk of the Virginia General Court.

To Martin Cockburn

Sir,   Mount Vernon May 3d 1786
    Being informed that you receive the lists of Taxable property in Truro Parish, I do, tho' late, send you that of mine.[1]
    Do you hire your Negro Tailor by the year? If so, on what terms? and is he now, or will he soon be, disengaged? My Compliments, in which Mrs Washington joins, are offered to Mrs Cockburn. With esteem—I am—Sir Yr most Obed. Servt
                                                            Go: Washington

ALS, NIC.
    Martin Cockburn, of Springfield in Fairfax County, who from 1770 to 1779 served on the Truro Parish vestry, was at this time tax commissioner for Fairfax County. His wife, Ann, was the daughter of Jeremiah Bronaugh.
    1. The lists of taxable property have not been found.

From Benjamin Lincoln

My dear General   Boston [May] 3d 1786
    I was yesterday honored with the receipt of your Excellencys favor of the 16th Ulto.[1]
    It is probable that Mr Lear will be with you by the first of June I expect him from Portsmouth New Hampshire in about six days he will soon after commence his journey for Virginia I hope & trust your Excellency will find him a Gentleman of an amiable character. With real esteem & affection I have the honor of being Your Excellencys most Obedient Servant
                                                            B: Lincoln

ALS, NN: Emmet Collection. Lincoln clearly dates this letter "March 3d," but it certainly was not written before Lincoln received GW's letter of 10 April. Its contents suggest it was written in early May. See Tobias Lear to GW, 7 May, and Lincoln to GW, 9 May.

1. No letter from GW to Lincoln of 16 April has been found, but Lincoln may well be referring to GW's letter of 10 April.

Letter not found: from Henry L. Charton, 5 May 1786. On 20 May GW wrote Charton: "The letter which you did me the favor to write to me from Philadelphia, on the 5th instt, came safely to hand."

Letter not found: to Battaile Muse, 6 May 1786. On 4 June Muse wrote GW: "Your Favour dated the 6th may Came To hand."[1]

1. Muse's letter of 4 June appears to be in response to GW's letter of 12 May which in turn was GW's response to Muse's letter of 6 May; Muse may have meant to cite GW's letter of 12 May rather than a missing letter of 6 May.

From Battaile Muse

Honourable Sir, Belvoir May 6th 1786

The waggons that stored my wheat on the roads Last winter I did not Expect would have brought the wheat To your Mill as they had neglected their duty so Long. at Last they have delivered it—which makes more than the Quantity Engaged—I shall be oblige to you To buy it at 5/6 ℔ Bushel[1] or to let it be ground for me I have sold Wheat to Colo Griffin at that price. I am Sir your Very Hble Servant

Battaile Muse

ALS, DLC:GW.

1. In Ledger B, 213, GW credits Muse between 17 Feb. and 6 May with £230.15 for 735 bushels of wheat. For GW's purchase of wheat from Muse in December 1785, see Muse to GW, 28 Nov., 10 Dec. 1785, 12 Jan. 1786, and GW to Muse, 16 Dec. 1785. GW wrote Muse on 12 May refusing Muse's offer to sell him the "surplus wheat," apparently fifty bushels belonging to Dr. Wilson Selden (see Muse to GW, 15 Nov. 1785, 4 June, 11 July 1786). At the same time, GW agreed to manufacture and pack flour for Muse, and Muse sent to GW's mill 500 bushels of wheat (GW to Muse, 12 May, 1 July, Muse to GW, 4 June). See also Muse to GW, 31 Aug., 26 Nov. 1786, and GW to Muse, 25 July, 1 Aug., and 4 Dec. 1786. Colonel Griffin may be Samuel Griffin of Williamsburg.

From Tobias Lear

Honored Sir   Boston 7th May 1786
     General Lincoln has favoured me with the perusal of your
Letter of the 10th Ulto wherein you mention your acceding to
the sum of two Hun[dre]d Dollars in addition to the Stipulations
mentioned in your last for my services for a year, and desire that
I may come on as soon as is convenient; if I find an opportunity
of going by Water I shall embrace it immediately and be with
your Excellency in about three week, but if an opportunity does
not offer in a few days I shall set off by the Stages, and very
probably be at Mount Vernon soon after you receive this.[1] I am
with sentiments of the greatest Respect your Excellency's most
Obedt & Hume Servt

                                              Tobias Lear

ALS, DLC:GW.
     1. Lear arrived at Mount Vernon on 29 May. He brought letters from Sam-
uel Haven and John Langdon (1741–1819). Langdon was president of New
Hampshire in 1785 and 1786, and both men were from Portsmouth. Lear also
brought a letter from Joseph Willard (1732–1804), the former president of
Harvard College. See also Benjamin Lincoln to GW, 9 May. The text of Langdon's letter, dated 5 May, reads: "Mr Tobias Lear, a relation of mine, will have
the honor of delivering this letter, which serves only to introduce him to your
Excellency's kindness, and protection. He called this morning, and informed
me that he should set out on Friday next for Virginia, where he is to be im-
ployed, and to make one of your Excellency's family. This young Gentleman
sustains a very fair Character, and it will give me the highest pleasure, should
he meet your Approbation: I am sure his goodness of heart will lead him to
make every exertion to please. With the most cordial wishes for your health,
and happiness" (DLC:GW).
     Samuel Haven wrote on 6 May: "Your well known candour will permit a
stranger to address a Line to your Excellency in Favour of a young gentleman
already recommended to your kind Notice by Gentlemen who have had the
honor of your Excellcy knowledge far more than I can pretend to boast.
     "Mr Lear is a Child of my Parish—And I am happy to say, has conducted,
from his Childhood to this manly period of his Life with Marks of Genius,
Modesty & Virtue—His Character thro' an Accademical Education & ever
since has been irreproachable I doubt not your Excellency will find him a
young Gentleman possest of Principles of the strickest honour, & integrity of
Heart—As We Esteem him much, We are very happy that the *great Disposer* of
all human Events has opened before him the Door of your Patronage. Permit
me Hond Sir to be numbered among the many Thousands who hail you as
the honoured Instrument of their Country's Salvation. deign to Accept a cordiallity of Duty, an affection to your *Excellency's* Person & Lady—in the fer-

vent & daily Prayers offered to Allmighty God for the rich abundance of divine Blessings, both Temporal & Spiritual on your Excellency & Lady and *all* who, under your Excellencys Guidance & Command have assisted in the present happy Revolution—by one who wishes to be so happy as to promote Virtue, & a Servant to that divine Lord whose Kingdom is not of this world—and who is with the highest Duty & Esteem your Excellcy most obedient Servant" (DLC:GW).

Willard's letter is dated 15 May: "Mr Lear, the Bearer of this, spent four years in this University, to very good advantage. He pursued his studies with diligence and success, and shone as a Scholar. His temper and deportment were amiable, his morals unblemished, and in all respects he approved himself to the Government of the University. Since taking his Bachelor's degree with us, which was at the Commencement in 1783. he has been in business, and has sustained a very fair character. I find that he is going to live in your family, in the capacity of your Secretary. From my acquaintance with him, I am persuaded, Sir, that you will find him agreeable; and I doubt not, he will fill his department to your satisfaction. Happy should I be, Sir, to see your Excellency in this part of America, where you first took the field, at the head of our armies: Happy to have it in my power personally to testify my esteem, veneration and gratitude to the Patriot and Hero, who, in the most disinterested manner, has gloriously and successfully asserted the liberties of his country, and established that independence, which not only secures the rights of the citizens of America, but has the happiest aspect upon the liberties and happiness of mankind" (DLC:GW).

GW waited for nearly a year, until 10 Mar. 1787, to acknowledge these letters.

To Thomas Cresap

Sir,   Mt Vernon 8th May 1786.

Your letter of the 8th of last month came to my hands just as I was leaving home for Richmond, which is the reason you have not received an earlier acknowledgment of it.[1]

I am not a member of, nor am I in any manner interested in the affairs of the Ohio Company—nor indeed do I know at this time, of whom it consists, further than of those claiming under, & mentioned by you—of Colo. Mason & of the heir of my brother Augustine, who lives at the distance of an hundred miles from me; & is one whom I scarcely ever saw.[2]

I feel myself much obliged by your polite attention in offering me a Lott at the mouth of the South branch; it will, I dare say, be a convenient spot, whereon to establish a Town. I am Sir, &c.

G. Washington

LB, DLC:GW.

Thomas Cresap (1694–c.1790), the prominent frontiersman who had lived in western Maryland since about 1730, was one of the organizing members of the Ohio Company in 1749.

1. Letter not found.

2. William Augustine Washington inherited Pope's Creek plantation (Wakefield) in Westmoreland County at the death in 1742 of his father, Augustine Washington. He lived at this time at Haywood across the creek from the site of Wakefield, which burned in 1780.

To Thomas Freeman

Sir,   Mo[un]t Vernon 8th May 1786

Being informed that Mrs Crawford is on the point of having her negroes sold to discharge a Debt due from her late husband, Colo. Crawford, to Mr James Cleveland, for whom you are Agent; I will, rather than such an event shall take place, agree to apply any money of mine, which may be in your hands, towards the discharge of the execution; and desire, in that case, you will receive such security as Mrs Crawford can give for reimbursing me.[1] I am Sir &c.

G: Washington

LB, DLC:GW.

1. See Hannah Crawford's earlier plea for help, 4 June 1784. See also her letter to GW of 16 Mar. 1787, written after the Virginia legislature on 9 Jan. 1787 had acted positively on her petition for aid as the widow of William Crawford. Crawford was killed while serving "his country during the late war" (*House of Delegates Journal, 1786–1790*, 83, 150). In 1775 GW sent James Cleveland out to his Ohio lands with a party of workers (see GW's instructions to Cleveland, March 1775, and Cleveland to GW, 12, 21 May 1775).

To Thomas Smith

Sir;   Mount Vernon 8th May 1786.

Vale Crawford died indebted to me—say One hundred pounds Virginia Curry—more or less. Previously thereto, he wrote me the letter dated Jacobs Creek, May 8th 1774[1] and accompanied it with the Bill of Sale herewith transmitted dated May 8th 1774.

Quære, Is this Bill now valid?

Will it secure my debt? This is all I want.

And can it be recovered without hazarding a defeat which may add cost without benefit.

If these points should be determined in the affirmative, I would wish you to prosecute my claim so far as to secure my debt, but not otherwise. In haste, but with much esteem—I am—Sir Yr Most Obedt Servt

Go: Washington

ALS, NhD; ADfS, owned (1975) by Dr. Calderon Home, New Orleans, La.; LB, DLC:GW.

1. Valentine Crawford wrote to GW on 6 and 7 May 1774. In the draft GW correctly identifies the letter as one of 6 May 1774. In his letter of 6 May Crawford wrote: "as you are Largeley Engaged for Me and So Kindley wase My Securety to the Sheriff I have Sent you a Bill of Sa⟨le⟩." In his diary entry for 8 May 1786, GW wrote: "In the Evening a Captn. Whaley from Yohiogany came in on some business respecting the Affairs of the deceased Val. Crawford and Hugh Stephenson; to whom I gave, under cover to Thos. Smith Esqr. (my Lawyer in that Country) a Bill of Sale and the letter wch. inclosed it which the said Vale. Crawford had sent me, in the Mo[nth] of May 1774 as Security for what he owed me, and to indemnify me for my engagements in his behalf— to see if they were valid, & would cover the debt he owed me, as they never had been recorded" (*Diaries*, 4:326). Smith was unable to act for GW in this matter, and so GW secured Charles Simms's services (see GW to Simms and to Smith, both 22 Sept. 1786, and John Minton to GW, 2 Mar. 1787). According to GW's account with Valentine Crawford in Ledger B, 27, Crawford on 13 Feb. 1775 owed only £35.10, which GW's clerk credits to Valentine Crawford "By settlement" at an unspecified date.

From Benjamin Lincoln

My dear general   Hingham [Mass.] May 9th 1786

Mr Lear will have the honor of delivering this. I have the highest expectations that his services will be acceptable. He wishes to pursue in his liesure hours, the study of the law; his want of books may retard his progress therein—Had I been acquainted with any Gentleman of the bar in your neighbourhood, I would have solicited the loan of some books for him, but, as I am not permit me to ask your Excellencys attention to this matter, hereby you will greatly serve my young friend and confer new obligations on me.[1]

I shall leave this part of the State in a few days for Passamaquady—we are attempting to make a settlement there—we shall
be near neighbours to the refugees If they do not quarrel among
themselves, they will I trust live in peace. I have the honor of
being My dear General with the highest esteem Your Excel-
lenceys Obedent humble servant

B. Lincoln

ALS, DLC:GW; AL (incomplete), MiDbGr. The first page of the incomplete
letter has only slightly different wording.

1. Lear wrote John Langdon from Mount Vernon on 24 July 1786: "As you
were so kind, upon my leaving Portsmouth, as to desire me to write to you,
and inform you of my welfare, and how I liked my situation here. I can with
pleasure assure you that I enjoy my health perfectly well, and find my situation
very agreeable. I have every attention paid me by His Excellency and all the
family that I can wish; the duty required of me is small, and agreeable: more
than one half of my time is at my own disposal, which I employ in reading the
Law; the General has been so good as to procure me the favr of any books, or
assistance, that I may need in the course of my reading, from Mr [Charles]
Lee a Lawyer in Alexandria, and he seems desireous upon every occasion to
promote whatever he thinks is agreeable to me" (NhHi: Langdon-Elwyn Family Papers). See Langdon's letter to GW recommending Lear, which is printed
in note 1, Lear to GW, 7 May.

Lincoln wrote GW the next day, 10 May: "My dear General[,] Mr Bowen
will have the honor of waiting upon your Excellency and delivering this. Having, some years since, lost his health he was induced to solicit but it was with
difficulty he obtained a release from his employment, as a minister of one of
the congregational Churches in Boston, as he shared largely in the affections
of his people—Being now much better he wishes to assume his character as a
public teacher, and that in some of the southern States, as their climate he
supposes would be more friendly to his constitution than a northern one. It is
with pleasure that I can recommend him to your Excellency as a Gentleman
of abilities, education, integrity, a lover of his country and fellow men—knowing that such a character will always meet your Excellencys kind attention I
have ventured to assure him that if he should set down in any part of your
country you would be his friend—I have the honor of being My dear General
with the most perfect esteem your Excellencys obt servant B. Lincoln"
(DLC:GW). GW does not record in his diary a visit from Penuel Bowen, who
was the former minister of New South Church in Boston and since 1783 a
shop owner in Boston. Bowen went to South Carolina in 1786. On 14 July
1788 he was installed rector of St. John's Parish, Collington, in South Carolina.
He died later in that year.

To Joseph Eckley

Sir, Mount Vernon 10th May 1786.

I have had the honor to receive your favor of the 20th ulto and its enclosure. I was indebted to Doctr Gordon before he left the Country, for the Boston Independant Chronicle; and am so since to your goodness for offering to continue them. The Doctr sent these papers unasked, after having read them himself (being a subscriber)—but as their continuation must be attended with expence & trouble, you would oblige me by withholding them. To be candid, my avocations are so numerous that I very rarely find time to look into Gazettes after they come to me. I feel myself, however not less indebted to your politeness, & obliging offer, by the non-acceptance of it. With respect I am Sir Your Most Obt and obliged Servant

G: Washington

LB, DLC:GW.

To Adrienne, Marquise de Lafayette

Madam, Mount Vernon 10th May 1786.

Of all the correspondencies with which I am honored, none has given me more pleasure than yours; none which I am more desireous of continuing, or more ambitious to deserve. What then my Dr Madam, must have been my mortification when, instead of receiving the letter you did me the honor to write to me on the 15th of April last year, in due time, it was not 'till sometime in the course of last month, that I received it at all, & the parcels with which you were pleased to accompany it. By mistake these parcels lay at Bordeaux a considerable time after they had arrived there, before it was discovered for whom they were intended, & then were sent by a Vessel which took a very circuitous voyage to the Country. I trouble you with this detail of matters by way of apology for what otherwise might appear a want of sensibility in me for your distinguished and valuable favors, than which nothing is, or can be more flattering & pleasing to my vanity.

The tokens of regard with which Miss de la Fayette & my name-sake have honored the young folks of this family, will ce-ment the friendship which seems to be rising in their tender breasts; & will encrease those flames of it which they have imbibed from their parents, to which nothing can add strength, but the endearments which flow from personal interviews, & the unreserved exchange of liberal sentiments. Will you not then Madam, afford them this opportunity? May we hope for it soon? If the assurances of the sincerest esteem & affection: if the varieties of uncultivated nature; the novelty of exchanging the gay & delightful scenes of Paris with which you are surrounded, for the rural amusements of a country in its infancy; if the warbling notes of the feathered songsters on our Lawns & Meads, can for a moment make you forget the melody of the Opera, & the pleasures of the Court—these, all invite you to give us this honour, & the opportunity of expressing to you personally, those sentiments of attachment & love with which you have inspired us.

The noon-tide of life is now passed with Mrs Washington & myself, and all we have to do is to spend the evening of our days in tranquillity, & glide gently down a stream which no human effort can ascend. We must therefore, however reluctantly it is done, forego the pleasures of such a visit as you kindly invite us to make. But the case with you, is far otherwise—Your days are in their me[r]idian brightness. In the natural order of things you have many years to come, in which you may endulge yourself in all the amusements which variety can afford, and different countries produce; & in receiving those testimonies of respect, which every one in the United States would wish to render you.

My Mother will receive the compliments you honor her with, as a flattering mark of your attention; & I shall have great pleasure in delivering them myself. My best wishes & vows are offered for you, & for the fruits of your love, & with every sentiment of respect & attachment I have the honor to be Madam, &c. &c.

G: Washington

LB, DLC:GW.

To Lafayette

My Dear Marquis,   Mount Vernon 10th May 1786.

The Letter which you did me the favor to write to me by Mr Barratt dated the 6th of Feby, together with the parcel & packages which accompanied it, came safely to hand; & for which I pray you to accept my grateful acknowledgments.

The account given of your tour thro' Prussia & other States of Germany, to Vienna & back; & of the Troops which you saw reviewed, in the pay of those Monarchs, at different places, is not less pleasing than it is interesting; & must have been as instructive as entertaining to yourself. Your reception at the Courts of Berlin, Vienna, & elsewhere must have been pleasing to you: to have been received by the King of Prussia, & Prince Henry his brother, (who as soldiers & politicians can yield the palm to none) with such marks of attention & distinction, was as indicative of their discernment, as it is of your merit, & will encrease my opinion of them. It is to be lamented however that great characters are seldom without a blot. That one man should tyranise over millions, will always be a shade in that of the former; whilst it is pleasing to hear that a due regard to the rights of mankind, is characteristic of the latter: I shall revere & love him for this trait of his character. To have viewed the several fields of Battle over which you passed, could not, among other sensations, have failed to excite this thought—here have fallen thousands of gallant spirits to satisfy the ambition of, or to support their sovereigns perhaps in acts of oppression or injustice!—melancholy reflection! For what wise purposes does Providence permit this? Is it as a scourge for mankind, or is it to prevent them from becoming too populous? If the latter, would not the fertile plains of the Western world receive the redundancy of the old.

For the several articles of intelligence with which you have been so good as to furnish me, & for your sentimts on European politics, I feel myself very much obliged—on these I can depend. Newspaper Accounts are too sterile, vague & contradictory, on which to form any opinion, or to claim even the smallest attention. The account of, & observations which you have made on the policy & practice of Great Britain at the other Courts of Europe, respecting those States; I was but too well informed &

convinced of before. Unhappily for us, tho' their Accounts are
greatly exagerated, yet our conduct has laid the foundation for
them. It is one of the evils of democratical governments that the
people, not always seeing & frequently mislead, must often feel
before they can act right—but then evils of this nature seldom
fail to work their own cure. It is to be lamented nevertheless that
the remedies are so slow, & that those who may wish to apply
them seasonably are not attended to before they suffer in person, in interest & in reputation. I am not without hopes that
matters will soon take a favourable turn in the fœderal constitution—the discerning part of the community have long since
seen the necessity of giving adequate powers to Congress for
national purposes; & the ignorant & designing must yield to it
'ere long. Several late Acts of the different Legislatures have a
tendency thereto; among these, the Impost which is now acceded to by every State in the Union, (tho' cloggd a little by that
of New York) will enable Congress to support the national credit
in pecuniary matters better than it has been; whilst a measure,
in which this state has taken the lead at its last session, will it is
to be hoped give efficient powers to that Body for all commercial
purposes. This is a nomination of some of its first characters to
meet other Commissioners from the several States in order to
consider of & decide upon such powers as shall be necessary for
the sovereign Power of them to act under; which are to be reported to the respective Legislatures at their autumnal sessions
for, it is to be hoped, final adoption: thereby avoiding those
tedious & futile deliberations which result from recommendations & partial concurrences; at the same time that it places it at
once in the power of Congress to meet European Nations upon
decisive & equal ground. All the Legislatures which I have heard
from have come into the proposition, & have made very judicious appointments. much good is expected from this measure,
and it is regretted by many that more objects were not embraced
by the Meeting. A General Convention is talked of by many for
the purpose of revising & correcting the defects of the fœderal
Government, but whilst this is the wish of some, it is the dread
of others from an opinion that matters are not yet sufficiently
ripe for such an event.

   The British still occupy our Posts to the Westward, & will, I am persuaded, continue to do so under one pretence or another, no matter how shallow, as long as they can: of this, from some circumstances which had occurred, I have been convinced since August 1783 & gave it as my opinion at that time, if not officially to Congress as the sovereign, at least to a number of its members that they might act accordingly. It is indeed evident to me, that they had it in contemplation to do this at the time of the Treaty; the expression of the Article which respects the evacuation of them, as well as the tenor of their conduct since relative to this business, is strongly masked with deception. I have not the smallest doubt but that every secret engine in their power is continually at work to inflame the Indian mind, with a view to keep it at variance with these States for the purpose of retarding our settlements to the Westward, & depriving us of the fur & peltry trade of that Country.

Your assurances my dear Marquis, respecting the male & female asses, are highly pleasing to me; I shall look for them with much expectation & great satisfaction, as a valuable acquisition, & important service. The Jack which I have already received from Spain, in appearance is fine; but his late royal master, tho' past his grand climacteric, cannot be less moved by female allurements than he is, or when prompted, can proceed with more deliberation & majestic solemnity to the work of procreation. The other Jack perished at Sea.

Mr Littlepage in his dispute with Mr Jay seems to have forgot his former situation. It is a pity, for he appears to be a young man of abilities—At the next meeting of the Potomac Company (which I believe will not be 'till August) I will communicate to them your sentiments respecting the terms on which a good Ingénieur des ponts & chaussées may be had & take their opinion thereon.

The benevolence of your heart my Dr Marqs is so conspicuous upon all occasions, that I never wonder at any fresh proofs of it; but your late purchase of an Estate in the Colony of Cayenne with a view of emancipating the slaves on it, is a generous and noble proof of your humanity. Would to God a like spirit would diffuse itself generally into the minds of the people of this country, but I despair of seeing it—some petitions were presented to the Assembly at its last Session, for the abolition of slavery, but they could scarcely obtain a reading. To set them afloat at once would, I really believe, be productive of much inconvenience & mischief; but by degrees it certainly might, & assuredly ought to be effected & that too by Legislative authority.

I give you the trouble of a letter to the Marqs de St Simon, in which I have requested to be presented to Mr de Menonville. The favourable terms in which you speak of Mr Jefferson gives me great pleasure: he is a man of whom I early imbibed the highest opinion—I am as much pleased therefore to meet confirmations of my discernment in these matters, as I am mortified when I find myself mistaken.

I send herewith the copies of your private Letters to me, promised in my last, & which have been since copied by your old aid.[1] As Mrs Washington & myself have both done ourselves the honor of writing to Madame de la Fayette, I shall not give you the trouble at this time of presenting my respects to her; but pray you to accept every good wish which this family can render for your health & every blessing this life can afford you. I cannot conclude without expressing to you the earnest enquiries & ardent wishes of your friends (among whom I claim to stand first) to see you in America, & of giving you repeated assurances of the sincerity of my friendship, & of the Affectionate regard with which I am &c. &c.

G: W——n

P.S. I had like to have forgotten a promise which I made in consequence of the enclos'd application from Colo. Carter—It was, that I would write to you for the wolf hound if to be had conveniently. The inducements, & the services you would render by this Act, will be more evident from the expression of the letter than from any thing I can say.[2]

The vocabulary for her imperial Majesty, I will use my best endeavours to have compleated—but she must have a little patience—the Indian tribes on the Ohio are numerous, dispersed & distant from those who are most likely to do the business properly.[3]

G: Washington

LB, DLC:GW. GW wrote another letter to Lafayette on 8 June covering this letter.

1. GW's "last" was dated 8 Nov. 1785. See note 4 of that document.

2. "Colo. Carter" is probably Charles Carter, Jr. (1733–1796), of Ludlow, in Stafford County. GW often corresponded with him regarding agricultural matters. For a full identification, see *Diaries*, 3:326. Carter had recently given GW grass seed (ibid., 4:326).

3. See Lafayette to GW, 10 Feb., and note 1 of that document.

From Samuel Powel

Dear Sir   Philadelphia 10 May 1786

You will readily acquit me of any Neglect in performing the Promise made in my last, of sending you the Essay on the Farm Yard which obtained the Præmium from the Society for promoting Agriculture, tho' I confess that Appearances do not seem in my Favor from the long Delay, when I tell you that it was not returned to the Society till the second of this Month. Some particulars in the Essay, as it was at first presented to the Society, appeared to want Elucidation. To give the Author an opportunity of rendering it as perfect as he was able, induced the returning of it to him, to clear up the obscurer parts, & make the whole plainer to the Capacit⟨*mutilated*⟩ Instruction it was principally ⟨*mutilated*⟩ These alterations & Corrections necessarily took up some Time.

Col. Morgan, of Princetown, I understand, conducts his Farm, in general, on the Principles which he has here laid down: at least he does so as far as his Circumstances will admit; & he is thought to be one of the best Farmers in America.

The Society have thought it expedient to continue their Præmium on this Subject; as they esteem the Object of it, namely the Perfection of the Barn-Yard, to be the Basis of all good Husbandry, & they are desirous to receive every Information that further Experiment, or the probable Theories of ingenious Persons, can suggest. To Col. Morgan they have adjudged their first Præmium, as an Evidence of the Sense they entertain of the Merit of his Essay, but are unwilling to preclude further Improvement, either by discontinuing their Praemium, or by pretending to offer the present Plan to their Countrymen as a perfect one.[1]

I ⟨*mutilated*⟩ me Pleasure to be of use to you, as far as lies in my Power. Mrs Powel requests to join her most sincere good

Wishes for Mrs Washington & yourself, to those of Dear Sir your most obedt humble Servt

Samuel Powel

ALS, DLC:GW.

1. For a description of the contest sponsored by the Philadelphia Agricultural Society, won by George Morgan for his "Essay on a Farm-Yard System," see Powel to GW, 16 Jan., n.1. The copy of Morgan's essay that Powel made for GW runs to eight manuscript pages including a drawing of the "Plan of the Buildings" of the barnyard (DLC:GW).

To Saint Simon-Montbléru

Sir,   Mt Vernon 10th May 1786.

I received with great pleasure (a few days ago in a letter from the Marquis de la Fayette) the news of your being in good health. The recollection of your gallant services & the happy moments I have had the honor to spend with you in this country, will always be dear to me.[1]

It appears by the Marquis's letter that the answer to a letter which you did me the honor to write to me (now more than two years) respecting the order of the Cincinnati, had never come to your hands. I cannot tell how to accot for it, as all the papers are in the hands of the Secretary General. I well remember however, that at the general meeting which was held at Philadelphia in May 1784, that I laid all the letters with which I had been favored on that subject, before the members which constituted it; and that the Secretary was ordered to communicate the determinations which that Meeting had come to, to the gentlemen who had written to the President—one of which was, that the members of the Society in France were to constitute a Meeting of themselves in order, among other things, to investigate the claims of those who conceived they were entitled to the order, & to decide on them accordingly; in as much as the general Meeting in this Country was not intended to be held oftener than triennially; & could not well at those times enter into the detail of a business which with more propriety would be taken up by the several State meetings, & the one it had just authorised to be held in France.[2]

If Mr de Menonville should happen to be with you, I pray

you to offer him my compliments, & to be assured yourself of the sentiments of esteem & respect with which, I have the honor to be &c.

G: Washington

LB, DLC:GW.
   1. See Lafayette to GW, 6 Feb., and GW to Lafayette, 10 May. See also Lafayette to GW, 9 Mar. 1784 (first letter), n.3.
   2. Apparently Saint-Simon-Montbléru's letter was not among these. See GW to Lafayette, 1 Sept. 1785, n.3.

To Thomas Ringgold Tilghman

Sir;   Mount Vernon May 10th 1786
   Being at Richmond when your favor of the 22d Ulto came to this place, is the reason of its having lain so long unacknowledged. I delayed not a moment after my return, to discharge the Ball[anc]e of your deceased Brother's acct against me, to Mr Watson, according to your request.
   As there were few men for whom I had a warmer friendship, or greater regard than for your Brother—Colonel Tilghman—when living; so, with much truth I can assure you, that, there a⟨re⟩ none whose death I could more sincerely have regretted. and I pray you, & his numerous friends to permit me to mingle my sorrows with theirs on this unexpected & melancholy occasion—and that they would accept my compliments of condolence on it, I am—Sir Yr most Obedt Hble Servt
                                                    Go: Washington

ALS, NN: Lee Kohns Memorial Collection; LB, DLC:GW.

From John Dandridge

Sir   New Kent Court house May—12th 1786
   About three weeks since, Mr Wm Holt of Williamsburg informed me that there were some Eastern shore beans lodged in my neighbourhood for him, & requested me to take them into my possession, & send you one half; which I now do in the bag connected with this letter—Mr Holt expected this would have

been done long before this, but the Gent. with whom the beans were lodged has been from home until within a few days.[1]

You will be so good as to inform my Aunt, that her acquaintances & relations are all well, except my Grandmother who is at present tormented with the rheumatism;[2] & present my Duty & affection—With sincere sentiments of respect & Esteem I am, Sir, yr Sert

Jn Dandridge

ALS, DLC:GW.

1. GW wrote in his diary on 20 May that he had "received from [William] Holt [d. 1791] of Williamsburg through the hands of Mr. Dandridge, about 6 gills of the Eastern shore Peas" and had "planted 3 Rows in the inclosure below the Stables" (*Diaries*, 4:333). For a description of this Eastern Shore (or Magothy Bay) bean, see ibid., 333–34.

2. John Dandridge's paternal grandmother, Frances Jones Dandridge, died in 1785; his maternal grandmother was the widow of Julius King Burbidge of Pamocra in New Kent County. His mother and father, Bartholomew and Mary Burbidge Dandridge, were living at Pamocra when his father died in 1785. John Dandridge also was living at Pamocra at the time of his death in 1799.

To Battaile Muse

Sir,   Mount Vernon 12th May 1786.

I have received your letter of the 6th instt but not inclining to take your surplus wheat, on purchase, will order it to be ground & packed, subject to your order—As you did not direct what kind of flour it should be made into—it will be fine only— unless you should in time direct otherwise.

I lost very considerably by the delay of your wheat—In the first of the Manufactury of it I had a brisk demand for my superfine flour at 40/ & 38/ pr Barrl and for that which has been lately ground I have not had more than 32/ offered—and this price for a small quantity only.[1]

The enclosed was brought to me (under cover) by the person whose name is mentioned therein and with whom I have agreed.[2] I am Sir yr Very Hble servt

Go: Washington

ALS (photocopy), NjP: Armstrong Collection; LB, DLC:GW. The ALS was sold at the Kende Galleries by Gimbel Brothers, item 205, in 1947.

1. See Muse to GW, 6 May, n.1.

2. The enclosure has not been identified.

From Samuel Purviance

Dear Sir   Baltimore 12th May 1786
The Packet inclosed with this came under Cover to me from a Mr Pike of Newbury Port, (a Person utterly unknown to Me) with a Request that I woud forward it to you—Shoud you have occasion to reply, Letters sent to me can be readily forwarded from hence, by Vessels bound to Boston or Newbury Port.[1]

I received the Letter which you was so obliging as to write me by Mr Neilson, for which I thank you: also your favour by Mr Harris, to whom I gave a Letter to my friend Mr Samuel Hughes, who has had the chief management of the Susquehanna Canal, and who gave him an Introduction to Mr Brindley, which I presume answerd his Expectations, as I learn Mr Brindley has since been down at James River.[2]

When the Commissioners appointed by your Assembly to examine the Navigation of the Kenhawa & James River, have executed that Bussin[es]s; you will greatly oblige me by a Communication of their report, or such part thereof as you may be at liberty to mention[3]—My Son who I informed you had traveled last Fall thro part of that country, on his return from Louisville, tells me it is 68 Miles from where he crossd the Kenhawa or New River, to Crows Ferry on James River, and that the whole of that distance is a better Waggon Road than he has traveled in any of these States, and the Passage across the Mountains in that Quarter very easey for full loaded Waggons: but I presume this is not the nearest Communication between the two Rivers.

I hope the Peace or treaty lately concluded with the Shawnese, will facilitate & encourage Settlements about the two Kenhaways, which may add to the Value of Land in that Quarter—I woud readily consent either to rent, or sell out on moderate terms, rather than be a means of retarding the Settlements. I am with great Respect Sir Your most Obedt & Very hble Servt
                                         Saml Purviance

ALS, DLC:GW.

1. See Nicholas Pike to GW, 25 March.

2. Neilson conveyed to Purviance GW's letter of 10 Mar. in answer to Purviance's letter of 6 Mar.; the letter sent by James Harris, who left Mount Vernon on 30 Mar., has not been found. Neilson may be Robert Neilson of Baltimore County, Maryland.

3. For the James River Company report, see Edmund Randolph to GW, and enclosure, 2 March.

Letter not found: from William Fitzhugh, Jr., of Maryland. On 15 May GW wrote Fitzhugh: "Your favor of the 13th came to me this day."

From Joseph Jones

Dr Sr   Richmond 14th may 1786.

Apprehending from the conversation that passed between us at the Bowling-green you might think as well as others a meeting of the assembly necessary to take into consideration the late proceeding of Congress respecting the System of revenue of the 18th of April 1783[1]—I beg leave to trouble you with a more accurate account of that business than I was then able to give you, tho' I think I then told you we had complied with the system as to the impost, but had departed from it with respect to the other branch of the revenue—but doubted whether if all the States had granted the impost Congress could execute that part without the other—I think also I said we had no official communication on the subject when I left Richmond, and that I conceived if Congress thought an earlier, than the usual, meeting of our assembly necessary, it shod have been desired. I find our act grants the impost fully, and goes to that subject only, and that the other was taken into the revenue law. after geting to Town and attending the Board on monday the 1st May I found the Govr had received a letter from our Delegates on the subject dated the 16th last month, from which I transcribe the following extract for your information "The representation of the 15th of Febry last upon the system of revenue of the 18th of april 1783 Has operated very successfully—N. york and Georgia are now the only States whose accession to the impost part of the system we have not received authentic information of, and the accession of the latter we have such information of, as leaves no doubt an authentic act will shortly come to hand—N. york has passed an act effecting a compliance but clogged with conditions and provisions which render it inadmissible—Your Excellency will observe that Virginia having in her act granted only the impost part of the System she stands of course in the representation of the 15th of Febry amongst ⟨those⟩ States who have not fully complied—We think it not amiss to inform you that most of the States, who have in any degree complied, have left out the supplementary funds. It will be to no usefull purpose for Virga to take the subject under consideration at an earlier period than the fall Session—whenever all the States have so formed their acts as to embrace the impost alone, that part of the System may go into effect, so far the act of Virginia is already competent to its operation, and it is not probable that her accession to the other part will become necessary before the fall."[2] Add to these observations what, if my memory does not deceive me, is a fact that the act of Pennsylvania cannot operate untill all the States adopt the whole of the system of 83, and you will be satisfied an earlier meeting of the assembly for the purpose of taking into consideration the business, is unnecessary. A ⟨wish to explain⟩ in this matter to you and through you to any other whose observations may lead to the subject, will I hope be to you a sufficient apology for troubling you with this letter[3]—with respectfull compliments to Mrs Washington I am Dr Sr yr aff. hum. sevt

Jos. Jones

ALS, DLC:GW.

Joseph Jones (1727–1805), who served in Congress for six years during the Revolution, had been a member of the house of delegates during the session that ended 21 Jan. 1786 and was now a member of the council of state.

1. GW spent the night of 28 April at Bowling Green on his return from Richmond (*Diaries*, 4:319).

2. Letter not found. There is no reference to the letter of the Virginia delegate to Congress in the minutes of the meeting on 1 May of the Virginia council (see *Journal of Virginia Council*, 3:544–46). The members of the Virginia delegation to the Congress in attendance in April 1786 were Edward Carrington, William Grayson, Henry Lee, and James Monroe (see *JCC*, 30:200).

3. GW acknowledged Jones's letter from Mount Vernon on 25 May in these terms: "My Dr Sir, I have been favored with, and thank you for your letter of the 14th inst:. The reasons which you have been at the trouble to assign for the Executive's not calling the assembly at an earlier period than the annual meeting, are very satisfactory; & I am much obliged to you for the recital of them, for I confess to you that I was not only among the number of those who expected this event, but under the publication of Congress of the 15th of Feby & my want of information of the precise state of matters in other States, was among those also who could not account for the postponement. It will always give me pleasure to hear from you, because it will afford me fresh occasion for assuring you of the sincere esteem & regard with which I am My Dr Sir &c. G: Washington" (LB, DLC:GW).

To William Fitzhugh, Jr.

Dear Sir,   Mount Vernon 15⟨th May 1786⟩

Your favor of the 13th came to me this day.[1] Particular attention shall be paid to the Mares which your Servant brought; and when my Jack is in the humour they shall derive all the benefits of his labours—for labour it appears to be. At present, tho' young, he follows what one may suppose to be the example of his late royal Master, who cannot, tho' past his grand climacterick, perform seldomer, or with more Majestic solemnity, than he does. However, I am not without hope, that when he becomes a little better acquainted with republican enjoyments, he will amend his manners, and fall into a better & more expeditious mode of doing business. If the case should be otherwise, I should have no disinclination to present his Catholic Majesty with as good a thing, as he gave me.

I am very sorry to hear of the accident which befel Colo. Fitzhugh in his late trip to Virginia; but, from the effect of it, I hope he will soon be perfectly recovered. I am happy in having it in my power to furnish the Colo. with a Bushel of the Barley, requested in your letter. A propos, are there any persons in your neighbourhood who raise Lambs for sale? My stock of sheep were so much neglected during my absence, that I would gladly buy one, or two hundred ewe lambs, and allow a good price for them, in order to get it up again. A line from you, when convenient, in answer to ⟨this query,⟩ would be obliging[2]—Mrs Washington ⟨& the⟩ rest of the family join me in every good wish to the Colo. his Lady & yourself. I am—Dr Sir Yr Most Obedt Servt

                                   Go: Washington

P.S. Please to present me to Colo. & Mrs Plater when you see them.[3]

ALS, anonymous donor; LB, DLC:GW; copies, CSmH, MdBJ. The words in angle brackets are taken from the letter-book copy.

1. Letter not found.

2. Fitzhugh and his father, Col. William Fitzhugh (1721–1798) of Rousby Hall in Maryland, who was nearly blind, were at Mount Vernon on 22 April. For the ensuing correspondence regarding lambs for GW and studs for William Fitzhugh, Sr.'s mares, see William Fitzhugh, Jr., to GW, 26 May, 15 June, GW to William Fitzhugh, Jr., 5 June, to William Fitzhugh, Sr., 2 July, William Fitzhugh, Sr., to GW, 1 July, and Peregrine Fitzhugh to GW, 10 July 1786.

3. George Plater and his wife, Elizabeth Rousby Plater (d. 1789), lived at Sotterly on the Patuxent in St. Mary's County, Maryland.

To John Rumney, Jr.

Sir;   Mount Vernon May 15th 1786

I am indebted to you for your favor of the 5th of September, and to Messrs Robinson, Sanderson and Rumney for their letter of the 28th of Jany in the present year. The last was accompanied with 1400 Flags, which came with very little breakage; and for your care of, and attention to which, I beg you to accept my sincere thanks.

On the 18th of Novr I enclosed you a Bill on Wakelin Welch Esqr. of London for £50 Sterg; and will, before Mr Sanderson leaves the Country, settle with him for the Ballance.

It gives me pleasure to hear that we may soon expect to see you in this Country again. With great esteem & regard—I am— Sir Yr most Obedt & Obliged Hble Servt

Go: Washington

ALS, ViMtV; LB, DLC:GW.

To Clement Biddle

Dear Sir   Mount Vernon May 18th 1786

Your favors of the 19th of Feby & 16th & 19th March, are before me; And would have been acknowledged Sooner, had any thing material, occurred.[1]

The Clover Seed, Boots &c. came in Season; but I must take care to be earlier in my application another year, as the Expence of getting heavy articles from Baltimore by land, comes high; I was charged forty odd Shillings for the Transportation of those Seeds, by the Stage, from that Place. I am nevertheless much obliged to you for forwarding of them in that manner; as the delay would have rendered the Seeds useless for Spring Sowing, & altogether defective, perhaps, by the Fall. I am obliged to your Good Father for the Trouble he was at in choosing them, they are very good, & pray you, to Offer my Complts & Thanks, to him therefor, & to Capt. Morris, for his kind present of a hunting horn, as I was unable to get One in Virginia, or at Baltimore.[2]

If you Should not have purchased Young's Tour Through Great Britain, before this Reaches you, be pleased to decline doing it, as I have just received a very Polite letter from that Gentleman, informing me of his having dispatched a Compleat Sett of his Works for my acceptance.[3]

The Person in whose Name the inclosed certificate has Issued, is owing me a considerable Sum, (indeed half the Flour, & Meal, for which the Certificate was granted belonged to me) & having requested that it may be Sold for what it will fetch, & his part of the Money applied to my Credit, I pray you to do it accordingly; but at the Same time, I must desire, as a Halfe the Property is my own, that if it Shall appear to you, to be for my Interest, that it Should be bought in again on my Accot, that you would do so. In either case, place the Amot to my Credit in your Books, Subject to a future disposition.[4]

I must be owing Messrs Robt Lewis & Sons (of Phila.) some Trifle on Accot of a Miller which they procured for me, last Year, but have never yet been able to get their Accot. Be so good as to know what the Amot is, & Pay it, the Inclosed Informs them thereof.[5]

I have Such a number of Gazettes crouded upon me, (many without orders) that they are not only Expensive, but realy useless; as my other avocations, will not afford me time to Read them oftentimes; & when I do attempt it, find them more troublesome, than Profitable. I have therefore to beg if you should get money into your hands, on Accot of the Inclosed Certificate, that you would be so good as to pay what I am owing to Messrs Dunlap & Claypoole;—Mr Oswald—& Mr Humphreys.

If they consider me, however, as engaged for the Year, I am content to let the matter run on, to the expiration of it; but as my Expences run high, it would be imprudent in me to encrease them unnecessarily.

I am in want of Glass (for a Particular purpose) & beg you would Send it to me, by the first opportunity, agreeably to the Inclosed Pattern, & Quantities.[6]

Is Linnen to be had cheap, at the Vendues in Philadelphia, for ready Money? And at what price, could the best dutch, or Strip'd Blanketts, be bought by the piece, of 15 or 16 in each, which I think is the usual number? I may want 200 of them. My Compliments in which Mrs Washington Joins, are Offred to Mrs Biddle, & I am. Dear Sir Your Mo. Obedt Hble Servt

Go: Washington

LS, in William Shaw's hand, PHi: Washington-Biddle Correspondence; LB, DLC:GW. The two signed letters are virtually identical.

1. None of these letters has been found.

2. GW sent his order for seed, shoes, boots, a hunting horn, and books on 10 February. John Biddle, Clement's father, settled in Philadelphia in 1730. Capt. Samuel Morris (1734–1812), a sporting man from a Quaker family, obtained eight hunting dogs for GW when GW was attending the Federal Convention in Philadelphia (Morris to GW, 21 Sept. 1787).

3. See GW to Biddle, 10 Feb., n.3. See also Biddle to GW, 25 June.

4. GW enclosed a document headed: "Copy of the Certificate sent to Colo. Biddle, 18th May 1786, assigned to G. W——n by Gilb[er]t Simpson." The certificate, no. 4958, "State of Pennsylvania May 18th 1785," reads: "On the final settlement of an account between the United States & Gilbert Simpson, there appeared to be due to him the sum of three hundred & thirty nine Dollars & fifty three ninetieths of a Dollar. I do therefore certify that the said sum is payable, with interest at six per cent from the fourth day of November 1780, to the said Gilbert Simpson, or bearer. (signed) Benja. Stelle Commissr" (DLC:GW). For an explanation of this, see GW to Biddle, 1 Feb. 1785, n.8.

5. See GW to Robert Lewis & Sons, this date.

6. The pattern has not been found.

To John Jay

Dear Sir,   Mount Vernon 18th May 1786.

In due course of Post, I have been honoured with your favours of the 2d & 16th of March; since which I have been a good deal engaged, and pretty much from home.

For the inclosure which accompanied the first, I thank you. Mr Littlepage seems to have forgot what had been his situation—What was due to you—and indeed what was necessary for his own character. And his Guardian I think, seems to have forgot every thing.

I coincide perfectly in sentiment with you, my dear Sir, that there are errors in our National Government which call for correction; loudly I will add; but I shall find my self happily mistaken if the remedies are at hand. We are certainly in a delicate situation, but my fear is that the people are not yet sufficiently misled to retract from error! To be plainer, I think there is more wickedness than ignorance, mixed with our councils. Under this impression, I scarcely know what opinion to entertain of a general Convention. That it is necessary to revise, and amend the articles of Confederation, I entertain *no* doubt; but what may be the consequences of such an attempt *is* doubtful. Yet, something must be done, or the fabrick must fall. It certainly is tottering! Ignorance & design, are difficult to combat. Out of these proceed illiberality, *improper* jealousies, and a train of evils which oftentimes, in republican governments, must be sorely felt before they can be removed. The former, that is ignorance, being a fit soil for the latter to work in, tools are employed which a generous mind would disdain to use; and which nothing but time, and their own puerile or wicked productions, can show the inefficacy and dangerous tendency of. I think often of our situation, and view it with concern. From the high ground on which we stood—from the plain path which invited our footsteps, to be so fallen!—so lost! is really mortifying. But virtue, I fear, has, in a great degree, taken its departure from our Land, and the want of disposition to do justice is the sourse of the national embarrassments; for under whatever guise or colourings are given to them, this, I apprehend, is the origin of the evils we now feel, & probably shall labour for sometime yet. With respectful Complimts to Mrs Jay—and sentiments of sincere friendship—I am—Dear Sir Yr most Obedt Hble Servt

Go: Washington

P.S. Will you do me the favor to forward the enclosed, with any dispatches of your own, for England?[1]

ALS, NNC; LB, DLC:GW.

1. This is a letter, which has not been found, from GW to Catharine Macaulay Graham. See Jay to GW, 27 June.

To Robert Lewis & Sons

Gentn   Mount Vernon 18th May 1786
    Waiting to be informed of what I stand indebted to you, is the cause of my not acknowledging sooner the receipt of your favor

of the 24th of May last year. I have now requested Colo. Biddle to enquire into, & to discharge what is due from me.[1]

I feel myself very much obliged to you for the trouble you have had in obtaining a miller for me. Mr Devenport seems to be a very honest, good kind of man; but as a miller, & as a person skilled in the art of keeping a mill in order, I think him much inferior to Roberts. In these points perhaps roberts had no superior; but his propensity to liquor, & his turbulent temper when under the intoxicating doses of it, were not to be borne. I have no trouble at all with Devenport; he is steady, orderly & quiet, & does, I believe, as well as he knows how. We have neither of us intimated any inclination to part; & if the reputation of my flour (which stood very high under Roberts's management) can be maintained, it is all I want.[2]

The Agreement which you entered into with him is perfectly satisfactory to me, & I thank you for your attention to the business.[3] With great esteem, I am Gentn &c.

G: Washington

LB, DLC:GW.

    1. See GW to Clement Biddle, this date.
    2. For GW's hiring of Joseph Davenport as his miller to replace William Roberts, see Robert Lewis & Sons to GW, 5 April 1785, and notes.
    3. GW's agreement with Davenport is dated 23 May 1785.

From Alexander Steel

Sir   Baltimore May 18, 1786

With the most perfect respect your Excellency will pardon the Liberty in sending the inclosed praying your Breaking (the seal) on my arrivall from Dublin, I was informed Doctor Sheal of Philidelphia removed to Canetuck, and died there; since the Peace—as his Family may reap some Benafit at Least £60 a year on only writing to settle A Balance for your Excellencys advice I now refer with regard to my answer for Europe; being Obliged by promise to write By the First vessell that sails for Ireland from here, (which is next week)[1] there is another Motive induces me Troubling your Excellency annexed to it Willm Osbrey Esqre Major of the Duke of Liensters regiment of Volunteers informs him my unhappy sittuation on my return to Europe[2]—at the Begining of our Contest with Britton, I was appointed a second

Lieutenant in Coll Spencers Regiment, Captn Weatherbys Company; Mr Brown who I gave him his warrant for first Lieut. on his raising so many men in Cumberland County West Jersey's and not Fulfilling his Promise, I was Displeased that he shou'd rank over me when I had given the appointment out of my own Hands. Promotion was not then my view what I had pledged my Honour for was then at stake and all my wish, under these circumstances untill after the Battle of Brandewine—a few days after we left Chester I informed Coll Spencer that I cou'd not think of Browns haveing the Command Over me, that raised Captn Weatherbys Company, but if the Captain had enlisted & Brown onely 3 out of (52) my Gold, not Paper, done the rest in Salem & Cumberland Counties—in this sittuation as second Lieutt I remained untill your Excellency crossed Dobbs Ferry, I was then determined on leaving the Regiment, Coll Spencer requested I woud not. I remained purely to Convince him my attatchment to the cause,[3] Coll Charles Stewart Finding I was determined on Leaving the Line a Gentn I shall ever Hold in the most perfect respect, requested I woud goe and take Charge of the Magazine at Trenton where I remained about 11 Months, when I received Colol Stewarts Letter that I must deliver up the Stores to Mr Stephen Lowry[4] and goe Immediately to East Town, to Superintend General Sullivans Army on the Western Expedition (It was Obeyd) to Genl Philemon Dickinson for my Conduct while there, to Coll Spencer while in the Line, General Hand and Coll Stewart I refer the whole of my conduct on the Expedition,[5] on my return Rheumatick pains Obliged me to goe to Cape May, for the Benefitt of my Health, and while there Colol Robt Taylor sent me word of some Gunn boats being at Clam Town, in consequence I sent him word I shou'd meet at Weaden River Bridge and there Consult the best mode of Surprizing them at Break of Day—but was to often the Case they receivd but one Fire when his Militia run and I being wounded made Prisoner was sent on board Captn Roaches Gun Boat, and Plundered of my Hatt, watch, coat, knee Buckles, and even the Broach out of my Shirt & then Handcuffed, in this sittuation I remained during their cruise of Seven weeks, during which time I was unhappy to see Captn Glisson Killed and a number of Genl Smallwoods men that had been sent out in the whale Boats for some private expedition cut almost to attems on their Board-

ing at the Tangier Islands.[6] Their Cruise being out I was
Brought to York, tho was happy in getting Captn Roach who
was Commidore of the Five Gunn boats Paroling all that Had
been taken during the whole of his Cruise, but repeatedly told
me it was out His power to parole me that he wished he had
Got Taylor along with me, untill he brought him to york) on my
arrivall their I was Brought to Admaral Digbeys Qrs where
Captn Roach and Him Had some private discourse, He sent for
me, and what will amaze your Excellency the Onely question he
asked me was what Country man are you Sir, (I informed him)
His reply was it is you and your Countrimen that are Carrying
on the Warr against your Royal Sovereign, for the Present you
must Goe to the Suger House, but Had not been there above 20
Minutes untill a Guard was sent to bring me to Provo (I remained only 17 Days their untill I was ordered on board the
Rhinocerous Guard Ship that lay at Governors Island for telling
Cunningham that if his Deputy ever attempted striking any of
our Men they shou'd serve me as they had done my acquaintance and very particular Friend Captn Joss Haady that they
Had taken at the Block House, Toms River; My answer was you
deserve the same;[7] in this sittuation from the 17th April 82 I
remained untill the Genl Exchange, and being informed of My
Fathers death I returned to Europe where I found ⟨1s.⟩ on account of my being in the American Service, I sensure him not,
he died in (1778) in Europe it was then Thought, that Genl
Howe & Burgoine woud sweep our Army before them, and our
Confiscating the Property of Loyalists and Toryes alone induced
him alterining his Will; Dubious we shou'd be Conquered, and
in the Body of His will says to my Eldest son Alexander Steel I
leave One Shilling for his being an Officer in the Rebell Army;
I therefore most respectfully hope your Excellency: will pardon
my presuming to request relative to my Conduct if an application to Congress wou'd serve me; Young I came into this Country with Letters of recommendation from Messrs Latouche; Gladowe & Compy Bankers in Dublin, the latter for whome I done
Business for all most Two years,[8] Brought with me £500 it went
the war comeing on so soon—must I lose a Property at home
and have no recompence here, it is sufficient to Break the Heart
of any man of Feeling, my all gone in Europe and nothing left
Here.

Your Excellency the Patron of Man as Sir Henry Flood Titles you;[9] alone I refer most Humbly requesting your Answer if I shall apply to Congress for any Kind of redress, Mr Haigh's Jeweller in Baltimore, Mr Smith Jeweller in Philidelphia, who both left Europe since, Peace can fully testify the Circumstances of my Father Mr William Steel Jeweller Dublin. Your Excellency will Permit me to be your Most Devoted & Obedt Servt

Alexr Steel

P.S. shou'd I be Honoured with an answer. I lodge at Mr Grants.[10]

ALS, DLC:GW.

1. Dr. Hugh Shiell (c.1760–1785), Steel's fellow Irishman, practiced medicine in Philadelphia during the Revolution before moving to Kentucky, where he was drowned while attempting to cross a river. GW returned the enclosure without opening it (GW to Steel, 25 May; see also note 2).

2. Steel seems to be saying that the enclosure was a letter from Maj. William Osbrey to Shiell and "annexed to it" was Osbrey's account of the "unhappy sittuation" that Steel met with upon his return to Dublin in 1783 after serving in the American army throughout the war only to learn that his father had disinherited him. Osbrey was major in the Dublin regiment, commanded by Col. William Robert Fitzgerald, 2d duke of Leinster (1749–1804).

3. On 23 Feb. 1777 Benjamin Weatherby (1747–1812) became captain and Steel became second lieutenant in a company which the two of them with David Brown raised in Salem and Cumberland counties, New Jersey. The company was in one of the Sixteen Additional Continental Regiments authorized by Congress in December 1776 and commanded by Col. Oliver Spencer (1736–1811). Steel became quartermaster for the New Jersey regiment in July 1777.

4. Charles Stewart, a colonel in the New Jersey militia, became commissary general of issues in New Jersey in June 1777. Steel served under him at the magazine at Trenton from the summer of 1778 to May 1779. Steel's successor at the magazine, Stephen Lowrey (Lowrie; 1747–1821), owned the Rising Sun Hotel in Trenton from 1779 to 1792.

5. Steel served as deputy commissary general of issues on the western expedition against the Six Nations led in 1779 by Maj. Gen. John Sullivan (1740–1795) of New Hampshire and Brig. Gen. James Clinton (1736–1812) of New York. Philemon Dickinson (d. 1809) of New Jersey and Edward Hand (d. 1802) commanded brigades in the Sullivan expedition.

6. Robert Taylor (d. 1789) was an officer in the Gloucester County militia. Clam Town is the present Tuckerton, N.J., near Little Egg Harbor. Wading (Weaden) River in New Jersey is an arm of Little Egg Harbor. Roach may have been Capt. William Roach. Smallwood was Gen. William Smallwood (d. 1792) of Maryland.

7. Rear Admiral Robert Digby (1732–1814) arrived in New York in Septem-

ber 1781 to take command of the British navy in North America. Sugar House was a notorious prison in New York City. William Cunningham (1717–1791), an Irishman, was provost marshal of the British prison in New York, called Provost Prison. Capt. Joshua Huddy (1735–1782) of the New Jersey state artillery was in command of the blockhouse at Toms River when on 24 Mar. 1782 the British captured it. On 12 April Huddy was hanged (see GW to Henry Knox and Gouverneur Morris, to John Hanson, both 20 April 1782, to Moses Hazen, 3 May 1782, and to William Livingston, 6 May 1782).

8. William George Digges La Touche (1747–1803) was head of the principal bank in Dublin.

9. Henry Flood (1732–1791) was an Irish reformer and noted orator.

10. Daniel Grant's Fountain Inn was a tavern on Light Lane in Baltimore.

To George Taylor, Jr.

Sir,   Mount Vernon 18th May 1786

You will excuse me I hope, for not having acknowledged the receipt of your favours of the 21st & 25th of Feby at an earlier period. The truth is, I have been much hurried, and a good deal from home, since they came to this place.

I thank you for your obliging attention to the apples, which were very good & arrived safely, and Mrs Washington joins me in thanking you also for your kind present of pickled & fried Oysters, which were very fine: This mark of your politeness is flattering, and we beg you to accept every good wish of ours in return. With esteem I am—Sir Yr most Obedt Servt

Go: Washington

ALS, ViMtV; LB, DLC:GW.

From Thomas Marshall

Dear Sir.   Fayette County 19th of May 1786

I have made inquiry concerning your entry which Mr Hite mentioned to you & can find nothing of it—I believe he must have been misstaken—I have seen him and ask'd him concerning it, but he can tell me nothing more about it than that he thought he had seen such a one.

Your warrant I have put into the hands of Mr John Obannon, formerly a Neighbor of mine, and now one of the Military Surveyors. He has promised to do his best for you & I think he may be depended on. I have made no particular bargain with him otherwise than assuring him that he shall be generously satisfyed for his trouble.[1]

I will this fall attend to the commission you honord me with respecting the Marquis La Fayette. & send on such of the articles as I can procure.[2] I have the honor to be with the most respectful esteem Dear Sir your most obedient servant

T. Marshall

ALS, DLC:GW. The letter was delivered to GW at Mount Vernon on 24 July 1786 (*Diaries*, 5:15).

1. GW gave to Marshall in May 1785 before Marshall's departure for Kentucky John Rootes's warrant for 3,000 acres assigned to GW in 1774. John O'Bannon (d. 1813), who went from Fauquier County to Kentucky in 1784, surveyed three tracts on the Little Miami for GW under the Rootes warrant and delivered them to GW in August 1788. See Marshall to GW, 12 May 1785, and notes, GW to Thomas Lewis, 1 Feb. 1784, n.5, and *Diaries*, 5:371–72. A survey of 977 acres on the Little Ohio by O'Bannon, dated 26 May–11 June 1788 is in OCCtH.

2. On 12 May 1785, shortly before he went out to the Kentucky region, Thomas Marshall wrote that he would be pleased to collect seeds of plants for GW as Lafayette had requested and that he would take out GW's "warr[an]t as Assignee of Rootes." On 27 Oct. 1787 he wrote GW about the seeds he had found and said that he was sending them to Mount Vernon by Rawleigh Colston.

From Robert Sanderson

Sir   Alexa[ndria] 19th May 1786

Inclosed I forward your Acct Current as it now stands. My Partners did not mean to make any Charge of Freight &c, which I much approve.[1] Your Letter to Sir Edwd Newenham shall be carefully forwarded.[2] Wishing you and your Lady a Long Continuance of Good Health I am Sir Your much Oblig'd & Very Hble Servt

Robt Sanderson

ALS, DLC:GW.

1. Sanderson was probably referring to the flags for the piazza at Mount Vernon shipped from Whitehaven by his partner, John Rumney, Jr. See Rumney to GW, 16 April.

2. GW's letter to Edward Newenham has not been found, but see his letter of 10 June 1786.

To Henry L. Charton

Sir   Mount Vernon 20th May 1786

The letter which you did me the favor to write to me from Philadelphia, on the 5th instt, came safely to hand; and would have received an early acknowledgmt had not frequent calls from home, and unavoidable business prevented it.[1]

I do not perceive, upon recurring to the subject, that I can be more explicit in the description of my Lands on the big Kanhawa, and on the Ohio, between the two Kanhawas, than I was when I had the pleasure of seeing you at this place.[2]

If I recollect rightly, I then informed you, that from the Accts given me of them by the Surveyor—from what I had seen of them myself (especially the tract on the big Kanhawa)—from every other sourse of information—and from my best knowledge & belief, there can be no finer land in that, or any other Country; or lands more abounding in natural advantages. The whole of them are washed by the rivers I have mentioned—are furnished with land streams fit for water works of various kinds—stored with meadow ground, which may be reclaimed in the cheapest, & most expeditious manner imaginable (by only cutting away trifling banks of earth, which have been formed by the Beaver)—and abound in fish & wild fowl of all kinds; as well as in every other sort of game, with wch the Country is filled. With respect to the quality of the soil, it may be conceived, that none can exceed it from this single circumstance, that it was the first choice of the whole Country thereabouts, after a thorough research of it, by an excellent judge—the late Colo. Crawford. As to the situation of them, none can be more advantageous; for lying about midway between the upper & lower settlements on the Ohio, the trade must pass by the Land, whilst the Occupants of it, equally convenient to both, might embrace the inland navigation of either the Potomack or James River as soon as they are made to communicate with the Western Waters; which no doubt will soon be effected, as both works have commenced. I think too, I should not be mistaken, were I to add, that ere long, a town of some importance will be established in the vicinity of these Lands—to wit—at the confluence of the big Kanhawa and Ohio; which is the point at which the trade to Richmond, & that which is carried to the Northern parts of this State, & to Maryland & Pensylvania, must seperate. But to go into a more minute detail in writing, of what has before been the subject of personal conversation, would be more tiresome than interesting; especially as it is by no means my wish that *any* purchaser whatsoever, should rely upon my acct of this matter, or on those of any others; but judge for himself, or themselves, in all matters.

When you asked me if I was disposed to sell these lands, I answered, and truly, that I had never had it in contemplation; because I well knew they would rise more in value than the purchase money would accumulate by interest. consequently—under these circumstances, it would be difficult, in the present moment, to fix on a price (that would be acceded to) that would be an equivalent for them hereafter. However, as I had no family—wished to live easy—and to spend the remainder of my days with as little trouble as possible, I said, I would part with them if a good price could be obtained. And this price being asked, I further observed, that my ideas of their value might easily be ascertained from the terms on which I had proposed to rent them (which I think you told me you had seen) one of which amounting in fact to an absolute sale, being on a lease for 999 years renewable, was, at Ten pounds this Currency (dollars at 6/) pr hundred acres, came to Forty shillings an acre allowing 5 pr Ct interest for the purchase. but I added, if any one person, or sett of Men, would take the whole, I would abate considerably in the price, & make the payments easy.

I therefore now inform you, that the lands (the Plats, & Patents of which I shewed you, & the titles to which are incontrovertable, free from those clashing interests and jarring disputes with which much of the property in that Country is replete) are in quantities, and situation, as follow:

1st	2314	Acres on the Ohio River; 3 or 4 Miles below the mouth of the little Kanhawa.
2d	2448	Acres on the said River, about 16 Miles below the former.
3d	4395	Acres on the same river just above the great bend in it, and below the other two.
4th	10,990	Acres on the big Kanhawa, (West side) beginning within 2 or 3 Miles of its conflux with the Ohio, & extending up the former 17 Miles.

5th	7276	Acres a little above this, on the East side of the same river Kanhawa.
6th	2000	Acres higher up the Kanhawa, West side, in the fork between Cole river and it.
7th	2950	Acres opposite thereto on the East side.
In all.	32373	Acres on both Rivers.

For these lands I would take Thirty thousand English Guineas (of the proper weight) or other specie current in this Country at an equivalent value. Two thousand five hundred of which to be paid at the execution of the Deeds, and the remainder in seven years therefrom, with an interest of five pr Ct pr Annum regularly paid at my Seat, till the principal sum shall be discharged.

I am not inclined to part with any of these Lands as an inducement to settle the rest. My mind is so much satisfied of the superior value of them, to most others, that there remns no doubt on it, of my obtaining my own terms when the Country populates, & the situation & local advantages of them unfold. These terms have already been promulgated, but I have not a copy of them by me, or I would send it to you. They were inserted in Dunlaps & Claypools Gazette about two years ago—at whose office it is propable a copy (if desired) might be had.[3] One of the considerations was, if my memory serves me, an exemption from the payment of rent three years—whilst the tenements were opening, and improvements making. This I am still inclined to allow. The rents were different, according to the term for which the leases were to be granted. If for twenty one years only, they were to commence, and end, at five pounds pr hundred Acres; for in that case the stipulated improvements being made I know that almost any rent might be had for the tenements thereafter—If on leases renewable every ten years forever, the rents were, in that case, to advance in a certain ratio to keep pace with the increasing value of the Land. And if given in the first instance for 999 years, as has been mentioned before, then the rent was to commence at Ten pounds pr hundred acres, which being in fact an alienation of the Fee, shewed my ideas of its present value, & the purchase money, as already mentioned. These as far as I can recite from memory, were the terms on which I offered to rent; and from which I feel no disposition to relax, unless, as in the case of a purchase, some one or more persons, would take the whole of[f] my hands at once, & become responsible for the rent—in which case the same motives might induce me to abate accordingly—as in the other instance.

I should have great pleasure in giving you such letters as you have asked to the Marquis de la Fayette and Chevalier de la Luzerne, but conceive they could only have an embarrassing operation—It is certainly as consistent with the policy of one Country to discourage depopulation, as it is for another to encourage emigrants. Considering the matter in this point of view I cannot suppose however well disposed either of the above Gentlemen may be to promote the interest of this Country, that they would do it at the expence of, and perhaps hazard of censure from their own. One of these Gentlemen too, being in the diplomatic, or Ministerial line, would, undoubtedly, be very cautious in expressing a sentiment favourable to a business of this kind. My best wishes however will accompany you in it, through all the stages; and with esteem—I am—Sir Yr Most Obedt Hble Ser⟨vt⟩

Go: Washington

P.S. I should be glad to hear whether this letter got to Philadelphia in time.

ALS, InHi; LB, DLC:GW.

1. Letter not found.

2. Henry L. Charton, "(a french Gentleman)," arrived at Mount Vernon on 18 Mar. with a letter of introduction from Patrick Henry dated 11 March. Henry's letter has not been found but reportedly contained information that Charton was joined in his plans to settle whites on the Ohio by Albert Gallatin and Savary de Valcoulon (*Diaries*, 4:295). See also GW to Charton, 22 July.

3. GW's advertisement of his Ohio land, dated [c.10] Mar. 1784, is printed in *Papers, Confederation Series*, 1:201–4.

To Neil Jamieson

Sir,   Mount Vernon 20th May 1786.

Messrs Balfour & Barraud of Norfolk died indebted to me in a pretty considerable sum. Meeting with Mr Newton a few days ago at richmond, he informed me that the books of that Company had been in the hands of a Mr Schau deceased, to whom you were an Executor; and that it was highly probable you could in this character, give me some clue by which I could recover my Debt; for he added, that he was certain money was due in and about Norfolk to Messrs Balfour & Barraud, & might be obtained if a list of the Debts cou'd be had.

My debt was contracted for flour sold these Gentlemen—This flour was for Mr Hanbury of London, & there can be little doubt of their connexion in trade; but whether of such a nature as to make the latter liable for the debt, I am unable to say.[1]

If my present application to you is improper, or likely to give you any trouble in affording me the requisite information, you will please to place the liberty I take, to a former acquaintance, and have the goodness to excuse it. I am Sir &c.

G. Washington

LB, DLC:GW.

1. For GW's efforts to collect the prewar debt of Balfour & Barraud Co., see GW to Thomas Newton, Jr., 3 Sept. 1785, n.4. Colt MacGregor answered GW's inquiries on behalf of Jamieson (see MacGregor to GW, 29 May).

To John Marsden Pintard

Sir,   Mount Vernon 20th May 1786.

Your favors of the 24th of January & 5th of Feby[1] are at hand; but I have heard nothing of the Vine slips mentioned therein, nor do I know where to direct my enquiries for them, as you do not mention the Port or State to which the Industry, Captn Gibson was bound For your good intentions however, I am as much indebted, as if the slips had actually been delivered to me.

It is to be hoped & much to be wished that the negotiations of Messrs Barclay & Lamb, at the Court of Morocco, & with the State of Algiers, may terminate favourably for America. Should they not, our trade will be exceedingly incommoded by the piratical states of the Mediterranean.[2]

At present, thro' the early attention of Messrs Jno. Searle & Co., & some others, (formerly my Correspondents in Madeira) together with the purchases I have occasionally made in this Country since the re-establishment of peace, I am more than usually well stocked with Madeira Wine. I am Sir &c.

G: Washington

LB, DLC:GW.

1. The letter of 5 Feb. has not been found.
2. See David Humphreys to GW, 1 Nov. 1785, n.1.

To Thomas Ridout

Sir,   Mount Vernon 20th May 1786.

Since my last dated the 20th of August, I have been favored with your letters of the 31st of Augt, 7th of Septr & 4th of Novembr in the past year.

The packages by the Peggy, Capt. Cuningham are safely arrived. I am sorry they should have given you any trouble, & am much obliged by your care of them.

I have paid Colo. Fitzgerald the full amount of the Wine & other articles wch were sent to me by Captn Smith; & am sorry to add that the quality of the Claret on proof, did not answer my expectation, & was far short of some other of the same cargo, wch I had drank at other places. I ascribe this however to chance; it may be my luck next time to get better, & therefore when your Vessel comes to this river again, I request that a gross of the best may be sent to me.

Excuse the liberty I take of addressing a packet containing papers of consequence, to your care for the Marqs de la Fayette, & a barrel;[1] to both of wch I ask your particular attention. I am Sir &c.

G: Washington

LB, DLC:GW.

1. The packet contained copies of Lafayette's letters. See GW to Lafayette, 10 May, n.1. The barrel contained hams that Mrs. Washington intended for Adrienne, the marquise (see GW to Lafayette, 8 June). W. B. Smith was master of Ridout's brig *Fanny*.

Letter not found: from Chastellux, 22 May 1786. On 18 Aug. GW wrote Chastellux about his "writing to me on the 22d of May."

From David Humphreys

New York May 23d 1786.

My last letter to you, My dear General, was dated in Febry at London and forwarded by Captain Clagget late of the Maryland line, in that I had the honor of informing you of my intention to return to America in the Spring, in this I have the pleasure to announce my safe arrival from L'Orient after a pleasant passage of 32 days—I am charged with Compliments & messages for your Excellency on the part of many of our friends in France; but have no news of considerable consequence to communicate.[1]

I propose setting out in three or four days on a visit to Connecticut & perhaps as Boston, this will occupy me for some weeks, after which I hope to have the pleasure of embracing you at Mount Vernon, and of remaining with you at least until the winter. I need not say how much felicity I anticipate on the occasion: nor how many thousands there are who would be envious of my situation. Nor am I little flattered with it. For although I have met with many flattering circumstances in my absence, yet certainly no gratification arising from them could come in competition with the consciousness of possessing no inconsiderable share in your friendship. My horses having been disposed of in my absence, I shall come either in the stages or by water, and will not hesitate to trespass on your goodness, by asking the favor of one of your horses when I may want to take the air on horseback.[2]

I beg my best respects may be given to Mrs Washington, my Compliments to the rest of your friends, & that you will ever consider in the number of those who are most sincerely attached to you, him who has the honor to be My dear General Your most obedient & Most humble Servant

D. Humphreys

ALS, DLC:GW.

1. Humphreys' letter from London is dated 11 Feb. 1786. Horatio Clagett (1756–1815), son of John Clagett (1713–1790) of Prince George's County, Md., served in the 3d and 5th Maryland regiments during the Revolution and was brevetted major in 1783. He lived in London after the Revolution.

2. Humphreys arrived at Mount Vernon on 24 July but remained only a month (*Diaries*, 5:14, 30).

From Josiah Parker

Dear sir   May 23rd 1786

Captn Nicholson has left with me a pair of Gold Fish which would have been sent to you before but feared to remove them dureing the Winter. I have now sent them to Genl Weedons care; to whom I Sent a box from New York last winter for you,[1] with great respect sir your most obedient Servt

J: Parker

ALS, DLC:GW.

1. Josiah Parker, the naval officer and collector for the port of Portsmouth, had in the past sent GW plants and seed from tidewater Virginia. See Parker to GW, 24–28 Feb. 1785.

From Daniel of St. Thomas Jenifer

Dear Sir.　　　　　　　　　　　　　　Annap[oli]s May 24th 1786

In a letter I received from Col. Fitzhugh dated the 17th Instant, He expresses a desire that my Answer to the Report of a Committee of the H. of Delegates against the late Intend[ant] should be transmitted to your Excelly & to Col. Mason. I do not know that it is worth your reading; but such as it is I send it to you. I shall only add to it, That the Chairman is a great Speculator, & was the man who drank bankruptcy to the Continental Money, & Confusion to Your Excellency & the American Army; yet these things are forgot, & the Man trusted. But it is said he is now sunk for ever.[1] With my most respectful compliments to your Lady & family I am my dear Sir Your ever Affectionate friend

　　　　　　　　　　　　　　　　Dan. of St Thos Jenifer

P.S. The Intends. Office being abolished by the Negative of the Senate—The office of state Agent has arose out of its ashes.[2]

ALS, DLC:GW.

1. Daniel St. Thomas Jenifer filled from its inception the office of the intendant of the revenue created in 1782 to introduce centralized control of Maryland's fiscal affairs. The enclosed pamphlet, printed at Annapolis in 1786 by Frederick Green, is entitled *The Report of the Committee Appointed to Inspect into the Books, Papers, and Accounts, of the Intendant of the Revenue, with His Answer, and the Resolutions of the House of Delegates Thereon* (DLC:GW). In the November 1785 session of the Maryland house of delegates, Jenifer presented his report on the twenty-second. On 9 Dec. the committee of claims expressed reservations about the report. A special committee was formed on 12 Dec. "to inspect into the books, papers, and accounts, of the intendant." The special committee delivered its report on 29 December. The house read Jenifer's "answer" to the report on 12 Jan. and on 14 Jan. the delegates by a vote of 32 to 22 decided that "the conduct of the said intendant" did not merit "their censure or disapprobation" (*Md. House of Delegates Proceedings*). This attack on the intendant coincided with the opening of the fight over paper money that convulsed Maryland politics through 1786 and into 1787, with Samuel Chase deeply involved in both controversies. Philip Key (1750–1820) of St. Mary's County, one of the three original members of the special committee among the five

who presented the report and whose name is listed first, was presumably the committee chairman. Key, educated in England, was a lawyer as well as a planter and merchant. On 4 June GW acknowledged receiving Jenifer's letter and the pamphlet: "Dear Sir, The Letter with which you favored me on the 24th ulto & the enclosures came to my hands by the last post; & I thank you for the information I have received from them. The Committee; by its report, seemed disposed to run you hard; but happily the House viewed matters in a different light, & rendered you the tribute of applause which was due to your services; which, as every circumstance that can contribute to your honor or satisfaction, has afforded me much pleasure, being Dr Sir Yr Mo: Obt &c. G: Washington" (LB, DLC:GW).

2. Jenifer was made state agent for special purposes—in effect was given the task of settling the affairs of the intendant's office—on 20 April 1786 and resigned on 7 Nov. 1788 (*Biographical Dictionary of the Maryland Legislature*, 2:485).

From Lafayette

My dear General,   Paris 24 May 1786.

While I Have to lament the distance which separates us, it is an additional, and an Heartfelt Mortification for me, to Hear so seldom from My Beloved and Respected friend—and Among the Many Reasons I Have to wish for a Greater intercourse Between my two Countries, I don't forget the Hope that More frequent Opportunities will increase the Number of your wellcome letters—this is Going By the packet, and will be either forwarded or delivered By M. duplessis, a Brigadier in the french service and Count d'estaing's intimate friend who intends settling in the State of Georgia—in case it is His good fortune to Come to Mount Vernon, I Beg leave to present Him to You and Mrs Washington[1]—I Have Recommended Him to general greene and I think that so far as Respects the Contract with the french Navy they may Be Useful to each other.

By a letter I Have just Received from Prince Henry, I find the Health of His Brother is declining Very fast—the New King of prussia will then Receive some proposals from the Emperor Respecting Baviera which will Be Rejected—The empress of Russia is More Anxious for the Attak of the ottoman Empire than Her imperial friend—they are to Meet, it is said, By the Next Spring in Krimée—the patriotic party prevails in Holland—But are not so United together as were to Be wished—I Have no

Great opinion of the pretended Commercial treaty Between france and Great Britain—this last Country is More Rancourous than ever towards America—they are far from adopting proper Regulations of Commerce, and still Less think of Giving Up the forts—there are only two ways to obtain them—Sword in Hand with a wiew to extend farther and then Ready I am. The other to shut up every port Against English Commerce until they Have Complied with the treaty—I don't think America Has much to fear in a War with england—and in Case she waits for a General one to see Her Claims forward she will not Have that opportunity probably for some years.

In my last letter I Have spoken to You of a Committee in which I am a Member, and of Course an Advocate for American Commerce—the Next packet will, I Hope, furnish you with some popular Resolutions—Great deal of time Has Been employed in examining the affair of tobacco—I did vigourously attak the farm Generale, and warmly expostulated for its destruction—But they can't be cut down, and must fall By the slower Method of Mines—in the Mean While mr Moriss's Bargain Has engrossed the Whole Consumption of france at such a price that no American Merchant Can find the like Any where—the ministry to palliate the evil Have obliged the farmers general to purchace Annually from twelve to fifteen thousand Hogs Heads of American tobacco, Besides mr Moriss's envoices, on the same Conditions which He Has obtained—By those Means Moriss's Contract will not Be Broken, But the Monopoly is in a Measure avoided, and it Has Been Resolved not to make any more Bargain of that kind.

in a few days, my dear General, I will go to the New Harbour of cherbourg and from thence, with the Minister of the Navy, to Brest and Rochefort—I will also visit My Country seat in Auvergne—perhaps make a tour through Holland—and Certainly spend the Month of September in Alsace with the french troops there are Under the inspection of My father in law the duke d'ayen—I will also examine the grounds of the last Campaign of Marechal de turenne.

The Queen is pregnant and will be laying in About the Month of july—Count de charlus, now Called duke de Castries, is Commander in second of the Gendarmerie which is Commanded by His father.[2]

Adieu, my dearest and Most Respected general, present my Respects and those of mde delafayette and family to mrs Washington and accept of them Yourself with that warm and paternal friendship with which I Have the Happiness to be Honoured By You—Remember me to Your Respected Mother, to all your Relations and our friends, and think often of your adoptive son who Has the Honour to be Most Respectfully and affectionately Your devoted friend

Lafayette

My Best Compliments to George.

ALS, PEL.
    1. See Mauduit du Plessis to GW, 20 July.
    2. The son, Armand-Charles-Augustin de La Croix, duc de Castries (1756–1804), participated in the siege at Yorktown.

To William Moultrie

Dr Sir,   Mount Vernon 25th May 1786.
    The Letter which your Excellency did me the honor to write to me, of the 7th ulto came safely to hand; & I should feel very happy if I could render the Company (who are engaged in the laudable & important design of opening a Cut between the rivers Cowper & Santee) any services.
    Mr Brindley, nephew to the celebrated person of that name who conducted the work of the Duke of Bridgewater & planned many others in England, possesses, I presume, more *practical* knowledge of Cuts & Locks for the improvement of inland navigation, than any man among us, as he was an executive officer (he says) many years under his uncle in this particular business: but he is, I know, engaged with the Susquehanna company, who are I believe (for I saw Mr Brindley about six weeks ago) in a critical part of their work. I have notwithstanding, written to a gentleman of my acquaintance who is not only a member of that Company, but one to whom the business is chiefly confided, & near the spot, to know if Mr Brindley's services can be dispensed with long enough to answer the purposes mentioned in your letter: his answer shall be forwarded as soon as it comes to my hands.[1]

It gives me pleasure to find a spirit for inland navigation prevailing so generally. No country is more capable of improvements in this way than our own—none which will be more benefited by them; & to begin well, as you justly observe, is all in all:
error in the commencement will not only be productive
of unnecessary expence, but, what is still worse, of discourage-
ments. It appears to me therefore, that if the cost of bringing
from Europe a professional man of tried & acknowledged abilities, is too heavy for one work; it might be good policy for several
Companies to unite in it; contributing in proportion to the esti-
mates & capital sums established by the several Acts. I see no
necessity for confining the services of such a person to a single
undertaking—one man may plan for twenty to execute; and the
distance from Delaware (between which & Chesapeak a cut is in
contemplation & Commissioners appointed by the two States to
agree on a plan) to the Cowper river is not so great but that one
person of activity might design for all between them, & visit the
whole three or four times a year.

This is only a thought of my own—I have no authority for
suggesting it; but for my private satisfaction had written both to
England & France, to know on what terms a person of competent skill could be obtained—& have received the following answer from my friend the Marqs de la Fayette; "There is no doubt
but what a good Engineer may be found in this country to conduct the work. France in this point exceeds England; & will have
I think every advantage but that of the language, which is something, altho' it may be supplied by an Interpreter. An application
from Mr Jefferson & myself to the Ministry, and more particularly an intimation that you set a value on that measure, will
ensure to us the choice of a good Engineer. They are different
from the military ones, and are called Ingènieurs des ponts &
chaussées—I think five hundred guineas a year while the business lasts, & an assurance not to loose his rank in France will be
sufficient to provide you with the gentleman you want."[2]

I have also received an acknowledgmt of the letter I had written to England; but the gentleman there goes no further than
to assure me he will make every necessary enquiry, & has no
doubt but that a person may be obtained. He says nothing however respecting the terms on which he could be had.[3] Mrs Washington joins me in compliments & every good wish for Mrs

Moultree & yourself. With great esteem & respect I am Dr Sir, &c.

G: Washington

LB, DLC:GW.

1. For James Brindley's work with the Susquehanna Company, see James Rumsey to GW, 29 Mar. 1786, n.1.

2. Lafayette's letter is dated 6 Feb. 1786.

3. See George William Fairfax to GW, 23 Jan. 1786.

To Samuel Powel

Dear Sir,   Mount Vernon May 25th 1786

The letter which you did me the honor to write to me on the 10th Instt came safely to hand, and claims my particular acknowledgments & thanks.

When I beheld the trouble I had given you, in the long transcript from the essay on the Farm-Yard, I was quite ashamed of the request I had made; but having no just plea to offer as an apology for it, I will rely on your goodness, rather than a lame excuse, for pardon.

The Society, in my opinion, have judged rightly, in resolving to continue their premium for the best Barn-Yard; for whatever merits Colo. Morgans essay may have, some thing, yet more perfect, may be hit upon; and this being, as you justly observe, the basis of all good Husbandry, too much encouragement cannot be given to men of ingenuity & industry to turn their thoughts to an object of this magnitude, to induce endeavours to improve it. It is from such attentions as these, by similar Societies, that Agriculture has been brought to the perfection it now is, in England; and this, certainly, is the readiest path, by which we can arrive at it here. Practices, founded on experience, are the best touch stones, & will prove our best guide & director, in all cases whatsoever.

Will Mrs Powell never visit her friends on James River?[1] Is it necessary to add how happy she, & you, would make Mrs Washington & myself, by taking this place in the rout? I hope not. but if it were, I could add the most unequivocal assurances of it. We unite in every good wish for you both, and I am—Dear Sir Yr Most Obedt and Obliged Hble Servt

Go: Washington

ALS, MWiW; LB, DLC:GW.
    1. Mrs. Powel's "friends" on the James River were probably her sister Mary Willing Byrd of Westover and her children.

To Alexander Steel

Sir,   Mount Vernon 25th May 1786.

As I have no information of Doctr Shiell's death, nor any connexion with his family or affairs; I return the letter which you sent me for him (and which came to hand last night only) unopened.[1] The Doctr married a lady of Newtown in Pennsylvania—a Miss Harris, and had connexions, I believe, in trade with some gentn in the City of Philada, but with whom they were formed, I am unable to inform you.[2]

Altho' I have no doubt but that the Account, rendered by you of your services & sufferings, is literally true; yet as they did not happen to fall within my own knowledge, there would be an impropriety in my certifying them. Indeed it has always been a maxim with me, to grant Certificates to no Officers in a subordinate character, who did not apply thro' the Colonel & genl officer under whom they had served; or from the head of the department in which they had acted if in the staff; the presumption being, tho' the fact in some instances might be otherwise, that I could only be acquainted with their characters & conduct thro' one or the other of these channels.

Congress have not, I believe, made provision for losses of property sustained in the course of the War, instances of which are without number; but for invalids & those who have been disabled they have, I believe, where the regular modes pointed out by their resolves, have been pursued, made allowances—but what, or how to come at them, I am unable to inform you, as this business never went thro' my hands. I am Sir, &c.

                                    G: Washington

LB, DLC:GW.
    1. See Steel to GW, 18 May.
    2. Dr. Hugh Shiell was married to Ann Harris Shiell (1760–1851), daughter of John and Hannah Stewart Harris.

From William Fitzhugh, Jr.

Dear Sir   Baltimore Town 26th May—1786.

Soon after I was honor'd with your Favor of the 15th, I had an opportunity of making an Enquiry respecting the sheep, you mentioned you were in want of—I find from one Cause or other, most of the Gentlemen who bred the best sheep have suffer'd a considerable Diminution of their Stock: so much that I am of opinion the Number you wish for, could not be obtain'd among the whole of them: On my application to Mr Edward Reynolds, he has been prevailed on to spare fifteen, perhaps twenty, of his best blooded Ewe Lambs: his Price is two Dollars each: lower than which none have been sold this season.[1] If the Number is worth your attention, and you approve of the Terms: the sooner it can be communicated with Convenience the better; as he has engaged to keep them until I receive your Determination. I think the Price Extravagant: but they are such as merit the highest recommendation and are to be met with in few places—my Fathers unsettled State in the Time of the war has been nearly fatal to his Flock of sheep: a little Time with proper attention, I hope will render it as valuable as ever—and if no accident intervenes, we shall have it in our Power the ensuing Spring, to offer you a blooded ram and a few Ewes: which by crossing with yours may be of great Improvement to them— The Barley you were so kind as to send over arrived very seasonably and safe—for which we return our Thanks. Be pleased to present me respectfully to Mrs Washington and the Family— with perfect Esteem and regard I have the honor to be Yr Excelly's mst obedt servt

Wm Fitzhugh Junr

ALS, DLC:GW.

1. Edward Reynolds was a planter in Calvert County, Maryland. For references to further correspondence, see note 2 in GW to Fitzhugh, 15 May.

To Thomas Newton, Jr.

Dr Sir,   Mount Vernon 26 May 1786.

Inclosed you have Peter Kerwins receipt for fifty barrels of super fine flour, which I beg you to sell to the best advantage, and remit what may be due to me, after deducting what I am owing to you.[1]

Twenty four of these fifty barrels are inspected; the others, tho' of equal quality, are not. The reason is, the bearer calling unexpectedly, & being in a hurry, would not allow time to get the Inspectors from Alexandria; I was obliged therefore to send them without, or miss the conveyance—the former I preferred, as I have been some time on the enquiry for a Vessel. The quality of the uninspected, my miller assures me, is at least equal to the inspected, being quite fresh. With esteem & regard I am &c.

G: Washington

LB, DLC:GW.

1. GW notes in his diary for this date that he sent the flour to Newton "by the sloop Tryal Peter Kirwin [Kerwin]" (*Diaries*, 4:336). The final entry in GW's account with Newton, and the only one after this date, is the receipt on 4 May 1787 of "a Bill upon Mr Colin McIver of Alexanda for [£]70.0.0" (Ledger B, 85). See also GW to Newton, 19 Aug. 1786, 11 Feb. 1787.

From James Tilghman

Dear Sir   Balt[imor]e May 26th 1786

In looking over poor Tench's Papers I found a bundle containing principally the letters that passed between him and the N. York committee of correspondence in 1776 I have sealed them up and if you chuse to make them a part of your Collection they shall be sent you by some safe hand[1] I am persuaded you Sir have had a share of the Sorrow his death occasioned pretty extensively—To myself the stroke was most severe For it is but justice to his memory to say that no man ever had a more dutiful and affectionate son—He made a great part of my happiness and his death has clouded my prospects exceedingly His Brother Thomas Ringgold Tilghman has taken his place in Mr Morris's business here And dare say will be ready and happy to supply it as well as he can in executing your commands here[2]— With my respectful compliments to Mrs Washington I am with great respect & regard Yr Most Obt hble sert

James Tilghman

A letter is just come to hand from an American friend of Tenchs in London, in which your name is mentioned and I take the

Liberty of inclosing you a Copy of the Paragraph If you think it worth your while to say any thing upon the Subject, I will transmit it to the Gentleman who writes the Letter with some degree of Anxiety. I know what pleasure poor Tench would have taken in setting the matter in it's proper light.

"I have had it in contemplation to write you for sometime past on Subject in which I find my self more and more interested I have endeavored to Shake it off from my mind, because I am persuaded that Genl Washington is too great in himself to be concerned at any calumny and his character too fair and pure to need any defence of mine I have the honor to be introduc'd to a party of Sages of which my Uncle is one that meet regularly at a Coffee house where they discuss politicks or subjects to communicate useful knowledge They are all of extensive knowledge and very sensible one in particular (a Mr Mauduit) is said to have written two of the best Pamphlets that ever appeared in England, is visited and consulted by the greatest personages. Mr Pitt in particular is fond of him and his opinions This Sett often mention our great & good General and commonly in *a proper* manner But seem to give Credit to a charge exhibited against him by young Asgyl, of illiberal treatment & cruelty towards himself. He alledges that a Gibbet was erected before his prison Window and often pointed in an insulting manner as good, and proper for him to atone for Huddy's death And many other insults all of whch he believes were countenanced by General Washington who was well inclined to execute the Sentence on him but was restrained by the French General Rochambeau. I have contended that it was entirely owing to the humane procrastination of our General that Capt. Asgill did not suffer the fate allotted him And that it was most happy to Genl W——'s good disposition that the French Court interposed so as to enable him to save Asgill and at the same time keep our Army in temper This affair is stated by Young Asgill and canvassed at the British Court as before related Now Sir not for General Washington's Sake who, as I observed before, is above it but for mine who take Pride in him as I believe every honest American Must, I request the favour that you would inform me fully on this Subject that I may be enabled to parry the only bad thrust made at our Salvator in my presence."[3]

ALS, DLC:GW; copy (incomplete), CtY: Humphreys Collection. As do other of
GW's correspondents, Tilghman tends to substitute blank spaces for periods.

James Tilghman (1716–1793) was a distinguished lawyer with whom GW
corresponded before the Revolution when Tilghman was a member of the
governor's council in Philadelphia and secretary of the Pennsylvania Land
Office. Tilghman retired to the Eastern Shore of Maryland during the Revolution. He had large landholdings in Queen Ann's, Talbot, and Kent counties in
Maryland as well as in Pennsylvania.

1. GW wrote Tilghman on 5 June declining his offer of Tench Tilghman's
correspondence with the New York committee of correspondence, but see
James Tilghman to GW, 7 July.

2. Thomas Ringgold Tilghman wrote GW from Baltimore on this date: "I
have been honored with your letter of the 10th & it is to repair in some degree
an omission, of which I recollect to have been guilty, that I take the Liberty of
addressing your Excellency a second time. Regard to the memory of my late
Brother, as well as respect to yourself, ought to have reminded me of offering
to supply the loss you have sustained in him, in the only way in which it is
possible for me, I mean in the ready & disinterested performance of such
services as you may have occasion for in this place. Permit me then, to assure
your Excellency that I shall be proud & happy to execute such commands as
you may occasionally think proper to honor me with . . . " (DLC:GW). GW
replied from Mount Vernon on 4 June: "Sir, I have to acknowledge the politeness of the offer contained in your letter of the 26th ulto—& to thank you for
tne disinterestedness of it. I shall have no scruple when occasion occurs to
accept (in the small way I am in) the services you obligingly tender me, as
proofs of my sensibility for your kindness, & as a testimony of my regard for
the memory of your deceased brother, who I knew took pleasure in obliging
me by acts of this nature. With great esteem, I am Sir &c. G: Washington"
(ALS, DLC:GW; LB, DLC:GW; printed copy, Thomas Birch's Sons, catalog
683, item 767, 1892).

3. For a description of the Asgill affair, see source note, Lebarbier to GW, 4
Mar. 1785. On 5 June GW gave Tilghman from memory a brief account of the
treatment that young Capt. Charles Asgill met with while under GW's sentence
of death in 1782, and on 7 July Tilghman declared himself completely satisfied
with GW's reply. After further thought, however, GW had Tobias Lear collect
and copy the documents in his possession relating to the Asgill affair, and he
sent them to David Humphreys with an eye to their publication (see GW to
Tilghman, 5 June, 20 July, 26 Dec. 1786, Tilghman to GW, 7 July, 2 Aug., 23
Sept. 1786, to Humphreys, 1 Sept., 22 Oct. 1786, and from Humphreys 9, 16
Nov. 1786; see also Richard Henry Lee to GW, 23 July 1785). According to
the incomplete copy of Tilghman's letter of 26 May, Tench Tilghman's friend
in London was named Henry Nichols. See also James Tilghman to GW, 2
Aug. 1786.

Letter not found: from Thomas Bedwell, 27 May 1786. GW wrote Bedwell on 7 June: "Your letter of the 27th ulto . . . I have received."

From William Grayson

Dear Sir   New York May 27th 1786.

I should have done myself the honor of writing to you sooner, if any thing had occurred at this place worth communicating: There has been a great dearth of foreign news, & till within a short time the representation has been so thin as to render it impracticable for Congress to undertake any matter of importance, although there are many which require their serious attention: Of late there has been a tolerably full representation but the time of Congress has been chiefly taken up with an investigation of the Connecticut cession of Western territory.

That State some time ago offered to cede all her claim to Western territory within the following limits Beg[innin]g 120 Miles Westwd of the Pennsylvania line at the beginning of the 42nd degree, extendg N. as far as two minutes of the 43rd, West to the Mississippi, the meanders thereof the same breadth; East to the beginning, reserving out of this cession the 120 Ms. between the ceded lands & the Pennsylvany line, with the jurisdiction of the same: this cession was at first much opposed, but Congress have at length agreed to accept it whenever the delegates of that State shall be authorized to make a proper deed; The consequence of which is I apprehend a clear loss of about six millions of acres to the United States & which had been already ceded by Virginia & N. York: for the Assembly of Connecticut now sitting will unquestionably open a land office, & the fœderal constitution has not given a Court in this instance: The advocat⟨es⟩ for this measure, urged, in favor of it's adoption that the claim of a powerful State although unsupported by right, was under present circumstances a disagreeable thing; & that sacrifices ought to be made for the public tranquility as well as to acquire an undisputable title to the residue; that Connecticut would settle it immediately, with emigrants well disposed to the Union, who would form a barrier not only against the Brittish but the Indian tribes upon the Wabash & lake Michigan; That the thick settlement they would immediately form, would enhance the value of the adjacent country and facilitate emigrations thereto.[1]

Some alterations have been made lately in the Land Ordnance; the surveyors are now allowed to survey by the magnetic Meridian, & are limited to the territory lying Southward of the

East & West line as described in the said ordnance; the navigable waters and the carrying places between them are made common highways & for ever free to the Atlantic States as well as any new States that may be created, witht any tax or impost thereon. An attempt was made to change the system altogether, but negatived; indeed the Eastern States & some others are so much attached to it, that I am satisfied no material alteration can ever be effected; the Geographer & surveyers have directions to proceed without delay to carry the Ordinance into execution, which I presume they will execute provided the Indians will permit them, of which however I have very great doubts.[2]

Mr Adams has informed Congress by letters lately recieved, that he has made a demand of the Posts, and has been refused; the Marquis of Caermarthen has given as a reason for refusal that many of the States in the Union have violated the treaty with respect to the debts; that the King of Gr. B. will comply with his engagements when the States shall shew a disposition to perform their part of the contract respecting this matter; the States not included in the accusation are N. Hamshire, R. Island, Connecticut N. Jersey & Delawar. I beg leave to inform you confidentially that there does not appear at present the most distant prospect of forming a treaty either with Spain or G. Brittain; That the treaty with Portugal is in a proper train; that peace can be procured with Tripoli & Tunis on reasonable terms, i.e. for 33,000 Guineas each, & probably with Morocco & Algiers for double that sum respectively if money can be loaned in Holland for that purpose. The late treaty with Algiers cost Spain one million three hundred thousand dollars. I found in Philada the book respecting Corks, which I committed to the care of Mr Fitzhugh son of the Fitzhugh of Mermian, which I hope you have recd.[3] My complimts to Mrs Washington & remain with the highest respect & esteem Yr Affect Hhble servt

William Grayson

ALS, DLC:GW.

1. After devoting a great deal of time to the question, Congress on 26 May approved Connecticut's claim to the disposal of about three million acres in the Ohio country, to be known as the Western Reserve, for the reimbursement of the people of Connecticut who had suffered losses from incursions of the British during the war (Gerlach, "Firmness and Prudence" 70–73; *JCC*, 30:310–11).

2. The vote rejecting the move toward a more fundamental change in the Land Ordinance of 1785 was taken on 11 May (ibid., 256–57).

3. On behalf of Congress John Jay sent instructions to John Adams dated 7 Mar. 1785 to protest Britain's failure to vacate the Northwest posts in accordance with the terms of the peace treaty. On 28 Feb. 1786, in his formal response to Adams's memorial of 30 Nov. 1785, the British foreign secretary, Francis Osborne, the marquess of Carmarthen (1751–1799), pointed to the failure of the American states to fulfill the articles of the treaty regarding repayment of British debts and the treatment of Loyalists. Adams wrote Congress on 4 Mar. 1786 enclosing copies of his memorial and Carmarthen's reply (*Secret Journals of Congress*, 4:185–89). See John Jay to GW, 27 June 1786, n.2. Col. William Fitzhugh (1725–1791) of Marmion in King George County had at least five sons.

From Colt MacGregor

Sir,   New York 29th May 1786

In absense of Mr Jamieson, who is at present in Halifax, I had the honor to receive your letter to him of 20th inst., and immediately enquired of Mr John Schaw's Legatee, who is still here, concerning the Books & Papers of Messrs Balfour & Barraud. I find that some years before Mr Schaw's death they were delivered up to Mr Walter Franklin of this place, who is also since dead; they came then into the hands of his brother Mr Samuel Franklin, who informs me, that he gave up the whole on 28th Novembr last to a Mr John Clapham, lately from England, in consequence of orders from Mr John Lloyd of London. Mr Clapham sett off immediately for Virginia taking the Books &ca with him, in order to effect some settlement of that Concern: I cannot find out what particular place he is now at, but presume you will be enabled to hear of him, thro' the medium of some friend at Norfolk.

Mr Samuel Franklin says that, Mr Hanbury of London was actually concerned with Balfour & Barraud, but he does not know how far that Connexion went. It is very probable Mr Jamieson can give more certain information on that head; and, as his Business to the Northward may detain him sometime, I shall by the first Conveyance, forward your letter, which I doubt not will be duly Answered. In the meantime; I thought it proper to convey what information I could collect; particularly, as Mr Clapham's stay in Virginia may be of short duration. I have the honor to be With the greatest respect Sir, Your most obdt hble Servt

Colt MacGregor

ALS, DLC:GW.

To Joseph Brown

Sir,   Mount Vernon 30th May 1786.

I have been favored with your letter of the 12th of September, & thank you for the prints which accompanied it, by the Ship Potomac which arrived safely.[1] The frames of these pictures are quite equal to my wishes, & you will please to accept my best acknowledgments of it; & assurances that an apology for their being inferior to those sent to Congress, was altogether unnecessary.

It gives me concern to learn from yourself, that the late War has been so injurious to your income, and so destructive of your hopes. My best wishes will attend any plan you may adopt for the perfect restoration of both. Of the obliging expressions of your letter, as they respect myself, I have a grateful sense, & am, Sir &c.

G: Washington

LB, DLC:GW.

Joseph Brown, a publisher in London, bought two bust-length portraits by Charles Willson Peale, one of GW and one of Nathanael Greene, which Peale had sent over "to get plates engraved" (Peale to Benjamin West, 10 Dec. 1783, in Miller, *Peale Papers*, 1:404–5). Brown had the English artist, Thomas Stothard, make "drawings based on the paintings, transforming the portraits into full-length figures and adding background details" and had Valentine Green engrave the mezzotints (Wick, *Graphic Portraits of Washington*, 31). On 12 Sept. Brown wrote to Greene, GW, and Charles Thomson, secretary of Congress, that he was sending to each of them copies of his engravings of the portraits of GW and Greene. See note 1. On 25 Nov. 1785 GW wrote Edward Newenham that he had "a mezzotinto print [of Nathanael Greene], sent to me a few days ago only, by the publisher a Mr Brown at No. 10 George Yard, Lombard street, London." Brown wrote Thomson on 15 April 1786 from London saying that he had received Thomson's acknowledgment of receipt of the two prints made for Congress. He also wrote: "I addressed a Letter by Captn Cooper to General Washington which was forwarded at same time; but as neither of those Gentn [GW nor Greene] have honored me by the least notice of either the prints, or the Letters I am apprehensive they have not been received"

(DNA:PCC, item 78). Brown's full-length portrait of GW, engraved by Valentine Green and published on 22 April 1785, shows GW standing by a cannon with the rear end of his horse to his right (Eisen, *Portraits of Washington*, 2:588). The two Peale portraits are in the Montclair (N.J.) Art Museum.

1. Brown's letter to GW of 12 Sept. 1785 has not been found, but the wording of Brown's letter to Nathanael Greene of that date indicates that he wrote identical letters to both men. The letter to Greene reads: "The reputation you deservedly acquired in the late War; a war which as a member of the Corporation of this City, I gave the utmost opposition to, long before I had the least apprehension that it would prove fatal to my Fortune, & cost me a situation in which as a Wholesale dealer I was clearing with great reputation near Two thousand Pounds ℔ annum: I say the honor you acquired induced me to be very sollicitous to posess myself of a good likeness of you; I obtained it of the late General [Joseph] Reid, who brot over half length portraits both of your Excellency & of General Washington: I have been happy in the idea that the likenesess are good, & engaging one of our most eminent Artists [Thomas Stothard] to draw them at Whole-length *I* sat for the deliniation of *your* Person.

"Those who have the honor of your Acquaintance assured me that they would make good prints; I therefore spared no expence to complete them & have done myself the pleasure to send one pair of them in a small Case ℔ the Edward Captn Cooper, bound for New York; they are addressed to the care of Chas. Thompson Esqr. who I have requested to take the trouble to forward them, to You; Give my leave to hope they will prove acceptable.

"I have also sent a pair of them dedicated to Congress, & framed in the best style I was capable of designing; I am exceedingly sorry, I could not before the Ships departure get yours & the pair I have sent to his Excellency General Washington, framed in the same manner as those are wch I have sent to Congress.

"America must for ever look up to your Excellencys as instruments in the hand of providence who rescued her from the tyrany of a corrupt Government. I therefore flatter myself when these prints are seen on your Continent that the number of orders I shall be honored with, will reimburse the expence attending the publication; at all events I have unspeakable pleasure in paying this tribute of respect to your distinguished merit—merit which has rendered you the admiration of the present Age & illustrious to posterity" (MiU-C). Charles Thomson enclosed this letter in his letter to Greene of 2 Dec. 1785.

Earlier, on 9 May 1785, Brown wrote Charles Thomson: "I have shiped a Case directed to you, containing one set of *Proof* impressions framed and glazed, of General Washington & General Green; in the same Case two other sets of prints of those illustrious Men, are packed, which I must request the favor of you to take the trouble to forward; viz. one set, to each of them, together wth Letters which it is my intention to take leave to write them, & shall inclose under cover to You" (DNA:PCC, item 78). On 3 Aug. Brown wrote Thomson that the prints did not reach the ship before it sailed, and so he "ordered them back, and perceiving that the countenance of General Washington could be improved in the print to a nearer resemblance of that benign chearfulness which distinguishes that excellent man, I had the plate altered;

The face is shortened, enlivened and in my opinion so much improved for the better that I do not regret my first disappointment" (DNA:PCC, item 123). In his letter of 12 Sept. 1785 to Thomson, Brown wrote that he was sending by the *Edward* "Two framed Impressions" of Greene and GW and expressed the hope that Congress "will do me the honor to accept these Impressions, and deem them worthy of being placed near the seat of their deliberations" (DNA:PCC, item 123).

Articles of Agreement with James Bloxham

[31 May 1786]

Articles of Agreement entered into this 31st day of May in the year 1786 between George Washington Esqr of the County of Fairfax and Commonwealth of Virginia of the one part, and James Bloxham lately from the Shire of Gloucester in the Kingdom of England Farmer of the other part. Witnesseth, That the said James Bloxham for and in consideration of the wages, allowances, and priviledges hereinafter mentioned, doth agree with, and oblige himself to serve, the said George Washington for the space of one year; to commence the first day of the present Month, in the capacity of a Farmer and Manager of such parts of Husbandry, as shall be committed to his charge; and will, to the utmost of his skill and abilities, order & direct the same (with the approbation of the said George Washington) to the best advantage. That he will, at all times, and upon all occasions, suggest such plans for the improvement of the said George Washingtons Farms, and the stocks of Horses, Cattle, Sheep, Hogs &ca which are on them as to him shall appear most conducive to his interest. Will keep regular Accts of the said Stock—and will strictly observe & follow all such orders and directions as he shall from time to time receive from his said employer; for this, and for other purposes. That when thereunto required, he will buy, at the expence of the said Washington, Cattle or Sheep for feeding, or for Store; and will dispose of the same, or any others, to the best advantage; attending particularly to the care & management of the Stock of every kind, both in Winter & Summer—as well those for the use and benefit of the Farms, and for family consumption, as those which may be fatted for Market. That he will use his utmost endeavours to encrease, and properly distribute, the Manure in the farms; and also will improve to the best of his judgment, the implements of husbandry necessary thereto—and will instruct, as occasion may require, and opportunities offer, the labourers therein how to Plow, Sow; Mow, Reap; Thatch; Ditch; Hedge &ca in the best manner. And generally, that he will consider the said Washingtons interest as his own, and use his true endeavour to promote it accordingly. In consideration whereof the said George Washington doth agree to pay the said James Bloxham Fifty Guineas for his years Services, to be compleated on the first day of May 1787; and will allow him the said Bloxham, ten guineas besides, towards defraying the expences of bringing his wife and family to this Country. That when they shall have arrived, he will provide him, & them, a decent and comfortable House to reside in, by themselves; will lend them two Cows for Milk—a Sow to raise Pigs for their own eating (but not to sell)—and give them as much Bran as is sufficient to brew Beer for his familys use. And moreover, will allow them for the part of the year which will remain after the arrival of his family and leaving his present board, at the rate of Six hundred pounds of Porke or Beef, and Eight hundred pounds of middling flour, per annum, and likewise a piece of ground sufficient for a Garden, and firewood. The said George Washington also agrees to provide the said James Bloxham with a horse to ride on for the purpose of superintending the business herein required—or, if the said Bloxham shall find his own horse, to allow pasturage & reasonable feed for him. Lastly, it is agreed between the said George Washington & James Bloxham, that if the said James should not return to England at the expiration of the year for which he now engages, and his conduct shall be such as to merit the approbation of the said George Washington, that then, and in those cases, his wages for the next year shall be Sixty Guineas; and the other allowances and priviledges the same as those of the present year. In testimony of all, and each of these Articles, and for the full and perfect compliance therewith, the parties to these presents hath interchangeably set their hands and Seals, and to the other, doth bind himself in the Sum of One hundred pounds Currt money of Virginia, the day and year first written.

Signed sealed &ca   Go: Washington
in the presence of   James Bloxham
Geo: A. Washington

ADS, DLC:GW. The document was docketed by GW.

After GW asked George William Fairfax to try to find for him an English farmer to oversee the farming at Mount Vernon, Fairfax directed James Bloxham to Mount Vernon with the strong recommendations of Bloxham's former employer, William Peacey (d. 1815) of Northleach in Gloucestershire. Bloxham arrived at Mount Vernon on 21 April with letters of recommendation in hand. In August Bloxham made clear his unhappiness with his situation in Virginia and his determination to return to England at the end of the year of service, but in the fall he changed his mind and sent for his family, who arrived in 1787. See GW to George William Fairfax, 30 June 1785, Fairfax to GW, 23 Jan. 1786, nn.1 and 2, GW to William Peacey, 5 Aug. 1786, and its enclosure, Bloxham to Peacey, 23 July 1786, GW to Peacey, 16 Nov. 1786, and *Diaries*, 4:315, 5:285.

To Alexander Spotswood

[May 1786]

my lame horse; and for the lent of the one which Austin rid up. Mr Hunter (of Alexandria) is so obliging as to take him down, to you, and will bring mine up, if he is fit to move. if not, I will wait until you may write me, as I had rather send for him than have him travelled as quick as he must do to accompany the Stage.[1]

Mrs Washington and the family here join me in every good wish for yourself, Mrs Spotswood and the rest of the family. With great estm & regard I am—Dr Sir Yr Most obedt & Affece Se⟨rvt⟩

Go: Washington

P.S. I pray your excuse for detaining your horse so long. to be honest, till I gave your letter a second reading, this day, I thought it was your request to have him sent down when mine came up—Why I should think so as there was no reason for it, and the letter contains no such request, is a little unaccountable—but this is the fact.[2] Yrs &ca G. W———n

ALS (incomplete), ViMtV.

1. On his return from Richmond GW "breakfasted at General Spotswoods" at New Post on the Rappahannock River in Spotsylvania County, on the morning of 29 April and wrote in his diary: "One of my Chariot Horses having got lame going to Richmond, but forced back to Genl. Spotswoods (not however

without much difficulty) was left there with a Servant who was ordered to proceed with him or a horse which Genl. Spotswood would lend in two days" (*Diaries*, 4:319). William Hunter, Jr., a merchant in Alexandria, had dinner at Mount Vernon on 14 May.

2. Spotswood's letter has not been found.

To Henry Knox

My dear Sir,   Mount Vernon June 1st 1786.

The Post of last week brougt me (by way of New York) a letter, of which the inclosed is a Copy. I transmit it, not only for your perusal, but for information, and advice.[1] All the papers respecting the Soci[e]ty of the Cincinnati being in possession of the Secretary Genl or the Assistant Secretary, and my memory very defective, I cannot speak with precision to Mr Jefferson, or decide on any thing which is pleasing to myself. From what I can recollect of the matter, all the Officers who chose to make use of Major L'Enfant's Agency to obtain the badge of the Society, not only commissioned him to bring them from France, but furnished him with the means. I did this myself for 6 or 8. He brought many more. I have some reason to beleive on a speculating Scheme; and demanded so much for them, as, if my Memory serves me, to disgust many Members of the Society, and induce them to apply to an Artist in Philadelphia, who, it was said, would not only execute them as well, (and without the defect which was discovered in the French ones) but furnish them cheaper. This and L'Enfant's misapplication of the money (if the fact is so) for those he did receive, may have been the Sources of the present difficulty. On the one hand, it will be very disagreeable to the American Officers to be freely spoken of on this occasion. On the other, it may not only be hard but distressing to comply with the demands of the Parisian Artisan, as we are not only unacquainted with the extent, but in some measure with the nature of them. What is become of L'Enfant? I have not seen him since the general Meeting of the Society which was held at Philadelphia in May 1784, nor, that I recollect, have heard of him 'till Mr Jefferson's Letter came to hand.[2]

Mrs Washington joins me in every affectionate wish for Mrs

Knox, yourself, & family. And with sentiments of the warmest friendship I am ever your's

Go: Washington

By forwarding the inclosed letter you will oblige G.W.

LS, in William Shaw's hand, NNGL; ADfS, Netherlands: Koninklijk Huisarchief. This is one of the rare drafts of a letter by GW from these years to have survived. Except for slight changes in capitalization and punctuation, and the omission of a letter in two words, the copy by GW's secretary, William Shaw, is entirely faithful to the draft. On the other hand, a comparison of GW's autograph letters in 1786 with the letter-book copies of these letters reveals that the copyists were often both inaccurate and careless.

1. GW is referring to Thomas Jefferson's letter of 7 Jan. 1786. See note 1 of that document.

2. See Knox's reply of 13 June, and notes.

From Richard Sprigg

Dear Sir   Strawberry Hill [Md.] June 1st 1786

In consequence of a polite Message I received from You through Col. Tilghman to send any She Asses to Your Jack—I requested Col. Mercer to send two that were at Marlbro—Now send a third to the care of Doctr Bowie at Piscataway from whence You will please send for it.

I shall be particularly obliged if You will except of the first produce from Her—then have Her covered again by the Jack for Me.[1]

By this opportunity You will receive a young bitch Spaniel— it is the second I attempted to send You from the English Bitch You may remember to have seen at my House in Annapolis. The first dyed on the Road.

Mr. Geo Diggs will send You some grass Seed from me.[2]

My Family desire their most respectfull Compts to You & Your Lady to whom You will please add those of Yr Most Obt Hume Sert

Richd Sprigg

ALS, DLC:GW.

1. Lt. Col. John Francis Mercer (1759–1821) was the son of John Mercer of Marlborough, in Stafford County, and Sprigg's son-in-law since 1785. Dr. Bowie may be F. John Bowie, who was a doctor and planter in Prince George's County, Maryland. See GW to Sprigg, 28 June.

2. George Digges (1743–1792) lived at Warburton Manor across the river from Mount Vernon.

To Mary Bristow

Madam,   Mount Vernon 2nd June 1786.

Though small were the Services I rendered you, consequent of your first application to me; yet it behoves me to add, in answer to your favor of the 15th of December last, that it was all I then had, or now have it in my power to offer. For having no share in the Legislative or Executive concerns of the Country, I could do no more than to bring your Petition before the former. This I did by a letter to the Governour inclosing it. What the ultimate determination of the Assembly was, respecting this matter, I am unable with precision, to inform you.[1] Generally, I was given to understand, that however hard the case might appear to be, it was to be ascribed to the nature of the contest in which we had been oppressively involved, and tho' to be lamented as a Misfortune, was not to be attributed as a fault in the Justice of this Country, since it was difficult, if not impracticable to draw a line between the promoters, and actors, and innocent Victims, of the War, in a national point of view. How far the reasoning is good I shall not take upon me to decide; but with much truth may assure you that I can readily enter into your feelings on this occasion, & sincerely wish that those who were the contrivers and abetters were alone to be the Sufferers by the War. I have the Honor to be, Madam, your most Obdt & very Huml. Servt

Go: Washington

LS, in Tobias Lear's hand, British Museum: Add. MSS 9828; LB, DLC:GW.

1. Mary Bristow's letter of 15 Dec. 1785 has not been found. The only known letter dated between January and June 1786 from GW to Gov. Patrick Henry is the one of 5 March. GW wrote that letter with regard to Henry's offer to send convicted felons to work for the Potomac River Company, and he does not refer to Mrs. Bristow's letter. The legislature adjourned on 21 Jan. 1786 and did not begin its next session until 23 Oct. 1786. For a summary account of the prolonged and unsuccessful efforts by the guardians and heirs of Robert Bristow to reclaim his confiscated property in Prince William County, see GW to Benjamin Harrison, 14 June 1784, n.1.

From Battaile Muse

Honorable Sir.   Berkeley C[ount]y—June 4th 1786
    Your Favour dated the 6th may Came To hand this morning
with Colo. Fairfaxes enclosed.[1]

    I did Every thing in my Power to get my wheat down as Quick
as Possable and I am sorry that you Loose by the Contract I
beleave Every Farmer and Planter In this Country will be disa-
pointed in their Expectations As Produce Sells so Very Lo we in
this Country Where Waggonage is so High see the Effects of
Such Lo prices as is now going[.] I have now in hand 1000 bushels wheat & 250 barrels Flour. I shall be oblige To you To dispose
of the Flour made from the 50 bushels wheat in your mill when
you Sell yours and place the amount of the Sale to my acct the
brand ⟨Lee⟩ if you do Not Chuos To make use of it—I shall be
Very thankfull if your miller would sell it for me this wheat is
the Property of Doctr Seldens I shall be much oblige to you To
say what you think I can give for it at your mill as some acct
must be returnd of it and I mean To allow the Docr a Just price
for it so as for me not To be Too great a Looser—my accts with
Him will be Closed for the Last years Transactions the first of
July next therefore I shall be thankfull to give me your oppinion
what the price should be.[2]

    I have not Collected as much money as to sattisfy my acct. as
soon as the Weather and roads gets better I expect To receive
again Something and what Ever I receive I shall Draw for in
your Favour in Alexandria If I can get my Tobacco down I expect To be at Mount Vernon the Last of July Should any thing
prevent me going down you shall hear From me by the Last of
July & If necessary before. in order To spurr up the Fauquier
Tenants I have Obtained Judgments on sundrie Replevey
Bonds Last Fauquier Court and have Told them I shall order
Executions out in July but as they are Poor and money Scarce I
Shall not order Executions unless I Find ⟨they⟩ are about To
remove out the County untill ⟨*mutilated*⟩ Spring only against Rector & Keyes if they do not Pay up well I shall order Executions
in July or august next agt those Two for good reasons.[3] it may
not be a miss To observe that Some of the Replevey Bonds were
Taken for more than is Justly due I have Promised the People

that I will settle with them Justly. I am Sir with great regard your Most Obedient Humble Servant

Battaile Muse

ALS, DLC:GW.
  1. Letter not found.
  2. See Muse to GW, 6 May, n.1.
  3. For the tenancy of David Keyes (Keas) on GW's lot no. 6 in Fauquier County, see Lists of Tenants, 18 Sept. 1785, n.15. Jacob Rector was a tenant on lot no. 3 of GW's Chattins Run tract (see Muse to GW, 28 Nov. 1785, n.6).

To John Fitzgerald

Dr Sir,   Mount Vernon 5th June 1786.
  Whatever number of servants you & Colo. Gilpin may think it advisable to purchase in behalf of the Potomac Company from the Ship which is just gone up, will meet my approbation; & I shall readily concur with you in price. There is a Black smith on board highly recommended, & one or two stone masons which may be useful at our works.[1]
  Have you received any precise account of the appearance or effect of the late fresh, at the great Falls? From the swell of the water & quantity of drift wood at this place, I am led to believe that it must have exceeded in height, any within the memory of man; which makes me anxious to hear from our works.[2]
  If there is anything which may require a meeting of the Directors, it would be convenient for me to attend (at any hour which may be named) on Wednesday next. I am Dr Sir, &c.

G: Washington

LB, DLC:GW.
  1. On Sunday, 4 June, GW "Received from on board the Brig Ann, from Ireland, two Servant Men for whom I had agreed yesterday—viz.—Thomas Ryan a Shoemaker, and Caven Bowe a Tayler . . . " (*Diaries*, 4:340; see also Ledger B, 227). Four days later the Georgetown merchant William Deakins, Jr., advertised for sale "on reasonable terms" 150 "very healthy indented servants" brought in the *Ann*, including "several valuable tradesmen" (*Virginia Journal and Alexandria Advertiser*). See Fitzgerald to GW, 6 June. See also GW to Thomas Johnson, 20 Dec. 1785.
  2. On 29 May GW "Found my Mill race broke in 3 or 4 places and nearly half my Tumbling dams at the head of it, carried away by the fresh, occasioned by the immoderate rains, which had fallen" (*Diaries*, 4:337).

To William Fitzhugh, Jr.

Dr Sir,   Mount Vernon 5th June 1786
     Your favor of the 26th ulto from Baltimore did not reach me
'till the 2d inst: I will take the ewe lambs at the price they are
offered by Mr Reynolds; but not knowing the age of them, or
when it may be proper to remove them, will wait 'till I hear from
you again before I send, which may be when the mares are taken
from this; & when I send, the money shall also go for Mr Reynolds's Lambs, & others, if more can be added to them of good
quality, at the same price.
     My Jack has favored one of your mares with a cover; which,
with three others, is the sum total of his performances to this
time. I do not intend to withhold my own mares more than
three days longer from Magnolio, in expectation of the Jacks
serving them. If Colo. Fitzhugh should incline to let his other
mare (if the Jack should not come to) go to the same horse, he
shall be heartily welcome to the use of him.[1] With very great
esteem I am &c.

                                                   G: Washington

LB, DLC:GW.
     1. See GW to Fitzhugh, 15 May, n.2.

From Charles MacIver

                                                        Alexandria
May it please your Excellency,   5th June 1786. 3 P.M.
     When I did myself the Honour to address your Excellency in
Octr 1784,[1] I expected, in a few Months, to have Money in
Pocket, wherewith to appear before your Excellency, and to intreat your Patronage on what I always deemed an Occasion worthy of it. I am disappointed wholly. The four inclosed Accots are
Samples of Disappointment on this Side of Potomac only.[2] If
ever I could be sordid enough to wish any Citizen of America
possessed of royal Revenues & Domains, it should be your Excellency; but as this is inconsistent with my Principles, I only
look to you with the cordial Respect due to a Fellow-citizen of
the most exalted Virtues; & so far I am ambitious to enjoy your
Countenance on the Subject of the Proposal irregularly laid be-

fore you in the inclosed Papers, which I have not Time to transcribe, because I shall want them again by the next Opportunity you have to Town, as I have promised to exhibit next Saturday.

The disaffected exert themselves against me, as they have no Favour to expect from one whose Misfortunes they have always insulted; whose Feelings they have always outraged. Numbers are misinformed, and because I deign not to be very explicite, support the first mentioned Class in supposing that I mean to be illiberal: and the Ladies, who did not attend my Lecture in 1778, are given to believe that I mean to treat them as a Satyrist. In this Emergency, I should be happy if your Excellency lived nigher, that I might endeavour to shew you I meant always to be an useful Citizen. If this appeared to your Excellency, you would perhaps countenance by your Presence.

I cannot find a Piece I wrote in May 1776, on the political Balance, practicable on Republican Principles. With candid Allowances, I wished to inclose it. It was in Opposition to a Party in Virginia.

I wrote several Pieces, for the Maryland Commitees and Conventions at the same Time; but cannot find them.

I never wished to be known as the Author of some Pieces wrote at that Time, because I wished them to be ascribed to Characters of Eminence, and of natural as well as political Attachements to the American Cause. Colo. William Fitzhugh of Maryland advertized for an Interview with the unknown Writer of one Piece; of which one Peter Carns tried to avail himself. But unfortunately he was then too deficient in the common Principles of Grammar, to gain much Credit.

I am somewhat disordered by necessary Attendance on a sickly Family, & hope your Excellency will not impute my Hurry to the least Disrespect; from which no Man can be more distant than, Your Excellency's most obedient & dutiful Servant

                                                        Chas MacIver

living at a House of Mr Hartshorn's, on Fairfax Street, betwixt Duke & Wilks Street.

ALS, DLC:GW.

1. The letter MacIver is referring to is printed above under the date November 1784. For GW's dealings with MacIver, see the source note of that document.

2. GW returned MacIver's enclosures to him on 7 June.

To John Rumney, Jr.

Sir;   Mount Vernon 5th June 1786.

Since my last of the 15th of May to Messrs Robertson Sanderson & Rumney, I have been favoured with your letter of the 16th of April by Captn Aitkinson—The cost of the Flags is finally settled, with other articles had from your store in Alexandria—and I again thank you for the trouble you have had in this business—more so—as neither Commission nor freight are charged, nor would be received—although I am very willing, and offered to pay both to Mr Sanderson.

The Flags came very reasonably and will answer my purposes very well though the workman did not keep to the sample in two or three respects—particularly on the thickness, and dressing of the Stones—some not being more than ¾ of an inch thick (scarcely that on one side) and none with the same polish of the pattern—enough however may be picked out of the whole to floor my Gallery which is all I wanted. With great esteem & regard—I am Dr Sir Yr Obedt Ser.

Go: Washington

ALS (photocopy), DLC:GW; LB, DLC:GW.

To James Tilghman

Dear Sir,   Mount Vernon 5th June 1786.

I have just had the pleasure to receive your favor of the 26th ulto. Of all the numerous acquaintances of your lately deceased son, & amidst all the sorrowings that are mingled on that melancholy occasion, I may venture to assert that (excepting those of his nearest relatives) none could have felt his death with more regret than I did—No one entertained a higher opinion of his worth, or had imbibed sentiments of greater friendship for him than I had done. That you, Sir, should have felt the keenest anguish for this loss, I can readily conceive, the ties of parental affection united with those of friendship, could not fail to have produced this effect. It is however a dispensation, the wisdom of which is inscrutable; and amidst all your grief, there is this consolation to be drawn, that while living, no man could be more esteemed—and since dead, none more lamented than Colo. Tilghman.

As his correspondence with the Com[mitt]ee of New York is not connected with any transactions of mine; so consequently, it is not necessary that the Papers to which you allude shou'd compose part of my public documents; but if they stand single, as they exhibit a trait of his public character, and, like all the rest of his transactions, will, I am persuaded, do honor to his understanding & probity, it may be desirable in this point of view to keep them alive by mixing them with mine; which undoubtedly will claim the attention of the Historian, who, if I mistake not, will upon an inspection of them, discover the illiberal ground on which the charge, mentioned in the extract of the letter you did me the honor to enclose me, is founded. That a calumny of this kind had been reported, I knew: I had laid my account for the calumnies of anonymous scriblers but I never before had conceived that such an one as is related, could have originated with, or met the countenance of Captn Asgill, whose situation often filled me with the keenest anguish. I felt for him on many accounts, & not the least, when viewing him as a man of humor & sentiment how unfortunate it was for him that a wretch who possesses neither, should be the means of causing in him a single pang, or a disagreeable sensation.[1] My favourable opinion of him, however, is forfeited if, being acquainted with these reports, he did not immediately contradict them. That I could not have given countenance to the insults which *he says* were offered to his person, especially the *grovelling* one of creating a gibbet before his prison window, will, I expect, readily be believed when I explicitly declare that I never heard of a single attempt to offer an insult, & that I had every reason to be convinced that he was treated by the officers around him with all the tenderness & every civility in their power. I would fain ask Captain Asgill how he could reconcile such belief (if his mind had been seriously impressed with it) to the continual indulgencies & procrastinations he had experienced? He will not, I presume, deny that he was admitted to his parole, within ten or twelve miles of the British lines; if not to a formal parole, to a confidence yet more unlimitted, by being permitted for the benefit of his health & the recreation of his mind, to ride, not only about the cantonment, but into the surrounding country for many miles, with his friend & companion Major Gordon constantly attending him. Would not these indulgencies have pointed a military character to the fountain from which they flow'd? Did he conceive that discipline was so lax in the American Army, as that *any* officer *in it* would have granted these liberties to a person confined by the express order of the commander in chief, unless authorised to do so by the same authority?[2] And to ascribe them to the interference of Count de Rochambeau, is as void of foundation as his other conjectures; for I do not recollect that a sentence ever passed between that General & me, directly or indirectly on the subject.

I was not without suspicions after the final liberation and return of Captn Asgill to New York, that his mind had been improperly impressed; or that he was defective in politeness. The treatment he had met with, in my conception, merited an acknowledgment. None however was offered, and I never sought for the cause.

This concise account of the treatment of Captn Asgill is given from a hasty recollection of the circumstances. If I had had time, and it was essential, by unpacking my papers & recurring to authentic files, I might have been more pointed, and full. It is in my power at any time to convince the unbiased mind that my conduct through the whole of this transaction was neither influenced by passion—guided by inhumanity—or under the controul of any interference whatsoever. I essayed every thing to save the innocent, and bring the guilty to punishment, with what success the impartial world must and hereafter certainly will ⟨decide⟩. With very great esteem & regard I have the honor to be Dear Sir Yr Most Obedt Servt

Go: Washington

ALS (incomplete photocopies), American Art Association bulletin, item no. 358, 3 May 1923, and Sotheby, Parke-Bernet catalog, item no. 188, 28 April 1981; LB, DLC:GW; copy (incomplete), CtY: Humphreys Collection. The first page of the manuscript, through the words "as they exhibit," is reproduced in the American Art Association bulletin; the last page beginning with the words "that he was defective in politeness," in the next to the last paragraph, is reproduced in the catalog of Sotheby, Parke-Bernet. David Humphreys' copy of the part of the letter dealing with the Asgill affair (see GW to Humphreys, 1 Sept. 1786) begins with the second paragraph and continues to the end. Although there is little difference between GW's text as it appears in the photocopies and the letter-book copy made later by GW's clerk, GW's text has been substituted here for the portions of the letter-book copy for which it is the original.
    1. See note 3 in Tilghman's letter of 26 May.

2. After reviewing his papers relating to the Asgill affair, GW realized his memory was faulty and acknowledged as much when writing to David Humphreys on 1 Sept.: ". . . it should seem . . . as if the loose and unguarded manner in which Captn Asgill was held, was sanctioned by me; whereas one of my letters to Colo. [Elias] Dayton condemns this conduct, and orders Asgill to be closely confined."

From John Fitzgerald

Dear Sir   Alexandria 6th June 1786

Soon after I was honor'd by the receipt of your letter this morning, I had an opportunity of seeing Colo. Gilpin & we have concluded to go up to George Town tomorrow[.] Colo. Deakins promises, in a letter received to day, that he will not part with any of them untill the Company, if they want any, have a choice.

From the mention made of the Blacksmith by Mr Dillon & others, I expect he will be very suitable for the Works, & also one or two of the Stone Masons[.] I think we had better not exceed the Number of 25 at this time, & not near so many unless appearances are very favorable.[1]

From the best accots I have been able to get from the falls, the fresh has not at any one time been higher than it was in the Spring, altho' both Potomack & Shenandoah were higher than they have been known since the year 1771, but fortunately, Potomack fell before Shenandoah began to rise so that the Violence of both did not Cooperate[.] In this part of the River the Easterly Winds which blew almost incessantly heighten'd the appearance of the fresh by the quantity of tide water which was driven up.

By first opportunity after my return I will inform you of what we have done. I am with affectionate Esteem Dear Sir Your Obed. Servant

                                    John Fitzgerald

ALS, DLC:GW. The letter was sent by William Shaw, who on this day "went up to Town on my business & returned in the Afternoon" (*Diaries*, 4:343).

1. See GW to Fitzgerald, 5 June, n.1.

From David Stuart

Dear Sir,   Abingdon 6th June—[17]86

As nothing could be transacted in a more favourable manner for the estate; than the way in which your account is settled, it must always be infinitely obliged to you—I assure you I am perfectly satisfyed[1]—with great regard I am, Dr Sir Your Obt Servt

D:d Stuart

ALS, DLC:GW.

1. What prompted this letter is not known. In March 1786 GW settled his account with the estate of John Parke Custis by acknowledging having received the balance due the estate. GW received payments due the Custis estate from the English firms of Robert Cary & Co. and Hanburys, interest due from Bank of England stock, Magnolio and another horse, oats and corn, amounting in all to £2,584.5.4 Virginia currency. This was mostly in payment of rents due on the dower plantations since Custis's death in 1781 (Ledger B, 224).

From Thornton Washington

Dr Sir   Mount Pleasant june 6th 1786

I must again trouble you respecting the two hundred acres of land whereon I now live though I fear I shall find the presant claim not so easily settled or so much to my satisfaction[1] it is among the surveys of the Hights lately recoverd by A soot in chancery which is certain as there is many now in being within the bounds of my neighbourhood that know it of A truth. John Smith whom I doubt not but you are acquainted at least with his charackter I mean Lawyer John as he is cald who married A daughter of A certain Lewis Thomas the first Purchaser of this land now claimed by the Hights John Smith says that Lewis Thomas he knows got A Bond of hite for the security of the land and gave his for the Payment of A certain sum of money which money he beleives never was Payd and he believes from this cause after Lord Fairfax became Proprietor and there was fresh warrants or grants for lands that People thinking the title of the Hights of non Effect they were careless of any papers or conveyances from Hight though he says he thinks that Hights bond is yet in being it may be in the hands of A certain George Johnstons Executors he being dead or otherways they might have been assigned by Johnston to your brother Lawrance as he was the

Purchaser of Johnston if so I suppose it may be in your hands I understand that there is to be A meeting of the Commissioners within this month for all Persons to come and Prove their rights if you have any papers relitive to the land that will be of service Pray send them.

I am informd that the Hights are to pay for improvements I have 350 acres Ajoining those without any house free from any claim of theirs but there is A mortgage of my fathers on it which I knew not when I purchasted it of him nor indeed untill since his death though I suppose I could venture to build there his estate being able to discharge the det it not excedind 600 with about 10 or 11 years interest I have just begun adding to my house the frame hauled if I must move it to my own land and begin A fresh I have but little time to get shelterd from the weather as I am informed we are to be turnd out of possesion 1st day of January[2] if this must be the case your kind offer of procuring me A workman will be if possible more acceptable.[3] offer my Respects to Your Lady I remain Sir with Esteem Yours

Thornton Washington

ALS, ViMtV.

1. In 1773 GW's brother Samuel secured from GW a tract of 180 acres of GW's Bullskin land. During the war Samuel turned the tract over to his son Thornton Washington. See note 3 in GW to James Nourse, 22 Jan. 1784. Thornton Washington wrote GW on 1 Aug. 1784 seeking GW's confirmation of his own title to this piece of land in Berkeley County where Thornton was living.

2. The challenge to Thornton Washington's (or GW's) title to his Bullskin land grew out of an old dispute between the Hite family and the Fairfax proprietors. The dispute arose after Jost Hite in 1731 by purchase and royal grant secured some 140,000 acres of Virginia land, much of it within the Fairfax Proprietary. Thomas, Lord Fairfax, persisted for decades in his refusal to confirm the Hite grants and appealed decisions of the Virginia General Court in 1769 and 1771, favorable to the Hites, to the Privy Council in London. The Hites renewed their suit after the Revolution, and, in May 1786, they obtained from the Virginia court of appeals affirmation of the favorable decisions handed down by the General Court of the colony in 1769 and 1771. For a more detailed summary of the pre-Revolutionary Hite-Fairfax dispute, see William Grayson to GW, 23 Sept. 1770, n.3. See also Editorial Note, *Hite v. Fairfax*, 5 May 1786, in Johnson and Cullen, *Marshall Papers*, 1:150–64.

When GW was acquiring a number of parcels of land in the early 1750s in the vicinity of Bullskin Run in Frederick County, he bought on 16–17 Mar. 1752, a 552-acre tract on Bullskin Run from George Johnston (d. 1766; Land Grant from Thomas, Lord Fairfax, source note, in *Papers, Colonial Series*, 1:47–

48). The 180 acres that Thornton Washington received from his father were a part of this tract. Johnston had bought the 552-acre tract from Lewis Thomas who in turn, GW assumed, had purchased it from Jost Hite. In 1770, after the Virginia General Court's decision in 1769 confirming the Hites' title to the land, William Grayson acting as GW's attorney got from Thomas Hite his acknowledgment that he had in hand Lewis Thomas's bond and would "relinquish his claim to the land provided I would undertake to pay the amount of the bond," which Grayson refused to do because he "conciev'd Thomas & his heirs were liable for it, & that the land was not subject to it in the hands of an assignee" (Grayson to GW, 23 Sept. 1770).

After receiving Thornton Washington's letter, GW wrote George Johnston's widow, Sarah McCarty Johnston Darrell, on 18 June, explaining the situation and asking her to search her papers for Jost Hite's bond of conveyance of the 552-acre tract to Lewis Thomas which should have been assigned to her deceased first husband, George Johnston. GW suggested to her that without this bond he might lose the land, but when he wrote Thornton Washington four days later, on 22 June, it was, he said, "quite immaterial" whether or not the bond was found by Mrs. Darrell, who in any case was away and unlikely to return soon. In answer to a comment by Battaile Muse on 11 July 1786 about the Hites' claims to some of GW's Bullskin land, GW summarized how matters stood in these terms: "Nor do I think the determination in favor of the Hites can possibly affect the other Land on Bullskin, because it is in proof that this Land was sold by old Joist Hite to one Lewis Thomas who sold it to Captn George Johnson and is so recited in the Deed from the Proprietors Office— In the former Trial these matters were adduced as evidence; which evidence I suppose is of record" (GW to Muse, 1 Aug.). According to Muse, "the Commissioners would hold a Court on the 4th day of September next In Winchester in order To Settle the wrights of the Lands" (Muse to GW, 11 July). GW's (and Thornton Washington's) title to the land was not challenged, but the decree of the court of May 1786 ushered in a generation of litigation over titles to land held in the Northern Neck of Virginia.

3. See GW to Thornton Washington, 22 June.

To Thomas Bedwell

Sir,   Mo[un]t Vernon 7th June 1786
    Your letter of the 27th ulto with the patterns enclosed, I have received.[1] I am sorry for the misfortunes which you have met with in the course of your business, & heartily wish that your future attempts to carry on any useful manufactory, may succeed; but I think Sir, that it would be presumption in me to recommend to any Gentleman in the State of South Carolina, a person from Philada with whom I have no acquaintance, and of whose abilities in his business I have not a complete knowledge.

I might with more propriety, venture to do it in my neighbour-hood, or in this State, than in South Carolina; but even here, I should not feel myself perfectly justified in doing it. Letters from some Gentlemen in Philadelphia to their friends in So. Carolina would, in my opinion, be more suitable, & have their proper effect. You will have my best wishes for the success of any attempt that may prove useful & beneficial to the Country. I am Sir, &c.

Go: Washington

LB, DLC:GW.

John Walters and Thomas Bedwell advertised in the *Pennsylvania Packet* (Philadelphia) on 13 Mar. 1775: "LINEN PRINTING In all its Branches, performed by the subscribers, at their Manufactory near the Three-Mile Store, on Germantown Road" (quoted in Harrold E. Gillingham, "Calico and Linen Printing in Philadelphia," *Pa. Mag. of Hist. and Biog.*, 52 [1928], 107–8).

1. Letter not found.

To Benjamin Lincoln

My Dr Sir,   Mount Vernon 7th June 1786

Inclosed is a copy of my last to you, soon after writing which I heard of Doctr Gordon's sailing. Not knowing who his Agent is, I again take the liberty of putting under this cover, the second Bill of exchange for him; & the original subscription paper on which the eleven pounds arose as part of the Bill (just mentioned) for forty two pounds which was the amount of both the Alexandria & Fredericksburgh subscriptions. As I have passed my receipts to the gentlemen who collected the money at the places above named; I wish the Doctors Agent—or Attorney if he has appointed one, would acknowledge the receipt of the Bill to me.[1]

Mr Lear arrived here a few days ago, & appears to be a genteel, well-behaved young man: he delivered me your letter, in consequence of which I applied to, & have received a promise from Charles Lee Esqr. (brother to the Colonel) to furnish him with such Law Books as he may have occasion for.[2] I wish you success in your Passamaquady undertaking, & with sentiments of very great esteem & regard, am My Dr Sir, &c.

G: Washington

LB, DLC:GW.

1. GW sent Lincoln on 20 April a list of those in Virginia subscribing to William Gordon's history of the Revolution and a bill of exchange for Gordon for the amount raised by subscription. See the response of Benjamin Lincoln, Jr., on 24 Sept., and note 1 of that document.

2. Charles Lee (1758–1815), the brother of Henry (Light-Horse Harry) Lee, Jr., practiced law in Alexandria and often handled legal matters for GW.

To Charles MacIver

Sir,   M[oun]t Vernon 7th June 1786

I received your letter of the 5th inst. together with the MSS. & other papers sent with it, which I have returned.

It gives me pleasure to see any attempts made towards improving literature & science, more especially when they tend to the immediate & particular advantage of this Country, & I should always wish to encourage & promote them: but I cannot with propriety enter into your plan, & offer you the encouragement you desire, as I am not so well acquainted with your character & abilities as many Gentlemen in Alexandria undoubtedly are, who will have an opportunity of attending your lectures, which I shall not; & are capable of giving your plan every encouragement which it deserves. I am Sir &c.

G: Washington

P.S. As the patterns & drawings may be useful to you on some other occasion, I return them.

LB, DLC:GW.

To Lafayette

My Dr Marqs   M[oun]t Vernon 8th June 1786.

You would be surprised at the old date of the letter herewith sent you, were I not to tell you that the vessel which carries it was to have sailed agreeably to the date, & by information was to do so every day since.[1] Nothing new has occurred since it was written, nor should I have given you the trouble of a second letter by the same ship, had I not forgotten to mention in my last that Mrs Washington had packed & sent for Madame de la Fayette's acceptance, a barrel of Virginia Hams. I do not know that they are better, or so good as you make in France but as they are of our own manufacture (and you know the Virginia Ladies value themselves on the goodness of their bacon), and we recollect that it is a dish of which you are fond, she prevailed on me to ask your's & Madame de la Fayette's acceptance of them.

I wanted to have accompanyed them with an anchor of old Peach brandy, but could not provide any which I thought of such a quality as would do credit to the distillery of this liquor, & therefore sent none;[2] and after all, both perhaps would have been better furniture for your Canteens on a long wet march, than for your table in Paris. It is unnecessary to repeat the assurances of the affection & regard with which I am &c. &c.

Go: Washington

LB, DLC:GW.

1. GW's earlier letter is dated 10 May. He wrote Thomas Ridout on 20 May that he was sending to him the letter and barrel for Lafayette. Ridout's brig *Fanny*, bound for Bordeaux, did not sail until late June (*Virginia Journal and Alexandria Advertiser*, 22 June).

2. An anker (anchor) was a keg holding ten old wine gallons.

To Edward Newenham

Dear Sir,   Mount Vernon 10th June 1786.

I cannot omit so good an opportunity as Mr Wallace affords, of addressing a few lines to you; altho' from the barrenness of the times I have little to say.[1]

Our Country is, at present, in peace; and measures are pursuing to give adequate powers to Congress to form such a commercial system as shall pervade, *equally*, every branch of the Union; without which we are unable to meet European powers on equal ground, and our trade with them will continue under many disadvantages.

I begin to despair (the season being so far advanced) of the pleasure of seeing you in Virginia this year, unless, instead of a Spring voyage, you should incline to make an Autumnal one. It would be but a repetition of former assurances were I to add, that I should be happy to see you in either, whenever your convenience, & the Affairs of Ireland will permit.

I little expected when I wrote you last, that Tharpe was to be the executive workman, of the ornamental parts in my new room. I had not, at the time, even heard of his arrival in this Country; but having engaged one Rawlins of Baltimore, in Maryland (lately from England) to finish it, I found, when he had brought his Men and Tools here, that Tharpe had been contracted with, and was the person on whom dependance was placed for the execution of the plan, on which we had agreed two or three months before. To this man I objected, till it became evident it must be *him*, or no *work*, there being no other, Rawlins said, who was competent to the undertaking. This being the case, and as the inconvenience of laying another year out of the room would have been very great, I consented to try him, on condition that Rawlins (who I believe has left off work himself) should superintend it closely—Tharpe has been here now more than Six weeks, and hitherto has demeaned himself soberly & well.[2] With great esteem & regard I have the honr to be Sir Yr Most Obedt & very Hble Servt

Go: Washington

ALS, PWacD: Sol Feinstone Collection, on deposit PPAmP; LB, DLC:GW.

1. On 30 Mar. GW wrote in his diary: "On my return home, found a Mr. Wallace, an Irish Gentlemen—some time since recommended to me by Mr. Edward Newenham, here" (*Diaries*, 4:301). Wallace sailed later in June in Thomas Ridout's *Fanny* (ibid., 349).

2. GW's most recent letter to Newenham, sent in May, is missing, but see GW to Newenham, 25 Nov. 1785. In the Huntington Library there is a receipt of 3 June from Richard Tharpe (Thorpe) for £24 Maryland currency, signed by him and GW, "on acct of work done to his new room."

From Gardoqui

Sir   New york 12th June 1786.

Upon the arrivall of my good freind Collo. Grayson I was puntualy honour'd with your Excellency's letter of the 20th Jany the contents whereof gave me the utmost satisfaction flattering myself with the continuance of your correspondence, to which I shall now add that you wou'd make free with, fully assur'd that nothing will be of so real pleasure than your freindly commands.

In a letter I had the honor to write to his Excellency Count of Floridablanca soon after I received your Excellency's, I had the pleasure to copy the polite paragraph by which you express'd your gratitude to his Majesty, so that I make no doubt but your Excellency's wishes have or will be complied with in the properest manner.

Spain does certainly afford some very particular curiosities both in Europe & their Americas, & the generosity of the King is always ready to satisfy the wishes of such deserving great characters as your Excellency. This subjectt leads me to take a liberty which I beg you wou'd excuse. Perhaps you have never had an oportunity to see his Majesty's *true* manufactur'd cloth so notted for its richness, call'd Vicuña, made of the wool of an animal of that name produced only in Buenos Aires. I have lately been honour'd with some, & I gladly embrace the present oportunity to send you a few yards that you may examine it, & that you wou'd do me the honor to usse it.

I wou'd not have taken such a liberty if I was not contious of the rarety of it, for even in Europe there is none but that which his Majesty grants it, so I repeatt that you wou'd excuse & accept it as a mark of the great consideration & regard I have the honor to subscribe Sir Your most obt Humble servt[1]

James Gardoqui

ALS, DLC:GW.

1. On 22 July Gardoqui, Spain's chargé d'affaires in the United States, wrote this covering letter: "Sir[,] What stands on the other side is what I had the honor to write your Excellency as soon as Collo. Grayson ynform'd me that he was to return soon, but finding that his dayly expectations are delay'd by his Employment, I take the liberty to send the present by my freind Collo. H. Lee with a small box containing the 6 yards of the Vicuña Cloth, that your Excellency may honor me with your opinion about it, observing to you that it is of the natural collor of the wooll. Your Excellency's wearing it & commanding me freely will be esteemed by Your mo. obt h[umbl]e Servt Gardoqui" (DLC:GW). Henry Lee, Jr., forwarded the letters and the vicuña cloth on 12 Aug.; GW wrote Gardoqui on 30 Aug. that he had received the letters and the cloth two days before.

Letter not found: to John Fitzgerald, 13 June 1786. Fitzgerald wrote GW on 13 June: "I am honoured with your letter of this date."

From John Fitzgerald

Dear Sir						Alexandria June 13th 1786

I am honoured with your letter of this date & am extremely sorry it is out of my power to meet you & Colo. Senf at the falls tomorrow as Mr Ridout's Brigg will then be clear for sailing & his dispatches are yet to be made out[.]¹ I have sent your letter to Colo. Gilpin & have no doubt but he will attend & I hope you & he will make any alterations in the Plan which may appear necessary to you without attending to the formality of a regular board. I am Dear sir Your mo. Obedt Servant

						John Fitzgerald

ALS, DLC:GW.
	1. Letter not found.

From Henry Knox

My dear Sir						New York 13 June 1786.

I have received your esteemed favor of the 1st instant, covering the copy of a letter from Mr Jefferson.

The Marquis de la Fayette also wrote to me concerning the affair of the eagles. The enclosed papers will fully inform you on the subject.¹

I have not the papers of the general society, they being with General Williams, therefore I cannot speak on the subject so accurately as I could wish. But I have communicated with Major LEnfant who is here, and the following is I beleive very nearly a true state of the case.

Major LEnfant conceived that the spirit of his instructions, directed that *the order* of the society should be presented to the french officers who were comprehended therein. Accordingly he did present to forty two Gentlemen of the french army, the Eagle, at the expence, and in the name of the American society. This measure was approved at the general meeting held in Philadelphia May 1784. Some advances of money were made to Major LEnfant, in 1783 previous to his departure for France, in order to enable him to procure the plate for the diploma dies &c. A committee of the general meeting examined Major LEnfants account, and reported a balance due to him of six hundred and thirty dollars, which report was accepted. The money is still due, and is all that is due from the Society of the Cincinnati, as a society.[2]

But Major LEnfant with a view to serve the american officers, and at the instances of some of them, brought over to America upwards of an hundred eagles, more than were subscribed for. I mean those for which you, myself and others gave him the money amounting to about forty. These eagles, together with those presented to the french officers, he obtained on ⟨*illegible*⟩ credit of six months. On his arrival in America he found that either the finances of the officers did not permit them to take the order, or an opinion that they were charged at too high a rate. Having bought them unconditionally he was in danger of having them remain on his hands, an event little short of ruin to him. He therefore was constrained to send them to different parts of the United States, and he did place most of them in the hands of officers in some of the States. Some yet remain unsold. In the State of South Carolina upwards of forty were furnished, and the Gentlemen paid the money into the hands of Major LEnfants Agent, but by some malarrangement LEnfant has not received it—His letter to the Marquis de lay Fayette expresses his situation fully—It appears to me that his wish to serve the American officers has involved him in his present embarrasments.

I confess I feel much concerned for him, and that my feelings are also strongly excited on account of the reputation of ourselves. For although as a society we are responsible only in a degree, yet some individuals who belong to the society have by their neglect in some instances, and non-payment in others, reduced not only Major LEnfant, but the whole society to a situation rather disagreable, as by an indelicate imputation the whole may suffer for the conduct of a part.

Although I have not the shadow of a fund for the purpose, I have offered to Major LEnfant, to pay the sum due from the general society. I should depend on Subscribtions to replace it to me. But he says that having entered into a contract with Mr Francastle the artist for the payment of the interest, and having made arrangements for that purpose, that he had much rather that the whole should rest as it is, untill the next general meeting to be held in May 1787. That he finds his fame committed, and being conscious of having acted from pure motives, he wishes to have an examination into the affair, and if he has acted right, that he may have the sense of the Society expressed thereon— He says that he shall write to the M. Fayette by the packet which will sail tomorrow, which will explain fully the matter. I shall also write to the Marquis, and inform him that the sum of 630 dollars still remain due to Major LEnfant—That I have offered to pay it to him, on behalf of the Society, but that he declines it for the reasons before given—But that if in the opinion of the Marquis the Society is in any degree likely to be injured by the arrangements Mr LEnfant has made, then to request he will pay the said 630 dollars to Mr Francastle, and that I will immediately on advice thereof replace the money to the Marquis.

I do not see what other measure can be taken at present. But if you should be of a different opinion, and will have the goodness to communicate it to me I shall be happy to conform to it.

I am persuaded, that Major LEnfant has ⟨conducted prudently⟩ here on the subject—although he may have incurred the expence of his residence here, on this very account, and perhaps have been obliged to appropriate the small sums of money he may from time to time received for the eagles for that purpose; yet he has not mentioned the circumstance, at least, I have not heard that he has. So much for Major LEnfant.

I blush my dear Sir, that I have been so remiss in writing to you. But I beg you to be persuaded that an apprehension of obliging you to answer me when it might but ill comport with your hea[l]th or convenience has been the principal cause of my omission I love and respect you, and the sentiment is deeply engraven on my heart—A line from you now and then, at your leisure will always afford me great happiness. I shall very shortly take the liberty to write you on our unsettled situation as a nation.

Mrs Knox Unites with me in presenting our affectionate respects to Mrs Washington—And I am very dear Sir Your ever affectionate friend and humble Servant

H. Knox

ALS, DLC:GW; ADfS, NNGL; copy, NNGL.

1. In DSoCi there is a copy of an extract of a letter from Lafayette, dated 11 Feb. 1786, enclosing a copy of a letter from L'Enfant to Lafayette, 2 Nov. 1785. The extract of the letter from Lafayette, which may have been a part of

the letter that he wrote to Knox, reads: "There is an Officer my dear Friend of which I must speak to you—while Major L'Enfant was here he ordered a number of Cincinnati Eagles to be made and took them away to sell them to the Officers, he now writes he cannot get paid and what money he can obtain is lost in expences to recover it. in a word, as you will see by the enclosed copy he refuses to pay what he has given his receipt for and imputes the failure to our officers. it has not yet made a great eclat, and Mr Francastel the workman has given me his last proposal herein enclosed. But Count Rochambeau to whom L'Enfant has already written intends calling for the money of those french officers to whom we gave the Badges as a present. I requested him to wave the measure telling that our Officer's could Know nothing of L'Enfants mismanagement until I had sent them a copy of his Letter—here therefore it is—and we must somehow or other arrange the bussiness, so as to take of the blame which this Letter of L'Enfants and a total refusal of payment could not but raise. I have written to the Major and to Mr Otto I think L'Enfant is at bottom an honest man, but I fear he has blundered himself into embarrassments and don't think it right that our affairs should be blamed for L'Enfants folly" (DSoCi).

2. For the arrangements made in October 1783 with Pierre-Charles L'Enfant to secure in Paris medals and engraved diplomas for the members of the Society of the Cincinnati, see Lafayette to GW, 10 Jan. 1784, n.3. For L'Enfant's report on his mission to France made to the Cincinnnati, see L'Enfant to GW, 29 April 1784. For the actions taken at the General Meeting of the Cincinnati in 1784 with regard to payments to L'Enfant, see the entries in Winthrop Sargent's Journal, 4–18 May 1784, in *Papers, Confederation Series*, 1:348–49. See also Thomas Jefferson to GW, 7 Jan. 1786, and note 1 of that document, and L'Enfant to GW, 6 Dec. 1786.

To William Moultrie

Dr Sir,   M[oun]t Vernon 14th June 1786.

Since I had the honor of writing to your Excellency last, I have been favored with the enclosed from Mr Hughes, in answer to mine respecting Mr Brindley. If you Sir, or the Board of Directors of the So. Carolina canal should incline to return the answer requested & will commit it to my care; I will be particularly attentive to it, as I shall have pleasure in obliging you, or them.[1] I have the honor to be &c.

G: Washington

LB, DLC:GW.

1. GW wrote to Moultrie on 25 May in response to Moultrie's request of 7 April for aid and advice regarding a project to connect by canal the Santee and Cooper rivers in South Carolina. Neither GW's letter to Samuel Hughes,

the manager of the Susquehanna canal project in Pennsylvania, nor the reply from Hughes has been found. Moultrie's reply to GW is dated 7 August.

From William Fitzhugh, Jr.

Dear Sir   Millmont Calvert [County, Md.] 15th June 1786
I have communicated to Mr Reynolds by Letter your Determination respecting the Ewe Lambs; since which he has not favord me with his Directions as to the Time of removing them—I mentioned to him that unless I received his particular Instructions on the subject—I should recommend it to you to let them remain with their Mothers until the last week in July; I therefore presume it meets his approbation: as there cannot be the least Doubt of his having received my Letter[1]—should you however think the Time late, it rests entirely with yourself, when you will send for them—It is improper to separate them too early from their Mothers; in which Case they frequently pine, and are injured in their growth—I wish I could flatter you with the smallest probability of your encreasing the Number to a Purchase of such as would be worth your Attention—The most eligible route to Mr Edward Reynolds's is from Mount Vernon to the Cross Roads near Piscataway about ten miles—thence to Lower Marlbro by the brick Church twenty miles, thence to the Bay side nine miles, where he now resides—He will meet with little Dificulty, whoever comes over, as the road is by no means intricate—My Father is much obliged by your Offer of Magnolio's Services: by choice he could not wish a finer horse to his mare—on a presumption—they will be sufficiently served by the last of this month, we shall about that Time send over for them—It will be unfortunate should the Jack's present Frigitity prove constitutional tho I am rather inclined to ascribe it to youth and the Change of Climate than any other Cause—for if he continues to grow to the age of twenty (a very general opinion) his early performance cannot be otherwise than highly flattering—My Father and Mother join me in best wishes to you your Lady and Family—with perfect Esteem and regard I have the honor to be yr Excelly mot Obedt Servant
                                        Wm Fitzhugh Junr

ALS, DLC:GW.
1. See GW to Fitzhugh, 15 May, and Fitzhugh to GW, 26 May. See also the other references in note 2 of GW's letter of 15 May.

From Charles MacIver

May it please your Excellency   Alexandria 17th June 1786.

It is with Reluctance, & almost by Compulsion that I trouble your Excellency so soon, & on so disagreeable an Occasion. On the 6th instant, my Wife sent me a pressing Message, desiring me to come out of Court, and speak to her on a very particular Occasion. It seems she had discovered one Charlotte, a House maid of your Excellency's, as we were afterwards informed,[1] dressed in Part of a Garment which was stole from her two Years ago. My Wife, inexperienced in the Tricks of the World, and under the Influence of natural Sympathies, had listened, in my Absence, to a Tale of feigned Distress, and given a Night's Quarters to a plausible, likely young woman. I would not turn her away on Sunday, & the third Day, my wife found her a tolerable Sempstress. On Tuesday she took a bold and desperate Resolution to carry off, at Midday, half an ass-load of Goods, including three elegant, well trimm'd Gowns, with aprons, &c. belonging to my Wife. In one Hour she was pursued thru different Ways, & almost overtaken at ⟨4⟩ Mile Run, when Chace was given to George-town, and ⟨*mutilated*⟩ towards the Falls. But the cunning Creature had got ⟨to⟩ Dr Stewarts Quarters,[2] where She Sold the Gown your Maid had, & the Apron belonging to it. The latter was taken from a Maid of Dr Stewart's at the Races in Octr 1784. If I rightly remember, she said her Husband had got it for putting the white Woman over Potomac. As the Negroe was afraid, she had Credit for supposed Candour, & was not troubled. I think she also informed us that another Negroe of Dr Stewart's bought the Gown, & sold it to a Negroe Woman belonging to your Excellency. This Gown was of Indian Chintz, white Ground, with Stripes and Figures of different Sorts of red, if not other Colours. The Work was curious & peculiar, an old Country Mantua-maker having been near a Week about it. My Wife says it is altered for the worse, particularly in the Flouncing which went all round the Tail. The Lining originally overshot the Chintz at the Sleeves, which used to be concealed by Cuffs, as they were very short. I understand the Boarder is turned upside down. My Wife wanted to take a nearer View of the Gown; but Mrs Charlotte, countenanced by another black Woman, to whom she appealed as a Lady of Character & Distinction, abused my Wife very grossly and threatened to beat her; nor would she *demean herself so much* as to be seen walking *with such* a Creature as my Wife, whom she called Suke, from Mrs Herbert's to Colo. Fitzgerald's. Mrs Herbert, hearing something of what passed, politely called in my Wife from such an unequal Contest.[3]

I have been much censured, by different People, for not making an Example of the Woman, and by some old Tories, in particular, for Reasons my Wife incautiously assigned as the Cause of my Delay. At first I tried to divert my Wife by telling her that all the Magestrates were engaged as Judges or Hearers at the Examination of the Rioters.[4] but, in Fact, it readily occurred to me, that Discretion should yield as much to your Excellency as ⟨cus⟩tom & Law gave to the most worthless Legislators ⟨in⟩ my native Country; especially when the State ⟨was⟩ not in the least Danger of suffering from the Incident of an insignificant Individual. When a Negroe Fellow of Dr Stewart's stole a fine shirt from my Wife, I thought that Gentleman competent to any Examination or Punishment the Matter deserved: and the Court of Fairfax would not have taken so much Trouble, nor given so much Satisfaction as that Gentleman—I am sorry to give your Excellency the Trouble of reading this Scrawl—When you have read it, you will, no doubt, direct some sensible Domestic to investigate the Matter, in such a Manner as it may appear to your Excellency to deserve. In the meantime I remain, with unalterable Respect, Your Excellency's most obedient and dutiful Servant

Chas MacIver

P.S. The Wench ask'd my Wife, if she could inform her what Sort of Lining the Gown had. The answer confounded the Wench, who then declared Mr Lund Washington bought it for her. My Wife told her his Word would be very good, and she would instantly go to him. The Wench instantly told her that would be needless, and asked her Companion if she had said any *Thing of*

Mr Washington's buying it. The Lady of Character & Distinction readily gave my Wife the Lie, and Charlotte threatened to flog my Wife, not without abusive & contemptuous Epithets; as if she[5] had been somewhat maudlin. Then again, the Overseer's Wife made the Gown. But Mrs Herbert Message suspended further Examination; and, as she thought of having the Matter examined by Mr Herbert, my Wife stayed with her till the Chariot ⟨w⟩ent out of Town.

ALS, DLC:GW. The cover indicates the letter was sent by John Fitzgerald.

1. In February GW lists a woman named Charlotte as one of the three seamstresses among the slaves at Home House farm at Mount Vernon (*Diaries*, 4:277).

2. This is David Stuart who had married John Parke Custis's widow.

3. Mrs. Herbert was Sarah Carlyle Herbert, daughter of John Carlyle and the wife of William Herbert.

4. On 24 June the justices of the Fairfax County court bound over to appear "at the next Grand Jury Court" Henry Low, Peter Williams, Amos Gore, John Burnham, and Michael Glass in order to answer charges of "having behaved in a disorderly and riotous manner on the saturday evening preceding whitsunday," i.e., 3 June (Fairfax County Order Book [1783–88], p. 247).

5. MacIver struck out "the Wench" here.

To Sarah McCarty Johnston Darrell

Madam   [Mount Vernon] 18th June 1786.

A tract of land which I bought of Captn Johnston (your deceas'd husband) lying on Bullskin in Frederick (now Berkeley) county, is, as well as a great many others, comprehended in the judgment lately obtained in the General Court in favor of the Hites; but may, it is said, be relieved from the consequences if it shall appear that this land was originally purchased from Hite.[1]

That the fact is so there can be no doubt, but the difficulty lies in proving it. It would seem by some papers in my hands that Captn Johnston bought the land, wch he sold me from one Lewis Thomas; & that Lewis Thomas bought it of old Jois Hite, father of the present complainants; who passed his Bond for the conveyance; which bond it further appears was assigned to Captn Johnston. Now, if this bond is to be found among the papers of Captn Johnston, for I have it not, it will render null &

void the claim of the Hites; unless it may be for the original purchase money (which was very trifling)—if it cannot be proven that it has been paid.

But if this bond is not in being, it is highly probable the Land will be lost.[2]

The person to whom I sold the land is now calling upon me—this will oblige me in turn to resort to the representations of Capt. Johnston of whom I purchased, & whose Deeds to me warrant it against the claim of every person whatsoever. But all these difficulties (except as to the original sum, which was to have been paid by Lewis Thomas to Hite) may be avoided if you fortunately should find among Captain Johnston's papers, the original bond from Hite to Thomas for conveyance of the land. It is for this reason I give you the trouble of the present application.

I am informed that commissioners are to meet some day this month, to receive such evidence as can be offered in favor of the present possessors of the land, without which the judgment will be final, I therefore pray that diligent search may be made for Hites Bond, which may prevent a heavy loss, as the land, with the improvements thereon, is now become very valuable. I am &c.

G: Washington

LB, DLC:GW.

Sarah McCarty Johnston Darrell was the daughter of Denis McCarty (d. 1742) who lived at Cedar Grove a short distance down the river from Mount Vernon. She was first married to George Johnston of Belvale, and after Johnston's death in 1766 she married, in 1771, Augustus Darrell of Fairfax County, who died the same year.

1. For a general discussion of the Hite challenge to some of GW's Bullskin land in Berkeley County, see Thornton Washington to GW, 6 June, n.2.

2. Elsewhere GW downplays the importance of Jost Hite's bond of conveyance to Lewis Thomas. See, for instance, GW to Thornton Washington, 22 June.

To Henry Lee, Jr.

My dear Sir,   Mount Vernon 18th June 1786

Under cover of your favor of the 21st of April, which came duly to hand, was a letter from Arthur Young Esqr. (author of the tours thro' G. Britain and Ireland, with observations on the husbandry of those Kingdoms) informing me that he had sent me a compleat sett of all his works. As these have never yet come to hand, nor any advice of them, you would do me a favor (if you can recollect of whom you received the letter) by enquiring whether, or not, it was accompanied with a parcel. Mr Young in his letter to me says, these books were sent to the care of Mr Athawes, Mercht of London; but why Mr Athawes should send the letter without the parcel—or either by way of New York—I cannot easily conceive, as there are vessels from London passing my door (the situation of which is well known to him) every day.[1]

The Winter & spring have been exceedingly opposed to our works at the Great Falls—The incessant rains often preventing, and at all times retarding, the removal of earth. The latter rains in May, which were continual for more than 20 days, have produced very calamitous effects in this Country; Half the Wheat (some say a great deal more) and 3/4ths of the rye, are blasted; and the ground surcharged to that degree with Water, as to have rendered plowing impracticable; which has involved the Indian corn *that did come up* so deeply in weeds & grass as to exhibit a melancholy prospect in level lands of this crop also.

The advantages with which the inland navigations of the rivers Potomack & James are pregnant, must strike every mind that reasons upon the subject; but there is, I perceive, a diversity of sentiment respecting the benefits, & the consequences which may flow from the free, & immediate use of the Mississipi. My opinion of this matter has been uniformly the same, & no light, in which I have been able to consider the subject, is likely to change it. It is, ⟨neither to⟩ relinquish, nor to push our claims to the navigation; but in the meanwhile to open *all* the communications which nature has afforded, between the Atlantic States and the Western territory, & to encourage the use of them to the utmost. In my judgment it is a matter of very serious concern to the well being of the former, to make it the interest of the latter to trade with them; without which, the ties of consanguinity which are weakening every day, will soon be no band; and we shall be no more a few years hence to the Inhabitants of that Country than the Spaniards or British are to them at this day; perhaps not so much—because commercial connections it is well known introduce others; and united, are difficult to be broken.

With the Spaniards these must take place, if the navigation of the Mississipi is opened. Clear I am that it would be for the interest of the western settlers as low down the Ohio as the big Kanhawa, & back to the Lakes, to bring their produce through one of the channels I have mentioned; but the way must be cleared, made easy, ⟨& obvious⟩ to them or else the ease with which people ⟨glide⟩ down the stream, will give a different bias to their thinking & acting. ⟨Whene⟩ver the New States become so populous, and so extended to the Westward as *really* to need it, there is no power that can deprive them of the use of the Mississipi. Why then should we, prematurely, urge a matter which is disagreeable to others, and may be attended with embarrassing consequences, if it is our interest to let it sleep? It may require some management to quiet the restless & impetuous spirits of Kentucke (of whose conduct I am more apprehensive in this business than I am of all the opposition that will be given by the Spaniards).

Mrs Washington & George & his wife join me in compliments & good wishes for Mrs Lee & yourself. With very great esteem & regard I am Dr Sir Yr affecte Hble Servt

Go: Washington

I will thank you for your care of the inclosed.[2]

ALS, ViHi; LB, DLC:GW. The words in angle brackets are taken from the letter-book copy. The ALS is torn.

1. Arthur Young's letter is dated 7 Jan. 1786. For the arrival of the Young volumes, see Thomas Fairfax to GW, 30 June.

2. See GW to David Humphreys, 20 June.

From Peter Dow

Sir   [Fairfax County] June 20th 1786

Mr Lund washington, applied to me yesterday, as also your young Man ⟨W.⟩ Shaw, to day for the Rent I owe you; I sincerely wish it had been in my power to discharge the same; but from an unforseen event, my Family coming in and drawing on me without advice for Some money; togather with my retirement from any kind of Trade to the Country, has rather embarrassed me at this Season till I can collect the growing Crop—If it were any way agreeable to your excellency I wou'd give Bond with

Security & Interest pay[abl]e in Six months.[1] I am Sir your Excellencys Most Obedent & Most hume Servant

Peter Dow

ALS, DLC:GW. The letter was sent "by Mr [William] Shaw," GW's secretary.

1. In 1782 GW bought a 376-acre tract on Hunting Creek from Peter Dow and others in order to exchange it for the 543-acre French–Dulany land on Dogue Run, but the exchange was not consummated until the fall of 1786 because of Penelope French's refusal to give up her lifetime right to the land on Dogue Run. In the meantime, Dow had been renting and continuing to live on the Hunting Creek tract. See George Clinton to GW, 27 Feb. 1784, source note, GW to Charles Lee, 20 Feb. 1785, *Diaries*, 4:84–85, and GW to William Triplett, 25 Sept. 1786, and notes.

To David Humphreys

My dear Humphreys   Mount Vernon 20th June 1786

Your letter from New York (as did the preceeding one from London) came duly to hand, & claim my particular acknowledgments.[1] On your return to America I sincerely congratulate you. I shall rejoice to see you at this place, & expecting it soon, shall add little at this time. The only design of this letter is to assure you, that you will have *no* occasion for Horses, for mine will always be at your service; & very little for a Servant, as your old acquaintance Will (now fit for little else) can whiten your head, & many idlers about the House can blacken your shoes; but in the latter case I entreat you to be governed wholly by your own inclination & convenience.

Not knowing at what place to direct for you, I send this under cover to Colo. Lee (to whom I have occasion to write)[2]—Mrs Washington & George & his wife join me in every good wish for you & I am ever yr sincere friend and Affe. Hble Servt

Go: Washington

ALS, ViMtV; LB, DLC:GW.

1. Humphreys' letter from New York is dated 23 May and that from London, 11 February.

2. See GW to Henry Lee, Jr., 18 June.

From André Michaux

Sir   Alex[andri]a 20th June 1786
　You will find herewith, the Seeds, that I Spoke of, to Your
Excelly Yesterday.[1] I will accept of the Offer, that you made me,
in Sending to your Care, the Collections that I Shall make in the
Distant Countries for the use of the King of France.[2]
　I Shall Esteem it a Happiness, If I Can Discover any thing,
that can be of any use to Your Excellency. I am very Respectfully
Sir Your Very Obedt & Very Humble Servt

A: Michaux
Botanist to his Most Christian Majesty

Translation, DLC:GW. Both the unaddressed letter and the endorsement are
in the hand of GW's secretary, William Shaw, who on 20 June "went up to
Alexandria on my business and returned in the afternoon" (*Diaries*, 4:351).
　1. Michaux visited Mount Vernon on Monday, 19 June, with letters of introduction from Lauzun and Lafayette and remained for dinner. GW recorded
in his diary on 29 June and 1 July the planting of the seed and plants sent
him by Michaux, which included seeds of the Jerusalem thorn and pyramidi-
cal cypress, pistachio nuts, evergreen buckthorn trees, *phillyrea latifolia* shrubs,
and golden chain trees (ibid., 354, 5:1).
　2. For Michaux's current activities in America, see Lafayette to GW, 3 Sept.
1785, n.1. For GW's earlier involvement in collecting seed and plants for Louis
XVI's gardens at Versailles, see Lafayette to GW, 17 Dec. 1784, Thomas Marshall to GW, 12 May 1785, and GW to Lafayette, 25 July 1785.

To Nicholas Pike

Sir,   Mount Vernon 20th June 1786
　Your letter of the 25th of March did not come to hand till
lately or it should have had an earlier acknowledgement.
　It gives me the highest satisfaction to find the Arts and Sci-
ences making a progress in any Country; but when I see them
advancing in the rising States of America I feel a peculiar pleasure: and in my opinion, every effort of Genius, and all attempts
towards improving useful knowledge ought to meet with encouragement in this Country. Your performance is of the most
useful and beneficial kind, and, from the opinion of those Gentlemen who have inspected it I have not the least doubt but that
it is a very valuable one.

I feel a grateful sense of the honour which you designed me by wishing to dedicate your Book to me, and would even sacrifice my own ideas of propriety respecting the matter so far as to comply with your request, if I thought that by a non-compliance I should discourage so good a work. But Sir, as there are several Characters in your part of the country who deservedly hold a high rank in the literary world, and whose names would add dignity to such a performance, it would be more proper (if I might presume to offer my opinion upon the matter) to dedicate your Book to them. I must therefore beg leave to decline the honour which you would do me, as I have before done in two or three cases of a similar kind. With the sincerest wishes for the success of your work, and much esteem I am Sir, Your Obdt Hume Servt

Go: Washington

LS, in Tobias Lear's hand, NNC; LB, DLC:GW.

To Clement Biddle

Dear Sir,   Mount Vernon June 21st 1786

Enclosed is a copy of my last—It is so long since it was dispatched (without an acknowledgment of it) that I begin to fear some accident must happened, altho' it was sent to the Post Office in Alexandria by a very safe hand. Should this be the case, I pray you to notify the Office of the loss of the Certificate which was enclosed, that neither principal nor interest may be paid to the bearer till there is an investigation of his, or her claim to it, is first had. For this reason I send you an exact copy of the certificate, taken from the original before it was enclosed. and wish that every proper step may be taken to recover it.[1]

Not being able to discover how the letter should get lost, and still hoping it is not, I do not, at this time, send you patterns for the glass then required, but will do so if necessary as soon as I hear from you. I am—Dear Sir Yr Most Obedt Hble Servt

Go: Washington

ALS, PHi: Washington-Biddle Correspondence; LB, DLC:GW.

1. See GW to Biddle, 18 May, and Biddle to GW, 25 June.

To Joseph Dashiell

Sir,   Mount Vernon 21st June 1786.

I thank you for requesting a skipper from the Eastern shore to call upon, & make me an offer of the posts & rails he had for sale. They were not however of a kind to answer my purposes (being for paling), nor should I incline to buy any unless they are *better* & are to be had *cheaper* than those wch might be taken from my own land.

To judge of the propriety of this, you wou'd oblige me Sir, by informing me on what terms Cypress posts 7 feet long, 5 inches by 6 at top, & 7 inches by 6 at bottom; (a stack a foot square making 4)—and Cypress plank 12 feet long, 6 wide & 1¼ inches thick, could be had delivered at my landing, supposing 500 of the first, & a proportional quantity of the latter for rails. I mention cypress on a supposition that it is a lasting wood for posts; but would be glad to know *also*, what the difference in price would be, between cypress & Pine, in the rails *only*.[1] I am &c.

G: Washington

LB, DLC:GW.

Joseph Dashiell (1736–c.1787), a planter and the owner of a sloop, was a justice of the peace in Worcester County, Maryland. He had represented the county in the lower house of the legislature as recently as 1785.

1. See Dashiell to GW, 20 July.

To Thornton Washington

Dr Thornton,   Mount Vernon June 22d 1786.

Mr Throckmorton delivered me your letter of the 6th inst:[1] I am under no apprehension that the title to the land on which you live can be affected by the decision lately had in favor of Messrs Hites & others. Such papers as I can readily find respecting this tract, I send you. The patent from the proprietors office, granted to Captn George Johnston of whom I bought the land, particularly recites that it was granted by Jois: Hite to Lewis Thomas. the deposition of John Smith taken, & admitted in the former trial, & I suppose is of record—with the copy of Lewis Thomas's bond passed for the payment there of—together with the statement subscribed by Colo. Grayson—places the whole business in my opinion in a very clear & unequivocal point of view. But if the Commissioners (which I can scarcely conceive) should be of a different way of thinking, I should be glad to have time to illucidate matters more fully.

Colo. Grayson you will perceive certifies that what he has signed is a true copy from the proceedings; in these it is expressly admitted by the complainants, that Js Hite did sell 425 acres; which upon a resurvey (possibly by adding a little of the barrens) measured 552 acres. Not having the original bond from Joist Hite to Lewis Thomas in my possession, I sent to the widow Darrell, formerly wife of Captn Johnston, to see if it could be found among his papers; but she was from home & not likely, my messenger was informed, to return soon—and very probably may be found as a deposit in the proprietors, as the Deed is expressly founded upon it. In my judgment it is quite immaterial where it is, as there is, besides the admission of the papers, the most uncontrovertible evidence of the sale to Thomas. By L. Thomas's bond to Joist Hite, it appears that the money was to have been paid, "at such time, that the said Joist Hite, his Heirs, Executors, Administrators or Assigns can obtain a good Patent from the office."

The only point therefore which can be disputed, according to my conception of the case, is, if the purchase money has never yet been paid, who is liable—the possessors of the land, or the persons to whom it was sold, or their representatives? Whether the decree of the Court goes to this point, or what powers are vested in the Commissioners respecting it I know not, never having seen the judgment, & having had but a very indistinct report of it.[2]

The Ship with servants happening to be becalmed opposite to my door, I sent on board to enquire for a Carpenter; only one stood upon the list—& he professing not to understand much of the business, I concluded he understood nothing of it, and therefore did not b[u]y him for you.[3] My best wishes attend you & your wife. I am Affectly yrs

G: Washington

LB, DLC:GW.

1. Albion Throckmorton of Frederick County and his wife Mildred Wash-

ington Throckmorton had dinner and spent the evening at Mount Vernon on 19 June (*Diaries*, 4:350). The copyist wrote "Jnr" instead of "Mr."

2. For a discussion of the Hites' challenge to GW's title to some of his Bull-skin land, see Thornton Washington to GW, 6 June, n.2. William Grayson's enclosed statement regarding the proceedings of a "former trial" undoubtedly refers to the trial before the Virginia General Court decided in 1771 (see Grayson to GW, 23 Sept. 1770).

3. See GW to John Fitzgerald, 5 June, n.1.

From William Foster

Sir   Bridlington Yorks[hir]e [England] 23 June 1786

In the Season of Warr when too often the voice of Humanity and the calls of Justice are stifled in the Rage and Tumult of the Contest, 'Twas Yours sir in the midst to exhibit that a delicate adherence to the Virtues of the mind may be united in the Breast of the Warrior and the Statesman.

In the beginning of the late unhappy dispute I was (not in Arms) taken going to Boston and carryed to your Camp at Cambridge, it was there I was indetted to you for personal Security and speedy Liberation, and it was in the Confidence of your Protection our Confinement was considerably alleviated.[1]

The Opportunity of a Relation passing near your door affords me the means of declaring to you how much I feel myself Sir Your obliged and Obedient servt

Wm Foster

ALS, DLC:GW.

1. William Foster was captain of the ship *Jenny* when it was captured in 1775 by the schooner *Lee*, John Manley captain. See William Bartlett to GW, 9, 11, 20 Dec. 1775, GW to John Hancock, 11 Dec. 1775, and notes of all these documents.

From George Fisher

Sir,   Philad[elphi]a 24 June, 1786

Agreeably to your orders I waited on Capt. Colfax for the Money which you informed me you had paid to him for me, being Eighty Dollars, but he told me, in direct Opposition to your Excellancy's words that he had never recd any such money. I also waited on Lt. Howe, and he had nothing for me neither.[1]

I think, in my humility, it is parculiarly hard that I should be kept out of what is so justly my due, & indeed what your Excellany paid to Men in Affluance to deliver to the poor. However from your Excellancy's benevolence & Charity I still hope to receive this Sum & leave to your Excellany the mode of recovering it. I continue with Mrs House in my old Station, as Cook, & where I hope I shall have the honor of receiving your Excellency's further information. I have the honor to be your Excellancy's most Obedient & Obliged Servant

George Fisher

LS, DLC:GW.

George Fisher, who in February 1777 enlisted in the 3d Pennsylvania Regiment, was transferred as a cook on 1 Jan. 1782 to the commander in chief's guards commanded by Capt. William Colfax. He was furloughed in Newburgh, N.Y., on 6 June 1783 and discharged on 3 Nov. 1783.

1. Bezaleel Howe was a lieutenant of GW's guards.

From Clement Biddle

Dear Sir   Phila[delphi]a June 25. 1786

I must appologize for my not acknowledgeing the receipt of your favour of 18 May Covering Certificates for 339⁵³/₉₀ Dollars but I was daily in expectation of our Opportunity to send the Glass which I did not meet till last week by the Dolphin Captain Stewart by whom I sent it with the receipt enclosed under cover to the care of Colo[ne]l Hooe & since then I have waited for this Conveyance by Major Gibbs.[1]

I now inclosed the Bill for the Glass also Mr Oswald's & Messrs Dunlap & Claypooles receipt for the papers which I have stopped them from sending—Mr Humphreys say he has no account against you I have also paid Messrs Lewis's Acct which is inclosed—Stelles Certificate would sell for 8/ in the pound as it now is that is £50.18.9 specie for the whole or you may draw 84 Dollars Interest in Indent & 6 p. Ct Interest in our paper money and then let it remain a funded Certificate of Pennsylvania.

I had not purchased the Tour through Great Britain as no New Book have arrived—Linen is not sold very low at our Vendues this season as but few Vessels have arrived from Ireland & will not till about September—Oznabrigs has been a scar[c]e Article & tho' I am within a few doors of the City Vendue I have seen none there for sale of a good quality but what was damaged and there are few striped Duffel Blankets for sale in the stores— nor do I think they can be had reasonable till October.

In answering your former Letter I have of course inclosed your favour of 20 Inst. just received.

Mrs Biddle begs to join in respectful Compliments to Mrs Washington with—Dr General yr Obedt & very Hume Servt

Clement Biddle

I shall keep the Certificate for your further Orders. I forwarded the Letter recd from Mr George Washington to Jamaica immediately.

ADfS, ViMtV: Clement Biddle Letterbook. In his letter to Biddle of 31 July, GW refers to Biddle's letter of 24, not 25, June.

1. Caleb Gibbs, formerly commander of GW's guards, arrived at Mount Vernon on 29 June and left on 1 July.

To George William Fairfax

dear Sir,   Mount Vernon June 25th 1786

Since I had the honor of writing to you in November last, I have been favoured with your letters of the 23d of June in the last, and 23d of Jany in the present year. The first was handed to me by Doctr Baynham, and the other by Mr James Bloxham.

Your conjectures respecting the fate of our letters, are, I am persuaded, too well founded. Such frequent miscarriages would not have resulted from negligence alone—but why after the prying eye of curiosity, or the malignant hope of trapanning an individual, or making useful discoveries were disappointed, the letters should not have been permitted to proceed to their address, is not easy to be conceived. Being well apprized of the delicacy of your situation I have studiously avoided every expression in all my letters which might, if known, have involved you in the smallest difficulty or embarrassment. It is wantonly unfeeling therefore to destroy, as well as to have inspected, such as were founded in friendship and so contained occurrences which related to the parties *only*, for their bases. In future I will always place my letters to you, under cover to Mr Athawes.[1]

In a former letter I informed you, that Mr Pine's reception in this Country had been favourable; and indicative of a plentiful harvest in the line of his profession. Consequent of your good report of this Gentleman, I furnished him with letters to many of the first characters in Philadelphia & Annapolis; & have every reason to believe that his success will not fall short of his expectations if it is not injured by any act of his own—against which his prudence will, no doubt, secure him.[2]

Though envy is not among the ingredients which compose my constitution, yet the picture you have drawn of your present habitation & mode of living, is enough to create strong desires in me to be a participator of the tranquillity and rural amusements you have described. I am gliding into the latter as fast as I can, being determined to make the remainder of my life easy let the world, or the concerns of it, go as they may; & I am not a little obliged to you, my good Sir, for the assurance of contributing to this by procuring me a Buck & Doe of the best English Deer; but if you have not already encountered this trouble I would now wish to relieve you from it, as Mr Ogle of Maryland has been so obliging as to present me Six fawns from his Park of English Deer at Bell-Air.[3] Of the forest Deer of this Country I have also procured six, two bucks & four Does—with these & tolerable care, I shall soon stock my small Paddock. In this release, I do not mean to acquit my good friend Mrs Fairfax of the offer she has made me. I will receive with great pleasure & gratitude the seeds of any Trees or shrubs which are not natives of this Country but reconcileable with the climate of it, that she may be so obliging as to send me; and while my attentions are bestowed on the nurture of them, it would, if any thing was necessary to do it, remind me of the happy moments I have spent in conversations on this and other subjects with that Lady at Belvoir.

My Friend in New England having, since the date of my letters to you, in November, engaged a young Gentlemn for me of decent appearance & respectable family as a tutor for the two little Custis's (who live with me), I have to pray that the trouble I was about to give you on this occasion may cease, and that the letter which I put under your cover for a Mr Chapman, may be burnt.[4]

I have now, my dear sir, to beg you to accept my particular thanks for the early attention which you paid to my request respecting a Farmer; and for directing Mr Bloxham to offer himself to me before he should engage with any other. The character given of him by Mr Peacy is full & ample, & his appearance and conversation being much in his favour, I have agreed to give him Sixty Guineas pr Ann. for his services, & find him and family in Provisions, a house to live in, a garden to work, and two Cows to furnish them with Milk. In consequence thereof he proposes to write for his wife and children to come to him. With his assistance & advice I shall be able to dispense with a Steward. I have now taken the management of my Farms into my own hands, and shall find employment & amusement if not profit, in conducting the business of them myself.

The Postscript to your letter of the 23d of Jany has given me pain, It would seem from the tenor of it as if you conceived I was not well pleased at your giving Mr Thos Corbin a letter of introduction to me; be assured my dear sir, nothing was ever further from me than to express such a sentiment. My intention, however incautiously it was communicated, was only to inform you that his brother Dick had determined to play nothing short of the whole game, & therefore was resolved to be as early with his narrative in this Country as Tom could be. And now, whilst I am upon this subject, let me once for all entreat you not to be so scrupulous, or backward in your introductions, for I can assure you with much truth that every occasion which affords the means of hearing from you & Mrs Fairfax will give pleasure in this family; & no person who shall bear your passport will be an unwelcome guest in it. So many come hither without proper introductions that it is a real satisfaction when I am able to discriminate. This will be the case when Mr Ansly, or any other shall present a letter from you to me—No inconvenience can arise from these things—my manner of living is plain and I do not mean to be put out of it—A glass of wine and a bit of mutton is always ready—such as will be content to partake of it are welcome—those who look for more will be disappointed, but no change will be effected by it.[5]

In every wish that can contribute to the happiness and pleasure of yourself & Lady Mrs Washington joins me—and with sincere regard and Affection I am—My dear Sir Yr Most Obedt Hble Sert

Go: Washington

ALS, MoSW; LB, DLC:GW. Presumably both this and the letter of 30 June were sent under cover of the letter to Athawes. Fairfax wrote on the back of the last sheet of GW's letter of this date: "those lrs from General Washington contain an account, and are about business: therefore kept."

1. GW wrote Samuel Athawes on 15 July: "Sir, The frequent miscarriages of letters from Colo. Fairfax to me, & vice versa, has induced him to request, & me to take the liberty of placing the enclosed under cover to you. I pray you to excuse it, & to be assured of the esteem with which, I am, Sir, &c. G: Washington" (LB, DLC:GW).

2. GW wrote Fairfax on 30 June 1785 about the American reception of the portrait painter Robert Edge Pine.

3. See Benjamin Ogle to GW, 20 Aug. 1785.

4. GW's letter to George Chapman is quoted in GW to Fairfax, 10 Nov. 1785, n.2.

5. See Fairfax to GW, 23 Jan. 1786, n.6. GW plainly misread "Ansly" for "Ansty" in Fairfax's letter.

From Alexander McCabe

Sir   Elizabeth Town [N.J.] June the 26th, 1786

I take the liberty to write to your Excelly about a gentleman that I have some letters for from Ireland, the Revd John Wallace. I am informd by a letter I recd a few days ago, that he is under an appointment of yr Excellency's as presedent of an academy in Verginea, I shall therefore be much Oblig'd if your Excellency will be so good to inform me what part of Verginea he is in.[1]

I hope your Excellency will excuse the freedom I take in enclosing a letter of Colonel Persse's of Roxborrow a gentleman of extensive fortune a particular friend & well[2] wisher of yours, was so the most precarious times in Ireland I could tell yr Excellency many Anecdotes of the Colonels good Sentiments love & Esteem for you. one in particular every day after dinner the first toaste was his Excy George Washington, he has compell'd yr greatest Enemies to do the same. There is no beautifull spot on his Estate but will bare your memory to the latest ages as they have some appellation from every Victorious Engagement your Excellency was in.[3]

Coll Persse begs to know how you are I am convinc'd he would rather receive a line from your Excellency than any honour the first Monarch in the universe could Confer on him I will write to the Coll when I receive your Excellencys ansr relative to Mr Wallace, will be much oblig'd if your Excellency will enclose back Coll Persse's letter to me. I am yr Excellency's most humble & most Obedient se⟨rvt⟩

Alexander McCabe

P.S. Please to direct to the Care of Jacob Cooke Esqr. Lancaster, State of Pennsylvania.

ALS, DLC:GW.
   Alexander McCabe has not been identified.
   1. John Wallace is probably the man who stayed at Mount Vernon from 30 Mar. to 3 April, and again on the night of 8 June (see *Diaries*, 4:301–3, 344, and GW to Edward Newenham, 10 June, n.1).
   2. McCabe wrote "fell."
   3. The letter from William Persse, whose estate Roxborough was in county Galway, has not been found, but see Persse to GW, 11 Oct. 1788, and GW to Persse, 2 Mar. 1789. A daughter of Persse married a son of Edward Newenham.

Letter not found: from William Brown, 27 June 1786. On 30 June GW wrote Brown "In answer to your favor of the 27th."

From John Jay

Dear Sir   Philadelphia 27 June 1786
   Being deputed by the Church Convention of New York, to attend a general one convened here, I brought with me your obliging Letter of the 18 ult. that I might devote the first Leisure Hour to the Pleasure of answering it.[1]
   Congress having freed the Papers of which the enclosed are Copies from Injunctions of Secrecy, and permitted the Delegates to make and send Extracts from them to their different States, I think myself at Liberty to transmit copies to you.
   These papers have been referred to me—some of the Facts are inaccurately stated, and improperly colored—but it is too true that the Treaty has been violated. on such occasions I think it better fairly to confess and correct Errors, than attempt to deceive ourselves & others by fallacious tho' plausible Palliations and Excuses. To oppose popular Prejudices, to censure the Proceedings and expose the Improprieties of States, is an unpleasant Task—but it must be done.[2]

Our affairs seem to lead to some crisis—some Revolution—
something that I cannot foresee, or conjecture. I am uneasy and
apprehensive—more so, than during the War—*Then* we had a
fixed Object, and tho the means and time of attaining it were
often problematical, yet I did firmly believe that we should ultimately succeed, because I was convinced that Justice was with
us. The Case is now altered—we are going and doing wrong,
and therefore I look forward to Evils and Calamities, but without being able to guess at the Instrument nature or measure of
them. That we shall again recover, and things again go well, I
have no Doubt—such a variety of circumstances would not almost miraculously have combined to liberate and make us a Nation for transient or unimportant Purposes—I therefore believe
we are yet to become a great and respectable People—but when
or how, the Spirit of Prophecy only can discern.

There doubtless is much Reason to think and to say that we
are woefully and in many Instances wickedly misled. private
Rage for Property suppresses public Considerations, & personal
rather than national Interests have become the great objects of
attention. Representative Bodies will ever be faithful Copies of
their originals, and generally exhibit a chequered assemblage
of Virtue and Vice, of Abilities and Weakness. The Mass of Men
are neither wise nor good—and the Virtue like the other Resources of a country can only be drawn to a point by strong
Circumstances ably managed, or strong government ably ad-
ministred. New governments have not the aid of Habit and hereditary Respect; & being generally the Result of preceding Tumult and confusion do not immediately acquire Stability or
Strength—Besides, in times of Commotion some Men will gain
confidence & Importance who merit neither; and who like political Mountebanks are less sollicitous about the Health of the
credulous Croud, than about making the most of their Nostrums & Prescriptions.

New York was rendered less fœderal, by the opinions of the
late President of Congress[3]—This is a singular tho' not unaccountable Fact—indeed human actions are seldom inexplicable.
What I most fear is, that the better kind of People—(by which I
mean the People who are orderly and industrious, who are content with their situations, and not uneasy in their Circumstances,) will be led by the Insecurity of Property, the Loss of

Confidence in their Rulers, & the Want of public Faith & Rectitude, to consider the Charms of Liberty as imaginary and delusive. A State of uncertainty and Fluctuation must disgust and alarm such Men, and prepare their Minds for almost any change that may promise them Quiet & Security.

Your letter to Mrs Macauley Graham is on the Way to her, enclosed in one from me to Mr Adams[4]—I forget the Name of the Vessel.

Be pleased to make my Compts to Mrs Washington, and be assured that I am with the greatest Respect & Esteem Dear Sir your obt & hble Servt

John Jay

ALS, DLC:GW.

1. The General Convention of the Episcopal church began in Philadelphia on 20 June.

2. Jay had begun work on a report documenting the failure of individual states to fulfill the terms of the treaty of peace with regard to the collection of British debts and the treatment of Loyalists. He presented it to Congress on 13 Oct. 1786, and the report is printed in *Secret Journals of Congress*, 4:185–287. The copies of "papers" that Jay sent to Washington in this letter may have included John Adams's memorial of 30 Nov. 1785 protesting the British occupation of the northwest forts, the British foreign secretary's countercharges of 28 Feb. 1786, and Adams's letter to Congress of 4 Mar. 1786 (see William Grayson to GW, 27 May 1786, n.3). In a letter to Adams on 1 Nov. 1786, Jay summed up his report to Congress: "The result of my inquiries into the conduct of the States relative to the treaty, is, that there has not been a single day since it took effect, on which it has not been violated in America, by one or other of the States" (Johnston, *Jay Papers*, 3:214–15).

3. Jay is referring to Richard Henry Lee, president of Congress in 1784 and 1785, who had become a vociferous opponent of the movement to strengthen the general government.

4. See GW to Jay, 18 May.

From Thomas West

Sir   Alexandria [Va.] 27th June 86

I am sorry that the papers you mention are not ready for your perusal but you may rest Assured that nothing shall be wanting on my part to bring those matters to a final conclusion. since I spoke to you last on the subject have selected a number of the decd Colo. Colvills Papers many of which are of consequence and shou'd have had the whole ready by this day had proper care been taken of them before they came under my care but in the course of two Weeks expect to be prepared[1] in the mean am sir yr most Obedt & very Hble Servt

Thos West

ALS, DLC:GW.

1. Thomas West was the son of John West, Jr., who until his death in 1777 was, like GW, one of the executors of the estate of Thomas Colvill, his wife's uncle who died in 1766. Thomas West, as his father's executor, wrote to GW about the Colvill estate as early as 1779, and GW replied from New Windsor, N.Y., on 5 July 1779: "Let me entreat you to have the accts of that Estate put in the best Order imaginable—and every voucher, Paper, and memorandum which tends to explain, or can any ways illucidate matters, carefully selected, as I am very anxious, or shall be so the moment it is in my power, to have a final settlement of my Executorship of that Estate in order to obtain a discharge from the trust." Despite West's promises on this day, it was not "two Weeks" but more than four months before Thomas West sent GW the papers relating to the Colvill estate (see GW to James Tilghman, 20 July 1786, and GW to Thomas West, 6 Nov. 1786). For a summary account of the complexities of the Colvill estate and the continuing efforts to settle it, see the notes in GW to John West, Jr., December 1767; see also GW to John Swan, 23 May 1785, and the references in notes 1 and 2 of that document, and Thomas Montgomerie to GW, 24 Oct. 1788, source note. GW continued to be involved in the settlement of the Colvill estate, but see his description of how matters stood in the late 1780s in his letter to John Rumney, 24 Jan. 1788.

From Rochambeau

Calais June the 28th 1786.

I come, my Dear General, to read in the public papers your letter to the general assembly of Virginia, by Which you refuse the fifty shares that have been, by it, offered to you.[1] there I have well Known again your character and your Virtues, and I am very glad to see in a corrupted age how they make Still a great account of this rare exemples of generosity. I come, my Dear general to make a turn in holland, this republick and yours are not much alike. in holland they have done, as god, of a heap of dirt the finest World that can be, by Strength of art and industry; your country, on the contrary, has received all the most generous natural gifts, but it remains yet to be done many things by the art to improve it, Which Should not require a long time With arms, and under the direction of my Dear general, if it Would follow them. further more, that republick of the Seven united provinces is at present in a great crisis between the patriot party and that of the Stathouder Which has Still Strength and credit.

my neighbours the Englishmen begin to restore themself of their Loss and are governed by a Wise man Who sets their finances in good order—our sovereign is gone to visit the harbour of *cherbourg*, he enjoys always in Europe of the consideration that his firm and moderate character inspire with generally. The King of Prussia is at the death, but he Shall have a successor that will continue him. in all, Europe appears to be quiet, and likely will not be disturbed, but after the death of the Elector of Bavaria, and it appears that all the politick prepares itself at that event.

Give me news of you, my Dear general, and be pursuaded of the tender interest that I take of and of the Eternal and Inviolable attachment With Which I have the honour to be My Dear General Your most obedient and very humble servant

le cte de Rochambeau

ALS, DLC:GW.
  1. See GW to Patrick Henry (second letter), 29 Oct. 1785.

To Richard Sprigg

Dr Sir,   Mount Vernon 28th June 1786.
    When your favor of the 1st inst: accompanying the she ass, came to this place, I was from home; both however arrived safe, but Doctr Bowie informed me by letter, that the bitch puppy was not brought to his house—nor have I heard anything more of the Asses which were at Marlbro'—nor of the grass seeds committed to the care of Mr Digges.[1]

I feel myself much obliged by your polite offer of the first fruits of your Jenny. Tho' in appearance quite unequal to the match—yet, like a true female, she was not to be terrified at the disproportionate size of her paramour—& having renewed the conflict twice or thrice, it is to be hoped the issue will be favourable. My best respects attend Mrs Sprigg & the rest of your family—With great esteem & regard I am Dr Sir &c.

Geo: Washington

LB, DLC:GW; printed version of the ALS, George D. Smith catalog, item 136, undated, p. 8. The catalog copy is clearly a faulty transcription.
1. See Sprigg's letter of 1 June. The letter to GW from Dr. Bowie has not been found.

To William Brown

Sir,   Mount Vernon 30th June 1786.
In answer to your favor of the 27th written at the request of the Trustees of the Alexandria Academy,[1] I have the honor to inform you that the education of boys for the purposes mentioned in my letter of the 17th of December, was what I had principally, if not wholly in view at that time. But if it shall appear to the Trustees that there are girls who may Fitly share the benefits of the institution, I will readily comprehend them in a ratio not to exceed one girl for four boys. With esteem & regard I am &c.

G: Washington

LB, DLC:GW.
1. Letter not found.

To George William Fairfax

My dear Sir   Mount Vernon 30th of June 1786
Better late than never, is an adage not less true, or less to be respected, because it is old.

The letter I am now about to write to you, ought to have been written many a day ago; but however strange it may seem, it is nevertheless true, that I have not had leizure (though more than two years have elapsed since my return to what the world calls retirement) to overhaul papers, & inspect transactions, which preceeded the revolution.

Having abundant reason to distrust my memory, I did not incline to write to you fully respecting the trust with which you had invested me, till I could go into a thorough examination of all the papers to which it had given birth; that I might not only satisfy you in the best manner the nature of the case would admit; but myself also with respect to the transactions. How, methinks I hear you say, could the inspection of these papers be a work of so much time? It would not, indeed, Sir, if the papers had been properly arranged, and my time had been more at my own disposal; but a house never clear of Company—a continual reference to me of old matters (with which I ought not to have been troubled)—& corrispondencies innumerable, following several hasty removals of my papers from book presses to Trunks, and thence into the Country when the British armed Vessels would make their appearance, had thrown the whole into such disorder & confusion that it was next to impossible to come at any paper that was wanting.[1]

I have now taken up the business with your letter of the first of Jany 1773, with which it commenced, and having gone through all the papers respecting it, from that date to the present moment, I am exceedingly sorry to find that the greater part of it has been managed so little for your interest, & so repugnant to my wishes. Till my Country called my Services to the field (in which I spent almost nine years,) I acted, in every respect for you as I should have done for myself; but after bidding adieu to my family & home (to which in case of adverse fortune I never expected to return) a general wreck of my affairs, as well as yours, succeeded—Aware of the probability of this, I perceive by the copy of a letter which I wrote to you from Cambridge the 26th of July 1775 (so soon as I had taken the command of the Army) that I informed you in strong terms of the indispensable necessity of appointing another Attorney, as I could not, from my then situation, give any attention to private concerns. A little before that, from Philadelphia, in a letter dated the 31st of May, I inclosed you several Bills which I then mentioned, and ever since have thought, were to the full amount of what I owed you, till the late investigation of the papers hath discovered that I am yet indebted to you in the sums of £169.12.6 for Goods bought at your Sale the 15th of August 1774, and £91.11.9 for those purchased at the subsequent one on the 5th of december following; which with some other credits, make the balle due to you £207.13.[2]

That I should have informed you in that letter, that the remittances were to the full amount of what I then owed is easily accounted for, and was proper at the time; because the sums just mentioned did not become due (according to the conditions of the sale) till twelve months thereafter; but why it should not have occured to me afterwards, is most difficult to solve; and is of no great importance to do it now; yet, I can assure you with much truth, that till within these few days I thought the accts betwn us were so near a ball[anc]e as to render it of little consequence when they were exhibited. I was led into this belief from two circumstances: first, having omitted to credit you in my Ledger by the amount of my purchases at the sales, I wanted that remembrancer of a fact which a variety of occurrances, & close attention to other matters had entirely obliterated. And 2d by having recurrence to the copies of my last letters to you, written after I had left home and which were always at hand, I was deceived by the information there given that the remittances were competent. The inclosed acct, commencing with the balle of the one transmitted the 6th of April 1775 does, I believe, comprehend every thing between us; for the balle I give you a draft on Wakelin Welch Esqr. of London for £155.14.9 Sterling.[3] I have drawn this at the legal exchange as settled by Act of Assembly, altho the currt exchange is 40 pr ct, which would have reduced the above sum to £148.6.5[.] I have allowed no interest on what I am owing you; The reasons I will frankly communicate. If they are not satisfactory, it may be drawn for hereafter. first, even if there had been any person appointed by you to have received the money from me when it became due, I could not have reconciled it with my conscience to have paid the nominal sum in paper bills of credit (which was the only money in circulation) thereby giving the shadow for the substance of a debt. 2d because I am, in a manner, rendered unable to do it by the ungenerous, not to say dishonest practices of most of my debtors, who paid me with a shilling or Sixpence in the pound, by which, & other means, I have sustained a loss of at least ten thousand pounds during my absence. and 3d because my creditors let their claims sleep till the annihilation of paper money and are now receiving, as indeed every person ought to do, specie, or its equivalent, to the full amount.

A Mode so unequal, has pressed hard upon me under the Deprivation of Crops, & want of a market for the little that were raised.

The Bonds that were taken at the Sales beforementioned were put into the hands of Mr Craven Peyton to collect, as appears by his receipt to Lund Washington of the 7th of April 1776; copy of which I will send Colo. Geo. Nicholas that he may see how they have been accounted for;[4] as I will also do the receipts from the same person for Colo. Stephen's bond for £230, and Majr McDonalds for £56.[5] The other Bonds remain where you informed me they were deposited, subject to the conditions, & directions, pointed to in your letter of the 10th of Jany 1774.

With respect to your Book Debts, my letters of the 10th of June, 20th of Augt, & 15th of Novr 1774 will have informed you of the difficulties which then occurred in every attempt that was made to collect the ballan[ce]s[6] & these difficulties encreased as often as they were thereafter renewed; nothing therefore could be done without going into Courts of Justice, which soon, thereafter, were shut; and were not opened before I left home; after which, upon the first intimation of your wish that Robt Carter Nicholas Esqr. or Colo. Fielding Lewis might be empowered to direct your affairs, I addressed both those Gentn on the subject. The latter, on acct of his declining state of health, desired to be excused; from the former I never got an answer. Equally unsuccessful was I in my application to his son, (after I had heard of his entering upon the duties of the trust) when I informed him that papers were in my possession which might be necessary for his government. In April last however, I saw Colo. Nicholas in Richmond, & repeating what I had before written, he assured me that every attempt to recover debts that were not reduced to specialties, were altogether unavailing; but that he would direct your Manager (Mr Muse) to receive the Books, Papers &ca from me.[7] As these were not necessary for any purposes he could have, and no inconvenience would attend their remaining with me (for they are in your own Escroitore) I thought it better, & advised, that they should remain here; which Colo. Nicholas readily consenting to, here they will be, till you may think proper otherwise to dispose of them. No settlement having been made of the Bloomery Accts by Messrs Adam & Campbell before I left home, though the matter was repeatedly pressed upon them as may appear by the letters which have passed, I was restrained by your instructions of the 31st of March 1774 from executing deeds for the Land belonging to that concern, & Colo. Carlyles bond depending upon this Settlement, as you will perceive by the letter before alluded to, remains as it did; for I have heard nothing of this business since my return.[8]

Among other papers which I have found in my researches is the inclosed letter from Mr Athawes. as it is of no use here, but may serve to compare with the transactions of that date respecting your estate in England, I send it.[9] The Pictures, for directions concerning which I applied in my letter of the 20th of Augt 1774 were (not having recd any before my departure) left standing at Belvoir; and, unfortunately, perished with the house.[10]

For the furniture of your blue room—which had been removed to this place (out of Mr Morton's way) during my absence—for which I intend to allow whatever you might think it was worth (as we were under the necessity, it seems, of using it)—and of which you have been pleased to request my acceptance, my grateful acknowledgements of thanks are due—but as it was used under full expectation of paying for it I am very willing, & ready to pay for it accordingly.[11]

There is, with the papers in my possession, a sealed packet endorsed "A copy of G.W. Fairfax's last Will and testament, which he begs not be opened untill his death is confirmed, or a subsequent one is produced" It shall remain sealed as desired; & be kept safe, unless you should incline to recall it.

I might, my dear Sir, have gone more into the detail of this business. I might have given you the corrispondencies between your Steward & your Collectr, & myself; & between me & others, respecting your concerns in this Country; but from the recurrence which I have had to the copies of my letters to you, I perceive it is sufficient to refer to them. The letters of the 25th of Septr 15th of Octr & 30th of Decr 177⟨3⟩—15th of May, 10th of June, 20th of Augt & 15th of Novr 1774—and 6th of Apl and 31st of May 1775 previous to my taking command of the Armys of America, contain a full, & accurate acct of every thing that had occurred relative to your business, which had fallen under my notice[12]—They transmitted copies of all the Accts which had been rendered to me by yr Steward & Collectr. They inclosed Bills which had been purchased with your money. And they gave an Acct of all the monies wch had been paid me for your use. And my letter of the 26th of July 1775 informed you of my then situation—the impracticability of my giving further attention to your business—& the indispensable necessity therefore of your employing another Attorney.

From that period, untill my return to Virga in the beginng of the year 1784, I remained in total ignorance of yr business; &

had *nearly* as little knowledge of my own. How much my own suffered in that space, I have already informed you; and I have reason to suspect, from what I have heard, that yours was not under the best management—Willis with his family are removed to the state of Georgia[13] & Peyton is dead—but all these matters you are, doubtlessly, informed of in a more regular & authentic way by Colo. Nicholas. With sentiments of very great regard & friendship, I am, My dear Sir, Yr Most Obedt & Affecte Hble Servant

Go: Washington

ALS, DLC:GW; LB, DLC:GW.

1. After his return to Mount Vernon at the end of 1783, GW was without a secretary until William Shaw began work in August 1785. This letter to Fairfax indicates that with Shaw's help GW had made real progress in sorting out his personal papers during the past year.

2. See the letters to which GW refers. For the sale of the furnishings at Belvoir on 15 Aug. 1774, see Francis Willis, Jr., to GW, 2 June 1774, n.4. For the sale of furniture, livestock, and equipment at Belvoir on 5 Dec. 1774, see Willis to GW, 6 Dec. 1774, n.2. See also GW's account with Fairfax, Ledger B, 66.

3. See GW to Fairfax, 31 May 1775, and Ledger B, 230. A copy of GW's holograph account with Fairfax dated June–17 Dec. 1774 and marked "E. Excepted pr Go: Washington April 6th 1775" (MnSM) is in CD-ROM:GW.

4. GW oversaw Fairfax's affairs in America until he left for Boston in 1775. Robert Carter Nicholas was then entrusted with the oversight of Fairfax's Virginia property, and at Nicholas's death in 1780 his son George Nicholas (c.1749–1799) took over. See Fairfax to GW, 23 Aug. 1784, n.1, and GW to Battaile Muse, 3 Nov. 1784, n.1. "A List of Bonds due The Honble George William Fairfax Esqr. the 15th day Augt 1775" is deposited at Mount Vernon. Craven Peyton's receipt at the bottom of the document dated 7 April 1776, reads: "Received of Mr Lund Washington the Bonds due The Hon'ble George William Fairfax Esqr. mentioned in the above List." GW's docket is on the reverse: "Craven Peyton's receipt for Bonds—taken at the Sale of Colo. Fairfax's Furniture &ca 7th April 1776." Craven Peyton (d. 1781) continued to serve as Fairfax's land agent after Fairfax left Virginia in 1773 (see GW to George William Fairfax, 10 Jan. 1774).

5. Colonel Stephen was Adam Stephen (c.1718–1791), and Major McDonald was perhaps Stephen's friend and Lord Fairfax's former agent, Angus McDonald (c.1727–1778) of Frederick County. See McDonald to GW, 8 Jan. 1774.

6. GW's letters to Fairfax of 20 Aug. and 15 Nov. 1774 have not been found.

7. Battaile Muse replaced Craven Peyton as Fairfax's land agent during the Revolution.

8. Fairfax's instructions of 31 Mar. 1774 have not been found. For an account of the efforts to sell a tract of Fairfax's land on the Shenandoah River in

Frederick County on which Fairfax and John Carlyle had built a bloomery, see Fairfax to GW, 10 Jan. 1774, n.9.

9. The letter from the London merchant who acted for Fairfax, Samuel Athawes, has not been found.

10. See note 6.

11. See note 5, Fairfax to GW, 23 June 1785. The Rev. Andrew Morton rented Belvoir in 1775 (see GW to Morton, 21 Dec. 1774).

12. GW's letters to Fairfax of 25 Sept., 30 Dec. 1773, 15 May, 20 Aug., 15 Nov. 1774, and 6 April 1775 have not been found.

13. Francis Willis, Jr., acted as estate manager for Fairfax until 1775.

From Thomas Fairfax

Sir   Annapolis 30th June: 1786

Mr Cary who Came Passenger with me does me the favor of taking charge of four Vols of Annals for you; they were Sent to me at London by Mr Young[1]—inclosed is two Letters from a Lady in London (one of which directed to Mr Lyons, shoud be much obliged to you to put in some good channel of Conveyance) also a Letter for Bloxham the Farmer who my uncle Sent out to you and who I hope to hear is Safely arrived—The Letter is from his wife and I dont doubt will give the poor man great pleasure.[2]

We have had a pretty good passage of about Seven weeks—when I parted with my uncle & aunt at bath, which was about the last of march, they were tolerable well and entrusted me with their most affecnt. good wishes to yrself and Mrs W——n—my uncle is amazingly Broke since he left this Country and I think in a very infirm State of health.[3]

I Shall defer any further Particulars till I have the pleasure of Seeing you and the interim I remain respectfully Sir, yr obedt humle Sert

Tho: Fairfax

ALS, DLC:GW.

1. For Arthur Young's gift to GW of his *Annals*, see GW to Biddle, 10 Feb. 1786, n.3. Wilson Cary (1760–1793), son of Wilson Miles Cary (1734–1817), of Ceelys and Carysbrook in Elizabeth City County, and Sarah Blair Cary (1739–1799), was the nephew of Sarah Cary Fairfax.

2. The "Lady in London" has not been identified. Mr. Lyons is perhaps Judge Peter Lyons (d. 1801; *Diaries*, 4:132).

3. George William Fairfax died on 3 April 1787.

From William Fitzhugh, Sr.

Dear Genral   [Calvert County, Md., c.1 July 1786]

My son William is now in Virga and If he Shou'd not have the Honor to wait on you, will address you on the subject of sheep— I advised that the Lambs shou'd not be taken sooner than the last week in July, because I know by experience it wou'd be Injurious to them—and Mr Edward Reynolds in the upper End of this County of Calvert, who promis'd 20, I doubt not will be Satisfied to deliver them at that time[1]—My son Pery was with me a few days ago, & offers his respectful Compts to you & your Lady—He says there are large flocks of Valuable Sheep, in the Circle of His residence on Kent Island, where He thinks he can Immediately procure for you One Hundred or more Good Ewe Lambs at 12/6—Dollars @ 7/6. and as the last week in July is not far distant, I suppose it will be agreeable to the farmers to keep in some until that time—Other wise he will recieve them into his Own Pasture, which is Large & fine, & on the Bayside Opposite to West River Neck, where a Mr Jackson keeps a Ferry & has a Large Commodious boat, & will be the most convenient Place for the Person You send, to Pass the Bay to recieve and return with the Lambs—On this subject If he shou'd Succeed, He has promised to write you directly on his return home, by two or three weeks Posts successively—and I presume will then Point out the best route for them[2]—I am much obliged to Your Excellency, for the Service of Magnolio to my Mares, in case the Young Spaniard shou'd have failed—The person who goes for them will Carry this Letter.[3]

The Wounds I recd by a fall from my carriage in Virga have confin'd me to the House ever since my return, until two days ago, when I began to Hobble about, but have still a disagreeable lameness in my leg—The Turkish or Polish Barley—which was sew'd about the 20th of October Last, became ripe & was Cut the 4th of this month—I send you a sample of the Grain, wch I think is fuller and better than any I have seen from spring seed-ing. it is true the last winter was very moderate, yet there were some severe Frosts in which it was observable, that the Barley Continued its growth and Verdure, at least as well, If not better, than the Wheat & Rye in the same season—from the experience I have had, I can entertain no doubt of its being Summer or Spring Barley, & by sewing in the fall, might Possibly be much hurt or even be destroy'd by a very Severe Winter—Yet I am of oppinion, that If sew'd under a furrow, about the last Week in October or first of Novr it wou'd generally stand the Winter, & yeild a greater Crop & of better Grain than if sewed in the Spring—still spring sewing If so Early as February or March it probably may produce better than I have had an Oppertunity of Observing—by the scrawl which I wish may be inteligable, You will see how hard I strive to make the last use of my Sight.

Mrs Fitzhugh Joins with me in Compts and best Wishes to you, your Lady & Family. I have the Honor to be with Perfect Esteem and respect Your Excellencys Affectionate & Oblig'd Humle Sert

Willm Fitzhugh

P.S. In S. Carrolina, they have Emitted Bills of Credit for £100.000—not to be a Tender for dischargeing Debts—it is sup-ported by an Association of Merchts who have subscrib'd for that Purpose.[4] W.F.

ALS, DLC:GW. The many random dots in the manuscript have been elimi-nated or converted into commas when appropriate. For the tentative dating of this letter, see GW to Fitzhugh, 2 July.

1. See William Fitzhugh, Jr., to GW, 15 June.
2. See Peregrine Fitzhugh to GW, 10 July.
3. The cover indicates the letter was carried "pr James," Fitzhugh's servant. See GW to Fitzhugh, 2 July.
4. The South Carolina legislature passed on 12 Oct. 1785 and amended on 12 Mar. 1786 "An Act to Establish a Medium of Circulation by way of Loan, and to Secure it's Credit and Utility" (*S.C. State Records: Journals of House of Representatives, 1785–1786*, 355). It provided for the state to issue £100,000 in paper currency to be lent on a credit of five years at 7 percent interest (ibid., items 20–30, pp. 699–700).

To Battaile Muse

Sir,   Mount Vernon 1st July 1786

I did not receive your Letter of the 4th of June seasonably enough to return an Answer so soon as you may have expected. I cannot inform you with any precision what the flour made of the 500 bushels of wheat sent to my mill is worth, as I am informed that flour has risen to the Northward, and the short crops of wheat this season will undoubtedly have a great effect upon the price of it. I should therefore think it advisable to let it lay a little longer till it can be disposed of to more advantage. It is customary at my Mill to receive the Bran in payment for the Barrels, packing &c.

I should be much obliged to you if you would draw in my favour as soon as possible after having the means in your hands[1] and let me know where I shall receive the money, as the number of workmen which I have employed, and sundry other matters call for a large and constant supply of Cash. I am Sir your Obdt Hume Servt

                                        Go: Washington

LS, in Tobias Lear's hand, NjMoNP.
    1. GW inserted "after having the means in your hands."

To Wakelin Welch

Sir,   Mount Vernon [c.1] July 1786.

Since my last of the 28th of Novr I have been favored with your letters of the 27th of Feby & 13th of March; & have receiv'd the paper hangings & watch by Capt. Andrews.[1] With the last Mrs Washington is well pleased, & I thank you in her name for your attention to the making of it.

If the stocks keep up, & there is not a moral certainty of their rising higher in a short time, it is my wish & desire that my interest in the Bank may be immediately sold, & the money arising therefrom made subject to my Drafts in your hands, some of which at 60 days sight may soon follow this letter.[2]

The footing on which you have placed the interest of my debt to you, is all I require. To stand on equal ground with others who owe money to the Merchants in England, & who were not so prompt in their payment of the principal as I have been, is all I aim at. Whatever the two Countries may finally decide with respect to interest, or whatever general agreement or compromise may be come to, between British Creditors and American Debtors, I am willing to abide by; nor should I again have touched upon this subject in this letter, had you not introduced a case which, in my opinion, has no similitude with the point in question. You say I have received interest at the Bank for the money which was there—granted: but (besides remarking that only part of this money was mine) permit me to ask if G: Britain was not enabled by means of the bank, to continue the war with this Country? whether this war did not deprive us of the means of paying our Debts? and whether the interest I received from this source did, or could bear any proportion to the losses I sustained by having my grain, my Tobacco & every article of produce rendered unsaleable & left to perish on my hands? However, I again repeat that I ask no discrimination of you in my favor, for had there been no stipulation by treaty to secure debts—nay more, had there even been an exemption by the Legislative authority, or practice of this Country against it, I would, from a conviction of the propriety & justice of the measure, have discharged my *original* debt to you.

But from the moment our Ports were shut, & our markets were stopped by the hostile fleets & armies of Great Britain, 'till the first were opened, & the others revived, I should, for the reasons I have (tho' very cursorily) assigned, have thought the interest during that epocha, stood upon a very different footing.

I am much obliged by the trouble you have taken to enquire into the nature of the connexion between the House of Messrs Hanbury & Co. and Balfour & Barraud.[3] I had no sanguine hopes of redress from that quarter, but as it seemed to be the *only* chance I was willing to try it. I am Sir, Your Mo: Obedient & very Hble Servt

G: Washington

LB, DLC:GW. The clerk dates the letter "July 1786"; GW's letter to Welch of 4 Aug. enclosing a copy of this letter makes clear that GW wrote it before forwarding his letter of 30 June under cover of a letter to Samuel Athawes dated 15 July.

1. Neither of the letters from Welch has been found.
2. For a discussion of the Custis stock in the Bank of England, half of which

GW and his wife acquired at the death of Martha Parke Custis and half of which went to John Parke Custis, see GW to Welch, 27 July 1784, n.2.

   3. See GW to Thomas Newton, Jr., 3 Sept. 1785.

To William Fitzhugh, Sr.

Dear Sir,   Mount Vernon 2d July 1786.

   Your letter without date was handed to me last night by your servant.[1] With one of your mares, he returns—the other I detain: the latter was among the very few which were early favoured by the Spaniard, but is not yet satisfied. The other, which went to Magnolio, my Groom seems confident is with foal, which is the reason of my sending her.

   A female ass which I have obtained lately, has excited desires in the Jack, to which he seemed almost a stranger; making use of her as an excitement, I have been able to get several mares served, which otherwise would have gone uncovered by him this Season: this expedient, unluckily, was hit upon too late for me, as I had put almost the whole of my mares to Magnolio before it was tried; it will be practiced with your mare that is left, & I hope with success.

   I have advised your Servant to try the mares he carries back by some horse in your neighbourhood, & if she should discover an inclination to him, to bring her to Magnolio when he returns for the other. If this should not happen before the latter end of this month when I shall send to Mr Reynolds for the ewe lambs, I will contrive your mare that far, unless you forbid it in the interim.

   I am much obliged to my good friend Perry for the trouble he is about to take by his enquiries for ewe lambs for me; & will give him an answer the moment he advises me of the result, which I shall be enabled to do as soon as I hear from Genl Smallwoods Manager, who sent me word that there were a number of Lambs belonging to the Genls Estate, which he believed were to be disposed of; about which he was desired to enquire & to let me know when the Govr came into Charles Coty which has happened.[2]

   I am much obliged to you for the sample of Barley. Mine that I sowed this Spring is come to nothing; occasioned I believe by the continual rains.

I am very sorry to hear of your long confinement by the fall you got in this State, but glad to find you are begining to over-come it. With every good wish for Mrs Fitzhugh, yourself & family, I am Dear sir &c.

Geo: Washington

LB, DLC:GW.

1. See Fitzhugh to GW, c.1 July.

2. See Peregrine Fitzhugh to GW, 10 July. Gov. William Smallwood held land adjacent to GW's in Charles County, Maryland.

From Henry Lee, Jr.

My dear Genl   New York July 3rd 1786

I had the honor of your letter four days past, and would have sooner replied but waited in the expectation of learning some-thing about the package you enquire after. The letter from Mr Arthur Young came in the packet, but was not accompanied by any thing else. The british Consul here tells me it is not custom-ary to send packages of any sort by the packets as they sail from Falmouth or Portsmouth 300 miles from London, but that they come in vessels directly from London—perhaps the letter is only meant as a letter of advice & that its copy will arrive in Potomac with the books, tho it is strange how Mr Athaws could think of sending the letter via New York. Unaccountable as the procedure appears I hope no loss may accrue, as Mr Young' works are the most valuable production of the sort extant. Solici-tous to gather all useful knowledge respecting farms & farming I sought this author out, on my arrival here, I could only obtain his tour thro Ireland, which I take the liberty to transmit to you now by favor of Doctr Griffith. Before my return it is very proba-ble you may receive the whole of the authors work, and these two volumes will in the mean time afford you an oppertu⟨nity⟩ of putting into practice Mr Youngs system of culture.[1]

If you should be in want of a new set of china it is in my power to procure a very genteel set, table & tea—what renders this china doubly valuable & handsome is the order of the eagle en-graved on it in honor of the Cincinnati—It has upwards of 306 pieces, and is offered at the prime cost, 150 dollars.[2]

Your reasoning on the navigation of the Missisippi is perfectly conformable to the prevalent doctrine on that subject in Congress. We are very solicitous to form a treaty with Spain for commercial purposes; indeed no nati[o]n in Europe can give us conditions so advantageous to our trade as that kingdom. The carrying business they are like ourselves in, & this common source of difficulty in adjusting commercial treatys between other nations does not apply to America & Spain. But my dear Genl I do not think you go far enough. Rather than defer longer the benefits of a free liberal system of trade with Spain, why not agree to the occlusion of the Mississippi. This occlusion will not, cannot exist longer than the infancy of the western emigrants, therefore to those people what is now done, cannot be important; to the atlantic states it is highly important, for we have no prospects of bringing to conclusion our negotiations with the Court of Madrid, but by yielding the navigation of the Missisipi—their Minister here, is under positive instructions on that point, in all other arrangements the Spanish Monarch will give to the States testimonys of his regard and friendship, & I verily beleive that if the above difficulty could be removed we should soon experience the advantages which would flow from a conn⟨ect⟩ion with Spain—Mrs Lee returns her most respectful compliments to the ladys of Mount-Vernon and repeats thro me, an offer she before made of executing any command which Mrs Washington may please to favor her with. I beg my return of esteem to Mrs Washington, and am with unalterable attachment and respect your most obt servt

Henry Lee jur

ALS, DLC:GW.

1. GW's letter inquiring about the Arthur Young volumes is dated 18 June. See also Young to GW, 7 Jan. 1786, n.2.

2. GW wrote Lee on 26 July asking him to buy the Cincinnati china that Samuel Shaw had brought from Canton in 1785. On 7 Aug. Lee purchased 302 pieces of the china from Constable, Rucker, & Co., and before the end of the month he sent it to Mount Vernon via Col. Josiah Parker at Norfolk. On 23 Aug. GW sent by David Humphreys £45.5 Virginia currency (150 dollars) to Lee in New York "to pay for a set of China bot for me there," and on 23 Sept. he paid six shillings for "Freight of China &c. from Norfolk" (Ledger B, 231, 235, Lee to GW, 7, 12 Aug., 8 Sept., 1 Oct. 1786, GW to Lee, 31 Oct. 1786, Josiah Parker to GW, 9 Sept. 1786). For a discussion of the acquisition of the Cincinnati china and its subsequent disposition, see Detweiler, *Washington's*

Chinaware, 81–97. For earlier references by GW to the Cincinnati china, see GW to Tench Tilghman, 17 Aug. 1785, n.2.

From Timothy Dwight

Greenfield, in Connecticut, July 5 1786

May it please your Excellency,

I have delayed an answer to your Excellency's letter, which I duly received,[1] from an expectation of having a conveyance by Col. Humphry's, of whose design to visit Mount Vernon I was early informed after the receipt.

Had the Conquest of Cannan been published, on the plan of a subscription, I should have taken the earliest opportunity to forward a paper of proposals to your Excellency. But that mode of supporting a publication, after repeated trials, has been found, in New England at least, to answer the purpose in view but indifferently.

A preposterous but habitual mode of considering the subject, partly derived from failures of publishing, or forwarding, the book proposed, has established a general conviction, thro'out this country, that a publisher is at liberty to purchase, or neglect, the book he has engaged to buy. For this reason, I followed the advice of my Friends, & determined to venture the work upon the Laws, which in most of the United States, secure to the writer a copyright in his productions.

Since I had the honour of addressing your Excellency, on this subject, the book, so far as I have been able to learn, has met with a friendly reception from the publick; more friendly, I confess, than my own hopes had ventured to presume. The pleasure I had derived from this quarter was not a little heightened by your Excellency's favourable opinion, & assurances that it is not unfavourably received in the neighborhood of Mount Vernon.

The natural carelessness of my character would easily explain, to my particular acquaintance, the omissions of date, & place, in my letter; but if I had been possessed of a character much more attentive, the feelings, with which I wrote, would have explained it to myself. It was written from New York, the last of October; & forwarded by a person, who engaged to convey the letter, &

books, by a very direct progress, to your Excellency. The partial miscarriage of that induced me more especially to wait for the present safe opportunity, by Lieut. Col. Humphrys. With the most respectful sentiments, I beg leave to subscribe myself, your Excellency's most obedient, & most humble servant,

Timothy Dwight

ALS, NIC.

1. GW's letter of 1 April 1786 to Dwight is printed as a note in Dwight's letter, October 1785.

Letter not found: from Edmund Randolph, 7 July 1786. On 12 July GW wrote Randolph: "Your letter of the 7th is this instant come to hand."

From James Tilghman

Dear Sir   Chester Town [Md.] July 7th 1786

I have the honour of your letter of the 5th of June. Altho' nothing can compensate the loss of My good Son, yet your kind condolence is a great consolation to me, as an honorable testimony of his Merit[.] When I go to Baltimore I will look out the papers I mentioned and inclose them to you[.] If I had wanted any Satisfaction of the falsity of Capt. Asgills insinuations, as I really did not, what you have been pleased to say on the occasion would have put an End my doubts[.] You do not say whether I am at liberty to transmit it to the Gentleman in London who is so anxious to be furnished with a vindication and I can not venture to do it without your express approbation[.] I know he has the matter so much at heart that it would be a great relief to him to be able to put it in the proper light to the small circle of Acquaintance, from whom he would wish to wipe off all manner of doubt[.] If I had your permission I should lay him under the prohibition of giving Copies or makeing any other use of it than a private Satisfaction to him-self and them.[1]

Since poor Tench's death I have taken up the matter of looking after Miss Andersons Legacy left by the will of Colo. Colville And this leads me to address you on that Subject[.] Her case is remarkably pityable[.] Her father left something handsome and her Mother had a valuable landed intrest in this Country and a great share of it ought to have come to her as the only surviving child of the family yet so it is that by the wretched indiscreet management of a Brother who was Executor to the father, And for whose debts the mother became security, every thing is totally sunk and lost and she is without any property save this Legacy[.] Happily for her she is not without good friends[.] She is a most worthy creature and claims the commiseration of every body acquainted with her Situation[.] I am induced to give my little assistance as well by the tyes of relationship as the impulse of humanity[.] Your letters to Tench upon the subject refer him for some information to a Mr West of Baltimore Exr of his Brother John West who was your colleague in the Executorship of Colo. Colville's Will and who it seems was the acting Executor[.] I have applyd to Mr West who writes me that he does not find any thing relative to the Legacy amongst his Brothers papers[.] He adds that Mrs Colville was left Executrix and that she living near Alexandria the Executors used to meet at her house where probably the papers relative to the Estate may have been deposited[.] He does not say whether Mrs Colville be living. It is likely she is not as I think she was not much younger than the Colo. with whom I had the pleasure to be intimate. The case being thus circumstanced I find myself under the necessity of applying to you in behalf of this worthy Young Lady as there is no other person left from whom the wanted information can be had[.] I beg you will believe that no man would be more tender of giving you any trouble than myself and I only wish you to take such measures at your Liesure as may in the End bring miss Anderson to the possession of what is due to her by Colo. Colvilles Will[.] To this I am persuaded you will be induced not more by the duty of your Executorship than your own humane feelings for this amiable young Lady.[2] With my respectful Compliments to Mrs Washington I have the honor to be with great regard yr Most obt hble servt

James Tilghman

ALS, DLC:GW; Tobias Lear's extract, CtY: Humphreys Collection. A period enclosed in brackets has been inserted in the places where Tilghman left a space to indicate the ending of a sentence. Only the first paragraph was extracted by Lear for David Humphreys (see GW to Humphreys, 1 Sept. 1786).

1. See Tilghman to GW, 26 May, n.3.

2. Earlier correspondence regarding Harriot Rebecca Anderson's plight and her inheritance from the Thomas Colvill estate includes letters from Ed-

ward Anderson to GW, 13 Aug. 1773, GW to Anderson, 10 Sept. 1773, Henry Hollyday to GW, 30 April 1785, Tench Tilghman to GW, 14 May 1785, and GW to Tench Tilghman, 23 May 1785. See also GW to James Tilghman, 20 July, 4 Dec. 1786, and James Tilghman to GW, 2 Aug., 23 Sept. 1786. For some of the ramifications of GW's involvement in the settlement of the Colvill estate beginning in 1767, see Thomas West to GW, 27 June 1786, n.1, and the references in that note.

Letter not found: from Maurice Desdevens, 8 July 1786. On 22 Aug. GW wrote Desdevens: "I have received your letter of the 8th of July."

To Thomas Johnson

Dear Sir,   M[oun]t Vernon 8th July, 1786
It was not 'till our return to the great Falls, that Colo. Gilpin and myself discovered the error of the propos'd meeting of the Directors of the Potomac Company at Alexandria on Monday preceding the first day of August. The general Meeting of the company it seems is, by Law, to be held on the first Monday in that month; & this not happening, in the present year, 'till the 7th day of it—we wish that the Meeting of Directors may take place on the Saturday before; of which I pray you to give Mr Lee notice.[1] I am &c.
                                                    G: Washington

LB, DLC:GW.
1. Johnson, George Gilpin, and GW had attended a meeting of the president and board of the Potomac River Company at Seneca Falls on 3 and 4 July. On Saturday, 5 Aug., GW went into Alexandria to meet with the directors of the company, but neither Johnson nor the other Maryland director, Thomas Sim Lee, appeared (*Diaries*, 5:22).

From Peregrine Fitzhugh

Dear General   Effingham Kent Island [Md.] July 10th 1786
Upon a Visit to my Father some little time ago I was informed by him you wanted a number of Ewe Lambs and as there was a prospect of my being able to make a considerable collection in my neighbourhood I promised to make enquiry on my return and address you upon the subject—this Letter is to comply with my promise to my Father and to execute a pleasing duty to

you[1]—If I had fortunately been acquainted with your desire a fortnight sooner it would have been in my power to have purchased for you an hundred fine lambs at 10s. each, this was done in my Absence by a Butcher from Baltimore who I found upon the Island at my return and who had purchased upwards of an hundred and fifty—This draught from the inhabitants has made my attempts to accomplish your wishes not so successful as I could wish—from 20 to 30 are all I have been able yet to engage, these are very good at 12/6 each, should you not yet have supplied yourself elsewhere and incline to have the above as you have a number at Mr Reynolds's if you will give me a week or ten days notice previous to your sending for them—I can without the least inconvenience send them across the Bay in my Boat and have them lodged with my Brother in Law Mr Saml Chew of Herring Bay which is only a few Miles from Mr Reynolds's to be delivered to your order[2]—My Father informed me you proposed sending over the last of the present month— as I can at any time collect the Lambs engaged here in a day so if I have timely notice of your inclination they can be in place by the forementioned period—I will still continue my enquiries and may very probably add to the number—A letter sent from Alexandria to Annapolis by the Post will meet a ready and quick Conveyance. Be pleased to offer Mrs Fitzhugh's and my respectful Compliments to Mrs Washington and permit me to add that I shall embrace with anxiety and pleasure every opportunity and am happy in this tho' a trifling one of testifying the very grateful sense I do and shall ever retain of your friendly services to me and the perfect respect with which I have the honor to be Dr General Yr aff. and obedt Servt

Peregne Fitzhugh

ALS, DLC:GW.

Peregrine Fitzhugh (1759–1810), son of William Fitzhugh, served in the 3d Continental Dragoons during the Revolution and in July 1781 was made aide-de-camp to GW. His wife Elizabeth (b. 1765) was the daughter of Samuel Chew who was living in Herring Bay, Anne Arundel County, Md., at the time of his death in 1786.

1. See William Fitzhugh, Sr., to GW, c.1 July.

2. Peregrine Fitzhugh's brother-in-law was Samuel Lloyd Chew (1756–1796).

From Richard Harrison

Sir,   Cork [Ireland] 10 July, 1786.
    Passing through Madrid some time since Mr Carmichael en-
charged me with two Toledo Blades for your Excelly which I
hoped for the pleasure of delivering in person. But the period
of my return to America being yet uncertain, I now commit
them with this to the care of Capt. Sullivan of the Union, bound
to Alexandria.[1] Wishing them safe, I have the honor to remain,
with the most perfect respect, Sir, Your most obt & humble
Servant
                                                    R. Harrison

Sprague transcript, DLC:GW.
    Richard Harrison was a partner in the Alexandria firm of Harrison & Hooe.
    1. Capt. Giles Sullivan of the ship *Union* dined at Mount Vernon on Sunday,
26 Nov. (*Diaries*, 5:71). GW wrote Harrison about the swords on 20 Nov. 1786.
It was William Carmichael, the United States agent in Madrid, with whom GW
mainly dealt in 1784 when he was seeking to acquire a Spanish jackass (see
especially Carmichael to GW, 3 Dec. 1784, n.1).

From Henry Lee, Jr.

My dear Genl   New york 11h July 1786
    Your friend and servant, the patriot and noble Greene is no
more—on the 19th June after 3 days fever he left this world.
    Universal grief reigns here—how hard the fate of the U.
States, to loose such a son in the middle of life—irreparable
loss—But he is gone, I am incapable to say more—May health
attend you my dear General Yours most affy
                                                    H. Lee junr

ALS, DLC:GW.
    Nathanael Greene died on 19 June at Mulberry Grove Plantation in Savan-
nah, Georgia. For a description of his final illness and death, see Jeremiah
Wadsworth to GW, 1 October.

From Battaile Muse

Honourable Sir,   Leesburg July 11th 1786
    your Favour dated the 1st of Instant I received on my way To
this place—the Lo prices given at Alexandria For Flour &c. has

prevented my going To that place before now agreeable To my Expectations when I last saw you—I have made but a small Collection since April, I am Indebted about Twenty pounds—I here Inclose and order on Colo. George Gilpin for the sum of fifty pounds—I do not Expect to receive any money on your acct untill about next November—as I am about To Make the Tenants Pay up their arrears I have thought it may not Be necessary To Trouble you with a Settlement until the accounts are nearer Closed—I Shall order an Execution next month agt Rector in Fauquier County for £130[1] the other Tenants are Too Poor To Execute untill their Crops Come in unless I hear they are about To remove in that Case and in every other I shall do as for my Self—your money Shall not Lie in my hands as Fast as I collect you shall receive. when the Flour is sold I shall be Glad To hear of the amount as the 50 bushels wheat I am To account For with Doctor W. C. Selden[2] I think it my duty To inform you that I have Been often Told that the Hites & Greens Claim your Tract of Land at the head of Bullskin and that Tract of 180 acres Lease To Bailey Joining To Lott Lee—the Commissioners will Be on those Lands next Month—and I was Informed by Colo. Geo. Nicholas that the Commissioners would hold a Court on the 4th day of September next In Winchester in order To Settle the wrights of the Lands—this Company Claims a great Part of Colo. Fairfaxes Lands in Berkeley—which I Suppose Colo. Fairfax will Loose—Colo. Nicholas informed me that Colo. Fairfaxes Tittle Papers was at Mount Vernon Should I have ocation for To Call for them can they be had without and order—Should you Come up in consequence of your Lands or send up I shall be much oblige To you To desire Mr Shaw To Examine Colo. Fairfaxes Deeds and To Favour me so Far as to have them Conveyed up before the 4th day of September I mean the Deed or deeds for the Tract where I Live—If Possable I expect To be down before the 10th day of august if so I shall waite on you.[3]

I have Settled the acct with Mr Crane for Bartletts Lott and have got Six pounds more than I Expected I enclose the acct for your Examination which I hope will please.[4]

I must beg leave To Trouble you in consequence of renting your Lands that have been Left by Insolvent Tenants. I have thought it Would be best To Advertise yours and Colo. Fairfax⟨es⟩ Lands in one advertisement—if you approve ⟨*mutilated*⟩ to make such Correction in the Advertisment as you think

Proper and desire the Printer to have 100 printed & I will Call
For them after hearing From you & will send them To all parts
Necessary—as Tenants Seldom see a News paper it may not be
of much advantage To advertise in them[5]—I will pay half the
Expense for Colo. Fairfax. I am Sir your Obedient and Very
Humble Servant

Battaile Muse

P.S. I have Sown some of ⟨the⟩ Clover Seed I Purchased for you
which come up Very well—⟨*mutilated*⟩ as before.[6] B.M.

ALS, DLC:GW.

1. This is Jacob Rector. See Muse to GW, 28 Nov. 1785, n.6.

2. See Muse to GW, 6 May 1786, n.1.

3. GW refutes this claim in a letter to Muse on 1 August. See Thornton
Washington to GW, 6 June, particularly note 2, and GW to Thornton Washington,
22 June 1786, for discussions of the problems posed by the Hites' land
claims. For the 180-acre, or 183-acre, lot leased to Samuel Bailey, see Lists of
Tenants, 18 Sept. 1785, n.8. For a detailed record of the Hite-Fairfax suit, see
Dickinson, *The Fairfax Proprietary*, 1–57.

4. Muse enclosed a "Memo. of Settlement Made this day with James Crane
Sheriff of Berkeley County—July 5th 1786." See also Lists of Tenants, 18 Sept.
1785, n.5.

5. GW wrote Muse on 1 Aug. that he had sent the advertisement to the
printer.

6. For the exchange between Muse and GW regarding clover seed sent to
GW by Muse, see GW to Muse, 5 Jan. 1786, n.3.

From Benjamin Ogle

Dr sr   Annapolis July 12 1786

It was not the least inconvenient to spare six fauns as I am at
present fully stocked, & I shall think you lucky if you raise half—
It would have been a very difficult matter to have got that number had I not this Spring forced the deer intirely out the
Woods & great part of the Park, tending it in Tobacco with a
view of laying it down in Grass in the fall it having grown over
with Sedge I hope you received the fauns safe.[1] I am Sr with
great Esteem Sincerely yrs

Ben. Ogle

ALS, DLC:GW.

1. GW exchanged letters with Ogle in 1785 regarding deer for GW's park
(GW to Ogle, 17 Aug. 1785; Ogle to GW, 20 Aug. 1785).

To Edmund Randolph

Dr Sir,   Mount Vernon 12th July 1786.
Your letter of the 7th is this instant come to hand.[1] Elizabeth &
Sarah, daughters of Michl Cresap, live I presume in Hampshire,
to the Sheriff of which I will direct the summons; tho' it is at a
hazard—having no other knowledge of the matter, than that
their mother married one Jacobs of that county. Luther Martin
lives in Maryland, and is I believe Attorney General of that
State—What is to be done in this case?[2]
I am exceedingly sorry to hear of your indisposition & loss. I
hope the change of air & exercise which you are about to take
will restore you to perfect health.[3] Be assured I shall have singular pleasure in seeing you at this place as you return from, or go
to Annapolis, being with great esteem & regard, Dr Sir &c.
                                                    G: Washington

LB, DLC:GW.
    1. Letter not found.
    2. This is with reference to the claims of Michael Cresap and his heirs to
GW's Round Bottom tract. See John Harvie to GW, 5 Aug. 1785, and notes.
See also GW to John Marshall, 15 Aug. 1788.
    3. Randolph wrote James Madison on 12 June that he had been "under the
severe regimen of blisters and purges, produced by four violent colds" (Rutland and Rachal, *Madison Papers*, 9:75–76). Elizabeth Nicholas Randolph gave
birth to their son, John Jennings Randolph, in October 1785; the baby died
suddenly in the summer of 1786.

From William Gordon

My dear Sir   London July 13. 1786
Your favour of Apr. 20th was forwarded from Boston in
May, & was received the beginning of this week, upon my returning from Ipswich in Suffolk, where I had the pleasure of
hearing that a complete farmer had been forwarded to you, in
whom I hope you will have satisfaction, though not capable of
filling up Mr Lund Washington's place. Such a steward as you
have described & wish to have, is not easily found; but your
friends, who are numerous even in this country, will be looking
out for one that will answer. Till you can happen of a person,
that is capable of taking off the additional burden from your

shoulders, it cannot be expected that you can be so frequent in corresponding as otherwise.

You have my most sincere thanks for the honour you have done me in subscribing & in promoting subscriptions; & must pray your Excellency to present my compliments to the Honle James Mercer, & make my acknowledgments to him for his paronage. My friend Jonathan Mason Esqr. of Boston or Mr James Jackson of Jamaica Plain, will transact the business of the bill. Doubt not but the gentlemen at Warren are possessed of more honour, than to attempt the payment of it in paper.[1] The step that Rhode Island has taken in issuing paper &c. must be reprobated by all who are both honest & judicious. Such measures instead of lessening will increase difficulties, & are like drinking water in the dropsy. The mention of the dropsy has reminded me of my intention to write about bilious complaints, with which your Lady is troubled. Being in company sometime back with an apothecary of my acquaintance & a clergyman, they were the subject of conversation. The clergyman mentioned the case of a gentlewoman whom he knew, that, after consulting the first physicians in England & trying the waters in different places & obtaining no cure, was effectually cured by taking the yolk of a new laid egg in the morning fasting, for some considerable time. The apothecary turning to me said, "I apprehend many of our disorders arise from the contents in the stomach being of such a nature, that they will not incorporate with each other; & I can easily conceive that the egg may be of service by producing that incorporation, as it mixes both with oil & water, & compounds each with itself in one mass." The thought pleased me, & the last friday while at Ipswich I made the following experiment. Having the yolk of a new laid egg, I procured the gall of a sheep hot out of the body, poured a quantity of the bile upon the egg, & with the motion of a tea spoon not exceeding the motion in the stomach, soon united the two bodies; upon that a good quantity of oil was added which was soon incorporated thro the like agitation; then followed a large portion of water, which succeeded as well. I then tried what effect salt of wormwood would have upon the mixture; it produced no fermentation whatsoever. The whole was left all night in the bason, & by morning the oil appeared to be much separated & risen to the top; but in the body such a mixture would have been subject to a continual motion & would not have cooled. Should your Lady be induced to try the effects of the yolk, it will afford me the greatest pleasure to hear that she is benefited by it, so as to have her complaints wholly removed.

Am glad that the key & its appendage are safe. Before I forget it, would observe that as your writing is probably known at the Post Office, & I am very obnoxious to the promoters of the late war, & they have too great influence in the cabinet, it may be best that when you honour me with a letter it should be directed by another hand, that there should be no suspicion of a correspondence, so that should I have occasion to write upon any particular subjects that may possibly turn up, such suspicion may not prevent my letters coming to Mount Vernon. The nation is loaded with taxes & what with these & the dearness of provision the people are hard put to it to procure a livelihood. There are at present fine prospects upon the ground—appearances of great plenty, except the article of apples which have failed in general.

We left Boston Apr. 16, but the wind changing we did not reach the grand bank of Newfoundland till the 4th of May. On the 5th we had a fine fair breeze, & from that day we had a most charming run to the channel. On the 26th we landed at Gravesend, took a post chaise & got to London in the ⟨late⟩ evening. It pleased God to grant us upon the whole a good voyage. We were sea sick only the first day; with no storms or tempests; met with no accidents; had plenty of good provision; were well accommodated; & enjoyed good company.

Upon our arrival found as many of our relations & friends living & in health, as could be reasonably expected after a sixteen years absence. A fortnight back the last tuesday, we paid a visit to Ipswich, where we were first settled & lived thirteen years. We were received with the greatest cordiality & affection; for they were opposed to the war & hearty Americans. The next saturday I set out for my native place Hitchin in Hertfordshire, to see my sister & a few other relations. I mean to finish all journeys before the month is out, that I may apply myself without interruption to the Work in Hand; but before I go to the press must wait till I have received from Mr Hazard at New York further accounts of subscriptions. The publications of the printers at Boston & elsewhere proved very injurious; but abuse & ingratitude, when persons are vexed at the disappointments they meet with; are nothing uncommon.[2] I shall guard against being warped by any provocations or favours from exercising faithfulness; & flatter myself that impartial judicious part of mankind will approve the goodness of my intentions & the uprightness of my conduct. I design doing myself the honour of writing shortly to the Marquis La Fayette. I have been almost in one continual hurry since my arrival; & shall be most heartily rejoiced when it is over. The plants you was so good as to send me I brought over; they are ⟨still⟩ alive shewing out near or at the root. They are at Newington about three miles from the city where we ⟨live⟩ with Mrs Gordons brother; but when you direct let it be at Mr Field's Apothecary No. 95 Newgate Street London. We are wholly at a loss as to our future settlement but the same kind Providence that has hitherto cared for us I desire to rely upon for comfort during my remaining pilgrimage. Should you think of any way in which I can be the least serviceable to you, pray you to do me the honour of imploying me. Mrs Gordon joins in most affectionate regards to your Excellency, your Lady, your friends at Alexandria, the last married couple (whose fruitfulness I wish to hear of) my young friend, Mr & Mrs Lund Washington, & whoever else of my acquaintance you may occasionally fall in with, particularly Dr Craik. I remain with the sincerest esteem, My dear Sir, Your most obedient & humble servant

William Gordon

ALS, DLC:GW.

1. Jonathan Mason (1725–1798), an affluent Boston merchant who was active in the Revolutionary cause, served as a selectman of Boston and a deacon in the Old South Church. He was married to Miriam Clark Mason. His son Jonathan Mason, Jr. (1756–1831), in 1786 was elected to represent Boston in the Massachusetts General Court and from 1799 to 1803 served as a United States senator. James Jackson may be either James Jackson, "formerly of Boston," who died near London in 1828 at the age of 93, or the Rev. J. Jackson who died in Boston in 1796 at the age of 83.

2. See Gordon to GW, 9 April 1786, n.2.

From Macarty de Marteigne

My Lord   Baltimore 18th July 1786

As a Father to this Country, You ought to be One, to those who had the Honour of defending it, I Served under the Com-

mand of Monsr le Compte, d'estaing, & was afterwards aboard
the Ship of Monsr le Marquis de Vaudreuil: My Brother Commanded the Magnifique, which the Pilote unluckily lost in Boston River, he has at the Same time the happiness to be adorned
with your Order, whc. I have not had. I now find myself, My
Lord, in this Country by the loss of a Ship, whc. I was aboard
of, & whc. Going into the Missisipi, without knowing that New
Orleans belongs at present to the Spaniards; a person is thought
little of in this Country, when in Distress, but that whc. embarrasses me most, is being without Succour in this Country. I have
had the Honour of Seeing the French Consul, who has not made
me the least offer of Assistance,[1] I hope more, from Addressing
myself to you, My lord, & am perswaded that you will make me
an Offer of your Assistance, & will not Abandonn a person in
Distress, & with these Sentiments, I have the Honour to be your
Excellys My lord Very Hble & Obedt servt

le Chevalier Macarty, Macteigue

Translation, from the French, DLC:GW; ALS, PHi: Gratz Collection. A transcript of the letter in French is in CD-ROM:GW.

The younger Macarty de Marteigne (Marteigue) was *lieutenant de vaisseau* in
Le Fendant, commanded by the marquis de Vaudreuil, while it was in American
waters between 1779 and 1781. He burned the palm of his left hand while
seeking to put out a fire on the ship during an engagement with a British
naval force off Grenada on 6 July 1779 (*Les combattants français de la guerre
américaine, 1778–1783* [Paris, 1903], 76).

1. Charles-François-Adrien le Paulinier, chevalier d'Annemours (d'Anmour;
b. 1742), left France for America in 1754 and came to the United States in
1777. He served as France's consul in Baltimore from 1779 to 1789.

From Edward Peyton

Sir,   Spotsylvania 18th July 1786
That your Excellency will be somewhat surprised, at the reception of this epistle is an event, natural to my expectations—
That it may be perused, with candor, and not be productive of
the least offence is the utmost of my wishes.

At the house of Mr Man Pages of Spotsylvania, I understood
your excellency was in want of an assistant in yr office—a person
had applied but was rejected on account of his assuming and
exorbitant demands; in consequence of which I have taken this
liberty. and should my writing suit any business, of your excel-

lency's, or if upon trial I have abilities suitable in any other department I shall esteem myself happy in your employ.[1]

As to demands I pretend not to any, only require an emolument adequate to the servises I might render.

For diligence and sobriety I can procure the testimony of Mr Wm Stanard—a Gentlman of indisputable veracity with whom I have lived near nine months as Tutor to his children and still remain in that capacity: but would prefer an employment wherein there is a greater variety.[2]

Should your excellency require a further Recommendation, I am sorry to say, it is out my power to furnish you with any: unless being subject to the capricious Necessitudes of Fortune will plead an advocate in my favor. if that would have any influence I can produce a certificate dated ten years back. If your excellency concieves this application merits an answer I shall esteem it an honour in recieving one, directed at the Post Office Fredricksburg. I am With Great Respect Your Excellency's Most Obedient Humble Servat

Edw: Peyton

ALS, DLC:GW.

1. Mann Page, Jr., lived at Mannsfield in Spotsylvania County. Tobias Lear arrived in June to replace William Shaw as GW's secretary. Peyton acted as a witness to two legal documents in Spotsylvania County in September 1786.

2. William Stanard of Spotsylvania, a minor when his father, Beverley Stanard, died in 1765, secured from John Lewis in 1787 six lots in the town of Fredericksburg (*Spotsylvania County Records*, 1:22, 409).

From Joseph Dashiell

Sir   Salisbury [Md.] 20th July 1786

I was Honourd a few days ago, with Yours of the 20th Ul[t]o. Obsarve the Content; I have made Inquiry & find that Good Cypress Posts, Could not be delivered with you, for less then Twelve shilling⟨s⟩ & six pence a hundred, & the rales at 15/ which is a price that I do not think they merit, as their is but Very little of that kind of Wood, that will last, in posts, so well as good Oak—and I Can find no One that will agree to furnish a quantity sooner then the Winter. I must Confess I would prefer

Ceader, Locase or good Post Oak, & I think Good Yellow pine rales Very Little Inferour to Cypress', altho I have no doubt that the rales would answer well, if the price was not so Very high. If you Should Incline to have pine rales, them of the best kind Can be delivered with you for 10/6 to 11/3.

If you should want any thing in the Plank or scantling way, I Should be happy to sarve you upon the lowest Termes, agreable to the quality. I have the Honr to be with the Gratest Respect yr Mo. Obt Hbe Servt

Joseph Dashiell

ALS, DLC:GW.

From Mauduit du Plessis

[New York, 20 July 1786]

I have the honour to transmit to your excellency, a letter that the marquis de la fayette had directed me, to hand you, requesting me, to Send it wery Soon.[1]

the Count D'Estaing has also, given me, one for your excellency, & flatted my Self to put it in your excellencys hands; but at present, I Send you a copy of it.[2]

I am Just arrived from france, on my way to Georgia, to take posession of a wery considerable tract of land which I have purchased at Paris, of M. John McQueen.[3]

this Calculated steep which I have taken with pleasure, makes me a Citizen of america, and, I Delight in believing that my children Shall imbibe from me the respect Justly due to a nation which has discovered So many virtues.

if I have taken great freedom in Speaking of my Self to your Excellency, my Design is to prove to you; that as an american Citezen, at this time, I have tittle to your good will; and that as a man my Self ⟨lone⟩ will be exceedingly flatered to present to your Excellency, my respect and hommage in these two Cases I pray your Excellency to recieve with Kindness my wishes to admired in Personn the whole assemblage of Virtues, in the calm retreat of mount vernon.

I Speack not your excellency, of Count D'Estaing, this man who has not his equal, in Europe, never mentions your name

but with sentiments fulls of admiration and the highest veneration, however your Excellency Well Knows his Perfict atta-
chement to you.

if your excellency will do me the honnoure to give me ad vice
of the reception, of the letter from the marquis de la Fayette, to
whom I Shall writte wery Soon, I pray you to adresse to me your
orders, to the Care of the Consul of france at philadelphia, and
where I Shall attend them[4]—I am with the highest respect your
excellency's Most obedient and Wery humble Servat.

Translation, DLC:GW; ALS, in French, advertised for sale in George D. Smith,
("American and Foreign Autographs"), item 147, no date. The translation was
docketed by GW and headed "traduction de ma Lettre au General washington."

Thomas-Antoine Mauduit du Plessis (1753–1791) began serving in the Continental army in 1777 and from 1780 served under Rochambeau. For his unhappy experiences in Georgia, see Mauduit du Plessis to GW, 12 Feb. 1787.

1. Lafayette wrote in his letter to GW of 24 May it would "be either forwarded or delivered by M. duplessis."

2. There are in DLC:GW three copies of d'Estaing's letter from Paris of 9
May, one in French signed by d'Estaing, one a translation by David Stuart
endorsed by GW, and another translation, also endorsed by GW, which may
be the "copy sent by du Plessis." The last of these reads: "Sir, One of my fellow
Soldiers, in the East Indies, whose least merit has been the Saving of my life,
Mr Duplessis, Brigadier of the King's armies, and ancient Governor of the
Island of St Vincents, will have the honour of remitting this Letter to your
Excellency; he intreats me to recommend him to you. An officer of Distinction,
who has placed a part of his fortune in a Country which owes all to your
eminent virtues, Stands in need of no other recommendation to your Excellency's favour, your are undoubtedly pleased when you see any one leave his
Country in order to participate of a happiness, to the foundation of which you
have been instrumental. Behold then a Soldier, who retires to live under the
Shadow of the tree which you have planted and Supported. Mr Duplessis, is
worthy of all the advantages that may result therefrom, by his Sentiments, I
dare answer for him, as for myself. To render hommage to the Great man
who has most wisely performed the greates[t] actions, admire the only and
respectable mortal who has produced the greatest resultats the human mind
is Capable of Conceiving, is the Desire of my friend⟨:⟩ He willingly undertakes
to present you my hommage and eternal attachment and respect with which
I am of your Excellency's The most humble and most obedient Servant Estaing."

GW did not acknowledge d'Estaing's letter until 19 Nov., when he wrote
from Mount Vernon: "Sir, I have had the honor of receiving your letter of the
9th of May; by the hands of Genl Duplissis who did me the honor to spend a
few days with me on his way to Georgia. I am highly obliged to you for introducing to my acquaintance a Gentleman of so much worth & merit: his own

personal qualifications are sufficient to ensure to him the regard and affection of all good men; but when to these are added his being the intimate friend and companion, & having preserved the life of Count d'Estaing, he will be doubly esteemed by every one who has the honor of knowing you. I sincerely wish that he may find the Country answerable to his expectation, & be induced to reside among us; if he should, America will make the valuable acquisition of a useful & worthy Citizen.

"I need not tell you, Sir, how happy I should be to have the honor of paying my respects to you in this Country. Every person who tastes the sweets of American liberty, must esteem & revere you, & those other great characters among our good allies, who by your noble & generous exertions, were highly instrumental in procuring it. I have the honor to be &a G: Washington" (LB, DLC:GW).

3. John McQueen (1751–1807), originally from South Carolina, moved to Georgia after the Revolution. He served in the legislature of both states and was a major land speculator. During the Revolution McQueen served in the navy and in the militia of South Carolina.

4. GW wrote to Mauduit du Plessis in answer to this letter of 20 July, from Mount Vernon, on 28 July: "Sir, It is with great pleasure I take the earliest opportunity of acknowledging the receipt of the letter you did me the honor to write to me from New York on the 20th inst:, accompanied by an original letter from M: le Marquis de la Fayette—& by the copy of one from Mr le Comte d'Estaing.

"Such ample testimonials of merit from such distinguished characters, cannot fail to ensure you the most grateful reception throughout America in general; but permit me Sir, to add for myself in particular, that I shall be unfeignedly happy in receiving you under the peaceful shades of Mount Vernon, & in seeking occasions to render you any services which it may be in my power to offer.

"In the mean time (as I hope soon to have the pleasure of seeing you personally) I will content myself with felicitating you on your safe arrival in the United States, while I congratulate my Country on the acquisition of so valuable & dignified a Citizen. With sentiments of perfect esteem & consideration I have the honor to be &c. Geo: Washington" (LB, DLC:GW). Mauduit du Plessis visited GW at Mount Vernon from 14 to 19 Aug. en route to Georgia.

Letter not found: to Leven Powell, 20 July 1786. On 12 Sept. Powell wrote GW: "I should have done myself the Pleasure of Answering your favor of the 20th of July earlier."

To James Tilghman

Dr Sir,   M[oun]t Vernon 20th July 1786.
    It will readily appear to you from the manner & evident marks of hurry with which the letter I had the honor to address

you last, was written, that it was only meant for your own perusal; but if the contents of it can afford any satisfaction to the gentleman who you say is anxious to be informed of the truth of the insinuations which have met Capt. Asgill's countenance, I have no objection to its being handed to him under the prohibition you have mentioned; for if that gentleman conceives that such tales will excite commiseration, he may be endulged in them 'till the touch stone of time & truth will reverberate upon him. I have already informed you that my letter was written from memory—I am persuaded, nevertheless, that nothing is contained therein, wch is not founded on facts; & that more might have been said to disprove the allegations.[1]

I am really sorry that it is not in my power yet, to give you any satisfaction respecting the affairs of Colo. Thos Colville's Estate; & of what can be done with the claim of Miss Anderson. No man can be more anxious than I am to bring these matters to *such a close* as will satisfy all parties, & exonerate myself. It is now many months, since I have pressed the eldest son, & I believe one of the Executors of Mr John West deceas'd, who was the principal acting Executor of J. Colvil, to furnish me, if he would not take the matter in hand himself, with all the papers of that Estate, that a final settlement, upon some principle or another, might be gone into. He always promised, but has never performed this—two months ago, he assured me I should have these papers in three weeks; at the end of which, I again applied & was as unsuccessful as before. His last assurance was, that he would bring them himself in a little time.[2]

As the concerns of this Estate have been intermixed & blended with Jno. Colvil's affairs, to whom Thomas was an Executor, & as both are in great confusion & perplexity—I mean as soon as I can get the papers, to put the whole into the hands of some gentleman of abilities & knowledge of the Law, to overhaul, digest & advise what is proper to be done in every matter for the fulfilment of the trust, & towards a final settlement: the result of which, so far as it respects Miss Anderson, you shall be informed of, so soon as I can speak with any decision on this point; for at present I am perhaps, as ignorant as you can be of the concerns of these Estates, & of what is proper to be done in behalf of the Legatees[3] & I am Dr Sir &a

G: Washington

LB, DLC:GW; Tobias Lear's extract, CtY: Humphreys Collection.
1. GW's letter is dated 5 June. See Tilghman to GW, 26 May, n.3.
2. Thomas West gave GW his "last assurance" on 27 June. See note 1 in West's letter of that date.
3. See Tilghman's response of 2 August.

Letter not found: from Metcalf Bowler, 21 July. On 19 Aug. GW wrote Bowler that he had "received your letter of the 21st of July."

To Henry L. Charton

Sir,   Mount Vernon 22d July 1786
The rude draughts herewith enclosed will, in some degree, comply with your request;[1] because it will shew the shape of the lands about which you have been treating. The Ship by which they are sent, heaving in sight before I had notice of its coming, I could do no more than send them in the unpolished state in which they are now handed to you.
The descriptions & situations of them you already have.
It may not be amiss to repeat, that the price set upon these lands, was on the supposition that the whole were to be taken; if part only is wanted (if I consent to separate them at all) the price by the acre, according to its situation & value, will be encreased; for to be relieved of the trouble of seating them was my principal motive & only inducement to offer them at a price which I conceived to be much under their intrinsic value. I have the honor to be &c.

Go: Washington

LB, DLC:GW.
1. See GW to Charton, 20 May.

To Battaile Muse

Sir:—   [Mount Vernon, 25 July 1786]
I want to change my seed wheat, but do not incline to sow any but of the white kind, I shall be ready to commence my seeding in a few days and if you have of this kind, ready, either of this, or the last year and will receive payment for it out of your collection of my Rents, I should be glad to have sent me from one to

three or four hundred Bushels.—I will give the Alexandria price at this time (be it what it may) or the price it may be hereafter, you at the moment, saying you are content with it—The Wheat must be clean & good & as I said before, white, & for the reason assigned I must have it sent to me immediately if at all; Pray let me know by Post what I have to trust to.[1] I am Sir Yr very Hble Servt

GEO WASHINGTON.

ALS, sold by Thomas Birch's Sons, item 12, catalog no. 683, 5–6 April 1892.
   1. See Muse's response, 31 July.

From Richard Thomas

Hond Sir   Charleston [S.C.] 25th July 1786
Your Letters of the 5th December 85 & 25th March 86 in answer to mine of 13th August & 10th December 85, are come safe to hand,[1] & should think myself wanting in gratitude to Your Excellency did I not instantly on the receipt of the last, acknowledge the due sence I have of the generosity & condescension you have been pleas'd to show on this occasion.

I was so unfortunate as not to get the first till the 5th of March, & should not have repeated my application had it arrived in the time there was the greatest reason to expect it, except in case of miscarriage, or some unavoidable delay.

I have to inform Your Excellency these Letters have sufficiently convinced me, as well as every other person to whom the affair has been communicated, that you are a stranger to the whole matter; and I cannot think a further examination necessary or justifiable, knowing the immaculate character in which Your Excellency is so eminently held by every Englishman.

I was actuated by no motive in this pursuit beyond a desire of discharging one of the duty's of humanity, not having any knowledge of Mr Richards, nor the least information how that premature report respecting the Executor was first brought into existance. As to the Estate I beleive there is some truth in: for by an enquiry among the Virginians here, I have found that Lawyer Haynes is still living, & resident in Meclenburgh County, where I am to suppose the Estate lies; a Letter has been sent, & an answer is daily expected: so if any further information will be satisfactory to Your Excellency, I will transmit it with a boundless pleasure. I have the Honour to be With Gratitude & Respect Hond Sir Your Excellency's Obedt Humble Servt

Richd Thomas

ALS, DLC:GW.
   1. GW's letter of 25 Mar. 1786 has not been found.

To William Grayson

Dear sir,   Mount Vernon 26th July 1786.

It is a fact that your favor of the 27th of May was long getting to me; but why it happened so, I am unable to inform you; as I generally send to the Post Office in Alexandria twice in every week.

Is it not among the most unaccountable things in nature that the representation of a great Country shou'd, generally, be so thin as not to be able to execute the functions of Government? To what is this to be ascribed? Is it the result of political manouvre in some States, or is it owing to supineness, or want of means?

Be the causes what they may, it is shameful & disgusting. In a word it hurts us; our character as a nation is dwindling; & what it must come to if a change should not soon take place, our enemies have foretold; for in truth we seem either not capable, or not willing to take care of ourselves.

For want, I suppose, of competent knowledge of the Connecticut claim to Western territory, the compromise which is made with her, appears to me to be a disadvantageous one for the Union; & if her right is not one of the motives (according to your account) for yielding to it, in my humble opinion, is exceedingly dangerous & bad; for upon such principles, *might*, not *right*, must ever prevail, & there will be no surety for anything.

I wish very sincerely that the Land Ordinance may answer the expectations of Congress. I had, & still have my doubts of the utility of the plan, but pray devoutly, that they may never be realized, as I am desireous of seeing it a productive branch of the revenue. That part which makes the waters & carrying places common highways, & free for all the States, is certainly valuable.

I thank you for the other articles of information; such as you have disclosed confidentially, you may rest assured will proceed no further, 'till it becomes public thro' other channels; & this shall always be the case with paragraphs which are so marked. The answer to the Memorial of Mr Adams, by Lord Carmarthen, I have seen at large. It was impolitic & unfortunate, if it was not unjust in these States to pass laws, which by fair construction might be considered as infractions of the treaty of peace.

It is good policy at all times, to place one's adversary in the wrong. Had we observed good faith, & the western Posts had then been withheld from us by G: Britain, we might have appealed to god & man for justice, & if there are any guarantees to the treaty, we might have called upon them to see it fulfilled. But now we cannot do this—tho' clear I am, that the reasons assigned by the British ministry are only ostensible—& that the Posts, under one pretence or another, were intended to have been detained, tho' no such acts had ever passed: but how different would our situation have been under such circumstances? With very sincere regard & Affection, I am Dr Sir, &ca

G: Washington

LB, DLC:GW.

To Henry Lee, Jr.

My Dr Sir,   Mount Vernon 26th July 1786

Your favors of the 3rd & 11th inst. are both at hand. The last came first—the first only two days ago. The Books by Mr Griffith are also received, & came in good order. My thanks for your kind intention of giving me the use of them 'till you return to Virginia are sincerely offered. Youngs tour thro' Ireland, I had myself purchased when in New York; and I have just received advice of the others at Annapolis, which I had been expecting, & had given you the trouble of enquireing after.

I am much obliged to you for the information respecting the China which is for sale in New York, with the order of the Cincinnati engraved on it; if it should not be disposed of before this letter reaches you, & you think a ready & safe conveyance can be had for it to Alexandria or this place, I would thank you for buying it for me. In this case, pray let me know the exchange between New York & London at 60 days sight, & I will by return of the Post, give you a good Bill for the sterlg amount of the 150 Dollars: or, by means of some of the merchts in Alexandria who have connexions in New York, I will forward an order on that place, to that amot.

If I stopped short of your ideas respecting the navigation of the Mississippi, or of what may be the opinions of Congress on this subject, it was not for want of coincidence of sentiment, but because I was ignorant at that time of the rubs which are in the way of your commercial treaty with Spain, & because I thought some address might be necessary to temporize with, and keep the settlement of Kentuckey in a state of quietness. At this moment that settlement is formidable—population is rapidly encreasing there. There are many ambitious & turbulent spirits among its inhabitants, who from the present difficulties in their intercourse with the Atlantic States, have turned their eyes to New Orleans, & may become riotous & ungovernable, if the hope of traffick with it is cut off by treaty. Notwithstanding if this cession is counterpoized, it may be a more favourable time for Congress to speak decisively to them, than when they have got stronger, but not sufficiently matured to force the passage of the Mississippi themselves; whilst the plans which are in agitation for opening communications with that territory, may, if successful, unfold to them new prospects, mutually beneficial to the old & new States.

All those matters, no doubt, will be duly considered by Congress, & a decision had on whichever side the advantages preponderate.

It was with very sincere regret I received the news of Genl Greens death. Life & the concerns of this world one would think are so uncertain, & so full of disappointments, that nothing is to be counted upon from human actions. Adieu, with sentiments of great regard & affection, I am Dr Sir &c.

G: Washington

LB, DLC:GW.

Letter not found: from Samuel Branden, 27 July 1786. On 20 Nov. GW wrote Branden that he had received "your letter of the 27th of July."

To Thomas Smith

Sir,   Mount Vernon July 28th 1786

It would be more tiresome than interesting, to assign reasons for my not having acknowledged the receipt of your letters of the 26th of Novr & 7th of Feby before this.[1] It may be sufficient to inform you, that they came duly to hand, though I had not the pleasure of seeing Majr McCormick whilst he was in Virginia, which I regretted, as I might have derived useful information from him respecting the views & expectations of the occupants of my Land in Washington County, at the sametime that I might, possibly, have engaged him, or through him some other, who would have made it a point to bring forward such testimony as would evince that preoccupancy of the tract in dispute was in me.[2] Without this I may fail in this particular, as it is not frequently found that people volunteer their services upon these occasions; but on the contrary, that they generally hang back from a desire of living (the idea is) in peace with their neighbours. for this reason I must refer you to the information given in my former letters, with a request that the evidences there named, may be summoned (if you think it necessary) to prove what has been advanced.

The instances of decision, of which you have made mention in your letter of the 26th of Novr in the Western Courts, are indicative of a favourable determination of my suit; and I would not depart from the legal ground on which I claim. Yet, as auxiliary, the proof of pre-occupancy would drive my opponants from what they conceive to be their stronghold, for it is on this (before what they call legal steps were taken by me) that they, I am persuaded, rest their cause. But why *all of them* should take this ground, when *most of them* emigrated to the Country after the *date* of my *Patent*, is misterious, & may comprehend more than I am aware of—for which reason, among others, if I could be ascertained of the precise time for the tryal, I would endeavor to be at it; especially as I have other calls in that Country, among wch to dispose of that Land, if the decision is favourable for me, and of my other Land where Simpson formerly lived, are most important.[3]

I have considered your remarks and wish it was in my power

to solve the doubts. My answers shall be candid, though the explications may be unfavourable.

However strange it may seem then, the fact nevertheless is, that Poseys Warrant was not dated till the 25th day of Novr 1773 (posterior, according to my opponants acct to their settlement)—This knowledge I have but lately obtained, and am exceedingly surprized at the fact, as the right was bought by me for this express purpose two or three years before, as you may perceive by the date of the Bond which is now in your possession. Of this it is necessary to apprize you, that if known to the defendants, you may be guarded against the force of it; as also that, the date of Colo. Crawfords deputation, is subsequent to their pretended Settlement.

The proof to the hand writing of Posey I have already furnished you with.

I believe there has been no entry in the Surveyors book of this tract; for I can find nothing there preceeding the record of the Survey; to what to ascribe this, I know not, except to a neglect of Office, or to the unacquaintedness of Colo. Crawford with business. The presumption is, that the preceeding steps to the issuing of the Patent, were legal, and such as satisfied this Government, under whose jurisdiction it then was. And this Government having stipulated in its cession to Pensylvania that the Grants it had made should be secured to the Proprietors, I cannot perceive upon what ground the validity of mine can be questioned without arraigning the conduct of a sister State in the management of her own internal concerns.[4]

The Council Books, as I have before informed you, were either distroyed by the enemy, or in a removal of the Papers so mislaid, as that no access can be had to them, consequently, it is not in my power to furnish you with an authenticated copy of the proclamation which takes of[f] the restriction in that of 1763.

If you should hear of any person who may want to purchase improved Land in the Counties of Fayette or Washington, I would thank you for letting them know that mine are for sale (as I have before mentioned to you). I want no more than the real value of them according to the credit which may be given and if you could help me to fix this by comparison of it with the

prices of Lands of equal quality, similarity of improvements, and
with the same advantages in the Counties they respectively lye
in, it would oblige me. The payments, being secured, shall be
made easy with respect to time I should be glad to hear that this
letter had got safe to your hands—information via Philadelphia
or Baltimore, by letter thrown into the Post Office, will be most
certain of a conveyance. With very great esteem I am Sir Yr
Most Obedt Hble Ser⟨vt⟩

                                              Go: Washington

ALS, NhD; LB, DLC:GW.
    1. Smith's letter of 26 Nov. 1785 has not been found.
    2. See George McCarmick to GW, 30 Oct. 1786, and GW to McCarmick, 27
Nov. 1786. For the eviction suits that Thomas Smith was handling for GW in
Washington County, Pa., with which this letter is concerned, see the editorial
note in Smith to GW, 9 Feb. 1785.
    3. For GW's final settlement with Gilbert Simpson in regard to ending
Simpson's management of GW's property, called Washington's Bottom, on the
west bank of the Youghiogheny River, see GW to Clement Biddle, 1 Feb.
1785, n.8.
    4. See Editorial Note, Smith to GW, 9 Feb. 1785.

From William Moultrie

Dear Sir   Charleston [S.C.] July 30. 1786
    The Gentleman who favors me with the delivery of this letter,
is the Honle Wm Drayton Esqr. Council for this State, he will be
on his return from the Federal Court, called to determine a dispute between this State & Georgia respecting their boundary
lines, he wishes to be introduced to your Excellency.[1] I have
therefore taken the liberty of giving him this letter of introduction.[2]
    Mrs Moultrie begs leave to join me in our best respects to Mrs
Washington. I have to honor to be Dr Sir Your Excelly Most Obt
hume Servt

                                              Willm Moultrie

ALS, PHi: Gratz Collection; Sprague transcript, DLC:GW.
    1. The South Carolinians William Drayton and Walter Izard (c.1750–1788)
arrived at Mount Vernon on 22 Oct. (*Diaries*, 5:55–56). GW's new secretary,
Tobias Lear, was present when GW told the South Carolinians what he remembered about the treachery of Benedict Arnold in 1780. In his diary entry for

22 Oct. Lear sets down his version of what GW said: "I confess I had a good opinion of Arnold before his treachery was brot to light; had that not been the case I should have had some reason to have suspected him sooner—for when he commanded in Philadelphia the Marquis de la Fayette brot accts from France of the armament which was to be sent to cooperate with us the ensuing Campaign. soon after this was known Arnold pretended to have some private business to transact for himself in Connecticut & on his way there he called at my quarters, & in the course of conversation expressed a desire of qu[i]tting Philadelphia & joining the Army the ensuing campaign. I told him that it was probable ⟨t[ha]t⟩ we should have a very active one & that if his wound & state of health would permit I should be extremely glad of his services with the army.

"He replied, that he did not think his wound would permit him to ⟨*illegible*⟩ persisted in his desire of being with the army. he went on to Connecticut & on his return called again upon me. he renewed his request of being with me next campaign & I made him same answer that I had done before. he again repeated that he did not think his wound would permit him to do active duty & intimated a desire to have the command at West point—I told him I did not think that would suit him so I should leave none in the Garrison but invaleeds because it would be entirely covered by the main Army. The Subject was dropt at that time & he returned to Philadelphia. It then appeared somewhat strange to me that a man of Arnolds known activity & enterprize should be desireous of taking so inactive a part. I however, thot no more of the matter. When the French troops arrived at Rhode Island—I had intilligence from New York that Genl Clinton intended to make an attack upon them before they could get themselves settled & fortified. in consequence of that, I was determined to attack New York which would be left pretty much exposed by his drawing off the troops, & accordingly formed my line of battle &c. and moved down with the whole army to King's ferry which we passed. Arnold came to camp at that time & having no command & consequently no quarters (all the houses thereabout being occupied by the Army) he was obligd to seek lodgings at some distance from Camp. While the Army was crossing at Kings ferry—I was going to see the last detachment over & met Arnold who asked me if I had thot of anything for him. I told him that he was to have the command of the light troops wh. was a post of honour & which his Rank entitled him to. upon this information his Countenance changed & he appeared to be quite fallen & instead of thanking me or expressing any pleasure at the appointment, never opened his mouth. I desired him to go on to my quarters & get something to refresh himself & I would meet him there soon. he did so—upon his arrival there, he found Colo. Tilghman, whom he took on one side & mentioning what I had told him, seemed to express a great uneasiness at it—as his leg he said, would not permit him to be long on horse back, & intimated a great desire to have the command at West point. when I returned to my Quarters, Col⟨o⟩. Tilghman informed me of what had passed between him & Arnold. I made no reply to it—but his behaviour struck me as strange & unaccountable. in the course of that Night, however, I recd information from New York that Genl Clinton had altered his plan & was debarking his troops. this information obliged me likewise to alter my disposition, (which was only

consequent of his) & return to my former station where I could better cover
the Country. I then determined to comply with Arnold's desire & accordingly
gave him the command of the Garrison at Wt Point. The things remained in this
situation about a fortnight, when I wrote to the Count Rochambeau desiring
to meet him at some intermediate place (as we could neither of us be long
enough from his respective command to visit the other) in order to lay ⟨the⟩
plan for the seige of York town—& proposed Hartford, where I accordingly
went & met the Count. On my return I met the Chevelier Luzern towards
evening within about 15 miles of W. point on his way to join ⟨*illegible*⟩ Rhode
[Island] which I intended to reach that night, but as he insi[s]ted upon turning
back with me to the next publick house, where in politness to him I could not
but tarry all night, determining however, to get to Wt Point to Breakfast—
very early, I sent off my baggage & desired Coll Hamilton to go forward &
inform Genl Arnold that I would breakfast with him—soon after he arrived at
Arnold's quarters, a letter was delivered to arnold which threw him into the
greatest confusion. he told Col. Hamilton that something reqd his immediate
attendance at the Garrison which was on the opposite sde of the River to his
quarters—& immediately ordered a horse for him to ride to the River, & the
Barge which he keep to cross, to be ready; & desired Majr Franks, his Aid, to
inform me when I should arrive, that he was gone over the River & wou'd
return immediatley. when I got to his quarters & not findg him there, I desird
Majr Franks to order me some breakfast, & as I intended to visit the fortifica-
tions I would see Genl Arnold there. After I had breakfasted—I went over the
River, & enquiring for Arnold, the Command⟨ing⟩ officer told me that he had
not been there—I likewise enqured at the several Redoubts but no one could
give me any information where he was. The impropriety of his Conduct when
he knew, I was to be there, struck me very forcably & my mind misgave me,
but I had not the least idea of the real cause. When I returned to Arnolds
Quarters about 2 hours after and told Colo. Hamilton that I had not seen
him—he gave me a paquet which had just arrived for me from Col. Jemmis-
son, which immediately brot the matter to light—I orderd Col. Hamilton to
mount his horse & proceed with the greatest dispatch to a post on the river
about ⟨*illegible*⟩. papers found upon him were in his possession. Colo. Jemmis-
son, when Andre was taken with these papers, could not beleive that Arnold
was a traitor but rather thought it was an imposition of the British in order to
destroy our Confidence in Arnold. he, however, immediately upon their being
taken, dispatched an express after me, ordering him to ride night & day till
he came up with me. the express went the lower road [(]which was the road
by which I had gone to Connecticut) expecting that I should return by the
same rout & that he sho'd meet me, but before he had proceeded far he was
informed that I was returning by the upper road. he then cut across the Country & followed in my tract till I arrived at Wt Point. he arrived about 2 hours
after & brot the above ⟨paqete *mutilated* Arnold gave orders *illegible*⟩ he ordered
his men (who were very cleaver fellows & some of the better sort of soldiery)
to proceed immediately on board the Vulture Sloop of war (as a flag) which
was lying down the river, saying that they must be very expeditious as he must
return in a short time to meet me, & promised them 2 Gallons of rum if they

wou'd exert themselves. they did accordingly; but when they got on board the ship, instead of their two Gals. of rum, he ordered the Cockswain to be called down into the Cabin & informed him that he & the men must consider themselves as prisoners. the Cocksman was very much astonished, told him that they came on board under sanction of a flag. he answd that was nothing to the purpose—they were prisoners; but the Captain had more generosity than this mean, pittiful scoundrel & told the Cocksman that he would take his parole for him to go on shore & get cloaths, & whatever else was wanted for him & his compannions. he accordingly came, got his cloths &c. & returned on board; when they got to New York, General Clinton, ashamed of so low & mean an action, set them all at Liberty" (AD, owned [1989] by Mrs. Helen Marie Taylor, Orange, Va.). The only portions of Lear's diary which have hitherto come to light are this entry of 22 Oct. 1786 along with the brief one for the following day and the entry containing Lear's well-known account of GW's death in 1799.

2. Drayton had in hand another letter from Charleston, one from John Rutledge (1739–1800) dated 7 Aug.: "Mr Drayton proposing to pay his Respects in person, to you, I take the Liberty of giving him this Line of Introduction—you will find him a gentleman—in every Respect—worthy of Attention" (PP).

To Clement Biddle

Dr Sir,   Mo[un]t Vernon 31th July 1786.

Majr Gibbes handed me your letter of the 24th ulto with the accounts enclosed.[1] Necessity alone ought to compel me to loose the difference between £50:18.9 and 339⁵³⁄₈₀ Dollars; because the last mentioned sum (but a very little while since) was, [(]if I recollect rightly) considered as the *specie* value of the Commissary's Certificates for which it was issued by Mr Stelle, and was accordingly so settled by the scale of depreciation. Notwithstanding, as I am entirely unacquainted with the fund upon which this certificate has issued, & what it may ultimately tend to, I must repeat my wish that you would act for me in this case, as you wou'd do for yourself. Laying out of the money will be no inducement to my selling the Certificate at an under value, if it is thought that it will finally be good, & the interest[2] can be received in the meanwhile. But as I never made paper money a study, having had nothing to do with any except old Continental (by which I have lost very considerably) I must rely upon your judgment more than on any direction I can give, for the disposition of Stelles certificate; always remembering that I am to give others credit for one moiety of what it would really fetch, *in specie*, & that their accots are to be credited by what you shall say to me on this head, it would sell for in this manner.[3]

When Blankets, Oznaburghs, Linnen of any kind, Paints, loaf sugar, Coffee, best Hyson Tea, or either of them, may happen to be low at the wholesale or vendue stores in Phila.; you would do me a kindness by giving me information of it; as, if I should not happen to be supplied at the time, I would immediately Commission you to make a purchase for me.

Do the Tanners in Philadelpa make leather that is stout, strong, & well adapted for Negros shoes? If so, what could Twenty five sides of Soal and the like quantity of upper (un-blacked)—or as much as would make 150 pair with three Soals, be bought for?

Be so good as to forward the enclosed by a safe conveyance— The one to Mr Smith respects a Law suit I have in the Western Country; the miscarriage, or delay of which, might be injurious to me.[4] My Compliments to Mrs Biddle—& with esteem I am, Dear Sir Yr most Obedt & very Hble Se⟨rvt⟩

Go: Washington

LB, DLC:GW; ALS, (incomplete photocopy), Sotheby, Parke-Bernet catalog no. 38131B, item 468, 25 Nov. 1975, item 468. According to the catalog, GW's letter is dated 31 July.

1. Biddle's letter is printed above under the date of 25 June, the date Biddle gives the surviving draft.

2. The remainder of the text is taken from the photocopy of the ALS.

3. See GW to Biddle, 18 May 1786, n.4.

4. GW's letter to Thomas Smith is dated 28 July.

To Lauzun

Monr le Duc,   Mo[un]t Vernon July 31st 1786.

I have had the honor to receive your letter to me of the 25th of Augt 1785. by the hand of Mr Michau, of whom it was introductory.[1] The scientific object which occasioned the voyage of that gentleman to America, his personal character, & the recommendation of the Duke de Lauzun, conspired to make me extremely happy in forming an acquaintance with him. I should be made still more so by his complete success in his botanical pursuits. Any assistance in my power will be most chearfully accorded as a tribute to his merit, & as a demonstration of the attachment & esteem with which I have the honor to be &c.

G: Washington

LB, DLC:GW.

1. Lauzun's letter is quoted in Lafayette to GW, 3 Sept. 1785, n.1, which see. See also André Michaux to GW, 20 June.

From Battaile Muse

Honourable Sir,   Berkeley C[oun]ty July 31st 1786

your Favour dated the 25th of Instant I this moment received—It's out of my Power To Furnish you with the Seed wheat in Time as the wet seasons will not give me Time To get out wheat for my own Seeding—besides if I had the wheat now out, I could not get it down for the want of waggons unless I give £4 a Tripp the price will not afford that deduction of waggonage—If your own wheat is but midling it's better To sow it as the wheat in Genl this year is Very Fowl—unless you can get from a neit Farmer—was I To send any it should be good—but it's out of my Power without Ingureing my Imployers—I expect To be at Alexandria next month if so, I shall call on you—I have not received one shillings since my last Letter wherein I enclosed and order on Colo. Gilpin for £50. I am sir Your Very Humble Servt

Battaile Muse

ALS, DLC:GW.

To Rochambeau

My dear Count,   Mount Vernon July 31st 1786.

I have been duly honored with the two letters you were pleased to write to me in the months of Jany and March last:[1] I need scarcely tell you that your communications always afford me the sincerest gratification—because they are always replete with the most friendly sentiments—because they insensibly bring to remembrance some circumstances of that pleasing & important period we so happily passed together—and because you frequently have it in your power to give such informations, as in my present retirement from the busy & political world cannot fail of being acceptable to me.

It must give pleasure to the friends of humanity even in this distant section of the globe to find that the clouds, which threatned to burst in a storm of war in Europe, have dissipated & left a still brighter political horizon. It is also to be hoped, that something will turn up to prevent, even at the death of the Elector of Bavaria or the King of Prussia, the effusion of human blood, for the acquisition of a little territory.

As the rage of conquest, which in the times of barbarity, stimulated nations to blood, has in a great degree ceased; as the objects which formerly gave birth to Wars are daily diminishing; and as mankind are becoming more enlightened & humanized, I cannot but flatter myself with the pleasing prospect that more liberal policies & more pacific systems will take place amongst them. To indulge this idea affords a soothing consolation to a philanthropic mind, insomuch that altho' it should be founded in illusion, one would hardly wish to be divested of an error, so grateful in itself & so innocent in its consequences.

The Treaty of Amity which has lately taken place between the King of Prussia & the United States marks a new æra in negotiation. It is perfectly original in many of its articles. It is the most liberal Treaty which has ever been entered into between independent Powers; and should its principles be considered hereafter as the basis of connection between nations, it will operate more fully to produce a general pacification than any measure hitherto attempted amongst mankind. Superadded to this, we may safely assert, that there is at present less war in the world than ever has been at any former period.

The British continue to hold the Posts ceded by the late Treaty of Peace to the United States. Each of these powers does not hesitate to criminate the other, by alledging some infractions of that Treaty. How the matter will terminate time must disclose. Every thing remains tranquil on this side of the Atlantic, except that the Savages sometimes commit a few trifling ravages on the frontiers.

General Green lately died at Savanna in Georgia. The Public, as well as his family & friends, has met with a severe loss. He was a great & good man indeed. With sentiments of the purest esteem & attachment, I have the honr to be, My dear Count, Yr most Obedt and affecte Hble Servt

Go: Washington

ALS, DLC: Rochambeau Papers; LB, DLC:GW.
　1. The day of the month is not given in Rochambeau's January letter; the other letter is dated 9 March.

To Antoine-Felix Wuibert

Sir,　　　　　　　　　　　　Mount Vernon 31st July 1786.

I have been favored with the receipt of triplicate copies of your polite letter dated at Cape-françois the 15th of Novr last.

While you do me the justice to acknowledge the zeal with which I desired & attempted to promote the interest of all the individuals composing the army I had formerly the honor to command; permit me to express my regret that, from peculiar circumstances, I had it not more fully in my power to attain that desirable object.

It was doubtless the intention of Congress to establish funds for the punctual payment of the interest as it became due on the public securities given to the officers & Soldiers of the Army for arrearages of pay & commutation: Their designs however have hitherto been unfortunately frustrated by the delinquency of some of the States, which could not be induced to comply with their requisition of 5 ⅌ Cent impost. All the States in the Union have at length granted that impost, but there are still some difficulties respecting the collection &c. Whenever these can be removed, it is to be hoped the interest will be regularly paid on your Certificates. In the mean time Congress are taking measures for surveying the Lands ceded to them; out of wch the officers & Soldiers will undoubtedly receive what has been promised.

Having, as you know sir, long since retired from all public employment, I have it not in my option to interfere with public measures by making recommendations. Indeed I do not think it probable that any Corps of Engineers will be established at present. But I am very happy in all events to find that you are so agreeably situated with an old acquaintance & friend.

As to medals & Diplomas for the Cincinnati, the former I believe are to be purchased in Philada, & the latter to be obtained
thro' the State Society of wch an officer is member. I have none
of either at my disposal. With sincere wishes for your health &
happiness, I remain Sir, &c.

G: Washington

LB, DLC:GW.

Articles of Agreement
with Thomas Mahony

[Mount Vernon, 1 August 1786]
An Agreement made this first day of August Anno Domini one
thousand seven hundred and eighty six between George Washington of the County of Fairfax of the one part, and Thomas
Mahony of the other part, Witnesseth; that the said Thomas Mahony, for the wages and priviledges herein after expressed doth
agree, and oblige himself to work one year from the date hereof
for the said George Washington as a House-Carpenter, Joiner,
and (when not employed in either of these) in other jobs which
he may be set about; and will, during said term, behave himself
quietly, soberly, and orderly in the family, pursuing the business
about which he may be employed with diligence and fidelity.

In consideration of these things well & truely performed and
done on the part of the said Thomas Mahony, the said George
Washington doth hereby oblige himself, his heirs, and Executors
to pay the said Thomas Mahony Thirty pounds in Specie for his
year's service (or as the same shall come due) estimating dollars
at six shillings each and other Gold and Silver in that proportion. And will furnish him the said Thomas Mahony with board,
washing, and lodging as he has been usually accustomed to in
the family; and will give him the same allowance of spirit with
which he had been served, and will do it weekly if the said
Thomas shall prefer it. That he will cause to be made four shirts
and two pair of Overalls (the linnen and materials to be found
by said Thomas) and will cause his shirts, stockings and linnen
to be mended as usual. That whilst he has a Taylor and Shoemaker in the family of his own, they shall, without any other cost

to the said Thomas than his finding the materials, mend and repair his body-cloathes and shoes. And moreover, will pay the publick taxes, and the County and parish levies—to which the said Thomas is exposed, and which will become due and, payable within the year for which he stands engaged. And lastly, will allow the said Thomas Mahony one day each quarter of the year (at such times as can be best spared) to provide himself with necessaries, and execute his own lawful business.[1] In testimony of all these things the parties have hereunto set their hands & seals this day and year first written.

Witness   Thomas Mahoney
Tobias Lear   G: Washington

DS, DLC:GW.

Subsequent articles of agreement with Mahony in DLC:GW are dated 15 April 1788 and 7 May 1789. Mahony continued to work for GW until 1792 (Ledger B, 236, 271, 331). The articles are in Tobias Lear's hand and are docketed by GW.

1. On this day GW entered into a similar agreement with Cornelius McDermott Roe, "as a Stone Mason, Bricklayer, and (when not employed in either of these) in other jobs which he may be set about." For a description of the agreement with McDermott Roe, see *Diaries*, 4:191; for its text, see CD-ROM:GW.

To Thomas Jefferson

Dear Sir,   Mount Vernon Augt 1st 1786.
The letters you did me the favor to write to me on the 4th & 7th of Jany have been duly received.

In answer to your obliging enquiries respecting the dress, attitude &ca which I would wish to have given to the Statue in question—I have only to observe that not having a sufficient knowledge in the art of sculpture to oppose my judgment to the taste of Connoisseiurs, I do not desire to dictate in the matter—on the contrary I shall be perfectly satisfied with whatever may be judged decent and proper. I should even scarcely have ventured to suggest that perhaps a servile adherence to the garb of antiquity might not be altogether so expedient as some little deviation in favor of the modern custom, if I had not learnt from Colo. Humphreys that this was a circumstance hinted in conversation by Mr West to Houdon. This taste, which has been introduced in painting by West, I understand is received with applause & prevails extensively.

I have taken some pains to enquire into the facts respecting the medals of the Cincinnati, which Majr L'Enfant purchased in France. It seems that when he went to Europe in 1783 he had money put into his hands to purchase a certain number, and that conceiving it to be consonant with the intentions of the Society, he purchased to a still greater amount—insomuch that a Committee of the Genl Meeting, upon examining his Acct reported a balle due to him of Six hundred & thirty dollars, wch report was accepted. This money is still due, and is all that is due from the Society of the Cincinnati as a Society. General Knox has offered to pay the amount to Majr L'Enfant, but as it has become a matter of some public discussion, the latter wished it might remain until the next Genl Meeting, which will be in May next. In the meantime Genl Knox (who is Secretary Genl) has, or will write fully on the Subject to the Marquis de la Fayette, from whom he has had a letter respecting the business.[1]

We have no news of importance And if we had, I should hardly be in the way of learning it; as I divide my time between the superintendence of opening the navigations of our rivers & attention to my private concerns. Indeed I am too much secluded from the world to know with certainty, what sensation the refusal of the British to deliver up the Western posts, has made on the public mind. I fear the edge of its sensibility is somewhat blunted. Fœderal measures are not yet universally adopted. New York, wch was as well disposed a State as any in the Union is said to have become in a degree antifœderal. Some other States are, in my opinion, falling into very foolish & wicked plans of emitting paper money. I cannot however give up my hopes & expectations that we shall 'ere long adopt a more liberal system of policy. What circumstances will lead, or what misfortunes will compel us to it, is more than can be told without the spirit of prophecy.

In the meantime the people are industrious, œconomy begins to prevail, and our internal governments are, in general, tolerably well administered.

You will probably have heard of the death of Genl Greene before this reaches you, in which case you will, in common with your Countrymen, have regretted the loss of so great and so honest a man. Genl McDougall, who was a brave Soldier & a disinterested patriot, is also dead—he belonged to the Legislature of his State, the last act of his life, was (after being carried on purpose to the Senate) to give his voice against the emission of a paper currency.[2] Colo. Tilghman, who was formerly of my family, died lately & left as fair a reputation as ever belonged to a human character. Thus some of the pillars of the revolution fall. Others are mouldering by insensible degrees. May our Country never want props to support the glorious fabrick! With sentiments of the highest esteem & regard, I have the honor to be Dear Sir Yr Most Obedt & very Hble Servt

Go: Washington

ALS, DLC: Jefferson Papers; LB, DLC:GW.

1. See Jefferson to GW, 7 Jan., n.1, and Knox to GW, 13 June.

2. Alexander McDougall (1732–1786), one of the leaders of the radical movement in New York before the Revolution, was made major general in the Continental army in 1777. He was a member of the New York senate from 1783 until his death.

To La Luzerne

Dr Sir,   Mount Vernon 1st Augt 1786

The letter you did me the honor to write to me on the 3d of Feby, has come safely to hand. Nothing could be more satisfactory to me than the friendly sentiments contained in it, & the generous manner in which you always interest yourself in the happiness & dignity of the United States.

I wish I had it in my power to inform you, that the several States had fully complied with all the wise requisitions which Congress has made to them on national subjects. But unfortunately for us, this is not yet the case. Altho' for my own part I do not cease to expect that this just policy will ultimately take effect. It is not the part of a good Citizen to despair of the republic: nor ought we to have calculated that our young Governments would have acquired, in so short a period, all the consistency & solidity, which it has been the work of ages to give to other nations. All the States however, have at length granted the impost; tho' unhappily some of them have granted it under such qualifications, as have hitherto prevented its operation. The greater part of the Union seems to be convinced of the necessity of fœderal measures, & of investing Congress with the power of regulating the commerce of the whole. The reasons you offer on this subject are certainly forcible, and I can not but hope will 'ere long have their due efficacy.

In other respects our internal Governments are daily acquiring strength. The laws have their fullest energy; justice is well administered; robbery, violence or murder is not heard of from N[e]w Hampshire to Georgia. The people at large (as far as I can learn) are more industrious than they were before the war. Œconomy begins, partly from necessity & partly from choice & habit, to prevail. The seeds of population are scattered over an immense tract of Western Country. In the old States wch were the theatres of hostility, it is wonderful to see how soon the ravages of war are repaired. Houses are rebuilt, fields enclosed, stocks of cattle which were destroyed are replaced, and many a desolated territory assumes again the chearful appearance of cultivation. In many places the vestiges of conflagration & ruin are hardly to be traced. The arts of peace, such as clearing of rivers, building of bridges, establishing conveniences for travelling &c. are assiduously promoted. In short the foundation of a great Empire is laid, and I please myself with a persuasion that Providence will not leave its work imperfect.

I am sensible that the picture of our situation, which has been exhibited in Europe since the Peace, has been of a very different complexion; but it must be remembered that all the unfavorable features have been much heightened by the medium of the English news papers thro' which they have been represented.

The British still continue to hold the Posts on our frontiers, & affect to charge us with some infractions of the Treaty. On the other hand we retort the accusation. What will be the consequences, is more than I can pretend to predict. To me, however, it appears that they are playing the same foolish game in commerce, that they have lately done in War; that their ill-judged impositions will eventually drive our ships from their Ports, wean our attachments to their manufactures & give to France decided advantages for a commercial connexion with us. To strengthen the alliance & promote the interests of France & America will ever be the favorite object of him, who has the honor to subscribe himself, with every sentiment of attachment, &c. &c.

G: Washington

LB, DLC:GW.

To Battaile Muse

Sir,   Mount Vernon Augt 1st 1786

Not till within these two days did your letter of the 11th of last Month get to my hands. I have sent your advertisement to the Printer and as soon as the number of copies are struck they shall be forwarded to you. My former letter containing my sentiments respecting the flour at my mill, I have done nothing in it since rather wishing that you would pursue your own judgment with respect to the sale than to derive any price from me. Neither wheat or flour has started in price that I have heard of as yet.

Your order for Fifty pounds on Colo. Geo. Gilpin which I hereby acknowledge the receipt of will be presented in a day or two.

The Hites can have no claim, I conceive, to the small tract of 183 Acres on which Bailey lives. that was a piece of land which lay waste, after all the surrounding Lands were taken up & Patented and granted without the interference of any one. Nor do I think the determination in favor of the Hites can possibly affect the other Land on Bullskin, because it is in proof that this Land was sold by old Joist Hite to one Lewis Thomas who sold it to Captn George Johnson and is so recited in the Deed from the Proprietors Office—In the former Trial these matters were adduced as evidence; which evidence I suppose is of record; I have in answer to a letter on this head, written to Thornton Washington who lives on part of the Land and who I hope (for I have no idea of attending the Commissioners) will take care of his as well as my interest in this business—if you can assist him in it I shall be obliged to you. I have not had time yet to examine Colo. Fairfax's Land Papers—nor would I incline to entrust them to any casual conveyance where their can be the remotest danger of delay or miscarriage—If you call here, as intimated, I will deliver them to you without the formallity of an order from Colo. Nicholas—your receipt for them will satisfy me.

I am very well-satisfied with your settlement with Mr Crane— and I am pleased to hear you had so much better luck with your Clover Seed than I had with that you sent me which was sowed as soon as I got it last fall in a piece of the best ground I had on purpose to raise Seed, not one of wch was up the middle of May when I put the same ground in Timothy—the disappointment I would not have sustained for fifty pounds because fifty pounds will not buy me as much Seed as I expected to raise from the four Acres on which I sowed the bushel of defective Seed which has occasioned me the loss of a Season. I am Sir your Very Hble Servt

Go: Washington

ALS, PWacD: Sol Feinstone Collection, on deposit PPAmP.

To John Marsden Pintard

Sir,   Mount Vernon 2d Augt 1786.
Since my last to you, the Industry Captn Gibson is arrived, but from the length of the voyage most of the articles you had the goodness to send me have perished The Figs were entirely lost, so were all the malmsey grape. Of the Muscat & Ver[delh]a, some showing signs of feeble life, I have with great care & attention recovered two of the cuttings. These have now put forth leaf, & I hope will do well.[1]

The wines with which I was furnished by Messrs Searle & Co. are of a very good quality, & came to hand in very good order—& supplied, I dare say, upon as good terms as they could have been had from any other House on the Island; these considerations, added to such as you have mentioned, will, I am persuaded, induce me to give it the preference, especially, as from the purport of your letter, you must be connected therewith.[2]

The negotiations which have been set on foot by Congress with the piratical States will, it is to be hoped, put an end to the apprehensions with which the american trade is labouring, from the conduct of those barbarians towards it. I am Sir, Your most Obedt Humble Servant

G: Washington

LB, DLC:GW.

1. GW wrote Pintard on 20 May. See also Pintard to GW, 24 Jan., and note 1.
2. See note 2, Pintard to GW, 24 January.

From John Sullivan

Augst 2d 1786

To his Excellency General Washington The humble Petition of John Sullivan Humbly Sheweth—That your Excellencys Petitioner is a Native of the County of Kerry in the Kingdom of Ireland that he had a Brother by the Mothers side whose name was Timothy Mahony who was Clerk to Mr Sullivan of Massachusets Bay as appears by the last Account that came from him.

That—Your Excellencys Petitioner has receiv'd an Account from Cork which was brought by an American Captain that his Brother Timothy is Dead & that he had left his effects in your Excellencys Care.

Your Excellencys Petitioner knowing he is the nearest of Kin to the said Timothy Mahony humbly begs pardon for thus intruding on your Excellencys goodness hoping you will be pleas'd to forgive his rudeness & let him know the truth of the Matter & your Petitioner as in Duty bound shall ever pray &c.

Your Petitioner humbly begs your Excellency will be so Condescending as to let him have an Answer Directd to be left at the Bell Goswell Street London.[1]

D, DLC:GW.

1. GW wrote from Mount Vernon on 28 Sept.: "Sir, I have received your letter of the 2d of Augt—In answer to it, I can only say that I have not the least knowledge of the person or circumstances mentioned therein, & never heard of either, but thro' your letter. I am Sir &c. G: Washington" (LB, DLC:GW).

From James Tilghman

Dear Sir,   Chester Town [Md.] Augt 2d 1786
   I am honoured with your letter of the 20th of July[.] When I transmit your Paragraph relating to Capt. Asgill, to Mr Nicols it shall be under the restriction mentioned[1]—I am perfectly satisfyed you will do every thing in your power [to] assist Miss Anderson in the Recovery of Colo. Colville's Legacy—and shall not trouble you any further on that head—My sorrows multiply[.] I have just heard that my Son Richard died on his passage from India to London and I have too much reason to fear the report is true[.][2] He was a credit to his family as was poor Tench[.] My Losses I must endeavor to bear[.] Submission is my part which I shall endeavor to act as well as I can. I have the honour to be with very sincere regard Yr Most obt hble Servt
                                                   James Tilghman

ALS, DLC:GW.
   1. See Tilghman to GW, 26 May, n.3.
   2. Richard Tilghman (b. 1746) studied at Eton and the Middle Temple and before the Revolution returned to England to live. The report proved to be untrue; Richard Tilghman lived until 1796.

To Henry Hill

Dr Sir,   Mount Vernon 3d Augt 1786.
   Inclosed is a letter for Messrs Lamar, Hill, Bissett & Co., and a draft for £43.12.4 on Wakelin Welch Esqr. of London, in payment for the Pipe of Madeira wine sent me by that House. If you accept the Bill please to return me the order with your signature. If you prefer the cash, let me know it, & I will get some gentleman in Alexandria who may have commercial connexions in Philada, to pay it.[1] My compliments if you please to Mrs Hill[2]—with great esteem & regard, I am, Dear Sir, &c.
                                                   G: Washington

LB, DLC:GW.
   1. See GW to Lamar, Hill, Bisset, & Co., this date.
   2. Hill's wife, Ann, was the sister of Gen. Samuel Meredith and of Mrs. George Clymer.

To Lamar, Hill, Bisset, & Co.

Gentn   Mount Vernon 3d Augt 1786.

Your favors of the 6th & 17th of December came duly to hand; & I have also received from Norfolk the pipe of Madeira wine which you addressed to the care of Doctr Taylor of that place for my use. I have not yet tasted it, but presume it is fine: it ought to be so, for the cost of it in the Island, besides the extra charges here, is £7.12.4 pr pipe more than the wines I had from Messrs Searle & Co. in April 1783; than which none, I think, could be better, for it was old, & of an excellent quality.[1]

I remit to Henry Hill Esqr. of Philada a draft for £43.12.4 on Wakelin Welch Esqr. of London, which is the amot of your order on me in favor of the above gentleman.[2] I am Gentn &c.

G: Washington

LB, DLC:GW.

1. See GW to John Marsden Pintard, 24 Jan. and 2 Aug. 1786.
2. See GW to Henry Hill, this date.

To Wakelin Welch

Sir,   Mount Vernon 4th Augt 1786.

The inclosed is a copy of my last letter to you, since which I have drawn upon you in favor of the honble Geo: Wm Fairfax for £155.14:9.—of Henry Hill Esqr. for £43.12.4 and of William Hartshorne Esqr. of this date for £47.12.6. which please to pay with my money in the Bank[1] & there by oblige Sir Your Most Obed. &c.

G: Washington

LB, DLC:GW.

1. GW's "last letter" has been dated c.1 July. See GW to George William Fairfax, 30 June, and GW to Henry Hill, 3 August. In his cash accounts GW notes paying on 5 Aug. £66.13.4 in Virginia currency to William Hartshorne for "my 1/4th Dividend of P[otomac] Co[mpany]" (Ledger B, 231). For his "money in the Bank," see GW to Welch, c.1 July, and the reference in note 2 of that document.

To William Peacey

Sir,   Mount Vernon, Virginia Augst 5th 1786

Excuse the liberty I take in putting the inclosed Letters under cover to you.[1] It is to oblige Mr James Bloxham who now lives with me, but who scarcely has sufficient knowledge of his own mind to determine whether to continue more than the present year (for which he is engaged) or not. In a word he seems rather to have expected to have found well organized farms, than that the end and design of my employing him was to make them so. He makes no allowances for the ravages of a nine year's war from which we are but just begining to emerge, nor does he consider that if our system of Husbandry had been as perfect as it may be found on your Farms, or in some of the best farming Counties in England, there would have been no occasion for his Services.

What the old man has written to you respecting the coming over of his wife—sending over plows, seeds, and so forth, I know not; because at different times he seems to be of different opinions. I can only add therefore, if his family are to come, and by the way of London, that it would be well for some person in their behalf to open a correspondence with Messrs Forrest & Stoddart—Merchan[t]s, of that place, who have Ships that pass by my door in their way to Alexandria, and would render the passage in one of them much more convenient & less expensive than to any other place; tho for a Vessel bound to Norfolk in this State (Virginia) or to Annapolis, Baltimore, or Patuxent in the neighbouring one of Maryland, it would not be very inconvenient. In case of her coming, whatever Impliments, Seeds, &c. may be requested by Mr Bloxham on my Acct had better be paid for by his Wife, and settled for here.[2]

I am sorry to be thus troublesome, but as Mr Bloxham considers you as his Benefactor, and Friend—has addressed one of his Letters to you—and his Wife, if she finally resolves to come, will stand in need of advise and assistance, it is necessary that the best mode should be suggested. A Ship from Bristol to either of the places above named, may probably, be more convenient than the rout by London, but of this you can judge better than I. I am Sir, Yr Most Obedt Humle Servt

Go: Washington

LS, in the hand of Tobias Lear, ViMtV; LB, DLC:GW.

1. For one of these letters, see the enclosure printed below.

2. For Bloxham's tenure as a farmer at Mount Vernon, see the note in Articles of Agreement with James Bloxham, 31 May 1786. Uriah Forrest and Benjamin Stoddert were merchants in Georgetown, Maryland.

Enclosure
James Bloxham to William Peacey

Vurginua July 23 1786

James Bloxham Sr this is to Inform you that I arived Safe att the Generls Washingtons the 23 of aprel which was Ester monday I have orderd for 10 Bushels of Sanfine Seed and other Seeds from you which the generel washington will aplie to you for and I should be glad if you would take the Best Care you Can to send it over good ass you Can for he have been Deseved in soom sanfire Seed from England which I recemend him to you and let me have good that the generel sends for of all sorts if posable and send it along with my Wife ass soon ass posable and I sould bee glad If you Could get a Clever Lille Deasant plow which must go whithout a weeal for the Land is not Level and to be shoor to make him Light and Desant and be Shoor to make him to turn the worke well for they have som most Shoking Plows that Ever was Seen in the world the land is Light and very Esey to plow they go with two horses only and Doble the Same ass our norflk plows But no weel but very light but they have no noshun of making of a plou to turn the work thay are very Stupet in thare ane Conscist but send on that is Light an Deasent and that it will turn the work well I Rot in my other Letter to my Wife to Com over but I thinks it not worth wile for I thinks thatt I Shall Not Stay no Longer then my yeare is up which is the forst of next may for things Are verey Desagreable to Do Bisnes it is in posuble for any man to Do Bisness in any form the Genral have a Bout 25 hundard akers of Clear Land under is own ⟨*illegible*⟩ing Ther is nothing agreble about the plase which I Can not Do no Bisnss on form nore no Credet but I have you Send the plow And the Seeds which the Genearel will Send for to you and send half a Doson of good Clean made sh⟨ap⟩sks for thay have nothing but woodon forks I have got on[e] or two made but in a very bad maner that I Should be glad to Show them a patrn and if my house is not Disposed of I should be glad if you would not for this Contey is verey pore and there is no Chance for any Body to Do any go[o]d and I Schould Be g[l]ad if you and my Brother Thomas would See if these velins would Com to any terms or I would go to any part of England to Be out of thare way But this Contruy will not Do for me but to be shore what the General have oferd in wages is prete Well he Gives for this year we have a Gred for 50 English ginues per yeare and Bord and washing and Lodging and if I Would Send for my wife and famly he would alow me ten Ginues towards thare Coming to this Contry an if I would Stay and to alow me 8 hundard Waite of flower and 6 hunderd Wait of pork and Bef and to alow me two milchs Cows for the youse of my famly and to alow me a Sow to Bred Som pigs for my on yous but Not to sell and to alow me a Comfortouble house to Liven but it apears to me not Any Inheretance the ar is another thing Which is very Disagreable tese Black Peope I am Rather in Danger of being posind among them which I think I shall Leeve the Contrey ass son Ass I Can But the General and I have agreed and articld for one yeare But my Wife may youse one Will A Bout Comming over But I hope Sr you I Hope Will Be A frend to my poor Deer Children and Wife and I Hope you will Remember my brother Thomas to a Sist them what he Can my hart have yarnd for my famly A Gret maney time and I think I am all most Like a Transpart But I hope that the Sun will Shine unon me wonce more the General hve Some very ⟨*illegible*⟩ Beut badly manedge and he never well have them no Better for he have a Sett of About him which I nor you would Be trobled with But the General is goot them and he must Keep them But they are a verey Desagreable People and I will Leave the Contry But I Should be glad of answwer Inmedally to Know how afares Stand and then I Sall be abetter Judge of the matter the General have Som very Good Shep which he sold for 40 shilings apes of thar money a English ginua is 28 Shiling of mney and I hope mrs and all the famly is Well and I have Whent there a greatt Dele Since I Laft England.[1]

And Lett me have a nanswer Imeadedly Rember me to all frends and no mor from me yr frend and well wisher

James Bloxham

ALS, DLC:GW.

1. On 2 Feb. 1787, after Bloxham had decided to remain at Mount Vernon and had sent for his wife and children, Peacey commented to GW: "James Bloxham's first Letter (in august) was ritten in Bad Spirits on acount of Being at so great a distance from his fammily."

To Wakelin Welch

Sir,   Mount Vernon 5th Augt 1786.

On the other side is a copy of my letter to you of this date[1] under cover to Arthur Young Esqr. of Bradford Hall, near Bury in Suffolk. The articles which I have written to him for are,

2 ploughs, with spare shares & coulters; & a mould to form others on.

A little of the best kind of cabbage seeds for field culture.

20 lb. of best Turnip seeds.

10 bushels of Sainfoin seeds.

8 Do of the winter Vetches.

2 Do of rye-grass Seeds.

50 lb. of Hop clover seed; & a little Burnet seed, if it is in estimation with Farmers.

Perhaps he may add a few seeds of other kinds—perhaps he may encrease the quantities above, & possibly add some other instruments of Husbandry, tho' I have written for none, nor have I reason to expect any, unless he may be disposed to send some very useful ones without waiting a request. It is also possible, tho' I have very little expectation of its happening, that he may engage me a common plough-man.

Your paying the cost of these things and forwarding them in a vessel for Potomac, will much oblige me; as it will to convey the letters herewith enclosed, to their respective addresses. I am &c.

G: Washington

LB, DLC:GW.

1. GW's other letter to Welch of 5 Aug. is printed in note 31, GW to Arthur Young, 6 August.

To Arthur Young

Sir,   Mount Vernon 6th Augt 1786
  I have had the honor to receive your letter of the 7th of Jany
from Bradford-Hall, in Suffolk, and thank you for the favor of
opening a correspondence, the advantages of which will be so
much in my favor.
  Agriculture has ever been amongst the most favourite[1] amusements of my life, though I never possessed much skill in the art,
and nine years total inattention to it,[2] has added nothing to a
knowledge which is best understood from[3] practice, but[4] with
the means you have been so obliging as to furnish me, I shall
return to it (though rather late in the day) with hope & confidence.[5]
  The system of Agriculture (if[6] the epithet of system can be
applied to it)[7] which is in use in this part of the United States, is
as unproductive to the practitioners[8] as it is ruinous[9] to the land-
holders.[10] Yet it is pertinaciously adhered to. To forsake it; to
pursue a course of husbandry which is altogether[11] different &
new to the gazing multitude, ever averse to novelty in matters
of this sort, & much attached to their old customs,[12] requires
resolution; and without a good practical guide, may be dangerous, because[13] of the many volumes which have been written on
this subject, few of them are founded on experimental knowledge—are verbose, contradictory, & bewildering. Your annals
shall be this guide.[14] The plan on which they are published,
gives them a reputation which inspires confidence; and for the
favor of sending them to me I pray you to accept my very best
acknowledgments. To continue them, will add much to the obligation.[15]
  To evince with what avidity, and with how little reserve I embrace the polite & friendly offer you have made me of supplying
me with "Men, Cattle, Tools, seeds, or any thing else that may
add to my rural amusement,"[16] I will give you, Sir, the trouble
of providing, and sending to the care of Wakelin Welch, Esqr. of
London, Mercht the following articles.
  Two of the simplest, & best constructed Plows for land which
is neither very heavy nor Sandy. To be drawn by two horses. To
have spare shares & Colters—and a mold[17] on which to form
new irons when the old ones are worn out, or will require re-
pairing.

I shall[18] take the liberty in this place to observe, that some years ago, from a description, or recommendation of[19] what was then called the Rotheram; or Patent Plow, I sent to England for one of them,[20] and till it began to wear, & was ruined by a bungling Country Smith that no plow could have done better work, or appeared to have gone[21] easier with two horses; but for want of a Mold (wch I had neglected to order with the Plow), it became useless after the irons which came in with it were much worn.

A little of the best kind of Cabbage seeds, for field culture.

20 lbs. of the best Turnip-Seeds, for Do.[22]

10 Bushels of Sainfoin Seeds.

8 Bushls of the Winter Vetches.

2 Bushls of Rye-grass Seeds.[23]

50 lbs of Hop clover seeds.

and

If it is decided (for much has been said for and against it), that Burnet, as an early food, is valuable, I should be glad of a[24] bushel of this seed also. Red clover seeds are[25] to be had on easy terms in this Country, but if there are any other kinds[26] of grass-seeds (not included in the above) that you may think valuable, especially[27] for early feeding or cutting, you would oblige me by adding a small quantity of the seeds, to put me in stock.[28] Early grasses, unless a species can be found that will stand[29] a hot Sun, and oftentimes severe droughts in the summer months, without much expence of cultivation, would suit our climate best.

You see, Sir, that without[30] ceremony, I avail myself of your kind offer; but if you should find in the course of our correspondence, that I am likely to become troublesome you can easily check me. Inclosed I give you an order on Wakelin Welch, Esqr. for the cost of such things as you may have the goodness to send me.[31] I do not at this time ask for any other implements of Husbandry than the Plows; but when I have read your annals (for they are but just come to hand) I may request more. In the meanwhile, permit me to ask what a good Plowman might[32] be had for, annual wages, to be found (being a single man) in board, washing, & lodging? The writers upon Husbandry estimate[33] the hire of labourers so differently in England, that it is not easy to discover from them whether one of the[34] class I am speaking of[35] would cost Eight, or Eighteen pounds a year. A good Plowman at low wages, would come very opportunely with the Plows here requested.

By means of the application I made[36] to my friend Mr Fairfax, of Bath, & through the medium of Mr Rack, a bailiff is sent to me, who, if he is acquainted with the best courses of cropping, will answer my purposes as a director or superintendant of my Farms.[37] He has the appearance of a plain honest Farmer; is industrious; and, from the character given of him by a Mr Peacy (with whom he has lived many years) is understanding in the management of Stock, & of most matters for which he is employed. How far his abilities may be equal to a pretty extensive concern, is questionable.[38] And what is still worse, he has come over with improper ideas; for instead of preparing his mind to meet[39] a ruinous course of Cropping, exhausted Lands, and numberless inconveniencies into which we had been thrown by an eight years War, he seems to have expected that he was coming to well organized Farms, &[40] that he was to have met Plows, Harrows, and all the other[41] impliments of Husbandry in as high taste[42] as the best farming Counties in England could have exhibited them.[43] How far his fortitude will enable him to encounter these disappointments, or his patience & perseverence will[44] carry him towards the work of[45] reform, remains to be decided.[46] With great esteem, I have the Honor to be, Sir, Yr Most Obedt[47] Hble Servt

Go: Washington

ALS, PPRF; ALS, marked "Duplicate," PPRF; LB, DLC:GW. When he wrote Young again on 16 Nov. 1786, GW enclosed the duplicate copy of this letter. Before making the duplicate, GW revised his retained copy, or draft, of the original letter, introducing scores of changes in wording, punctuation, and spelling. These alterations are reflected both in the duplicate sent to Young and in the letter-book copy made years later by one of GW's clerks. As so few of the drafts or retained copies of the letters that GW wrote have survived, the assumption is that his clerks discarded GW's drafts after entering the letters in letter books, mostly in the 1790s. The discarded drafts must have numbered in the hundreds each year in the 1780s. Consequently, although there are many other clues in GW's papers to his method of composition and to his close attention to language, we are almost entirely missing the evidence to be derived from his drafts of letters. For this reason, the substantive changes in language that he made in preparing the duplicate letter are noted here as they appear in the duplicate letter sent to Young.

1. Favoured *for* favourite.
2. Dereliction *for* total inattention to it.
3. Only to be perfected by *for* best understood from.
4. But *deleted, and period inserted.*

5. More alacrity than ever *for* hope & confidence.
6. It merits *inserted.*
7. Can be applied to it *deleted.*
8. Cultivator *for* practitioners.
9. Injurious *for* ruinous.
10. Land-holder *for* land-holders.
11. Entirely *for* altogether.
12. The customs of their fore fathers *for* their old customs.
13. Unprofitable: for *for* dangerous, because.
14. Under these impressions, I shall make choice of your annals as my Preceptor and guide *for* Your annals shall be this guide.
15. See Young to GW, 7 Jan. 1786, n.2.
16. Amusements *for* amusement.
17. (If the ploughs are of this kind) *inserted.*
18. Will *for* shall.
19. Thereof which I had somewhere met with, I sent to England for *for* of.
20. I sent to England for one of them *deleted.*
21. Run *for* gone.
22. Ten pounds each, of the three best sorts of Turnips Seed for feeding in succession, through the Season *for* 20 lbs. of the best Turnip-Seeds, for Do.
23. Ray grass *for* Rye-grass.
24. One *for* I should be glad of a.
25. Seed is *for* seeds are.
26. Sorts *for* kinds.
27. Particularly *for* especially.
28. Each, that I may get into a stock of it *for* the seeds, to put me in stock.
29. Wihsand *for* will Stand.
30. Any *inserted.*
31. In his letter to Wakelin Welch of 5 Aug., GW sent a second letter of the same date to Welch, this copy of which went "under cover to Arthur Young" on 6 Aug.: "Sir, Arthur Young Esqr. of Bury, in Suffolk, having been so obliging as to offer to procure for me Implements of Husbandry, seeds &c.—I have accepted his kindness with much pleasure, because he is a competent judge of the first, and will be careful that the latter are good of their several kinds—a thing of much consequence, & which does not often happen with seeds imported into this country from Europe.

"I have requested him to forward these articles to your care, & to draw upon you for the amount.

"Let me entreat your particular attention to them, with a request that the Captn of the Vessel on board which they are shipped may be sollicited to keep the seeds in the Cabbin—or out of the Ship's hold at any rate—as they never fail to heat & spoil when put there. I am Sir &c. G: Washington" (LB, DLC:GW).
32. Cd *for* might.
33. Speak of *for* estimate.
34. This *for* the.
35. I am speaking of *deleted.*

36. I made *deleted*.
37. See George William Fairfax to GW, 23 Jan. 1786, n.1.
38. May be questioned *for* is questionable.
39. For *for* to meet.
40. Period *inserted*; & *deleted*.
41. Different *for* other.
42. Perfection *for* taste.
43. Would have been able to exhibit *for* could have exhibited them.
44. Will *deleted*.
45. Effecting a *for* the work of.
46. See GW to William Peacey, 5 Aug. 1786, n.1.
47. And obliged *inserted*.

From Henry Lee, Jr.

My dear Genl   newyork 7h august [17]86
I had the pleasure of hearing from you last week, and have complied with your wishes respecting the china. No conveyance at present offers for Alexandria, but every day presents one to norfolk, from which place the correspondance up your river is frequent. I intend unless I should meet with a vessel for potomac, to send the box to Col. Parker naval officer at norfolk, and ask his special attention to forwarding it to Alexandria or Mount Vernon.[1] At the same time I will send a small box put into my Care for You by Mr Gardoqui—I have had it some time and waited to know your intention ⟨as⟩ to the china, that the same conveyance might take both.[2] If you have an opportunity to convey my Young, (as the books are useless to you) to Mr R. H. Lee you will oblige me by doing it.[3]
The Mississippi business is very important and full of difficulty—In the debilitated condition of the fœderal government, it is unwise to risk the offence of any part of the empire, unless to effect great good. My mind has no doubt of the extensive good consequences that would result to the Union from a commercial connexion with Spain, & I am also clear, that in agreeing to the occlusion of the Navigation of the Mississippi, we give in fact nothing, for the moment our western country become populous & capable, they will seize by force what may have been ⟨yielded⟩ by treaty. Till that period, the river can not be used but by permission of Spain, whose exclusive system of policy, never

will grant such permission—Then to be sure, we only give, what we can not use—But the source of all the coils which press these States is the inefficiency of the fœderal government—This can not be altered & remedied but by consent of the states.

Already in every state the amplification of the powers of the Union have too many enemys. Should therefore a treaty take place between Congress & Spain occluding for a term the navigation of the Mississippi, in return for advantages very great, but not so great to the whole as to a part, I apprehend it would give such a tent for popular declaimers, that the great object viz. bracing the fœderal government may be thwarted, and thus in pursuing a lesser, we loose a greater good.

I forwarded by the last post ⟨some⟩ public information some intelligence lately received from Mr Jefferson & I have also sent an extract of a letter from Mr Randall from Algiers—these two papers comprehend all the news here—I transmit the gazette of the day.[4] Bills on ⟨tender⟩ at 60 days sight fluctuate in their value from six to seven per cent præmium—the cost of the china is 150 dollars besides the incidental charge of freight to Norfolk, which can not be much.[5] my best wishes for the health & happiness of Mount Vernon, in which Mrs Lee unites. Most respectfully yours

H: Lee junr

ALS, DLC:GW.

1. GW wrote to Lee on 26 July agreeing to buy the Cincinnati china.

2. The box from Gardoqui was the vicuña cloth. See Gardoqui to GW, 12 June, n.1. For the Cincinnati china, see Lee to GW, 3 July, n.2.

3. Lee indicated in his letter of 3 July that he was sending Young's *Tour in Ireland* to GW.

4. These enclosures have not been identified.

5. Lee enclosed the receipt from Constable, Rucker, & Co., of New York, dated 7 Aug., of £60 for a 302-piece service of "Cincinnati china" (DLC:GW).

From William Moultrie

Dear Sir,   Charleston South Carolina Aug. 7 1786

I am honored with your favor of the 14th June last, with Mr Hughes's letter inclosed.

I must beg leave to apologize for the trouble I have given you in this business of ours.

Your Excellency's obliging offer to forward a letter to Mr Brindley has induced me to give you this further trouble, by inclosing you a letter for him.[1] I have the Honor to be Dear Sir Your Excellency's Most Obedt Humble Servant

Willm Moultrie

ALS, NN: Emmet Collection; Sprague transcript, DLC:GW.

1. The enclosed letter from William Moultrie to James Brindley reads: "Charleston, South Carolina, August 7, 1786—by a letter from Mr. Hughes to General Washington, the Company for the Inland Navigation, are informed that the Susquehannah Company have given you permission to be absent for four months in the next winter, and that you have authorized Mr. Hughes to say that you will be in Charleston in December next. The Board of Directors have requested of me to urge your coming, and sooner if possible to South Carolina to take a view and give your opinion upon the probability of opening the communication between Santee and Cooper Rivers, they are perfectly satisfied with the knowledge and abilities you are possessed of in that branch of business and they are therefore unwilling to begin the great work, until you have surveyed and marked out the ground for the carrying of it into execution, and I assure you that every expense attending your coming here shall be paid you as also full compensation for your trouble, etc.—William Moultrie" (printed, Gary Hendershott's catalog, n.p., n.d.). GW forwarded Moultrie's letter on 16 Sept. from Mount Vernon: "Sir, The enclosed came under cover to me from Govr Moultre of So. Carolina. If you chuse to return an answer thro' the same Channel, it shall be my care to forward it safely. I am Sir Yr Very Hble Servt Go: Washington" (facsimile, Hendershott catalog, p. 4).

Potomac Company Annual Report

Alexandria Augst 7. 1786

The president and directors of the Potomac Company beg leave to report that they have called for four dividends on the several subscriptions as follows—the 1st of 5 pCt[,] 2—2[,] 3—10[,] and 4—10[,] Amounting in the whole to Twelve thousand four Hundred & thirty Pounds Sterling, of which there has been paid, Five thousand Nine hundred & forty pounds Sterling. The several expenditures will appear by the Treasurers account, who has in hand One thousand Six Hundred Thirty Six pounds 13/7 Virginia Currency equal to One thousand Two hundred Twenty Seven pounds 10/2 Sterling.

With respect to the business we beg leave to refer to the Secretary's Books which contain all our orders relating thereto.[1]

In consequence of these orders the Work has been carryed on at the Seneca and Shenandoah Falls while the Waters were low enough to admit of it—after the River rose too high, the hands were removed to the Great Falls, where a considerable progress has been made in cutting a Canal, and the most of the men are still employed on account of the uncommon wett Season.

We beg leave to remind the Subscribers that this is the day appointed by Law for electing a President & Directors for the ensuing Year.

In behalf of the Directors

Go: Washington P.

DS, NIC.

1. In his diary entry regarding the meeting of the Potomac River Company in Alexandria on Monday, 7 Aug., GW wrote: "The Accts. of the Directors were exhibited and a Genl. report made but for want of the Secretarys Books which were locked up, and he absent the Orders and other proceedings referred to in that report could not be exhibited" (*Diaries*, 5:22).

Letter not found: from Thomas Smith, 9 Aug. 1786. GW wrote Smith on 22 Sept. that his letter "to me from Philadelphia the 9th Ulto came duly to hand."

To Armand

Dr Marquis,   Mo[un]t Vernon 10th Augt 1786.

I am to acknowledge the receipt of the agreeable letter you did me the honor to write to me on the 20th of Jany, & at the same time to congratulate you on the happy event announced in it.

Permit me to assure you that nothing affords me more satisfaction than to receive good news of my friends; and you must allow me the liberty of considering your marriage to an amiable lady, with a handsome fortune, in that point of light.

Indeed I was not surprized at this, because I knew the merits of the Marqs de la Rouerie entitled him to such a connexion. But I must confess, I was a little pleased, if not surprized, to find him think quite like an American on the subject of matrimony & domestic felicity. For in my estimation more permanent & genuine happiness is to be found in the sequestered walks of connubial life, than in the giddy rounds of promiscuous pleasure, or the more tumultuous and imposing scenes of successful ambition.

This sentiment will account, in a degree, for my not making a visit to Europe: other reasons may conspire to prevent me from enjoying the heart-felt satisfaction I shou'd experience in embracing my friends on that continent. Their kind sollicitude & invitations are, however, entitled to my cordial acknowledgments; & you may be persuaded, it will not be among the least of my regrets on this occasion, that the circumstances preclude me from receiving the *welcome*, & witnessing the *happiness*, I should expect to meet with at the Château de la rouerie.

I enter so little into disquisitions of politics, that I could hardly do justice to the subject, should I undertake to dilate upon it. I have understood, in general, that Congress have taken arrangements for the payment of the interest due on Securities given to foreigners who served in their Army. A timely & efficacious application to the States will, I hope, in future produce more punctuality, & supercede the necessity of any interference on my part, which it appears to me would be improper on many accounts.

Mrs Washington desires her compliments may be made acceptable to Madame la Marquise de la rouerie & yourself; with a similar request, I have the honor to remain &c.

G: Washington

LB, DLC:GW.

From Matthew Whiting

Dear Sir   Snow Hill 10th Augt 1786
I recd yours and am very sorry that it did not come ten days sooner as I had parted with all the money that I had by me however the first that comes into my hands will take care to pay you. Should of been glad to of let you had wheat for sowing if I had any that I could recommend. I had parted with all my old wheat and the new I think but very Indifferent.[1] I am with Complements to your good Lady and am Dear Sir Yr mo. Obt Hble Servant

M. Whiting

ALS, DLC:GW.

Matthew Whiting (d. 1810) lived at Snow Hill on Bull Run in Prince William County.

1. GW received on 8 Dec. 1772 £250 from Whiting, leaving £27.8.8 still due. See GW to Fielding Lewis, 20 April 1773, n.2, and Ledger B, 109. The account was settled on 27 May 1787 "By a Bill drawn by Wm Hunter Junr Esqr. upon Robt Morris Esqr. for £50 Pensylviania Currency" (Ledger B, 109).

From John Ariss

Sir   Berkeley [County] 12th August 1786

I am now to inform your Excellency that a Mr John Beale came to my house on the 3th Instant and deliver'd me a Decree of the High Court of Chancery, Hites & others, against the Executors & heirs, of Thos Lord Fairfax Decd, and that on Thursday the 10th the Commissioners With Colo. John Green & Mr Isaac Hite came to my house and Asked me What Improvements was on the Lands Suppos'd to be in dispute and which was Once Surveyed by Colo. Thos Marshall. my Answer was that I had been Informd by James McCormack that Saw the Line Run that Between 2 & 300 Acres was on the Backside of that Line & that their was no Improvement on it but about 200 Acres of Clear'd Land & which was now fenced in. They Further informd me that They were to Meet at Winchester the 4th day of September, in Order for the Different persons to put in their Claims for the Lands in dispute.[1] I thougt it my duty to Inform your Excellency of the Above. I am, Sir Your Excellencys Most Obt Hbe Servt

Jno. Ariss

ALS, DLC:GW.

1. John Ariss rented a 700-acre tract of GW's Bullskin land in April 1786. See Ariss to GW, 5 Aug. 1784, n.2. For the Hites's claims to some of GW's land in Berkeley County, see Thornton Washington to GW, 6 June 1786, n.2.

From Henry Lee, Jr.

dear Genl   New York 12h Aug. 1786

Since writing my last I have an opportunity of sending the small box given to me by Mr Gardoqui for you under care of Mr Wilson of Petersburgh by the stage, to be delivered to Mr C.

Lee. I prefer this conveyance to the one intended, & now enclose the letter which accompanyed the box.[1] It is probable that the China will leave New York for Norfolk next week. I am most respectfully Yours

Henry Lee Junr

ALS, DLC:GW.

1. See Gardoqui to GW, 12 June, n.1. This was the attorney Charles Lee in Alexandria. Wilson has not been identified.

To John Francis Mercer

Dr Sir, Mount Vernon 12th Augt 1786.

The Clerks notes in the Suits ordered by you on the Bonds taken at Colo. Geo: Mercer's sale, are (many of them) brought against me; some of wch without adverting thereto, I have paid, supposing them to have arisen on distresses made by Mr Muse for my rents.[1] A few days ago a Bill from the Clerk, I believe, of Berkley, was handed to me amounting to near six hundred pounds of Tobacco, which not being convenient for me to pay, was returned. I shall be obliged to you in future when writs are ordered, to direct these notes into some other channel. I am threatened also (as you may see by the enclosed) in another manner on the same Accot.[2]

I am led from these circumstances to hope that the suits have been, or soon will be productive; for, tho' painful to reiterate, the fact is that I am *really* in want of money.[3] The almost total loss of my Corn last year, the scantiness of my Crop of wheat this (in which I am only a common sufferer) & the probable destruction of my Corn by the Chinch-bug, in which I stand almost alone, deprives me of all hope of aid from these sources; which is the more distressing to me as I am at this time involved in more than common expence to finish my house & to make the repairs which were found wanting when it come to be examined. I am Dr Sir Your Obt Hble Servt

Go: Washington

LB, DLC:GW.

1. For a description of the sale of George Mercer's Virginia property conducted by GW in November 1774, see GW to John Tayloe, 30 Nov. 1774, n.2. See also Statement concerning George Mercer's Estate, 1 Feb. 1789, printed below.

2. This letter to GW is dated from Alexandria 27 July: "Sir May it please your Excellency, inclosed is a Clerks Note from Berkeley office for 595 lb. Tobacco due the Estate of Mr William Pres⟨el⟩ decd being sent by Me with many others of the kind to collect by his Exors the amount of which @ 12/6 ℔ Ct may it please your Excellency to send ℔ Bearer, and am with all Respect your Excellencys most obt and humble Servt James Meyler" (DLC:GW). Meyler wrote at the bottom: "Amot £3.14.4½."

3. For the debt of the Mercer estate, see GW to John Francis Mercer, 8 July 1784, n.1. For Mercer's proposal regarding payment on the estate debt, see GW to Mercer, 9 Sept. 1786. GW's legal and financial involvement with the Mercers, which began with his marriage to Martha Custis and extended into the 1790s, derived, first, from the loan of £2,100 to John Mercer in 1758 by Martha Custis and, second, from GW's management of the sale of George Mercer's Virginia property in 1774. John Mercer died in 1768, and his son George Mercer died in 1784 after living abroad since the early 1760s. After the Revolution John Francis Mercer took over the management of the affairs of his father's estate from his elder half brother James Mercer. GW's letters to John Francis Mercer during the next three years rang changes on GW's need for money and on the failure of Mercer, who had married the Maryland heiress Sophia Sprigg, to make good his repeated promises to make substantial payments on the estate debt which still stood at more than £900 in May 1791 (Ledger B, 221). None of John Francis Mercer's letters in these exchanges has been found.

From Edward Newenham

Bell Champe near Dublin
Dear Sir, August 12th 1786
May I presume to solicit your friendship in obtaining the wish of a whole family; Viz.; to have one of them honoured by the Congress of American Patriots—The idea originated with my Son—he is so good and virtuous a young Man, that I can boldly assert, he never will dishonour any confidence reposed in him— he has been warm in yours and your Countrys cause from the beginning; his future life is fixed at Marsailles, where his fortune is vested; his third Sister is married there—he wants no sallery—it is the honor he solicits for.

I cannot express how anxious I am to obtain his wish—the mode I have adopted is novel but it occurred to me as the most respectfull; I have acquainted Doctr Franklin and Mr Jay with this affair, and had time been allowed, I am confident that the Marquis De Fayette would write most warmly in our favor, but as this is the only opportunity, of a safe conveyance, that I can have for some time, I could not delay it—the Ship Dublin Packet Captain Alcorn, sails tomorrow, for Philadelphia, and this will be committed to his care.[1]

Copy (extract), PPAmP: Franklin Papers; copy, DNA: RG 59, Domestic Letters. The copy of the extract in the Benjamin Franklin Papers was enclosed by GW in his letter to Franklin of 3 Nov. 1786 and was endorsed by GW: "Extract of a letter from Sir Edward Newenham to Geo: Washington."

1. Newenham wrote to Benjamin Franklin on 10 July 1786 asking that Franklin intercede with Congress to secure for his son Robert O'Callahan Newenham an appointment as United States consul at the port of Marseilles. Newenham wrote Franklin that he had invested for his son: "*all* his [son's] fortune in the Trade of that rising City, where he will spend the rest of his Days." Newenham expanded on his son's qualifications for such an honor and pointed to his own support of and aid to the American cause during the war. Newenham wrote to Franklin again at this time, on 12 Aug., enclosing a letter from Lady Newenham extolling her son, and letters from himself to the president and members of Congress. On 21 Nov. 1786 Franklin forwarded to John Jay these letters and the extract of GW's letter, with a noncommittal covering letter, copies of all of which are in DNA: RG 59, Domestic Letters. GW may have received in Newenham's letter to himself of 12 Aug. copies of Newenham's petitions to Congress which Franklin forwarded to Congress (see GW to Franklin, 3 Nov. 1786). For GW's subsequent correspondence with Newenham about this matter, see his letters to Newenham of 10 Mar., 20 April, and 25 Dec. 1787.

From Clement Biddle

[Philadelphia] August 13th 1786.

I have before me your Esteemed favour of 31st Ulto—at present there is a Suspension of paying the Indents for Interest of Certificates in this State, owing to a misunderstanding between the Controller of our State and the Treasury Board. but it is supposed that it will before long be settled when I will draw the Indents for Interest on the Certificate of 339^{53}⁄₉₀ D[ollar]s which you sent me as they will be usefull to you for paying Taxes in Virginia after which I will Loan the Certificate to our State— draw one years Interest in our paper Money and return you the State Certificate—this mode I conceive to be most for your Interest, as the State Certificate will afterwards draw Interest here every Six Months, yet the price of your Certificate of which kind, hundreds are bought here and sold here daily, don't vary Sixpence in the pound from what I advised you in Case of actual

Sale—But for a Settlement with the person you received it from I have stated an Account of the Specie Value at the time I wrote you the 24th of June last.

At present there is by no means a plenty of goods at this Market especially of the kinds you mention—Blankets, Oznabrigs and Linen are realy scarce & will be so till our fall Vessels arrive—Paints may sometimes be had at Vendue Cheap, but only the Close of Sales of that article and those insorted, but Hyson Tea is plenty and very good at or under two Dollars but a Superior kind from 17/6 to 20/ p. lb.—Inclosed is an answer from Arthur Howell who is reckoned an honest Tanner respecting the price of Leather—I delivered your Letter into the hands of Mr Thomas Smith who happened to be in Town and I forward you his answer herewith.[1]

As he was going through Lancaster I put your Letter for that place in his Charge—Mrs Biddle joins in respectful Compliments to Mrs Washington—I am—dr General &c.

C. Biddle

ADfS, ViMtV: Clement Biddle Letterbook.

1. GW's letter to Thomas Smith is dated 28 July. Smith's response has not been found.

From John Witherspoon

Sir   Tusculum near Princeton [N.J.] August 14. 1786

I am induced to give you the following Trouble at the Desire of a Friend. It is said there is a presbyterian Congregation in your Neighbourhood Poeheek which wants a Minister that Col. George Mason is a Member of the Congregation & that you are some times there yourself. There is a Gentleman lately come recommended to me from Scotland Mr James Wilson who if invited would probably accept of it. He is of an excellent Character by his Recommendations to me & since he has been here has justified it by his Behaviour. I am wholly uncertain whether you chuse to interest Yourself in Such a Matter at all but if you do & send any Notice to me I will attend to it.[1] My respectful Compliments to Mrs Washington. I am Sir your most obed. & humble Servant

Jno. Witherspoon

ALS, DLC:GW.
   1. See GW's response, 23 August.

To Theodorick Bland

Dear Sir,   Mount Vernon 15th Augt 1786.

    By Colo. Fitzhugh I had the satisfaction to receive the humorous accot you were pleased to give me of your nocturnal journey to Fredericksburg. I recollect very well, the Lady whom you mention to have had for a fellow traveller, & if you should chance to be in her company again, I should be much obliged by your presenting my compliments to her. The even tenor of my life (in which I can expect to meet with few extraordinary adventures) as well as my long seclusion in a great measure, from the exhilirating scenes of mixed society, must be an apology for my not attempting (with such provocatives to gaiety) to say some more sprightly things in reply to the brilliancy of her dialogue; or the vivacity with which you have reported it. I commend you, however, for passing the time in as merry a manner as you possibly could; it is assuredly better to go laughing than crying thro' the rough journey of life.[1]

    I have mentioned your request to Colo. Humphreys, who is still at Mt Vernon & who has put a copy of his last poem into my hands to be forwarded with his compliments to you. He has farther desired me to inform you, in answer to the civil things you have said of it, that he feels himself singularly happy whenever he finds that his works are honored with the approbation of men of taste & liberallity. He regrets that he cannot send you the copy of a former poem, which after being several times reprinted in Europe, has lately been translated by the Marqs de Chastellux, & received with a great deal of applause at Paris.[2]

    I shall always be happy to give & receive communications on improvements in farming, & the various branches of agriculture. This is in my opinion, an object of infinite importance to the country; I consider it to be the proper source of American wealth & happiness. Whose streams might become more copious & diffusive, if gentlemen of leisure and capacity would turn their attention to it, & bring the result of their experiments together? Nothing but cultivation is wanting—our lot has certainly destined a good Country for our inheritance—we begin already to attract the notice of foreigners of distinction. A French general officer whose name is Du Plessis is now at Mount Vernon on his way to Georgia, with a design to settle there—as a farmer.

Sequestered as I am, from the bustlings & intrigues of the world, in the calm walks of private life; I can hardly flatter myself with being able to give much light or assistance, to those who may be engag'd in passing thro' the dark & thorny paths of politics. I can only repeat what I have formerly told my countrymen in a very serious manner "that honesty will be found, on every experiment, the best policy." How far arguments deduced from *this topic*, and from the *present alarming troubles* in Rhode Island, can with pertinancy & force be made use of against any attempts to procure a paper currency in the State, I leave to your judgment to decide. The advantages which are to be derived from Seminaries of learning—from the improvement of our roads—a proper establishment of our militia—the extension of inland navigation &c. must have struck you in too forcible a manner to need a remembrancer.

My sentiments respecting fœderal measures, in general, are so well known that it is unnecessary to reiterate them.

The two Mrs Washingtons & my nephew join in compliments with me to Mrs Bland & yourself, & I am &c.

G: Washington

LB, DLC:GW.

Theodorick Bland (1742–1790) of Prince George County was a doctor, trained in Edinburgh. He was a colonel in the Continental army from 1776 to 1779 and a member of Congress from 1781 to 1783. He was married to Martha Daingerfield, who after Bland's death married in 1792 Nathan Blodget.

1. William Fitzhugh of Chatham visited Mount Vernon on 8 August. No letter from Bland dated at this time has been found, and "the Lady" has not been identified.

2. Before Humphreys returned from Europe, Chastellux translated into French and published Humphreys' poem "Address to the Armies of the United States of America." The poem became very popular in the United States. Humphreys' "last poem" was either his "An Epistle to Dr. Dwight" written in 1784 or "The Shepherd: A Song." For the poem he wrote while at Mount Vernon at this time, see Humphreys to GW, 24 Sept. 1786, n.6.

To John Jay

Dear Sir   Mount Vernon 15th Augt 1786

I have to thank you very sincerely for your interesting letter of the 27th of June, as well as for the other communications you had the goodness to make at the same time.

I am sorry to be assured, of what indeed I had little doubt before, that we have been guilty of violating the treaty in some instances. What a misfortune it is the British should have so well grounded a pretext for their palpable infractions?—and what a disgraceful part, out of the choice of difficulties before us, are we to act?

Your sentiments, that our affairs are drawing rapidly to a crisis, accord with my own. What the event will be is also beyond the reach of my foresight. We have errors to correct. We have probably had too good an opinion of human nature in forming our confederation. Experience has taught us, that men will not adopt & carry into execution, measures the best calculated for their own good without the intervention of a coercive power. I do not conceive we can exist long as a nation, without having lodged somewhere a power which will pervade the whole Union in as energetic a manner, as the authority of the different state governments extends over the several States. To be fearful of vesting Congress, constituted as that body is, with ample authorities for national purposes, appears to me the very climax of popular absurdity and madness. Could Congress exert them for the detriment of the public without injuring themselves in an equal or greater proportion? Are not their interests inseperably connected with those of their constituents? By the rotation of appointment must they not mingle frequently with the mass of citizens? Is it not rather to be apprehended, if they were possessed of the powers before described, that the individual members would be induced to use them, on many occasions, very timidly & inefficatiously for fear of loosing their popularity & future election? We must take human nature as we find it. Perfection falls not to the share of mortals. Many are of opinion that Congress have too frequently made use of the suppliant humble tone of requisition, in applications to the States, when they had a right to assume their imperial dignity and command obedience. Be that as it may, requisitions are a perfect nihility, where thirteen sovereign, independent⟨,⟩ disunited States are in the habit of discussing & refusing compliance with them at their option. Requisitions are actually little better than a jest and a bye word through out the Land. If you tell the Legislatures they have violated the treaty of peace and invaded the prerogatives of the confederacy they will laugh in your face. What then is to be done? Things cannot go on in the same train forever. It is much to be feared, as you observe, that the better kind of people being disgusted with the circumstances will have their minds prepared for any revolution whatever. We are apt to run from one extreme into another. To anticipate & prevent disasterous contingencies would be the part of wisdom & patriotism.

What astonishing changes a few years are capable of producing! I am told that even respectable characters speak of a monarchical form of government without horror. From thinking proceeds speaking, thence to acting is often but a single step. But how irrevocable & tremendous! What a triumph for the advocates of despotism to find that we are incapable of governing ourselves, and that systems founded on the basis of equal liberty are merely ideal & falacious! Would to God that wise measures may be taken in time to avert the consequences we have but too much reason to apprehend.

Retired as I am from the world, I frankly acknowledge I cannot feel myself an unconcerned spectator. Yet having happily assisted in bringing the ship into port & having been fairly discharged; it is not my business to embark again on a sea of troubles. Nor could it be expected that my sentiments and opinions would have much weight on the minds of my Countrymen—they have been neglected, tho' given as a last legacy in the most solemn manner.[1] I had then perhaps some claims to public attention. I consider myself as having none at present. With sentiments of sincere esteem & friendship I am, my dear Sir, Yr most Obedt & Affecte Hble Servant

Go: Washington

ALS, Great Britain: Windsor Castle; LB, DLC:GW. The letter-book copy is dated 1 August. GW's letter was bound in the volume that John Jay (1817–1894) presented to the Prince of Wales on 10 Oct. 1860. It is docketed "Gen. Washington 15 Augt 1786 an[swere]d 7 Jan. 1787." Jay's letter of 7 Jan., deposited in DLC:GW, is printed below.

1. See GW's Address to Congress on Resigning His Commission, 23 Dec. 1783, in Fitzpatrick, *Writings of Washington*, 27:284–86.

To Lafayette

My Dr Marqs   Mount Vernon 15th Augt 1786.

I will not conceal that my numerous correspondencies are daily becoming irksome to me; yet I always receive your letters with augmenting satisfaction, and therefore rejoice with you in the measures which are likely to be productive of a more frequent intercourse between our two nations. Thus, motives of a private as well as of a public nature conspire to give me pleasure, in finding that the active policy of France is preparing to take advantage of the supine stupidity of England, with respect to our commerce.

While the latter by its impolitic duties & restrictions is driving our Ships incessantly from its harbours; the former seems by the invitations it is giving to stretch forth the friendly hand to invite them into its Ports. I am happy in a conviction that there may be established between France & the U.S., such a mature intercourse of good offices & reciprocal interests as cannot fail to be attended with the happiest consequences. Nations are not influenced as individuals may be, by disinterested friendships: but when it is their interest to live in amity, we have little reason to apprehend any rupture. This principle of union can hardly exist in a more distingushed manner between two Nations, than it does between France & the United States. There are many articles of manufacture which we stand absolutely in need of & shall continue to have occasion for so long as we remain an agricultural peoples, which will be while lands are so cheap & plenty, that is to say, for ages to come. In the meantime we shall have large quantities of timber, fish, oil, wheat, Tobo, rice, Indigo &c. to dispose of: Money we have not. Now it is obvious that we must have recourse for the Goods & manufactures we may want, to the nation which will enable us to pay for them, by receiving our Produce in return. Our commerce with any of the great manufacturing Kingdoms of Europe will therefore be in proportion to the facility of making remittance, which such manufacturing nation may think proper to afford us. On the other hand, France has occasion for many of our productions & raw materials—let her judge whether it is most expedient to receive them by direct importation & to pay for them in goods; or to obtain them thro' the circuitous channel of Britain & to pay for them in money as she formerly did.

I know that Britain arrogantly expects we will sell our produce whereever we can find a Market & bring the money to purchase goods from her; I know that she vainly hopes to retain what share she pleases in our trade, in consequence of our prejudices in favor of her fashions & manufactures; but these are illusions which will vanish & disappoint her, as the dreams of conquest have already done. Experience is constantly teaching us that these predilections were founded in error. We find the quality & price of the French goods we receive in many instances, to be better than the quality & price of the English. Time & a more thorough acquaintance with the business may be necessary to instruct your Merchants in the choice & assortment of Goods necessary for such a country. As to an ability for giving credit, in which the English merchants boast a superiority, I am confident it would be happy for America if the practice could be entirely abolished.

However unimportant America may be considered at present, & however Britain may affect to despise her trade, there will assuredly come a day when this country will have some weight in the scale of Empires. While connected with us as Colonies only, was not Britain the first power in the World? Since the dissolution of that connexion, does not France occupy the same illustrious place? Your successful endeavours my Dr Marqs, to promote the interests of your two Countries (as you justly call them) must give you the most unadulterated satisfaction: be assured the measures which have been lately taken with regard to the two Articles of *Oil* & *Tobacco*, have tended very much to endear you to your fellow Citizens on this side of the Atlantic.

Altho' I pretend to no peculiar information respecting commercial affairs, nor any foresight into the scenes of futurity; yet as the member of an infant-empire, as a Philanthropist by character, and (if I may be allowed the expression) as a Citizen of the great republic of humanity at large; I cannot help turning my attention sometimes to this subject. I would be understood to mean, I cannot avoid reflecting with pleasure on the probable influence that commerce may here after have on human manners & society in general. On these occasions I consider how mankind may be connected like one great family in fraternal ties—I endulge a fond, perhaps an enthusiastic idea, that as the world is evidently much less barbarous than it has been, its melioration must still be progressive—that nations are becoming more humanized in their policy—that the subjects of ambition & causes for hostility are daily diminishing—and in fine, that the period is not very remote when the benefits of a liberal & free commerce will, pretty generally, succeed to the devastations & horrors of war. Some of the late treaties which have been entered into, & particularly that between the King of Prussia & the U[nite]d States, seem to constitute a new era in negotiation, & to promise the happy consequences I have just now been mentioning.

But let me ask you My Dr Marquis, in such an enlightened, in such a liberal age, how is it possible the great maritime powers of Europe should submit to pay an annual tribute to the little piratical States of Barbary. Would to Heaven we had a navy able to reform those enimies to mankind, or crush them into nonexistence.

I forbear to enter into a discussion of our domestic Politics, because there is little interesting to be said upon them, & perhaps it is best to be silent, since I could not disguise or palliate where I might think them erroneous. The British still hold the frontier Posts, & are determined to do so. The Indians commit some trifling ravages, but there is nothing like a general or even open war. You will have heard what a loss we have met with by the death of poor Genl Green. General McDougal & Colo. Tilghman are also dead.

It is a great satisfaction to have it in my power to pay some attention to Monsr Du Plessis, by whom I had the happiness of receiving your last letter: he is now at Mount Vernon on his way to Georgia.

You will see by the length to which I have extended this letter, that I can never find myself weary of conversing with you. Adieu, my Dr Marqs—Mrs Washington & the family desire to be most respectfully presented to Mad[am]e de la Fayette—to whom, I pray you also to offer my very best homage; & to believe that I am, My Dr Marqs &c. &c. &c.

G: Washington

LB, DLC:GW.

To David Stuart

Dear Sir, Mount Vernon Augt 15th 1786
Mrs Washington is prevented from dining with you tomorrow by the arrival of a French Gentleman of Rank—Genl Duplessis—who is introduced, and very warmly recommended to me by the Count de Estaing, the Marqs de la Fayette &ca—in consequence I have persuaded Colo. Humphreys to Postpone his visit to Abingdon. Wishing to shew this Gentleman (Genl Duplessis) all the Civilities in my power, I should be glad if you & Mrs Stuart would dine with us tomorrow. other Company are also invited from Alexandria at Dinner, at this time.[1] That Mrs Stuart may be accomodated, George's Phæton, & a pair of my horses (two others being sent to Fredericksburgh) is carried up by Charles.[2] Yrs affectly

Go: Washington

ALS, sold in 1992 by Christie, Manson & Woods International, Inc.
   1. In his entry for 16 Aug. GW wrote: "Colonels [John] Fitzgerald and [William] Lyles Mr. Brailsford (an English Gentleman) and Mr. [Joseph Marie] Perrin came here to dinner" (*Diaries*, 5:27). Perrin was a Frenchman living in Alexandria.
   2. Charles may be GW's Muddy Hole farm slave, but it is more likely that he is a slave of George Augustine Washington's of that name.

From John Peck

Sir, Piscataway [Md.], 16 August, 1786
In compliance with the enclosed resolve I have the honor to transmit the Diplomas of the Cincinnati of New-Jersey. It would have afforded me inexpressible satisfaction to have presented them in person, but the duty I owe the nearest connextion in life requires that I should dispense with that happiness.[1] I am Sir With the highest respect & esteem Your Most Obedient Very Humb. Servt

Jno. Peck

ALS, DLC:GW. A copy of the letter, marked "Duplicate," has an asterisk before "resolve" referring to the notation: "An extract of the resolve of the Society signed by the Secretary." Peck enclosed the duplicate in a letter to GW of 5 Mar. 1787. GW docketed the letter "From Captn Jno. Peck." In DLC:GW, dated 4 July 1786 (misfiled 4 July 1788), there is an excerpt of the minutes of

the New Jersey Society of the Cincinnati containing the resolve, signed by
Andrew Hunter, that Peck be authorized to obtain GW's signature to eighty diplomas.

John Peck (c.1754–c.1795), formerly of New Jersey, had replaced his
Princeton classmate Philip Fithian in 1774 as tutor to Robert Carter's children
at Nomini Hall in Westmoreland County. He later married Anne Tasker Carter, his former pupil, and lived in Richmond County at Bladensfield which
had been formerly a part of the Nomini Hall plantation. He was probably the
John Peck who joined the 2d New Jersey Regiment as a second lieutenant in
November 1776 and retired in 1783 as a brevet captain.

1. Horatio Clagett wrote GW from Piscataway on 4 Sept.: "The Bearer will
deliver you a Bundle that was left with me by a Mr Peck, late an Officer of the
Jersey line, who is now in Virginia, and will do himself the honor to call on
you in a few days on his Return to Jersey" (DLC:GW). Peck wrote again to
GW, from Robert Carter's Nomini Hall, on 4 September.

To Clement Biddle

Dr Sir,   Mount Vernon 18th Augt 1786.
This letter serves to acknowledge the receipt of your favor of
the 13th & to inform you that I have this day, sent a small box
to Alexandria to go from thence by the Packet, or first conveyance to Philada to your address. It contains two window curtains
which I pray you to get new dyed of the same color, *green*, &
returned to me as soon as may be.

I am obliged by your care of my letters; & thank you for the
attention paid to the other requests of my former letter.[1] The
price of Mr Howells leather is not cheaper than it is sold at in
Alexandria, & the freight would make it come higher. I am Dear
Sir &c. &c.

G: Washington

LB, DLC:GW.
1. See GW to Biddle, 31 July.

To Chastellux

My dear Marquis   Mount Vernon 18th Augt 1786
I cannot omit to seize the earliest occasion, to acknowledge
the receipt of the very affectionate letter you did me the honor
of writing to me on the 22d of May;[1] as well as to thank you

for the *present* of your Travels in America and the Translation of
Colonel Humphreys' Poem,[2] all of which came safely to hand by
the same conveyance.

Knowing as I did, the candour liberality & philanthropy of
the Marquis de Chastellux, I was prepared to disbelieve any im-
putations that might militate against those amiable qualities. For
characters & habits are not easily taken up, or suddenly laid
aside. Nor does that mild species of philosophy, which aims at
promoting human happiness, ever belye itself by deviating from
the generous & godlike pursuit. Having, notwithstanding, understood that some misrepresentations, of the work in question,
had been circulated; I was happy to learn that you had taken
the most effectual method to put a stop to their circulation, by
publishing a more ample and correct Edition. Colo. Humphreys
(who spent some weeks at Mount Vernon) confirmed me in the
sentiment, by giving a most flattering account of the whole performance. He has also put into my hands the translation of that
part in which you say such, & so many Handsome things of me;
that (altho' no sceptic on ordinary occasions) I may perhaps be
allowed to doubt whether your friendship & partiality, have not,
in this one instance, acquired an ascendency over your cooler
judgement.

Having been thus unwarily, and I may be permitted to add,
almost unavoidably betrayed into a kind of necessity to speak of
myself, and not wishing to resume that subject, I chuse to close
it forever by observing; that as, on the one hand, I consider it as
an indubitable mark of mean-spiritedness & pitiful vanity to
court applause from the pen or tongue of man; so on the other,
I believe it to be a proof of false modesty or an unworthy affecta-
tion of humility to appear altogether insensible to the *commenda-
tions* of the virtuous & enlightened part of our species. Perhaps
nothing can excite more perfect harmony in the soul, than to
have this string vibrate in unison with the internal consciousness
of rectitude in our intentions, and an humble hope of approbation from the supreme disposer of all things.

I have communicated to Colo. Humphreys that paragraph in
your letter which announces the very favourable reception his
Poem has met with in France. Upon the principles I have just
laid down he cannot be indifferent to the applauses of so enlightened a nation, nor to the suffrages of the King & Queen

who have been pleased to honour it with their royal approbation.

We have no news on this side the Atlantic, worth the pains of
sending across it—The Country is recovering rapidly from the
ravages of War—The seeds of population are Scattered far in
the wilderness—Agriculture is prosecuted with industry—The
works of peace such as opening rivers, buildg bridges &ca are
carried on with spirit—Trade is not so successful as we could
wish—Our state govermts are well administered—Some objects
in our fœderal system might probably be altered for the better.
I rely much on the good sense of my Countrymen & trust that
a superintending Providence will disappoint the hopes of our
enemies—With sentiments of the sincerest friendship I am, my
dear Marqs Yr Obedt and Affecte Servt

Go: Washington

ALS, CSmH; LB, DLC:GW; copy, ScC; French translation, CSmH.
1. Letter not found.
2. For David Humphreys' poem, see GW to Theodorick Bland, 15 Aug.,
n.2. The complete revised edition of Chastellux's book was published in Paris
in April 1786 in two volumes under the title *Voyages de M. le Marquis de
Chastellux dans l'Amérique Septentrionale Dans les Années 1780, 1781 & 1782*
(Chastellux, *Travels in North America*, 1:25–29).

Letter not found: to Josiah Parker, 18 Aug. 1786. On 9 Sept. Parker
wrote GW: "Your favor of the 18th Ultimo reached me a few days
since."

To Metcalf Bowler

Sir,   Mount Vernon 19th Augt 1786.

I have received your letter of the 21st of July together with
the Treatise on Agriculture & practical Husbandry.[1] I consider
the latter as a mark of attention which merits my warmest acknowledgments.

It is a subject highly worthy the attention of every gentleman
in this country who has leisure, abilities, or opportunity to improve it. It is the only source from which we can at present draw
any real or permanent advantage; & in my opinion it must be a
great (if not the sole) means of our attaining to that degree of

respectability & importance which we ought to hold in the world. I am Sir &c.

G: Washington

LB, DLC:GW.
Metcalf Bowler (1726–1789) before the Revolution was a leading commercial figure in Rhode Island and from 1767 to 1776 the speaker of the house in its assembly. In 1786 he published in Providence *A Treatise on Agriculture and Practical Husbandry. Designed for the Information of Landowners and Farmers. With a Brief Account of the Advantages Arising from the New Method of Culture Practised in Europe*. The eighty-eight-page volume was in GW's library at Mount Vernon at the time of his death.
1. Letter not found.

To Thomas Newton, Jr.

Dr Sir,   Mo[un]t Vernon 19th Augt 1786.

Inclosed is a duplicate of my letter to you of the 26th of May which was forwarded by Peter Kirwins[1] who received fifty barrels of superfine Flour to be deliver'd to you at Norfolk. It is now almost three months since the flour was sent: as I have not heard from you, and am unacquainted with Mr Kirwin, I do not know whether it has come to your hands or not. If you have received it, & it is sold, I should be glad to know what it sold for; if it is not sold, should wish to know what it will sell for, as, from the short crops of wheat, I think it must now fetch a pretty good price. I am Dr Sir &c.

G: Washington

LB, DLC:GW.
1. The copyist wrote "Peter Virwins" and, below, "Mr Virwin."

To William Hunter, Jr.

Monday Morng [Mount Vernon, 20 August 1786]

G: Washington presents his Compliments to Mr Hunter and would thank him for recommending the letters herewith sent to the particular care of his Corrispondent at Havre de Grass, to be forwarded by him to Paris.[1]

AL, ViMtV.

1. GW wrote to Lafayette on 15 Aug. and to Chastellux on 18 August. This is Havre de Grace, Md., on Chesapeake Bay.

To Thomas Hutchins

Sir,   Mount Vernon 20th Augt 1786.

You will see by the enclosed letter from the Marqs de la Fayette to me, that the Empress of Russia is desirous of obtaining some authentic documents respecting the languages of the natives of this Country, for the purpose of compiling an universal Dictionary. As I have thought no person was more in condition to accomplish that essential service for the republic of letters than yourself, I have taken the liberty of transmitting a specimen of the vocabulary to you, together with a request that you will do me the favor of paying as early & accurate attention to the completion of the matter, as your avocations will admit. Persuaded that a gentleman of your taste for science in general, & particularly of your capacity for acquiring the information in question, will enter upon the task with pleasure, I make no apology for troubling you with it. Nor do I think it necessary to add any thing farther, than that it may be expedient to extend the vocabulary as far as, with the aid of your friends, you conveniently can; & that the greatest possible precision & exactitude will be indispensable in committing the Indian words to paper, by a just orthography.[1] With sentiments of esteem & regard I have the honor to be &c.

G: Washington

LB, DLC:GW. GW wrote the same letter to George Morgan on this date, a copy of which is in NcD: Thomas Gibbes Morgan Papers. The Morgan letter was printed in the Washington, Pa., *Reporter*, 27 April 1938, and the ALS was advertised and quoted in part in Parke-Bernet catalog 1385, item 372, November 1952.

1. See Lafayette to GW, 10 Feb., n.1. See also Hutchins's response of 8 November.

From William Jackson

My dear General,   Philadelphia August 20. 1786

It was not till last evening I discovered that a packet, which I had done myself the honor to address to you by a private conveyance, had been forgotten by the person to whom it was entrusted. To prevent a similar accident, and to avoid any farther delay, I take the liberty to forward the enclosed pamphlets (which are transmitted at the request of our State Society) by post.

Unable to decline, though very unequal to fulfil, the task which was assigned me on the fourth of July—I hope it will be unnecessary to bespeak your indulgence of an essay produced at the pressing instance of friends, whose partiality prejudiced their discernment.[1] With every wish for your happiness, which the most respectful esteem and affection can suggest, I am, my dear General Your obliged obedient Servant

W. Jackson.

ALS, DLC:GW.

1. William Jackson's *An Oration to Commemorate the Independence of the United States* (Philadelphia, 1786) was not listed in the inventory of GW's library taken after his death, but on 28 Sept. GW acknowledged its receipt in these terms: "Dear Sir, I have received your letter of the 20th Ulto together with the Pamphlets enclosed. I consider your sending the latter to me as a mark of attention which deserves my warmest acknowledgments.

"I cannot join with you in thinking that the partiality of your friends, in assigning to you so honorable a task, prejudiced their discernment. The subject is noble, the field extensive; and I think it must be highly satisfactory, and indeed flattering to a man, that his performance, upon such an occasion, is approved of by men of taste & judgment. With sentimts of great esteem & regard I am—Dear Sir Yr Obedt Hble Servt Go: Washington" (ALS, PHi: Washington Manuscripts).

Letter not found: from John Francis Mercer, 20 Aug. 1786. On 9 Sept. GW wrote Mercer: "Your favor of the 20th ulto did not reach me till about the first inst."

From James Monroe

Dear General   New York Augt 20. 1786

May I take the liberty of our former acquaintance to confer with you freely upon the following propositions—You seem'd satisfied with those presented to the view of Congress on friday by Colo. Grayson viz. that exports be admitted down the Missisippi to N. Orleans as an *entrepot*—to pay there a duty of 2½ pr centm or more if necessary to the crown of Spain ad valorem, to be carried thence in Sp[anis]h, American & french vessels to other countries—that imports be prohibited[1]—in short that any arrangments on this subject be made w[hic]h shall hold up the U.S. to those people, our ultra-montane brethren, as the patrons of their interest, and not give the sanction of Congress to a measure which suspends for a day expressly their just rights— with these objects in view we will go as far as those who are the most anxious to obtain a Spanish treaty & cultivate the good wishes of that branch of the house of Bourbon—the point then upon which I wish particularly to consult you is simply this— the puting the negotiation of this treaty in the hands of Mr Jefferson & Mr Adams, that the former be instructed to repair to Madrid under the mediation of France for that purpose in character of Envoy extraordinary. This I presume may be done without giving offence to the gentn here, either Mr Jay or Gardoqui, since it is in difficulties of this kind the usage of courts to proceed thus & this line of negotiation must be particularly respectful to the court of Spain as it will be the highest evidence of our disposition of it as will form the manner as the terms upon which we are willing to make the treaty. Without this believe me I have the most satisfactory evidence nothing will be done—Mr Jay has within my knowledge since Decr last been negotiating with Congress to repeal his instructions (or rather with particular members) so as to occlude the Missisippi, & not with Spain to open it[2]—I trust you have sufficient knowledge of me to be satisfied I wo'd not make this allegation if I had not the most satisfactory evidence in my own mind of what I say—This evidence you shall possess whenever you please—I therefore calculate with certainty upon losing every thing whilst the business is in his hands—If in this free communication, I deviate from any of those rules of friendship & respect I have always entertain'd for you, & which I mean this as an evidence of, you will attribute it to no motive of that kind since I am not influenc'd by it—I am dear Sir with real esteem & regard yr very humble servt

Jas Monroe

ALS, DLC:GW.

James Monroe (1758–1831) was at this time a member of Congress from Virginia.

1. The Virginia delegates Monroe and William Grayson presented a motion to this effect on 18 Aug. (Burnett, *Letters*, 8:440–42).

2. Negotiations between Foreign Secretary John Jay and Don Diego de Gardoqui to form a treaty between the United States and Spain began in the summer of 1785 after the arrival of the Spanish envoy in New York in May. Congress's instructions to Jay were to secure the free navigation of the Mississippi River and the 31° latitude as the boundary between the United States and Spanish Florida. Jay, like GW, had come to believe it imprudent to demand the immediate opening of the Mississippi, and on 3 Aug. 1786 he appeared before Congress to argue that while the United States should continue to assert its right of navigation on the Mississippi, it should agree not to exercise that right for the time being. The storm of opposition this aroused in the South and West made ratification of any treaty negotiated by Jay and Gardoqui impossible. For other attacks at this time by Monroe on the Jay-Gardoqui negotiations, see his letters to James Madison, 31 May, 10 Aug. 1786 (Rutland and Rachal, *Madison Papers*, 9:68–73, 91–92), to Thomas Jefferson, 16 June, 16 July, 19 Aug. 1786 (Boyd, *Jefferson Papers*, 9:652–55, 10:142–22, 274–79), and, especially, to Patrick Henry, 12 Aug. 1786 (Hamilton, *Writings of Monroe*, 1:144–51).

To Henry Knox

Dr Sir   Mount Vernon 21st Augt 1786

The inclosed letter I received a short time since. As I am wholly unacquainted with the writer, & circumstances therein mentioned; I can only say, that if the facts are such as there alledged, I think the sufferer is entitled to some redress; but how far it may be in the power of Congress to comply with petitions of this nature I am not able to say. You undoubtedly know much better than I do, & I am sure your exertions will never be wanting to have justice done to those who have suffered by adhering to the cause of our Country.[1] I am Dr Sir &c. &c.

G: Washington

LB, DLC:GW.

1. The letter from Maurice Desdevens has not been found. Knox wrote GW on 23 Oct. that Desdevens had "been teizing congress for a number of years" and had "received considerable emoluments therefrom," even though Knox had never "been convinced of his services for the Union." Desdevens, a Canadian commissioned captain by Gen. Richard Montgomery in 1775, petitioned

Congress more than a dozen times between 26 Mar. 1781 and 21 July 1786 for various forms of compensation. Acting on Desdevens's petition of 10 July 1786 that all the papers he had previously submitted in support of his claims for compensation be considered by a committee, Congress voted on 12 July 1786 that Desdevens's claims "be referred to the board of treasury" (*JCC*, 30:397–98; 29:497–98). GW wrote Desdevens from Mount Vernon on 22 Aug.: "Sir, I have received your letter of the 8th of July, setting forth the misfortunes which you met with in the late war: As I have wholly laid aside public business, I can do nothing respecting the matter; but think that if the circumstances are such as you have mentioned, you ought to have some redress. I have written to Genl Knox upon the subject, who, I dare say, will do every thing in his power for you, consistently with propriety & justice. I am Sir, &c. G: Washington" (DLC:GW).

From Samuel Powel

Dear Sir   Philadelphia 21st August 1786

I have now to acknowlege the Receipt of your Letter, of May 25, in Answer to mine inclosing Col. Morgan's Essay. I beg you will not imagine that the transcribing it was troublesome to me. The Pleasure arising from a Communication in which you were interested abundantly compensated for the Time employed in making it; &, I hope, I need not add that I shall think myself happy to be of use to you on any Occasion.

Dr Griffith delivered me your Letter of the 5th of April. I should have been pleased to have had it in my Power to have furthered his Views with Convenience to myself; but, to have fallen in with his Plans, I must have withdrawn from the national Bank, what would have [been] requisite to accomplish them. Had my Situation corresponded to his Wishes your Recommendation would have proved an additional Inducement.

Mrs Powel begs Leave to join me in offering our best Thanks to you & Mrs Washington for your obliging Invitation. Be assured that should we ever determine upon visiting Virginia, the pleasure of paying you a Visit will not be the least of the Gratifications we should expect to derive from such a Journey.[1] Our best Wishes attend you both, and I am Dear Sir, Your most obedt humble Servt

Samuel Powel

ALS, DLC:GW.

1. Elizabeth Powel added a postscript: "Altho I well know that a Postscript is by no means essential to a Gentleman's Letter, yet I am willing to avail myself

of Mr Powels Permission of adding one to his. Tho I am sensible your Time may be more satisfactorily employed than by attending to the Ladies Concerns, yet allow me to arrest your Attention so long as to request the Favor of you to forward the enclosed Letter to my Friend Mrs Fitzhugh. I am at a Loss for her Address, at this Season of the Year, well knowing she annually ⟨q⟩uits Fredricksburg for the more cool & healthy Residence of Colo. Meade. My Satisfaction is compleat every Time that I can renew to you the Sentiments of Esteem & Affection with which I am Your sincere Friend Eliza Powel." Richard Kidder Meade's wife, the former Ann Randolph of Chatsworth, was the niece of William Fitzhugh of Chatham, near Fredericksburg. The Meades lived at Lucky Hit near the Blue Ridge Mountains in Frederick, now in Clarke County. The Meades' first child, Ann Randolph Meade, was born at Chatham in 1781 and named for Mrs. Fitzhugh, also a Randolph. See Brown, *Annals of Clarke County*, 1:196–205.

Letter not found: from Samuel Vaughan, 22 Aug. 1786. On 12 Sept. GW wrote Vaughan: "A few days ago I had the honor to receive your favor of the 22d ulto."

To Jonathan Loring Austin

Sir,   Mo[un]t Vernon 23d Augt 1786.
    I have received your Oration of the 4th of July, which you did me the honor to send me; & am much obliged to you for so polite a mark of attention. I have perused it with a great deal of pleasure, & hope that the anniversary of that day will ever be commemorated in this Country as the era from which we may date our happiness & importance.[1] I am Sir, &c.
                                                       Go. Washington

LB, DLC:GW.
    1. The *Oration Delivered July 4, 1786, at the Request of the Inhabitants of Boston* (Boston, 1786) by Jonathan Loring Austin (1748–1826) was listed in the inventory of GW's library taken after his death. Austin spent most of the war in the employ of the American commissioner in Paris. He at this time was a partner of his brother Benjamin Austin (1752–1829) in a mercantile firm in Boston.

To John Witherspoon

Revd Sir,   Mount Vernon 23d Augt 1786.
    The last Post brought me your favor of the 14th. You have been misinformed, respecting the congregation of Pohick. It is of the Episcopal Church & at this time has an incumbent; of

which I give you the earliest notice for the information of Mr Wilson.

A Church above this, formerly under the same ministry, is, I believe, unprovided; but of what religion the people thereabout *now* are, I am unable to say—most probably a medlay; as they have had Methodist, & Baptist preachers of all kinds among them.[1] With respect, I am Sir, &c.

G: Washington

LB, DLC:GW.

1. Lee Massey, who had been rector of Truro Parish since 1767, seems to have remained officially the rector until his death in 1814, although he ceased to preach because of a speech impairment (Slaughter, *Truro Parish*, 93; Goodwin, *Colonial Church in Virginia*, 292). Services were held only sporadically at Pohick, the Lower Church in the parish, after the Revolution, and ministers seem to have been brought in from time to time to preach. GW notes that he attended Pohick on 2 Oct. 1785 when James Thomson, minister of Leeds Parish in Fauquier County, preached. He attended again in 1786 and 1788 (*Diaries*, 4:200, 5:51–52, 411). Ministers' salaries were no longer paid by parish taxes but rather by subscription of members of the individual churches.

The Upper Church of Truro Parish, usually called Payne's Church, was in a less densely populated area and seems to have been little used after the Revolution. Baptists took possession of the abandoned church early in the nineteenth century and used it until the winter of 1862–63 when Federal troops tore it down in order to build chimneys and hearths for their camp from its bricks (Slaughter, *Truro Parish*, 68–69).

From George Lewis

Dr Sir   Bath 25th of August [17]86

By the particular request of Doctor Lemare, I have examin'd your houses at this place, and from the discription which the Doctor sayes you gave him of them he is induced to think you have been impos'd on[.] this supposition prompts him to wish of me an accurate and impartial discription of them, in there present situation. On viewing the houses I find them to be two of logs 19 by 17 each, hew'd inside and out, in hight what they call here, Story and half, cover'd wth long shingles, one of them floor'd above and below with a wall'd Cellar, which the Doctor sayes was intended for a Stable to contain nine horses; I think four might stand in it and no more; the other house has a floor above only, some stone under one end and side. The other logs lay on the ground; this house has a Chimney but Slightly built, and from appearances must certainly burn the house whenever there is a warm fire made in the harth. in Short the houses are esteem'd badly built, and of bad timber. The Doctor call'd in a Workman to examine the work, who agreed in opinion that it was badly done.[1]

I hope to have it in my power to pay you a visit with Mrs Lewis this fall, she is at this place for her health, and has receiv'd considerable benifit from the trip, and flatters herself another season will be the means of establishing her halth,[2] she joins me in Love to my Aunt and yourself. Am Dr Sir with the warmest esteem and Afft. Yr

G. Lewis

ALS, with a postscript from John Augustine Washington, DLC:GW.

George Lewis (1757–1821), a son of Fielding Lewis and GW's sister, Betty Washington Lewis, was married to Catherine Daingerfield Lewis (1764–1820) of Spotsylvania County.

1. According to his diary entry of 6 Sept. 1784, when GW entered an agreement with James Rumsey for Rumsey to build at Bath (Berkeley Springs) a two-story dwelling house, 36 by 24 feet, and a kitchen and stable, each 18 by 22 feet, GW specified how the structures should be built (*Diaries*, 4:9–11). John Augustine Washington appended this statement to Lewis's letter: "Doctr Lemare who is living in Genl Washingtons House at Bath, and much attached to his interest, conceiving the work not to be done properly, and agreeable to bargain prevailed on Mr G. Lewis to examine it, and has also requested me since to do the same, I find the work executed as our young Freind has stated it—I flatter my self with the pleasure of seeing the Genl the latter end of Septr at Mt Vernon and am Most sincerely & affy his affe Brother J. A. Washington." See also Jean Le Mayeur to GW, 28 Aug., and James Rumsey to GW, 19 September.

2. The George Lewises, who had lived for a time in Frederick County, were now living near Fredericksburg.

To Thornton Washington

Dear Thornton, Mount Vernon Augt 25th 1786

I wrote so fully to you at the time I inclosed the Papers which respected the Land on which you live, that I did not intend to have said any thing more on the subject of Hites claim—but the other day one of the Tenants on the same land (living near the head spring of Bullskin) informed me that he had been forewarned from sowing Winter grain on his place. It will behove you, to make use of all the means I put in your power to oppose their claim. I think they were ample if properly set to view, against every other claim than the original purchase money. If therefore you do not exert yourself in bringing these forward with such other lights as can be thrown upon them, you may not only suffer yourself, but will disappoint me; for relying entirely on you I have taken no step to oppose the late decision of the General Court, or high Court of chancery in which the matter was determined. I understand that Commissioners are appointed who are to examine the legal objections to the judgment, where there are any. It would be well for you therefore not only to appear before these—but to get some able Lawyer to consider the papers I sent you, state the case with all the advantages it admits—and if allowed—appear in support of it. I have applied, as I wrote you in my last that I should do, to the representative of George Johnston (of whom I bought the Land) for the Original Bond of Joist Hite, but it is not to be found among his Papers—and ought in my opinion to be searched after in the Proprietors Office; It being highly probable it was deposited there, as the Deed from thence recites that the Land was purchased from Hite by Thomas of whom Johnston had it.[1]

I wish to hear from you, and to know precisely what has been, or is likely to be done, in this business. A letter thrown into the line of the Winchester Post will come safe, and is better than private opportunities when the conveyance is not direct to the person. My best wishes attend you & your wife, in which the family here all join. I am affectionately Yrs

Go: Washington

P.S. If your Uncle John is in Berkeley, be governed by his advice in the mode of proceeding which may be best for you to adopt in exhibiting your right before the Commissioners.

ALS (photocopy), CSfBo. The original, owned by the Bohemian Club, in 1991 could not be found.

1. See Thornton Washington to GW, 6 June 1786.

From Jean Le Mayeur

sir   Bath August 28. 1786.

i should have wrote thre weks ago to your Excellancy had not mr Rumsey deceivd me in his departure from this place. probably he suspected my informing you of the situation of your Building—which he has not done well—Colo. jno. washington and Mr Georges Lewes agree with me in oppinion of mr Rumsey performance.[1]

should your Excellancy proper to write to me i shall get it at the post office in philadelphia as i Expect to be there in ten or twelve days at farthest—and i hope to be at mountvernon by the first days of octobr when i Entend to Give to General a narration of all the civilities i have recived from Generl smallwood but for that i make him fine Gentleman in transplanting front teeth in his head. of which he wrot me he is Extremely satisfay.[2]

i Shall refers to Mr Randolph ow will set of from here in 5 or 6 days on his way to mountvernon, & for the news at Bath.[3]

i hope Lady Washington and Major and all Washingtons are well. I have the honour to be with Great Respect and veneration of your Excellancy his most obt and humle serviteur

                                               j. Le Mayeur

ALS, DLC:GW.

1. See George Lewis to GW, 25 August.

2. William Smallwood at this time was governor of Maryland. Le Mayeur, who had been at Mount Vernon in July, returned on 14 Dec. (*Diaries*, 5:1, 78).

3. Edmund Randolph stopped at Mount Vernon on 16 Sept. on his return from the Annapolis Convention, but not from Frederick County.

To James Hill

Sir,   Mo[un]t Vernon 29th Augt 1786.

I have been in continual expectation ever since my return to private life (now near three years) of receiving a statement of the accots between us. This not having yet happened, and finding sums which I expected were due to me (especially in the case of Mr Newton of Norfolk from whom I thought a large balance was due to me) charged as having been paid to you, it makes it indispensably necessary for me to be furnished with a precise & compleat accot of all the transactions of my business which had been committed to your care from the date of the last settlement which I made with you myself, to the present moment. Shewing, if monies have been paid to others on myself, the sums, & by what authority it was done. Without these it is impossible for me to adjust my own accounts, or bring my business to a close with others.[1] I pray you therefore not to delay complying with this request, & it will oblige yrs &c.

G: Washington

LB, DLC:GW.

James Hill (1736–1802) of Springfield in King William County paid taxes on 642½ acres and twenty-two slaves in that county in 1782.

1. Hill was hired by GW in March 1772 to manage the Custis lands in the York River area in place of Joseph Valentine who died the previous year. See Hill to GW, 9 Dec. 1771, and notes to that document, and Cash Accounts, March 1772, n.2. On 27 Oct. 1778 GW wrote Hill that he no longer needed a manager and that Hill was to send any money he had collected for GW and John Parke Custis to Lund Washington at Mount Vernon. At the same time GW requested an exact account of all Hill's expenditures and everything sold from the estate, "since the last Acct which I settled with you myself" (DLC:GW). This last settlement with GW was undoubtedly the one recorded on 28 Aug. 1775 in Hill's accounts with GW (see Hill to GW, 1 Feb. 1787, n.1): "To Cash paid you in Wmsbg the 16th June 1774 which has been Omitted ℈ acco.[—]£147.1.⟨3⟩." For GW's complaints during the Revolution about Hill's stewardship and his delay in accounting for money collected for the estate, see especially GW to Burwell Bassett, 22 April 1779. For the balance GW thought was due from Thomas Newton, Jr., of Norfolk, see GW to Newton, 3 Sept. 1785, and notes 1 and 2 of that document. For Hill's explanation of his actions in winding up his stewardship of the Custis estate, see Hill to GW, 24 Sept. 1786 and 1 Feb. 1787.

To Gardoqui

Sir,   Mount Vernon 30th Augt 1786.

The day before yesterday gave me the honor of your Excellency's favor, written on the 12th of June, with a postscript thereto of the 22d of July. It was accompanied by the cloth made of the wool of the Vicuna, which indeed is of a softness & richness which I have never seen before, & is truly worthy of being called his Majesty's *true* manufactured cloth. For your Excellency's goodness in presenting me with this specimen of it, I pray you to accept my best acknowledgements. I received it Sir, as a mark

of your polite attention to me, & shall wear it with much pleasure as a memento thereof. The color is really beautiful, & being
natural can never fade.

I feel myself much indebted to your Excelly for communicating the testimonies of my gratitude to the King, thro' the medium of His Excelly Count de Florida Blanca, for his royal present of the Jack Asses; one of which arrived very safe, & promises
to be a most valuable animal. I am endeavouring to provide a
female, that the advantages which are to be derived from this
Jack may not end with *his* life.

I can omit no occasion of assuring your Excellency of the high
sense I entertain of the many marks of polite attention I have
received from you; nor of the pleasure I should feel in the honor
of expressing it at this seat of my retirement from public life, if
you should ever feel an inclination to make an excursion into
the middle States. I have the honor to be &c.

G: Washington

LB, DLC:GW.

From Battaile Muse

Honourable Sir,   Alexandria Augt 31st 1786
Ten days Billious Fever and wet weather prevented my arriveing at this place untill yesterday—My weak state—wet
weather—and Being obliged To Winchester next Monday prevented My waiting on you at this Time, I expect To be down
Some Time in October at which Time I hope I shall be able To
waite on you To represent the Sittuation of your Business in my
Care—I do not Expect To receive any money untill Late in the
fall as the Tenants depend on the Sales of this years crops To
raise money—I have been Fortunate in geting £20.6.0 from Mr
R. Rutherford—the Ballance of his note He Prayes Indulgence
on untill next year[1]—your acct is now Indebted To me about
my Commision. I shall be much oblige To you To Contrive Some
of the Enclosed Advertisements Towards Port Tobacco—your
Ferry and mill—also Please To get Mr Shaw To date them Sept
1st[.] after my return from the Commissioners at Winchester I
shall write you about your Lands, the Commissioners and Colo.

Hite was at my House—they were of opinion your Lands are Safe Never the less I shall attend them as well on your acct as Colo. Fairfaxes.[2]

Colo. Charles Washington desired me To Enquire of you whether you Should have Ocation to Call for money soon for the Expences of Colo. S. Washington's Sons at this place as the Estate is Likely to be distressed for £800 by a Colo. Alexander[3]— all the money that can be raised Colo. Washington desires To be applyed To Save the Estate unless your Sittuation require money—I am Sir your Obedient Humble Servant.

Battaile Muse

I shall be Thankfull If you will Sell my Flour with yours & give me Credit for it—I am as before.[4] B.M.

ALS, DLC:GW.

1. In Muse's Accounts as Rental Agent (see source note, Lists of Tenants, 18 Sept. 1785), he records this payment from Robert Rutherford on 22 Aug., "in part of His note of Hand."

2. See Muse to GW, 11 July, and GW to Muse, 1 August.

3. See GW to Charles Washington, 14 Feb. 1787, and note 2 of that document.

4. See GW to Muse, 6 May, n.1.

To George Gilpin and John Fitzgerald

Gentn,   Mount Vernon 1st Septr 1786.

Nothing but sickness would have prevented my attendance at the Seneca Falls on Monday next agreeably to appointment. On sunday last (occasioned by an imprudent act) I was seized by an ague & fever. on Tuesday & yesterday they returned with great violence, with scarce any intermission of the fever. Whether the Doctors efforts will baffle them tomorrow, remains to be determined; but at any rate he thinks it would be improper for me to leave home. The fevers, moreover, have made such havock of my mouth, nose & chin that I am unable to put a razor to my face. Thus circumstanced, I have given up all idea of meeting the Board the 4th instant.[1]

Besides the business which is the immediate occasion of this meeting, it might be well, as we are every day thrown back in our operations on the bed of the river, to prepare the draft of a Petition which will be necessary to hand to the respective Assemblies for prolongation of the time for that part of the undertaking; and, as there may be difficulties in the way yet unforeseen, I should incline to enlarge it to the greatest extent it is thought we can obtain.[2] I submit for consideration also, the propriety (if the waters should get low enough in the course of the Fall) of a thorough investigation of the river, by a skilful person, from the Shannondoah falls to Fort Cumberland at least; that by having the matter fully before us, we may be enabled to form some precise judgment of the difficulties which lie in the way, & prepare for them accordingly.

As I cannot do greater justice to the sentiments of the Company respecting its approbation of the conduct of the Directors, than it conveyed by the Address of the Committee, I have the honor of forwarding a copy of that letter to me, which I beg the favor of you, Gentn, to lay before the Board at the Meeting which is about to take place.[3] With great esteem & regard, I am Gentn &c.

G: Washington

LB, DLC:GW.

1. GW sent for Dr. James Craik on Thursday, 31 Aug., and Craik prescribed quinine. The fever, which struck on alternate days, failed to return on Saturday, 2 Sept., which would have been his fourth "fit day." GW makes no further reference in his diaries to his illness, and on 9 Sept. he wrote Fitzgerald that he was "tolerably well again." See *Diaries*, 5:32–34. The two Maryland trustees of the Potomac River Company, Thomas Johnson and Thomas Sim Lee, both also were ill, and so no meeting of the trustees was held on 4 September.

2. See GW to David Stuart, 5 Nov., n.1.

3. A committee of the Potomac Company at Alexandria composed of David Stuart, Charles Simms, and James Keith, directed this address of 15 Aug. to GW at Mount Vernon: "Sir, The Industry & Attention with which the Attempt to make the Potomack navagable, has been prosecuted by you, & the Gentlemen united with you in Office; have excited feelings in the breasts of the Company, which can only be estimated by those, who are acquainted with the extensive national utility of the work, & the unpatriotic Indolence which retards similar designs in this State.

"Be assured Sir, that while the Company is strongly impressed with Gratitude towards the Directors, for their Assiduity, the happy Influence of your Presidency, is deeply engraved on every mind. The fidelity, & accuracy, with which the treasurers accounts have been kept, merit also their Notice, & sincere thanks.

"It is with Pleasure Sir, we impart to you these sentiments in behalf of the Company, & beg you will do us the honour of communicating them to the above Gentlemen" (DLC:GW).

In addition to sending a copy of the address to Gilpin and Fitzgerald, GW on the same day forwarded a copy to the company's treasurer, William Hartshorne: "Sir, The enclosed Address to me, from a Committee of the Potomac Company, will convey the sense of that company on the fidelity & accuracy with which your accots have been kept, in the fullest & clearest manner. I have great pleasure in communicating these sentiments, & with very great esteem & regard, I am Sir &c. G: Washington" (LB, DLC:GW).

Later in the day Hartshorne responded: "Your favor of the 1st inst. I recd enclosing the Address from a Committee of the Potomac Company to you as president of the directors, in which I think they have expressed the Sentiments of the Company respecting yourself and them—And I think myself highly honored by the obliging manner in which they are pleased to Notice my Services as Treasurer of the Company—It shall be my endeavor to merit a continuance of the same confidence and I return you my thanks for the honor you have done me, in furnishing me with the Address, in which I am mentioned in such terms of approbation as are very pleasing to me" (DLC:GW).

To David Humphreys

My dear Humphreys,   Mount Vernon Septr 1st 1786.

Enclosed are all the documents Mr Lear could find respecting the confinement, & treatment under it, of Captain Asgill. For want of recurrence to them before I wrote to Mr Tilghman, I perceive that a bad memory had run me into an error in my narrative of the latter, in one particular. For it should seem by that, as if the loose and unguarded manner in which Captn Asgill was held, was sanctioned by me; whereas one of my letters to Colo. Dayton condemns this conduct, and orders Asgill to be closely confined. Mr Lear has given all the letters at length. Extracts might have answered. But I judged it better, that the whole tenor of the Correspondence should appear, that no part might seem to be hidden. I well remember Major Gordon's attending Asgill; and by one of my letters to Dayton it is evident that Gordon had written to me; but my letter-books have registered no reply.

In what manner it would be best to bring this matter before the Publik eye I am at a loss, and leave it to you to determine under a consideration of the circumstances which are as fully communicated as the documents in my hands will enable me to do. There is one mystery in the business which I cannot develop, nor is there any papers in my possession which explain it. Hazen was ordered to send an unconditional prisoner. Asgill comes. Hazen or some other must have given information of a Leiutenant Turner. (under the former description) Turner is ordered on, but never came. Why? I am unable to say; nor is there any letter from Hazen (to be found) that accounts for a noncompliance with this order. If I had not too many causes to distrust my memory I should ascribe it to there having been no such Officer—or that he was also under capitulation, for Captn Shaack seems to have been held as a proper victim after this.

I will write as soon as I am able to Mr Tilghman requesting him to withold my first acct of Asgill's treatment, from his corrispondent in England, promising an authentic one from original papers. It may however have passed him, in that case, it will be necessary for me to say something to reconcile my own Accts.[1]

I write to you with a very aching head, and disordered frame, and Mr Lear will copy the letter. Saturday last, by an imprudent act, I brought on an ague and fever on Sunday, which returned with violence Tuesday & Thursday; and if Doctor Craik's efforts are ineffectual, I shall have them again this day. The family join me in every good wish for you. It is unnecessary to assure you of the friendship & affection with which I am yr's

Go: Washington

P.S. We have found Gordon's letters.[2] They contain a remonstrance and demand of Asgill as an officer protected by the Capitulation of York-Town. This I suppose is the reason they were never answered.

LS, in Tobias Lear's hand, NN: Emmet Collection; LB, DLC:GW.

1. In November Humphreys sent GW the piece that he wrote, and had arranged to have printed, in defense of GW's handling of the Asgill affair. See Humphreys to GW, 16 Nov., n.1.

2. The only letter which has been found from Maj. James Gordon of the 80th Regiment of Foot is dated 27 May 1782.

To James Tilghman

Dr Sir; Mount Vernon 2d Septr 1786.

If the Account I handed to you respecting the treatment of Captn Asgill (in confinement) has not passed from you, I should be obliged to you for withholding, & suffering no copies to be taken from it; to counteract such an injurious & ill founded calumny which obtains credit as it rolls on.[1]

I have it in contemplation to inspect my registers, & to give something from authentic documents relative to this matter. The former being drawn up in a hasty manner, & from memory, may contain something inconsistent with the latter, which will be substantiated.[2] With great esteem & regard, I am Dr Sir, &c.

G: Washington

LB, DLC:GW.

1. See GW to Tilghman, 20 July, and Tilghman to GW, 23 September. The words following the semicolon clearly should be a part of the first sentence in the next paragraph, as presumably they were in GW's own version.

2. See GW to David Humphreys, 1 September.

From John Peck

Sir,   Nomony-Hall, 4th Septr 1786.

Since I had the honor of addressing you from Piscataway,[1] I have been confined by a severe intermittant which has rendered me unable to attend to the business of the Cincinnati, or indeed any other.

If the Diplomas are ready would thank you to forward them by Mr Elwood, agreeably to a written request which he will deliver for that purpose.[2] I am, Sir, With Sentiments of the most perfect respect Your Very Humb. Servt

Jno. Peck

ALS, DLC:GW. Peck enclosed a "Duplicate" of this letter in his letter to GW of 5 Mar. 1787 (DLC:GW).

1. Peck's earlier letter is dated 16 August. Nomini Hall was the place of Peck's father-in-law Robert Carter (1728–1804) in Westmoreland County.

2. John Ellwood (Elwood), Jr., was captain of the sloop *Charming Polly*, the Philadelphia packet boat that made regular runs to Alexandria.

From James Rumsey

Dr General.   Alexandria Septr 5th 1786

I was Verry Sorry to hear that it was Sickness prevented you from Comeing to The meeting at Seneca, Govenor Johnson and

Lee was also Sick and Could not attend therefore Their was no
Board. It would Oblige me much if The next meeting was to be
at the great falls as their is Several persons whose presence will
Be Nescessary that Objects to going Over to the maryland Side
an account of the Bad attention to that ferry, and Dearness of it,
I am Convinced that the maryland gentlemen would wish to See
the works at the great falls, and therefore think that they will
have no Objection to meeting their.[1]

Inclosed is an account of the Expence of your Buildings at
Bath It amounts to a Considerable Sum higher than I Expected
the ac[c]t is Stated in penns. Currencey. The Stone work of the
Celler is Extended at an astablished price that I had from Every
person that I had work of that kind Done for, when I found
Every thing. The underpinning the kitchen and kitchen Chimney I Estamated at ten pounds ten Shillings a particular account
of it Being Neglected, But I Beleive it To Be Set Loe, The nails,
Glass Locks and hinges are high, But they are at the prices that
we was Obliged to give at Bath for them, I am not Quite as To
the amount of the money I have Receivd of you But I think it is
as follows,—Viz.

paid to Mr Herbert	£40.0.0
my first Devidend to potomack Co.	3.6.8
Receivd for Rent of houses	9.0.0
paid me at your house	20.0.0
	72.6.8

I am not Very Clear but the money I got at your house was
twenty five pounds but I gave a Receipt for it which will Show
the amt[2]—the Boat will be tryed this week on the Oreginal
plann you Shall Immediately Hear what Suckcess[3]—I am with
Every Sentyment of Regard your most obt Very hbl. Servt

James Rumsey

ALS, DLC:GW.

1. The board of directors of the Potomac River Company met at the Great
Falls of the Potomac on 2–4 Oct. (see *Diaries*, 5:47–48). See also GW to George
Gilpin and John Fitzgerald, 1 Sept., n.1.

2. GW engaged Rumsey in 1784 to build for him at Bath (Berkeley Springs)
a two-story house and outbuildings. See *Diaries*, 4:9–12, and Rumsey to GW, 5
June 1785, 10 Mar. 1785, and Rumsey to GW, 24 June 1785. For reports critical of Rumsey's work, see George Lewis to GW, 25 Aug. 1786, and Jean Le
Mayeur to GW, 28 Aug. 1786. Rumsey's enclosed account of the costs for erect-

ing the structures shows a total charge of £104.9.1. The largest items were £16.16.8 for "33 & ⅔ perches of Stone work in Celler wall @10/ ," £18.19.6 to pay Thomas Beard for carpentry work on the house, £10.10 for "under pining kitchen & Building Chimney," and £12 to the carpenter for building the kitchen. A transcription of Rumsey's account is in CD-ROM:GW. Rumsey also enclosed in this letter a receipt from Thomas Beard for the carpentry work done on the house.

3. GW viewed the model of Rumsey's mechanical boat at Berkeley Springs in September 1784 and gave Rumsey a certificate dated 7 Sept. 1784 attesting to the boat's efficacy. He thereafter maintained a lively interest in Rumsey's progress, or lack of, in perfecting his boat. See GW to Rumsey, 31 Jan. 1786, and note 1 of that document.

From Henry Lee, Jr.

My dear Genl   New York Sept. 8th 1786

By Col. Humphrey I had the pleasure to receive your letter acknowledging the receipt of the china account paid here by me, and at the same time got one hundred and fifty dollars payment in full for the money advanced. Before this Mr Gardoquis box must have reached you; it was sent to the care of Mr C. Lee in Alexandria and I hope your China has also got to hand—It had left this for Norfolk addressed to Colo. Parker before your letter respecting the mode of conveyance got to me, or I should have obeyed your wishes.[1]

The period seems to be fast approaching when the people of these U. States must determine to establish a permanent capable government or submit to the horrors of anarchy and licentiousness—How wise would it be, how happy for us all, if this change could be made in friendship, and conducted by reason. But such is the tardiness of the virtuous and worthy part of society in matters of this importance, and such the conceit & zeal of the vicious, that it is to be apprehended that wickedness and audacity will triumph over honor & honesty—The enclosed proclamation just come to hand will shew you the temper of the eastern people[2]—it is not confined to one state or to one part of a state, but pervades the whole. The decay of their commerce leaves the lower order unemployed, idleness in this body, and the intriguing exe[r]tions of another class whose desperate fortunes are remediable only by the ruin of society produce schemes portending the dissolution of order & good government—Weak and feeble governments are not adequate to resist such high handed offences—Is it not then strange that the sober part of mankind will continue to prefer this incertitude & precariousness, because their jealousys are alarmed and their envy encited when they see the officers of the Nation possessing that power which is indispensably necessary to chastise evil and reward virtue. But thus it is, and thus it has been, and from hence it follows that almost every Nation we read off, have drank deep of the miserys which flow from despotism or licentiousness—the happy medium is difficult to practice.

I am very unhappy to hear by Mr Shaw that your health declines; I must hope he is mistaken and cannot help thinking so, as Col. Humphreys tells me that you look very hearty, and use vigorous exercise[3]—if the potomac navigation succeeds in the manner these gentlemen mention, it is another strong evidence that difficultys vanish as they are approached, and will be a strong argument among the politicians, in favor of the spanish treaty and the occlusion of the Mississippi—Mrs Lee joins me in most respectful compliments to Mount-Vernon—with unceasing and affectionate attachment I am dear Genl your Most ob. h. ser.

Henry Lee Junr

ALS, DLC:GW.

1. GW's letter has not been found. See Lee to GW, 3 July, n.2.

2. The enclosure may be a copy of the resolutions adopted at Hatfield, Mass., on 25 Aug. by delegates from towns in Hampshire County listing many of the grievances that became the rallying cries of the Shaysites in the fall and winter. A copy of the resolves is in Minot, *History of the Insurrections in Massachusetts*, 34–37. They were printed in the *Hampshire Herald* as early as 5 September.

3. David Humphreys left Mount Vernon on 23 Aug. for Alexandria and New York. William Shaw, GW's former secretary, spent the night of 24 Aug. at Mount Vernon and on the next day "went to Alexandria after breakfast in order to proceed to the Northward to embark at Philadelphia for the West Inds." (*Diaries*, 5:30). GW wrote to David Humphreys about his illness on 1 Sept. (see also GW to George Gilpin and John Fitzgerald, 1 Sept., n.1).

To John Fitzgerald

Dear Sir,   Mount Vernon Septr 9th 1786.

Have you heard from Annapolis since Monday? Have the Commercial Commissioners met? Have they proceeded to business? How long is it supposed their Session will last? and is it likely they will do anything effectual?[1]

Is Colo. Gilpin returned? Was there a meeting of the Board? What was the result of the enquiry into the charges exhibited against Stuart?[2]

I hope Mrs Fitzgerald & yourself are quite recovered. I am tolerably well again, but obliged to make use of Scissars instead of a Razor, for part of my face, when shaving. I am Dr Sir Yr obedt Hble Servt

Go: Washington

ALS, PWacD: Sol Feinstone Collection, on deposit PPAmP.

1. Delegates from five states met in Annapolis 11–14 September. See David Stuart to GW, 18 Dec. 1785, n.3.

2. The meeting of the trustees of the Potomac River Company was not held. See GW to George Gilpin and John Fitzgerald, 1 Sept., n.1, and James Rumsey to GW, 5 September. At their meeting of 2–4 Oct., the trustees of the Potomac Company examined the charges of James Rumsey against Richardson Stewart (Stuart), the former assistant manager of the Potomac River Company who had succeeded Rumsey in July as manager, and found them "malignant, envious, & trifling" (*Diaries*, 5:48).

From Henry Hill

Dear Sir   Philad[elphi]a 9th Sepr 1786

Being much in the Country with Mrs Hill who is yet almost confin'd by indisposition, my acknowlegements of your favor of the 3d past will come later than could happen through want of Attention[1]—This I am certain will appear on all occasions where my respect can avail you any thing.

No payment could be more acceptable than your Bill which I remitted by the last packet on the 6th instt tho' I had a good mind to convert it into Cash & therewith build part of the walls of my new house in town, that if possible your Claims to the best reception in it might be strengthened, but they appear'd already quite sufficient.

I must leave my Madeira friends to account for the difference of price in the two wines you imported, and shall only observe that age however essential to the perfection of an original good growth, exposes a mean one, as appeard by some wine we lately tasted here that came by China & shipd I believe for the best by the house you allude to.

You will find no small difference in comparing the two qualities or I shall have greatly err'd in my Expectations—& if so I request you will candidly undeceive me. With the most Affectionate respect to you & Mrs Washington I am Sir Your obedt humb. Servt

Henry Hill

ALS, DLC:GW.

1. GW's letter is dated 3 August.

To John Francis Mercer

Dear Sir,   Mount Vernon 9th Sep. 1786.

Your favor of the 20th ulto did not reach me till about the first inst. It found me in a fever, from which I am now but sufficiently recovered to attend to business. I mention this to shew that I had it not in my power to give an answer to your propositions sooner.[1]

With respect to the first, I never mean (unless some particular circumstances should compel me to it) to possess another slave by purchase; it being among my first wishes to see some plan adopted, by the legislature by which slavery in this Country may be abolished by slow, sure, & imperceptable degrees.[2] With respect to the 2d, I never did, nor never intend to purchase a military certificate; I see no difference it makes with you (if it is one of the funds allotted for the discharge of my claim) who the purchaser is. If the depreciation is 3 for 1 only, you will have it in your power whilst you are at the receipt of Custom—Richmond—where it is said the great regulator of this business (Greaves) resides, to convert them into specie at that rate. If the difference is more, there would be no propriety, if I inclined to deal in them at all, in my taking them at that exchange.[3]

I shall rely upon your promise of two hundred pounds in five weeks from the date of your letter. It will enable me to pay the workmen which have been employed abt this house all the Spring & Summer, (some of whom are here still).[4] But there are two debts, which press hard upon me. One of which, if there is no other resource, I must sell Land or Negroes to discharge. It is owing to Govr Clinton of New York, who was so obliging as to borrow, & became my Security for £2500 to answer some calls of mine. This sum was to be returned in twelve months from the conclusion of Peace. For the remains of it, about eight hundred pounds York C[urrenc]y I am now paying an interest of seven Pr Ct; but the high interest (tho' more than any estate can bear) I should not regard, if my credit was not at stake to comply with the conditions of the loan.[5] The other debt, tho' I know the person to whom it is due wants it, and I am equally anxious to pay it, might be put off a while longer. This sum is larger than the other.[6] I am Dr Sir Yr Most Obedt Hble Servt

Go: Washington

ALS, CStbKML; LB, DLC:GW.

1. Letter not found.

2. In the end, after extensive correspondence, GW and Mercer reached a mutual agreement that GW would take no slaves in payment of the debt owed him by the estate of John Mercer. See GW to John Francis Mercer, 1 Feb. 1787. For the estate debt, see GW to John Francis Mercer, 8 July 1784, n.1.

3. GW ultimately agreed to accept military certificates in payment of the Mercer estate debt, but it is not apparent from GW's accounts, or from this correspondence, what if any certificates he received from Mercer. See GW to Mercer 6, 24 Nov., 5, 19 Dec. 1786, 1 Feb. 1787, and Ledger B, 221.

4. Mercer paid £200 on 16 Oct. (Ledger B, 221).

5. GW paid George Clinton in June 1787 (GW to Clinton, 9 June 1787). For the Clinton loan, see Clinton to GW, 27 Feb. 1784, source note.

6. GW was probably referring to what he owed George Clinton for their joint purchase of land in upstate New York. See GW to Clinton, 5 Nov. 1786, and the references in note 2 of that document.

From Josiah Parker

Dear Sir   Portsmouth September 9th 1786

Your favor of the 18th Ultimo reached me a few days since, and a day or two after the china arrived from New York, which shall be sent by the first safe Conveyance to your seat on potowmack.[1] I lamented much the death of one of the pair of Gold fish, as I am sensible they would have bred had you have provided them an enclosure in a runing pool. I deemed it best to send them to Fredricksburg as the Captain of the Packet promised especial care of them & the conveyance from thence might have been very easy by puting them in a Bucket ⅓rd full of Spring Water. they require no food but the surface of the Water, that should be shifted dayly if they are confined. I have a pair which I am sure would increase if they were at liberty. Should they, I shall do myself the honor of offering you a share or should one of them die the other will be sent to you. they are beautiful little fish and in this Country a real curiosity.

I did not expect you would have troubled yourself to have answered my letter of the 23rd May as it was only a companion for the box from New York, and I am very sensible that you can have very little leisure to attend to every little transaction. Its enough for me to be satisfied with your doing me the honor of transacting any little matter for you here which will ever give me pleasure to attend to. I have one wish very much at heart which is that you sometimes cast your Eyes to this part of the Country and further the Canal business as the importance of it to us here & to the Community in general as well as you who have property in the neighbourhood must be particularly conspicuous—a Single Visit from you with an explanation of the advantages attending a canal would give it more credence than any patronage it can expect from this quarter: I am very sensible that if a proper conveyance was made from the head of Pasquotank throug the lake and to empty its waters into the Southern Branch of Elizabeth River that the waters would be fresh enough to kill the Worm—the only Enemy to our harbour.[2] Let me pray you to believe that this long scrawl is not intended to draw you into an Answer, unless you should find a leisure moment, when you can thing of any thing to say, or any thing that I can do for you. May you live long and be happy is the wish of My dear Sir your obliged, humble Servant

J: Parker

ALS, DLC:GW. The letter was sent by "Post."

1. Letter not found. For the Cincinnati china, see Henry Lee to GW, 3 July, n.2.

2. For the proposal to build the Elizabeth River Canal in the Dismal Swamp, see Patrick Henry to GW, 11 Nov. 1785, n.2.

From Thomas Ridout

Sir,   Bordeaux, 10 Septemr 1786

I had the Honor to receive, the 1st Ulto your Excellency's letter of the 20 May, together with the Packet & Barrel for the

Marquis de la Fayette—the former I forwarded him immediately pr post, & I sent the Barrel last week in very good condition. I could not get it sooner from the Custom House & Brokers.

The wine you are pleased to order will be sent you by the next opportunity for the Potowmack & I hope it will be such as will please you.

As I propose revisiting America very soon my Friends. Mess. W. & N. Johnston of this place will transact my Business during my absence & will with pleasure execute any orders you may have in this place.

I have the Honor to be with the greatest respect Your Excellency's Most Obedient Humble Servant

Thos Ridout

ALS, DLC:GW.

From Leven Powell

Dear Sir   Loudoun Sepr 12th 1786.

I should have done myself the Pleasure of Answering your favor of the 20th of July earlier, if I had not then expected it would have been in my power to send you the Timothy seed wrote for in the course of a few weeks; for immediately upon the receipt of your letter I sent to a man in Frederick much to be depended on & from whom I have hitherto been supply'd, who readily engaged your Quantity.[1]

Eight or ten days ago I had information from him that he had secured a sufficiency of Timothy, but the continual rains had prevented his getting the seed out.

We have now an appearance of fair weather & I do expect it here in a few days, but as my son informs me it will be more agreeable to you not to take it, I shall endeavour to dispose of it in the mean time, if I cannot do so I shall immediately upon its coming to hand send it down to him.

He informs me you wish to know whether I can purchase 100 or 150 Bushels of Buck wheat for you.[2]

I can readily get you either of those Quantities of the New Crop which will soon be in & which I presume will be in time for your purpose. Be pleased to inform me the exact Quantity & when you will want it[3] & be assured it will give me pleasure to serve you in that or any other respect in my power & that I am with due regard Dear Sir yr Obt & Hble Servt

Leven Powell

ALS, DLC:GW.

1. Letter not found.

2. The Mr. Powell who was at Mount Vernon on 23 July was probably William H. Powell (d. 1802), the oldest son of Leven Powell of Loudoun County. Young Powell had recently opened a general merchandise store in Alexandria.

3. For the continuing correspondence regarding the supply of buckwheat for GW, see GW to Powell, 30 Sept., 21 Dec. 1786, and Powell to GW, 8 April, 18 Dec. 1787.

To Samuel Vaughan

Dr Sir,   Mount Vernon 12th Septr 1786.

A few days ago I had the honor to receive your favor of the 22d ulto.[1]

At the same time that I regret not having had the pleasure of testifying under my own roof the respect & regard I had imbibed for your Lady & family before their departure from this Continent, I beg you to be assured that every wish which I can offer for a short & agreeable passage, & happy meetings with their friends in England, attends them. Although I can now no longer look for the pleasure of the Ladies companies at this seat of my retirement, I will not despair of seeing you at it, when it can be made to comport with your other pursuits. It is unnecessary I persuade myself to repeat the assurances of the pleasure it would give me you, or such of your family as remain in this Country, here, or of the sincere esteem & respect with which I have the honor to be &c.

G: Washington

LB, DLC:GW.

1. Letter not found.

From Charles Lee

Sir   Alexandria Sepr 13. 1786

This is accompanied with instruments of writing which I hope you will find agreeable to your intentions.[1]

Mr Lund Washington is said not to have qualified as exr of

Manley in which case he need not be a party to the deed but I conceive it necessary that he should in open court renounce the execution thereof and that his renunciation should be recorded if already this has not been done—After this the deed of Manleys exrs as drawn by me ought to be executed and not before Mr L. Washington's renunciation—If Mr L. Washington ever did qualify as exr of Manley, he must be a party to the deed.[2]

Mrs Sanford having some time ago qualified as exr it became necessary to make her a party and this occasions her husband to be joined with her in the deed.[3]

One of Manleys children having arrived to full age has not altered the trust.

The lease to Robertson not having been recorded, it is void in law and equity against purchasers without notice, and in the present case void in law if the assignment accepted from Mrs French shall not make it valid, which I think it will do.

The clause in that lease respecting the nonpayment of rent doth not avoid or forfeit the lease, till there be a demand of the rent and an actual reentry for the non payment thereof.

You have by Mrs French's assignment the same power over Robertson that she had. To save trouble I joined in the same deed the assignment of Robertson's lease and the demise of the residue of Mrs French's estate in the plantation & slaves.[4] I have the honor to be with every sentiment of esteem and respect your most obed. hble serv.

Charles Lee

P.S. A blank is left in Triplett and Sanfords deed for the name of the patentee because the deeds to Manley mention Nicholas Spencer and your letter Spencer and Washington which you will please to fill up as may be right. C. Lee

ALS, DLC:GW.

1. The "instruments of writing" are undoubtedly a draft of the deed from Harrison Manley's executors to GW, finally dated and signed on 22 Sept., and a draft of the deed from Penelope Manley French to GW. For GW's efforts to acquire the two French-Dulany tracts on Dogue Run, see George Clinton to GW, 27 Feb. 1784, and GW to Charles Lee, 20 Feb. 1785, and note 1 of that document. See also *Diaries*, 4:84–85, 93, 5:32–33, 37–38, 40, 52, 57, and GW to William Triplett, 25 Sept., and notes. For the locations of the Manley and French-Dulany tracts, see *Diaries*, 1:240.

2. By his will Harrison Manley left his wife Margaret Barry Manley the use

of the estate during her lifetime. Should she remarry, the estate was to be divided equally among herself, her son, John, and her daughters, Sarah, Mary, and Penelope. The will provided, however, that: "If my Executors Should Judge it Proper to Sell or Dispose of any or all my Lands, that they be hereby Authorized to make Sale of all my Lands and the money Arriseing from the above mentioned Lands to be Laid out by my Executors on the Purchase of other Lands or Slaves, or Applyed to such uses as my Executors Shall Judge proper for the Benfett of my Wife and Children." The executors named by Manley were "my Loveing Wife Margret Manley My Brother William Triplett and my Brother Thomas Triplett and my Friend Lund Washington" (Fairfax County Will Book C-1 [1767–76], 215–16, ViFaCt).

3. Harrison Manley's widow Margaret was by this time remarried. Her husband Edward Sanford was a silversmith in Alexandria. The deed transferring the property was signed on 22 Sept. 1786 by William Triplett, Margaret Sanford, and Edward Sanford. The other qualified executor, Thomas Triplett, had died in 1780. GW paid £426 for the land (Fairfax County Deed Book Q [1785–88], 295–98, ViFaCt).

4. John Robertson (died c.1791), a son of James Robertson, Sr. (died c.1769), of Fairfax County, was a tenant on the French-Dulany land that GW was attempting to acquire. GW had received a deed on 21 Feb. 1785 from Benjamin and Elizabeth French Dulany for the two tracts totaling about 552 acres and had in exchange given the Dulanys a deed for approximately 376 acres on a branch of Hunting Creek near Alexandria which he had bought in 1782 for this purpose from Robert Adam, Peter Dow, and Colin McIver (Fairfax County Deed Book P [1784–85], 311–21, ViFaCt). Elizabeth Dulany's mother, Penelope French, was continuing to present obstacles to GW's leasing her own life rights in the property. John Robertson had received on 1 Jan. 1784 a seven-year lease on the land from Mrs. French and Benjamin Dulany, for which he was to pay £136 per annum, including the use of Mrs. French's twenty-four slaves living on the land. GW wanted to obtain not only a lease for Mrs. French's lifetime but also to be assigned the remainder of Robertson's lease. On 18 Oct. 1786 Mrs. French finally signed a deed whereby GW was to pay her £136 per annum for the remainder of Robinson's lease and then £150 per annum for the land and rental of the slaves. She stipulated in the deed that the slaves were not to be removed from the county and were to be well treated (Fairfax County Deed Book Q [1785–88], 392–96, ViFaCt).

From Comtesse d'Anterroche

General,   18th Septr 1786

Fame has informed me that you are the friend of humanity— that your generous heart delights in doing good. I take the liberty to claim your protection for the Chevalier D'Anterroches my son, who is settled in Elizabeth Town, near New York. Altho'

I have no right to make a request of this nature, which is altogether an idea of my own; yet whoever dares to accuse me of imprudence, has never experienced, as you have General, the force of sensibility. If, from the feelings of a heart alive to the misfortunes of others, you deign to give my Son access to you, he will himself have the honor to relate his history to you—a history painful & affecting to a Soul so delicate as your's—You must have the goodness to desire him to come to you, because he is ignorant of my resolution to write to you; & that you may take an interest in him, I dare to assure you General that you will find him an engaging man, a comely man, & a man who can render himself beloved & esteemed; You will be touched with his misfortunes & distresses, and the more, I dare say, as his birth is distinguished in this kingdom, as having descended from a family of military men who have borne high Command—he bears a name well known both in church & State—the D'anterroches have from time immemorial held an elevated rank. For these 12 years my Son has groaned under the weight of Misfortunes, & has thereby given me great pain—the time has appeared long to us both, & we have no prospect of terminating our sufferings unless you lend your aid—It requires an Arm powerful as your's, General, to succour us—I trust in you who are as good as you are great—all the world admires you, & you have only to say the word to change our Condition; I wait for that with the most lively impatience; I already perceive General that the hours of Affliction glide off more gently—but to pass them as those of prosperity, nature will not permit—Alass! who can feel the sufferings of a Child as poignantly as a Mother—my soul, deeply wounded, knows no repose! Restore it to that tranquility which it has lost, & which I perceive is so necessary for it—you will make it compleatly happy if you comply with my earnest prayers—I will not enter into a detail of what concerns my son, he will do it himself if you will permit him; permit him & give him an opportunity, & you shall be informed of every thing.

Mr Otto Charge des Affaires de France in New-York has passed the highest encomiums upon his good behaviour—he can give you, General, the same favourable account of him; all the people of distinction who have seen him in your country speak of him in the same manner—I beseech you to interest yourself so far in him as to give him an existance, whether in America or in France—you can easily do it in either. What would I not do myself to effect what I ask of you—if nothing would procure it but my life I would give that—Altho' my Husband, Good man, loves his son dearly, yet he is so oppressed by Age that he is incapable of doing as he would—he tells me that he wishes him all happiness, & if he could obtain it he should partake of it with him—You have too much penetration not to see all the uneasiness which so long an absence & at so great a distance must have given his friends[1]—You, General, can do what he would have you—you are powerful in your own Country, & there is nothing at our Court that would be refused you—Your own Genius furnishes resources—your penetrating Eye discovers all—you will not suffer my son & his family to suffer longer in your latitude—being once informed of their situation. By applying to the Court of France you may obtain for him a lucrative employment which will make him & his family easy— he will then be induced to return & you will give a son to his Mother, a Citizen to his Country, & enable a man to give aid & succour to his Parents who have much need of it; all this is worthy of you—Take the trouble of conferring with him—I entreat you to compleat my wishes, (if the time is not yet arrived in which I shall have the sweet satisfaction of seeing my son) by succouring & supporting him—&, when he may come to you, by shewing him this letter which is no equivocal proof of my tender sollicitude for him—& may your benefactions cause the tears of Joy & Gratitude to flow instead of those of sorrow which we have shed for 12 years past.[2] I have the Honor to be with respect, General, Yr very humble & obedient Servt.

De chauni Comtisse D'anterroches.

My Address is the Comtisse de Chauni D'Anterroches at her house at Puydarnac near—[3]

If you do me the honor of Answering this, I request you to address to Mr Van Berchem of Nantes in Brittany—a City of France—he is an eminent Merchant, a man of merit & will take care of it for me.

Translation, DLC:GW; LS, in French, DLC:GW; copy, in French, DLC:GW. The signed letter in French is included in CD-ROM:GW. The copy, marked "Dupa," is in another hand, and varies somewhat in spelling of names and some words from the LS.

1. From time to time, the translator takes the liberty of abbreviating what the comtesse wrote. For instance: "You have too much penetration not to see all the uneasiness which so long an absence & at so great a distance must have given his friends" is a translation of: "vous avés trop de pénétration pour ne pas imaginér tout ce qu'une longue absience et un grand èloignement fait pèrdre dans lésprit dès autres parens, lés absiens ont tor. ha. il nen cera pas ainsi d'une mère. pourait-èlle oublier le fruit de cès entrailles, hé, que puis je seule retirée depuis lage de vingt ans dans une campagne, d'ou je nay pas bougé, à sens lieux de la capitale, sens secours, menant une vie privée."

2. Jeanne-Françoise Teyssier (Tessier) de Chauny, comtesse d'Anterroche (d'Anterroches), wife of Jean-Pierre, comte d'Anterroche, renewed her plea to GW on 16 Nov. in these terms: "General, I have already done myself the honor of writing to you in behalf of an unfortunate Son, who resides at Elizabeth Town near N. York—I ardently beg your protection for him General. Suffer a Child to be recommended to you by a distressed mother—For pity, grant him your Countenance. His family, out of their good will towards him, have thought of granting him a small establishment in America, or if he will return to France, a pension—provided that he can come I do not know but it will be best—the objects here may excite his powers. they (his family) will think better of him, & I beleive he will gain much by being in his Country; with your recommendations he would be received by them with open Arms, & if you will take the trouble to recommend him to our Court he will be very happy. You have a soul so sensible that I do not despair of your granting my request—A great man, as you are, loves, & seeks occasions to do good. To give a Son to his mother, a citizen to his Country is an action worthy of you—But how shall I be reunited to this Son? that embarrasses & disturbes me—lighten this weight—reunite him with his Wife & Children. I address myself to heaven for you with eyes bathed in tears of gratitude & with the most ardent & tender vows—change, change my days of tribulation & anguish into days of calmness & serenity—I have no hope but in you, & I do not doubt but you will do every thing to gratify my desires. I imagine that the sending him a sum of money to buy Goods will lead him to think of himself—I have the Honor to be with respect—General—Yr most Hbe & Obedt Servt de chaunae comptess d'anterroches.

"P.S. I would not however take upon myself to bring my son over here unless it is perfectly agreeable to him. I ask your protection for him General—You can do every thing in America, in France & every where" (DLC:GW; a transcription of the ALS, CSmH, is in CD-ROM:GW). She wrote similar pleas for help to Lafayette, Benjamin Franklin, and Thomas Jefferson. Her son Joseph-Louis, chevalier d'Anterroche (1753–1814), came to America in 1777. In 1780 he married Mary Vanderpoel, daughter of David Vanderpoel of Elizabethtown, N.J. (Emeline G. Pierson, "Some Records of the French in Elizabethtown," *Proceedings of the New Jersey Historical Society*, 2d ser., 13 [1895], 163–70).

3. In the original this is: "mon adrèsse èst la comtèsse de chaunac d'anterroches; a son chateau du puydarnac prè tulle bas limousin, par paris et limoges."

From James Rumsey

Dr General   Shepherd town Septr 19th 1786
   When I wrote you from alexandria on the Sixth Inst[1] I was
on my way to the Southward and Did not Return to this place
untill Last Evening which was the Reason you Did not hear from
me Sooner what Suckcess we had in the Experiment I mentioned to you in that Letter that We Expected to have with the
Boat. Mr Barnes got her Readey on Saterday the 9th Inst and
put about three tuns of Stone in her and Could not avoid Take-
ing in nine or ten persons that was waiting To See her Tryed
which made near four tuns on Board, when he Set out, the River
being a Little up was in his favor as it was not naturally Rapid
where tryal was made, he went up about two hundred yards
Greatly to the Satisfaction and Admiration of the Spectators, But
not so to himself, for the following Reasons, first the machinery
Being fixed on But one Boat, Instead of two, as first Intended
prevented her from going So Steady as She Ought To have
Done, the people on Board Shouting and Running Backward
and forward aded much to this Inconvenance, In the next place
the poles, or Shovers, was made of Wood w'th Iron Spikes at
their Lower End, to Sink them, which Spikes proved too Light,
and Caused the poles Very frequently to Slip on the Bottom,
But the Greatest Deterrent was, that when a pole got a good
holt on One Side and not on the Other, it had a Tendencey to
give Her a Heel, which would throw part of the wheel out of
water, which weakned the power, and would often Loosen the
foot of the pole, so as to make it Slip. These Inconvenanceys Mr
Barnes Related to me, they were what I too much Expected
from a tryal with one Boat, But not haveing time, nor yet being
Able to Build another at the present, was therefore Obliged to
Risk the one, It was on wensday on my way Up that I got these
accounts from Mr Barnes, we then went on Board for an Other
Experiment, But the water had got So Lowe that It Did not
move But Little more than Two miles per hour, which by my
Calculations I had caused only sufficient to overcome the fric-
tion of the Machine, we Moved up Slowly for Sum distance during which time two or three persons (acquaintances) Colected
on the Shore and Informed me that many Others would be
Down Very Soon I Therefore thought it Best to put to Shore

and take of[f] Sum of the Macheinery, as the first Impression Received of her going was favourable, the Current then ⟨too Slack⟩ To Impress them again with an Openion that She would make much progress, the Company Came Down and Insisted much on Seeing her go. I Excused myself from it, Altho almost Induced to push up to pains falls which was not far Above us But on Considering the Lightness of our poles and the Strenth of the Current in (that place) I Doubted their Sinking, Besides there is (you know) many Rocks in that place that Lye But Little under water that might Break the wheel, and Spectators Generally give their openion according to what they See, without *any* alowance for Accidents, which Determined me not to attempt It Publicly, nor have I made any farther Experiment Since. It is Evedant from what has Been Done that She would make a tolarable progress in all Currents that is Strait and Clear of Rocks, and moves three miles per hour, or upwards, But will go But Slow in Currents Under that Velocity. It is also Certain that It will never Answer a Valuable purpos Except when put upon two Boats (as it Cannot be Steady on One) In which Case their is not the Least Doubt But it will answer Every purpos that was Ever Expected from it. I Cannot with propriety Expect you to Come to See her in her present Situation, But if you would wish to See he⟨r⟩ Before any alteration is made, and will Let me hea⟨r⟩ It by a Line, I will bring her Down to Sum Conveni⟨ent⟩ place and will Send you word where to Come to See her.[2] I am Sir with great Regard your most abt and Very hbe Servt

James Rumsey

ALS, DLC:GW. On the cover Rumsey wrote "Honourd by Capt. [Abel] Westfall."

1. Rumsey dated his letter from Alexandria 5 Sept., not 6 September.

2. See GW to Rumsey, 31 Jan. 1786, n.1. Joseph Barnes (Barns) of Berkeley County, Rumsey's brother-in-law, built the boats for Rumsey and acted as Rumsey's mechanic.

To Charles Simms

Dear Sir,   Mt Vernon—22d Septr 1786.

I now sit down to avail myself of your friendly offer of serving me whilst you are on your Western tour.

I give you the trouble of some letters. That to Mr Smith I leave open for your perusal. Please to seal before delivering it.[1] Mr Smith has my Patent—Posey's Bond on which my military Right was founded, and on which the Warrant for surveying issued—together with every other publick & private document which could be obtained in evidence of the regularity and legality of my claim. The plea of the Defendants will be, I know, that I cannot trace any steps of regular & authentic proceedings back to their occupancy. For, say they, you can find no entry on the Surveyor's books, nor on the records of Council previous to the survey, which is the first legal process you can adduce; and this is not dated 'till Feby, when our settlement of the land was in the month of October preceeding. Nay more, your warrant of survey, which was laid upon this land, received date in Novr subsequent (by a month) to our settlement. The latter (under the Rose) I believe is the fact, and is as unaccountable, as it may be unlucky, as my purchase from Posey (for the express purpose of covering this Tract) was made, as will appear by the Bond, (if my memory has not deceived me) in the year 1770. This difference, if it is not founded in mistake, is altogether incomprehensible, as the land was explored & surveyed for me the first time, in the fall of 1770, or early in the following year: And this right, as I have before observed, was intended as the legal security of it. The first & second surveys—or in other words the legal return of the first differing in dates, were both made by Captn (afterwards Col.) Crawford. The first was made whilst his Commission was local—given for the express purpose of surveying 200,000 Acres granted by Mr Dinwiddie's proclamation, to the officers & soldiers of the *first* Virga regiment. The second, or as I have before mentioned, the return, was made after he had received a deputation under Mr Thos Lewis for Augusta, in which County the land was supposed to lye—and this I believe, did not happen 'till Feby 1774—consequently the date was made subsequent to the date of the deputation.

Upon these grounds, *my legal title*, I am convinced will be disputed, with a view to establish their Occupancy; but there is an Act (an authentic copy of which I have sent Mr Smith) which legalizes the surveys of Crawford from the period he first held a Commission from the College.[2] But for Arguments sake, supposing my Patent, & every thing which led to the obtainment

were mere nullities: and my military claim out of the question—
had I not an equal right with any other Citizen or subject to
obtain land in that Country? It cannot be laid to my charge that
I have been either a monopolizer or a Land-Jobber, for I never
sold a foot of land in the Country, nor am I possessed of an acre
West of the Alligany (and the quantity comparatively speaking,
is small) that I do not hold under military rights, except the
Tract at what is called Washington's bottom, and about 2 or 300
Acres at the Great Meadows; both of which I purchased. The
latter at a high price—And that I surveyed this land before the
Defendts ever saw it, built one or more Cabbins thereon before
they came into the Country; hired people to live on it, gave them
repeated notices of my right at their first coming, & warnings
afterwards of the consequences of their usurpations, are facts;
but whether evidence can *now* be obtained in support of all of
them, is questionable; as the two Crawfords who were my principal agents in that Country, are both dead; others knowing to the
transactions, removed; and a third set unwilling, I have no
doubt, to come forward. Yet, under all these disadvantages,
Charles Morgan will be able (or I am mistaken) to prove that the
survey was made a year or two before the Defendts pretend any
claim to occupancy (the date of which requires better proof than
their assertion)—and I think he is the most likely person to
prove also that there were Cabbins erected thereon for my benefit—claims, antecedent to those of the Defendts purchased by
Crawford on my accot to avoid disputes—A man hired to live
on the land to keep others off it—and that frequent notices were
given to them of the lands being mine, & admonishing them to
quit it. Marcus Stephenson must be knowing to many, if not all,
of these curcunstances, but a spell of sickness I have been told
has impaired his memory, and may have rendered him an unfit
evidence. Major Lite, & George McCormick, or the Brother who
married Colo. Crawfords Daughter, cannot, I should think be
unacquainted with many of these facts.[3] There can be no question of Colo. Cannon's testifying to what I have recited in my
letter to Mr Smith, because I had the information from his own
mouth, & he is a Gentleman of Credit. I should think it strange
indeed, if Colo. Jno. Stephenson from his intimacy & connection
with Colo. Crawford, is not privy to most of these things—possibly Mrs Crawford may be as strong an evidence to some points

as any one—Captn Swearingin also seemed to have knowledge of them.

The reason of my being so particular with you, my good Sir, is, that if any of these people should fall in your way, & upon enquiry it shall be found that they possess the knowledge I conceive of these transactions, but are unwilling to come forward, that effectual steps may be taken to compel them. There is reason to apprehend that an oath *only* will extort from *some of them* all they do know. Colo. Cannon, Chas Morgan, Marcus Stephenson (if he has recollection enough), & perhaps Majr Lite, must be more intimately acquainted with Colo. Crawfords proceedings on my behalf in the early stages of this business, than any others. Morgan or Lite surveyed the Land; M. Stephenson carried the chain, &, I believe made the improvements. What G. McCormick & Captn Swearingin can say in the case, I know not—both I believe would willingly serve me, & would point out if they are acquainted with them, the evidences that may be essential on the tryal if it shall be found necessary for me to attack on this ground.[4]

The enclosure No. 2 contains some queries which were put to Mr Smith, but not answered—tho' touched upon by him as appears by his letter No. 3. I will thank you for doing what shall seem necessary in this business. There is an open Accot between Vale Crawford & me, by which it appears that he is about £100— in my debt. Conscious of this, & of my engagements for him— unsollicited, he wrote me the letter & sent me the Bill of sale referred to in my letter to Mr Smith of the 8th of May last, & now in his trust.[5]

My Lands in Pennsylvania (west of the Laurel-hill) have been so unproductive of every thing but vexation and trouble, that I am resolved to sell them at long or short credit, as may best suit the purchaser, provided I can get near the value of them. The tract where the Mill is, lying in Fayette County, & commonly called Washington's bottom, contains about 1650 acres. The one in dispute, lying in Washington County, contains about 2,800 acres. The defendants were a long time deliberating on eligibility of giving me 25/ pr acre, rather than to engage in a Law Suit; but finally chose the latter: they must give more now if I oust[6] them. Should you hear of any purchasers, or if you could discover the price it is probable obtain for them, you would render me a service by the communication. Inclosed are several advertisements—one of which I pray you to have set up at the Court Houses of the County in which the Lands lie—at Pittsburgh, and at such other places as you may think best.[7]

I give you the trouble of proving (I believe before a Magistrate) the power of attorney which I have executed before you, and to send it with my letter inclosed to Major Thomas Freeman who does business for me in that county.[8]

I paid Mr Smith, at the time the Ejectments were brought, some where about £20. If you could by indirect or other means, discover what would be proper compensation for his trouble in this business, I should be much obliged by it. I have had in the course of my life, so little to do with Law & Lawyers, that I feel myself extreamly awkward in these matters.[9] With sentiments of great esteem & regard I am Dr Sir &c.

G: Washington

L (incomplete), DLC:GW; LB, DLC:GW. The incomplete copy, in the hand of Tobias Lear who had recently become GW's secretary, comprises the first three paragraphs printed here; the remainder is taken from the letter-book copy.

During the Revolution Charles Simms moved from the Pittsburgh area to Alexandria, where he was practicing law in 1786.

1. GW's letter to Thomas Smith is also dated 22 September.

2. The background to the Millers Run ejectment suits, which Thomas Smith tried for GW in Washington County, Pa., on 24–26 Oct. 1786, is given in the editorial note, Thomas Smith to GW, 9 Feb. 1785.

3. Major Lite is undoubtedly Daniel Leet (1748–1830) who had a commission as an assistant surveyor of Yohogania County under William Crawford. His designation "Major" probably came from his acting as brigade major to Crawford's ill-fated expedition against the Indians in 1782.

4. For the identity of these men and their relationship to GW, see Thomas Smith to GW, 9 Feb. 1785, and notes.

5. GW made his "queries" regarding Valentine Crawford's debt in his letter to Thomas Smith on 8 May 1786, and Smith's response came in his missing letter of 9 Aug. 1786 (see GW to Smith, 22 Sept.). For Valentine Crawford's debt to GW, see GW to Smith, 8 May 1786, n.1.

6. The copyist wrote "cost."

7. Following the letter to Charles Simms in GW's letter book is this "Copy of an Advertisement": "The Subscriber would sell his land in Fayette County, State of Pennsylvania, containing about 1650 acres—distinguished, commonly, by the name of Washington's Bottom.

"Also, About 2800 acres on Miller's run, a branch of Shirtee, in Washington Coty & State aforesaid, if the Ejectments now depending are decided in his favor.

"The credit may be long or short according to the price given.

"To describe these Lands is needless, as the presumption, & wish of the proprietor is, that those who incline to purchase, would examine them well.

"Majr Thos Freeman will show the land in Fayette County; & Majr Geo: McCormick the other tract. G: W——n" (DLC:GW). The advertisement is dated "Virginia 22d Septr 1786."

8. See GW to Tobias Lear, 30 Nov. 1786, n.6.

9. See GW to Tobias Lear, 30 Nov. 1786, n.11.

To Thomas Smith

Sir   Mount Vernon Septr 22d 1786.

The letter which you did me the favor of writing to me from Philadelphia the 9th Ulto came duly to hand.[1]

A fever, of which I am but just well recovered, makes me fearful of encountering the bad roads & disagreeable accommodations between this & the Western Country at this season. Other circumstances too, rendering it inconvenient for me to be from home at this time, have combined, to set aside the Journey I had it in contemplation to make to the Court of Nisi-prius to be holden in Washington County, State of Pennsylvania, on the 23d of next month. Nor, upon a revision of the notes with which I have furnished you, do I see wherein I could add aught to them were I to be present at the Tryal. The summoning of a Jury so long before the merits of the Cause will come *legally* before it, is, in my opinion, very much against me; for there can be no doubt but that every indirect (if not direct) means which the Defendts & their friends can adopt will be used to impress the members who constitute it with all the circumstances favourable to their claims. However, if it is an event to be regretted, it is equally unavoidable, as it is constitutional.

There were proclamations (as I have observed upon a former occasion) and Orders of Council in this State, previous to the Revolution, which, could they have been adduced, might have subserved my cause, as much as it would have appeared from them that tho' military rights were recognized, and warrants of survey were actually issued by the Executive previously to the occupancy of the Defendts, yet, that their settlement of the lands which were considered as appertaining to the State of Virginia was expressly contrary to a pointed proclamation, & consequently must not only have been illegal, but highly unwarrantable, as it was an invasion of private right (for the Defendts do not deny having been informed that the land was surveyed for me) as well as a contempt of publick Authority; however, the records of these proceedings are lost, as you will find by the authenticated certificate which has been heretofore sent you.

My opinion of the case, as I have mentioned in a former letter, is, that the *legal* title ought to be strenuously insisted upon: and that the Deed, as it was the last solemn act of the Government should be considered as conclusive evidence of the regularity of the antecedent proceedings; it being a fact well known in this Country, that by the removal of the records from Williamsburgh, whilst the Enemy were manœuvering in the state, many of them were lost or destroyed. To argue otherwise is to arraign the Conduct of the Government in the management of our internal policy; And I do not know under or by what authority the State of Pensylvania can *now* after having made a solemn compact with this State, by which she engages to confirm all legal & established titles, go into such an enquiry. But if notwithstanding, from the complexion of matters it should be conceived that the plea of preoccupancy is likely to have weight, I would *then*, as if to shew that *even on that ground* the Defendts stand hindmost, call evidence to prove that the land was surveyed for me before they came into the Country—That a Cabbin, if no more, (for one remained in 1784) was built on the land before they ever saw it—That Colo. Cannon had fixed himself thereon before them, but discovering traces of a regular survey, & upon enquiry, finding it was made for me, quit it, after having done some work thereon—That the Defendts were also told that the land belonged to me (whilst they were in the act of settling upon it)—and were repeatedly informed of it afterwards, and admonished by publick notices & private intimations of the hazard they ran, as I was determined (as soon as my publick duty would allow me to attend to my private concerns) to assert my right to the land. These all are indubitable facts; but where the evidences are, or by what means they can be drawn forward to prove them, are questions which I am unable to solve, unless Colo. Crawford's letters will be admitted, & those persons whom I have named in the notes formerly sent you, will make them appear.[2]

As I have confided this Cause entirely to your management, I should, if Mr Ross's abilities had not spoke so powerfully in his favour, have been perfectly well pleased at your choice of him as a Coadjutor. With talents such as you describe, I cannot but be highly satisfied therewith.[3]

My Friend Colo. Simm, who will do me the favor of presenting this letter to you, is called to the Western Courts in your State on some business of his own. He perfectly understands the Laws of this State—the practices of our Courts—and the principles of our Land-Office—and may be able to communicate much useful information. You may place entire confidence in him: safely trusting him with all the communications I have made to you, & with a sight of the papers if he should incline to see them.[4]

I am much obliged to you for the information respecting the bill of sale from Val[entin]e Crawford. At the time of my writing to you on this business I was quite ignorant of the Agency you had in the matter on behalf of another, the declaration of which will, I hope, be an apology for my application to you in a case where you were Council for another. I have requested the favor of Colo. Simm to do, or cause to be done what shall appear just & proper in this case—To secure my debt is all the inducement I have for resorting to the Bill of Sale.[5]

I ought, my good Sir, to have recollected the trouble you have had in this Business 'ere this, and I intended to have compensated it out of the funds I had in that Country; but in truth, they have been very unproductive—however, if you will be so obliging as to inform me by Colo. Simm with *what* sum I can equal your expectations I will resort to other means to lodge it in Philadelphia for you. With very great esteem & regard I am Sir Yr Most Obedt Hble Servt

Go: Washington

LS, in Tobias Lear's hand, NhD; LB, DLC:GW.

1. Letter not found.

2. See Thomas Smith to GW, 9 Feb. 1785, and notes, particularly the editorial note; but see also GW to Smith, 14 July, 10 Sept., 7 Dec. 1785, 8 May, 28 July 1786, and Smith to GW, 17 Nov. 1785, 7 Feb. 1786. Lear wrote "personos" for "persons."

3. James Ross assisted Smith at the trial in October 1786, and in 1788 GW paid him £50 for his services, the same fee that he paid Smith (Ledger B, 259).

4. See GW to Charles Simms, this date.

5. See GW to Simms, this date, n.4.

To Clement Biddle

Dr Sir,   Mount Vernon 23d Septr 1786.

It is sometime since my window curtains were sent to you to get dyed; I should be glad to have them back as soon as an opportunity offers of forwarding them to me. Let me beg you to send by Mr Porter, (who will deliver you this letter) if he can bring it, or with the curtains if he cannot—16 yards of Stuff of the same kind & colour of the curtains, to cover two dozen chairs, the front of which will require cloth near 2½ feet wide, & the hinder part near two feet: this I fear is wider than that kind of Stuff generally is, but it is to be hoped that the gores which come off the latter, will be sufficient for the former.[1]

Do the prices of the articles mention'd in my former letter still keep up? I pray you to cause the enclosed Advertisement to be published three weeks in one of your Gazette's which has the most general circulation.[2] With great esteem, I am Dr Sir &c.

G: Washington

P.S. Add if you please 3500 good brass nails for the chairs.

LB, DLC:GW.

   1. GW wrote Biddle about the curtains on 18 August. Biddle wrote GW on 15 Oct. that he was sending the dyed curtains and additional material to the care of Thomas Porter of Porter & Ingraham in Alexandria.

   2. See GW to Charles Simms, 22 Sept., n.6.

From James Tilghman

Dear & honred Sir   Chester Town [Md.] Sept 23d 1786

I yesterday received your favour of the 2d of this month which came in time to stop the transmissal of your Paragraph relating to Capt. Asgils confinement I had not met with any opportunity proper for the Conveyance of it And you may relye on its not being known to any person living but myself.

Miss Anderson furnished me with a letter from Mr John West to Mr Hollyday, which may afford you some insight in this matter of the Legacy by Col. Colvilles will I send you a Copy.[1] I am with much respect yr most obt hble Servt

James Tilghman

ALS, DLC:GW.

1. Tilghman wrote GW on 7 July about Harriot Anderson and her need for her legacy from the Thomas Colvill estate. For references to the earlier correspondence about Miss Anderson and her legacy, which includes a letter to GW from her uncle Henry Hollyday, of 30 April 1785, see Tilghman to GW, 7 July, n.2. The enclosed letter to Hollyday, dated 7 Feb. 1776, was from John West, Jr., another trustee of the Colvill estate (DLC:GW).

From James Hill

Sir   King William Sepr 24th 1786

Your favor of the 29th August came to my hands a few days ago, & in answer thereto, I have long since closed all my Accots respecting such of your Business as had been committed to my Care & delivered up the Books & papers to Mr posey & the late Bartho. Dandridge Esqrs it is now out of my power to comply with your request, The first Book in which I kept the Accounts of Mr Custis's Estate, as well as yours, I delivered to Mr Posey when he first took Possession & entered on the Management of that Estate, and I then procured another Book for the purpose of keeping your Accounts, but when I was called on early in the year 1779 by Mr Posey to bring my Transactions of your business in Mr Davenports & my care to a close, I directed Mr Davenport to Accot with Mr Posey & I did the same on my part. and having paid such sums of Money that came into my hands of yours to him, that Book with some Vouchers remained in my hands until a Settlement was about to take place Between Mr Dandridge & Mr Posey, when Mr Dandridge wrote to me for this Book & all the papers in my hands which I delivered to him in presence of Mr James Quarles.[1]

With respect to Mr Newton I never received a Shilling of him that I recollect on your Accot. it appears by my Pocket Memo. Book that he gave me an Order on one Jacob Williams in Williamsburg for £180—on your Accot which I received at two paymts the first £50—the 12th day of Augt 1778 which I paid the same day to Mr Lund Washington in Williamsburg. and the Second £130—the 3rd day July 1779 which I also paid the same day to Mr posey.[2] I am with respect your mo. Obdt Servt

James Hill

ALS, DLC:GW.

1. For GW's letter to John Price Posey, manager of John Parke Custis's lands, instructing him to wind up GW's business affairs which had been in the hands of Hill and Joseph Davenport, see Posey to GW, 27 Jan. 1787, n.2. James Quarles was probably one of the several men of that name who lived at Woodbury in King William County, and he may have been the James Quarles who served as a captain in the 2d Virginia State Regiment during the Revolution. James Quarles was the clerk who made the copy of Hill's accounts enclosed in his letter of 1 Feb. 1787 to GW (see note 1 of that document).

2. Jacob Williams, a baker, was listed in 1782 as head of a household of six whites and two blacks in the borough of Norfolk. In GW's account with Lund Washington, Lund recorded £50 credited "To Jacob Williams in part of a Debt contracted by Mr Thos Newton for Flour Sold at Norfolk & left with Mr Hill to Collect" (Ledger B, 154). In his accounts with GW (see note 1), Hill recorded on 2 July 1779 the payment of £130 received from Williams and paid to Posey. Posey's letter of 27 Jan. 1787 to GW mentions this last payment.

From David Humphreys

My dear General, Hartford [Conn.], Septr 24th 1786

I had the pleasure, before I left New York, to receive your favor containing the enclosures respecting Asgil's affair, and am taking measures for their publication[1]—Interested, as I feel myself in your wellfare & happiness, I could not but be extremely affected by the account of your ill-health; and beg you will let me know in what condition your health is, as I shall not find myself at ease until I hear of its re-establishment.

Not having found in my journey Genl Knox, (who was at the eastward) or any of our particular friends, with whom I might converse unreservedly on the subject of the Cincinnati; I have delayed writing to you until I could have an opportunity of advising with Colo. Trumbull, Colo. Wadsworth & Mr Trumbull of this town—and now I have to inform, that it is their unanimous sentiment, it would not be of any good consequence, or even advisable for you to attend the next General Meeting. Agreeably to your desire in this case, I forward you the draft of a circular letter, of which you will, of course, My dear General, make such use as you shall judge most expedient, either by altering, suppressing, or communicating it. I am sensible the subject is a very delicate one, that it will be discussed by posterity as well as by the present age, and that you have much to lose & nothing to gain by it in their estimation—Under this persuasion, caution was the primary point, & it has consequently been the object to avoid as much as possible, every thing that will be obnoxious to censure on the part of the public as well as of the Society. Whatever communication is made, it ought to have the property of a two-edged weapon, & to cut both ways.[2] We have had a State Meeting at New Haven since my return, in which, I found there was no disposition to adopt the Institution as altered and amended—I moved therefore to postpone the discussion until after the next General Meeting, this was unanimously carried, and they appointed Genl Parsons, Col. Wadsworth, Mr Pomeroy, Dr Styles (Presidt of the College) & myself their Delegates. Having learnt it was wished & expected the General Meeting would be holden at New York, I have ventured to propose that place accordingly.[3]

As to the subject of politics, they wear so unpleasing an aspect, I hardly dare enter into a disquisition of them. You will have seen by the public papers that every thing is in a state of confusion in the Massachusetts. Our freind Cobb, who is both a General of Militia & a judge of the Court in the County where he resides, is much celebrated for having said, "he would die as a General, or sit as a Judge." This was indeed a patriotic sentiment. His firmness in principles, & example in conduct effected a suppression of the mob—but the Court was adjourned in consequence of the Governor's order. I have just now seen an account of the tumults in New Hampshire: Genl Sullivan has behaved nobly, & put a period to a very considerable insurrection, without the effusion of blood.[4] Rhode Island continues in a state of phrenzy & division on account of their paper currency. A useful example to such of their neighbours as wish to profit by it. This State, which seems rather more tranquil & better disposed than those before mentioned, has had an election of representatives for the Assembly since my arrival. More gentlemen lately belonging to the Army, have been elected than on any former occasion. Amongst these are Genl Huntington, Colos. Wadsworth, Wyllys, Bradly, myself, & many others who may be personally unknown to you. But what appears most singular & proves some revolution of sentiment, is, that Major Judd, who 3 years ago was driven by an armed Mob out of the town to which he belonged on account of commutation, should now have a seat in the Assembly from the same town.[5]

The Assembly will sit at New Haven, through the months of Octr & Novr at which place, I request you will advise me of the receipt of this letter. Colo. Trumbull is in town & desires to be presented most affectionately to yourself, Mrs Washington & the family at Mt Vernon. For myself, having wrote a poem expressive of the satisfaction I experienced in my residence there, & having since been told by some better judges than myself, it is not destitute of merit, I take the liberty of offering a Copy & wish it may be acceptable to my amiable & dear friends under your roof[6]—they are entitled to all my gratitude for their hospitality & freindship—to you, My dear Genl, I need only say that no one is more entirely & sincerely devoted than your faithful friend & hble Servt

D: Humphreys

ALS, DLC:GW.

1. See GW to Humphreys, 1 Sept., and Humphreys to GW, 16 Nov. 1786.

2. GW's circular letter of 31 Oct. 1786 to the Society of the Cincinnati, setting the triennial General Meeting of the Society in Philadelphia in May 1787 and announcing both his intention not to attend and his unwillingness to continue as president, is printed below.

3. Humphreys was present at the General Meeting in 1784 when under GW's prodding the society's Institution, or constitution, was "altered and amended." Samuel Holden Parsons, who was elected a delegate, did not attend the meeting in 1784. Ralph Pomeroy (1737–1816) reached the rank of lieutenant in the Continental army before retiring in 1781. Only Humphreys and Parsons attended the Cincinnati meeting in Philadelphia in May 1787. See also Jeremiah Wadsworth's letter to GW of 1 October.

4. Except for Henry Lee's allusion to "the temper of the eastern people" on 8 Sept., this is the first reference in GW's surviving correspondence to the disturbances in Massachusetts which were to erupt in Shays' Rebellion in the winter. GW's main informants about developments in Massachusetts during the winter were Congress's secretary of the army, Gen. Henry Knox, and the leader of the Massachusetts forces raised to put down the insurrection, Gen. Benjamin Lincoln. Henry Lee, Jr., also wrote GW regularly from Congress about developments. David Cobb, formerly one of GW's military aides, was at this time a major general in the Massachusetts militia and a judge of the court of common pleas in Bristol County. Others have improved on Humphreys' version of Cobb's statement when threatened by the insurrectionists: "I will sit as a judge, or I will die as a general."

5. Jedediah Huntington (1743–1818), a Harvard graduate and a merchant in Norwich, Conn., who was made a brigadier general in the Continental army in 1777, was one of the committee of four who drew up the Institution of the Society of the Cincinnati in 1783. Samuel Wyllys (d. 1823) served in a number

of Connecticut units during the Revolution and was colonel of the 3d Connecticut Regiment when he retired in January 1781. Philip Burr Bradley retired as colonel of the 1st Connecticut Regiment in January 1781. William Judd until 1781 was a captain in the 3d Connecticut Regiment.

6. One of the twelve stanzas of Humphreys' "Mount Vernon: An Ode" in *Miscellaneous Works*, 223–25, reads:

> Let others sing his deeds in arms,
> A nation sav'd, and conquest's charms:
> Posterity shall hear,
> 'Twas mine, return'd from Europe's courts,
> To share his thoughts, partake his sports,
> And soothe his partial ear.

From Benjamin Lincoln, Jr.

Sir   Boston Sep. 24 1786

Enclosed is one of two Bills sent on to my father by your Excellency to be handed to the Agent of Dr Gorden. This was done immediately on the receipt of them and Mr Mason the agent forwarded the first directly to the drawers for acceptance of payment. Being altogether in the paper money system of that State they were willing to discharge the draught in that currency but in no other. Many efforts have been made to perswade them to be honest and honourable but to no purpose. It was with difficulty that a protest could be obtained and it was finally taken by a Justice of the Peace who appears to be quite a stranger to the business. My father being obliged to be much absent left this business to my care. I wish it was in my power to render your Excellency a more agreeable account of it.

I requested the agent to give me a receipt for the bills. He was unwilling to do this being uncertain as to their payment and in expectation every day of either receiving the monies or the bills protested. He was finally obliged in order to have the matter closed to attend to the business in person.[1] I have the honour to be with the highest respect your Excellencys most obedient servant

Benj. Lincoln Jun.

ALS, DLC:GW.

Benjamin Lincoln, Jr. (1756–1788), the eldest of six sons and five daughters, was an attorney at law in Boston. General Lincoln wrote GW on 9 and 20 Jan. 1788 of his son's final illness and death on 17 January.

1. On 20 April and again on 7 June 1786, GW sent Benjamin Lincoln bills of exchange for £42 sterling drawn by Josiah Watson & Co. of Alexandria on the Rhode Island firm Cromel & Caleb Child. This was the amount collected in Virginia by subscription to William Gordon's proposed history of the American Revolution, about two-thirds collected in Alexandria and the rest in Fredericksburg. The proceeds were to be paid to the agent of William Gordon, whom GW assumed had already sailed for England, and Gordon's agent, Jonathan Mason, was to give GW a receipt for the amount. After receiving from Benjamin Lincoln, Jr., the protested bill, GW had Josiah Watson draw another set of bills which GW sent to young Lincoln. See GW to William Gordon, 20 April, and to Benjamin Lincoln, Jr., 9 November.

To William Triplett

Sir,   Mount Vernon 25th Septr 1786.

If Mr Lund Washington has not misconceived the conversation which passed between you & me the day you lay ill in bed; or if you understood the matter in the same light he seems to have done, I find there is another mistake between us respecting Mrs French's land, which it behooves me to clear up as soon as possible.[1]

He thinks you asked me if I meant to take the Land for the term of robinson's lease; and that I answered yes. If such a question, & such an answer passed, we must some how or other have been at cross purposes; for clear & evident it might be, even to yourself, that I could have no intention of being concerned with the land at all, unless it was for Mrs French's life. You may well recollect Sir, that I declared this in explicit terms in the conversation I had with you at my own house, & assigned reasons for it to you—namely—that if I got this and Mr Manley's Land, it was my intention to blend them & my other plantations together, & to form entire new ones out of the whole; that I meant to go into an entire new course of cropping, & would lay off my fields accordingly in a permanent & lasting form by Ditches & Hedges; & that it was for this reason I was desireous of knowing this fall (before I went into such arrangement & expence) whether I had any chance of getting these places or not, because it might be too late afterwards to make any change in my plan. With this object in view, I must have been insane to have taken the plantation for the remainder of Robinson's lease only; first, because it is uncertain whether I could get possession of the land

or not, never having exchanged a word with Robinson on the
subject, nor never intending to do it unless I had got the place
to myself entirely; and, secondly, if I did, because I should not
probably be able to compleat the plan of enclosures by the time
the Lease would expire. What situation should I be in then? A
new bargain under every disadvantage to make, or go back to
my former grounds?

In the latter case all my labour & expence would have been
thrown away & my whole plan defeated. In the former (that is
supposing Robinson could not be got off by fair means, and Mr
Lee is of opinion, which opinion I had in my pocket at the time
I call'd upon you in expectation of meeting Mrs French that
without a regular demand of rent & reentry, which might be a
tedious & expensive process in Courts, the Lease cannot be set
aside)—under these circumstances I say, I should have made
myself liable for the payment of Robinson's rent, without deriv-
ing a single advantage. Will any body think this reasonable; or
suppose that whilst I retain my senses, I would do it?

As I do not recollect that in the course of my life I ever forfeited my word, or broke a promise made to any one, I have
been thus particular to evince (if you understand the matter in
the same light that Lund Washington did) that I was not attending to, or did not understand the question.

I am sorry any mistake has happened, & to convince you &
Mrs French that through the whole of this business, I meant to
act upon fair, open & honorable grounds, I will, as mistakes have
taken place, & as there is a difference of opinion respecting the
annual value of the Lands & negroes, leave it to any person of
her own choosing (Major Little if she pleases) to say, whether
the rent after the expiration of Robinson's lease shall be £136 or
£150 pr ann: if he thinks one too much & the other too little,
any sum between. Mrs French has declared that she neither
wanted, nor would take more than the intrinsic worth of the
place. I on the word of a man of honor declare that I do not
desire it for a farthing less than the value; for to make money
by it was never my object; but we differ in our sentiments of this.
Is there any mode then so fair, as for an impartial person to see
the place, and to hear what Mrs French, or you in her behalf &
myself will say on the subject, & then to decide according to his
best judgment from the facts? And can there be anything more

favourable to her wishes than to have this determined by her friend in whom she places, I presume, implicit confidence? I never exchanged a word directly nor indirectly with Major Little on the subject; but believing him to be a gentleman who will decide according to the dictates of his judgment, I am not afraid to entrust the matter to him, notwithstanding the family connexion between him & Mrs French.[2] In a word, I am so conscious of the rectitude of my intentions in the whole of this business, that it is a matter of the most perfect indifference to me, to whom it is left; and tho' it may be supposed I have some sinister views in saying it, yet without the gift of prophecy, I will venture to pronounce, that if Mrs French misses me as a Tenant, she will repent, long before Robinson's Lease expires, for having done so: for I can assure her from an experience of more than twenty five years that there is a very wide difference between getting Tenants & getting rents. She may get a dozen of the first (& I have not the smallest doubt but she may); but if there is one among them who (having no other dependence than the produce of the Plantation) who will pay her the latter without hard working & pinching her negroes, & a great deal of trouble & vexation to her, I shall be more mistaken than I ever was in any thing of the kind in my life.

This may not appear so to her at first view; because it is but too common to compare things without attending enough to the circumstances of them. I have no doubt but that Mrs French thinks it very strange that I should receive £120 a year rent from Mr Dulany, & scruple to give her £150 for rather more land, and twenty odd negroes: but has she considered that the one is accompanied by no charge except the land tax, & the other with many & heavy ones?[3] And do not every body who have Meadows, & have ever made an estimate of their value, know that an acre of tolerable good grass will pay all the expences of cutting, curing & stacking, & will put at least 40/ in the owner's pocket annually? What then has Mr Dulany to do more than to keep up his fences to pay the rent? By his Advertisement of pasturage for Horses at 3/ pr week he has [   ] acres.[4] Suppose it [   ] only the Meadow alone without a single hand, will yield him at least [   ] pr ann. Is there a single acre of land on Mrs French's plantation, from which, (besides cropping, so precarious) this is to be expected? Is there a single acre which can be converted into meadow? Is not the Land much worn, greatly exhausted & gullied in many places? None can deny it. But why need I enumerate or dwell on these things? Have I not put the matter upon as fair a footing as a man possibly can do? If Mrs French wants no more than the value, as she has declared, what objection can she have to Majr Little's saying what that value is? If this proposition is acceded to the sooner it is communicated to me the better. I have never yet opened my mouth to Robinson on the subject of his Lease, nor never intended to do it unless I had got the Plantation for Mrs French's life. When I sent the papers to Mr Lee to draw the writings, I asked his opinion of the lease which he gave, to the effect already mentioned.[5]

It was for my private satisfaction I asked it, for as I told you before & now repeat, I never had an intention to get him off otherwise than by fair means, this year or any other. This year will convince him, or I am mistaken, that his inevitable ruin (if he has any thing to loose) will follow his holding it another year, if it is not the case already. With esteem, I am Sir &c.

G: Washington

LB, DLC:GW.

William Triplett (1730–1803) was the elder son of Thomas (d. 1737) and Sarah Harrison Triplett (1708–1785). After Thomas Triplett's death, his widow married John Manley, and among her children by this second marriage were Penelope Manley French, Sarah Manley Little, and Harrison Manley. William Triplett lived at Round Hill, built on the part of the original Harrison patent inherited by his mother. He and his brother Thomas Triplett (1732–1780) furnished labor and materials for construction of many of the buildings in the lower part of Fairfax County. In 1758 William Triplett did some remodeling on the Mount Vernon mansion house and in 1760 built two dependencies "in the Front of my House . . . and running Walls for Pallisades to them from the Great house & from the Great House to the Wash House and Kitchen also" (*Diaries*, 1:258). See also *Papers, Colonial Series*, 5:390–91, 328–29, 449–50, 6:19–20.

1. For the French-Dulany land, see Charles Lee to GW, 13 Sept., and notes 1 and 4 of that document.

2. Col. Charles Little (1744–1813) of Cleesh was married to Mrs. French's sister Mary Manley Little.

3. GW drew up, probably at this time, the following memorandum (AD, DLC:GW): "Estimate of the cost of Mrs French's Land and Negroes on Dogue Creek—compared with the produce by which it will be seen what the Tenant is to expect

Rent   <u>£136. 0. 0</u>

Cloathing. 4 Men & 6 Women—viz.

60 Ells best Germn Oznbgs @ 16d.		£ 4. 0. 0
50 yds best Cotton	2/6	6. 5. 0
10 pair of Shoes	6/	3.
Repairing do at least		1.
10 pair plaid Stockings	2/6	1. 5.

Blankets—Suppose 5 only in the year for the whole 23 Negroes
     @ 10/   <u>2.10.</u>

     18. 0. 0

13 Young Negroes will cost at least half what is here charged for
     the old ones—but it shall be set down at 1/3 only   <u>6.</u>

     24.

Feeding—23 Negroes—viz.—

3 Barls of Corn each, comes to 69 Barrl and this @ 12/6 is	43. 2. 6
Fish—say 10 Barrls @ 15/	7.10. 0
Meat now and then—suppose 500 weight in all @ 30/	7.10.
Milk, fat, &ca cannot be had without cost—but say nothg	

     <u>58. 2. 6</u>

Doctr—Suppose one is called only 6 times a year—the visits alone, without Medicine, will cost	6. 0. 0
Midwife—twice a year is the least	1. 0.
Taxes—Of the Land (this may be reduced to a certainty, but as I do not know what the assessment is) I will call it only £10	10. 0. 0
10 Working hands—and the Over[see]r @ 20/	11. 0. 0
13 Young Negroes @ 10/	6.10. 0

     27.10. 0

Levies—County & Parish—mine last year was 37 lbs. of Tobo pr
     Poll—11 of these is 407 lbs. wch @ 16/8 prC. comes to   <u>3. 7.10</u>

Horses. This Plantation will require at least 6 for Plowing—These
     if good cannot be bought for less than £12 a piece which comes
     to £72 the interest for which cannot be less than 10 pr Ct be-
     cause by accidents & natural decay you cant calculate upon their
     services more if so much as 7 yrs—10 pr Ct then comes to   7. 4. 0

Feeding these horses will require at least 6 Barrls of Corn for
     each—this amounts to 36 Barls—@ 12/6—is   22. 0. 0

Plows, Cart, & their gears will cost at least—£4 pr Ann.   <u>4. 0. 0</u>

     33. 4. 0

Tools for the Negroes—these are generally estimated at 20 a hand   10.

Smiths & Carpenters Work will, I should suppose, amt to at least
     £4 pr ann.   4. 0.

Wheat for Sowing. Suppose 80 Acres—or 100,000 Cornhills;
     which is as much as 10 hands (6 of them breeding Women can
     attend) to be laid down in Wheat—this will take 80 Bls of
     Seed— @ 5/— comes to   20. 0.

Overseers Wages—&ca

If he is worth having, and standing wages is given to him his
price will not be less than £35 pr ann. If he receives part of the
Crop it will be a deduction from the produce below—on the
credit side   35. 0.
Meat for Do not less than 500 lbs. @ 30/   7.10.
Corn—at least 5 Barls— if a family perhaps a great deal more but
call it 5 Barls only at 2/6   3. 2. 6
                                                                           45.12.
                                                                          368.16.

note, Besides the above expenditures which are certain, and unavoidable, there are many others, such, as Harvesting which will
only be thought of as they occur, but wch, nevertheless, will be
drawbacks.

now, let us see what it is probable this plantation will produce
annually. Wheat & Corn, or Corn & Tobacco are the usual
Crops. Where all 3 are attempted—the whole I believe, are generally injured and the profit not greater unless the expence in
harvesting the wheat is done by hired hands
80 Acres of Corn, or 100,000 Corn hills for a gang chiefly composed of breeding women will, it is presumed be thought full
enough. this at 2½ Barrls to the 1000 wch I am sure is more
than the Land will yield makes 250 Bls—@ 12/6 is   156. 5.
80 Acres, or 100,000 Corn hills in Wheat at 7 bushls to the Acre
(more than anybody in this Neighbourhood gets) is 560
Bushls—This at 5/— comes to   140.
                                  or
Instead of Wheat, suppose Tobo is made, 1200 lbs. a share it is
presumed is as much as can be expected—This wd be 12
Hhds—@ 20/—wd be £120.
                          amt of Crops   £296. 5.
                          Loss to the Tenant   72.11.
                                                        £368.16.   ”
On the side of the second page of the document is an illegible comment in
an unknown hand.
    4. In the *Virginia Journal, and Alexandria Advertiser,* beginning 24 Aug., Ben-
jamin Dulany placed the following advertisement: "Meadow Pasture[.] I WILL
take to pasture twenty or thirty Horses, at three shillings per week, the money
to be paid weekly. The grass is at this time from six to eight inches in height
throughout the meadow, which contains from fifty to sixty acres. There is
a good fence round the meadow, but will not be answerable for accidents or
escapes."
    5. For Penelope French's ultimate signing of a lifetime lease to GW, see
Charles Lee to GW, 13 Sept., n.4. On 24 Oct. GW and the tenant John Robertson signed an agreement, or "Memorandum." By the terms of the agreement
Robertson consented to give up the use of the land and slaves on or before 1
Jan. 1787, but in the meantime GW would be allowed to use some of the

laborers not being employed in getting in Robertson's current crops, in order to make preparations for the planting of GW's crops for the following year. GW agreed to let Robertson have the use of a tenement on the land "now in the occupation of a certain Peter Pool" rent free for 1787 with the option of renting it the following year. GW also agreed to buy most of Robertson's horses and cows, paying the money to Mrs. French in order to exonerate Robertson from rent or arrearage of rent due at the end of his lease. In addition GW agreed to let Robertson have the use of the fishery on Clifton's Neck for the upcoming shad and herring season for £12.10 (ADS, DLC:GW). See also *Diaries*, 5:52, 57.

From Bushrod Washington

Bushfield, September 27th [1786]
We have lately instituted a society in these lower counties, called the *Patriotic Society*. As it is something new, and there are a few men both good and sensible who disapprove of it, it will be a high gratification to me to know your sentiments of it, if you will be so kind as to communicate them. The object of the institution is to inquire into the state of public affairs; to consider in what the true happiness of the people consists, and what are the evils which have pursued, and still continue to molest us; the means of attaining the former, and escaping the latter; to inquire into the conduct of those, who represent us, and to give them our sentiments upon those laws, which ought to be or are already made.

It will also be a considerable object to instil principles of frugality into the minds of the people, both by precept and example. If any real good should result from such a society, we hope similar ones will be generally instituted through the State; and, if so, they may establish a very formidable check upon evil-disposed men, who, clothed with power, make interested motives, and not public good, the rule of their conduct. These are the general outlines of the institution; and, whether in the event it may be beneficial or not, I think that it has taken its rise in virtuous motives. We have had a considerable meeting of the most sensible and respectable gentlemen in this part of the country, and another is to be held on Tuesday next, previous to the meeting of the Assembly. Our design is to hold another as soon as the Assembly has risen; the first to instruct our delegates what they ought to do, the next to inquire what they have done.[1]

L (incomplete), Sparks, *Writings*, 9:199–200. The extract is printed as a note in GW's letter to Bushrod Washington of 30 September.

1. The following notice appeared in the *Virginia Gazette, or the American Advertiser* (Richmond): "*At a Meeting of the* PATRIOTIC SOCIETY *at* RICHMOND *Court-house, on Tuesday* Oct. 3, 1786, *the following resolutions were unanimously agreed to.*

'The Patriotic Society upon mature reflection, being fully convinced, that the only method in the power of the people, honestly and effectually to relieve themselves from the oppression of public and private debt, is, by spirited exertions of industry, to encrease the productions of the country, and by a strict frugality, and avoiding all dissipation, to lessen their expences, which will necessarily leave them the means (much wished for) of removing their embarrassments. We do therefore pledge ourselves by our *examples*, to encourage and promote industry, frugality, œconomy.

'And whereas, the dependence of this country upon foreigners, for almost every necessary and conveniency of life, must, as has ever been the case in other countries, tend to its impoverishment and weakness.

'We further declare, that we shall be at all times ready, by every encouragement in our power, to promote every well founded scheme of trade or manufactures, the profits of which shall arise and center with our own citizens.'" For further correspondence with regard to Bushrod Washington's Patriotic Society, see GW to Bushrod Washington, 30 Sept., Bushrod Washington to GW, 31 Oct., and GW to Bushrod Washington, 15 Nov. 1786.

From William Gordon

My dear Sir   Stoke Newington [England] Sepr 28. 1786
     It is with concern I learn, that the old leaven, which brought on the late American troubles, still exists in the present ministry; & that so many falsehoods are propagated to keep up an unfriendly disposition toward the United States, & no more pains taken to contradict them. Among other reports it is said, that the settlement at Kentucky is made up wholly of the scum & refuse of the continent; that the people are opposed to the Congress; & that they are attached to the British government. I wish your Excellency to furnish me with the best account of their numbers, their characters & quality; & of their political attachments, that so I may insert the same in one of the news-papers, if it should serve to put down, what I suppose to be idle stories respecting them.
     You will probably have heard, before this can come to hand, that my friend durst not offer the bill, you was so obliging as to

forward, for fear of having it paid in paper. The Rhode Islanders & others have been very wrong, in my judgment, while they have attempted introducing a paper currency. After the late experience, it might have been thought, that they would not run again, so soon, upon the same rock.[1]

The Dutch seem to be upon the eve of a civil war. The friends of liberty are determined, if possible, to let the common people into a share of the government, & to overthrow the aristocratic junto. They mean not to set aside the Stadtholder; but to reduce his power within narrower limits, & to have a mixt government. However should the Prince of Orange interest himself in attempting to frustrate the patriots, it may provoke them to carry their views so far as even to set him aside. The prospect is but gloomy, as to the inhabitants of the United Provinces. Should a civil war break out, & the parties be nearly matched, there will, most probably, be more dreadful scenes by far than what America was acquainted with, in the late contest. I had the happiness of being exempted from the great difficulties with which others were pressed; but heard & knew enough of what my fellow citizens suffered, so that I desire ever to be at a distance from the seat of war.

Allow me to mention, that I have a nephew by Mrs Gordon's side, named Field, who, the next month, finishes his apprenticeship after having faithfully & steadily served the noted Messrs Nairne & Blunt opticians, mathematical instrument makers &c. &c. &c. He has made himself master of every branch.[2] I can recommend him as being a good hand, & such as has given his masters great satisfaction. He will set up for himself. Your countenance should you want any articles in his way, & interest among your friends on his behalf, will be a fresh favour done me.

I am not yet settled; but hope to be fixed in the neighbourhood of London. Any letter directed to me at Mr Thos Field's No. 11. Cornhill will go near to find me. We are for the present about three miles from London; but before I can receive an answer, may be some where in the city. Would have your letter be under cover & directed by another hand, & sealed with another seal, that it may not be known at the Post Office that we correspond, lest the runners of government should suppress or peep into your letters. I have learnt, that one of the former secretaries gave me the name of arch-rebel, & that the letters in my hand writing were stopt. Mrs Gordon joins in best regards to your Excellency, your Lady, my young friend, Dr Stewart Lady & children. Pray my respects to Mr & Mrs Lund Washington. I remain with the greatest Esteem Your Excellency's sincere friend & humble servant

William Gordon

ALS, DLC:GW.
  1. See Benjamin Lincoln, Jr., to GW, 24 September.
  2. Gordon wrote GW on 16 Feb. 1789: "Mrs Gordon's nephew Mr John Field [Jr.], being now settled in a house his father has built for him I have made bold to send you four of his cards."

To Leven Powell

Dear Sir,—   MOUNT VERNON, 30th Sept., 1786.

I have received your favor of the 12th inst. Some mistake must have happened in delivering my message to your agent respecting the Timothy seed, I never wished to decline taking the whole; having saved 14 or 15 Bushels of seed myself more than I expected to do, less than I desired you to procure for me would have sufficed, say half; but I am equally willing & ready to take the whole, if it is provided. Be it more or less, I should be glad to receive it soon, that having it in possession I may use it as occasion presents.

I will take 100 Bushels of Buckwheat, the new crop I shall prefer, as it is for seed next year. This also I should be glad to have in my own possession for the reason above.—Not being much acquainted with the culture of this crop, you would do me a favor, by informing me of the best time or times for sowing it, for the different uses it is applied, how much seed is usually given to the acre & what cultivation it generally receives.

If you will accompany the seed with an acct. of the cost, I will pay the amount to your agent. With much esteem & regard, I am Dr. Sir, Yr. Obedt. & Hble. Servt.

GO. WASHINGTON.

"The Leven Powell Correspondence—1775–1787," *John P. Branch Historical Papers of Randolph-Macon College*, 2 (1902), 137.

To Bushrod Washington

Dear Bushrod,   Mount Vernon 30th Sepr 86.

I was from home when your Servant arrived, found him in a hurry to be gone when I returned, have company in the house, and am on the eve of a journey up the river, to meet the Directors of the Potomack Company. These things combining, will not allow me time to give any explicit answer to the question you have propounded.[1]

Generally speaking, I have seen as much evil as good result from such societies as you describe the constitution of yours to be—they are a kind of emperium emperio, and as often clog, as facilitate public measures. I am no friend to instructions, except in local matters which are wholly or in a great measure confined to the County of the Delegate. To me, it appears a much wiser, & more politic conduct, to chuse able & honest representatives, & leave them in all national questions to determine from the evidence of reason, and the facts which shall be adduced, when internal & external information is given to them in a collective sta⟨te⟩. What certainty is there that societies in a corner, or remote part of a state, can possess all that knowledge which is necessary for them to decide on many important questions which may come before an Assembly? What reason is there to expect that the Society itself may be accordant in opinion on such subjects? May not a few members of this society (more sagacious & designing than the rest) direct the measures of it to private views of their own? May not this embarrass an honest, able Delegate who hears the voice of his Country from all quarters, and thwart public measures?

These are first thoughts, but I give no decided opinion. Societies nearly similar to such as you speak of, have lately been formed in Massachusetts-bay. What has been the consequence? Why they have declared the Senate useless—many other parts of the Constution unnecessary. Saleries of public Officers burthensome &ca—To point out the defects of the Constitution in a decent way (if any existed) was proper enough—but they have done more. They first vote the Courts of Justice in the present circumstances of the State oppressive. And next, by violence, stop them. Which has occasioned a very solemn proclamation & appeal from the Governor to the people. You may say that no such matters are in contemplation by your Society. Granted. A snow ball gathers by rolling. Possibly a line may be drawn between occasional meetings for special purposes, & a standing Society to direct with local views & partial information, the affairs of the nation, which cannot be well understood but by a large & comparative view of circumstances. Where is this so likely to enter as in the general Assembly of the people? What figure then must a delegate make who comes there with his hands tied, & his judgment forestalled? His very instructors perhaps (if they had nothing sinister in view) were they present at all the information & arguments which would come forward, might be the first to change sentiments.

Hurried as this letter is, I am sensible I am writing to you upon a very important subject. I have no time to copy, correct, or even to peruse it; for which reason I could wish to have it, or a copy returned to me. George & his wife set off yesterday for the Races at Fredericksburgh. The rest of the family are well & join in love & good wishes for all at Bushfield with Dear Bushrod Yr Affecte

Go: Washington

ALS, anonymous donor; LB, DLC:GW.
    1. Bushrod Washington's letter is dated 27 September.

To George Augustine Washington

Dear George,   Mount Vernon 30th Sep. 17[86]
    Giles bringing the enclosed from Alexandria & presuming it was on the business he was sent about, I opened it before I discovered the mistake.[1]

Endeavor among other things you were to have enquired after, to engage me some Pompion (Pumpkin) seed. and ask if a good kind of sweet Potatoe seed can be had in case I should not be able to get enough in this part of the Country to plant an Acre of ground next Spring—this may properly be introduced into my course of experiments next season. We remain as you left us & join in best wishes for you & Fanny; & Compliments to all friends. I am Yrs Affectionately

Go: Washington

ALS, MnHi. The date in the heading is partly torn off; George Augustine Washington, who was visiting in Fredericksburg, dockets the letter: "30th Sept. 1786."

1. Giles was GW's coachman. George Augustine Washington and his wife Frances Bassett Washington left for Fredericksburg on 29 Sept., returning on 9 October.

From Henry Hill, Jr.

Dear Sir   Philad[elphi]a 1st Octo. 1786.

The Bill of exchange omitted in my last is now inclosed with a receipt in full—& your letters were duely forwarded.[1]

I lately had the pleasure of hearing Mr King's harangue to our Assembly, on the Subject of the Commission with which he & Mr Monro were charged by Congress. It was truely, to the best of my judgment adapted to insure applause even from an Attic Audience.

Virginia appeared in the most advantageous light—Should her liberal support of the Union be Withdrawn, & Pennsylva. refuse her's—he represented wth wonderful effect what would become of our State regulations—of the renown of our heroes & patriots—they wou'd all be swept away—and utterly lost!

The impression made on the House in favor of the point "supplicated" was remarkably tho' tacitly confess'd and had the Members individually been question'd on the Spot whether the impost should be granted without reserves no one doubts it would have succeeded—They chose however on cool Deliberation to refer the important business to the next Assembly— Whether or not such a measure is practicable appears very doubtful.[2] I am with our best Compliments to Mrs Washington Dear Sir Your most obedt hble servt

Henry Hill

ALS, DLC:GW.

1. Hill wrote on 9 Sept. in answer to GW's letter of 3 August.

2. On 14 Aug. Congress appointed Rufus King of Massachusetts and James Monroe to go from New York to the Pennsylvania legislature "to explain to them more fully the embarrassed state of the public finances, and to recommend it to the said state to repeal the clause in her act granting the impost, which suspends its operation until all the states shall have granted the supplementary funds" (*JCC*, 31:512–13, 515). King and Monroe attended the Penn-

sylvania legislature on 13 Sept. and were back in New York on 25 Sept., having succeeded in their mission (see Monroe to James Madison, 12 Sept., 29 Sept., in Rutland and Rachal, *Madison Papers*, 9:122–24, 134–35). Hill at this time was a member of the supreme executive council of Pennsylvania.

From Henry Lee, Jr.

dear Genl   [1 October 1786]
    I have not written to you for a long time having nothing important or agreable to communicate.
    Nor have I now any thing agreable, but alas the reverse.
    The commotions which have for some time past distracted the two eastern states, have risen in Massachusetts to an alarming height—In New Hampshire the firmness of their President the late General Sullivan has dissipated the troubles in that state—I enclose a full narration of his decided conduct, and the effects which it produced.[1] But affairs are in a very different situation in Massachusetts—After various insults to government, by stopping the courts of justice &c., the insurgents have in a very formidable shape taken possession of the town of Springfield, at which place the supreme court was sitting—The friends to government arrayed under the Militia General of the district Shephard in support the court, but their exertions were not effectual—the court removed and broke up, the insurgents continue possessed of the town & General Shepherd has retired to the United States arsenal one mile from Springfield—this Arsenal contains a very important share of our munitions of war.[2] Congress have sent their Secretary of this department, General Knox to take the best measures in his power in concert with government for the safety of the Arsenal. What renders the conduct of the insurgents more alarming is that they behave with decency & manage with system, they are encamped and regularly supplied with provisions by their friends & have lately given orders to the delegates in Assembly from their particular towns, not to attend the meeting of the Legislature.
    It must give you pleasure to hear in this very distressing scene the late officers & soldiers are on the side of government unanimously—the Insurgents it is said are conducted by a Captain of the late army, who continued but a small period in service & possessed a very reputable Character.

This event produces much suggestion as to its causes—Some attribute it to the weight of taxes and the decay of commerce, which has produced universal idleness.

Others, to British councils[,] the vicinity of Vermont & the fondness for Novelty which always has & ever will possess more or less influence on Man. The next accounts will I hope produce favorable intelligence, but present appearances do not justify this hope.

Has your china arrived, & does it please Mrs Washington. Be pleased to present my best respects to her and accept the repetition of my unceasing regard with which—I have the honor to be most sincerely your ob. ser.

Henry Lee Junr

ALS, DLC:GW; copy, MH: Lee Family Papers.

1. Enraged by the failure of the New Hampshire legislature to respond to their petitions for economic relief and by false rumors that confiscated land was to be returned to the Loyalists, more than a hundred armed farmers descended on the legislature in Exeter on 20 Sept., where they were faced down by Gen. John Sullivan, president of the state, and on the next day were put to flight or captured by a force of militia. The enclosed account of the incident has not been identified. The fullest contemporary account of the Exeter riot is to be found in William Plumer's letters of 20 and 21 Sept. 1786 to John Hale, in *Publications of Col. Soc. of Mass.*, 11:390–96.

2. William Shepherd (1737–1817) was major general of the 4th division of the Massachusetts militia. For reference to his role in putting down Shays' Rebellion, see editorial note in Benjamin Lincoln to GW, 4 Dec. 1786–4 Mar. 1787.

From Jeremiah Wadsworth

Dear Sir   Hartford [Conn.] October 1. 1786

Finding among General Greens letters one to you which has some expressions that are desponding and hearing that reports are circulated that his death was ocasioned by his troubles, I have taken the liberty to write you on the subject. the report which was circulated respecting Mrs Greene which gave so much pain to the Generals, & her friends: I believe never reachd his Ears: if it did he certainly never gave the least credit to it— as imedeately after it was circulated and believed here (that they had parted), they came together to my House and I never saw more unaffected fondness and attachment than existed between them at that time. I soon after spent a Week with them at New Port where thier was the same appearance and as I have been minutely informed of all General Greens other concerns and consulted by him respecting the affairs of Banks and all his other embarrasments[1]—I am persuaded no person on Earth better knew his inmost thoughts than I did I am persuaded he was just before his death, or rather before he fell sick—in better Spirits than he had ever been before, since his arriveing with his family in Georgia—as he had good prospects of geting clear of his troubles with the crediters of Banks & Co. and a Contract with the French Nation for Timber was so nearly compleated as to promise him sufficient funds for all his other purposes. Mr Miller a Young Gentleman who went with him to Georgia & lived on terms of intimacy & confidence with him assures me the General was in good Spirits and that he is persuaded he died of a fever in the Head which might have been removed if the Physicians had understood his disorder he had for some time before had an inflamation in one Eye—which was almost done away, when he was Sezed at table with a Violent pain in his Eye & Head which forced him to retire, a fever ensued the Symptoms increased and a few days put an end to his existance. I am my selfe persuaded that something of the apperplectick kind was the cause of his death as I was informed that the day after one of the important actions to the Southward he was taken suddenly with a disorder in the head which deprived him of sence & motion for some time and those about him best Skilled in the healing art—pronounced it an appoplexy[2]—Col. Humphreys informs me you did not know that the General had received your answer to his letter respecting Capt. Gun[.] I find it among his private letters and am not a little pleased to find your sentiments on that subject corresponding with my own, communicated about the same time, in answer to his letter to me on that subject. Mrs Greene & her Children are at present at New Port—Mrs Greene Mr E. Rutledge[3] & my selfe are his Executors if we get clear of his obligations for Banks & Cos. their will be a competency for her & the Children if not their situation will be very disagreeable as I am on this subject it may be proper to mention to you the cause of the Generals being so involved for those people, as I find he has been calumniated on that account—After his contract with Banks & Co. to feed the troops under his command made with all the precautions possible having first advised with the ruleing powers of the State & knowing that he had been censured before, respecting a bargain made (or said to be made) by his permission—and the Army having been some time fed on this Contract the Contractors were found to be greatly indebted & oblidged to Stop unless the Genl woud secure their Creditors This he consented to do on condition they sent a Man to receive the Monies to be paid to the Contractors for their Supplies at Phila which they agreeing to he became bound with the Contractors for large Sums—Banks the principal contractor & executive Man of the Company had the Address to draw all the Money but a trifle and apply it to other purposes—whereby the General was left liable—by various discoveries since made it appears their was much p[r]emeditated Villany and I am sorry to find among some of the actors or consentors to this sceme of fraud & Villany, some whose obligations were great to Gen. Greene—I am almost persuaded that to be serviceable to mankind has something creminal in it—as I find—no instance of any Mans being greatly serviceable to his Country who is rewarded even with sincere thanks—& few where some punishment is not inflicted, private gratitude may possibly be in existance among the human Race but is rare indeed—I beg pardon for troubling You with this long letter—but I am persuaded you will forgive me as my intentions are to rescue the character of my deceased friend from any unjust reproach. I am dear Sir with sentiments of the greatest Esteem your most obedent & most Humle Servánt

Jere. Wadsworth

⟨Inte⟩nded to have copied this letter in a fairer hand but want of time forbids I hope your Exey will be able to decypher it.

ALS, DLC:GW. A number of the period-like marks in the manuscript clearly were not intended as periods and have been deleted or converted to commas.

1. GW wrote Gen. Nathanael Greene on 20 May 1785 commiserating with him about his problems arising out of his dealings with John Banks & Co. for army supplies during the war and supporting the stand he took when challenged by James Gunn. Wadsworth is referring to rumors that circulated in New England of infidelity on the part of Catharine Littlefield Greene at the time General Greene took extended trips to South Carolina and Georgia in 1784 and 1785, leaving his wife behind in Newport, R.I., with their four children. See Isaac Briggs to Joseph Thomas, 23 Nov. 1785, *Ga. Hist. Quart.*, 12 (June 1928), 179–82.

2. When Greene died on 19 June 1786, Gen. Anthony Wayne was with him at Mulberry Grove plantation near Savannah, where Greene and his family had been living. Phineas Miller, a young man recommended to the Greenes by Ezra Stiles, went to Georgia with them in 1785 as tutor for their children. Miller's marriage to Mrs. Greene in Philadelphia in May 1796 was witnessed by GW and Mrs. Washington.

3. Edward Rutledge (1749–1800) and his brother John became particular friends of both General and Mrs. Greene when John Rutledge's house in Charleston served as Greene's headquarters in 1782.

To John Augustine Washington

Dear Brother,   Mount Vernon Octr 1st 1786

If you receive *this* letter at *this* place before I return home, it is to observe how singular it is that I should always be from home or upon the eve of leaving it, when you come here.[1]

An appointment which cannot be dispensed with (and which was made *by myself* before I had any intimation of your intention of taking this on your way down) obliges me to the Great, & perhaps the little Falls to a meeting of the Board of Directors. That (besides doing matters of smaller moment) we may fix a plan for the Winter operation & labour of our hands—determine the nature & ⟨mutilated⟩ Great Falls ⟨mutilated⟩ four Directors presented. A pointed summons is gone out for the present meeting which cannot be delayed without doing injury to the interest of the Company.[2]

I wished to see you on many Accts. One, to know what report is made respecting the Hites claim of the Land on which Thornton Washington lives—& thence up to the head spring. I sent Thornton all my papers respecting this business, and have written to him *three* or *four* times on the subject; but he has not vouchsafed to give me an answer or even to have acknowledged the receipt of my Papers on which the title depends.[3] Such is the inattention, and remissness of persons unaccustomed to regularity in business. If you can give me any information of what the Hites, or the Commissioner, have done in this case it will enable ⟨mutilated en⟩closed. It relates to some of your Land, or the Lands of Saml or Charles. Of what use it may be to either of you I know not. To me it is of none.[4]

I do not think it probable that I shall be returned before

thursday—possibly (according to the business which may come before the Directors) it may be longer. Very affectionately—I remain Yrs

Go: Washington

ALS, owned (1972) by Dr. Joseph Fields, Williamsburg, Virginia.

1. GW found his brother at Mount Vernon when he returned from Great Falls on 4 October. John Augustine Washington remained until 7 Oct., when the two parted for the last time. GW learned on 10 Jan. of the unexpected death of his "beloved Brother" (*Diaries*, 5:93).

2. GW arrived on the morning of 2 Oct. at the Great Falls for the meeting of the directors of the Potomac River Company. After hearing and dismissing the charges of James Rumsey against the new manager of the company, Richardson Stewart, the directors agreed to a petition of the Maryland and Virginia assemblies for an extension of the time allowed to complete the improvement of navigation above the Great Falls. They then "Directed the Manager respecting the Winter Work for the hands" before finishing up "about three oclock" on 4 Oct. (*Diaries*, 5:48).

3. See Thornton Washington to GW, 6 June, n.2.

4. The enclosure has not been identified. The mutilated portions of the letter are where repairs have been made at the fold.

Letter not found: from John Francis Mercer, 4 Oct. 1786. On 6 Nov. GW wrote Mercer about receiving "your letter of the 4th Ulto."

Letter not found: from Rawleigh Colston, 5 Oct. 1786. On 10 Nov. Colston wrote GW: "I had the honour of writing your Excellency on the 5th of October last."

From William Hickman

Sir.   Frederick County October 5th 1786

In consequence of my being Assured by Mr Rawleigh Coulston that the right of a Judgment Obtained against Mr William Ireland Junr in the General Court of Maryland in May last, as my Security in a Bond granted to your Excellency in November 1774 for two Tracts of Land I purchased at the sale of the Estate of George Mercer Esquire; I have sold to that Gentleman, among other property one of those Tracts, known and discribed in the plott by No. 7 I therefore request your Excellency will make a Deed for the same to Mr Coulston which when Executed you will please lodge in the Hands of Mr James Keith or some other Gentleman in Alexandria—with Instructions to hold the same until such time as Mr Coulston may be able to produce satisfactory vouchers to evince his being Intitled to receive the money due on the above Judgment; the Races happening Next week will offer I presume an Opportunity of procuring a Sufficient number of Gentlemen from this & Berkeley County to witness the Deeds, which I believe will be more agreeable to Mr Coulston, as he would wish the Deed Recorded in this County in which the land lay & himself resides: or If a Deed for Land lying in another County can with propriety be Recorded in Fairfax, Your Excellency will please procure such Witnesses as may with most convenience be called upon in that Court for proof: Mr Ireland who has an Assignment of your Bond for conveyance of those Lands will deliver it up, on Your Excellencys makeing the Deed to Mr Coulston for No. 7 & a Deed to me for the Lott called No. 1 which you will be pleased to do in the same manner with respect to the witnesses.[1] I am Sir With the Greatest Respect Your Obedient Hbe Servt

William Hickman

Sir. Since closeing the foregoing, Mr Ireland has thought it Imprudent to give up the Assignment of your Bond of Conveyance for the Lott No. 1 which was made him for his security in case Judgment should go against him, you will therefore be pleased to Renew your Bond for the Conveyance of that Lott to me, or take such writings from him as will, exonerate you from the Obligation of makeing a Title for the Lott No. 7 & let the old Bond remain as it is (which I think will be mo⟨*mutilated*⟩) as by renewal, it would divest me of any right. I am Sorry to give your Excellency so much trouble in this matter, but as my Long Infirmity, Mr Irelands particular & distressed Situation, & the Channel in which the business have been conducted seems to constrain us to intrude on your Excellencys Good nature, I hope you will excuse the freedom of my request. With Due respect
William Hickman

ALS, DLC:GW.

1. At the sale of George Mercer's tract of land on the Shenandoah River in Frederick County, which GW conducted and accepted bonds for payment from the purchasers, William Hickman of that county bought two lots, num-

bers 1 and 7. He and his wife Jane conveyed lot no. 7 to Rawleigh Colston in May 1788. Edward Snickers bought lot no. 1 from Hickman (Chappelear, "Early Landowners"; Edward Snickers to GW, 17 May 1784, n.1; Rawleigh Colston to GW, 10 Nov. 1786; GW to Rawleigh Colston, 4 Dec. 1786; GW to John Francis Mercer, 24 Nov. 1786).

To Thomas Snowden

Gentn   Mount Vernon 7th Octr 1786.
Agreeably to the enclosed List, be so good as to send to your Correspondent at Alexandria for my use a Ton of Iron; & order it not to be mixed with any other Iron—I am Gentlemen, Yr obt & Hble Servt

G. Washington

LB, DLC:GW. The heading is: "To Messrs Snowdon."
Thomas Snowden (1751–1803) inherited the furnaces and ironworks that he operated in Prince George's County, Maryland. See also GW to George Augustine Washington, 27 May 1787.

From Lafayette

My dear General.   Paris october the 8th [1786]
This Will Be presented By Mr le Coulteux a Relation to the Respectable House of french Merchants By that Name who is Going to Settle in America—I Beg You to Honour Him With Your patronage and Advices.[1]

Not Knowing when this Will Reach You I only add My Respects Most Affectionate to Mrs Washington—Remember me to George, to the Young ones, to all friends.

A treaty of Commerce is Signed Between france and England Who are to treat Each other like the Most favoured *European* Nation—Which Will not interfere With the Views of the United States. With those Sentiments of Respect and love which My dear general Knows to Be So deeply Rooted in my filial Heart I Have the Honour to be Your Most affectionate friend

Lafayette

ALS, PEL.
1. Louis Le Couteulx became an American citizen in Philadelphia in July 1787 (Couteulx to Timothy Pickering, 9 Oct. 1800, quoted in Syrett, *Hamilton*

Papers, 25:241–42). See also Thomas Jefferson to Charles Thomson, 20 Sept. 1786 (Boyd, *Jefferson Papers*, 10:395). There is no indication that Couteulx visited Mount Vernon. I. L. and C. Le Couteulx was a French banking house about which Thomas Jefferson wrote GW on 14 Nov. 1786 (ibid., 531–35).

Letter not found: from Thomas Freeman, 9 Oct. 1786. On 18 Dec. Freeman wrote GW: "I imagine you did not receive mine of the 9th October."

From Catharine Sawbridge Macaulay Graham

Sir   Knightsbridge near London Octbr 10. [17]86
  By some of those unlucky incidents which attend the passage cross the Atlantic the letter with which you honored me dated Jan. 10 did not reach me till the latter end of June last.
  There are few persons in Europe who would not be highly flattered by a correspondence with General Washington but when this gratification which from the consideration of popular eminence must be felt by every vulgar mind is enlarged by a Genuine taste for moral excelence it raises the most lively Sentiments of self complacency and gratitude.
  When I returned from Mount Vernon to Philadelphia I had the pleasure of seeing a Portrait which bore the strongest resemblance to the original of any I had seen, if you favor me with another letter you will do me great pleasure if you will inform me whether Mr Pine is much advanced in his grand designs of pourtraying the Capital events of the civil wars and whether he is likely to succeed in his attempt.[1]
  Give me leave Sir to return you our thanks for those obliging and benevolent sentiments with which your letter is replete.
  We present our best respects to Mrs Washington our best compliments and good wishes to the aimable pair who have united their fortunes since our departure from America and our love to the little people whom we sincerely hope will both in their different characters afford an ample recompense for the benevolent care and culture they have received. I have the honor to be Sir with those sentiments which your virtues and goodness are so well calculated to inspire Your Most Obednt And Most Obliged Humble Servnt
                              Cath: Macaulay Graham

ALS, PHi: Gratz Collection; Sprague transcript, DLC:GW.

1. In May 1785 Robert Edge Pine was at Mount Vernon painting the portraits of GW and Mrs. Washington, Fanny Bassett, and the Custis grandchildren. For Pine's proposed "Portraits of the Persons and Places" involving "the most interesting Events of the late War," see Francis Hopkinson to GW, 19 April 1785, and note 1 of that document.

From Henry Lee, Jr.

My dear Genl   Newyork 11th Ocr [17]86

In the full confidence you receive my letters as testimonials of my unceasing respect, and from a solicitude to acquaint you with all material contingencys in the administration of our national affairs, that you may be able to form your judgement on authentic documents, and consequently that your opinions being bottomed on truth may not fail to produce the most beneficial effects to our country, I again address you, and mean to confine myself to one subject, which will I apprehend soon become the topic of public debate. Among the defects which degrade the constitution of the fœderal government is the physical impossibility of secrecy in the sovereignty, therefore it is often necessary to make confidential communications, when they serve to correct the circulation of erroneous informations on subjects of national concern which in their nature is secret, but from the cause just mentioned become public. Considering myself therefore at full liberty to give you a history of this business, I will do it with brevity.

We are told here that the decided difference which prevailed in Congress on the proposed treaty with Spain is generally understood in every part of the Union, and it is suggested that the project of the treaty will become the subject of deliberation in the Assembly of Virga.

True it is that this affair unfortunately produced an intemperance common in democratic bodys & always injurious to the interest of the public; for to judge wisely on systems & measures, the mind ought to be free from prejudice & warmth, and influenced by a full deliberate view of the general effects of such system & measures.

The eastern states consider a commercial connexion with

Spain, as the only remedy for the distresses which oppress their citizens, most of which they say flow from the decay of their commerce. Their delegates have consequently zealously pressed the formation of this connexion, as the only effectual mode to revive the trade of their country. In this opinion they have been joined by two of the middle states. On the other hand, Virginia has with equal zeal opposed the connection, because the project involves expressly the disuse of the navigation of the Mississippi for a given time, & eventually they think will sacrifice our right to it. The delegation is under injunctions from the State on this subject—They have acted in obedience to their instructions & myself excepted in conformity to their private sentiments. I confess that I am by no means convinced of the justice or policy of our instructions & very much apprehend, unless they are repealed by the present Assembly the fatal effects of discord in council will be experienced by the U. States in a very high degree.

The project submitted by the Secretary for foreign affairs was founded as well as I can recollect on the following principles—
1st The commerce between the U. S. & the King of Spain to be founded on the principles of perfect reciprocity, which reciprocity to be diffused in all the sub-regulations.

2d The trade to be confined to his Catholic Majestys European dominions.

3d The bona fide manufactures & produce of the respective countrys imported into either, to be subject to the same dutys as are paid by the citizens and subjects of the two Nations.

4th A Tariff to be established by convention within one year after the ratification of the treaty ascertaining the necessary dutys, to be imposed.

5th Mast & timber annually requisite for the Navy of Spain to be bought from the Merchants of the U. States in preference, provided they are equal in price and quality.

There are some other matters which I forget—In consideration of the advantages of this treaty the U. S. stipulate to forbear for the term of the treaty the use of the river M.

The boundarys will be (in case of treaty) established as fixed in the definitive treaty of peace between the U. States and G. Britain.

The article of tobacco is excepted in the project being the produce of Spanish colonies & is to continue on the present footing, which is favorable.

Thus have I delineated to You the outlines of the proposed plan.

Among the many arguments used by the advocates for the treaty I will mention only one which I think ought to be known. They say that the right of the navigation of the M. is disputed, that the use of that right is now suspended & can not be possessed, but by force, or by treaty; and that a forbearance of the use on our part, is a confirmation of our right the use of which right will be in due time possessed in consequence of the present project without putting our claim to the issue of war, which is always precarious, & for which we are totally unprepared.

Should this matter come before our Assembly, much will depend on Mr Masons sentiments.

So many reasons founded on true policy will arise in a full investigation of this subject, that I can not but hope that the state of Virginia will consider a treaty with Spain on the principles of the project, essentially necessary to her political happiness, and to her commercial aggrandizement.[1]

The sedition in Massachusetts is in some degree subsided, but is not I fear extinguished.

Col. Monroe who was an aid in Lord Stirlings family, a delegate from Virginia in Congress will in a few days return home with his lady.

He means to do himself the honor to pay his respects to Mount-Vernon in his way.[2] My best respects to Mrs Washington: with the most affectionate attachment I have the honor to be your h: ser.

Henry Lee Junr

ALS, DLC:GW.

1. See James Monroe to GW, 20 Aug., n.2.

2. James Monroe and his wife, and James Madison as well, spent the nights of 23 and 24 Oct. at Mount Vernon.

From Fielding Lewis, Jr.

Bloomsbery Fredarick [County]

Deare Uncle Octbr 11th [17]86

Haveing made a purchase of a lot in Rectortown Fauquair County, and am desierous of building thareon on as good tirms a possable—made me petition you for a little timber, as your land lyes near the Town and your Tennents are willing I Should have it with your Approbation[1]—your Answer—with Complyance will Grately Oblige your Affectionate Nephiw

Fielding Lewis

N.B. My Kindest Respects to my Aunt. F.L.

ALS, CSmH.

1. Fielding Lewis, Jr., lived with his wife and children in Frederick County where he had secured land from his father. He wrote GW in 1784 saying he was confined in jail for debt and asking his uncle for a loan, which GW refused to give (Lewis to GW, 22 Feb. 1784; GW to Lewis, 27 Feb. 1784). See also GW to Lewis, 4 Dec. 1786.

From James Manning

Sir New York 11th Octr 1786

I beg leave to introduce to your notice the Bearer, Mr Joseph Jenckes of Providence in the State of Rhode Island. He is son of Mr John Jenckes of that Town, of a good family. He was educated under me, and I have ever considered him as a young Gentleman of real worth, as a man of principle. With mercantile views he has removed to the State of Virginia. As a stranger it may be of advantage to him to have his character known to your Excellency, whose known goodness prompts you to serve & encourage real merit.[1] I beg pardon for intruding upon your Excellency, and have the honour to be Sir Your very Humble Servt

James Manning

ALS, DLC:GW.

James Manning (1738–1791), president of Rhode Island College (Brown University) since its founding in 1765, was at this time representing Rhode Island in Congress.

1. Joseph, John, and Crawford Jenckes by April 1787 were partners in a firm called Jenckes, Winsor & Co., with a store on King Street in Alexandria. See also John Brown to GW, 1 November.

To Edmund Randolph

Dr Sir,   [c.12 October 1786]

By Doctr Stuart I return the books you were so obliging as to allow me the reading of: by him also I send you the Travels of the Marqs de Chastellux, for your perusal.[1]

I felt for your disappointment the day you left this, & hope no accidents intervened afterwards to give further interruption to your journey. Unknowing of the quantity of rain which had fallen in the course of the night, I was never more surprized than in a ride I took to some of my plantations an hour or two after you went away, to find every place deluged.

I[2]

LB (incomplete), DLC:GW.

1. Randolph stopped at Mount Vernon on 16–18 Sept., with his wife and two children, after attending the Annapolis Convention.

2. The next page of the letter book is missing.

From Clement Biddle

[Philadelphia] October 15th 1786.

The Box with the Curtains did not arrive till about twelve days ago when I put them into the hands of a Dyer who has finished them but was obliged to rip them as they could not be dyed and pressed without it—they are packed in the same box in which they Came together with 16 yards of the same kind of Stuff as near as I could make it & 3500 Brass nails—the box is Ship'd on board the Sloop Polly Capt. Ellwood for Alexandria and the bill of Loading delivered to Mr Porter to whom it is Consigned there to forward.[1]

I funded your Certificate amount £127.6.11 Pennsylvania Currency having first received 84^{50}⁄90 Dollars in Indents which are inclosed & will be usefull to you towards payment of Taxes in your State.

I have also received for 1 years Interest from this

State to April 1st	7.12.9
and for 6 months Do	3.16.4
	£11. 9.1

The two last Sums in paper money equal to ¹⁄₁₀ in value less than Specie which is to your Credit and the Certificate remains for your orders—It will draw Interest here every Six Months and is in your name[2]—But one Vessel has arrived this fall from London & the Blankets Oznabrigs and other articles are by no means plenty or to be purchased here lower than I think you may get them in Virginia—The Advertisement of Lands is in Dunlap & Claypoole's Paper which I think has the most general Circulation & I furnished a Copy to the members of Assembly where they lay, who was returning hom[e].[3] Mrs Biddle begs that her best respects may be presented to Mrs Washington. &c. &c.

Clement Biddle

ADfS, ViMtV: Clement Biddle Letterbook.
1. See GW to Biddle, 23 September.
2. See GW to Biddle, 18 May, n.4.
3. See GW to Charles Simms, 22 Sept., n.7.

From Henry Lee, Jr.

My dear Genl   New York 17th oct. [17]86
In my last letter I detailed the eastern commotions and communicated my apprehensions of their objects & issue.[1]

G. Knox has just returned from thence and his report grounded on his own knowledge is replete with melancholy information—a majority of the people of Massachusetts are in opposition to the government, some of their leaders *avow* the *subversion* of it to be their object together with the abolition of debts, the division of property and re-union with G. Britain[2]—In all the eastern states the same temper prevails more or less, and will certainly break forth whenever the opportune moment may arrive—the mal-contents are in close connexion with Vermont—& that district it is beleived is in negotiation with the Governor of Canada—In one word my dear Genl we are all in dire apprehension that a beginning of anarchy with all its calamitys has approached, & have no means to stop the dreadful work. Individuals suggest the propriety of inviting you from Congress to pay us a visit, knowing your unbounded influence & beleiving that your appearance among the seditious might bring them back to peace & reconciliation—This is only a *surmise* & I take the liberty to mention it to you that should the conjuncture of affairs Induce Congress to make this request you may have some previous time to make up your mind—In great hurry & real distress I am yours affecy

H: Lee Junr

ALS, DLC:GW.
    1. Lee's last letter was dated 11 October.
    2. Henry Knox wrote GW at length on 23 Oct. about the situation in Massachusetts.

Letter not found: from John Francis Mercer, 21 Oct. 1786. On 6 Nov. GW wrote Mercer of the delivery of "Your letter of 21st Ulto."

Letter not found: to Thomas Peters, 21 Oct. 1786. On 18 Nov. 1786 Peters wrote GW: "I have the pleasure of recieving your favour of the 21 of Oct."

To David Humphreys

My dear Humphreys   Mount Vernon 22d Octr 1786
    Your favor of the 24th ulto came to my hands about the middle of this month. For the enclosures it containd I pray you to receive my warmest acknowledgements and thanks. The poem, tho' I profess not to be a connoisseur in these kind of writings, appears pretty in my eye, and has sentiment and elegance which must, I think, render it pleasing to others.
    With respect to the circular letter, I see not cause for suppressing or altering any part, except as to the place of meeting. Philadelphia, in my opinion, has the advantage of New York on three accts 1st as being more central—2d because there are passage boats which ply regularly, and are well fitted between the more Southern States and the former, by which[1] the Delegates, if they chuse that mode of travelling, may be accomodated, and 3d it would seem to me that this body & Congress sitting in the same place, at the same time, will not be very pleasing.[2] ⟨When you have digested your Thoughts for publication, in the case of Captn Asgill, I would thank you for a copy of them; having arrested the account I had furnished Mr Tilghman, with an assurance of a more authentic one for his friend in England.⟩[3]
    I am pleased with the choice of delegates which were made at your State meeting, and wish the representatives of all the State Societies may appear at the General meeting with as good dispo-

sitions as I persuade myself they will. It gives me pleasure also to hear that so many officers are sent to your Assembly. I am persuaded they will carry with them more liberality of sentiment than is to be found among any other class of citizens.

The speech of our friend Cobb was noble, worthy of a patriot, & himself, as was the conduct of Gen. Sullivan. But for Gods sake tell me, what is the cause of all these commotions? Do they proceed from licenciousness, British influence disseminated by the Tories, or real grievances which admit of redress? If the latter, why has the remedy been delayed till the public mind had become so much agitated, & why yet postponed? If the former, why are not the powers of government tried at once? It is as well to be without them, as not to live under their exercise. ⟨Commotions of this sort, like snow-balls, gather strength as they roll, if there is no opposition in the way to divide & crumble them.

Do write me fully, I beseech you, on these matters; not only with respect to facts, but as to opinions of their tendency & issues.⟩ I am really mortified beyond expression that in the moment of our Acknowledged Independence we should, by our conduct, verify the predictions of our transatlantic foe, & render ourselves ridiculous & contemptible in the eyes of all Europe. ⟨My health (I thank you for the enquiry) is restored to me; & all under this roof join me in most affectionate regards, & regretting that your letter has held out no idea of visiting it again this winter—as you gave us hope of doing when you left us.

To all the gentn of my acquaintance who may happen to be in your circle, I beg to be remembered with sincere regard. To assure you of the sincerity of my friendship for you, would be unnecessary; as you must I think be perfectly satisfied of the high esteem and affection with which, I am &c. &c.

G: Washington⟩

ALS (incomplete photocopy; incomplete transcription), Maggs Brothers catalog no. 457, 1924; LB, DLC:GW. The text printed here is taken from the catalog photocopy and transcription, with the missing portions, enclosed in angle brackets, supplied from the letter book.

1. The photocopy ends at this point.

2. GW's circular letter to the Society of the Cincinnati, printed below, is dated 31 October.

3. For the publication of Humphreys' account of the Asgill affair, see Humphreys to GW, 16 Nov. 1786, n.1.

To Jeremiah Wadsworth

Dear Sir,   Mount Vernon 22d Oct. 1786

I have received and thank you for the communications in your letter of the 1st instt. It has given me much satisfaction, to find that the letter I had written to my much lamented friend Genl Greene (respecting his affair with Captn Gun) had reached his hands. Had the case been otherwise, and he had harboured a suspicion of my inattention or neglect, the knowledge of it, would have given me real pain.

Persuaded as I always have been of Genl Greene's integrity and worth, I spurned those reports which tended to calumniate his conduct in the connection with Banks; being perfectly convinced that whenever the matter should be investigated, his motives for entering into it would appear pure & unimpeachable. I was not without my fears though that he might suffer in a pecuniary way by his engagement with this man. I would fain hope however that the case may, ultimately, be otherwise; and that upon a final settlement of his affairs there will be a handsome competency for Mrs Greene and the Children. But should the case be otherwise, and Mrs Greene, yourself, and Mr Rutlidge would think proper to entrust my namesake G: Washington Greene to my care, I will give him as good an education as this Country (I mean the United States) will afford, and will bring him up to either of the genteel professions that his frds may chuse, or his own inclination shall lead him to pursue, at my own cost & expence.[1]

I Condole very sincerely with Mrs Greene (to whom please to tender my respects) and the rest of General Greenes friends on the loss the public, as well as his family, has sustained by the death of this valuable character—especially at this crisis—when the political machine seems pregnant with the most awful events.

My compliments if you please to Mrs Wadsworth, and any of my old acquaintance who may happen to compose your circle. With much esteem & regd I am—Dear Sir Yr most Obedt Servt

Go: Washington

ALS, CtHWa; LB (incomplete), DLC:GW.

1. George Washington Greene, who was born in the winter of 1776–77, began his formal education in 1781 under the care of John Witherspoon in

Princeton. At the time of his father's death, he was living with his parents at Mulberry Grove plantation near Savannah, where Phineas Miller was serving as tutor to the Greene children. Catharine Greene decided to accept an offer from Lafayette to take young George into his household and provide for his education, and in May 1788 the 12-year-old boy sailed for France under the care of Joel Barlow. Shortly after his return to Georgia more than four years later, George Washington Greene in the spring of 1793 drowned in the Savannah River after his canoe capsized (Stegeman and Stegeman, *Caty*, 92–93, 130– 31, 161–62).

From Henry Knox

My dear sir.   New York 23 October 1786
   I have long intended myself the pleasure of visiting you at Mount Vernon, and although, I have not given up that hope, and shall probably gratify it in the Course of next month, yet I cannot longer delay presenting myself to the remembrance of my truly respected and beloved general, whose friendship I shall ever esteem among the most valuable circumstances of my existence.[1]
   Conscious of affection, and beleiving it to be reciprocal in your breast, I have had no apprehensions of my silence being misconstrued. I know the perplexity occasioned by your numerous correspondents and was unwilling to add to it. Besides which, I have lately been once far eastward of Boston, on private business, and was no sooner returned here, than the commotions in Massachusetts hurried me back to Boston on a public account.
   Our political machine constituted of thirteen independent sovereignties, have been constantly operating against each other, and against the federal head, ever since the peace—The powers of Congress are utterly inadequate to preserve the balance between the respective States, and oblige them to do those things which are essential to their own welfare, and for the general good. The human mind in the local legislatures seems to be exerted, to prevent the federal constitution from having any beneficial effects. The machine works inversly to the public good in all its parts. Not only is State, against State, and all against the federal head, but the States within themselves possess the name only without having the essential concomitant of government, the power of preserving the peace; the protection of the liberty and property of the citizens.

On the first impression of Faction and licentiousness the fine theoretic government of Massachusetts has given way, and its laws arrested and trampled under foot. Men at a distance, who have admired our systems of government, unfounded in nature, are apt to accuse the rulers, and say that taxes have been assessed too high and collected too rigidly—This is a deception equal to any that has hitherto been entertained. It is indeed a fact, that high taxes are the ostensible cause of the commotions, but that they are the real cause is as far remote from truth as light from darkness. The people who are the insurgents have never paid any, or but very little taxes—But they see the weakness of government; They feel at once their own poverty, compared with the opulent, and their own force, and they are determined to make use of the latter, in order to remedy the former. Their creed is "That the property of the United States has been protected from the confiscations of Britain by the joint exertions of all, and therefore ought to be the common property of all. And he that attempts opposition to this creed is an enemy to equity and justice, and ought to be swept from off the face of the earth." In a word they are determined to annihilate all debts public and private and have agrarian Laws which are easily effected by the means of unfunded paper money which shall be a tender in all cases whatever.

The numbers of these people may amount in massachusetts to about one fifth part of several populous counties, and to them may be collected, people of similar sentiments, from the States of Rhode Island, Connecticut and New Hampshire so as to constitute a body of 12 or 15000 desperate & unprincipled men— They are cheiffly of the Young and active part of the community, more easily collected than perhaps Kept together afterwards— But they will probably commit overt acts of treason which will compel them to embody for their own safety—once embodied they will be constrained to submit to discipline for the same reason. Having proceeded to this length for which they are now ripe, we shall have a formidable rebellion against reason, the principles of all government, and the very name of liberty. This dreadful situation has alarmed every man of principle and property in New England—They start as from a dream, and ask what has been the Cause of our delusion? What is to afford us security against the violence of lawless men? Our government must be braced, changed, or altered to secure our lives and property. We imagined that the mildness of our government and *the virtue* of the people were so correspondent, that we were not as other nations requiring brutal force to support the laws— But we find that we are men, actual men, possessing all the turbulent passions belonging to that animal and that we must have a government proper and adequate to him—The people of Massachusetts for instance, are far advanced in this doctrine, and the men of reflection, & principle, are determined to endevor to establish a government which shall have the power to protect them in their lawful pursuits, and which will be efficient in all cases of internal commotions or foreign invasions—They mean that liberty shall be the basis, a liberty resulting from the equal and firm administration of the laws. They wish for a general government of unity as they see the local legislatures, must naturally and necessarily tend to retard and frustrate all general government.

We have arrived at that point of time in which we are forced to see our national humiliation, and that a progression in this line, cannot be productive of happiness either public or private—something is wanting and something must be done or we shall be involved in all the horror of faction and civil war without a prospect of its termination—Every tried friend to the liberties of his country is bound to reflect, and to step forward to prevent the dreadful consequences which will result from a government of events—Unless this is done we shall be liable to be ruled by an Arbitrary and Capricious armed tyranny, whose word and will must be law.

The indians on the frontiers are giving indisputable evidence of their hostile dispositions. Congress anxiously desirous of averting the evils on the frontiers, have unanimously agreed to augment the troops now in service to a legionary Corps of 2040 Men. The additionals are to be raised as follows

	Connecticut	180
	R. Island	120
Infantry and artilly	Massachusetts	660
	New Hampshire	260
Cavalry	Maryland	60
	Virginia	60
		1340

This measure is important, and will tend to strengthning the principle of government as well as to defend the frontiers—I mention the idea of strengthning government confidentially but the State of Massachusetts requires the greatest assistance, & Congress are fully impressed with the importance supporting her with great exertions.[2]

I received your favor respecting Desdevans who has been teizing congress for a number of years—He is now at lake champlain—I never have been convinced of his services for the Union, although he has received considerable emoluments therefrom.[3]

The death of our common & invaluable friend genl Greene, has been too melancholy and affecting a theme to write upon.

Mrs Knox has lately presented me with another daughter, who with its mother are in good health—She unites with me in presenting to Mrs Washington and yourself the most affectionate respects. I am my dear Sir with ardent wishes for your permanent and perfect felicity Your sincere friend, and much obliged humble Servant

                                             H. Knox

ALS, DLC:GW; ADf, NNGL.
   1. Knox did not visit Mount Vernon at this time.
   2. See *JCC*, 31:892–93.
   3. For Maurice Desdevens's request to GW, see GW to Knox, 21 Aug., n.1.

From Joseph Mandrillon

General   Amsterdam [Holland] 24th Octr 1786.
   Your Excellency gave me reason to hope in your last letter, that if the Statutes of the Cincinnati permitted it, you would do me the pleasure, Sir, to propose me in the next Assembly of 1787.[1]

Permit me to repeat to your Excellency how much I shall feel myself flattered by being connected, by a new bond, to a Count[r]y & to Citizens who have had so much of my devotion & admiration. In consequence, I take the liberty, Mr President, to send you my address to that illustrious Assembly.[2] It will be peculiarly agreeable to me to appear there under Aspices so respectable as those of your Excellency. If I am so happy as to obtain this favour, it will be equally agreeable to me to announce it to the Marquis de la Fayette, who will be charmed at my adoption.[3]

I understand that each member contributes something towards establishing a fund for the releif of the Widows & families of those who perished in the defence of their County. Think, Sir, how happy I shall be in taking a part in that humane & patriotic Contribution!

I have lately had a visit from Colo. Vernon, who travels with Milady Hamilton & returned to England.[4] We conversed much upon American affairs & particularly about your Excellency whose Virtues he admires as much as myself—What pleasure did I feel in conversing with a person who was so well acquainted with America & her Liberator!

Accept (with the enclosed Verses)[5] the Assurances of profound respect with which I shall never cease to have the Honor to be Your Excellency's Most Hble & most Obedt Servt

Mandrillon

I recommend to your care the list of the Members which I have made mention of in my Memorial. Accept, I beseech you, before hand, of my Gratitude for it. I wait only for that to publish a new Edition of my work.

Translation, DLC:GW; ALS, in French, DSoCi. Both Mandrillon's letter and his address to the Society of the Cincinnati are endorsed: "Read in Genl Meeting [or Meetg] May 18th '87." The ALS is in CD-ROM:GW.

1. GW wrote Mandrillon on 22 Aug. 1785. For a description of the correspondence between GW and Mandrillon, see the source note in Mandrillon to GW, 11 June 1784.

2. The translation of Mandrillon's enclosed address to the Society of the Cincinnati is in DLC:GW and is printed in Hume, *Society of the Cincinnati*, 260–61. Mandrillon asks for honorary membership in the society or to be given "the title of your *Historiographer*, and to print in french (at the end of a new edition of the *American Spectator* which I shall publish this current year of 1787) every thing which concerns the Rules and regulations of your illustrious Society" (ibid., 260).

3. The translator omitted this paragraph: "Souffrez, Monsieur, j'ajoute qu'un membre de plus en Europe ne sauroit devenir d'aucune conséquence pour l'Amerique, et qu'il est souvent des cas où l'on fait taire pour un moment la sévérité des loix & des statuts, surtout quand il sagit de ne faire que le bien."

4. "Colo. Vernon" may be the "Mr Vernon" mentioned by GW in a letter to Henry Knox of 8 Oct. 1783 introducing a Polish nobleman who was "travelling the Continent for his amusement." Traveling with him was "Mr Vernon, an

English Gentleman lately from Europe." "Milady Hamilton" was probably Elizabeth Gunning (1734–1790), a famous beauty who entered into a clandestine marriage with James, sixth duke of Hamilton, in 1752. After Hamilton's death she married in 1759 John Campbell, marquis of Lorne, heir to the dukedom of Argyle, but she seems to have called herself duchess of Hamilton, the superior title, until 1770 when Lorne became duke of Argyle. In 1776 she was created Baroness Hamilton of Hambleton in her own right. She suffered from consumption and beginning in 1760 spent much time in Italy and France, frequently traveling with a large retinue. Col. Vernon may have been traveling with her at this time. According to a London newspaper the duchess through her two marriages came "from being . . . a private lady" to have "no less than 26 [or 28] peerages in three kingdoms [France, Scotland, and England], viz. five duchies, six marquisates, six counties, two viscounties, and nine baronies" (Lewis, *Walpole Correspondence*, 23:247, n.10).

5. The "enclosed Verses" have not been found. They may have been included in his *Fragmens de politique et de littérature* that Mandrillon sent GW in 1788 (Mandrillon to GW, 25 Oct. 1788, n.1.).

From John Henry

Octobr 25th 1786.

A submission to intrusion is a tribute which exalted Characters must expect will be exacted from them, and that often founded in Ignorance, or Impudence, yet sometimes from admiration of the Character address'd. to this last, I shall rely on your Excellencys known Philanthropy to attribute the freedom of the person that now presumes to approach you, who flatters himself his mite of Respect, will not be the less welcome because cloathed in the garb of Humility.

Doctor Stewart, who does me the favour to take charge of this, will deliver to your Excelly in the shape of a Salt Cellar, a peice of antiquity; thought to be so, by the once possessor Oliver Cromwell; a great, but not a good man—happy he who unites both Characters, in the sweetest of all retribution, that which arises from within.[1]

I request your Excellencys acceptance of it, and trust to your gracious feelings to excuse this intrusion; Reverence and Respect guide the Pen, and your generous heart will let those plead my pardon—I shall have, I hope, the Pride to hand down to my Childrens Children, the Happiness of boasting when they open the Page of History, where this glorious revolution shall be recorded, that the amiable founder of it, amidst the applause of surrounding Millions, condescended to accept a trifle from their Humble Progenitor.

May the Almighty bless and preserve you and yours, may you live long and Happy, and when called from hence, may you enjoy an eternal seat in those mansions of the Good where reigns silence and peace for evermore, prays, with the warmest zeal, Your Excellencys devoted Hble Servt

John Henry

ALS, DLC:GW.

Patrick Henry's son John was a captain in the Continental army when in June 1778 his "ill state of health obliged him to quit the service" (GW to Patrick Henry, 13 Sept. 1778), but it seems unlikely that it was he who sent Oliver Cromwell's "Salt Cellar" to GW. Nor does it seem likely that the sender was John Henry (1750–1798) of Dorchester County, Md., who at this time was in New York attending Congress as a delegate from Maryland.

1. David Stuart was in Richmond attending the session of the house of delegates as a representative from Fairfax County. The session ended on 11 Jan., and on 13 Jan. GW recorded that "About 8 Oclock in the evening Doctr. Stuart on his return from the General Assembly at Richmond . . . came in" (*Diaries*, 5:94). GW wrote John Henry from Mount Vernon on 23 Jan. 1787: "Sir, Your letter of the 26th of October, & the piece of Antiquity accompanying it, I received by the hands of Doctr Stuart on the 13th inst: You will be pleased to accept of my thanks for your politeness in sending me the latter which, on account of it's antiquity & having been once the property of so remarkable a character as Oliver Cromwell, would undoubtedly render it pleasing to almost any one, and to an antiquary, perhaps invaluable. I am Sir Your Most Obedt hble Servant G: Washington" (LB, DLC:GW).

From William Hull

Sir   Newton [Mass.] 25th October 1786

At the Request of a Number of Gentlemen in this State, & many of them Officers in the late American Army, I take the Liberty of addressing your Excellency on a Subject, which they conceive of very great Importance to them—Your Excellency has doubtless seen the Articles of Association formed in this State for the purpose of making a Settlement in the Western Country on the Ohio[1]—A very considerable Number have subscribed to that Association and it is their Intention to carry it into Effect next Summer—As your Excellency has a perfect Knowledge of that Country, and we are persuaded, a Disposition to oblige those who were your Companions during the War, they have requested me to solicit your Advice with respect to the best Mode of effecting their Plan—Any Communications which I shall have the Honor to receive, will be laid before those who intend to be adventurers, at their next meeting, which will soon take place—As there are many Persons possessing considerable Property, whose Intention it is to transfer that Property and remove their Families to that Country, they wish to do it in such a Way as will conduce most to their Interest. Cows particularly will be very necessary, & driving them such a distance will be injurious to them & attended with considerable Expence—They wish to know whether it would not be more eligible to ship them in some part of Connecticutt and land them at Alexandria or some other place at the Southward, & from there drive them by Land—If so they would wish to know the particular place where it would be most convenient to land them, the Distance from that place to Fort-Pitt, the Situation of the Roads, & a variety of other Circumstances which will occur to your Excellency—They likewise wish to know whether there is a Furnace at Fort Pitt, or in that Country, where they can procure Iron Ware, & indeed whether they can purchase such Articles as will be necessary for their comfortable Existance, or whether it will be best for them to carry them from N. England. Any general Hints, which your Excellency will please to give on the Subject will be very gratefully received by those who feel the strongest Affection to your Person, & the sincerest Wishes for your Happiness, & still place Confidence in that Friendship which was so eminently distinguished during the War As an apology for this Letter, perhaps it may not be amiss to mention, that at the last Meeting, they appointed me one of their Committee to conduct the Business[2]—With my sincerest Wishes for the Health & Happiness of Mrs Washington, permit me to rank myself among those who feel the warmest Attachment to your Excellency, & to subscribe myself your most affectionate Friend

William Hull

ALS, DLC:GW.

William Hull (1753–1825) of Derby, Conn., graduated from Yale College and practiced law before the Revolution. During the war he served in the Massachusetts forces, rising to the rank of lieutenant colonel before leaving the service in June 1784. President Jefferson in 1805 made Hull governor of the Michigan Territory, and in 1812 President Madison gave him the rank of brigadier general to lead forces in Michigan against Canada. After Hull surrendered his army, a court-martial found him guilty of cowardice and neglect of duty and sentenced him to death, a sentence which Madison remanded.

1. Rufus Putnam and Benjamin Tupper held the organizational meeting of the Ohio Company in Boston beginning 1 Mar. 1786. The "Articles of Agreement Entered into by the Subscribers for Constituting an Association by the Name of the Ohio Company" are printed in Cutler, *Life of Cutler*, 1:181–86. See Rufus Putnam to GW, 5 April 1784, and notes.

2. On 4 Mar. "the convention resolved, that Colonel Hull, Major Sargent, and Captain [John] Mills be a committee to transact the necessary business of The Ohio Company until the directors are chosen" (ibid., 186). GW responded from Mount Vernon on 20 Nov. in these terms: "Dear Sir, I have received your letter of the 25th of October. I only write now to acknowledge the receipt of it, & to inform you that I shall be happy to do anything in my power to forward the settlement which you mention, or to oblige, in any way, any of my Compatriots in the field.

"As soon as I have collected all the necessary & useful information I can respecting the matter, (which I will endeavour to do) I will with pleasure communicate it to you; for at present my knowledge of the Western Country is more general, than particular, especially in the parts of it to which I presume you have turned your eyes. From Fort Pitt, downwards as low as the Great Kanhawa I have a pretty accurate knowledge of the climate, soil &c.; but below this river, & west of the ohio my ideas are borrowed. I am Sir &c. G: Washington" (LB, DLC:GW). See also GW to Tobias Lear, 30 November. But see GW to Hull, 29 Dec. 1786.

Letter not found: from Presley Neville, 25 Oct. 1786. On 27 Nov. GW wrote Neville thanking him for "your letter of the 25th ulto from the Court House of Washington."

To George Augustine Washington

Dear George,   Mount Vernon 25th Octor 1786.
It is natural for young married people, who are launching into life, to look forward to a permanent establishment. If they are prudent, they will be *reasonably* sollicitous to provide for those who come after, & have a right to look to them for support.

It is also natural for those who have passed the meridian of life, & are descending into the shades of darkness, to make arrangements for the disposal of the property of which they are possessed. The first of these observations will apply to you; & the second to myself. I have no doubt but that you & Fanny are as happy & contented in this family as circumstances will admit. Yet, something is still wanting to make that situation more stable & pleasing.

It is well known that the expensive manner in which I am as it were involuntarily compelled to live, will admit of no diminution of my income, nor could it be expected if I now had, or ever should have descendants, that I either would, or ought in justice to deprive them of what the laws of nature & the laws of the land, if left to themselves, have declared to be their inheritance. The first however is not the case at present; and the second, not likely to be so hereafter.

Under this statement then, I may add that it is my present intention to give you at my death, my *landed* property in the neck, containing by estimation between two & three thousand acres, by purchases from Wm Clifton and George Brent, and that the reasons why I communicate this matter to you at this time, are that you may, if you chuse it, seat the negroes which Colo. Bassett has promised you upon that part of the cleared land, on which Saml Johnson formerly lived; And under this expectation & prospect, that you may, when it perfectly suits your inclination & convenience, be preparing for, and building thereon by degrees.[1]

You may say, or think perhaps, that as there is a contingency tacked to this intimation, the offer is too precarious to hazard the expence of building; but if Mrs Washington should survive me, there is a moral certainty of my dying without issue; & should I be the longest liver, the matter in my opinion, is hardly less certain; for while I retain the faculty of reasoning, I shall never marry a girl; & it is not probable that I should have children by a woman of an age suitable to my own, should I be disposed to enter into a second marriage.[2] However, that there may be no possibility of your sustaining a loss, the matter may rest on the footing of compensation. I do therefore hereby declare it to be, & it is my express meaning, that, if by the event before alluded to, or any other by which you may be deprived of the fee-simple in the lands herein mentioned, (unless a full equivalent is given in lieu thereof) that I will pay the cost of any buildings which you may erect on the premises. The use of the Plantation, it is presumed, will be adequate for the fences with which it may be enclosed, & for the labour arising from the cultivation—nothing therefore need be said on that head.

Here then, the prospect of a permanent inheritance is placed in the opposite scale of possible disappointment, & you are to judge for yourself.

I have been thus particular, because I would be clearly understood; because it is not my wish to deceive, & because I would not raise an expectation not warranted from the premises, by fair deduction.

Johnson's plantation, as I believe, yes know, is destitute of fencing, but there is timber at hand. The cleared land, whatever may have been the original quality of it, now is, by use, & more so by abuse, much gullied & in bad condition; but as there is a sufficiency of it for the hands you will get, it may soon by care, good management, & a proper course of cropping, be recovered.

One thing more & I will close this letter. Do not infer from my proposing it to you to build, that I meant it as a hint for you to prepare another home—I had no such idea. To point you to a settlement which you might make at leizure, & with convenience was all I had in view. More than once, I have informed you that in proportion as age & its concomitants encrease upon me, I shall stand in need of some person in whose industry & integrity I can confide for assistance. The double ties by which you are connected with this family (to say nothing of the favourable opinion we have of you) by marriage union, have placed you differently from any other of my relations for this purpose; because no other married couple could give, or probably would receive the same satisfaction by living in it that you and Fanny do. But whether you remain in the same house, or at a future day may remove to the place proposed, your services will be convenient & essential to me; because with your aid I shall be able to manage my concerns without having recourse to a Steward, which comports neither with my interest nor inclination to employ. With very affectionate regard I am—Yrs

G: Washington

LB, DLC:GW; copy, DLC:GW.

1. In 1760 GW acquired 1,806 acres at Mount Vernon from William Clifton and 238 acres from George Brent. See The Growth of Mount Vernon, 1754–

86 in *Diaries*, 1:240–42. For further references to the slaves given to George Augustine Washington's father-in-law, Burwell Bassett, see George Augustine Washington to GW, 25 Oct. 1786, and, perhaps, 3 Feb. 1786. George Augustine Washington predeceased GW.

2. Eugene E. Prussing reported that a tradition persisted in Masonic circles that Martha Washington would have required corrective surgery to conceive children after her marriage to GW (memorandum of Charles C. Wall, 24 Jan. 1975, ViMtV).

From George Augustine Washington

Honor'd Uncle   Mount Vernon Octr 25th 1786
 I find it impossible to give expression to my feelings adequate to the warmth of gratitude which Your favor of this morning has excited. I know however it is not Your wish to receive laboured acknowledgements, and I will endeavour to offer no more (in this way) than will shew my deep sence of a new and extraordinary instance of regrard, in addition to the weighty obligations of being advanced in early life by Your patronage—supported in my circumstances, and placed in the happy situation of improvement from Your example and advice. I shall be sunk to worthless depravity e'er any one of these are blot'ed from my memory, or e'er a day passes that the remembrance of them does not induce fervent prayers for Your happiness and for Your being long spared to me and humanity—Both Fanny and myself are happier in this family than we could be in any other or I am persuaded in a house of our own, yet the prospect of those helpless dependants whom nature and duty teaches us to be solicitous for, renders it prudent to make arrangements for obviating the inconvenience that may arise from an increase to Your family. The Negroes Colo. Bassett will give me, cannot I am persuaded be so advantageously disposed of as in the way You so generously and kindly offer. To know that my services contribute in the smallest degree to Your satisfaction, or ease, is a circumstance highly pleasing, and a strict obedience to Your wishes will ever be a governing principal with Your truely affectionate Nephew

Geo: A. Washington

ALS, ViMtV.

From Lafayette

My dear General   Paris October the 26th 1786
To one who So tenderly loves You, who So Happily Enjoyed
the times We Have past together, and Who Never, on any part
of the Globe, Even in His own House, Could feel Himself so
Perfectly at Home, as in Your family, it Must Be Confessed that
an irregular lengthty Correspondance is far insufficient—I Beseech You in the Name of our friendship, of that Paternal Concern of Yours for My Happiness, Not to Miss Any Opportunity
to let me Hear from My dear General.

I Have Been travelling through Some Garrison towns, in
order to preserve the Habit of Seeing troops and their tactics—
Now am Mostly at fontainebleau where the Court is Residing
for a few weecks—The inclosed letter from the Minister to Mr
jefferson will, I Hope, prove Agreable to the United States[1]—
our Committees will Go on this Winter, and I will Endeavour to
propose Such Measures as May be thought Advantageous—Mr
jefferson is a Most able and Respected Representative, and Such
a Man as Makes me Happy to Be His Aid de Camp—Congress
Have Made a choice Very favourable to their affairs.

The treaty of Commerce betwen france and England is Made
But not Yet Ratified—they are to treat each other like the Most
favoured *European* Nation—So that America is Safe—News-
papers Will Acquaint You With the dutch Quarrels—it is
Strange to See So Many people, So Angry, on So Small a Spot,
without Bloodshed—But Parties are At the Same time Sup-
ported in their Claims, and Cramped in their Motions By the
Neighbouring powers—france Sides with the Patriots—the New
King of prussia interest Himself in Behalf of the Stat Holder His
Brother in law—and So does England Under Hand—But the
Republicans are So Strong, and the State Holder is Such a Block
Head, that it will turn out to the Advantage of the former[2]—No
Present Appearance of a War in Germany—The Russians and
turks are Quarrelling, But will not So Soon Make a War—the
Empress is Going to Krimée, where it is Said She will Meet the
Emperor—She Had Givin Me polite Hints that I Should go to
Pete[r]sburg—I Have Answered With a demand of a Permission
to Go to Krimée Which Has Been Granted—So that, (if the af-
fair of the forts, Which I think Must be taken does not More

Agreably employ me)³ I will Set out the last days of february for Krimée, and Return by Constantinople and the Archipelago—I will Refer to the Hints Given in a former letter about those forts which, if timely Advertised, Would Carry me Quite a different, and Much More pleasing Course.

I Have Been So Much Affected, My dear General, and So deeply Mourning for the Heavy loss which the United States, and ourselves particularly Have Had to Support, While Our Great and Good friend Gal Greene Has be Snatched from a Country to Which He Was an Honour; that I feel a Confort in Condoling With one Who Knew So well His Value, and Will of Course So much Have lamented the loss[.] There is Between Mr jefferson and Mr Adams a diversity of Opinion Respecting the Algerines Adams thinks a peace Should Be purchased from them—Mr jefferson finds it as cheap and More Honourable to Cruize Against them—I incline to the later opinion, and think it possible to form an Alliance Betwen the United States, Naples, Rome, Venice, Portugal and Some other powers—Each Giving a Sum of Monney Not Very large—Whereby a Common Armament May distress the Algerines into Any terms—Congress ought to Give Mr jefferson and Adams Ample powers to Stipulate in their Names for Such a Confederacy.⁴

You will Be pleased to Hear that I Have Great Hopes to See the affairs of the Protestants in this Kingdom put on a Better footing—not Such by far as it ought to Be—But Much Mended from the Absurd, and Cruel laws of lewis the fourteenth.⁵

I Hope Your jack Ass, with two females, and a few pheasants and Red partridges have Arrived Safe.

Adieu, My dear general, My Best and tenderest Respects wait on Mrs Washington—Remember me to the one who was formerly Master tub, and Now Must Be a Big Boy, and also to the Young ladies—Be pleased to Pay My Affectionate Compliments to George and His lady, to doctor and Mrs Stuart, doctor Craig, doctor Griffith, Your Brothers, Mrs Lewis, to Your Venerable Mother, to all our friends, and often think of Your Most devoted friend, Your Adoptive Son who with all the affection and Respect Which You know are so deeply Rooted in His Heart Has the Honour to Be My dear General, Yours

Lafayette

A New instance of the Goodness of the State of Virginia Has Been Given me, by the placing of My Bust at the Hôtel de ville of this City—the Situation of the other Bust will Be the More pleasing to Me as While it places me within the Capitol of the State, I will Be eternally By the Side of, and paying an Everlasting Homage to the Statue of My Beloved General.[6]

I Have Received the Hams, and am much obliged to that kind attention of Mrs Washington—the first was introduced three days ago at a dinner Composed of Americans, Where our friend Chattelux Had Been invited—They Arrived in the Best order— Mde delafayette and the little family Beg their Best Respects to Mrs Washington and Yourself.[7]

ALS, PEL.

1. The letter of Charles-Alexandre de Calonne, comptroller general of finances, to Thomas Jefferson, dated 22 Oct., ratifies the general regulations for Franco-American trade as approved by Lafayette's American committee (Boyd, *Jefferson Papers*, 10:474–78).

2. Frederica Sophia Wilhelmina, the sister of Frederick William II of Prussia, and her husband, the stadtholder William V of Orange, were extremely unpopular with the Patriot, or Republican, party in the Netherlands.

3. Lafayette wrote GW on 24 May 1786: "There are only two ways to obtain them [the northwest forts]—Sword in hand with a wiew to extend farther and then ready I am."

4. See Julian Boyd's editorial note for Jefferson's Proposed Concert of Powers against the Barbary States, July–December 1786, ibid., 560–68.

5. See the earlier exchange between Lafayette and GW regarding Lafayette's disapproval of the treatment of French Protestants, Lafayette to GW, 11 May 1785, and GW to Lafayette, 1 Sept. 1785.

6. Lafayette is referring to the Houdon bust of himself which was placed in the Virginia capitol with Houdon's statue of GW.

7. See GW to Lafayette, 8 June 1786.

Letter not found: to Clement Biddle, 28 Oct. 1786. On 5 Nov. Biddle wrote GW: "I have your Esteemed favour of 28th ulto."

From John Leigh

Norfolk Octr 30th 1786

I trust that your Excellency will pardon the liberty which I have taken with your Name, when the Circumstances are made known to you which induc'd me thus to conduct myself.

While I was engag'd in the Study of Medicine at the University of Edinburgh, the Professors offer'd a premium to any Student there, who shou'd write the best Dissertation on Opium; I enter'd immediately the List of Competitors, and was so fortunate as to gain the premium—Having effected this, my Friends advisd me to publish my Work, as the Subject was new, and containd many Experiments never before made. Sensible of the great benefits which every infant Production must experience by having a Protector, whose Name is sufficient to claim for it the Attention and favour of the World, and sensible also that there was no One on the Continent so well calculated to effect this as your Excellency—I was led to take the liberty of Dedicating my Work to you, a Copy of which will now accompany this Letter, begging for your Excellency's Patronage and support.[1] I have the Honor to subscribe myself, Your Excellency's most Obd. and very Hble Servt

J. Leigh

ALS, DLC:GW.

1. John Leigh's 144-page book, *An Experimental Inquiry into the Properties of Opium, and Its Effects on Living Subjects: with Observations on Its History, Preparations and Uses. Being the Disputation Which Gained the Harveian Prize for the Year 1785* (Edinburgh, 1786), was in GW's library at the time of his death. Leigh, a native of King William County, was listed as a student at the College of William and Mary in 1769, and in his book on opium he identifies himself as a medical doctor. On 9 Jan. 1787 GW wrote Leigh from Mount Vernon: "Sir, I received your letter of the 30th of October, together with your Dissertation on opinion [opium]. You will please Sir, to accept my thanks for the honor which you did me in the dedication of your work. Altho' I am not desireous of compliments of this kind, & have put off several applications which have been made to dedicate literary productions to me, yet I should always wish to encourage every useful and beneficial performance as much as is in my power. I am Sir &c. G: Washington" (LB, DLC:GW).

From George McCarmick

[c.30 October 1786]

I take Pleasure to wright to your Exallecy that you have Gaind all your land on millers Run—the persons who lives on the land are Determined to Go off amadetely. and will not lye—it wood be well a nuff not to Destress them any more—I do not think the land Can be Sold yet. money is So Scares here—Charles

Morgan is to meet me On the land Next friday to Runrou[n]d
it and mark the lines plane—if the men Should move off, it
wood be Nessery to Git Sombody to live on the lands to keep
the fence and plantations in Good order. and to Rent them, till
the[y] Can be Sold. I think the best way to Sell them, wood be
to Sell them in 2[,] 3 or 4 hundred Acres lotts—the[y] wood Sell
better and for more—how Ever I leve that to your own good
Judgment I have Shown them your Advertisement before the
tryall which the[y] laft at but have Cryed Sence—the Sooner the
land Could be taken Care off it would be the better, to appoint
Som body to take Care for you—I Expect a Number of men this
winter from the Jarseys to by lands—here I have Sold my land
to Sum Jarsey men nere your lands at 16/3 d. pr acre one half
Down and the other to be paid in Six months. but the land is
not as Good as yours I Dont think you Can Get more than
twenty Shillings pr acre—to Get Good pay[1]—I will do any thing
I can to oblidge you in the land—I can do nothing in Mr Lund
washington Land before Next fall; there is no dought but he
will Get his land then, the people who lives on his land will not
Give up[2]—which I wish you to inform him—the Judges paid
the Strictest Regards to our Virginia Rights—and any persons
who has any Just Clame under Virginia wright there is not the
lest Dought but he will have his lands Secured to him. this Judgments of the Judges has fritened all the Cohees[3] from Steelling
of Lands.

AL, DLC:GW. Some of the dots scattered through the text have been made
commas, and others have been eliminated. "Hond by Mr [Battaile] Mues" is
written on the cover.

1. George McCarmick, who lived in the area, was GW's agent for renting or
selling the land in the Millers Run tract under dispute in Washington County,
Pennsylvania. The lawyer in charge of the Millers Run eviction suits, Thomas
Smith, wrote GW on 7 Nov. confirming that he had secured favorable verdicts
in the trials held on 24, 25, and 26 October.

2. For Lund Washington's western landholdings, see Gilbert Simpson to
GW, 14 June 1773, n.3.

3. "Cohee" was a term often applied to people in the western parts of Virginia and Pennsylvania by those in the more settled eastern parts.

To the Society of the Cincinnati

Sir,   Mount Vernon in Virginia 31st Octo. 1786

I take this early opportunity, in my character of President of the Cincinnati, of announcing to you, that the triennial General Meeting of the Society is to be convened at the City of Philadelphia[1] on the first Monday of May in the year 1787.

As it will not be in my power (for reasons which I shall have the honor of immediately communicating) to attend the next General Meeting; and as it may become more and more inconvenient for me to be absent from my Farms,[2] or to receive appointments which will divert me from my private affairs; I think it proper also to acquaint you, for the information of your Delegates to the General Meeting, that it is my desire not to be re-elected to the Presidency, since I should find myself under the necessity of declining the acceptance of it.

The numerous applications for information, advice, or assistance which are made to me in consequence of my military command; the multiplicity of my correspondencies in this Country as well as in many parts of Europe; the variety & perplexity of my own private concerns, which, having been much deranged by my absence through the war, demand my entire & unremitting attention; the arduousness of the task, in which I have been as it were unavoidably engaged, of superintending the opening the navigation of the great rivers in this State; the natural desire of tranquility and relaxation from business, which almost every one experiences at my time of life, particularly after having acted (during a considerable period) as no idle spectator in uncommonly busy & important scenes; and the present imbecility of my health, occasioned by a violent attack of the fever & ague, succeeded by rheumatick pains (to which till of late I have been an entire stranger);[3] will, I doubt not, be considered as reasons of sufficient validity to justify my conduct in the present instance.

Although the whole of these reasons could not have before operated; yet, in conformity to my determination of passing the remainder of my days in a state of retirement, I should certainly have refused to accept the office of President with which I was honored in 1784, but from an apprehension that my refusal, at that time, might have been misrepresented as a kind of dereliction of the Society on my part, or imputed to a disapprobation of the principles on which it was then established. To convince the opposers of the Institution, should any such remain, that this was not the fact; and to give no colourable pretext for unreasonable attacks; I prevailed upon myself to accept the appointment with a view of holding it only until the next election: before which time I expected the jealousy that had been excited, would subside—and this, I am happy to be informed, has universally taken place.

Highly approving as I do, the principles on which the Society is now constituted; and pleased to find, so far as I have been able to learn from reiterated enquiries, that is is acceptable to the good people of the United States in general; it only remains for me to express the sense I entertain of the honor conferred by the last General Meeting in electing me their President, and to implore in future the benediction of Heaven on the virtuous Associates in this illustrious Institution.

During the residue of my continuance in Office, I shall be constantly ready to sign such *Diplomas* as may be requisite for the members of your State Society, being sincerely desirous of giving every possible proof of attachment, esteem, & affection for them; as well as of demonstrating the sentiments of perfect consideration & respect with which I have the honor to be Sir Yr most Obedt and most Hble Servt

Go: Washington

P.S. I have thought it expedient to forward a transcript of this circular address to Majr Genl Gates, Vice President of the Society: In order that the General Meeting may suffer no embarrassment for want of an official character to preside at the opening of it. G.W.[4]

ALS, NHi: Gates Papers; Df, in David Humphreys' hand, DLC:GW; DfS, RHi. Humphreys sent his draft of the circular letter to GW on 24 September. The emendations that GW made are noted. The draft is dated 31 Oct. as are the copies, signed by GW, which he sent to Gen. Horatio Gates as the vice-president of the Society of the Cincinnati and to the presidents of the individual state societies.

1. GW changed this from "New York" in the draft to "Philadelphia."
2. In the draft, this reads "plantations" instead of "farms."
3. GW inserted in the draft the passage beginning with "succeeded by."
4. On 8 Nov. GW enclosed in a letter to William Heth from Mount Vernon

the circular letter with a covering letter to General Gates. The letter to Heth reads: "Dr Sir, Taking it for granted that Genl Gates will be at the proposed meeting of the Society of the Cincinnati, in Richmond the [   ] inst:—I beg the favor of you to deliver the enclosed letter to him. If he should not be there—present it if you please to the Vice President of the State Society, for the information of the Meeting; with a request that it may be forwarded after-wards to Genl Gates, by a safe conveyance, as Vice President of the Genl Meet-ing—With esteem & regard I am Dr Sir &c. G: Washington" (LB, DLC:GW).

GW's letter to Gates, also dated 8 Nov., reads: "Sir[,] Expecting this letter will be handed to you in Richmond, at the meeting summoned to be holden there the 15th inst.—you will please to receive the enclosure in your dble capacity of Vice-President of the General Meeting of the Society of the Cincin-nati—and President of the said Society for this State (Virginia). I am—Sir Yr most Obedt Hble Servt Go: Washington" (ALS, NHi: Gates Papers; LB, DLC:GW). See also George Weedon to GW, 17 Nov., and GW to Weedon, 29 December.

To Henry Lee, Jr.

Dear Sir,   Mount Vernon 31st October 1786.

I am indebted to you for your several favors of the 1st 11th & 17th instt, and shall reply to them in the order of their dates: But first let me thank you for the interesting communications imparted in them.

The picture which you have drawn, & the accts which are published, of the commotions & temper of numerous bodies in the Eastern States, are equally to be lamented and deprecated. They exhibit a melancholy proof of what our trans atlantic foe have predicted; and of another thing perhaps, which is still more to be regretted, and is yet more unaccountable; that man-kind left to themselves are unfit for their own government. I am mortified beyond expression whenever I view the clouds which have spread over the brightest morn that ever dawned upon any Country. In a word, I am lost in amazement, when I behold what intriegueing; the interested views of desperate characters; Jealousy; & ignorance of the Minor part, are capable of effecting as a scurge on the major part of our fellow citizens of the Union: for it is hardly to be imagined that the great body of the people tho' they will not act[1] can be so enveloped in darkness, or short sighted as not to see the rays of a distant sun through all this mist of intoxication & folly.

You talk, my good Sir, of employing influence to appease the tumults in Massachusetts—I know not where that influence is to be found; and if attainable, that it would be a proper remedy for the disorders. Influence is no government. Let us have one by which our lives, liberties, and properties will be secured, or let us know the worst at once. Under these impressions, my humble opinion is, that there is a call for decision. Know precisely what the Insurgents aim at. If they have real grievances, redress them, *if possible*, or acknowledge the justice of their complaints and your inability of doing it, in the present moment. If they have not, employ the force of government against them at once. If this is inadequate, *all* will be convinced that the superstructure is bad, or wants support. To be more exposed in the eyes of the world & more contemptible than we already are, is hardly possible. To delay one of the other of these, is to exasperate in one case, and to give confidence in the other; and will add to their numbers; for like Snow-balls, such bodies encrease by every movement, unless there is something in the way to obstruct, & crumble them before the weight is too great & irrisistable.

These are my sentiments. Precedents are dangerous things. Let the reins of government then be braced in time[2] & held with a steady hand; & every violation of the constitution be reprehended. If defective, let it be amended, but not suffered to be trampled on whilst it has an existence.

With respect to the navigation of the Mississipi, you already know my sentiments thereon. They have been uniformly the same, and as I have observed to you in a former letter, are controverted by one consideration *only* of weight; and that is the operation the occlusion of it may have on the minds of the Western Settlers; who will not consider the subject in a relative point of view, or on a comprehensive scale; and may be influenced by the demagagues of the Country to acts of extravagence & desperation, under a popular declamation that their interests are sacrificed. Colonel Mason is at present in a fit of the Gout, what his sentiments on the subject are, I know not, nor whether he will be able to attend the Assembly during the present Session. For some reasons (unnecessary to mention) I am inclined to believe he will advocate the navigation of that river.[3] But in all matters of great national moment the only true line of conduct—in my opinion—is dispassionately to compare the advantages & disadvantages of the measure proposed, and decide from the ponderancy. The lesser evil (where there is a choice of them) should always yield to the greater. What benefits (more than we now enjoy) are to be derived from such a Treaty as you have delineated with Spain, I am not enough of a Commercial man to give any opinion on.

The China came to hand without much damage; and I thank you for your attention in procuring & forwarding of it to me. Mrs Washington joins me in best wishes for Mrs Lee and yourself and I am very affectionately Dear Sir Yr most Obedt & Obliged Hble Servant

Go: Washington

ALS (incomplete), Vi; ALS (incomplete), NN: Washington Collection; LB, DLC:GW. The first four sheets of the manuscript are at the Virginia State Library; the last is in the New York Public Library.

1. GW inserted "of the Minor part," "as a scurge," and "tho' they will not act."

2. GW inserted "in time."

3. George Mason wrote John Fitzgerald on 28 Nov.: "I have had the longest, & most severe Fit of the Gout, I ever experienced; having been constantly confined for more than a month. . . . If it pleases God to restore me tollerable Health, I will still attend the Assembly; there being several things in Agitation there, which I think will be very injurious to the public" (Rutland, *Mason Papers*, 2:858–59). Mason, who was one of the two delegates for Fairfax County, did not attend the general assembly in its session of 16 Oct. 1786 to 11 Jan. 1787. Mason refers to rumors of a new Port Act as among the "things in Agitation," but the navigation of the Mississippi was the more divisive issue during the session (see Madison to GW, 1 Nov.).

From George McCarmick

Sir   Octbr 31th 1786

I here inform you of the two Expedition against the Indians. the Seventeenth of Sept. Genl Clark Crossed the ohio River at the falls, to Go up the wawbash River, with aleven hundred and Eighty men and artilrey. the artilarey went up the wawbash and the men and Cattle and baggage went by land—Colo. lowgan Crossed the ohio, the first Day of Octobr with Eight hundred and Seventy men at the Mought of limestone, to Go to the Shawneys towns. brice Virgan was present when the Started—there is no accounts arived here yit what Sucksess the have had[1]—my Son John McCarmick, on his way from Detroyet ther Come with Simon Gurty and Colo. Brant to the upper Sunduskey on there way to the Grat Shawney town to a Grat Counsell, which was to be the fifteenth of Octbr he parted with them the tenth, which we all Expect that Colo. Lowgan, will take them in there Counsell; there is but ⟨a majr⟩ and Sixty men of the british, at Detroyet[2]—my Son went there with a Drove of Cattle and was there about two weeks—I ashoure you that these accounts Can be Relyed on And beg leve to Subscribe my Self your freend and Most hum. Sart

Go: McCarmick

N.B. I hope you will Excuse me for feeing of Mr Ross for you he is the first Loyer in this part of the world, and was the Most Ablest Loyer at your tryall—and laid Down Sulch points of law that Could no be Got Over. G.M.

ALS, DLC:GW. See source note in McCarmick to GW, c.30 October.

1. Gen. George Rogers Clark assembled the Kentucky militia on the Ohio opposite Louisville and on 14 Sept. ordered Col. John Logan to attack the Shawnee towns on the Great Miami. Logan burned a number of towns and killed ten chiefs. Clark established an unauthorized garrison at Vincennes and illegally seized private property, which led to his repudiation by Gov. Edmund Randolph and the Virginia council (see George Muter to James Madison, 20 Feb. 1787, and notes 10, 11, and 12 of that document in Rutland and Rachal, *Madison Papers*, 9:279–84). In 1779 Brice Virgin was living in Ohio County, one of the three counties formed in 1776 from the West Augusta District of Virginia.

2. Simon Girty and Joseph Brant were on their way to the Shawnee town of Wakotomica for a grand council of the Iroquois and their allies when Logan's raid prevented the meeting. Brant had a leading role in the council held in Detroit in December 1786.

To William Moultrie

Dr Sir, Mount Vernon 31st Octor 1786.

As soon as your Excellency's favor of the 7th of Augt, came to my hands, I forwarded the enclosure therein, to Mr Brindley, under cover to Saml Hughes Esqr. Herewith you will receive their answers.

Presuming that your Excelly is President of the Society of the

Cincinnati in the State of South Carolina, I have the honor of addressing the enclosed circular letter to you. If I am mistaken, I pray you to forward it to the right person.[1] Mrs Washington joins me in every good wish for Mrs Moultree & yourself, & with sentiments of great regard & respect, I have the honor to be &c.

G: Washington

P.S. Permit me to request the favor of you to direct the blank cover herewith sent, to the President of the Georgia Society of the Cincinnati, & cause it to be forwarded by the first safe conveyance that may offer. G: W——n

LB, DLC:GW.

1. See GW's circular letter to the Society of the Cincinnati, this date.

From Bushrod Washington

[31 October 1786]

The motives which gave birth to the Society, were these. We conceived, that in a government where the voice and sentiments of the people are delivered by representation, the few who are elected to speak these sentiments are the servants of the electors; that in grand points of national concern, the people are the best judges of their wants, their own interests, and can more sensibly feel those evils, which they wish to be corrected; that upon these two principles they have a right to instruct their delegates; and that silence at a time when they had reason to apprehend a conduct in these servants contrary to their wishes would be highly criminal. We thought that an appearance of corruption was discoverable in the mass of the people, or, what is as bad, a total insensibility to their public interest. Persuaded of this, and equally convinced that this inattention proceeded more from the want of information than from want of real virtue, a number of the principal gentlemen in these four counties determined to assemble, for the purpose of inquiring and deliberating upon such subjects as were of the most interesting consequence, and to communicate their sentiments to the people in the form of instructions; which, if approved by them, are signed and sent to their delegates; if otherwise, they continue only the opinion of a few, and can have no weight.

The people's attention being thus awakened to their public concerns, they are led to investigate the causes of those evils which oppress them, and to endeavor by some method to relieve them. The most uninquiring mind must, when put in action, perceive that the defect is either in the manners of the people, or in the misconduct of those, who, being intrusted to form salutary laws, have adopted the most destructive measures. The evil when seen may easily be removed; and unless the majority of the people are vitiated, which can hardly be the case, they would certainly be led to apply the only two possible remedies; the one, to exert more zeal in making a judicious choice of delegates; the other, to reform their manners. I am fully convinced that nothing could be more effective of the prosperity of this country, than the method you have pointed out of electing honest and able representatives. To recommend this to the attention of the people is a principal object with this Society.[1]

Thus you will perceive, that this institution assumes no other power, than that of recommending to the people an attention to their own interests, and of furnishing them with the sentiments and opinions of a few, which they may either reject or adopt. It is true, that a few designing men might creep into these societies; but I should hope that a majority will be virtuous. If this should be the case, their recommendation may have happy consequences; if the majority should unhappily be vicious, they are but the opinions of a few expressed collectively. In this, however, I am resolved, that as soon as I perceive that other motives than those of the public good influence their conduct, I will quit them.

Sparks, *Writings*, 9:200–201. Sparks prints this fragment as a note to GW's letter to Bushrod Washington of 30 September.

1. See Bushrod Washington to GW, 27 Sept., and GW to Bushrod Washington, 30 September.

From John Brown

My Dear Sir   Providence [R.I.] 1st Novemr 1786
    Tho' its a long time since I have had the pleasure of seeing or hearing from you, my continued esteem for your Person &

Character prompts me to address you in favour of a Mr Joseph
Jenckes a young Gentleman of about 22 years of age who went
from this place to Alexandria in September last with Intention
to set down in Business there in the mercantile Line under the
Firm of Jenckes Winsor & Co. provided he liked the Country
and found due encouragement, his Father being one of the first
Families in this State wishes his Son might be indulged with your
smiles, and I do assure you from the small acquaintance I have
had with the young Gentleman I can with propriety & do recommend him as a substantial and deserving young Gentleman,[1]
any little notice you may make it convenient to show him will be
gratefully acknowleged by him, his Friends & your Obt Humble Servt

John Brown

P.S. Dr Sr As I have ever had sanguine expections of your success in the promotion & utility of the canal you have so laudably
undertaken I shall be exceedingly obliged, if not too much
Trouble, you'll please to advise me how far you have succeeded,
what number of men are employed on the work &c. &c. &c.[2]

LS, owned (1985) by Mr. Thomas Krasean, Indianapolis, Indiana.
    1. See James Manning to GW, 11 Oct., n.1.
    2. On 22 Mar. 1785 Elkanah Watson wrote GW on behalf of John Brown at
a time when the great Providence merchant had "it seriously in contemplation
to lay the foundation of a new City between the first falls & Alexandria" in
Virginia.

From David Humphreys

My dear General   New Haven Novr 1st 1786
    I wrote your Excellency some time ago from Hartford & en-
closed you the draft of a letter on the subject we talked of when
I left Mount Vernon. I hope you have duly received it, tho' I
shall not be free from anxiety until I know with certainty that
has been the case.[1]
    When I wrote that letter, I was in hopes that it might have
been in my power before this time, to give you a favorable account of the complexion of politics in this State. It is true we
have done some negative good—we have prevented an emission
of a Paper money and Tender Acts from taking place: But I am
sorry to say, we have done nothing in aid of the fœderal Govern-

ment. The only Requisition of Congress we have complied with, is a recent one for raising Troops, on account of an Indian war, as is given out. But some conjecture for other purposes. The Assembly has this day given me the Command of A Regt part to be raised in this State & a part in the other New England States. I have been advised by our friends to accept it for the present: which I shall accordingly do.

The troubles in Massachusetts still continue. Government is prostrated in the dust. And it is much to be feared that there is not energy enough in that State, to reestablish the civil Powers. The leaders of the Mob, whose fortune & measures are desperate, are strengthening themselves daily, & it is expected that they will soon take possession of the Continental Magazine at Springfield: in which there are from ten to fifteen thousand stand of Arms in excellent order.

A general want of compliance with the requisitions of Congress for money, seems to prognosticate that we are rapidly advancing to a Crisis. The wheels of the great political Machine can scarcely continue to move much longer, under their present embarrassment. Congress, I am told, are seriously alarmed, & hardly know which way to turn or what to expect. Indeed, my dear General, nothing but a good Providence can extricate us from our present difficulties, & prevent some terrible convulsion.

In case of civil discord, I have already told you, it was seriously my opinion that you could not remain neuter—and that you would be obliged, in self defence, to take part on one side or the other: or withdraw from this Continent. Your friends are of the same opinion: and I believe you are convinced, that it is impossible to have more disinterested & zealous friends than those who have been about your person.

I write with the more confidence; as this letter will be delivered by Mr Austin & Mr Morse, two young Clergimen, educated at this University, who are travelling to the southern part of the Union, for the sake of acquiring knowledge of their own Country[2]—I beg leave to recommend them to your Civilities & to assure you, in offering my best respects to Mrs Washington & the family, how sincerely I am my dear Genl your friend & Hble Servt

D. Humphreys

ALS, DLC:GW.

1. Humphreys enclosed in his letter of 24 Sept. a draft of a circular letter to the Society of the Cincinnati, a nearly identical version of which, dated 31 Oct., GW sent to Horatio Gates, vice-president of the society, as well as to the presidents of all the individual state societies.

2. Jedediah Morse (1761–1826), who had already published his first book on geography, arrived at Mount Vernon on 27 Nov. en route to Georgia. Samuel Austin, a recipient of a Master of Arts degree from Yale College in 1783, decided not to accompany Morse.

From James Madison

Dear Sir   Richmond Novr 1. 1786

I have been here too short a time as yet to have collected fully the politics of the Session. In general appearances are favorable. On the question for a paper emission the measure was this day rejected in emphatical terms by a majority of 84 vs 17. The affair of the Missisippi is but imperfectly known.[1] I find that its influence on the federal spirit will not be less than was apprehended. The Western members will not be long silent on the subject. I inculcate a hope that the views of Congress may yet be changed, and that it would be rash to suffer the alarm to interfere with the policy of amending the Confederacy. The sense of the House has not yet been tried on the latter point. The Report from the Deputies to Annapolis lies on the Table, and I hope will be called for before the business of the Mississippi begins to ferment.[2] Mr Henry has signified his wish not to be reelected, but will not be in the Assembly. The Attorney & R. H. Lee are in nomination for his successor. The former will probably be appointed, in which case the contest for that vacancy will lie between Col. Innis & Mr Marshal. The nominations for Cong[res]s are as usual numerous. There being no Senate yet it is uncertain when any of these appointments will take place.[3] With the sincerest affection & the highest esteem I am Dear Sir Yr Obedt & humble Servt

Js Madison Jr

ALS, DLC:GW; signed copy, in Madison's hand, DLC: Madison Papers.

1. Madison later annotated this sentence: "Mr. [John] Jay's project for shutting it for 25 years" (Rutland and Rachal, *Madison Papers*, 9:156). See James Monroe to GW, 20 Aug. 1786, n.2.

2. For reference to the report of the Annapolis Convention drafted by Alexander Hamilton, see note 1 of GW to John Jay, 16 Mar. 1786.

3. Edmund Randolph was elected governor of Virginia on 7 Nov. to replace Patrick Henry. James Innes, who at this time was a delegate to the house from Williamsburg, was chosen on 23 Nov. to become attorney general in the place of Randolph. John Marshall represented Fauquier County in the house of delegates in 1785 and would represent Henrico County again in 1787, but he was not a member in 1786.

To Benjamin Franklin

Dr Sir   Mount Vernon 3d Novr 1786

The letter, of which I have the honor to enclose your Excellency an extract, & the Addresses, came to my hands a few days since. Whether the latter are originals or copies, & whether any steps have been taken in compliance with Sir Edwd Newenham's wishes, you can better decide than I. Also, if there has not, what is best to be done with the application.

If I mistake not, this case militates with a resolve of Congress, which declares that none but Citizens of these United States shall hold Consular appointments under it; but how far the singularity of the application, from such a character, & under such an enumeration of circumstances; may occasion a departure therefrom (if my belief is founded) is not for me to determine.[1]

This letter to you, My good Sir, is the first move I have made in this business; & I will await your sentiments before I make another. I am, as I hope you will always believe me to be, with the greatest respect & regard, Dr Sir, &c.

G: Washington

LB, DLC:GW; copy, DNA: RG 59, Domestic Letters. Receiving no answer, GW sent Franklin a copy of this letter on 11 Feb. 1787.

1. For Sir Edward Newenham's attempt to enlist the aid of GW and Franklin in securing a consulship for his son, see Newenham to GW, 12 Aug., and note 1 of that document.

Letter not found: from Theodorick Bland, 4 Nov. 1786. On 18 Nov. GW wrote Bland of "the receipt of your obliging favors of the 4th & 9th inst."

From Lamar, Hill, Bisset, & Co.

Sir   Madeira 4 Novr 1786

We have been favoured with your's of the 3d of last August, and have to return you our best thanks for your polite attention to our sundry letters. Mr Hill acknowledges to us the receipt of your bill upon Wakelin Welch Esqre for £43.12.4 stg.[1]

We observe with infinite concern what you have mentioned in regard to the high cost of your pipe of wine, and as to an old correspondent, are desirous of giving you every satisfaction in this respect in our power.

You will permit us therefore to remark Sir, that the shipping prices of the different denominations of wine are annually fixed upon at a meeting of the Consul and factory, at a season of the year, namely the last day of December, when the new wines are already clear, and a competent judgement can be formed of their quality and quantity; upon which two circumstances the shipping prices are principally dependent.

To these prices every member of the British factory subscribes, and from these they cannot deviate without a manifest breach of promise. It has been moreover the long established custom of all the houses here to charge twenty shillings sterling per annum for every year's additional age a pipe of wine acquires in our lodges—a charge infinitely inadequate to the expence incurred by leakage and frequent racking of the wine.

During the years 1782, 3, & 4 the shipping price of particular wine was £31 stlg per pipe of 110 gallons, which is the Common gauge of a Madeira pipe. In December, 84, the vintage having proved extremely short, and the quality of the wines not very generally good, it was deemed necessary by the Factory to raise the price of our first quality from the above price to £34 stlg: at which it still continues. The pipe we had the pleasure of shipping you last December, was of the age of 3 years, and of the large or Barbadoes gauge, that is instead of holding 110 gallons, contained 120;[2] the difference of which measure is always calculated at 10 per cent—These charges, together with the insurance thereon, and the additional cost of the case, were all specifically mentioned in the letter we had on that occasion the honour of addressing to you, and to which ⟨we⟩ take the liberty of referring you. The difference between the shipping price in the year 83, and 85, is too obvious to be insisted on—We shall be sincerely happy Sir if this statement of the case will clear us from having acted with impropriety in the above respect, in the opinion of a person whose correspondence we have every reason to esteem—We have the honour to be Sir—your obt servants

Lamar Hill Bisset & Co.

LS, DLC:GW.

   1. GW wrote to Henry Hill on 3 August. See Hill's letters to GW of 9 Sept. and 1 October.

   2. For Lamar, Hill, Bisset, & Co.'s correspondence regarding this wine, see their letter to GW of 6 Dec. 1785, and note 2 of that document.

From Clement Biddle

Novemr 5th 1786

I have your Esteemed favour of 28th ulto.[1] It is scarcely possible to get the Clover seed by the bushel from the farmers or Graziers who bring it to Market—those who are Accustomed to gathering it for sale having a Constant Market with the Retailers will give them a preference & in getting it from them you are sure of the best seed—it is just now coming in & the Retailers tell me they can shortly Supply a quantity @ 14d. or 15d. the pound, they sell by the dozen or twenty pounds at 18d. The present year has not been very favourable for Barley but the Brewers will chuse the best they have for seed—but expect a profusion in the produce they giving the Highest price & they Charge no more for it than they pay the Farmers which is this year 6/ and about a penny ℔ Bushel Cuttage—Reuben Haines one of our first Brewers has promised that I shall have one hundred Bushels of the Right Spring Barley & I have informed him I should make no engagement that you would send the Produce of it here, but if you did it should be offered to him he giving the highest price[2]—No such Coarse Goods as you mention have been in any quantity for Sale at Vendue. Yrs &ca

Clement Biddle

ADfS, ViMtV: Clement Biddle Letterbook. Biddle may have written over the 5 in "Novemr 5th" to make it a 6.

   1. Letter not found.

2. Reuben Haines (d. 1793) was a partner in the Philadelphia brewing firm of Haines, Twelff, & Company. See GW to Biddle, 3 Dec. 1787.

To George Clinton

Dear Sir,   Mount Vernon Novr 5th 1786

Not having heard, or not recollecting who the President of the Society of the Cincinnati in the State of New York is, I take the liberty of giving you the trouble of the enclosed.[1]

I am endeavouring by the sale of Land, to raise money to pay for my Moiety of the purchase on the Mohawk River—So soon as this is effected I will write your Excellency more fully.[2] In the meantime, with every good wish for Mrs Clinton and the rest of your family, in which Mrs Washington cordially unites I am Dear Sir Yr Most Obedt and Affecte Hble Servt

                              Go: Washington

ALS (photocopy), NjP: Armstrong Collection; LB, DLC:GW. The ALS was offered for sale by Goodspeed's Book Shop, catalog 592, item 142.

1. See GW's circular letter to the Society of the Cincinnati, 31 October.

2. For GW's joint purchase with Clinton in 1784 of a large tract of land in upstate New York, see GW to Clinton, 25 Nov. 1784, and note 2 of that document. GW sent his payment to Clinton in June 1787 (see GW to Clinton, 9 June 1787).

From James McHenry

My dear General.   Baltimore 5 Novr 1786

I have just received from L'orient by the Iris, a present from the Marquiss de la Fayette for your Excellency, of a Jack ass two mules some pheasants and partridges, which I shall after some days rest forward to your Excellency. The reason for giving you so early information is to request you send two careful servants to assist in conducting them to your seat. I imagine I must send the birds by water. If I do not hear from you in a reasonable time I shall take the necessary steps to ensure their safe conduct.[1]

This present comes under circumstances which does honor to the Marquiss. The King of Spain makes a present like a poor man—the Marquiss like a prince. With sencere affection I am Dr General yours

                              James McHenry

ALS, PHi: Gratz Collection.

1. Lafayette refers to the jackass and two jennys and the birds in his letter to GW of 26 October. For further references to the transporting of Lafayette's gifts from Baltimore to Mount Vernon, see GW to McHenry, 11, 29 Nov., McHenry to GW, 13, 18 Nov., and GW to Lafayette, 19 November.

To James Madison

My dear Sir,   Mount Vernon 5th Novr 1786.

I thank you for the communications in your letter of the first instt. The decision of the House on the question respecting a paper emission, is portentous I hope, of an auspicious Session. It may certainly be classed among the important questions of the present day; and merited the serious consideration of the Assembly. Fain would I hope, that the great, & most important of all objects—the fœderal governmt—may be considered with that calm & deliberate attention which the magnitude of it so loudly calls for at this critical moment.

Let prejudices, unreasonable jealousies, and local interest yield to reason and liberality. Let us look to our National character, and to things beyond the present period. No Morn ever dawned more favourable than ours did—and no day was ever more clouded than the present! Wisdom, & good examples are necessary at this time to rescue the political machine from the impending storm. Virginia has now an opportunity to set the latter, and has enough of the former, I hope, to take the lead in promoting this great & arduous work. Without some alteration in our political creed, the superstructure we have been seven years raising at the expence of much blood and treasure, must fall. We are fast verging to anarchy & confusion! A letter which I have just received from Genl Knox, who had just returned from Massachusetts (whither he had been sent by congress consequent of the commotion in that State) is replete with melancholy information of the temper & designs of a considerable part of that people. among other things he says, "there creed is, that the property of the United States, has been protected from confiscation of Britain by the joint exertions of *all*, and therefore ought to be the *common property* of all. And he that attempts opposition to this creed is an enemy to equity & justice, & ought to be swept from off the face of the Earth." again "They are determined to anihilate all debts public & private, and have Agrarian Laws, which are easily effected by the means of un-funded paper money which shall be a tender in all cases what-ever." He adds. "The numbers of these people amount in Massa-chusetts to about one fifth part of several populous Counties, and to them may be collected, people of similar sentiments from the States of Rhode Island, Connecticut, & New Hampsh⟨ire⟩ so as to constitute a body of twelve or fifteen thousand desperate, and unprincipled men. They are chiefly of the young & active part of the Commun⟨ity⟩.[1]

How melancholy is the reflection that in so short a space, we should have made such large strides towards fulfill⟨ing⟩ the pre-diction of our transatlantic foes!—"leave them to themselves, and their government will soon dissolve." Will not the wise & good strive hard to avert this evil? Or will their supineness suffer ignorance, and the arts of selfinterested designing disaffected & desperate characters, to involve this rising empire in wretch-edness & contempt? What stronger evidence can be given of the want of energy in our governments than these disorders? If there exists not a power to check them, what security has a man of life, liberty, or property? To you, I am sure I need not add aught on this subject, the consequences of a lax, or inefficient government, are too obvious to be dwelt on. Thirteen Sover-eignties pulling against each other, and all tugging at the fœderal head, will soon bring ruin on the whole; whereas a lib-eral, and energetic Constitution, well guarded & closely watched, to prevent incroachments, might restore us to that de-gree of respectability & consequence, to which we had a fair claim, & the brightest prospect of attaining—With sentiments of the sincerest esteem & regard I am—Dear Sir Yr Most Obedt & Affecte Hble Servt

Go: Washington

ALS (photocopy), CSmH; LB, DLC:GW. The ALS was reported sold in the *New York Times*, 7 Dec. 1892.

1. See Henry Knox to GW, 23 October.

To David Stuart

Dear Sir, Mount Vernon 5th Novr 1786

Enclosed is a petition from the Directors of the Potomack Company to our Assembly which they request you to present; and to use your endeavors to obtain the prolongation which is therein prayed for.[1] The Assembly need be under no apprehension of unnecessary delay. Interest and inclination will equally prompt the Company to dispatch. To shorten the time required may occasion a contrariety in the Acts of the different Assemblies, & would create confusion, trouble & delay in the business. We hope therefore no attempt will be made to do this.

As the petition recites the causes which have given rise to the application, and the facts enumerated are notorious, I shall add nothing in support of it.

I also give you the trouble of a small matter which concerns myself only. It is, if you shall see no impropriety from the lapse of time (which is injurious only to myself) to offer the enclosed certificates when you shall find a fit opportunity, for payment.

The circumstances are these. In the year 1774 I bought a number of Servants, hired many freemen, and sent Negroes to the Ohio for the purpose of saving, and improving my Military Lands, agreeably to the Laws then existing. The Indian disturbances wch obliged Lord Dunmore to embody and March the Militia into that Country, checked my operations; and the seizure of part of my goods (as will appear by these Certificates) compelled me the year following to encounter the same expence, trouble & difficulty I had done the preceeding one. And no Assembly happening that could take cognizance of such Claims before my departure from this State (in May 1775) the Certificates during my absence, and the frequent removal of my papers (to keep them from the hands of the enemy) got so intermixed as not to be found till very lately. If these circumstances which are truely related, are insufficient to obtain compensation for them without subjecting the application to much disputation, I had rather undergo the loss, than the mortification of an opposition to a measure that is merely personal.[2]

As we are to be made rich by the Magity Bay-Pea, might it not be well for you to enquire how and in what manner this great good is to be effected. Particularly when they are to be sowed—

the quantity required for an Acre—Preparation of the ground & nature of the Soil best adapted for them. Whether they are to be plowed in as a manure, and in what stage of their growth; or whether the leaf alone when fallen, is sufficient to answer this purpose. The best method of saving the Seed, and the quantity to be had from an Acre, &ca &ca—Mr Savage, or some of the Gentlemen from the Eastern shore can, no doubt, give full information on all these heads.

Will you be so good as to enquire if spring Barley can be had—in what quantity, at what price, and how it could be got here. The family all join me in best wishes for you—Mrs Stuart who is here, and will put a letter under cover with this, will tell you, I presume, that she and the Children are all well. I am— Dear Sir Yr Most Obedt & Affecte Servt

Go: Washington

P.S. If you could inform me what Sum, and at what time I may depend upon the Estate of Mr Custis for it, you would oblige me. My want of money presses. I must sell something if I cannot receive part of what is due to me.[3]

G: W——n

ALS (photocopy), DLC: McGarrah Collection; LB, DLC:GW. The ALS was offered for sale in 1890 by Libbie, item 956.

1. The president and trustees of the Potomac River Company met at the Great Falls of the Potomac on 2 and 3 Oct. and before adjourning on 4 Oct. adopted this petition to the Virginia and Maryland legislatures: "The humble petition of the President and Directors of the Potomac Company, in behalf of the said Company, showeth:

"That in and by the acts of the said 'Assemblies,' for opening and extending the navigation of Potomac River, it is provided and enacted, 'That in case the said company should not begin the work mentioned in the said Act, within one year after the company should be formed; or if the navigation should not be made and improved between the *Great Falls* and *Fort Cumberland*, in the manner hereinbefore mentioned, within three years after the said company should be formed, then the said company should not be entitled to any benefit, privilege, or advantage, under the said Act.'

"That your petitioners conceive the intention of the Legislatures in limiting the company to three years, after its formation, for making and improving the navigation between the Great Falls and Fort Cumberland, was to prevent any unnecessary delay in executing the work, and on the presumption that the time allowed was fully sufficient to effect it in the common and usual course of the seasons.

"That the said company have entered on the work, within the time limited, and prosecuted the same, at great expense, with unremitted assiduity, with such prospect of success, that they hope and expect to complete the whole navigation within the ten years allowed; but that the latter part of the summer, and the fall of 1785, were so unfavorable, that the hands employed in the bed of the river, above the *Great Falls*, were often drove from their work by the rises of the water, and frequently kept out for several days together, so that the work could not proceed as was wished and expected. And the last summer hath proved so very rainy, that the water has constantly kept up too high to permit any work to be done in the bed of the river; though the company retained a considerable number of men in their service through the whole of the last winter, with the view of being prepared to enter on the work with great force, about the 20th of June, the time that the water is commonly low enough for such purpose; and thus, by extraordinary exertion, to retrieve the unavoidable loss of time in the preceding year.

"Your petitioners, therefore, on behalf of the said company, pray that acts of the said Assemblies may be passed whereby the said company may be indulged with time till the seventeenth day of November, 1790, or such other time as to your Honors shall seem reasonable for making and improving the navigation between the Great Falls and Fort Cumberland. And your petitioners, &c. In behalf of the Board, Signed, G. WASHINGTON, *President*" (printed in Pickell, *A New Chapter*, 177–78). Both legislatures acted promptly. See Thomas Johnson to GW, 7 Dec., and Stuart to GW, 25 December. See also GW to George Gilpin and John Fitzgerald, 1 Sept., and GW to Johnson, 12 November.

2. For GW's attempts to make good his claims to his military lands on the Ohio and the Great Kanawha by sending people out, see Robert Adam to GW, 9 Jan. 1774, n.2, and GW to James Cleveland, 10 Jan. 1775, and notes. For further correspondence at this time regarding these certificates, see Stuart to GW, 8, 13 Nov., 19 Dec., and GW to Stuart, 19, 24 November.

3. GW was supposed to receive £525 annually for the dower lands rented by the estate of John Parke Custis. The Custis estate was under the general management of Stuart as the husband of Custis's widow, Eleanor Calvert Custis Stuart.

To Elias Dayton

Dear Sir,   Mount Vernon Novr 6th 1786

Presuming you are Presidt of the Society of the Cincinnati in the State of New Jersey, I give you the trouble of the enclosed address. If I am mistaken, you will be so good as to hand it to the right person.[1]

Months ago, I received a number of blank Diplomas for my Signature, which was affixed & held in readiness for Mr Peck or his order. No call has yet been for them. If a good conveyance should offer, I will forward them; but I am not much in the way of meeting this.[2] With great esteem and regard I am Dr Sir Yr Most Obedt Hble Ser.

Go: Washington

ALS, CSmH.

    1. See GW to the Society of the Cincinnati, 31 Oct. 1786.

    2. See John Peck to GW, 16 Aug. and 4 Sept. 1786. GW seems not to have received Peck's letter of 4 September.

To John Francis Mercer

Dear Sir,   Mount Vernon 6th Novr 1786

    It was not till after you had left this place that I received your letter of the 4th Ulto.[1] Altho' I have great repugnance to encreasing my Slaves by purchase, yet as it seems so inconvenient to you to make payment by other modes than those you have proposed, and so injurious as not to be accomplished at a less loss than 50 or more prCt; I will take Six or more Negroes of you, if you can spare such as will answer my purposes, upon the terms offered in your former letter. The Negroes I want are males. Three or four young fellows for Ditchers; and the like number of well grown lads for artificers. It is with you to determine, whether you can supply me with such Negroes. If you agree to do it, and will appoint a time, I would send for them; relying on your word that the whole are healthy, and none of them addicted to running away. The latter I abominate—and unhealthy negroes—women, or Children, would not suit my purposes on *any terms*.

    If you accede to this proposition I will extend it. I will take all the good, & merchantable Wheat, & Indian Corn you may have for sale, at a reasonable price (the first immedly—the latter at a proper time)—and Military certificates of this State, for the Balle of my claim; at the difference that *really* exists between them and specie; altho I never intended to possess one of them on *any terms* whatever in a depreciated State. If these proposals are agreeable to you in *all* their parts, I should be glad to receive a decided and speedy answer; because in that case I will no longer look to you for the means of discharging those debts I have enumerated to you, and to do which I am exceedingly anxious, but will endeavor without more delay, to sell Land to enable me to pay them.[2]

I had written thus far when Colo. Simm called on his way from Chas County Court to obtain some information respecting your suit against Combs. I was naturally led by the interest I *thought* I had in this business, to enquire into the state of it, & was told if Mr Ellzey's absence did not impede the sitting of Loudoun Court, he expected next week to obtain judgments for more than a thousand pounds; but guess Sir what my surprize must have been, when he added, that every shilling of this money was assigned to a Mr Colston, and authority given to receive it as fast as it could be recovered![3] I had flattered myself that my forbearance for near fifteen years, and the disposition I have discovered since the negotiation of the business seems to have got into your hands (to accomodate my wants as much as I possibly could to your convenience) merited more candid treatment. You cannot I think have forgotten the repeated assurances you have given me, that the moneis arising from this fund shd be sacredly appropriated to the discharge of my claim, whilst any of it remained. If this were possible, your letters in my possession would explicitly remind you of them. A conduct so extremely unfair, ungenerous, & disingenuous, I could not suffer to pass unnoticed.[4]

I send herewith the remainder of the blank Deeds which were formerly put into my hands by your Brother, James Mercer Esq., as also the survey, & partition of the Shanondoah tract (into the Lotts by which the Land was sold) that you may fill them up as occasion may require. If it is *absolutely* necessary for me to sign the Deeds for ⟨conveyance of these⟩ Lotts, ⟨now⟩ the business by a decree of the high Court of Chancery is taken out of my hands and put into yours, I will do it; otherwise, having stronger reasons than ever against resuming any agency in this business I would wish to decline it.[5] I am—Sir Yr Most Obedt Hble Servt

Go: Washington

Your letter of the 21st Ulto requesting me to execute a Deed to Mr Rawleigh Colston, for the lott no. 7, has been delivered to me.[6] You now will receive the only Deeds in my possession, and the Survey of the Shanondoah tract; and can do with them as circumstance may require. If it is indispensably necessary for me to convey the title & you shall accompany the return of the Deed with authority for me to do so I will go to Alexaa & execute it before evidences who will prove it in Fredk Ct.

ALS, NjP: de Coppet Collection; LB, DLC:GW.

1. Letter not found. Mercer, his wife Sophia Sprigg Mercer, and their son Richard (b. 19 Nov. 1785) spent the night at Mount Vernon on 15 Oct. (*Diaries*, 5:52).

2. For GW's negotiations with Mercer about payment of the Mercer estate's debt to GW with slaves and military certificates, see GW to Mercer, 9 Sept. 1786, n.3.

3. GW notes no visits to Mount Vernon at this time by Col. Charles Simms; he does record visits in August and September (*Diaries*, 5:19, 38, 41). For questions arising about the transfer to Rawleigh Colston of a lot on the Shenandoah River bought by William Hickman at the George Mercer sale in 1774, see William Hickman to GW, 5 Oct. 1786, and the references in note 1 of that document. William Ellzey (d. 1796) was a lawyer living in Loudoun County. Combs may have been either Joseph Combs who once had operated the ferry and ordinary at Ashby's Gap on the Shenandoah River in Frederick County or John J. Combes, a merchant in Alexandria.

4. For the debt of the Mercer estate, see GW to John Francis Mercer, 8 July 1784, n.1.

5. For the sale of George Mercer's tract on the Shenandoah in 1774, see Edward Snickers to GW, 17 May 1784, n.1. For GW's explanation of his exact legal position with regard to conveyance of these lots on the Shenandoah, see his letter to Rawleigh Colston, 4 Dec. 1786.

6. Letter not found.

To Thomas West

Sir,   Mt Vernon 6th Novr 1786.

From the *last* application which was made to you, I expected the papers so long promised, a fortnight ago. If you have any objection to my receiving them in order to effect a final settlement of the Admn of Colo. Thos Colvill's Estate, I beg you will have candour enough to declare it; that I may know what further steps are necessary for me to take to bring this business to a close.

I think I have been ungenteely treated, to be put off seven months in obtaining what was promised in three weeks, & reiterated several times since. I have had repeated applications made to me, as well from the Debtors to, as the Creditors of that Estate, for settlements, & could do no more than assure the applicants that the moment I was furnished with the necessary documents, I shou'd be ready to proceed to the business. I am anxious to do this on many accots; one of which is, that unfavorable suspicions will result from these delays.[1] My wish is to avoid them. I am &c.

G: Washington

LB, DLC:GW.
    1. See West to GW, 27 June 1786.

To Benjamin Lincoln

My Dr Sir,   Mount Vernon 7th Novr 1786.

I have, I think, seen your name mentioned as President of the Society of the Cincinnati in the State of Massachusetts. For this reason I give you the trouble of the enclosed address.[1]

I hope your wishes were fully accomplished in your Eastern trip. Are your people getting mad? are we to have the goodly fabrick that eight years were spent in rearing, pulled over our heads? What is the cause of all these commotions? When & how is it to end?[2] I need not tell you how much I am My dear Sir Yr most obedt & affect Hble Servant

Go: Washington

ALS, owned (1992) by Mr. Ralph G. Newman, Inc., Chicago, Ill.; LB, DLC:GW.
    1. See GW to the Society of the Cincinnati, 31 Oct. 1786.
    2. See Lincoln's reply of 4 Dec. 1786–4 Mar. 1787.

From Thomas Smith

Sir,   Bedford [Pa.] 7th November 1786

As the Bearer is going immediately to Alexandria & keeps the Post Office there I lay hold of the opportunity to inform you that on the 24th 25th & 26th Days of October, the Ejectments which I had the honour of bringing for You against James Scott & 12 others for Lands on Miller's Run, were tried at Washington at Nisi Prius, & I have the very great pleasure to inform you that Verdicts have been given in your favour in every one of them[1]—your satisfaction upon this occasion may be equal to, but cannot exceed mine—I never was more agitated, between hopes & fears, in any cause in which I have been engaged: I had, during the War, been repeatedly chosen into almost every honourable office which my fellow Citizens could bestow; to which my *merit* gave me no pretensions, & which must therefore have been the more flattering to my *vanity*; but believe me Sir when I assure you that I am more proud of having it said that General Washington selected me as his Counsel in an affair of this importance, than of all the distinguished stations in which I had been so often placed.

I had good information that James Scott Junr had the most plausible claim, & that he was the ringleader or director of the rest; I therefore resolved to take the Bull by the Horns, & removed the Ejectments into the Supreme Court in such order, as to have it in my power to try the Ejectment against him before the rest, reserving the Rule; so that had any unforeseen point turned up against me, I could try the rest or not as I pleased.

That Trial therefore was ordered on, on the 24th after Dinner & lasted that afternoon—the next Day, & till 11 o'Clock in the forenoon of the 26th when the Jury gave a Verdict for the Plaintiff; I thought the other Defendants would have confessed Judgments, & would not have been so mad as to have risqued weaker causes before the same jury; but I was mistaken, every one of them insisted on having a trial nay. each would have demanded a separate trial; but as I had consolidated the Ejectments against these Defendants, they were obliged to try them all together, & the trial did not last long. I take it for granted that many of the Jury wished it had been in their power to have given Verdicts for the Defendants; I knew that we had very strong prejudices, artfully fomented, to encounter—I had applied to the Court to name the jury at a Time when the Bench was filled with such of the Justices as I believed would make out the most impartial list, which it was possible to obtain; The Defendants pretended that I had taken an advantage of them, & refused to strike the Jury (as it is called)—I can truly say that I only wished to have an *impartial* & dispassionate jury, which I believed I could not otherwise obtain, & therefore I gave them notice to attend me a certain Day at the Prothonotary's Office in Philadelphia to strike—they thereupon agreed that it should be done on the spot—I took down the Jury list to Philadelphia myself (having other business there)—brought up the proper Process—informed myself of what witnesses might eventually be necessary, and even *served* the Subpœnas on as many as attended the preceeding County Court.

I was assisted by Mr Ross in a very masterly manner—we had consulted together before I had the honour of receiving your Letter, by Col. Sims, & it gave us satisfaction that we had agreed to conduct the trial upon the Plan pointed out in that Letter, & that I had transcribed & brought up the cases from the Books, which were not to be had at Washington, to support the points on which you directed us to rely.[2]

In the Letter last alluded to, you desired me to inform you with what sum you can equal my expectations, & that you will lodge it for me in Philadelphia—I have had motives in conducting this business, far more forcible than pecuniary considerations—& therefore I trust you will pardon me if I decline naming any sum—Mr Washington, who was at Fayette County with you, or Col. Sims, will readily point out what is usual on such occasions, & Mr Ross (to whom I have promised to divide with him what I receive) & I will be perfectly satisfied—I hardly know how to express myself—let me assure you that I do not wish to receive a large fee.[3]

I will take your Papers to Carlisle & will send them from thence to such place, either in Philadelphia, or Baltimore, as you will please to point out.

I believe that the Defendants in the Ejectments will be with you soon ⟨to⟩ endeavuour to do what they ought to have done when you made them the Offer—I verily believe that it was more their misfortune than their fault that they then rejected it. You have now *thirteen* Plantations—some of them well improved—I take it for granted that the improvements increase the value of the Land much more than all the expences of the Ejectments—those who mad[e] them are now reduced to indigence—they have put in Crops this season, which are now in the ground—they wish to be permitted to take the grain away— to give this hint may be improper in me—to say more would be presumptuous.

Orders for obtaining Possession cannot be Issued till the Supreme Court sits in January, it will be necessary that you appoint an agent in that Country to take Possession & to Lease the Lands for you—otherwise the fences & even the buildings will probably be burn'd or otherwise destroyed.[4]

Major Freeman put into my hands several small Bonds due to you to put in suit. I have recovered most of the Money & paid it over to him—he says he has some others, which when the Money shall be recovered I will pay in like manner—he seems to be as attentive to your interest as to his own.[5]

I Pray you to excuse the Length of this Letter—it is written during the hurry of the Court here, & therefore I had not time to make it *shorter*, nor to write so fully as I wished. I have the honour to be with the utmost respect Sir your very humble & most obedient Servant

Thomas Smith

P.S. Nothing can excuse me for writing to you in this desultory & hasty manner but my belief that you wish to have the earliest information respecting the event: There was a gentleman who left Washington-Town after I knew that the Jury had agreed in the first Verdict, & was going down into Virginia near to mount Vernon—Col. Nevill, at my desire, requested him to stay 'till they should give in their Verdict in Court; but he would not, his business requiring him to be at a certain place by a certain hour.[6]

ALS, DLC:GW.

1. For a discussion of the ejectment suits brought for GW by Smith against the tenants, or squatters, on GW's Millers Run tract in Washington County, Pa., see the editorial note in Smith to GW, 9 Feb. 1785. James Scott, Jr., who served as spokesman for the Millers Run tenants when GW confronted them in September 1784, was considered by Smith to be their leader. *Nisi prius* courts tried cases before a jury.

2. See GW to Smith, 22 Sept. 1786.

3. Smith and James Ross (1762–1847) in 1788 each accepted £50 as his fee (Smith to GW, 5 Feb. 1788; Ledger B, 259).

4. GW wrote John Cannon on 28 Nov. 1786 asking him to manage his Millers Run land and giving him authority to rent or lease it to those who were living on it. GW's present manager, George McCarmick, who was leaving the area, gave GW the same advice as Smith regarding the tenants and disposition of the land (McCarmick to GW, c.30 Oct. 1786).

5. In December Thomas Freeman, who as GW's land agent exercised general supervision in Pennsylvania over Washington's Bottom and GW's tract at Great Meadows, reported having paid Smith a total of £12 since 2 Sept. 1786 (Freeman to GW, 18 Dec., n.6).

6. Presley Neville, formerly of Frederick County in Virginia, lived at Wood-

ville, his place on Chartiers Creek below Pittsburgh near GW's Millers Run property (*Diaries*, 4:30). See also GW to Neville, 27 November.

Letter not found: to James Tilton, 7 Nov. 1786. On 15 Feb. 1787 Tilton wrote GW that he had received "your circular letter of the 31 Octr 1786 together with your private favour dated the 7th Novr following."

From Thomas Hutchins

Buffaloe Rivulet 4 Miles below Mingo Old Town
Sir   Ohio County 8th Novr 1786

Your Excellency's Favour of the 20th of August (accompanied by the Marquis de la Fayette's Letter, and a specimen of a Vocabulary) I was honoured with on the 23rd of October at my Camp west of Ohio River about ten Miles up a Rivulet called Indian Weeling. My not having earlier made this acknowledgement is to be attributed to my secluded situation in the Wilderness untill the date of this Epistle when I reached this place on my return to the Inhabitants. The honour of your Excellency's correspondence, and the favourable sentiments you are pleased to entertain of my poor abilities, entitles you to my most grateful returns, which are now very sincerely and respectfully tendered. I perfectly agree with your Excellency, that the greatest possible precision and exactitude will be indispensible in committing the Indian words to paper by a just Orthography. And were my abilities equal to my inclinations your expectations should be amply fulfilled; but the more I reflect on the difficulties unavoidably attending the fixing a Criterion to Systemize a rude Language, or even to ascertain a true standard for its Orthography, I am but the more convinced of my incapacity to effect so arduous a task. And however anxiously solicitous I am, and shall at all Times be, to contribute my Mite to the service of the republick of Letters, permit me to say, that a requisition of this nature from any other than your Excellency, could not have prevailed with me, overwhelmed as I am with the business of my department, to have attended to it at this Time. But as it will always afford me real pleasure to execute any Commands you may be pleased to honour me with and relying on your Candour for such defects as will unavoidably attend my most Zealous endeavours, I am imboldened to assure your Excellency, that every ef-

fort in my power shall be cheerfully and expeditiously exerted
to make the Vocabulary as extensive and perfect as my avocations, and those of my Friends, whose aid I shall solicit, will enable me. I shall be detained here untill the four Ranges which
were surveyed into Townships in the course of the summer (supposed to contain upwards of seven hundred thousand Acres) are
deliniated on paper which will probably be about the commencement of the ensuing Year the Time I have fixed for my
departure for New York. I expect my return to this Country
again will be early next Spring, when my endeavours to carry
the Ordinance of Congress into effect, will, I hope, be attended
with more favourable consequences than I have yet experienced.[1] With every sentiment of perfect esteem and respect I
have the honour to be Your Excellency's Most obedient and
most humble servant

Tho: Hutchins

ALS, DLC:GW.
    1. In September 1785 the party of surveyors from the various states under
the direction of Thomas Hutchins as Geographer of the United States began
the survey of the seven ranges in the Northwest Territory in accordance with
the terms of the Land Ordinance of 1785. See Benjamin Tupper to GW, 26
Oct. 1785. The surveyors returned to complete the survey in the summer
of 1786.

From James Madison

Dear Sir   Richm[on]d Novr 8th 1786
    I am just honoured with your favor of the 5th inst: The intelli-
gence from Genl Knox is gloomy indeed, but is less so than the
colours in which I had it thro' another channel.[1] If the lessons
which it inculcates should not work the proper impressions on
the American Public, it will be a proof that our case is desperate.
Judging from the present temper and apparent views of our
Assembly, I have some ground for leaning to the side of Hope.
The vote against Paper money has been followed by two others
of great importance. By one of them sundry petitions for
applying a scale of depreciation to the Military Certificates was
unanimously rejected. By the other the expediency of complying
with the Recomm[end]ation from Annapolis in favor of a general revision of the federal system was *unanimously* agreed to. A

bill for the purpose is now depending and in a form which attests the most federal spirit. As no opposition has been yet made and it is ready for the third reading, I expect it will soon be before the public.[2] It has been thought advisable to give this subject a very solemn dress, and all the weight which could be derived from a single State. This idea will also be pursued in the selection of characters to represent Virga in the federal Convention. You will infer our earnestness on this point from the liberty which will be used of placing your name at the head of them. How far this liberty may correspond with the ideas by which you ought to be governed will be best decided where it must ultimately be decided. In every event it will assist powerfully in marking the zeal of our Legislature, and its opinion of the magnitude of the occasion. Mr Randolph has been elected successor to Mr Henry. He had 73 votes.[3] Col. Bland had 28 & R. H. Lee 22. The Delegation to Congress drops Col. H. Lee, a circumstance which gives much pain to those who attend to the mortification in which it must involve a man of sensibility. I am even yet to learn the ground of the extensive disapprobation which has shewn itself.[4] I am Dear Sir most respectfully & Affecty Yr Obedt & hble servt

J. Madison Jr.

ALS, DLC:GW; signed copy, in Madison's hand, DLC: Madison Papers.

1. Madison is referring to his letters from Henry Lee of 19 and 25 October.

2. Madison's "A Bill For appointing deputies from the Commonwlth. to a Convention proposed to be held in the City of Philada. in May next for the purpose of revising the federal Constitution" was introduced in the house of delegates on 6 November. The house passed the bill on 9 Nov. and the senate on 23 Nov. (Rutland and Rachal, *Madison Papers*, 9:164).

3. The editors of the *Madison Papers* take the number to be *79* instead of *73*. In his file copy, Madison wrote *77*. He also changed Bland's total from *28* to *26* (ibid., 166–67).

4. Madison wrote Henry Lee on 9 Nov. expressing his regret that the house of delegates had not reelected Lee to Congress as was customary until a man had served for three years. Madison wrote Lee again on 23 Nov. to refute Lee's charge that he was involved in the rejection of Lee by the delegates. On 4 Dec. Madison wrote Thomas Jefferson: "Col. H. Lee of the last delegation was dropt. The causes were different I believe & not very accurately known to me. One of them is said to have been his supposed heterodoxy touching the Mississppi" (ibid., 189–92). See David Stuart's explanation of the rejection of Lee in his letter to GW of this date (8 Nov.). When Joseph Jones refused to serve, the house on 1 Dec. reelected Lee.

From David Stuart

Dear Sir,   Richmond 8th Novr [17]86

It gives me much pleasure to inform you, of the very auspicious manner, in which the serious entrance on business this Session, has been marked—Tho' it is not much short of a month now, since our meeting, no business of importance was introduced 'till the last week—You will learn the issue of this, from the inclosed vote—The strong language in which this off spring of iniquity is condemned, will it is hoped have some operation on future Legislatures, and by banishing the idea of it from among the people, be the means of encouraging industry and œconomy, the true sources of public happiness—From a conception that the vote on this subject might have some effect on the policy of other States, where the measure is not yet adopted; the Printer was ordered to publish it, with a request to the Printers throughout the Continent to do the same.[1]

As a further proof of the high regard, which seems at present to prevail for the preservation of national faith, I have to inform you, that an attempt to reduce the Certificates by a scale, has been unanimously rejected. The ease with which these two bugbears have been removed, gives me a hope, that a similar propriety will characterise all the proceedings of the present Assembly.

You have no doubt heard, that the Attorney was a Candidate for the chief Magistracy—As there has never been a Senate before yesterday, the election for this place, and Delegates to Congress was made—The Attorney was chosen by a great majority—the other Candidates were R. H: Lee, and Coll Bland—The Delegates to Congress are Messrs Maddison, Gresham, Carrington, R: H: Lee, and Jos: Jones—Coll Lee you observe is left out—It appears that this proceeded from an opinion generally prevailing, of his very embarrassed circumstances; to which, his election to Congress, served as an Asylum[2]—Tho' sorry therefore for his ill-luck, yet the principle from whence it proceeded, cannot be reprobated.

Many claims for impressed property have been laid before us and admitted, and the act for giving further time to bring in such claims has been revived—It cannot therefore be doubted, but the claims which you have would be good—But it is time, if you wish anything to be done with them that they should be sent down[3]—I have lost all hope of the assistance of my Collegue— the certain repeal of the Port-Bill, will be the consequence of his arrival, as it appears to have numerous foes, that need an able leader[4]—From the progress made to-day in two acts, one for immediately empowering Commissioners to meet, for the purpose of fixing on similar taxes, on imported articles, with the States of Maryd & Pennsylvania; and the other, agreeable to the recommendation of the Commissioners at Annapolis, there can be little doubt of their ultimately passing—The subject of the latter Commission, the amending the articles of the Confederation, is important and delicate, but absolutely necessary—From some conversation with Mr Maddison on this business, I have reason to think you will be requested to act on it[5]—I beg leave to remind you of the petition from the Potomac Company, which was thought necessary—the time for such business will soon expire.[6]

If not disappointed by Messrs Page & Baylor, I hope to be able to pay you a pretty considerable part of the sum due you by Christmass—they have made me a faithful promise of paying a considerable sum at that time—I have not heard yet from Mr Savage on the Eastern Shore—but hope, he will have the annual rent for that estate also ready.[7]

I inclose to you, a view of the taxes recieved at the treasury— Having nothing further at present to communicate, I must conclude with an offer of my respects to Mrs Washington and the family at Mt Vernon.[8] I am Dr Sir with great regard Your Obt Servt

Dd Stuart

ALS, DLC:GW.

1. On 1 Nov. the Virginia lower house rejected the issuing of paper money by a vote of 85 to 17 as "unjust, impolitic and destructive of public and private confidence" (*House of Delegates Journal, 1786–1790*). Stuart enclosed a printed extract of the house journal showing the vote on the bill.

2. See James Madison to GW, this date, and notes. "Gresham" is William Grayson. Joseph Jones refused to serve, and Henry Lee, Jr., was reelected in his place.

3. See GW to Stuart, 5 Nov., n.2.

4. George Mason, the other Fairfax County delegate, did not attend this session, but he attacked the Port Act in a broadside. James Madison wrote Thomas Jefferson on 4 Dec. that "the repeal were he [Mason] present would be morally certain" (Rutland and Rachal, *Madison Papers*, 9:189–92). The mo-

tion to repeal the Port Act was rejected on 11 Dec. by a vote of 69 to 35, but the act was later amended to increase the number of ports of entry from five to seven (*House of Delegates Journal, 1786–1790*; Rutland, *Mason Papers*, 2:859–64; 12 Hening 320–23).

5. See James Madison to GW, this date, n.2.

6. See GW to Stuart, 5 Nov., n.1.

7. See GW to Stuart, 5 Nov., n.3.

8. Madison wrote to Jefferson on 4 Dec. 1786 that the fruits of the tax measure of 1785 "are bitterly tasted now. Our Treasury is empty, no supplies have gone to the federal treasury, and our internal embarrassments torment us exceedingly" (Rutland and Rachal, *Madison Papers*, 9:189–92). The enclosed broadside giving the tax receipts from 1782 to 1786 is in DLC:GW.

From Peter Trenor

Petersburgh 8th Novr 1786

The inclosed Memorial I received from Mrs Ann Ennis of the City of Dublin which I expected to have had the Honour of handing your Excellency on my Way to Baltimore where I purposed going on my leaving Ireland—but calling here & meeting a market for my Goods prevents my having that Honour.[1]

Your Excellency will perceive by said Memorial that the Will of the Late Doctor Willm Savage, with many other Papers relative thereto were in the hands of a Captain Brereton of Baltimore which I presume he informed your Excellency of—if your Excellency will be so obliging as to inform me by Post (at Messrs *Gordon & Keans* Portsmouth Virginia,) whether or not you have any Effects in your hands to discharge Mrs Ennis's demand—and what sum she may expect—at same time if your Excellency will be so good, as to send me an order either on Philadelpha, New York, Baltimore or Portsmouth—for what you think proper to remit her—shall send you a receipt for same—& if required shall give your Excellency such Security for delivering of same as you may require.[2]

In expectation of having the Honour of hearing from your Excellency before my return to Dublin (which expect will be in the Course of three Weeks.[)] I am your Excellency's most Obed. Servt

Peter Trenor

ALS, DLC:GW.

1. The text of Ann [Anne] Ennis's memorial "To his Excellency General Washington," dated at Dublin, 12 July 1786, is: "The Memorial of Ann Ennis

Widow of Richd Ennis late of the City of Dublin Gentn Deced Sheweth That
your Memoralist Some few Years ago when Mrs Margt Savage Wife to Doctr
Wm Savage late of Virginia Lived in Dublin, Supported the said Mrs Savage &
Supplied her with every necessary possible to make her live Comfortably when
in Dublin.

"That your Memts paid & Expended for Necessarys for the Support of said
Mrs Savage upwards of fifty Guineas which Sum remains justly due and owing
to your Memorts by the Heirs & Representatives of the said Mrs Savage.

"That the said Mrs Savage Shortly before She left Dublin, duly made &
publishd her last will and testament which will after the accot of her Death
came to Dublin, was duly provd and Registerd in the Courts of Record for
Such in the City of Dublin—That the said Mrs Savage often Inform'd Your
Memort that She was formerly Wife to Doctr [Charles] Green of Virgina
Deced—who had left an Estate of upwards of £500 ℔ year to your Excellency
in trust & for the purpose of paying to his Widow (then the said Mrs Savage),
the sum of £100 Sterg ℔ year During her life, which Estate your Excellency is
now in possession of and the said Mrs Savage Informed Your Memoralist that
there were due her by your Excellency thirteen years annuity of the said Sum
of £100 Stg ℔ year left to her by her late Husband the said Wm Green which
Sum was in your Excellencys hands for her Use—and that your Excellency
would pay the same to any person She would will it to.

"That the said Mrs Savage by her Said Will among other Legacys left to
your Memot the Sum of £150—& to her Husband the sd Richd Ennis the Sum
of £100—& all the said Debt She owed & said Legacy to be paid out of the
Sum remain'g in your hands of her annuity due her as aforesaid, and said Mrs
Savage left to your Excell'y the Sum of £100—& to Col: [Bryan] Fairfax £50 &
appointed your Excellency & said Col. Fairfax Executors to her said Will.

"That your Memot had the Honour to write to your Excellency about 18
Mons ago—Informing you of the above Matters & that the said Will of the
said Mrs Savage with Many other papers relative thereto were in the hands
of Captn [Thomas] Brereton of Baltimore for the Inspection & Use of your
Excellency & Col. Fairfax—but your Memt has not Since had the honour of
hearing any thing from Your Excell'y or any other person in regard to the said
Mrs Savages affairs.

"That your Memot being now a Widow and in *reduced needy Circumstances*
She Humbly Hopes your Excellency will take her Case into your kind Consideration and order her paymt of the 50 Guineas justly due to Memots which
She Paid for the Support of the said Mrs Savage when in Dublin—and also
order her the amount of the said Legacys bequeathd to her and her Husband
by the said Mrs Savage in her Said will to which will your Excelly is
Trustee & Executor.

"That Memoralist fearing her Letters has & might Miscarry has requested
a friend of hers to have this Memorial Deliverd to your Excell'y and to Request
an answer thereto.

"Therefore your Memt Humbly Hopes [(]as She was a good friend to the
said Mrs Savage) Your Excelly will be so good as to grant a favourable answer
to this Memorial by Inform'g the Bearer whether or not Memot will get the
said 50 Gs. due her or any of the said Legacy so bequeathd to her—and if

your Excelly will pay any of the said Money to the Bearer Peter Trenor his Receipt on this Memorial will be Sufft & will be allowd & acknowledged by Your Excelly Most Obedt Servt Anne Ennis" (DLC:GW).

For GW's response to Mrs. Ennis's memorial, see his letter to her of 15 Nov. 1786. The outlines of the long continuing Savage affair are set out in Henry Lee and Daniel Payne to GW, 24 April 1767, n.1.

2. See Thomas Brereton to GW, 12 April 1786, and GW to Brereton, 20 April 1786. For references to fuller discussions of the Savage affair, see note 1 in Brereton's letter of 12 April.

Letter not found: from Theodorick Bland, 9 Nov. 1786. On 18 Nov. GW wrote Bland of "the receipt of your obliging favors of the 4th & 9th inst."

From William Deakins, Jr.

Sir.   Geo[rge] Town [Md.] Novr 9th 1786
You will find by the Inclosed I had procured you 10 Bushels Spelts but the Waggoner on his Way down from F. Town lossed one of the Baggs Containing 3½ Bushels. the other two Baggs Containing 6½ Bushels I have sent to the Care of Mr Wm Hartshorn in Alexandria to be delivered to your Order.[1] I am Very Respectfully Sir Your Obt Servt

Will Deakins Junr

P.S. I have engaged a part of the Poland Oats & will take care to get the whole you Want—W.D.[2]

ALS, ViMtV; Sprague transcript, DLC:GW.
    1. "F. Town" is Frederick, Maryland. The enclosed account shows a charge of £1.5 for the grain.
    2. See Deakins to GW, 10 Jan. 1787.

From David Humphreys

My dear General.   New Haven [Conn.] Novr 9th 1786
I have this moment been honored with your letter of the 22nd of Octr & am thereby relieved from some anxiety for fear mine of the 24th of Septr had miscarried. For the reasons you mention, I think it will be best that the General Meeting of the Cincinnati should be holden at Philadelphia. I am happy that the enclosures have met with your approbation.

A few days ago, I addressed a letter to you by Messrs Morse & Austin. the latter has since concluded not to go to the Southward—by the former I expect still to have an opportunity of forwarding this. Having been pressed in time, & not having kept any copy I can hardly recollect distinctly what I have written in the letter before referred to. I only remember that I had been much mortified by the ignorance & perverseness of some of the leading members, or Demagogues, in our Assembly; and that I gave no very favorable picture of our situation or prospects.[1]

As to your question, my dear General, respecting the cause & origin of those commotions; I hardly find myself in condition to give a certain answer. If, from all the informations I have been able to obtain, I might be authorised to hazard an opinion, I should attribute them to all the three causes which you have suggested. In Massachusetts, particularly, I believe there are a few real greivances: and also some wicked agents, or emissaries, who have been busy in magnifying the positive evils, & fomenting causeless jealousies & disturbances—but it rather appears to me, that there is a licencious spirit prevailing among many of the people; a levelling principle; a desire of change; & a wish to annihilate all debts public & private. The Assembly of that State are occupied in removing all the real subjects of hardship & complaint. They have likewise passed a new Riot Act, & given some indications of spirit in support of Government. But still the preparations & systematic arrangements on the part of the Mob do not cease. You will have seen by the Speech of Mr King before that Legislature that Congress consider themselves as the Guarantor of each State Government, & bound to interfere in its support under certain circumstances.[2]

I refer you to Mr Morse, the bearer of this, for particulars concerning this State—I will send by the next Post the Papers respecting Asgill.[3] Tho' I shall not see Mt Vernon this winter, my affections are centered there, being in sincerity your most zealous friend & Humble Servant

D. Humphreys

ALS, DLC:GW.

1. Humphreys' letter is dated 1 November.

2. At the end of his report of 11 Oct. to the Massachusetts house of representatives on the recent actions of the Congress, Rufus King "spoke of the commotions now existing in Massachusetts. This was viewed by Congress, as

the most important subject that ever came before that respectable assembly. Every member considered himself as personally interested in it. . . . There was a league subsisting between the States of America, to oppose every force that should arise against either of them. The United States would not be inactive on such an occasion" (*Boston Magazine* [September and October 1786], 3:405, reprinted in Burnett, *Letters*, 8:478–81).

3. Humphreys sent GW on 16 Nov. a copy of the printed piece on the Asgill affair that he had written.

To Benjamin Lincoln, Jr.

Sir,   Mount Vernon 9th Novr 1786.
I have received your letter of the 24th of Septr, together with the bill enclosed.

You will receive with this, the first of another sett of Bills, which Mr Watson the Drawer not only very readily gave, but likewise allowed interest upon the protested Bill, altho' it is not customary to do so here, upon inland Bills of exchange. I shall forward the others next week, & you will be so good as to have them handed to Doctr Gordon's agent as soon as may be.[1]

I am sorry that the Doctrs commission has given his friends so much trouble; tho' it can not be imputed to him, but must be considered as one of the lightest evils resulting from a paper currency. I am &c.

G: Washington

LB, DLC:GW; copy (typescript), dated 10 Nov., PVFHi.
1. For a summary of the difficulties GW encountered in transferring to William Gordon the funds raised in Virginia by subscription to Gordon's projected history of the American Revolution, see note 1 in Lincoln's letter to GW of 24 September.

From Ezra Stiles

Sir   Yale College [Conn.] Nov. 9. 1786.
Permit me to ask your Acceptance of an Election Sermon, which the Reverend Mr Morse a Tutor in this College will have the Honor to present to you.[1] I know you must feel sollicitous for the Tumults in Massachusetts. They are doubtless magnified at a Distance. I confide in it that there is Wisdom in the Legislature of that State sufficient to rectify the public Disorders and

recover the public Peace and Tranquillity. Perhaps all Things are cooperating & conspiring to effect the public Conviction of the Expediency & Necessity of a Cession of further Powers to Congress, adequate to the political Administration of a new and great Republic, to whose Origination your great Services have so highly contributed.[2] I have the Honor to be, Sir, Your most obedt Very hble servt

Ezra Stiles

ALS, DLC:GW.

1. Ezra Stiles (1727–1795), president of Yale College, sent GW a copy of the second, corrected edition of his *The United States Elevated to Glory and Honor*, a sermon that he delivered at the annual election on 8 May 1783 before Gov. Jonathan Trumbull and the Connecticut legislature in Hartford. This edition was printed at Worcester, Mass., by Isaiah Thomas in 1785, and GW's copy is inscribed by Stiles, "General Washington, Ezra Stiles." Stiles earlier had presented GW with the initial edition printed in 1783 in New Haven by Thomas & Samuel Green. He inscribed this: "His Excellency General Washington, from his most humble Servt Ezra Stiles" (Griffin, *Boston Athenæum Collection*, 194).

2. GW's acknowledgment of this letter and its enclosures is printed in note 1, Stiles to GW, 7 Feb. 1787.

From Rawleigh Colston

Winchester Nov: 10th 1786

I had the honour of writing your Excellency on the 5th of October last by one Mr Ireland on the Subject of a conveyance of the land you Sold Mr William Hickman, which letter I am informed you received; but having heard nothing from Mr Ireland Since, I am at a loss to know how the business has been Settled.[1] I am informed by my friend Mr Wright, that your Excellency had Some Conversation with Col. Mercer on this Subject, and that he did not determine you in respect to his having assigned Messrs Hickman & Irelands bond to me—a conduct I am unable to account for, as he knew an application had been made to you for a conveyance of the land—Your Excellency may rest assured I have his written assignment in date the 14th of Octo. 1785, with his receipt in full for the consideration—Being induced from the great Scarcity of money, and consequently the loss which those Gentlemen must sustain in being compelled to part with their property—to accept lands & negroes in payment, I wrote Mr Stone the lawyer to discharge Mr Ireland on his producing a certificate from your Excellency of your having executed deeds to me for the land the want of which may subject him to great inconvenience, as I could not think of releasing him from execution, without an assurance from you that a title should be made me to the land—I shall thank your Excellency to favour me with a few lines on this Subject, advising what Steps you have taken and whether any thing is likely to Obstruct a conveyance—as I cannot obtain possession of the property—till that is effected.[2] I have the Hon. to be Your Excellencys mo. & Obdt

Rawleigh Colston

ALS, ViHi.

Rawleigh (Raleigh) Colston (d. 1823) was living in Winchester as early as 1778 and was elected to the vestry there in 1785 and was one of the trustees of the Winchester academy when it was established in 1786. His wife was the sister of John Marshall.

1. Colston's letter has not been found, but see William Hickman to GW, 5 October.

2. See William Hickman to GW, 5 Oct., n.1, GW to John Francis Mercer, 6, 24 Nov., and GW to Colston, 4 December. Mr. Wright may be Matthew Wright, a merchant in Winchester. Mr. Stone may be Thomas Stone (1743–1787), who lived for several years before the Revolution in Frederick County, Md., but he also may be either John Hoskins Stone (1750–1804) or Michael Jenifer Stone (1747–1812). All three men were lawyers and natives of Charles County, Maryland.

From Nathaniel Smith

Sir,   Baltimore 10th November. 1786

From the difficulty I have met in the Settlement of my Accounts with the State of Maryland, & a hope that your Opinion on the Matters pending between the said State and myself, would tend to Obviate that difficulty, I have taken the freedom to Trouble you with the present letter—I would in the first place beg leave to Acquaint you Sir, that I entered into the Service of the Contenant in January 1776 and was appointed to the Command of a Company of light Infantry but when we begun to raise the men, I was directed to take the Command of a Company of Artillery and Stationed at the Fort on Whetson Point—at the latter part of 1776 & beginning of 1777 another Company was raised & placed under my direction; and the State then gave

me a Majors Commission and the Chief Command of the Fort.
In 1778 The Assembly resolved a Company of men from those
under me should, be drawn & Commanded by Capt Richard
Dorsey should march to join the Continantal Army—and at the
Same time passed further Resolves, that all officers and Soldiers
at Annapolis and Baltimore Should have and enjoy every priv-
iledge of those in the Contenantal Service.[1]

In the month of September 1779 Govener Johnson Sent for
me and Acquainted me, the Assembly had Ordered the Remainder of the Artillery to join the Troops then under your Command and Asked me if I was Willing to march with them, I told
him I was if I could have my Rank agreable to the Resolves of
1778—he said it could not be done—I observed to him that it
would be hard for me to Serve under one of my former Serjants,
(Leiutenant Colonel Strobach then of the Pensilvania line)[2] in
which he agreed with me, and Added that Somthing would be
done for the Supernumerary Officers who Could not be employed in those Companies—In the Resolves it is Said "The Govener & Council are directed to Recomend the Supernumerary
Officers to his Excellency General Washington and that they
Should be in full pay until they enter into the Contenantal Service"—Now what I would particularly Request of you Sir, is to
inform me wheather you Reciv'd any Recmmendatory letter
Concerning myself or any other Supernumerary Officer, of the
Artillery of this State.

With Some difficulty, I Obtained my depreciation Up to September 1779 the time the last of the Troops ware Ordered to
March—About two years past I handed in a Memorial to Our
Assembly—A Committee was appointed to Set on it—who reported, the Memorial was Just, and that I ought to be Allowed,
the Commutation pay—the Senate passed it & Ordered the Intendant of Finance to Settle with & pay me for all Services done
as Major of Artillery and for Some as Commissary for prisoners
of War. The latter the Intendant did but refused adjusting the
former.

As I entend presenting another Memorial this Session of Assembly, I would beg your Answer, not only as to my Recmmend-
ations but your Opinion wheather I am not entitled by the Resolves to full pay to the end of the War or the Commutation, or
Boath.[3] I Crave your pardon for the Liberty taken in this and

am with the most profound. Veneration Sir, your Most Obedient Humble Servant

Nathaniel Smith

ALS, DLC:GW. Meaningless dots between words have been eliminated.

1. Capt. Richard Dorsey's independent company of the Maryland artillery on 30 May 1778 became a part of the 1st Continental Artillery. Dorsey was wounded and taken captive at the Battle of Camden on 16 Aug. 1780.

2. Lt. Col. John Martin Strobagh of Pennsylvania became lieutenant colonel of the 4th Continental Artillery Regiment in March 1777 and died 2 Dec. 1778.

3. At the bottom of Smith's letter James McHenry endorsed it in these words: "It will give me great pleasure if your Excellency can recollect any circumstance which may be applied to Mr Smiths interest. He is a worthy citizen and was a diligent and useful officer." On 12 Nov. Samuel Purviance of Baltimore wrote this letter in support of Smith's claims: "Sir My Friend & Neighbour Major Nathl Smith, who served as Commander of the Artillery in this Place in the late War, has found many difficulties in obtaining a Settlement of his Claims against the State of Maryland, which occasions his application to you for some Information, which he conceives might remove the Objections made to his Accounts—Lest you shoud have forgot his Name or Station, he requests me to mention him on this Occasion to your Excellency; which I do with the more pleasure, from a long & perfect knowledge of his Merits & public Spirit thro. the late War, for which I conceive he has not been duely rewarded. If you can render him any Service in the establishment of his Claims, You will serve a worthy Man, whose little Fortune, and the Interests of his family have been sacrificd by his attentions to the Service of his Country. I am with the greatest respect Sir Your most hble Servt Saml Purviance" (DLC:GW).

GW responded to Purviance from Mount Vernon on 20 Nov.: "Sir, Your letter of the 12th instant came duly to hand. I should be very happy if it was in my power to render your friend Majr Smith any service by giving him the information which he desires; but as I do not remember to have received any recommendatory letter which he alludes to, nor have any knowledge of the payment of the Officers of the Continental Army, much less of those who were in the pay of their respective States, I cannot do it; however desirous I may be of obliging the deserving soldier or worthy Citizen. I am &c. G: Washington" (LB, DLC:GW). On the same day GW wrote Smith: "Sir, I have received your letter of the 10th inst: am sorry that it is not in my power to give you the information which you desire; as I do not remember to have received any recommendatory letter concerning yourself or any other supernumerary officer, of the Artillery of your State.

"Having wholly laid aside public business, I am not able to say anything with certainty, even respecting the payment of the officers & soldiers who were in the Continental service, much less of those who were in the pay of their respective States. I am &c. G: Washington" (LB, DLC:GW). For Smith's application for office under the new federal government, see Smith to GW, 10 July 1789.

From Henry Lee, Jr.

My dear General   Novr 11th [17]86 N-york

I have your letter of the 31st octr besides the pleasure we all feel in knowing the health of Mount Vernon I am delighted and edified by your sentiments—This moment Genl Knox & Mr King left me having perused the part of your letr which respects the Insurgents—They expressed the highest satisfaction in finding that your retirement had not abated your affectionate zeal for the prosperity of every part of the empire.

Every day brings new information of the designs & preparations of the Malcontents—they are training their people, have officered some considerable bodys & are forming connexions with their neighboring states and the Vermontese—A convention has assembled to devise ways & Means of supporting their military arrangements, & of doing such other things as may be necessary for the prosecution of their intentions—We have authentic information that they contemplate a re-union with G. Britain, & it is not improbable but that the convention now sitting will formally make propositions of this nature to Lord Dorchester (Sir Guy Carleton) who is arrived at Quebec with plenipotentiary powers as Governor General of British america—they also declare their willingness to establish an imperial government in the U-States and I beleive could they be indulged with their favorite wish abolition of debts they would chearfully enter into the plan of a fœderal government assimilating the British government. In some matters these people certainly think right, altho they act wrong—A continuance of our present feeble political form is pregnant with daily evils & must drive us at last to a change—then it would be wise that this necessary alterati[o]n should be effected in peace & governed by reason, not left to passion & accident. If the insurgents would submit to government, & by constitutional exertions induce their state to commence this change, they woud benefit themselves their country & the Union—Good management might perhaps produce this wholesome conduct, but it is too probable that desperate & intriguing men may pursue private objects only.

I enclose you a piece signed Belisarius—He is said to be Baron Steuben—this encites universal wonder.[1]

I hope to see you & your lady next month. Our united love &

respects to Mount Vernon—Adieu with most affectionate regard
your h. s.

H: Lee junr

ALS, DLC:GW.

1. General Steuben's article which filled two columns of the New York *Daily Advertiser* on 1 Nov. 1786 is signed "Bellisaurius." Steuben argues against the use of Continental troops to put down Daniel Shays' Rebellion.

To James McHenry

My dear Sir,   Mount Verno⟨n, 11th Novr 1786⟩

I met your favor of the 5th, in Alexandria yesterday. Today I dispatch one of my Overseers and two Servants for the Jack & Mules which are arrived at Baltimore. The Pheasants & Partridges, I pray you to procure a passage for them by Water, in the Packet. To bring them by Land would be troublesome, & might perhaps be dangerous for them.

Be so good as to let me know the expence of these importations, and the cost of their detention in Baltimore. It shall be immediately paid, with many thanks to you, for your obliging attention to the business.

If you have any particular information from my good friend the Marquis de la Fayette respecting the above things, I shall be obliged to ⟨you⟩ for it; his letter to me takes ⟨no not⟩ice of them, altho' I had for some time been expecting one Jack and two she Asses through his medium—but by no means as a present.

One of the Servants who accompany's my Overseer, belongs to the Honble William Drayton of Charleston So. Ca. This Gentn spent a day or two here on his return from New York, and at Dumfries (proceeding on) the above fellow run away from him & came here. He goes to Baltimore under the impression of assisting in bringing the Jack & Mules home, but the real design of sending him there is to have him shipped for Charleston, if the Packet (which I am informed is regularly established betwn that place & Baltimore,) or any other vessel is on the point of sailing for the former. Mr Drayton will readily pay the Captn for his passage, and the other incidental expences, having intimated this in a letter to my Nephew; but if any doubt is entertained of it, I will see it done.

Under this rela⟨tion of⟩ Circumstances attending ⟨*mutilated*⟩ way, I would beg of you, ⟨my good⟩ Sir, (if an opportunity presents) to have him shipped, & previously secured. The fellow *pretends* a willingness to return to his master, but I think it would be unsafe to trust to this, especially as he has discovered an inclination to get back to Philadelphia (with a view *he says* of taking a passage from thence).[1]

Why will you not make a small excursion to see an old ac⟨quain⟩tance. It is unnecessary I ⟨should⟩ assure you of the pleasure it ⟨would⟩ give Yr Obedt & affecte Hble Ser⟨vt⟩

Go: Washington

P.S. Engage the Master of the Packet Boat to drop the Birds at this place as he passes by—otherwise I shall have to send to Alexandria for them.

ALS, photocopy furnished (1989) by Margaret Williams, Smith College; LB, DLC:GW. The upper corner of the manuscript is torn; the words and letters in angle brackets are taken from the letter-book copy.

1. It was the overseer John Fairfax whom GW sent to Baltimore for the birds and animals. Presumably Fairfax and GW's servant returned with Frenchman Jaques Campion, who conducted the jackass and jennies to Mount Vernon. See *Diaries*, 5:65, and McHenry to GW, 13, 18 November. William Drayton and Ralph Izard spent the nights of 22 and 23 Oct. at Mount Vernon when en route from New York to Charleston, South Carolina. GW wrote Drayton on 20 Nov. that his slave had run away after GW had sent him to Baltimore under the care of Fairfax; but Edward Moyston wrote GW on 4 April 1787 from Philadelphia: "Mr Drayton's Negro having given himself to me, I have transmitted him home to his Master. . . ."

To Thomas Johnson

Dr Sir,   Mount Vernon 12th Novr 1786.

On a supposition that you are now at Annapolis, the Petition of the Directors of the Potomac Company, is enclosed to your care. A Duplicate has been forwarded to the Assembly of this State. The fate of it I have not heard, but entertain no doubt of its favorable reception, as there are many auspicious proofs of liberality & justice already exhibited in the proceedings of it this Session.[1]

I hope the same spirit will mark the proceedings of yours.[2] The want of energy in the fœderal government; the pulling of one State, & parts of States against another; and the commotions among the Eastern People, have sunk our national character much below par; & have brought our politics and credit to the brink of a precipice. A step or two more must plunge us into inextricable ruin. Liberality, justice & unanimity in these States, wch do not appear to have drank so deep of the cup of folly, may yet retrieve our affairs; but no time is to be lost in essaying the reparation of them.

I have written to no gentlemen in your Assembly respecting the Potomac business but yourself—the justice of the case & your management of it, will ensure success. With great regard & respect, I am Dr Sir &c.

G: Washington

LB, DLC:GW; Bacon-Foster, *Development of Patomac Route*, 44.

1 See GW to David Stuart, 5 Nov., n.1.

2. The printed letter is misdated 15 Oct. 1784, and while much of the text is identical to the letter-book copy, there are sufficient differences in the remainder of this paragraph to quote the printed version taken from the ALS: "The want of energy in the Federal government—the pulling of one State & party of States against another & the commotion amongst the Eastern people have sunk our national character much below par; and has brought our politics and credit to the brink of a precipice; a step or two further must plunge us into a Sea of Troubles, perhaps anarchy and confusion. I trust that a proper sense of justice & unanimity in those States which have not drunk so deep of the cup of folly may yet retrieve our affairs. But no time is to be lost in essaying them."

From James McHenry

My dear General	Baltimore 13 Nov. 1786

I received your letter by Mr Fairfax yesterday noon.[1] The Marquiss who does nothing by halves has paid every expence incurred by his present till its arrival at this place as well as the wages and passage of their conductor, one Campion. While here the asses have been carefully attended by my own servants in my own stable, not caring to trust them to the hostler of a tavern, or from under my own eye. I expect to be able to send the birds by Mortimers packet; and shall engage a fit person to take charge of them to your own door, provided it should appear necessary upon examining the vessel and character of the seamen.

Campion will deliver you a letter from the Marquiss. What do you conjecture from his appointment to the Indies?[2]

It would give me infinite pleasure to spend a few days at Mount Vernon, and to pay my respects to you and Mrs Washington in your place of peace and hospitality; which I shall certainly do unless the growing demands of a family should lay in a more urgent claim to my time. I want much to talk to you about a memoir of things and transactions in which you have been particularly concerned and which I think ought to be prepared for publication.[3] I would have it to comprehend your whole past life. A general history of the revolution does not admit of what I mean. It would suspend the narration of the history if inserted entire; or it would lose its own peculiar effect, if interwoven with the revolution. The pieces of a diamond may be disposed to advantage, but it is most valuable when entire and its lustre most penetrating. This diamond ought not to be lost nor divided tho' to ornament a crown. I am my dear Genl yours most affy

James McHenry

ADfS, DLC: James McHenry Papers. The ALS was lost in transit to Mount Vernon (see note 2).

1. GW's letter is dated 11 November.

2. Jaques Campion lost this letter from McHenry to GW between Baltimore and Mount Vernon. Campion insisted to GW that Lafayette had not entrusted him with a letter to GW. Lafayette's letter to GW of 26 Oct. 1786 seems to support this. See McHenry to GW, 18 Nov., GW to McHenry, 29 Nov., and GW to Lafayette, 19 November.

3. The remainder of the letter has many lines crossed out and rephrasing written in.

Letter not found: from Edward Newenham, 13 Nov. 1786. On 20 April 1787 GW wrote Newenham that he had been "honoured with your favours of the 13th and 25th of November last."

From David Stuart

Dear Sir,   Rich[mon]d Novr 13th 1786

I am informed by Mr Pendelton one of the Auditors, that it is unnecessary to lay your claims before the legislature—that by the law lately revived, they will be paid in Certificates, when passed by the Court of Fairfax. I therefore send them up to you, that you may have this done at the next Court—After which, you will be pleased to forward them on, again to me—You will see Pendletons advise noticed, at the bottom of the largest claim.[1]

Information is just recieved here, that the Indians have met with a considerable defeat from Logan, one of Clarke's officers.[2] The treaty reported to be made with Spain, respecting the navigation of the Mississippi, gives much displeasure here—Governor Henry in particular, is much incensed at it. If it is possible to defeat it, it will be done; and our members in Congress, will be instructed to that effect.[3]

I informed you in my last, what were my expectations of getting money—if not disappointed in these, I shall certainly be able to pay you, the greater part of the sum due you. If I should be able to dispose of the corn, made on the estates of New Kent & King William; I shall be able to pay you at the same time, your annuity—There is some probability that Mr Newton of Norfolk will buy it immediately[4]—I shall attend to the enquiries you have suggested, and also to the one from Mrs Washington. I am Dr Sir with great regard your Obt Serv:

                                                    Dd Stuart

ALS, DLC:GW.

1. See GW to Stuart, 5 Nov., n.2.

2. In October Col. John Logan made a devastating attack on the Shawnee towns on the Great Miami, which brought retaliations and further conflict. See George McCarmick to GW, 31 October.

3. James Madison reported to Thomas Jefferson on 4 Dec.: "The project for bartering the Missipi to Spain was brought before the Assembly. . . . The report of it having reached the ears of the Western Representatives, as many of them as were on the spot, backed by a number of the late officers, presented a Memorial, full of consternation & complaint; in consequence of which some very pointed resolutions by way of instruction to the Delegates in Congs. were *unanimously* entered into by the House of Delegates" (Rutland and Rachal, *Madison Papers*, 9:189–92; see also Resolutions Reaffirming American Rights to Navigate the Mississippi, ibid., 181–84, and *House of Delegates Journal, 1786–1790*, 17 Nov.). See Madison's similar report to GW on 7 December.

4. See GW to Stuart, 5 Nov., n.3.

To Robert Alexander

Sir,   Mount Vernon 14th Novr 1786

Fifteen months ago I informed you in as explicit language as I was master of, of my want of the money you are indebted to me. I have waited (considering the urgency of my call) with patience to see if you would comply with the demand: But no disposition having yet appeared in you to do this; I find myself under the disagreeable necessity of informing you, that unless you name a time not far distant for payment, & secure the same to me without delay, that I shall (tho' very reluctantly, as I think you have abundant reason to conclude from my long forbearance) have recourse to the most effectual mode the Law will give me to obtain justice.

It will avail nothing Sir, for you to repeat to me the claim you have upon Mr Custis's Estate. This, independent of the Law suit, is, I am told, very trifling; but were it otherwise, his affairs & mine now are, & have long been as distinct as yours & mine. If justice is denied you there, seek it; but let it be no plea for withholding my money which ought to have been refunded to me twelve or fifteen years ago, before your dealings with Mr Custis came into existence.[1] I am &c.

G: Washington

LB, DLC:GW.

Robert Alexander (d. 1793) of Alexandria was the son of Col. Gerard Alexander (d. 1761).

1. For the land deal in which GW in the fall of 1769 advanced Robert Alexander £500 to purchase land in Charles County, Md., see Thomas Hanson Marshall to GW, 18 June 1769, n.1. By the time Col. William Lyle assumed the Alexander debt on 30 April 1789, the debt, with interest, had reached £795.15.4 (Ledger A, 352; Ledger B, 41). For a full discussion of John Parke Custis's purchase from Alexander in July 1778 of the plantation on the Potomac River which he named Abingdon and the continuing dispute over the terms of the purchase, see David Stuart to GW, 14 July 1789, n.7.

From Thomas Jefferson

Sir   Paris Nov. 14. 1786

The house of Le Coulteux, which for centuries has been the wealthiest of this place, has it in contemplation to establish a great company for the fur trade. they propose that partners interested one half in the establishment should be American citizens, born & residing in the U.S. yet if I understood them rightly they expect that that half of the company which resides here should make the greatest part, or perhaps the whole of the advances, while those on our side the water should superintend the details. they had at first thought of Baltimore as the center of their American transactions. I have pointed out to them the advantages of Alexandria for this purpose. they have concluded to take information as to Baltimore, Philadelphia & N. york for a principal deposit, & having no correspondent at Alexandria, have asked me to procure a state of the advantages of that place, as also to get a recommendation of the best merchant there to be adopted as partner & head of the business there. skill, punctuality & integrity are the requisites in such a character. they will decide on their whole information as to the place for their principal factory. being unwilling that Alexandria should lose it's pretensions, I have undertaken to procure them information as to that place. if they undertake this trade at all, it will be on so great a scale as to decide the current of the Indian trade to the place they adopt. I have no acquaintance at Alexandria or in it's neighborhood. but believing you would feel an interest in it from the same motives which I do, I venture to ask the favor of you to recommend to me a proper merchant for their purpose, & to engage some well informed person to send me a representation of the advantages of Alexandria as the principal deposit for the fur trade.[1]

The author of the Political part of the Encyclopedie methodique desired me to examine his article 'Etats unis.' I did so. I found it a tissue of errors. for in truth they know nothing about us here. particularly however the article 'Cincinnati' was a mere Philippic against that institution: in which it appeared that there was an utter ignorance of facts & motives. I gave him notes on it. he reformed it as he supposed & sent it again to me to revise. in this reformed state Colo. Humphreys saw it. I found it necessary to write that article for him. before I gave it to him I showed it to the Marq. de la fayette who made a correction or two. I then sent it to the author. he used the materials, mixing a great deal of his own with them. in a work which is sure of going down to the latest posterity I thought it material to set facts to rights as much as possible. the author was well disposed: but could not entirely get the better of his original bias. I send you the Article as ultimately published. if you find any material errors in it & will be so good as to inform me of them, I shall probably have opportunities of setting this author to rights.[2] what has heretofore passed between us on this institution, makes it my duty to mention to you that I have never heard a person in Europe, learned or unlearned, express his thoughts on this institution, who did not consider it as dishonourable & destructive to our governments, and that every writing which has come out since my arrival here, in which it is mentioned, considers it, even as now reformed, as the germ whose development is one day to destroy the fabric we have reared. I did not apprehend this while I had American ideas only. but I confess that what I have seen in Europe has brought me over to that opinion: & that tho' this day may be at some distance, beyond the reach of our lives perhaps, yet it will certainly come, when, a single fibre left of this institution, will provide an hereditary aristocracy which will change the form of our governments from the best to the worst in the world. to know the mass of evil which flows from this fatal source, a person must be in France, he must see the finest soil, the finest climate, the most compact state, the most benevolent character of people, & every earthly advantage combined, insufficient to prevent this scourge from rendering existence a curse to 24 out of 25 parts of the inhabitants of this country. with us the branches of this institution cover all the states. the Southern ones at this time are aristocratical in their disposition: and that that spirit should grow & extend itself, is within the natural order of things. I do not flatter myself with the immortality of our governments: but I shall think little also of their longevity unless this germ of destruction be taken out. when the society themselves shall weigh the possibility of evil against the impossibility of any good to proceed from this institution, I cannot help hoping they will eradicate it. I know they wish the permanence of our governments as much as any individuals composing them. an interruption here & the departure of the gentlemen by whom I send this obliges me to conclude it, with assurances of the sincere respect & esteem with which I have the honor to be Dear Sir Your most obedt & most humble servt

Th. Jefferson

ALS, DLC:GW; LB, DLC: Jefferson Papers.

1. Lafayette wrote GW about Louis Couteulx on 8 October. See note 1 of that document.

2. Jefferson is referring to Jean Nicolas Démeunier's "Essai sur les Etats-Unis" in the *Encyclopédie Méthodique*. GW sent the copy of the article to Henry Knox on 27 April 1787, the day after he received it. For Jefferson's role in the writing of the article in the *Encyclopédie* relating to the United States, see "The Article on the United States in the *Encyclopédie Méthodique*" in Boyd, *Jefferson Papers*, 10:3–65.

From James Tilghman

Dear honoured Sir   Chester Town Maryland Novr 14th 1786

In the Draught of an Incription for Colo. Tilghman's Tomb I have taken the Liberty of mentioning your name in the manner you will perceive by the inclosed Copy of the Draught.[1] But I would not have the inscription made till it should have the honor of your approbation. You will be pleased to do me the favour to peruse it and give me Your Opinion of it's Propriety. I have the honor to be with much respect Yr Most Obt Servt

James Tilghman

ALS, DLC:GW.

1. Tilghman's draft for the inscription on his son's tombstone reads: "Beneath this Stone are laid / The Remains of a Good Man / Colo. Tench Tilghman / Who died April the 18th 1786 / In the 43d year of his life / He took an early and active part / In the great Contest that secured / The Independence of the United States of America / He was Aid de Camp to / His Excellency General Washington / Commander in Chief of the American armies / And was honored with his friendship and Confidence / And / He was one of those / Whose merits were distinguished / and / honorably reward[ed] / By the Congress." The inscription on the tomb in the graveyard in Baltimore on Lombard Street between Green and Paca is identical except for the beginning and end. The actual inscription begins: "In Memory of Tench Tilghman, who died April 18th 1786, In the 42nd year of his age, Very much lamented." It ends: "But Still more to his Praise He was A Good man."

To Anne Ennis

Madam,   Mount Vernon 15th Novr 1786.

Your letter, or memorial dated the 12th of July in Dublin, came to my hands yesterday under cover of a letter from Mr Peter Trenor of the 8th inst.[1]

The Memorial mis-states several facts—one of them materially; for I have not, nor never had one shilling of the late Mrs Savage's property in my hands: on the contrary, merely to relieve that Lady from the distress she represented herself to be in, I sent her in the year [   ] a Bill for £[   ] which sum is yet due to me.[2] The circumstances attending that unfortunate Lady & her Estate are these. Her first husband, the Revd Chas Green, left all his property real & personal to her, estimated at about £5000 current money of this State: not in trust, as you set forth, but at her absolute disposal. When she was about to enter into her second marriage, with Doctr Savage, she previously thereto made this Estate over to him, securing an annuity of £100 currency, for the term of her life, if it should be demanded: and it was this sum, which was secured to her by a trust-bond to Bryan Fairfax Esqr. & myself. The unhappy differences which soon arose, & occasioned a separation between the Doctor & her, obliged Mr Fairfax & myself, in order to obtain support for Mrs Savage, to put the Bond in suit. The Doctor (who I believe might very properly be classed among the worst of men) made use of every subterfuge, & practiced all the chicanery of the Law to postpone the payment; which he was well enabled to do, as there was a suspension of our Courts of justice consequent of the dispute with Great Britain. However, when no longer able to stave off judgment at Common Law, he threw the matter into the high Court of Chancery of this State, where it now is. We are encouraged by our Lawyers to expect a final issue of the business in a term or two more; but what reliance is to be placed on these assurances, is not for me to decide.

As soon as the money is finally recovered, & in the hands of Mr Fairfax & myself, we have neither the power nor inclination to withhold it one moment from the Executors of the deceased Mrs Savage; but it will readily occur to you Madam, that for our security, there must be an attested Copy of the Will, under the Seal of the Corporation where it is recorded, annexed to a regular power of attorney (to be proved in this Country) from the Executors to some person here, to receive the money from us. It is the business of the Executors—not the Trustees, to settle the accounts & pay the legacies of the Testator.[3]

I have never seen any *authentic* copy of the Will. In the one which was shewn to me by a Mr Moore of Baltimore I was not

named as an Executor;[4] If I had, it would not have been agreeable to me to have acted. I am, Madam &c.

G: Washington

LB, DLC:GW.

1. Mrs. Ennis's memorial is printed in note 1 of Peter Trenor's letter of 8 November.
2. On 27 Jan. 1772 GW sent Margaret Savage £53.
3. See note 2, Trenor to GW, 8 November.
4. This was William Moore. See Hanna Moore to GW, 20 Jan. 1785, n.2.

To Bushrod Washington

Dear Bushrod,   Mount Vernon Novr 15th 1786.
Your letter of the 31st of Octr in reply to mine of the 30th of
Septr came safe to hand.

It was not the intention of my former letter either to con-
demn, or give my voice in favor of the Patriotic Society of which
you are a member. I offered observations, under the information you gave of it, the weight of which were to be considered.
As first thoughts they were undigested, and might be very erroneous.

That representatives ought to be the mouth of their constituents, I do not deny; nor do I mean to call in question the right
of the latter to instruct them. It is to the embarrassment into
which they may be thrown by these instructions in *National matters* that my objection lyes. In speaking of National matters I look
to the Fœderal government which in my opinion it is the interest
of every state to support, & to do it as there are a variety of
interests in the Union there must be a yielding of the parts to
coalesce the whole. Now a county, a district—or even a state
might decide on a measure though apparently for the benefit of
it in its seperate & unconnected state which may be repugnant
to the interest of the nation, and eventually so the state itself: as
a part of the Confederation. If then members go instructed to
the Assembly from the different districts all the requisitions of
Congress repugnant to the sense of them—and all the lights
which they may receive from the Communications of that body
to the Legislature must be unavailing altho. the nature and necessity of them when the reasons therefor are expounded are as

self evident as our existance. In local matters, which concern the district—or in things which respect the internal police of the state, there may be no impropriety in instructions. In National matters also, the sense (under the view they have of them) but not the Law of the district may be given leaving the Delegates to judge from the nature of the case and the evidence before them which can only be received from Congress to the Executive & will be brought before them in their assembled capacity.

The instructions of your Society as far as they have gone accord with my sentiments, except in the article of Commutables. Here if I understand the meaning and design of the clause I disagree to it most clearly—for if the intention of it is to leave it optional in the person taxed to pay any staple commodity (Tobacco would be least exceptionable) in lieu of specie, the people will be burthened—a few speculators enriched—and the public not benefited. Have we not had a recent, and glaring instance of this in the course of the war, in the provision tax? Did not the people pay this in some way or other—perhaps badly—and was the Army, for whose benefit it was laid the better for it? Can any instance be given where the public has sold Tobacco, Hemp, Flour, or any other commodity upon as good terms as individuals have done? Who is this to serve? Is there a man to be found who, having any of the staple commodities to sell that will say he cannot get a *reasonable* price for them? Must there not be places of deposit for these commutables? Collectors, storekeepers, &ca, &ca employed? Rely on it, these will sink one half the tax and a parcel of speculators will possess themselves of the other half, to the injury of the people, & deception of the public. It is to similar measures of this, we owe the present depravity of morals, and abound in so many designing characters.[1]

Among the great objects which you took into consideration at your meeting in Richmond, how came it to pass that you never turned your eyes towards the inefficiency of the Fœderal government, so as to instruct your Delegates to accede to the propositions of the Commissioners lately convened at Annapolis—or to devise some other mode to give it that energy which is necessary to support a national character? Every man who considers the present Constitution of it, and sees to what it is verging, trembles and deprecates the event. The fabrick which took nine years (at the expence of much blood and treasure) to erect, now totters to the foundation, and without support must soon fall.

The determination of your Society to promote frugality & industry by example—to encourage manufactures—& to discountenance dissipation is highly praiseworthy. These and premiums for the most useful discoveries in Agriculture within your district—The most profitable course of cropping—and the best method of fencing to save timber &ca would soon make you a rich & happy people. With every good wish for you and yours in which your Aunt joins me I am—Dear Bushrod Yr Affecte

Go: Washington

ALS, anonymous donor; LB, DLC:GW.

1. For GW's own argument against acceptance by the state of Virginia of tobacco for specie payments, see GW to James Madison, 16 December.

To Wakelin Welch

Sir,   M[oun]t Vernon 15th Novr 1786

I take the liberty of giving you the trouble of forwarding the enclosed letters to their addresses. I have again requested the favor of Mr Young to send me a few Seeds: the cost may be about Ten pounds, more or less; for the amount of which, & other small matters, (should he think proper to add them) I pray you to honor his Draft.[1]

You would do me a singular favor by engaging the Captain who has charge of the Vessel by which they may be sent, to put them in the Cabbin or steerage. If they go into the hold of the vessel, the destruction of the seeds will be followed by a disappointment which would be of infinitely more importance to me than the cost of them.

Messrs Forrest & Stoddard have ships which pass by my door: so have Messrs Drusina Ridder & Clark. I persuade myself the masters of any of these would so far oblige me as to be attentive to your recommendation of them: Captn Johns of the Potomac Planter I am sure would.

I have a Farmer who was sent to me from Gloucestershire in England by a friend of mine at Bath. He has now written for his wife to come to him, with her children, & to bring with her some seeds, implements of Husbandry &ca, to this Country. Bristol is their nearest Port, but opportunities from thence to this river rarely happening, I have recommended it to their friend & patron Mr Peacy, to open a correspondence with you, or the House of Messrs Forrest & Stoddard of London, that she may be advised of the sailing of a vessel from that place to this river as a more speedy & certain mode of conveyance; your compliance therein would be very pleasing to me, & very serviceable to an honest, old English farmer.[2] I am &c. &c.

G: Washington

LB, DLC:GW.

1. See GW's letter to Arthur Young of this date. GW also probably enclosed his letter of this date to Anne Ennis for forwarding, and perhaps his letter to William Peacey of 16 Nov. as well.

2. See GW to William Peacey, 16 November.

To Arthur Young

Sir,   Mount Vernon in Virginia 15th of Novembr 1786

The enclosed is a duplicate of the letter I had the honor of writing to you the 6th of August.[1]

The evil genius of the Vessel by which it was sent (which had detained her many weeks in this Country after the letters intended to go by her were ready, agreeably to the owners appointment) pursued her to Sea, and obliged the Captain (when many days out) by the leaky condition in which she appeared, to return to an American Port. The uncertainty of his conduct with respect to the letters, is the apology I offer for giving you the trouble of the enclosed.

Since the date of it, I have had much satisfaction in perusing the Annals of Agriculture which you did me the favor to send me. If the testimony of my approbation, Sir, of your disinterested conduct & perseverence in publishing so useful and beneficial a work (than which nothing in my opinion can be more conducive to the welfare of your Country) will add aught to the satisfaction you must feel from the conscious discharge of this interesting duty to it, I give it with equal willingness and sincerity.

In addition to the articles which my last requested the favor of you to procure for me, I pray you to have the goodness of forwarding what follows—

Eight bushels of what you call velvet wheat, of which I perceive you are an admirer. (The Books being at a Book binders, I may have mis-called this Wheat.)

Four Bushels of Beans of the kind you most approve for the purposes of a Farm.

Four bushels of the best kind of Spring Barley.

Eight bushels of the best kind of Oats—and

Eight Bushels of Sainfoin seed—all to be in good Sacks.

My Soil will come under the description of Loam; with a hard clay, or (if it had as much of the properties as the appearance, might be denominated) marl, from eighteen Inches to three feet below the surface. The heaviest soil I have would hardly be called a stiff or binding Clay in Engld—and none of it is a blowing sand. The sort which approaches nearest the former, is a light gray—and that to the latter, of a yellow red. In a word the staple has been good, but by use & abuse it is brought into bad condition. I have added this information, Sir, that you may be better able to decide on the kind of Seed most proper for my Farms.

Permit me to ask one thing more. It is to favor me with your opinion, and a plan, of the most compleat & useful Farm yard, for Farms of about 500 Acres. In this I mean to comprehend the Barn, and every appurtenance which ought to be annexed to the yard. The simplest and most œconomical plan would be preferred, provided the requisites are all included. Mr Welch will answer your draught for the cost of these articles, as before. He is advised of it.[2] I have the honor to be Sir Yr most Obedt and most Hble Servt

Go: Washington

ALS, PPRF; LB, DLC:GW.

1. See the source note in GW's letter of 6 August.
2. GW wrote Wakelin Welch on this day.

From David Humphreys

My dear General   New Haven [Conn.] Novr 16th 1786

I have written you twice within these few days, and agreeably to the promise in my last, I have now the honor of enclosing papers containing the state of facts respecting Captn Asgill's confinement—I have no fear but that the truth will become generally known, I hope it is digested & printed in a manner that will be acceptable to you.[1] I would have sent you several of the late papers from the same press, which contained performances written by Mr Trumbull, Mr Barlow & myself, in a style & manner for wit & humour, I believe, somewhat superior to common News-paper publications: but the demand has been so uncommonly great for those papers that there is not a single one to be obtained. In some instances, the force of ridicule has been found of more efficacy than the force of argument, against the Antifederalists & Advocates for Mobs & Conventions. It was pleasant enough to observe how some leading Men, of erroneous politics, were stung to the soul, by shafts of satire.[2]

I perceive Sir Guy Carleton, who is made Lord Dorchester, has just arrived in Canada, with Billy Smith for Cheif Justice of that Province: this does not appear to forebode any great good to us.[3] It continues to be suggested in conversation & print, that Emissaries are employed to scatter the seeds of discord among the citizens of the United States—tho' I do not think the British too virtuous or liberal for such conduct, I cannot say that I have seen sufficient evidence to convince me that their Cabinet has adopted that system—it is not improbable, however, that officious Individuals, while they gratified their own private revenge, should have thought this work would not be disagreeable to their Government, even if unsanctioned by it.

The Assembly of Massachusetts seem disposed to redress all the real & even pretended greivances, under which their Constituents are supposed to labour; after which, it is hoped & expected they will adopt a line of conduct, pointedly vigorous & decided. On the strength of this expectation or something else, the Governor already talks *very big*.

I am informed that Genl Harry Jackson, is appointed Commandant of the Continental Regt to be raised in that State, &

that Gibbs is appointed one of the Majors, I have not heard who
are subjects of other appointments.[4]

The Rendezvous of my Regt is at Hartford, where I may probably be the greater part of the Winter.[5] Tho. I shall not have the
felicity of eating Christmas Pies at Mount Vernon, I hope & trust
my former exploits in that way will not be forgotten—To the two
Mrs Washingtons, to my friends the Major & Mr Lear be pleased
to present me affectionately. At one time or another I hope to
have the satisfaction of testifying personally how much & how
ardently, I have the honor to be Your sincere friend & Humble
Servant

D. Humphreys

ALS, DLC:GW.

    1. Humphreys' letters are dated 1 and 9 November. For GW's correspon-
dence in 1786 regarding the Asgill affair, see James Tilghman to GW, 26 May
1786, n.3. Humphreys' essay, "The Conduct of General Washington Respecting the Confinement of Captain Asgill placed in the True Point of Light," was
published on this day, 16 Nov., in the *New-Haven Gazette and the Connecticut
Magazine*. Humphreys' Asgill piece was reprinted in January and February
1787 in the *Columbian Magazine: or Monthly Miscellany* (1:205–9, 253–55). Humphreys' letter to the printers, dated at New Haven on 6 Nov., which serves to
introduce the excerpts from the letters and papers sent to him by GW, reads:
"WHEN I was in England, last winter, I heard suggestions that the treatment
captain Asgill experienced, during his confinement, was unneccessarily rigor-
ous, and as such reflected discredit on the Americans. Having myself belonged
to the family of the commander in chief, at that period, and having been acquainted with the minutest circumstance relative to that unpleasant affair, I
had no hesitation in utterly denying that there was a particle of veracity in
those illiberal suggestions. On my return to Mount Vernon, this summer, I
mentioned the subject to general Washington. He shewed me a communication from London, addressed to col. Tilghman, which, arriving just after the
death of that most amiable character, had been forwarded by his father to the
general—by the latter I was also indulged with a sight of his answer. I desired
to be permitted to take copies of these papers, together with transcripts from
all the original letters and orders respecting captain Asgill. Of these I am
now possessed.

    "Anxious that the circulation of truth should be co-extensive with the fals-
hoods which have been assiduously propagated; and desirous that the facts
may be placed in a true point of view before the eyes of the present age, and
even of posterity, I have determined, without consulting any one, to charge
myself with their publication. It is for this purpose, I request you to insert the
inclosed *documents*, for the authenticity of which I hold myself responsible to
the public."

    2. Humphreys, Joel Barlow (1754–1812), and John Trumbull (1750–1831),

known as the Connecticut Wits, were in 1786 and 1787 publishing their satiric prose and verse, *The Anarchiad*, in the *New-Haven Gazette and the Connecticut Magazine*.

3. William Smith (1728–1793), the New York Loyalist who was a distinguished lawyer, legal scholar, and historian of provincial New York, left for England when the British evacuated New York in 1783. His appointment as chief justice of Canada is dated 1 Sept. 1785. Smith held the office until his death.

4. Col. Henry Jackson, brevetted brigadier general in the Massachusetts forces in 1783, was left in command of the remnants of the Continental army at West Point when Maj. Gen. Henry Knox departed for Boston in January 1784. See Henry Knox to GW, 3 Jan. 1784, and notes. Caleb Gibbs (c.1750–1818) of Marblehead, Mass., was captain of GW's guards from 1776 to 1780; he remained in the Continental army until June 1784 as major of the 1st American Regiment under Colonel Jackson. The only role Jackson and his force played during Shays' Rebellion was to protect the federal arsenal at Springfield after any danger to it had dissipated.

5. See Humphreys to GW, 28 Feb. 1787.

Letter not found: to James McHenry, 16 Nov. 1786. McHenry wrote GW on 18 Nov.: "I received your letter of the 16th this evening."

To William Peacey

Sir,   Mount Vernon Novr 16th 1786

Enclosed, I give you the trouble of receiving the Copy of a letter I had the honor of writing to you in behalf of Mr James Bloxham. Since the date of it he has agreed to remain another year with me, and has written (as he informs me) in decided terms for his Wife & family to come to him, & bring with them the seeds & Implements which are enumerated in the enclosed Letters.[1]

As Vessels from Bristol (though the nearest shipping port to her) do not often come to this River, or to any convenient place of debarkation, it would be better I conceive for her, to resolve on a Passage from London alone—And if you, Sir, in her behalf, would open a Corrispondence with either Messrs Forrest & Stoddard, or with Wakelin Welch Esqr. of that City (to the last of whom I have written on the subject)[2] I am persuaded a passage could be obtained, & the time fixed for her to be there. Mr Bloxham places so much confidence in your friendship for him, & patronage of his family, that I have no scruple in suggesting these ideas to you, though it is a liberty I should not have taken under any other Circumstances.

If his wife brings seeds it cannot be too strongly impressed upon her, to keep them out of the Ship's hold, for they will certainly heat & spoil if put there. Mr Bloxham informs me that there is a young man of the name of Caleb Hall who is desirous of coming to this Country—I have mentioned to the old man the terms on which I would employ this Hall; I have no doubt of his finding the Country answerable to his expectations, and his coming might be very satisfactory and serviceable to Mrs Bloxham and her children on the passage, & previous to their embarkation.[3] I have the honor to be Sir yr most obedt & Hble Servt

                                        Go: Washington

LS, in Tobias Lear's hand, PHi: Washington Manuscripts; LB, DLC:GW.

1. See GW to Peacey, 5 Aug., and the enclosed letter from Bloxham to Peacey, 23 July 1786. For an account of Bloxham's career at Mount Vernon, see the note in Articles of Agreement with James Bloxham, 31 May 1786.

2. GW wrote Wakelin Welch on 15 November. See also GW to Peacey, 5 August.

3. In his diary entry for 13 Nov., GW wrote: "Told James Bloxham, my Farmer, who was about to write to England for his Wife & family, and who proposed the measure that he might write to one Caleb Hall a Neighbour of his in Gloucestershire (who had expressed a desire to come to this Country, and who he said was a compleat Wheel Wright, Waggon builder, and Plow & Hurdle maker) that I wd. give him 25 Guineas a year for his Services . . . " (*Diaries*, 5:66). Peacey wrote GW on 2 Feb. 1787 that "Caleb Hall have not made up his Mind to Leve this Kingdom." GW replied on 7 Jan. 1788 that he was "not sorry that Caleb Hall did not come out," for he had "proposed his coming more to please Bloxham . . . than from a want of his services myself."

Letter not found: to Peter Trenor, 16 Nov. 1786. On 1 Oct. 1792, Trenor wrote to GW and referred to "what your Excellency mentioned in yours of 16th November 1786." On 29 Jan. 1790 Trenor cites the letter as being written 15 Nov. 1786.

From George Weedon

Sir   Richmond November 17th 1786
    Your circular Letter of the 31t of October having been communicated to the annual Meeting of the Virginia Cincinnati,

they have directed me to assure you, that while they regret the loss the Society sustains by your relinquishing the Presidency, they are fully sensible of the justness of those motives which have determined your Retreat. They lament however, that to the causes which might have operated to produce this resolution before, is added a more afflicting one, the ill state of your health. They can never sufficiently express their gratitude for the patronage you afforded the Society in its insecure and infant state; and they trust that they shall never deviate from those principles of their constitution, which, as they procured your approbation, must dispel every idea of jelousy from the minds of the good People of these United States. They receive with pleasure the information of your being ready to sign Diplomas during your continuance in Office; as they apprehend those Papers might lose much of their value, in the opinion of the members, if marked with any other signature—This circumstance induces them to wish that you could be prevailed upon, to sacrifice so much of your valuable time to the interests of the Institution, as might be necessary for this purpose, without subjecting yourself to any other duty of the Presidency; supposing that the other labours of the Office, might without inconveniency be transferr'd to the Vice President of the Society—I have the honor to be with much esteem Your obt Servt

G. Weedon Prest

LS, DLC:GW.

To Theodorick Bland

Dr Sir,   Mount Vernon 18th Novr 1786.

Several matters in which I have been pretty closely engaged, having prevented my sending to the Post office with my usual regularity, is the cause of my not having got, & of course acknowledged, the receipt of your obliging favors of the 4th & 9th inst: earlier than I now do. By ascribing this delay to the true cause, I shall stand acquitted of all seeming inattention.[1]

Permit me now, Sir, to thank you for the interesting communications in your letters, & to express to you the sincere pleasure with which I am filled at hearing that the acts of the present Session are marked with wisdom, justice & liberality. The critical situation of our affairs calls for the most vigorous display of these virtues, & it is much to be wished that so good an example from so respectable a State will be attended with the most salutary consequences to the Union.

No man entertains a higher sense of the necessity of revising the fœderal System, & supporting its government, than I do; nor would any man more readily depart from a prescribed line of conduct to effect this, than myself, in any matters I am competent to. With these sentiments & under such impressions, notwithstanding my having bid adieu to the public walks of life in a public manner, I should, if the partiality of my Country had called me to the service you allude to in your letter of the 9th, have yielded assent, not from an opinion that I could have answered their purposes better, or with equability to many that might have been named, but to evince my gratitude for the numberless instances of the confidence they have placed in me, & my obedience to their call.

But a recent act of mine has put it out of my power, if this honor is intended me, to accept it consistently.

You know Sir, I was first appointed, & have since been rechosen, President of the Society of the Cincinnati; the last time much against my inclination. The triennial Genl Meeting of this Body is to be held in Philadelphia the first Monday in May next. The peculiar situation of my private concerns—the necessity of paying some attention to them; love of retirement, & a wish to enjoy a mind at ease; rheumatic pains which I begin to feel very sensibly, with some other considerations, induced me to address a circular Letter, dated the latter end of October, to the several State societies, informing them of my intention not to be at the next Genl Meeting, & desiring not to be rechosen. The Vice President is also informed of these matters, that the business may not be impeded on account of my absence. Under these circumstances you will readily perceive the impropriety there would be in my informing so worthy & respectable a part of the community as the late Officers of the American army, of the reasons which militate against my attendance at this Meeting, & to appear there at the same moment on another occasion.[2]

I thank you for the Cutting-box. The Drill-plough I promised to have made for you has been ready some time, & wou'd have been sent to the care of Mr Newton 'ere this; but the hourly expectation of receiving the Timothy seed I promised to obtain for you, induced me to keep it (as I did not imagine you would apply it to any use 'till the Spring) 'till both should go together. My best respects to Mrs Bland. I am Dr Sir, &c.

G: Washington

LB, DLC:GW.
1. Letters not found.
2. GW's circular to the Cincinnati, presented above, is dated 31 October.

From Gardoqui

Sir   New york 18th Novr 1786.

I received in course the honor of your Excellency's favor under 30th Augt to which I did not reply puntualy for want of subjectt, but haveing now that of the enclos'd letter which was sent to me by the Count of Floridablanca for your Excellency I gladly embrace the oportunity, haveing taken the liberty to add in it a translation in English for fear of your Excellency's being at a loss to understand it being in Spanish.[1]

It gave me the utmost pleasure to find that the Vicuña Cloth meritted your aprobation & that your Excellency wou'd wear it: As a memento of my regard & great consideration for your Excellency's great qualities, is what I wish you wou'd do it, & I further beg your Excellency wou'd make free & command me as a sincere well wisher to the great monument you have erected in the States & as an attach'd freind to them & your Excellency. I am glad to hear that your Excellency is so much pleas'd with the Jack Ass, & that he promises so valuable. I don't dare to affirm that I shall be able to provide your Excellency with the female you want for him, but I can assure you that I have already taken such measures as may probably produce what you want, & I will further promise your Excellency that I shall ℞ first Packett write my freind General Galvez to send me such female if to be had in the Dominions he governs, so that upon the whole I hope to help your Excellency in your wishes.

Accept my most gratefull thanks for your Excellency's repeated invitation to Mount Vernon I shall certainly embrace it if my business shou'd permitt me, but I have lately understood that it was probable your Excellency wou'd favor Philadelphia with a visitt next spring. I sincerely wish it may prove so as I shou'd not loosse a day in setting out for the honor of waiting on your Excellency. I wou'd at the same time communicate you my earnest wishes to join the States & my country in a firm & permanent good freindship, but I am truly concern'd that some of your worthy Gentn will not understand their own Interest. I repeatt their own Interest because my noble Master repays generously any good step, whereas the reverse, is the only way to deprive themselves of that fruitt which they hope to reap by the negative.

Excuse my noble General if I have got into an improper subjectt, but I have been, am & will be a true freind to your United States, & am certain that what I hint will be to the advantage of those immidiately concern'd in the western lands & that any contrary effectt will putt an everlasting impediment to all manner of intercourse. Pardon me & beleive me to be with the highest consideration & respectt Your Excellency's most Obedt humble Servt

James Gardoqui

ALS, DLC:GW.

1. The original letter from Floridablanca, dated 1 Sept. 1786 at San Ildefonso in Spain, is in the Gratz Collection, PHi. There are two translations of his letter in DLC:GW, both docketed by GW. The text of the translation that is headed "Translation of the annexed letter," which was sent to him by Gardoqui (see GW to Gardoqui, 1 Dec. 1786), reads: "The King has heard with a particular satisfaction the Kind expressions of your Excellency's Reply regarding the Jack Ass which his Majesty order'd to send to your Excellency. It will give great pleasure to his Majesty that oportunities of a higer nature may offer to prove the great esteem he entertains of your Excellency's personal merit singular virtues & other Circumstances. I am also glad of the present oportunity to assure your Excellency of my particular esteem & of the truth with which I pray God may preserve your Excellency's life for many years. Sir Your Excellency's assur'd Servent The Count of Floridablanca."

From James McHenry

My Dear General.   Baltimore 18th Novr 1786

I received your letter of the 16th this evening and am extremely sorry at the loss of the French mans pocket book; but I flatter myself that your name being on the letters will be a means of recovering it.[1]

With respect to Campion the conductor of the asses he has no other claim to your consideration than as a faithful servant. I collect from himself that he is an expert swordsman, and that his father is chief cook to the French King. You will see also his character by the inclosed bill for his boarding which he left for me to discharge. I mention these circumstances that you may be at no loss for his quality.[2]

The Marquis does not write to me himself about the asses or birds; but Poirey his secretary, tells me that every expence attending their transportation to this place with the passage of Campion, has been paid, and requests me to take the necessary steps to aid him in conveying them to your Excellency, alleging that the Marquiss at the time of his writing was at Strasburg. In additon to this the Mesrs Berards of L'orient who were entrusted with their embarkation recommended them to my care and speaks of them as a present from the marquiss.

I shall be uneasy till I hear that the pocket book is found: for I imagine there may be in it some confidential information. With great affection I am Dr Gen. Yours

James McHenry

Mortimer the bearer of this takes with him to your Excellency 7 Pheasants and 2 partridges being the number left by Mr. Campion. One of the pheasants died in this town while under his care. I have provided Mortimer with every necessary provision for them, and wish them safe to your Excellency.

ALS, DLC:GW.

1. Letter not found. McHenry wrote GW again on 19 Nov., with this explanation in the first paragraph: "I wrote you last night by Mortimer who sailed this morning with the birds, it being just a possible case that his packet may arrive before the post." The remainder of the letter is almost identical to this letter of 18 Nov. and is not printed here. The one addition of information is noted below. For the losing of McHenry's letter by Jaques Campion, see McHenry to GW, 13 Nov., n.2.

2. In his letter of 19 Nov. McHenry adds this about Campion: "He intends to teach the small-sword when he returns to this place should he meet with encouragement." In his missing letter of 16 Nov. to McHenry, GW evidently raised questions about Jaques Campion's social status, but in the end he decided "it best to err on the safe side, and therefore took him to my table" (GW to McHenry, 29 Nov.).

To James Madison

My Dr Sir,   Mount Vernon 18th Novr 1786.

Not having sent to the Post Office with my usual regularity, your favor of the 8th did not reach me in time for an earlier acknowledgment than of this date.

It gives me the most sensible pleasure to hear that the Acts of the present Session, are marked with wisdom, justice & liberality. They are the palladium of good policy, & the only paths that lead to national happiness. Would to God every State would let these be the leading features of their constituent characters: those threatening clouds which seem ready to burst on the Confederacy, would soon dispel. The unanimity with which the Bill was received, for appointing Commissioners agreeably to the recommendation of the Convention at Annapolis; and the uninterrupted progress it has met with since, are indications of a favourable issue. It is a measure of equal necessity & magnitude; & may be the spring of reanimation.

Altho' I have bid a public adieu to the public walks of life, & had resolved never more to tread that theatre; yet, if upon an occasion so interesting to the well-being of the Confederacy it should have been the wish of the Assembly that I should have been an associate in the business of revising the fœderal System; I should, from a sense of the obligation I am under for repeated proofs of confidence in me, more than from any opinion I should have entertained of my usefulness, have obeyed its call; but it is now out of my power to do this with any degree of consistency—the cause I will mention.

I presume you heard Sir, that I was first appointed & have since been rechosen President of the Society of the Cincinnati; & you may have understood also that the triennial Genl Meeting of this body is to be held in Philada the first monday in May next. Some particular reasons combining with the peculiar situation of my private concerns; the necessity of paying attention to them; a wish for retirement & relaxation from public cares, and rheumatic pains which I begin to feel very sensibly, induced me on the 31st ulto to address a circular letter to each State society informing them of my intention not to be at the next Meeting, & of my desire not to be rechosen President. The Vice

President is also informed of this, that the business of the Society may not be impeded by my absence. Under these circumstances it will readily be perceived that I could not appear at the same time & place on any other occasion, with out giving offence to a very respectable & deserving part of the Community—the late officers of the American Army.

I feel as you do for our acquaintance Colo. Lee; better never have delegated, than left him out; unless some glaring impropriety of conduct has been ascribed to him. I hear with pleasure that you are in the new choice. With sentiments of the highest esteem & affectn I am &c.

G: Washington

LB, DLC:GW.

From Thomas Peters

Sir   Baltim[or]e Novr 18th 1786

I have the pleasure of recieving your favour of the 21 of Oct.[1] you mention you are desireous of having procurd 50 bushls of Spring Barley. I have none by me at present, but if it can be procurd which I have no doubt of you may depend on its being sent you in time for sowing in the Spring. I should suppose 50 Bushls will be but a very small quantity if you have no Objection I will send you 100 Bushls and engage to take the produce of it. I believe that kind will answer this Climate, I procurd last Spring for Col. Lloyd Mr Bordley & some others some of the same but they have kept the whole produce, for sowing in the Spring.[2]

We should be willing to engage with you for 5000 Bushls Yearly at 5s. per Bushl this Currency if you find it will Answer your purpose, which I am confident it will from what I heard of the Fertility of your Land, I think they will turn out at least 35 bushls per Acre upon an average, which I think is more than any other Crop from the same Lands will produce; the Farmers here are troubled much in Cleaning the Barley for want of method. I will send you a small machine which will not Cost more than Ten shilling which will ⟨*illegible*⟩ & Clean in the hands of one man more than five could without such; should there be any Barley in your neighbourhood I shall be very glad to purchase it. Permit me to present my respectfull Compliments to Mrs Washington & ⟨subscribe⟩ myself with esteem & regard Your very humble Servant

Thos Peters

ALS, DLC:GW.

Thomas Peters came to Baltimore from Philadelphia at the end of the Revolution and built a brewery. He advertised on 3 Nov. 1786 in the *Maryland Journal and Baltimore Advertiser*: "GOOD BARLEY WANTED, For which a good Price will be given, at *Thomas Peters* and *Co*'s Brewery, On the lower End of Jones's Falls, Baltimore."

1. Letter not found.

2. John Beale Bordley and Edward Lloyd of Wye House, Talbot County, were among the leading planters of Maryland. For further correspondence with Peters about barley, see GW to Peters, 4 Dec. 1786, 20 Jan. 1787, 16 Sept. 1788, and Peters to GW, 3 Feb. 1787.

To Samuel Vaughan

My Dr Sir,   Mount Vernon 18th Novr 1786.

The obligations you are continually laying me under, are so great that I am quite overwhelmed & perfectly ashamed of myself for receiving them, notwithstanding your politeness leaves me without a choice. The picture of a battle in Germany, & the Jarrs came very safe. The first is fine: the latter is also fine and exceedingly handsome—they shall occupy the place you have named for them.[1]

May I hope Sir, that you have heard of the safe arrival of your Lady & family in England. Every occasion which informs me of your health and happiness, is pleasing to me; but none would equal that of testifying under my own roof the sentiments of perfect esteem & regard, with which I have the honor &c.

G: Washington

LB, DLC:GW.

1. Samuel Vaughan, who at this time was living in Philadelphia, sent the vases to be placed in the New Room on the marble mantelpiece that he had given GW in 1784. The picture was to be hung above it. The dark blue porcelain vases, made in Worcester and decorated with African animals and pastoral scenes, remain in place at Mount Vernon (Detweiler, *Washington's Chinaware*, 97–102).

To Lafayette

My Dr Marqs   Mount Vernon 19th Novr 1786.

On thursday last I received in very good order, from Baltimore, under the care of Monsr Compoint, the most valuable things you could have sent me, a Jack & two she Asses, all of which are very fine. The Pheasants & Partridges are coming round by water; for these also I pray you to accept my thanks. Words, my dear Marquis, will not do justice to my feelings, when I acknowledge the obligation I am under for the trouble & pains you have taken to procure, & forward these valuable Animals to me.

Monsr Compoint having brought no letter from you to me; having no instructions or orders to produce—and having lost with his pocket book a letter from your old aid Mr McHenry to me, which might have contained some information; I am left entirely in the dark with respect to the cost of the Asses in Malta, & the expences attending them since. I therefore pray you My Dr Marquis, to furnish me with an Accot of them as soon as possible, that I may delay no time in remitting you the amount.[1]

As this letter is only intended to give you the earliest advice of the safe arrival of Monr Compoint & his charges, I shall, as the Vessel by which it goes is now passing my door, add no more than those assurances, which you will ever believe me sincere in, of being with the most affectionate regard, yrs &c. &c.

G: Washington

LB, DLC:GW.

1. See James McHenry to GW, 5 Nov., and the other letters referred to in note 1 of that document. A draft of the lost letter of 13 Nov. is printed above.

To James Mercer

Dear Sir,   Mount Vernon Novr 19th 1786

I was informed by your Brother, Colo. Jno. Mercer, who with his family were here on their way to Annapolis; that by some discovery which had been lately made, it appears that Messrs Niell McCooll & Blair, had not a legal right to dispose of the moiety of the four mile run tract, which belonged to Colo.

George Mercer. This defect, I presume, can easily be remedied, as you are his Executor and heir at law. It is indifferent to me, to whom I pay the purchase money, if I am properly acquitted and assured of the title. I shall be obliged to you, therefore, to pass such a deed of confirmation for the moiety of the Land purchased from the above named persons, as to you shall seem proper. You drew the Deed from them to me, and have, I doubt not, the necessary documents for the one now asked. If not, I would furnish such papers as are in my possession. My wish is, to have all matters of this kind made clear, before I go hence, that no disputes may arise hereafter.[1] With very great esteem & regard I am—Dear Sir Yr most Obedt & Affee Ser⟨vt⟩

Go: Washington

ALS, owned (1977) by Mr. Nicholas H. Morley, Miami, Fla.; LB, DLC:GW.

1. For GW's acquisition of the Mercers' Four Mile Run tract in 1774, see GW to James Mercer, 12 Dec. 1774, n.3. There is this notation at the end of GW's account with the estate of John Mercer: "[The attorneys of George Mercer's creditors] proceeded to sell the sd George Mercer's moity of a Tract of Land in Fairfax County in Virginia near four mile Run which the sd Geo. Mercer held in common with his brother James Mercer and that George Washington did purchase from the Attornies aforesaid the Moity of Land aforesaid in the Conveyance of which the said James Mercer also joined with the sd attorneys, and the sd George Washington gave his Bond therefor, payable to sd attorneys on their assigns for £450 Va Cy but the sd George Mercer dying in London in 1784 without having returned to this Country, the sd James Mercer became heir and manager of the property of the sd George Mercer decd and he the sd James Mercer doubting the Validity of the power under which sd moity of Land near four mile Run, was sold, Conveyed by a Deed dated 22d of May 1787 to the sd George Washington the whole of sd tract of Land, including the moity of George Mercer & his own; the sd George Washington having also then purchased the moity of sd James Mercer and on the same day of May 1787 the sd James Mercer & John Francis Mercer did give unto the sd George Washington a Bond of indemnification to relieve the sd George Washington from the payment of the Bond of £450 given as aforesaid [to the attorneys of George Mercer's creditors] on condition of the sd Geo. Washington giving credit therefor to the Estate of Jno. Mercer decd which was accordingly done . . . " (Ledger B, 221). See also GW to James Mercer, 15 Mar. 1787.

James Mercer docketed this letter: "Washington Genl Novr 1786—abt Lands he purchased of McCoull & Blair attornies for Lindo & Cazenove—Memo. Lindo & Cazonove had no Title, but to avoid all disputes—and to do justice I sold the same Land to the General & for the same price & if Lindo & Cazenove recover the Money I am to repay the Genl. N.B. to enhance the value I discoun⟨t⟩ed the values. 729£ with the Genl out of Jno. Mercers Bond to him. Charge this to J. Fras Mercer."

To Edmund Randolph

Dr Sir,   Mount Vernon 19th Novr 1786

It gave me great pleasure to hear that the voice of the Country had been directed to you as chief magistrate of this Commonwealth, & that you had accepted the appointment.

Our affairs seem to be drawing to an awful crisis: it is necessary therefore that the abilities of every man should be drawn into action in a public line, to rescue them if possible from impending ruin. As no one seems more fully impressed with the necessity of adopting such measures than yourself, so none is better qualified to be entrusted with the reins of Government. I congratulate you on this occasion, and with sincere regard & respect am, Dr Sir, &c. &c.

G: Washington

LB, DLC:GW.

To David Stuart

Dear Sir,   Mount Vernon 19th Novr 1786.

I have been favoured with your letters of the 8th & 13th Instt; but not having sent to the Post Office with my usual regularity, I did not receive them so soon as I might have done from the date of the former.

I thank you for the interesting communications in both. It gives me sincere pleasure to find that the proceedings of the present Assembly are marked with wisdom, liberality & Justice. These are the surest walks to public, & private happiness. The display of which by so respectable a part of the Union, at so important a crisis, will, I hope, be influencial, and attended with happy consequences.

However delicate the revision of the federal system may appear, it is a work of indispensable necessity. The present constitution is inadequate. The superstructure totters to its foundations, and without helps, will bury us in its ruins. Although I never more intended to appear on a public theatre, and had in a public manner bid adieu to public life; yet, if the voice of my Country had called me to this important duty, I might, in obedience to the repeated instances of its affection & confidence, have dispensed with these objections, but another now exists which would render my acceptance of this appointment impracticable, with any degree of consistency—It is this. The triennial General Meeting of the Society of the Cincinnati is to be holden in Philadelphia the first Monday in May next. Many reasons combining—some of a public, some of a private nature, to render it unpleasing, & inconvenient for me to attend it; I did on the 31st Ulto address a circular letter to the State Societies, informing them of my intention not to be there, and desiring that I might no longer be rechosen President. The Vice Presidt (Gates) has also been informed thereof, that the business of the meeting might not be impeded on acct of my absence. Under these circumstances, I could not be in Philadelphia precisely at the same moment on another occasion, without giving offence to a worthy, & respectable part of the American community, the late Officers of the American Army.

I will do as you advise with respect to the Certificates, & trouble you with them again.[1] Colo. Mason, it is said, expresses an inclination to give his attendance but I question much his leavg Gunston this Wintr.

Pray what is become of that Superlative Villain, Posey? It has been reported here, that he is run off to Georgia. By a letter I have just received from Mr Hill, I find that the whole produce of my Estate below from the year 1774 together with the moneis which Hill received from others on my acct, has got into that abandoned wretches hands, not one shilling of which, I presume, will ever be got out of them.[2] All here join me in sincere good wishes for you—And I am Yr Affecte Hble Servt

Go: Washington

ALS, PHi: Dreer Collection; LB, DLC:GW.

1. See GW to Stuart, 5 Nov., n.2.

2. GW must be referring to James Hill's letter of 24 September. See also Stuart to GW, 19 December.

To Samuel Branden

Sir,   Mount Vernon 20th Novr 1786.

I have received by Captn Bartlet, your letter of the 27th of July.[1] The Ass arrived safe, & the other Articles agreably to the

Bill of lading. I am much obliged to you Sir, for your attention in executing my comm[issio]n, & the polite manner in which you offer me your future services. The Ass is undoubtedly one of the best kind that could be procured at Surinam; but I do not find it charged in your accot—If you will be so good as to let me know the price of it by the first opportunity, the money shall be remitted to you.[2] I am &c.

G: Washington

LB, DLC:GW.
    1. Letter not found.
    2. See John Fitzgerald to GW, 7 Feb. 1786, and note.

To William Drayton

Sir,   Mount Vernon 20th Novr 1786.
    I wish it was in my power to give you a more favourable acct of your Servant Jack than what follows.

After his absenting himself from you at Dumfries (as I believe my Nephew has already informed you) he came here, & remained quietly till the 12th; when being informed by some Gentlemen from Baltimore that a Packet from that place was on the point of Sailing for Charleston, I sent him under the care of a trusty Overseer to be shipped to you—requesting a friend of mine in the Town to engage a passage, & provide every thing necessary for him on ship board. When they arrived at Baltimore, unfortunately, the Vessel was hove down; it became necessary therefore to commit him to Goal for security, but before this could be effected (there being some demur on the part of the Goaler to receive him without the order of a Majestrate, which occasioned delay, & gave an opportunity to escape) he embraced a moment favourable thereto, to accomplish it. Diligent, but ineffectual search was instantly made, & it is supposed to arrive at Philadelphia, is his object.

The Gentleman to whose care I sent him, has promised every endeavor in his power to apprehend him, but it is not easy to do this where there are numbers that had rather facilitate the escape of slaves, than apprehend them when runaways. I hope your journey was not much incommoded by this untoward step of your Waiter.[1] With Sentiments of great esteem I am—Sir Yr Most Obedt Hble Serv⟨t⟩

Go: Washington

ALS, NjMoNP; LB, DLC:GW.

1. GW wrote James McHenry on 11 Nov. asking him to arrange the shipment of Drayton's servant back to South Carolina. See note 1 of that document.

From William Hansbrough

To his Excellency General Washington   Novm. the 20th 1786

I have to inform your Excellency that I ly under the unhapiness of being distresd at this time by Mr Mause for the rents that I am in debt to you for the non payment of the rents I owe for the teniment of land I now live on[1] If your Excellency will be kind enough to take a likely Negro Woman twenty eight years of agee it will much relieve me at this time I hope your Excellency will not destroy one tenant for the misconduct of others I have but the one Negroe Woman and if she is sold by public sale she will Not sell for the rents by reason of the scarcity of money therefore I hope your Excellency will have Compassion on me at this time or Else I am Entirely ruind Its please god to afflict my family with reumatism that I have no assistance but that Negroe Woman but I freely will give her up Mr Rector and my self have made up and pd fourty too pounds I have sold 22 bushels of small grain on the place I live on and if your Excellency thinks proper Ill give up the place as it is in good repair or I freely give up the Negroe therefore I hope your Excellency Will have Compassion as you see Cause my affects will be sold the 23d instant without some relief at your hands[2]—This from your destresd tenant

W. Hansbrough

ALS, DLC:GW.

1. For Hansbrough's tenancy on lot no. 3 of GW's Chattins Run land in Fauquier County and for Bataille Muse's dealings with him, see GW to Muse, 18 Sept. 1785, n.8, and Muse to GW, 28 Nov. 1785, n.6. Hansbrough enclosed this testimonial: "We the subscribers Doth herby Certifie that the bearer hereof William Hansbrough is an honest man and a Goode Neighbour as farr as his circumstances will allow and hath now livd in this Neighbourhood Now above Twelve Years Without the Least suspition of any gilt or Defrading any person

out of theire Rite And As he hath always behaved well we should be glad to have him continued[.] given under our hands this 19 day of Novmbr 1786." The names of Samuel Cocks, William Stephens, Benjamin Rust, Solomon Nickols, John Watts, James Strother, and Samuel Rust are affixed.

2. GW responded from Mount Vernon on 22 Nov.: "Sir, I have just received your letter of the 20th inst: & can only inform you that I have nothing to do with respect to the collection of my rents in your part of the Country. I have given it wholly to Mr Muse, to act as he shall think proper; but have directed him to distress no one without sufficient cause. He will be able to judge of the validity of your reasons for not paying the rent wch is due from you, & will act accordingly. I am, &c. G: Washington" (LB, DLC:GW).

To Richard Harrison

Sir,   Mount Vernon 20th Novr 1786.

I have received your Letter of the 10th of July together with the two Toledo Blades sent by Captn Sullivan.

I am much obliged to Mr Carmichael for this polite mark of attention to me; but hope I shall have no occasion to use them. I should have been happy Sir, to have received them from you in person; but as your business will not yet permit you to return to your native Country, I must postpone the pleasure of seeing you to a future day, tho' I hope not a very distant one. I am Sir &c.

                     G: Washington

LB, DLC:GW.

Letter not found: from John Francis Mercer, 20 Nov. 1786. On 24 Nov. GW wrote Mercer that "Your servant" has "this moment put your letter of the 20th inst. into my hands."

Letter not found: from Jabez Bowen, 23 Nov. 1786. On 9 Jan. 1787 GW wrote Bowen: "I have received your letter of the 23d of Novr."

From Benjamin Tupper

Sir   Mingo Bottom—Ohio county Novr 23rd 1786

I did myself the honor at the close of the Season last year to give your Excellency a hint, with respect to our ill success we have been in some measure more fortunate the last season and

have completed four ranges of Townships[1]—four more are begun, some of which were not far proceded on, by reason of certain information reciev'd, of the hostile disposition of the Indians in particular with respect to the Surveyors—but by a kind
hand of providence thier schemes have been frustrated & no
special accident has happend'd to either of the Surveyors—we
are now on our return to visit our Wives and Sweat-hearts. I
still entertain my former enthusiastic notions with respect to this
Country, & firmly beleive that the beneficent, divine being, hath
reserved this country as an Asylum for the neglected & perse-
cuted soldiers of the late American Army, in particular those of
the eastern states—I am returning home with as full a determination, to encourage a speedy settlement here, as though nothing had between us & the Indians—I hope I may not be instrumental of leading my friends to special danger or destruction.

As I have but a few minutes to write, I beg leave to refer your
Excellency to the bearer, William McMahen Esquire a Member
of the Assembly of your state for the County of Ohio, who is
thoroughly acquainted with the affairs of this country and has
been exceedingly serviceable to the surveyors.[2]

Colonels Sproat & Sherman present thier most respectful
compliments to your Excellency.[3] My son Anselm who was my
Adjutant, wishes to present his most profound respects. I wish
to be remberd to Mrs Washington in such terms as will express
the greatest respect—Colonel Humphries & all my acquaintance in that part, I remember with singular pleasure—I have
the honor to be Your Excellency's Most Obedient Most Humble servant

                                                    Benjn Tupper

ALS, DLC:GW.

1. See Tupper to GW, 26 Oct. 1785.

2. William McMahan represented Ohio in the Virginia house of delegates
from 1786 through 1791, except in 1790; GW does not record in his diary a
visit from McMahan.

3. Ebenezer Sproat (Sprout; 1752–1805), who served in the Massachusetts
regiments during the Revolution and was brevetted colonel in 1783, was the
surveyor for Rhode Island of the seven ranges in the Northwest Territory. See
Tupper to GW, 26 Oct. 1785, n.1. Sproat is fully identified in the note of his
letter to GW of 9 July 1789. Isaac Sherman was the surveyor from Connecticut.

To John Francis Mercer

Sir,   Mount Vernon 24th Novr 1786.

Your servant having this moment put your letter of the 20th inst. into my hands, & appearing to be in great haste; I shall not detain him, especially as it is neither my wish nor intention to enter on the justification of my last to you.[1]

The evidence, on which the charge of unfairness &ca was grounded, you have enclosed in Colo. Symm's own hand writing—(the amount of the other bonds in his possession appeared to me to be very trifleing)—The propriety, or impropriety of this charge, after this transcript & information is given, you are to judge; & whether Combs's bond is not among those assigned to Mr Colston. Hickmans, a considerable debt, must also have been under this predicament—or Colston's application to me for a Deed was very improper.

I would fain hope that there is not a greater impropriety in my receiving interest on a bonded debt, which lay years without having any part of the principal on interest paid, than is to be found in others; especially when the very fund you assured me should be applied to the payment thereof, you are recovering with interest. But I will have done with this subject, & never more shall give you the trouble of hearing further observations of mine thereon. What rough expression of mine to you at Richmond has been industriously reported, is for me yet to learn. Your letter conveys the first most distant hint I have ever heard of the matter; I certainly ought therefore to stand acquitted of having any agency in the circulation of it, if I was so ungenteel as to have offered any.

I profess an entire ignorance of the real difference between military Certificates & specie; for never having had inclination or intention to deal in them, & rarely going from home, I have not been in the way of obtaining information on this subject. Nevertheless, I will take two thousand pounds of *Virginia military Certificates* at the price you offer, viz: four for one, so as to discharge five hundred pounds of my claim; & I will take 400 or more barrels of Indian Corn, provided a price is now *fixed* that I can obtain it at—& for your information I add that any quantity, I am told, may be had at 10/ Maryland Cury per barrel—Colo. Hooe thinks less.

If this price accords with your ideas, in order to ascertain the point decidedly, I will give it; but assure you at the same time that your disposing of it to any other & paying the amot in money to me, would be quite as agreeable to me. Your accommodation was all I had in view—my own Crop is, I presume, adequate to my consumption. With respect to the negroes, I conclude it is not in my power to answer your wishes—because it is as much against my own inclination as it can be against your's, to hurt the feelings of those unhappy people by a separation of man and wife, or of families; because no others than such as I enumerated in my last will answer my purposes, & because the price exceeds what I *supposed* Negroes would sell for in ready money; for, in this as with Certificates, having had no intention to buy, I have made no enquiry into the price they sold at; but conceived that for ready money the best labouring negroes (which are the kind I wanted) might have been had for £60—£70—or at most £75. Upon the whole then, for the balance, I must take payment in the manner formerly mentioned by you at this place—unless you should think that young Bob (who has only a father without a wife) Tom the baker, Nessey & David, & James & Valentine (if of sufficient size to go to trades) could be separated without much uneasiness, & the prices of them, if not really the ready money prices, cou'd be abated.[2]

Your reply to this letter soon would be satisfactory, for I have just hired a compleat Ditcher with a view of putting several hands under him, and wish to know my prospects for it.[3] I am Sir &c.

G: Washington

P.S. I rece'd, enclosed in your letter, 2 half Joes, & 7 guineas—in part payment, I presume, of the 15 guineas lent you.[4] G. W——n

LB, DLC:GW.

1. Letter not found. GW's letter to Mercer is dated 6 November.

2. For these negotiations to settle the Mercer estate debt, see GW to Mercer, 9 Sept., 6 Nov., and notes.

3. GW's articles of agreement with James Lawson, "Ditcher," dated 18 Nov., is in DLC:GW and CD-ROM:GW.

4. GW notes in his ledger on 16 Oct. "cash lent Colo. Jno. Mercer 15 Guineas, to be retd in 10 days" (Ledger B, 221). "Colo. Jno. Mercer, his Lady & child . . . and their nurse" spent the night of 15 Oct. at Mount Vernon and on

16 Oct. "crossed the River after breakfast on their way to Annapolis" (*Diaries*, 5:52).

From Edmund Randolph

Dear sir   Richmond Novr 24. 1786

I am sensibly affected by your friendly congratulations. You will readily, I hope, believe, that I class them among the auspicious events of my life.[1]

But in truth more difficulties are in prospect, than prudence ought to have prompted me to encounter. The nerves of government seem unstrung, both in energy and money, and the fashion of the day is to calumniate the best services, if unsuccessful. What then am *I* to expect? Not much of approbation, I fear; I must be content to ward off censure. However I shall expose myself to these risques without shrinking, and make the motives atone for the miscarriages in the execution.

I am also to thank you for the travels of general Chastellux. Except in his observations on the natural bridge, he perhaps has lost by this composition the rank, which he deservedly acquired by his essay on public felicity. I will return them by Dr Stewart.

Upon leaving Mount Vernon, we were alarmed at the intelligence from almost every watercourse. Our real wish was to go back; but the terror of meeting the general court unprepared put every other consideration to flight.[2]

The part, which I purposed to take in your affair with the Hites, would have been perfectly consistent with my duty to them. But my new arrangement has rendered it unnecessary to enter now into the detail, as my lips are closed as to a profession, which from the earliest moment of my life I abominated, and from which I was determined to escape, as soon as I was possessed of a competence.[3]

On friday, the 1st of decr, I shall become a member of the executive. During my existence as such, I shall trouble you with many communications. I am Dear sir with the most sincere affection your Obliged humble serv:

Edm: Randolph

ALS, DLC:GW.

1. GW congratulated Randolph on 19 Nov. upon his being elected governor of Virginia.

2. Randolph left Mount Vernon on the morning of 18 Sept. after a heavy rainfall the night before (GW to Randolph, c.12 Oct.).

3. For GW's problems with the Hites, see Thornton Washington to GW, 6 June 1786, n.2.

To David Stuart

Dear Sir;   Mount Vernon 24 Nov. 1786

Enclosed I return the certificates with the Clerks signature of their having passed the Court of Fairfax. What is further necessary I shall rely upon you to have done.[1]

Mrs Washington owes Mrs Randolph (the Governors Lady) a bill of 10/ for books bought & sent to the Children of this family, which she requests the favor of you to pay for; and to procure & send to her an Almanack and half a pound of Nutmegs[;] of the latter Alexandria furnishes none, or next to it, at an enormous price.

What price is corn like to bear below? I hope I am under no necessity to buy; but Col. Mercer wanting me to take this article in part payment of a debt he is owing me, I want to be informed of the present, and what will probably be the future price of this, sometime hence (say the spring) seeing Gentlemen from all parts you will be able to get the best information on this head[2]— Inform me also, if you please What price Wheat & Flour now bears or is like to bear? A Waggon of yours delivered a load of Wheat at my Mill the other day, unaccompanyed by any message; my Miller has asked what was to be done with it, and I really could not tell him—I have recollection of your having spoke to me about Wheat, but whether it was to sell it to me, or to grind it for your use I cannot charge my memory—either will be agreeable to me, as you shall chuse. I wish to be informed soon—and if the former the quantity and price of it.

We have nothing new in these parts but a change of weather; being locked up in snow. All join in best wishes and I am—Dear Sir Yr affecte & obedt Hble ⟨Servt⟩

                            Go: Washington

P.S. Since writing the above, I am told that the load of Wheat mentioned in this letter, was only 17½ Bushels & intended for your familys use & that it was most miserably cleaned.

ALS (typescript), LNHT.
1. See GW to Stuart, 5 Nov., n.2.
2. See GW to John Francis Mercer, 6 November.

Letter not found: from Edward Newenham, 25 Nov. 1786. On 20 April 1787 GW wrote Newenham that he had "been honoured with your favours of the 13th and 25th of November last."

From Battaile Muse

Honourable Sir,   Berkeley C[oun]ty Novr 26th 1786

The Flour in your mill I wish To be sold if you are In want of money at what Ever price it will Fetch—I Paid Doctr Selden for the 50 bushels of wheat 5/6 ℔ bushel amounting To £13.15.0 in Augt Last in order To Close Our accts at that Time—as Colo. Gilpin gave that price For the remainder of the Crop I allow'd it To the Doctr I had reather be Considerable Looser than you should not be paid the Sum of £13.15.0 as I owe it and It stands Charged in your acct[.] when you Sell Flour From your mill I wish it To be Sold at any rate.[1]

I heard From the Sheriff of Fauquier County Yesterday—the Execution in His hands against Rector the Money Cannot be made yet—For want of buyers at His Sales—I shall go down my Self the week after Next To See into all your affairs in that County and If that Execution Can be Settled I will Contrive the money To you Immediately after it Falls into my hands about £90.[2] This is the only Prospect I have For money untill next spring—one Charles Rector that Took the place Let to Enock Ashby run away while I was below £83.2.0 in Debt—He has moved To Frederick County. John Thompson that Left His place Last Spring owes £40 & odd pounds. He lives in Fauquier Cty at this time—but Proposes To Leave the County. these People were Too Poor to Bear distress For such sums—as no one would buy their Little & Security they Could not give To Replevey their goods. those People Aught To be Corrected, To be made Examples off—If you approve I will bring Suits against them and on their Confessing Judgemts For Cost & one For the Sum 20£ & the other For £10 its Likely they may be able To Pay those Sums—I wish them To be made Pay Some thing, as they have behaved Very Ill[3]—Colo. Kennaday will not Pay—am I To Sue Him or return your acct[4] Please write To me your desire on acct of those three Persons. You have good Proof For your Claims as they all have Frequently assumed the Payments To me—as To Colo. Kennaday Debt—I am not anxious About; but the other Two, I wish To be Punnished a Little For their Wickedness, and deter other Tenants From behaving with Such Ingratitude—their is now three Widows on your Tract of Land—Ashbys bend—Lemart Deermant & Keys; these three Widows will be and Incumbrance on your Interest—I shall act Humainly with them and will Spurr them on To Industry and waite For your Particular directions respecting them. unless I am of opinion they do not act Providently in the Interim.[5]

If I Continue to have my heath I Expect To have your accts in my hands Properly Known by Next May. I am Sir your Very Humble Servant—

Battaile Muse

ALS, DLC:GW.

1. See GW to Muse, 6 May, n.1.

2. For Muse's dealings with Jacob Rector, GW's tenant on lot 3 of his Chattins Run tract, see Muse to GW, 28 Nov. 1785, n.6. See also William Hansbrough to GW, 20 Nov. 1786.

3. John Thompson and Charles Rector had been tenants on lots 1 and 2 of GW's Chattins Run tract. See notes 4 and 5, Muse to GW, 28 Nov. 1785.

4. See GW to Muse, 8 Mar. 1786, n.3.

5. For the land parcels on which the widows of Lewis Lemart (Ann), James Dermont, and David Keyes (Margaret) lived, see Lists of Tenants, 18 Sept. 1785, nn.19, 24, and 15.

To Richard Butler

Dr Sir,   Mount Vernon 27th Novr 1786.

I have been requested by the Marqs de la Fayette, in behalf of the Empress of Russia, to obtain a vocabulary of the languages of the Ohio Indians.

Previous to my hearing of your appointment as superintendant of Indian Affairs in that District, I had transmitted to Captn Hutchins a copy of the Marquis's letter, containing the above request; conceiving that it would be much in his power, from the opportunities which would present themselves whilst

he was surveying the western Lands, to do this; & praying him
to lend his aid to effect the work for this respectable character.

Since I have heard of your appointment to the above trust, &
know to what intercourse with the Indians it must lead, I have
resolved to ask the favor of your assistance also. If Capt. Hutchins is on the Ohio, he will shew you the paper which was transmitted to me by the Marquis, and which I forwarded to him. If
he is not, it may be sufficient to inform you that it was no more
than to insert English words & the names of things in one column—& the Indian therefor in others on the same line, under
the different heads of Delaware, Shawanees, Wiendots, &c. &c.[1]

Your appointment gave me pleasure, as every thing will do
wch contributes to your satisfaction and emolument, because I
have a sincere regard for you. In your leisure hours, whilst you
remain on the Ohio in discharge of the trust reposed in you, I
should be glad to know the real temper & designs of the Western
Indians, & the situation of affairs in that Country together with
the politics of the people. And as I am anxious to learn with
as much precision as your indubitable information goes to, the
nature of the navigation of Bever Creek; the distance, & what
kind of portage there is between it & Cuyahoga, or any other
nearer navigable water of Lake Erie, and the nature of the navigation of the latter: and also the navigation of the Muskingum—
the distance & sort of portage across to the navigable waters of
Cuyahoga or Sandusky, & the kind of navigation therein—you
would do me an acceptable favor to hand them to me, with the
computed distances from the river Ohio by each of these routs,
to the lake itself.[2]

If you should not write to me by the return of the Bearer, I
would beg leave to add that there is no way so certain of conveying letters to me, as to enclose them to your correspondent
in Philadelphia, 'till a more direct Post is established with this
part of the Country, accompanied by a request to him to put
them in the Post office. Private conveyances, (unless by a person
coming immediately to my house) I have always found the most
tedious & most uncertain: from Philada letters will reach me,
frost permitting, in three or four days.

If you are at Pittsburgh, this letter will be presented to you by
Mr Lear, a deserving young gentleman who lives with me, &
whom I beg leave to recommend to your civilities. He is sent by

me to see the situation of my property on Miller's run (lately recover'd) & to adopt some measures for the preservation & security of it.[3] With sincere esteem & regard, I am Dr Sir &c.

G: Washington

LB, DLC:GW.

Richard Butler (b. 1743), an Irishman, was second-in-command of Arthur St. Clair's disastrous expedition of 1791 and was killed in the surprise attack of the Western Indians on 4 Nov. of that year. On 14 Aug. 1786 he was made Indian Superintendent of the Northern District.

1. See GW to Thomas Hutchins, 20 Aug., and Hutchins to GW, 8 Nov. 1786. See also Lafayette to GW, 10 Feb. 1786. Butler sent GW the Indian vocabulary on 30 Nov. 1787.

2. See Butler to GW, 30 Nov. 1787.

3. For Tobias Lear's mission, see GW to Lear, 30 November.

To Robert Townsend Hooe

Dr Sir,   Mount Vernon 27th Novr 1786.

The plank I want is to floor a room 24 by 32 feet. It must be 24 feet long & 1½ inches thick—all of a colour, and entirely free from Knots & sap. More than the nett quantity is requisite, for allowances. If it were seasoned, so much the better; but this is hardly to be expected in plank of this particular kind.[1]

If Mr Swift can supply me, it will be better than to send to the Eastern shore; if he can not, I then beg the favor of you to engage Messrs Peterson & Taylor (I think the names are) to furnish me agreeably to the above Memo[randu]m—as soon as possible[2]—With much esteem, I am &ca

G: Washington

LB, DLC:GW.

1. This was for the flooring of the New Room at Mount Vernon. See GW to George Digges, 28 December.

2. Jonathan Swift (d. 1824) was a merchant in Alexandria, who in September 1785 married Ann Roberdeau. GW in 1788 bought lumber from the firm of Peterson & Taylor in Alexandria. The enclosed memorandum has not been found.

To George McCarmick

Sir,   Mount Vernon 27th Novr 1786.
I have received your letter of the 31st of October, & thank you for the information contained therein. Since which I have obtained a full account of the decisions in my favor against the settlers of my Land on Miller's run, from Mr Smith.[1]

Altho' those people have little right to look to me for favor or indulgences, & were told, if they run me to the expence of a Law suit, that they were not to expect any; yet as they are now in my power, it is not my wish or intention to distress them more than the recovery of my property obliges me. They may therefore continue on their respective places either as Tenants at an equitable rent which shall be deemed reasonable between man & man, or as pur-chasers, if the terms can be agreed on between us; but they, nor no others will ever get it for 20/ ℔ acre: this is five shillings less ℔ acre, than these people would have given whilst the matter was in dispute, could we have agreed on the security & times of payment. It will be a matter of indifference to me whether I sell the Land altogether, or in parcels of 2, 3, 4 or 500 acres, provided in the latter cases the price is proportioned to the quality of the Land & the improvements thereon; & provided also that it is laid off in regular form & in such a manner as not to injure the rest. Nor should I be very sollicitous about the payments, if the principal is well secured & the interest regularly paid at my house without giving me any trouble in the collection of it. For if this should be the case, I would immediately put the Bond or Bonds in suit. A part of the purchase money I should require down, or at a short period—perhaps one fourth. On these terms also I would dispose of my land in Fayette county, near Yohoghaney.

If I had known that you had removed from your former place of abode near my Land, to Cat-fish, I should not have taken the liberty of referring those who might wish to become purchasers of it, to you to shew them the land, as it was too inconvenient for you to do it; but would have requested this favor of Colo. Cannon, who lives more convenient. The same cause prevents my requesting you to have an eye to it now. It could only suit a person who lives near, & can know almost every day, what is doing on the places, to take charge of them if the present occupants are determined to remove. But if your Jersey friends or others should want to become pur-chasers, you might oblige them & me too by letting them know that my lands are for sale.[2]

If it was really necessary to have the out lines of the Tract run, in order to ascertain the boundaries of it, I am very willing to pay the expence; but the course by which this was done ought to have been taken from the Patent as the final act.

I am much obliged to you for the information respecting the expeditions of Genl Clarke &c., & for the account from Detroit.[3] I wish, most sincerely, that the first may answer the purpose of giving peace to the Western Settlements.

Mr Lear, a young Gentleman who lives with me, & who is the bearer of this letter, will probably deliver it.[4] If he should stand in need of your advice or assistance, I pray you to give it to him. I am Sir &c.

G: Washington

LB, DLC:GW.

1. McCarmick wrote two letters to GW in October, one dated 31 Oct. and the other without the day of the month (dated c.30 Oct., above); he is referring here to the latter. Thomas Smith wrote on 7 Nov. about the verdicts in the Millers Run ejectment suits.

2. See GW to John Cannon, 28 November.

3. See McCarmick to GW, 31 October.

4. See GW to Lear, 30 November.

To Philip Marsteller

Sir,   Mo[un]t Vernon 27th Novr 1786.

I send my Barge for the German family with which I agreed on Saturday last, & for their necessaraies if they have any to bring. As I have no body about me who can converse with them in their own language, I pray you to inform them that it will be necessary they should exert themselves to learn English; that their residences in the room into which they will be first introduced may be temporary, as they probably will be removed from it as soon as I can conveniently provide another place (on *this Estate*) for them to live in; that they will have provisions given to them to dress in the manner they like best; that they may obtain vegetables, out of my Garden by applying to the Gardener, to eat with their meat—and lastly, that I wish to impress upon them in strong terms the propriety of diligent attention to their duty, as I shall expect this of them, & shall myself be hurt if their idle conduct obliges me to remind them of a breach of their contract.[1]

As there is no hurry in the case, I will take a more leisure moment to write to you on the matter hinted to you already.[2] I am Sir, &c.

G: Washington

P.S. Pray ask, & let me know if the man understands thatching houses with straw.

LB, DLC:GW.

1. Philip Marsteller, a merchant in Alexandria, obtained for GW a German family named Overdonck; they were brought to Mount Vernon on this date as indentured servants. See Marsteller to GW, this date.

2. GW wrote to Marsteller on 15 Dec. about the possibility of Marsteller's acting as his commission agent in Alexandria to purchase for him goods and material at reduced prices.

From Philip Marsteller

Sr   Alexa[ndria] Novr 27th 1786

I recd your favor of this date and agreeable to Request have fully explain'd to them the Contents thereof, and hartily wish their behavior may merit your Attention.

I enclose the Indentures Signed on the part of the Servants, your part Sr after being Signed will belong to them. Col. Hooe informs me that the Laws of the State do not require the like Transactions to be done before a Majestrate therefore have not applied to any.[1] The Man does not understand Thatching, that being a Trade in the old Country—but the Woman Says she understands making Cheese according to the Custom of her Country, which comes very near to the mode of making English Cheese, by what I could learn from her[2]—Your further Commands shall always be attended to Sir By Your Very Humle Servt

P. Marsteller

ALS, DLC:GW.

1. The Virginia law relating to foreign indentured servants specified that their "contract of service shall be assignable by the master to any person to whom the servant shall, in the presence of a justice of the peace, freely consent that it shall be assigned" (12 Hening 190–91).

2. On his first day at Mount Vernon, 28 Nov., Daniel Overdonck was set to work "ditching" (*Diaries*, 5:73). Overdonck remained with GW at least until July 1788.

To Presley Neville

Dr Sir,　　　　　　　　　　Mount Vernon 27th Novr 1786.

Accept my thanks for the information given me in your letter of the 25th ulto from the Court House of Washington, respecting the decision of one of my Ejectments. I have, since, been informed by Mr Smith, of the favorable issue of the whole, and of the necessity there is of my paying immediate attention to the Tenements to prevent the waste & damage which otherwise will follow.[1]

Consequent of this advice I send Mr Lear, a young gentleman who lives with me, into that Country to take such measures for the preservation of my property as the exigency of the case, when investigated, may require. As it is more than probable he will see you, your friendly information of matters respecting this business, & advice to him would highly oblige me; as also your civilities to him.

Altho' the present occupants have little right to look to me for indulgences, & were told not to expect them; yet, as they are now in my power, it is neither my wish nor intention to distress them further than the recovery of my property from their usurpation, must unavoidably involve them in. They may therefore become Tenants upon terms equitable between man & man, or purchasers—it being my intention to dispose of the Land, from a conviction that property at the distance that is from the proprietor of it, never can be converted to uses so beneficial as the money arising from the sales; because those in whose fidelity & care we can depend, are too independent, & generally have too much business of their own to attend to smaller matters; & others who are less qualified, & more ready to accept trusts of this sort, are too apt to abuse them: this I have found to my cost.

As Pittsburgh is a point to which emigrants from the northern & Eastern States, & foreigners almost universally, direct their first steps, you would do me a favor to let those who may enquire for cultivated places in your presence, know that that tract, as well as the other (commonly called Washington's bottom) in Fayette county, are for sale. I would sell them altogether, or in parcels; but not, by the latter mode, in such a manner as to injure the sale of the rest. I would also give credit for the whole or greatest part of the purchase money, provided the principal is well secured, & the interest arising therefrom regularly paid at my own house without trouble or delay. You would oblige me too, my good Sir, by giving me your candid opinion of the value, or in other words, what these Lands ought to sell for upon the terms here mentioned.

If your Father is in that country now, I beg to be remembered to him & to Mrs Nevill.[2] With esteem and regard, I am Dear Sir &c.

G: Washington

LB, DLC:GW.

1. Neville's letter has not been found; Thomas Smith's letter is dated 7 November.

2. John Neville (1731–1803) lived at Bower Hill across Chartiers Creek from his son's place.

To John Cannon

Sir,   Mount Vernon 28th Novr 1786.

I have just been advised by Mr Smith, my Counsel, of the favorable issue of the Ejectments I was compelled to bring for the recovery of my land in your neighbourhood; and of the necessity there is for me to appoint an agent to take care of my interest therein.

As I am not acquainted with any one, who lives near the land, in whom I could place such entire confidence as yourself, permit me to ask if you could make it convenient to take charge of this Tract, so far as to see that each tenement, for the preservation of it, has some person living thereon, upon the best terms you can get them. And that you may not conceive, Sir, that I mean to give you trouble without compensation, I beg leave to inform you, that whatever you may think adequate to the former, I will readily allow.

Altho' the present occupants of it have little reason to expect favor or indulgences at my hands, yet as they are now in my power, I do not wish to distress them further than the repossession of my Land, & common justice to myself naturally tends to. I am willing therefore that they should remain on their respective places at such a rent as shall appear reasonable & just between man & man; & this I am perfectly willing you should fix, without considering, or in any degree attending to the loss I have sustained by being kept out of my property for more than twelve years. If you should incline to undertake this trust in my behalf, I shall be well satisfied with these or any other Tenants, for the ensuing year; a longer term, I do not at present incline to let the Tenements for, as it is my intention to sell the land if I can obtain what I conceive it is worth, & would not encumber it with Leases.

From the present scarcity of money I know it would sell low for ready cash, or on short credit; but permit me to ask your candid opinion of its real worth—& what you think it would sell for if credit was given for three fourths of the purchase money, three, four, or five years, with interest to be regularly & punctually paid at my own house during that term; & whether you conceive it would be most advantageous for me to sell it by the tract, or in parcels of one, two, three, four, or five hundred acres, as may be most convenient to the purchasers?[1]

Mr Lear who lives with me, and who I expect will deliver this letter to you, will, if it is necessary, explain any matter that I may be deficient in.[2]

I beg leave to recommend him to your civilities, & friendly advice what steps he had best take in this business, if you should be disinclined to engage in it yourself. With esteem, I am Sir, Your mo: Obt Servt

G: Washington

LB, DLC:GW.

John Cannon (d. 1799), who was a justice of the peace in Washington County, Pa., owned about eight hundred acres on Chartiers Creek into which Millers Run flowed.

1. Cannon was to replace George McCarmick as GW's agent to deal with his Millers Run property. See McCarmick to GW, c.30 Oct., and GW to McCarmick, 27 November.

2. See GW to Tobias Lear, 30 November.

To Thomas Freeman

Sir,   Mo[un]t Vernon 28th Novr 1786.

Mr Smith having advised me of the decisions in my favor at the Nisi prius Court held for the county of Washington; & of the necessity there is for my sending, or appointing some person on the spot to attend to my interest in the recovered lands; I have, as you appeared fixed on a removal to Kentuckey in the Spring, & with difficulty could be induced to continue the management of my business in your neighbourhood 'till now, sent Mr Lear, who lives with me, to examine into the situation of the Tenements—views of the present occupants, & on the spot to make such arrangements in my behalf, as the exigency of the case may require.[1] He will call upon you in his way out, or in; & by him I should be glad to know what has been done with my Negroes: if sold—to whom, on what credit & for what sum. I wish also to know whether you have received any more of my money; & in that case, how it has been applied: if any is coming to me Mr Lear will afford a safe conveyance for it. I want also to know, in what situation, under whose occupation, & what the expectations are from my land near you—especially the place lately occupied by Simpson; and in what condition the Mill is.[2] I would not wish to have any of the places not already under Leases, engaged for more than one year, because, as I am determined to sell the land if I can obtain a price adequate to what I conceive to be the worth of it, it might be considered as an incumbrance. To keep the buildings & fences in good repair may be essential, even if I gain nothing by the rents.

Considering the present scarcity of money, I am sensible it would not answer to sell for ready Cash; but what do you suppose the track near you would fetch if three, four, or five years credit (paying interest) should be given for three fourths of the purchase money? And what difference do you think there would be in the amount of the sales, between selling the tract entire, or by the Lotts as now laid off—or in three, four, or five hundred-acre parcels? If any person should apply to you for information respecting this Land & the terms, I would accommodate them in this manner; & with respect to price, I want no more pr acre than such kind of land, with such credit sells at in the same part of the country. I am &c.

Go: Washington

LB, DLC:GW.

1. GW made Thomas Freeman his land agent in Pennsylvania in September 1784, but he had asked George McCarmick and, more recently, John Cannon to act for him with regard to the Millers Run tract in Washington County (GW to Freeman, 23 Sept. 1784; GW to McCarmick, 27 Nov. 1786; GW to Tobias Lear, 30 Nov. 1786).

2. For Freeman's report on the Washington's Bottom tract in Fayette County and on the sale of the slaves there, see Freeman to GW, 18 Dec. 1786, and note 1 of that document. See also GW to Tobias Lear, 30 Nov. 1786.

To John Stephenson

Dr Sir, Mo[un]t Vernon 28th Novr 1786.

This Letter will be handed to you by Mr Lear a young gentleman who lives with me, & who will pass a receipt in discharge of any money you may pay him on my Account. I hope it will be convenient for you to discharge the whole, for it should be remembered that I have lain a long time out of what you are owing me, & that I can no more do without than another. My expenses are high, and my calls great, or I should not have reminded you so often of what I had hoped you would have paid with out any intimation of my wants.[1] With best wishes for you & yours, I am &c.

G: Washington

LB, DLC:GW.

1. GW wrote in his diary for 8 May 1786 that he gave Benjamin Wooley "the Statement of my Acct. with Colo. John, and the deceased Hugh Stephenson, which, in behalf of the latter, he promised to pay, and to obtain the other moiety from the first" (*Diaries*, 4:326). GW wrote Thomas Smith on 23 Sept. 1789 that the Stephenson account showed the Stephenson brothers owed him £70.10 in Virginia currency.

To James McHenry

Dear Sir, Mount Vernon 29th Novr 1786

Your letters of the 18th by the Packet, & 19th by the Post, are both at hand—The Birds were landed yesterday. A Patridge died on the passage.

If Monsr Campion's information is to be depended on, he had no letter from the Marquis de la Fayette or any other character in France, for me; nothing confidential therefore could have been disclosed by the loss of his pocket book, unless it was deposited in your letter. His acct is, that he was ordered to repair to L'Orient with the Asses & Birds, from whence *he* & *they* were to be shipped by the Messrs Barauds. That the Marquis told him, letters should follow, and he supposes they will arrive in the French Packet.[1]

By Monsr Campion I send the guinea you paid for his board; if there are any charges yet behind, I wish to be informed of them that they may be immediately paid. My sincere thanks are due to you, my dear Sir, for your kind attention to this business. Having received no intimation at, or previous to the arrival of Monsr Campion respecting the light in which he ought to be viewed, I thought it best to err on the safe side, and therefore took him to my table, where he has conducted himself with modesty & propriety.

Under full conviction that the Asses were never intended as a present, and that the Chinese Pheasants (instead of costing 16 Gu[inea]s a pair as the Baltimore paragraphist has anounced to the public) came from the Kings Aviary as a present to the Marquis for me (for so says Monsr Campion) I am concerned that such information should have been exhibited in a public gazette as appeared in the B. Pap. for it may be viewed as a contrivance to bespeak, what I should industriously have endeavoured to avoid, had I supposed it was so meant;—a present.[2] Was this publication confined to Maryland, or even the United States there would not be so much in it; but as these paragraphs for want of other matter to fill a Paper, are handed from one to another, and ultimately get into the British & French Gazettes; the Marquis will entertain a queer idea of it, if nothing more is meant than what was promised, & expected— that is—to be the instrument through the medium of Adml de Suffran (Govr of the Island of Malta, or head of the Order) of procuring & forwarding them from that place to me. That he should have paid all the expences which attended the getting, and shipping them is beyond a doubt—It could not well be otherwise, as their procuration was a doubtful essay. As I have not however received a single line respecting these animals, I do not undertake to contradict the report, but think the evidence of it—the cost—&ca appears to have been too slight to hand it in such a dress to the public.[3] With sincere esteem & regard I am—Dear Sir Yr most Obedt & affecte Servant

Go: Washington

ALS, MWeHM; LB, DLC:GW.

1. See McHenry to GW, 13 Nov., n.2.

2. This paragraph appeared in the *Maryland Journal, and Baltimore Advertiser* on 10 Nov.: "We are informed that the Jack-Ass, and two she Asses, with the foreign Pheasants and Partridges, which arrived in the Iris, on the 7th Inst. from L'Orient, is a Present from the Honourable the Marquis de la Fayette to His Excellency General Washington. The Asses are from two to three Years old, and cost at Malta Three Hundred Guineas.—The Silver and Golden Pheasants of China are beautiful Birds, and cost Sixteen Guineas each. But this is not all; every Expence attending their Transportation has been paid, and a careful Person employed, at a handsome Salary, to present them to the General."

3. GW received Lafayette's letter of 26 Oct. telling him of his gift of the birds and animals. See also McHenry to GW, 5 Nov., n.1.

To Tobias Lear

Mount Vernon Novr 30th 1786
Instructions for Mr Lear

You will proceed to Pittsburgh by the following rout—Leesburgh, Keys' Ferry, Bath, Old Town and Fort Cumberland. From the latter pursue the new road by the Turkey foot to Colo. John Stephenson (commonly called Stinson) wch is on the road to Pittsburgh.

When you are at Bath enquire the way to a piece of Land I have on the river about 14 Miles above the town on the way to Old Town and see if it is in the occupation of any one, and on what terms it is held. A Colo. Bruin in Bath, or a Mr McCraken near the Land will I expect be able to give you information on this head.[1]

When you arrive at Colo. Stephenson's you will deliver the letter which is addressed to him & receive what money he may be in circumstances or inclination to pay you on my acct.[2]

At Pittsburgh I expect you will find General Butler to whom you have a letter and from whom it is probable you may receive an answer. If he is not there leave the letter for him in the care of his brother (who lives at that place) or some other.[3]

Colo. Nevill lives at a place called Shirtees six miles below

Pittsburgh and I believe not much out of the road to my Land on Millers run (lately recovered) or to Colo. Cannons in the vicinity of it.

You will converse fully and freely with Colo. Nevill on the points touched on in my letter—hear his sentiments on them—and find out if you can how far and with what cordiallity he is disposed to serve me in providing Tenants and securing the Rents of the newly recovered Lands—You will be able to learn from him also whether Colo. Cannon is at home or at the Assembly in Philadelphia—probably Colo. Nevill will ride there with you in the former case, or to the land in the latter one—The condition the last is in you will examine and inform the residents thereon of the person I have named as my Agent—and though they have little right to expect favor from me, yet I have no inclination to distress them more than can be avoided.[4]

As Colo. Canon lives near my land & is esteemed a worthy and respectable character it would be more convenient and perhaps better—every thing considered—that he should superintend my tenants than any other person—but if he declines it and Colo. Nevill discovers an inclination to serve me in this business he would be my next choice—and Major McCarmick the third—In case either of the first (in the order they are named) should incline to accept this trust there will be no necessity for you to deliver the letter to the latter in person if he should not fall in your way.[5]

The name of the person accepting the trust must be inserted in the blank power herewith given you.[6]

You will endeavor to discover from those to whom I have written as also from others what probably is the highest price that can be obtained for the two tracts I wish to dispose of—viz.— that on Millers run in Washington County containing about 3000 Acres—and that on Yohiogany (commonly called Washingtons bottom) in Fayette County of 1650 Acres giving the credits & receiving the payments in the manner mentioned in my letters—& if you should find that none are of opinion that the first will exceed 30/ pr Acre and the other 40/ both Pensyla Curry you may give it out that although I have not named the prices of these tracts in my letters yet you have good reason to believe and indeed to know that if these prices could be averaged (in case the Lands are sold in parcels) that I would be content therewith and assurances might be given of my disposing of them on these terms.

After having finished the business which takes you to Washington County, return home by the way of my other Land in Fayette County the condition of which I wish you to examine over and above the Acct you will receive from Major Freeman[7] & then return in by Braddock Road at the Great Meadows lying on which I have a small tract which sometimes has and at other times has not a tenant (though no rent has ever yet been paid me for it) See in what state & Condition this tenement is in.[8]

Your road from hence will cross the No. Branch of Potomack above Fort Cumberland and pass through Rumney and thence to Winchester where you will deliver my letter to Mr White and receive the money due from Genl Lees Estate to me if he inclines to pay it.[9]

In this trip you will have an opportunity of satisfying yourself fully with respect to Colo. Hulls enquiries which I wish you to do[10]—and also what the legal fees of my Lawyers are in the ejectments lately decided in my favor that I may know better what to add to them.[11]

If Major Freeman can give any Acct of the suit (an ejectment I believe it is) brought by my Brother Colo. Jno. Washington in Fayette Court I should be glad if you would obtain it that I communicate the same to him.[12] Wishing you good health and as pleasant a journey as can be expected from the Season I am your sincere friend

Go: Washington

ALS, CSmH; ADfS, DLC:GW.

1. In September 1784 GW visited his 240-acre tract of land in Hampshire County, "on the Virginia side" of the Potomac, which he had secured from Lord Fairfax in 1753, and found it "exceedingly rich." At that time, he "requested a Mr. McCracken at whose House I fed my horses, and got a snack, & whose Land joins mine—to offer mine to any who might apply for £10 the first year, £15 the next, and £25 the third" (*Diaries*, 4:14). For the possible identity of McCracken, see ibid., 16. Peter Bryan Bruin (d. 1827) had served throughout the Revolution, eventually reaching the rank of major in the 7th Virginia Regiment. He later moved to Bayou Pierre above Natchez and was appointed by John Adams one of the three judges of the Mississippi Territory.

2. See GW to John Stephenson, 28 November.

3. See GW to Richard Butler, 27 November.

4. See GW to Presley Neville, 27 Nov., and to John Cannon, 28 November.

5. See GW to John Cannon, 13 April 1787.

6. There is in DLC:GW a draft of a document, dated 30 Nov. 1786 and in GW's hand, which begins: "I do by these presents constitute and appoint [   ] my agent and lawful attorney for the purpose of Renting my Lands on Millers run in Washington County & State of Pensylvania." The final version of the document, also in GW's hand and signed by him, witnessed by Tobias Lear, with "Colonel John Canon" written in the blank space by Lear, was owned in 1991 by Gallery of History, Las Vegas, Nevada.

7. See GW to Thomas Freeman, 28 Nov., and Freeman to GW, 18 December.

8. For GW's Great Meadows tract, see GW to John Lewis, 14 Feb. 1784, n.2, and references.

9. GW's letter to the attorney, Alexander White, who acted as the attorney of Gen. Charles Lee's sister, Sidney Lee, in the settlement of his American estate, has not been found, but see White to GW, 29 April 1786.

10. See William Hull to GW, 25 Oct., and note 2 of that document in which GW's response of 20 Nov. is printed. See also GW to Hull, 29 December.

11. For GW's payment of attorney's fees to Thomas Smith, see GW to Smith, 5 Mar. 1788, and Ledger B, 259.

12. See Thomas Freeman to GW, 18 December.

To Gardoqui

Sir,   Mount Vernon 1st Decr 1786.

I have had the honor to receive the letter which your Excellency did me the favor of writing to me on the 18th ulto together with the enclosure from the Prime minister of Spain, for which, and the translation, I pray you to accept my grateful thanks.

Besides the pleasure I feel in making these acknowledgements, one object that prompts me to them at this early period, is, to beg that your Excely will not take the trouble of being instrumental in procuring for me a She Ass (by means of which I might preserve the breed of the valuable Jack I received as a present from his Catholic Majesty). At all times & under any circumstances, I shou'd have been perfectly ashamed if an unguarded expression of mine should have been the cause of giving you trouble, but more so in the present. When I had the honor of addressing you last, I had actually sent to Surinam, where I was informed very good, though not of the first race of these animals, were to be had, for a she one; & besides, thro' the medium of my good friend the Marqs de la Fayette, I had assurances & the further prospect of obtaining one or two from the Island of Malta. I am quite unhappy therefore lest the information in my former letter, that "I am endeavouring to provide a female that the advantages which are to be derived from this Jack may not end with his life," should have been construed an expression of a wish that your Excely would employ your influence to effect this purpose, & it is the inducement which has hastened me to an explanation & correction of the indigested manner in which information was communicated.[1]

Rheumatic pains, with which of late I have been a good deal afflicted, and some other causes, will render it inconvenient for me to be in Philada in May next as seems to be expected, & where one of my first pleasures would have been to have paid my respects to your Excellency.

It will be to be regretted if a contrariety of sentiments respecting the navigation of the Mississippi should impede that harmony & mutual intercourse of interests so essential between nations whose territories border on each other. I would fain hope therefore that the true & reciprocal benefits of Spain & the United States, in this case, as well as in all others which may arise between them, will be cooly & dispassionately considered before the ultimatum on either side is fixed. There is no ground on which treaties can be formed that will be found permanent or satisfactory, unless they have these for their basis: but however necessary it may be to inculcate this doctrine upon others, your Excellency I am sure is too much of a politician to need the remark, & too much of a friend to these States to insist upon any measure, which the essential interests of your Nation, or the orders of your Court, may not have dictated; incompatible therewith. With very great consideration & respect I have the honor to be &c.

G: Washington

LB, DLC:GW.

1. GW is referring to his letter to Gardoqui of 30 August. For GW's efforts to secure a jenny from Surinam, see John Fitzgerald to GW, 7 Feb. 1786, and notes.

From James Maury

Sir,   Liverpoole 3 Decr 1786

Being lately arrived here from Virginia & fixed in the commercial Line, I beg Leave most respectfully to tender you my best Services: at the same Time assuring you, that, trade ⟨being⟩ out of the Question, I shall count myself singularly honored by your Commands and particularly obliged by your condescending to favor me with an opportunity of evincing the desire I have to be useful to you.[1] I have the Honor to be with the highest Respect your excellencys most obedient & most humble Servt

James Maury[2]

ALS, DLC:GW.

In July 1786 James Maury (1745–1840) left Fredericksburg, where he had been a merchant, for Liverpool.

1. GW wrote on 24 Feb.: "Sir, I have received your letter of the 3d of Octr [December] and am much oblige to you for the very polite manner in which you tenter me your services. As I have wholly discontinued the cultivation of Tobaco it is not probable that I shall have any business to transact in the mercantile line in your quarter—but if I should at any time have occasion for any thing from Liverpool or therabouts I shall take the liberty of applying to you—Wishing you much happiness and great success in you business. I am Sir yr mt Obedt Hle Sert G. Washington" (LB, DLC:GW).

2. Maury has written at the bottom of the page "Tobaccoe 2¼ @ 4[;] stemed 3½ [@] 5."

Letter not found: from Charles Carter, 4 Dec. 1786. GW wrote Carter on 10 Jan. 1787: "I should have presented you with an earlier acknowledgement of your favor of the 4th ulto."

To Rawleigh Colston

Sir,   Mo[un]t Vernon 4th Decr 1786.

Your favor of the 10th of Novembr, (which did not reach me 'till within these three days) as well as the former by Mr Ireland, came safe to hand.[1]

Mr Wright, whom I saw at Alexandria, will have informed you, that as the business respecting the affairs of the deceased Colo. *George* Mercer was transferred by a decree of the high Court of Chancery, from me to Colo. *John* Mercer; & the Bonds & other papers assigned over to the latter, that it lay with

him to settle the accounts & to decide on the propriety of making conveyances. The Deeds were only with-held 'till payment
of the consideration money should be made, or satisfactory security should be given for the doing of it—and that (if it was necessary for me to do it at all) I could make no conveyance without
his express direction; this being necessary, for my justification.
And this I also repeated to Mr Ireland in emphatic terms.[2]

Since these conversations I have received a line from Colo.
John Mercer requesting me to execute a Deed to you for one of
the Lotts sold Mr Hickman; but as the Deeds for conveyance of
these lands are much out of the usual form, (there being many
parties to them) & all the papers respecting the business now
out of my possession, I have, in answer to this request, desired
him if it is *indispensably* necessary for me as the seller to convey,
to have the deed (for there were some blank ones left) filled
up & sent to me with authority for me to sign, & no delay should
be found on my part.[3] Having thus explained my sentiments
of, & agency in this business, you will readily perceive to what
quarter your future applications are to be directed. Considering
the light in which Mr Ireland stood, I gave him a statement of
the case in writing, that Mr Stone might act in it agreeably to
the dictates of his own judgment, or the orders of Colo. Mercer,
with respect to the execution. I am Sir &c.

G: Washington

LB, DLC:GW.

1. "The former by Mr Ireland," dated 5 Oct., has not been found.

2. See Colston to GW, 10 Nov., and the references in note 2 of that document.

3. John Francis Mercer wrote GW on 20 Nov., but GW probably is referring
to Mercer's letter of 21 October. See GW to Mercer, 6 and 26 November.

To Fielding Lewis, Jr.

Sir,   M[oun]t Vernon 4th Decr 1786.

Your letter of the 11th of Octor never came to my hands 'till
yesterday. Altho' your disrespectful conduct towards me, in
coming into this country & spending weeks therein without ever
coming near me, entitles you to very little notice or favor from
me; yet I consent that you may get timber from off my Land in

Fauquier County to build a house on your Lott in Recter town. Having granted this, now let me ask you what your views were in purchasing a Lott in a place which, I presume, originated with, & will end in two or three Gin Shops, which probably will exist no longer than they serve to ruin the proprietors, & those who make the most frequent applications to them.[1] I am &c.

G: Washington

LB, DLC:GW.
 1. See GW to Battaile Muse, this date.

From Benjamin Lincoln

Editorial Note

General Lincoln did not complete this extended account of Shays' Rebellion for GW until 4 Mar. 1787, a month after he had defeated and dispersed Daniel Shays' followers at Petersham on 4 February. Hence Lincoln's letter, to which GW responded on 23 Mar. 1787, served for GW not as a running report but as a recapitulation of developments in Massachusetts. It was primarily Henry Knox, the secretary at war, who kept GW informed from New York of events as they unfolded in New England during the winter. For a time in January, Knox was writing to GW by every post, enclosing firsthand accounts from Lincoln and others of the progress of the campaign against the insurgents in western Massachusetts.

During the summer of 1786 the farmers in the rural towns of western Massachusetts expressed their growing discontent with their condition and with the government in Boston. The towns petitioned the General Court and called county conventions to press for economic relief, usually demanding paper currency and tender laws. By September the more radical of the protesters had moved to the forcible closure in some counties of the courts of common pleas through which debts were collected. Before the end of the month both Henry Lee in New York and David Humphreys in Connecticut had written GW about these developments in Massachusetts, which they found alarming, and by early October the Virginia newspapers were printing detailed reports from Boston. On 23 Oct., on the same day that Knox sent GW his first report, GW first expressed in writing, in a letter to Humphreys, his bewilderment and anger that Americans could turn against and seek to overthrow a government of their own making.

The Massachusetts General Court met on 22 Oct. to begin the session in which it sought without success to deal with the growing unrest and violence in the western counties of the state. To pacify the farmers, it enacted legislation to increase somewhat the supply of money and to give debtors some additional protection from their creditors; to restore order, it passed a new riot act and gave the governor broad powers to lift habeas corpus. As Lincoln makes clear in the part of his letter written on 4 Dec., neither of these stratagems worked. Within two weeks of the adjournment of the legislature on 18 Nov., the Shaysites had twice prevented the court from sitting in Winchester, and on 20 Dec. they kept the court closed at Springfield.

Gov. James Bowdoin on 4 Jan. 1787 ordered 4,400 troops to be raised and put under the command of General Lincoln, and on 19 Jan. he gave Lincoln his marching orders. In the portion of his letter to GW written on 22 Feb., Lincoln gives a succinct and lucid account of what ensued: his march with his army from Boston to Worcester on 19 Jan.; the wild flight of Shays' assembled forces at Springfield on 25 Jan. after Gen. William Shepard's Hampshire militia fired on them in defense of the federal arsenal; Lincoln's dogging of Shays' forces back and forth between Hadley, Northampton, Amherst, and Pelham; and Lincoln's night march of 3 Feb. in a snowstorm to Petersham culminating the next day in the capture of the remnants of Shays' forces, except for those who scattered and fled into the woods.

Lincoln writes the last portion of his letter, dated 4 Mar., to tell of the Shaysite raid from New York on Stockbridge at the end of February and to express misgivings about the disqualifying act passed by the General Court in mid-February placing severe disabilities on all who had taken up arms. Both GW and Henry Knox, to whom Lincoln sent a copy of this eloquent appeal for tolerance and generosity, shared Lincoln's views, which were to prevail after the election of John Hancock as governor in April.

Hingham [Mass.]

My dear General,   Decr 4th 1786[–4 Mar. 1787]

I was honored by the reciept of your favour of the 7th Ulto, and your circular address by one of the last Posts.

I wish your Excellency had not in so decided a manner expressed your determination to retire from the head of the order of Cincinnati. I shall communicate your address to our delegates at the next general meeting, and to our State society.

I have made three trips into the eastern country this year, partly on public and partly on private business. I have one son now there and another will probably go there next spring. I think it a good country and that young men may sit down in it with flattering prospects. Since the last Spring we have erected two saw mills on a large scale, and have established a number of settlers. We have frequent applications for lots and shall soon obtain the number of families we are obliged to settle, (viz. sixty in six years). From the situation of the two Townships which were bought by Mr Russel, Mr Lowell and myself, the settlement of them will be easy for the lands are so indented by rivers and bays that we lie about seventy miles on navigable waters; and there are not one hundred acres in the fifty thousand which will be five miles from such waters. Our people who have been bred near the sea are fond of settling as near to it as possible. It is a Country which abounds with fish of almost every kind, and the waters are covered with fowls. The lands will be friendly to the growth of wheat rye, barley, oats, hemp and flax, but not much so to indian corn. Indeed I am so pleased with the country that I frequently wish myself there where I might be free from the present noise and tumults.[1] but I cannot leave this part of the state at present, for notwithstanding the resolutions I had formed ever to decline entering again into public life, I was persuaded by my friends to take the command of the first division of militia in this state. I am now busily employed in organizing it &c. This business, which would at all times be a duty, is especially so now, when the State is convulsed, and the bands of government, in some parts of it, are cast off.[2]

I cannot therefore be surprized to hear your Excellency enquire "are your people getting mad? are we to have the goodly fabric, that eight years were spent in raising, pulled over our heads? what is the cause of all these commotions? when and how will they end?" Altho' I cannot pretend to give a full and compleat answer to them, yet I will make some observations which shall involve in them the best answers to the several questions in my power to give.

"Are your people getting mad?" Many of them appear to be absolutely so, if an attempt to annihilate our present constitution and dissolve the present government can be considered as evidences of insanity.

"Are we to have the goodly fabric, that eight years were spent in rearing, pulled over our heads?" There is great danger that it will be so, I think; unless the tottering system shall be supported by arms, and even then a government which has no other basis than the point of the bayonet, should one be suspended thereon, is so totally different from the one established, at least in idea, by the different States that if we must have recourse to the sad experiment of arms it can hardly be said that we have supported "the goodly fabric." In this view of the matter it may be "pulled over our heads." This probably will be the case, for there doth not appear to be virtue enough among the people to preserve a perfect republican government.

"What is the cause of all these commotions?" The causes are too many and too various for me to pretend to trace and point them out. I shall therefore only mention some of those which appear to be the principle ones. Among those I may rank the ease with which property was acquired, with which credit was obtained, and debts were discharged in the time of the War. Hence people were diverted from their usual industry and œconomy. A luxuriant mode of living crept into vogue, and soon that income, by which the expences of all should as much as possible be limited, was no longer considered as having any thing to do with the question at what expence families ought to live, or rather which they ought not to have exceeded. The moment the day arrived when all discovered that things were fast returning back into their original channels, that the industrious were to reap the fruits of their industry, and that the indolent and improvident would soon experience the evils of their idleness and sloth. Very many startled at the idea, and instead of attempting to subject themselves to such a line of conduct, which duty to the public, and a regard to their own happiness evidently pointed out, they contemplated how they should evade the necessity of reforming their system and of changing their present mode of life, they first complained of Commutation, of the weight of public taxes, of the insupportable debt of the union, of the scarcity of money, and of the cruelty of suffering the private creditors to call for their just dues. This catalogue of complaints was listened to by many. County conventions were formed, and the cry for Paper Money, subject to depreciation, as was declared by some of their public resolves, was the clamour of the day. But notwithstanding instructions to members of the General Court and petitions from different quarters, the majority of that body were opposed to the measures. Failing of their point, the disaffected in the first place, attempted, and in many instances succeeded, to stop the courts of Law and to suspend the operations of government. This they hoped to do untill they could by force sap the foundations of our constitution, and bring into the Legislature creatures of their own by which they could mould a government at pleasure, and make it subservient to all their purposes, and when an end should thereby be put to public and private debts, the Agrarian law might follow with ease. In short the want of industry, œconomy, and common honesty seem to be the causes of the present commotions.

It is impossible for me to determine "when and how they will end," as I see little probability that they will be brought to a period, and the dignity of government supported without bloodshed. When a single drop is drawn, the most prophetic spirit will not, in my opinion, be able to determine when it will cease flowing. The proportion of debtors run high in this State. Too many of them are against the government. The men of property, and the holders of the public securities are generally supporters of our present constitution. Few of these have been in the field, and it remains quite problematical whether they will in time so fully discover their own interests as they shall be induced thereby to lend for a season part of their property for the security of the remainder. If these classes of men should not turn out on the broad scale with spirit, and the insurgents should take the field and keep it, our Constitution will be overturned, and the fœderal government broken in upon by lopping off one branch essential to the well being of the whole. This cannot be submitted to by the United States with impunity. They must send force to our aid: when this shall be collected they will be equal to *all* purposes.

The insurgents have now every advantage. If we move in force against them, we move under the direction of the civil authority, and we cannot act but by the direction of it. After the riot-act has been read and one hour elapsed they may disperse if they think proper; and the next day assemble again in another place. So they may conduct themselves in perfect security from day to day untill a favorable moment shall offer, after the well affected to government are worn out, for them to commence the attack. Had the last General Court declared the disaffected counties in a state of Rebellion, they would have placed the contest upon a different footing, and the Rebels might have been soon crushed. They did not do it. What they will do at their next session, which will be in February next, is quite uncertain, and must remain, "with the time when and the manner how these commotions are to end," concealed from me in the unturned pages of futurity.

Feby 22 1787   Thus far I had written as early as December, and should have forwarded the letter at that time, but had some hopes that the Governour and Council would take some measures for crushing the Insurgents. This however hung in suspence untill the beginning of January. It was then agreed to raise two thousand men in the Counties of Suffolk, Essex, and Middlesex, and four companies of Artillery; twelve hundred men in the County of Hampshire; and twelve hundred men in the County of Worcester. The command of the troops was to be given to me being the first Major General in the State. At this moment, when every part of the system was digested, and nothing remained but the offering the order to raise the men, and carry it into execution, information was received from the Commissary General that the necessary supplies could not be obtained without a considerable sum in cash, which was not within the power of the Treasurer to borrow. On my hearing this from the Governour, I went immediately to a club of the first characters in Boston who met that night, and layed before them a full state of matters, and suggested to them the importance of their becoming loaners of part of their property if they wished to secure the remainder. A Subscription was set on foot in the morning, headed by the Governour. Before night the cloud which twenty four hours before hung over us disappeared as we had an assurance of obtaining the sum we wanted.[3]

Orders were then issued for raising the men. They were directed to rendezvous at different places on the 18th and 19th of January. The objects to [be] embraced by the force called into the field, your Excellency will learn from the following Instructions from the Governor.

Sir,   Boston January 19th 1787—
    You will take the command of the Militia detached in obedience to my Orders of the fourth instant. The great objects to be effected are to protect the Judicial Courts, particularly those next to be holden in

the County of Worcester, if the Justices of said Courts should request your aid; to assist the civil Magistrates in executing the Laws, and in repelling or apprehending all and every such person and persons as shall in a hostile manner attempt or enterprize, the destruction detriment or annoyance of this Commonwealth: and also to aid them in apprehending the disturbers of the public peace, as well as all such persons as may be named in the State Warrants, that have been, or shall be committed to any civil Officer or Officers, or to any other person to execute.

If to these important ends the Militia already ordered out should in your opinion be incompetent, you will call on the Major Generals for further and effectual aid. If you can rely on their attachment to Government, you will in the first instance call on the Militia in the neighbourhood of your Camp.

I cannot minutely point out to you the particular line you shall pursue in executing these Orders: but would observe in general, that if to answer the aforesaid valuable purposes you shall judge it necessary to march a respectable force through the Western Counties, you will in that case do it. This would give confidence to the well affected; would aid and protect the civil Officers in executing their duty, and would convince the misguided of the abilities of Government, and its determination to pursue every legal and constitutional measure for restoring peace and order to the Commonwealth.

You are to consider yourself in all your military offensive operations constantly as under the direction of the civil Officer, saving where any armed force shall appear and oppose your marching to execute these Orders.

That I may be fully acquainted with all the proceedings of the armed force under your command, and with all matters that respect the great objects to be effected, you will please to give me regular information by every post; and for immediate and necessary intelligence, you will order the Quarter Master General to provide the necessary expences.

On these attempts to restore system and order, I wish the smiles of Heaven; and that you may have an agreeable command, the most perfect success, and a speedy and safe return; and am with much esteem, Sir, Your most obedient Servant James Bowdoin.[4]

We commenced our march in the morning of the 20th for Worcester, where the Court of Common Pleas, and Court of the general Session of the peace were to set on the 23d, which Courts we were ordered to protect. They opened and compleated their business Thursday morning.

Shays did not point his force to any object untill the 24th.

Then he took a post from which he could suddenly strike the Public Magazine which seemed to be his object. He covered his men at Wilbraham six miles south of it, while Day remained with his at West Springfield. They were jointly to have made an attack on the Magazine at 4 oClock P.M. January 25th, one of the Letters from Day to Shays was intercepted which would have delayed Shays's movements. He came on in open column, was repeatedly warned of his danger by General Shepard, and finally if he progressed in any degree farther he would fire upon him. He moved, and the General fired over him, hoping to deter him from proceeding, but to no effect. He then fired two pieces into his column which he attempted to display. By these shots three men were killed, and a number wounded. His people were thrown into the utmost confusion, and dispersed for a time but soon collected as they were not followed by General Shepard, who could have destroyed a great proportion of them had he been disposed to do it.

Shays' dispersion led me to make a very rapid march for the relief of Shepard, who was apprehensive for the safety of the stores, and for the Inhabitants, and for the town of Springfield. I threw one regiment and some Horse into his camp in the night of the 26th. Shays having filed off about six miles to right, I arrived with the main body of the troops at noon the 27th. The men were immediately quartered, and took some refreshment. In this time: I had an opportunity of learning the situation of the Insurgents. Part of them were on the East and part on the West side of Connecticut River: those on the East were commanded by Shays, and those on the West by Day, who had placed his guard on the West bank of the River, and another at Agawaam River. Shays had placed his guards on the East bank of the River so that they had cut off all communication to the town of Springfield from the North and the West in the common routs. It was with the greatest difficulty that new ones could be formed as the snow was very deep. Hereby many of our supplies fell into their hands. In this situation I could not think of remaining one night. I ordered the troops under arms at 3 oClock, tho' many of them had been so from one in the morning. Part of them with the light Horse, I moved up the River on the ice with an intention to prevent the junction of Shays and Day; and if that was not attempted, to cut off Day's retreat. With the other part of the troops I moved across the river in front of his guard. They soon turned out and retreated to his main body. They retreated before us about half a mile, then made some disposition to attack, but soon left that post and retreated to a high peace of ground in their rear where they were met by the light Horse. Thence they fled in every direction, but most of them the same evening reached Northampton. This left Shays' right uncovered and induced him to move the same night to Amherst about 20 miles North of Springfield. At 3 oClock of the morning of the 29th we moved towards Amherst, where Shays had been joined by Day. On our arrival in the borders of the town the rear of Shays' force left it; some few fell into our hands. He then took post at Pelham East from Amherst: We filed off to the left, and took post in Hadley and Hatfield, on the River. He had now taken a very strong position. The ground he was well acquainted with, being the town in which he lived. On the morning of the 30th I sent him the following address.

Head quarters Hadley Jan 30th 1787
Whether you are convinced or not, of your error in flying to arms, I am fully persuaded, that before this hour, you have the fullest conviction on your own mind that you are not able to execute your original purposes.

Your resources are few, your force is inconsiderable, and hourly decreasing from the disaffection of your men. You are in a post where you have neither cover nor supplies, and in a situation in which you can neither give aid to your friends, nor discomfort to the supporters of good order and government. Under these circumstances, you cannot hesitate a moment, to disband your deluded followers. If you should not, I must approach and apprehend the most influential characters among you. Should you attempt to fire upon the troops of government, the consequences might be fatal to many of your men the least guilty. To prevent bloodshed, you will communicate to your privates that if they will instantly lay down their arms, surrender themselves to government, and take and subscribe the oath of allegiance to this Commonwealth, they shall be recommended to the General Court for mercy. If you should either withhold this information from them, or suffer your people to fire upon our approach, you must be answerable for all the ills, which may exist in consequence thereof.

To Capt. Shays & the other Officers commanding the men in arms against the Government of this Commonwealth.

This was delivered by General Putnam and two other Gentlemen, all of whom were of my family; and brought the same day the following answer.

Pelham Jany 30th 1787—

To General Lincoln Commanding the Government Troops at Hadley.

Sir

The people Assembled in Arms from the Counties of Middlesex, Worcester, Hampshire & Berkshire taking into serious Consideration the purport of the Flag just Received—

Return for Answer, that however unjustifiable the measure may be, which the people have adopted, in having recourse to Arms, Various Circumstances have induced them thereto, we are Sensible of the Embarrasments the people are under, but that Virtue which truly Charaterises the Citizens of a Republican Government hath hitherto marked our paths with a Degree of Innocence, & we wish & trust it will still be the Case, at the same time the people are willing to lay down their Arms on the Condition of a General Pardon, and Return to their respective homes as they are unwilling to Stain the Land which we in the late war purchased at so dear a rate with the Blood of our Brethren and Neighbours, therefore we pray that Hostilities may Cease on your part untill our united Prayers may be presented to the General Court, & we receive an Answer, as a person is gone for that purpose, if this Request may be complied with, Government shall meet with no interruption from the people, but let each Army Occupy the posts where they now are. Daniel Shays Capt.[5]

The following is an extract from a Letter I wrote the 30th to the Governour.[6]

Dear Sir,

I have had many applications from towns pretty much in the language of those made to your Excellency and Council. I have given them all the same answer, that I cannot suspend our operations, and if they wish to prevent the shedding of blood, they must apply to Shays to disband his troops. He is recieving daily supplies of provisions, and some few recruits. It will be difficult, if not impossible to put an end to such disorders, unless a Rebellion is declared to exist. Shays and his abettors must be treated as open enemies; the sooner it is done, the better: for if we drive him from one strong post, he flies to another; In these movements he could not be supported, if he was not comforted by the many disaffected in the Counties.

I hope the General Court will not hesitate, but come to the point at once; and act with that decision and firmness, which in my opinion a regard to the well being of the State so manifestly demands.

I had constant applications from Committees, and Selectmen of the several towns in the Counties of Worcester and Hampshire, praying that the effusion of blood may be avoided; while the real design, as was supposed, of these applications was to stay our operations untill a new Court should be elected. They had no doubt if they could keep up their influence untill another choice of the Legislature and the Executive that matters might be moulded in General Court to their wishes. This to avoid was the duty of Government. As all these applications breathed the same spirit, the same answer was given to them. The following is a copy.

Gentlemen, I have felt too sensibly for the distresses of those unhappy men who have been deluded to rise in arms against their Country, in violation of every principle of duty, not to have most seriously contemplated, how they might be reclaimed without bloodshed. Hitherto our men have been restrained from firing. Shays has been notified of his danger, and of the consequences which must ensue should he fire upon the troops of Government. His men have been invited to return to their homes, and lay down their arms. I hope they will attend to the advice.

I think those Towns which sincerely wish to put an end to this rebellion, might render essential services in effecting so desirable an object. They should by their advice recall their men now in arms, they should aid in apprehending all abettors of them, and all who are yeilding them any comfort and supplies. This would reduce them to submission, and prevent the horrors so much feared.

On the 31st I received the following application from Shays and others.

Pelham Jan. 31st 1787—
The Honorable General Lincoln. Sir, as the officers of the People now Convened in Defence of their rights and Priveleges, have sent a Petition to the General Court for the sole Purpose of accomodation of our Present unhappy affairs, we justly expect, that the Hostilities May cease on both sides untill we have a return from our Legislature.

Your Honnor therefore will Please to Give us an answer.

Frans Stone, Chairman
Pr order of the Committee   Daniel Shays, Captain
  for Reconciliation   Adam Wheeler, Captain

I returned the following answer.

Hadley Jan. 31st 1787—
Gentlemen, Your request is totally inadmissible, as no powers are delegated to me which would justify a delay of my operations. Hostilities I have not commenced.

I have again to warn the people in arms against Government, immediately to disband, as they would avoid the ill consequences which may ensue, should they be inattentive to this caution.[7]

In this position I remained refreshing the troops who had suffered very severe fatigue. This also gave time for the several Towns to use their influence with their own people to return, if they thought proper to use it: and to circulate among Shays' men that they would be recommended for a pardon if they would come in, and lay down their arms. The 2d of Febuary I was induced to reconnoitre Shays' post on his right, left, and rear. I had recieved information by General Putnam before, that we could not approach him in front. I intended to have approached him on the 3d inst. This reconnoitreing gave him an alarm. At 3 oClock in the morning of the 3d, I recieved an application from Wheeler, that he wished to confer with General Putnam. His request was granted.[8] He seemed to have no object but his personal safety. No encouragement being given him in this head, he returned a little after noon. In the evening of the same day, I was informed that Shays had left his ground, and had pointed his rout toward Petersham in the County of Worcester, where he intended to make a stand as a number of Towns in the vicinity had engaged to support him. Our troops were put in motion at 8 o Clock. The first part of the night was pleasant, and the weather clement; but between two and three o Clock in the morning, the wind shifting to the Westward, it became very cold and squally, with considerable snow. The wind immediately arose very high, and with the light snow which fell the day before and was falling, the paths were soon filled up, the men became fatigued, and they were in a part of the country where they could not be covered in the distance of eight miles, and the cold was so increased, that they could not halt in the road to refresh themselves. Under these circumstances they were obliged to continue their march. We reached Petersham about 9 o Clock in the morning exceedingly fatigued with a march of thirty miles, part of it in a deep snow and in a most violent storm; when this abated, the cold increased and a great proportion of our men were frozen in some part or other, but none dangerously. We approached nearly the centre of the Town where Shays had covered his men; and had we not been prevented from the steepness of a large hill at our entrance, and the depth of the snow from throwing our men rapidly into it we should have arrested very probably one half this force; for they were so surprized as it was that they had not time to call in their out-parties, or even their guards. About 150 fell into our hands, and none escaped but by the most precipitate flight in different directions.

Thus that body of men who were a few days before offering the grossest insults to the best Citizens of this Commonwealth and were menacing even Government itself, were now nearly dispersed, without the shedding of blood but in an instance or two where the Insurgents rushed on their own destruction. That so little has been shed is owing in a measure to the patience and obedience, the zeal and the fortitude in our troops, which would have done honour to veterans. A different line of conduct which Shays flattered his troops would have been followed, would have given them support, and led them to acts of violence, whilst it must have buoyed up the hopes of their abettors, and stimulated them to greater exertions.

At this time I recieved the proceedings of the General Court. They have acted with a degree of decision and firmness which do them honour. I think your Excellency will be pleased to have their doings added.[9]

* * * * * * *

Having distressed the main body of the insurgents, our next attention was so to disseminate our force thro' the disaffected Counties, as to break the little knots of those in arms which were collected in various parts of the Counties, and were taking up, confining, and plundering all who fell into their hands who in their opinion were "freinds to government," as they called them. A body of troops were retained in the County of Worcester; a regiment left in the County of Hampshire, besides a guard to the public Magazine at Springfield. With three regiments I came on to this place. I found the people in general had been in arms, or had been abettors of those who were, and that their obstinacy was not exceeded by anything but by their ignorance of their own situation. I at once threw detachments into different parts of the County, for the purpose of protecting the freinds to Government and apprehending those who had been in arms against it. This business is pretty fully accomplished, and there are no Insurgents together in arms in the State.

There are many parties in the neighbouring States lurking near the borders of this. They are poisoning the minds of a class among them. It is now time for those States to exert themselves in apprehending such characters, for they fan the coals, and will kindle the flame of rebellion whereever they go.

The time for which the Militia engaged to serve expires with this day. We are raising two regiments to remain in service for four months in obedience to the following resolves.[10]

* * * * * * * *

That your Excellency may have a knowledge of the doings of our Legislature which I think will some day or other make a rich page in History, I have subjoined the following Acts.[11]

* * * * * * * *

Although I revere the doings of our General Court, yet I think in one instance or two they have gone too far. The following observations on one of their laws, I have submitted to the consideration of a private Friend in Boston, and they are added to this letter, by which nothing more is intended, than as the reading it may serve as an hour of amusement to your Excellency.

When a State whose Constitution is like ours, has been convulsed by intestine broils; when the bands of Government have in any part of it been thrown off, and Rebellion has for a time stalked unmolested: when the most affectionate neighbours become in consequence hereof, divided in sentiment on the question in dispute, and warmly espouse the opinions they hold; when even the Father arms against the Son, and the son against the Father, the powers of Government may be exerted; and crush the Rebellion, but to reclaim its citizens, to bring them back fully to a sense of their duty, and to establish anew those principles, which lead them to embrace the Government with affection, must require the wisdom, the patience & the address of the Legislature.

Love and Fear are the bonds of civil Society. Love is the noblest incentive to obedience; a Government supported hereon is certainly the most desireable, and ensures the first degrees of happiness which can be derived from civil compact. Such a Government as this is always wounded, when any thing shall exist which makes it necessary to apply to the fears of the governed. This never will be done by a wise administration, unless the General Good renders it indespensible, and it will be removed the first moment it can be, consistently with the common safety.

The spirit of Rebellion is now nearly crushed in this State, and the opposition to Government is hourly decreasing. This therefore is the most critical moment yet seen. Punishment must be such, and be so far extended as thereby others shall be detered from repeating such acts of outrage in future, and care must be taken that they do not extend beyond a certain degree the necessity of which must be acknowledged by all. In her right hand Government must hold out such terms of mercy in the hour of success, with such evident marks of a disposition to forgive as shall apply to the feelings of the delinquents, beget in them such sentiments of gratitude and love by which they will be led to embrace with the highest cordiality that Government which they have attempted to trample under foot. This example in Government will have its influence upon Individuals, and be productive of the best Effects among contending Neighbours & divided Families.

These are sentiments which I suppose have their foundation in truth; and in the belief of them, I have been led to examine with some attention the late Act of the General Court, by which certain Characters are for a time disfranchised. Although I think the conduct of the Legislature will make a rich page in History, yet I cannot but suppose, that if the number of the disfranchised had been less, the public peace would have been equally safe, and the general good promoted.

The Act includes so great a description of persons that in its operation many Towns will be disfranchised. This will injure the whole, for multiplied disorders must be experienced under such circumstances.

The people who have been in Arms against Government and their Abettors, have complained, and do now complain that grievances do exist, and that they ought to have redress. We have invariably said to them, you are wrong in flying to Arms; you should seek redress in a Constitutional way, & wait the decision of the Legislature. These observations were undoubtedly just, but will they not now complain, and say, that we have cut them off from all hope of redress, from that quarter, for we have denied them a representation in that Legislative body, by whose Laws they must be governed.

While they are in this situation, they never will be reconciled to Government, nor will they submit to the terms of it, from any other Motive than fear excited by a constant military armed force extended over them. While these distinctions are made, the subjects of them will remain invidious, and their will be no affection existing among Inhabitants of the same Neighbourhood, or Families, where they have thought and acted differently. Those who have been opposers to Government will view with a jealous eye, those who have been supporters of it, and consider them as the cause which produced the disqualifying act, and who are now keeping it alive. Many never will submit to it, they will rather leave the State than do it. If we could reconcile ourselves to this loss, and on this account make no objection, yet these people will leave behind them near and dear connections who will feel themselves wounded through their Friends.

The influence of these people is so fully checked that we have nothing to apprehend from them now, but their Individual Votes. When this is the case, to express fears from that quarter is impolitic. Admit that some of these very people should obtain a seat in the Assembly the next year, we have nothing to fear from the measure: so far from that I think it would produce the most salutary Effects.

For my own part I wish, that those Insurgents who should secure a pardon, were at liberty to exercise all the rights of good Citizens; for I believe it to be the only way which can be adopted to make them good Members of Society, and to reconcile them to that Government under which we wish them to live. If we are now afraid of their weight and they are for a given time deprived of certain privileges, they will come forth hereafter with redoubled vigour. I think we have much more to fear from a certain supiness which has seized on a great proportion of our Citizens, who have been totally inattentive to the exercise of those rights conveyed to them by the Constitution of this Commonwealth. If the good people of the State will not exert themselves in the appointment of proper Characters for the Executive and Legislative branches of Government, no disfranchising acts will ever make us a happy & a well governed people.

I cannot therefore on the whole but think, that if the opposers to Government, had been disqualified, on a pardon from serving as jurors on the trial of those who had been in sentiment with them, that we should have been perfectly safe. For as I observed before these people have now no influence as a body, and their individual votes are not to be dreaded, for we certainly shall not admit the idea, that the Majority is with them in their political sentiments; if thus, how, upon republican principles, can we justly exclude them from the right of Governing.

March 4th

The parties I mentioned to your Excellency which were lurking on the borders of this State; remained inactive for some time with a hope and expectation as their leaders taught them to believe, that they should be reinforced from different quarters, and they were credulous enough to expect aid from Canada. Thus matters remained untill the Morning of the 27th Ulto when there appeared about 120 of them in Stockbridge who were in a very defenseless state, besides they were compleatly surprized. The Insurgents took a number of the leading Characters, in that Town, plundered many of the Inhabitants, & stole a number of Horses; They then, flushed with success proceeded on to Barrington; on their approach the well affected Militia retired before them towards Sheffield, and were met by the Militia of that Town commanded by Colo. Ashley. The halt the Insurgents made in Barrington gave time for the Lenox & Stockbridge Militia to collect and follow them. Colo. Ashley having collected about Eighty Men, came to a resolution to march in pursuit of the rebels, & to attack them where he should find them; he very soon fell in with them. They were marching in files, had their prisoners in the centre. Their front division formed a line on one side of the road, that left our prisoners in the front of the rear. It is said they did not form; that the whole were routed before they had time to do it; two or three Men on a side were killed & a number wounded; among them one Hamlen, Commander of the party; his wounds are dangerous; as they retreated they fell into the hands of the Militia from Stock-bridge & Lenox which were pursuing. About seventy of them have been taken: some are coming in and surrendering them-selves.[12]

This Action has had very happy Effects upon the people of this County; it has given them great spirits, and they begin to discover that state of mind which they enjoyed before the Rebel-lion existed, by which the Friends of government in this part of the County have been exceedingly born down.

The parties, which a few days since, were lurking on the bor-ders of this State, in Connecticut & New York, are very much dispersed, from causes not certainly known by us here. It is said they have been dispersed by the Authority of those govern-ments. The Rebels are retiring to Vermont, & are making their way Northerly, Shays and Wiley were by the last accounts at Otter Creek, and Parsons on his rout to that place. The leaders having left those deluded people, many of them will, I think, return, while others will endeavour to gain settlements in Vermont.

The State has much yet to do. The Supreme Judicial Court will meet in this County on the third Tuesday of this Month for the trial of these offenders. To preserve a line, which shall give security to the Citizens & dignity to the State, without incurring the censure of the World for being too cruel, may be difficult to draw. Where they hold out terms of pardon it should be done with a good grace, they should at the same time manifest a dis-position, to embrace cordially all who are truely penitent & give unequivocal proofs of reformation.

A proper address and attention will soon restore these Count-ies not only to Government and Order, but to that love and friendship, without which none can be long happy in civil So-ciety.

The regiments I mentioned before, are nearly full, one of them will be here in a few days; as soon as they are compleated and the necessary arrangements are made, I shall return home to the prosecution of the subject which engaged my attention the last year, that in the Eastern Country; my Friends tell me that I have just enthusiasm enough for such a project; what they call the Effects of enthusiasm to me appears the result of my best judgment.

I know this long letter may trespass upon your Excellency's time, did I not feel a responsibility to your Excellency when ever I enter on a military enterprize, and an Obligation to report as a duty I owe to your Excellency & to myself, I should have been silent, as I know your Excellencys time is constantly engrossed in pursuits which have for their object, the best interest & happiness of Mankind. I have the honor of being My dear general with perfect esteem your Excellencys most obedient & most humble servant—

B. Lincoln

LS, DLC:GW; ADf (incomplete), MHi: Benjamin Lincoln Papers. The documents which Lincoln enclosed and which are described in the notes are included in CD-ROM:GW.

1. Earlier in 1786 Lincoln joined the Boston merchants Thomas Russell and John Lowell in purchasing two Maine townships fronting on Passamaquoddy Bay and sent his 23-year-old son Theodore to supervise the development of the property.

2. Lincoln received his appointment as the senior major general of the Massachusetts militia in December 1785, with the request that he make recommendations regarding the military establishment of the state (Mattern, "Benjamin Lincoln," 317–18).

3. For the location of the text of these orders of the Massachusetts governor and his council, see Feer, *Shays's Rebellion*, 348, n.1. For other sources of information regarding the raising of money to support Lincoln's army, see ibid., 356, n.1.

4. Bowdoin's orders of 19 Jan. to Lincoln are printed in Minot's *History of the Massachusetts Insurrections*, 99–101. (Minot sent GW a copy of his history in August 1788. See George Richards Minot to GW, 7 Aug., and GW to Minot, 28 Aug. 1788.)

5. This exchange of letters is printed in ibid., 118–21.

6. Henry Knox sent to GW on 8 Feb. a copy of this letter from Lincoln to Bowdoin.

7. See ibid., 121–22.

8. Rufus Putnam, who had been Daniel Shays' commanding officer during the Revolution, met with Shays in early January 1787.

9. Lincoln includes here three documents: the senate's response of 4 Feb. to Governor Bowdoin's message to the General Court at the opening of its session on 3 Feb., and two senate resolutions regarding Shays' Rebellion, adopted on 4 February. In its letter, the senate expressed approval of the steps the governor had taken to oppose the insurgents and promised him continuing support for his policies. In the first of the senate's resolutions, it was "Resolved that this Court approve of General lincoln's conduct in his overtures of recommending certain descriptions of Insurgents to the clemency of Government, and that the Governor be, and he hereby is authorized and empowered in the name of the General Court to promise a pardon under such disqualifi-

cations as may hereafter be provided, to such private Soldiers, and others who act in the capacity of non-commissioned Officers, as have been, or now are in arms against the Commonwealth, with such exceptions as he, or the General Officer commanding the troops may judge necessary—provided they shall deliver up their arms, and take and subscribe the oath of allegiance to this Commonwealth, within such time as shall or may be limited by his Excellency for that purpose." The second resolution spelled out the misdeeds of the insurgents and "solemnly" declared "that a horrid and unnatural Rebellion and War has been openly and traiterously raised and levied against this Commonwealth."

10. Lincoln inserted here two senate resolutions, one of 8 Feb. and the other of 17 February. The first authorized "the Commander in Chief of this Commonwealth . . . to give immediate orders for the enlistment of such a number of men as he shall judge necessary . . . , not exceeding fifteen hundred, to serve for the space of four months . . . ." The one of 17 Feb. requested the governor to send General Lincoln £300 with which to recruit the men authorized in the resolution of 8 February.

11. The first of the acts of the legislature that Lincoln includes here is the act of 6 Feb. appropriating £40,000 of "the revenue of the Impost and Excise" to pay the charges of Lincoln's forces, including the militia, in putting down Shays' Rebellion. This is followed by Governor Bowdoin's proclamation calling for the arrest of Daniel Shays, Luke Day, Adam Wheeler, and Eli Parsons as "the principles in, and abettors and supporters of this unnatural unprovoked and wicked Rebellion." The third document inserted here is the act of the General Court placing restrictions on those privates and noncommissioned officers among the insurgents who would earn a pardon by laying down their arms and taking an oath of allegiance: those pardoned "shall not [for the next three years] serve as Jurors, be eligible to any Town-office, or any other office under the Government of this Commonwealth, and shall be disqualified from holding or exercising the employments of School-Masters, Inn-Keepers or Retailers of spirituous liquors, or either of them, or giving their votes for the same term of time, for any officer, civil or military, within this Commonwealth." After 1 May 1788 an individual could apply to the General Court to lift any or all such disqualifications (see editorial note). Finally, there is a copy of a senate resolution of 17 Feb. providing for a speedup in the collection of taxes.

12. For the raid from New York led by Perez Hamlin into Massachusetts at Stockbridge and the clash with John Ashley's Sheffield militia, see Feer, *Shays's Rebellion*, 402–4, and notes 1 and 2 on p. 404.

To Battaile Muse

Sir,   Mount Vernon 4th Decr 1786
    As the fifty Bushels of Wheat stands as an article of charge at 5/6 in your account against me, it may remain so as a final settlement of the matter—Although I have no flour at present for

sale and have made no enquiry into the price of this article, I do not suppose I shall either loose or gain much in so small a quantity by fixing the Wheat at this price.[1]

With respect to the persons named in your letter of the 26th Ulto (which is just come to hand) I can only repeat what I have often done before, in substance—and that is that it is my wish to obtain justice to myself but not to act with that rigor in effecting it as to bring ruin or even considerable distress upon poor families—rather than do this I would relinquish my claim; but in all cases of this kind I would endeavor to draw a line between inablility & dishonesty; where the former appears with good dispositions to the latter and to industry I would wish lenient measures may be used[;] where the intention appears fraudulent, no indulgence should be given. These being my sentiments you can apply them to the cases of Rector &c. Thompson as your own judgment under the circumstances as related, shall dictate; keeping the old proverb in view not to—"Sue a beggar and catch a Louse." This adage may apply also to Colo. Kennedy—otherwise if he will not give you security for paying the ballance of my account—in six months or even twelve months (as long as he has assumed the payment, for without this, he might have plead the Act) I would Sue him without further delay.[2]

All these difficulties & losses have arisen from Rents lying over unpaid from year to year; for which reason I am determined that my Rents in future shall be punctually discharged unless there is some interposition of Providence which calls for forbearance. The best Landlord, I am perfectly convinced is he who never suffers two Rents to become due on the same tenement.

In the enclosed (which I request You to forward) I have consented to Fielding Lewis getting timber (if the Tenants having Leases are willing) to build him a house in *Rector Town*, but what use he means to put it to afterwards will, I dare say, puzzle him to tell.[3] I am Sir Your Obt Servt

G. Washington

LS, in George Augustine Washington's hand, NjMoNP; LB, DLC:GW. The address on the cover is in GW's hand.

1. See GW to Muse, 6 May, n.1.

2. For Muse's efforts to collect the debt owed by David Kennedy, see GW to Muse, 8 Mar. 1786, n.3.

3. GW's letter to Fielding Lewis, Jr., is dated 4 December.

To Thomas Peters

Sir,   Mount Vernon 4th Decr 1786
Your letter of the 18th Ulto came duly to hand. From the number of fruitless enquiries I had made for *spring* Barley before I applied to you, and the intervention between the date of my letter and your answer being pretty considerable I despaired of obtaining any of this grain, and therefore seeded the ground which was at first designated for this Crop with Wheat & Rye. I have also since heard that many Gentlemen who have tried it (especially some on West River where I know the Lands are very fine and such as I conceived were well adapted for this grain) do not find it answerable to their expectations—Nevertheless as I wish to divide my seedtime and am desirous of sowing Clover and other grasses with Barley in preference to other grain I would gladly take fifty bushels of it and will depend *absolutely* upon *you* for this quantity which I pray may be sent me as soon as it can be procured, by the Packet. With respect to the latter I am anxious because having the seed in my possession I can lay out & prepare accordingly & not postpone my Oat season in expectation of a Barley one and be disappointed at last of the latter as was the case last year.

If I find this essay likely to answer my expectations I shall be better able to talk with you on a Contract. The Barley may be accompanied by the Machine you spoke of as eligable for cleaning it; and I shall thank you for sending one accordingly. Let me know decidedly if you please whether I may depend upon the above quantity of Barley in the manner mentioned—I have it now in my power (for it is offered to me) to get what I want from a Brewer in Philadelphia but I may even fail here if my engagement with him is delayed long for your answer.[1]

Can *good* Clover seed (not imported seed for that rarely is so) be bought at Baltimore? In what quantity and at what price? There is not, I believe a bushel of Barley of any kind in this neighbourhood for sale—A Mr Wales who Brews in Alexandria procures all of this he can. I am Sir Yr most Obedt Hble Servt
                                        Go: Washington

ALS, NN: Emmet Collection; LB, DLC:GW.
   1. See Clement Biddle to GW, 5 Nov., and GW to Biddle, 5 December.

From Francisco Rendón

Dear General   Philadelphia 4th december 1786.

Having received orders from my Sovereign to repair immediately to Court to give an account of my stewardship & receive
his Royal orders, I cannot quit this Country without taking the
most affectionate leave of your Excellency, and expressing my
gratitude for the friendship with which you have repaid the high
Veneration and sincere attachment which I have always entertained for your person & character. I would have wished it had
been in my power to take your commands before my departure,
but it is so sudden that I have not time to alow myself the satisfaction. It will be to me a heartfull pleasure in giving an account
to his Majesty of the distinguished Character of America, to ex-
patiate particularly on the private Virtues of Genl Washington,
and to delineate to the best of Kings the picture of the best of
Citizens, I am sure that this is the light in which you will please
him best; others have already taught him to admire your talents,
and publick Virtues, it will be my business to teach him to love
your Person. I leave this Country with a heart full of affection
for its inhabitants & full of gratitude for the affection & friendship they have shewn me, with this disposition you may judge,
whether I shall let an opportunity escape of being useful to
America; alow me to repeat my wishes that you may all your life
enjoy that happiness which you have insured to thousands. With
the most perfect Respect and Esteem I have the honor to be sir
your most humble & most obedt servt &ca

Francisco Rendon

P.S. If I could be of any use to you in Spain, I shall be happy to
receive your orders which you may direct to me under cover of
Mr Carmichael, I cannot yet give up the hope of seing this
Country again, and I think it very probable that I shall once
more revisit my old friends of America. Present my best respects
to your Lady and my good friend Majr Whashington.

ALS, DLC:GW.

To James Tilghman

Dr Sir,   Mount Vernon 4th Decr 1786
Your favor of the 14th ulto is but just come to hand, or an earlier reply shou'd have been made to it.

The inscription intended for the Tomb of my deceased friend meets my entire approbation; for I can assure you Sir, with much truth, that after I had opportunities of becoming well acquainted with his worth, no man enjoyed a greater share of my esteem, affection & confidence than Colo. Tilghman.

I now transmit you, for the satisfaction of the friend of your deceas'd son, a statement of the conduct which was observed towards Capt: Asgill during his confinement, by which his illiberality & want of candour will fully appear. These extracts are taken from authentic records, & contain every sentence wherein the name of that officer is mentioned according to my best knowledge & belief.[1]

At length, with much difficulty, I have got all the papers which are to be found, respecting the affairs of the deceased Colo. Thos Colvill, from the son of the principal acting Executor of the Will of that Gentleman. I have put them into the hands of a skilful lawyer to make, if possible, a proper statement of them for final settlement; and as soon as I can speak to any good purpose you shall again hear from me respecting the claim of Miss Anderson.[2] With great esteem, I am &c.

                                        G: Washington

LB, DLC:GW.
1. See David Humphreys to GW, 16 Nov., n.1.
2. Tilghman wrote GW on 7 July 1786 about Harriot Rebecca Anderson's legacy from the Colvill estate. See note 2 of that document. For the difficulties GW recently had in getting in hand the papers relating to the Colvill estate, see GW to Thomas West, 6 November. See also Charles Little to GW, 15 December.

To Clement Biddle

Dear Sir,   Mount Vernon 5th Decr 1786.
Your letters of the 15th of Octr and 5th of Novr are both before me, and I shall reply to them in their order.

For your trouble in negotiating my Certificate I thank you.

If it is necessary (in order) that you may receive the half yearly interest thereon I would wish you to keep it. If you can draw this without it may be sent to me. In the meantime inform me if you please if this certificate can be converted into cash, and upon what terms? that if I should have occasion to make any purchases in Philadelphia I may know the amount of this fund. The Indents to the amount of 84⁵³⁄₉₀ Dollars I have recd and note the credit you have given me for the year & halfs interest.[1]

The Curtains, stuff, & Nails are safe at hand and will answer very well.

The uncertainty of getting good *spring* Barley (for I had made many fruitless enquiries in this State & the parts of Maryland bordering on it before I wrote to you)[2] induced me to put the ground which I had first allotted for this grain into Wheat & rye but if you could procure & send to me by one of the the first vessels bound from your port to Alexandria fifty bushels I will yet find as much ground as will receive this quantity of Seed or if you have engaged one hundred bushls of this grain from Mr Haines as the expression of your letter seems to impart I will readily take it, but would not chuse to be under any promise to supply him with the produce of it—1st because being uncertain of the yield and inclining to go pretty largely upon it if I find it likely to answer my purpose I shall want a good deal for seed another year—and 2d because the frieght around it is to be feared would sink too deep into the sales to render me any profit upon a small quantity.

The Clover seed (as I conceived this had been a productive year of it) is high—yet I would beg you to send me 300 weight— as soon as I know the precise cost of this and the Barley the money shall be remitted—or if you have any dealings in Alexandria & an order on me would answer your purposes equally well it shall be immediately paid. If it is the same thing to Mr Haines whether I take 50 or 100 Bushls of Barley I should under the circumstances already mentioned prefer the ⟨former⟩ quantity.[3] It is so essential to every Farmer to have his seeds by him that I would urge in the strongest terms that these now required be sent me by the first good *Water* conveyance. The uncertainties & disappointments I met with last spring will always make me anxious to obtain all my seeds long before the season for sowing them shall have arrived—At any rate let me know by Post what I have to expect. Best wishes attend Mrs Biddle & your family. I am—Dr Sir Yr most Obedt Hble Servt

Go: Washington

ALS, PHi: Washington Manuscripts; LB, DLC:GW.
    1. See Biddle to GW, 15 Oct., and note 2 of that document.
    2. See, for instance, Thomas Peters to GW, 18 November.
    3. The word in angle brackets is taken from the letter-book copy.

To John Francis Mercer

Sir,   Mount Vernon 5th Decr 1786.

As I have not yet received a reply to my last letter, but, since the date of it, have made some enquiry into the prices of negroes at the ready money sales of them, I take the liberty of informing you, previously to your writing, or my receiving an answer to the above letter, that as it is not likely we shall agree on a price, (in case you should be disposed to spare such negroes as would have answered my purposes) it is my wish to save you the trouble of adding any thing more on the subject of them. Such as I pointed at might have been useful to me; but as I have no desire of adding to my present number by purchase, to accommodate you was the object I had principally in view, but I cannot think of allowing more to effect this, than the same kind of negroes would command at a sale of ready money, because in fact it is a discount of ready money, & for that species of property which I have no inclination to possess. I mention the matter now lest the intimation of such sentiments after an acquiescence with my proposal, should you have been thereto disposed, might be construed a disposition to take advantage of circumstances to reduce the price; rather than a thought of this kind should be entertained, my choice is to await the money in any manner you shall please to offer it.[1]

It was Mr Hunter not Colo. Hooe, that gave the information respecting the price of Corn, as mentioned in my last—I correct the mistake therefore then made, that there may be no representation suspected in the accot.

As I assured you in my last that I had bid adieu to the altercation respecting the appropriation of the money arising from the

Bonds in suit—so I can assure you I have no other motive for enclosing Mr Colston's letter, which only came to my hands the day before yesterday than to let you see his sollicitude to obtain a Deed for the land for which he has paid the consideration money—and to repeat the assurances of my last, that if it is essential for me to execute the Deed, I am ready to do it when it is presented, & I am properly authorised by you so to do.[2] I am Sir, &c.

G: Washington

LB, DLC:GW.

1. See GW to John Francis Mercer, 24 November. See also GW to Mercer, 19 December.

2. GW had only recently received Rawleigh Colston's letter of 10 November. See GW to Colston, 4 December.

Letter not found: from Bourdon, 6 Dec. 1786. On 8 Jan. 1788 GW wrote Bourdon: "I have recd your letter of the 6th of Decr 1786."

From L'Enfant

sir   new york december 6th 1786.

the inclosed memorial which my actual circumstances has mad necessary, rendering it usless I should enter here into any of the particular of its content I confine myself with requesting your Excellency will Excuse the length of it. unable to be concise in an explanation where in it is essential to me to give account of the differents sensations which actuated me I have need of much Indulgence[1]—and the good testimony of your Excellency being alone to persuad of my real principles in such an extraordinary a conjuncture I calim its suport with the more Confidence that I promise myself from your goodness as well as from the details which I take the liberty to submit to you that if in juging me after the event I am found culpable it will at any rate be only of too much Confidence and liberality and convinced I did not bring my self into so unfortunate a situation but through a wish to give a truly brotherly proof of my affection to the interest of the Cincinnati—your Excellency being placed to apprise the valu of the sacrifices which I have made will do me the justice to belive that if I have not done honor to the Engagements which I have been induced to contract in france for the Cincinnati it has not been from a want of my own good will neither through fear that the incapacity of the fund, of the society to reimburse would Expose me to remain the dupe of my advances—had my fortune allowed me to make an immediate sacrifice or could the present State of my personal resources enable me to borrow a sum such as would be necessary to do honor to the principal to gether with the interest of the sum of the advances that have been made to me in france for the society and also to reimburs the loans to which I have been forced to have recourse here I would not hesitate one moment to pay both the one and the other. a regard to my self as well as for the society which it is my wish not to bring in to the question acting conjunctly would surely led me to that measure, but it is with regret I see that with personal means in view—the actual derangement of my affair how ever Cross my inclination so ⟨far⟩ has to oblige me to intrud upon your Excellency by a relation of facts which nothing but the necessity of exculpating myself from charges which seem authorised by my failure to discharge those Engagements which by accident are become personal could only make me resolve to bring to light.

doubtless I ought to have begun this address by an apology for my apparant negligence in not having taken some opportunity during my residence here to have paid my respect to your Excellency agreable to the permission which you so complaisantly gave me—but full of the subject on which I have the honor to address you, it appeared most proper to explain my motives—and then Confiding in your Excellency sensibility of the cause which have taken from me the power of undertaking a journey to virginie I flater myself your Excellency will remain persuaded that this dissappointment has not little added to the bittereness of many other unhappiness. with the most profound respect I have the honor to be sir your Excellency most humble & obedient servant

P. ch. L'Enfant

P.S. a picture directed to your Excellency and which has been left to me, in the cours of last summer, by mr Snelf Col. in the service of the so. carolina—has not been forwarded to your Excellency for want of a direct opportunity by watter which had appeared to us to be the much proper way of conveyance I had proposed to my self being the bearer of it but circumstances not permitting I should if your Excellency will give me directions which way I may send it I will comply.[2]

ALS, DSoCi.

1. The enclosed memorial, running to more than fifty manuscript pages, is in DSoCi and transcribed in CD-ROM:GW. The memorial is L'Enfant's formal statement regarding his financial difficulties arising out of his mission to Paris to have emblems made for members of the Society of the Cincinnati. It is written in much the same style and vein as the letter printed here and includes little or no additional information. See Thomas Jefferson to GW, 7 Jan. 1786, n.1, and Henry Knox to GW, 13 June 1786.

2. See GW to L'Enfant, 1 Jan. 1787, postscript, and note 1. "Mr Snelf" is Christian Senf.

From Edmund Randolph

Sir   Richmond December 6th 1786

By the inclosed Act you will readily discover, that the Assembly are alarmed at the Storms, which threaten the United States.[1] What our enemies have foretold, seems to be hastening to its accomplishment; and cannot be frustrated but by an instantaneous zealous & steady Union among the friends of the fœderal Government: To you I need not press our present dangers. The inefficiency of Congress you have often felt in your Official Character: the increasing langour of our associated republics you hourly see: and a dissolution would be I know to you a source of the deepest mortification.

I freely then intreat you to accept the Unanimous appointment of the General Assembly, to the Convention at Philadelphia. For the gloomy prospect still admits one ray of hope, that those, who began, carried on & consummated the revolution, can yet rescue America from the impending ruin. I have the honor Sir to be with the sincerest Esteem & respect Your most obedt Servant

Edm: Randolph

LS, DLC:GW.

1. In addition to a printed copy of "An Act for Appointing Deputies from this Commonwealth to a Convention Proposed to be Held in the City of Philadelphia in May next, for the Purpose of Revising the Fœderal Constitution," Randolph enclosed copies made by both the clerk of the house of delegates

and the senate of the record of the election of the seven delegates to the convention. GW did not receive Randolph's letter until 20 Dec. (GW to Randolph, 21 Dec.).

To David Stuart

Dear Sir,   Mount Vernon 6th Decr 1786

If Mr Newton of Norfolk should offer you money on my acct, I wd thank you for bringing it.

I have a tenant—one Edward Williams—who I want to punish, because I believe him to be a bad man. I pray you therefore to send me a General Court Writ for him. The case I shall relate—and leave the nature of the writ, & quantum of damages to be filled up by better judges than myself—to frighten—not really to hurt him, is my object.

The case is. He pulls down my fences which are good, and adjoining to him, to let *his stock*, into my Inclosures for the benefit of better pastures than his own. The consequence is, that besides the injury I sustain by having my pastures a common; *my stock* go out and get into his fields, which have not lawful fences, and are there maimed and killed—One Hog of near 200 weight his people were caught in the act of killing; several others of equal size are missing, & no doubt is entertained of their having shared this fate—My wish therefore is to lay the damages high to scare him.[1] I pray you to pay Mr Hopkins ten or 15/ wch I owe him for some service rendered me in the payment of a fee for recording a Deed in the General Ct.[2] What are you about below?—we hear nothing from you now! The Maryld session will be warm. Paper money the cause! The disturbances in Massachusetts have not subsided, on the contrary are growing more systematic—They are alarming, & the evils, if possible, should be averted. To suppose, if they are suffered to go on, they can be kept at the distance they now are, from us, is idle. Fire, where there is inflamable matter, very rarely stops; and nothing is more certain than that, it is better to prevent misfortunes, than to apply remedies when they have happened. I am sincerely & Affecty Yrs

Go: Washington

ALS, PVF.

1. Edward Williams had been a tenant on the neck at Mount Vernon since GW bought it from William Clifton in 1760. GW "bought his lease for 20 pds. and some other priviledges" in February 1787 (*Diaries*, 5:103). See also GW to George Gilpin, 24 Jan. 1787.

2. See GW to John Hopkins, 1 May 1786, n.2.

From Thomas Johnson

sir.   Annapolis 7 Dec. 1786.

I am now able to inclose you a Copy of the Potomack Bill passed both Houses of our Assembly without any Opposition—if there should have any Deviation been made by the Virginia Assembly from the Application we made I beleive I can readily obtain a correspondent Alteration here if it should be necessary.[1]

It has occurred to me that Mr Smith on being furnished with a little pine plank and a Joiner might in a few Days have a Model made of the Locks for the Great Falls so as to exhibit the actual Effect in Miniature[2] I profess it would give me Satisfaction as well perhaps as some degree of pleasure to the other Gent. and might possibly render even Smiths Ideas more correct on the Subject by shewing in Time a defect, if there is any, in his plan—The Winter is so unpromising that I expect we shall be very still till the Spring but if agreeable to the Gent. of Virga, it is so to Mr Lee I wish Brindley to assist and advise on the Survey and Tract at the Little Falls from what Colo. Gilpin said I think we may expect Brindley is disposed to assist us and what would be liberal for his Trouble may be very usefully laid out.

The necessary Demands of Congress our own poverty and want of Spirit—the Distractions to the Eastward and our Rage for paper Money make my Time pass away here heavily enough—I am afraid I shall learn in the latter part of my Life that Americans are not so good as I thought them—a Lesson much against my Will. I am my dear sir With great Truth & Affection Your most obedt Servt

Th: Johnson

ALS, DLC:GW.

1. For the act passed by the Maryland legislature regarding the Potomac River Company, see GW to David Stuart, 5 Nov., n.1.

2. This may be James Smith who in 1788 succeeded Richardson Stewart as manager of the Potomac River Company. See GW to George Gilpin, 29 May 1786.

From James Madison

Dear Sir   Richmond Decr 7th 1786
Notwithstanding the communications in your favor of the
18th Ult: which has remained till now to be acknowledged, it
was the opinion of every judicious friend whom I consulted that
your name could not be spared from the Deputation to the
Meeting in May in Philada. It was supposed that in the first
place, the peculiarity of the mission and its acknowledged pre-
eminence over every other public object, may possibly reconcile
your undertaking it, with the respect which is justly due & which
you wish to pay to the late officers of the army; and in the second
place that although you should find that or any other consideration an obstacle to your attendance on the service, the advantage of having your name in the front of the appointment as a
mark of the earnestness of Virginia, and an invitation to the
most select characters from every part of the Confederacy, ought
at all events to be made use of. In these sentiments I own I fully
concurred, and flatter myself that they will at least apologize for
my departure from those held out in your letter. I even flatter
myself that they will merit a serious consideration with yourself,
whether the difficulties which you enumerate ought not to give
way to them.[1]
The Affair of the Mississippi which was brought before the
Assembly in a long Memorial from the Western Members &
some of the Officers, has undergone a full consideration of both
houses. The Resolutions printed in the papers, were agreed to
unanimously in the H. of Delegates. In the Senate I am told the
language was objected to by some members as too pointed. They
certainly express in substance the decided Sence of this Country
at this time on the subject, and were offered in the place of some
which went much farther and which were in other respects exceptionable. I am entirely convinced from what I observe here,
that unless the project of Congs can be reversed, the hopes of
carrying this State into a proper federal system will be demol-
ished. Many of our most federal leading men are extremely
soured with what has already passed. Mr Henry, who has been
hitherto the Champion of the federal cause, has become a cold
advocate, and in the event of an actual sacrifice of the Misspi by
Congress, will unquestionably go over to the opposite side. I

have a letter from Col. Grayson of late date which tells me that nothing further has been done in Congs and one from Mr Clarke of N. Jersey, which informs me that he expected every hour, instructions from his Legislature for reversing the vote given by the Delegates of that State in favor of the Project.[2]

The temper of the Assembly at the beginning of the Session augured an escape of every measure this year, not consonant to the proper principles of Legislation. I fear now that the conclusion will contradict the promising outset. In admitting Tobo for a commutable, we perhaps swerved a little from the line in which we set out. I acquiesed in the measure myself, as a prudential compliance with the clamours within doors & without, and as a probable means of obviating more hurtful experiments. I find however now that it either had no such tendency, or that schemes were in embrio which I was not aware of.[3] A bill for establishing district Courts has been clogged with a plan for installing all debts now due, so as to make them payable in three annual portions. What the fate of the experiment will be I know not. It seems pretty certain that if it fails the bill will fail with it. It is urged in support of this measure that it will be favorable to debtors & creditors both, and that without it, the bill for accelerating Justice would ruin the former, and endanger the public repose. The objections are so numerous and of such a nature, that I shall myself give up the bill rather than pay such a price for it.[4] With unfeigned affection & the higst respt, I am Dr Sr Yr Obedt hble servt

Js Madison Jr

ALS, PHi: Gratz Collection; signed copy, in Madison's hand, DLC: Madison Papers.

1. In response to Madison's allusions on 8 Nov. to the intention of the legislature to place GW's name at the head of a list of delegates from Virginia to the federal convention in Philadelphia, GW wrote Madison on 18 Nov. that he would not be able to obey the "call" of the legislature with "any degree of consistency" because he had notified the Society of the Cincinnati that he would be unable to attend its General Meeting to be held in Philadelphia at the same time as the federal convention. GW subsequently wrote to a number of others to express his misgivings about attending the constitutional convention (see, for examples, his letters to David Stuart, 19 Nov. 1786, to David Humphreys, 26 Dec. 1786, and to Henry Knox, 3 Feb. 1787).

2. For Madison's report to Thomas Jefferson on 4 Dec. of the action of the house of delegates regarding the Mississippi River, see David Stuart to GW, 13

Nov. 1786, n.3. William Grayson's letter to Madison is dated 22 Nov., and Abraham Clark's, 23 November.

3. The tax bill provided that duties to be paid in specie could be paid in tobacco at its market price. GW was unmoved by Madison's explanation of his vote and expressed his opposition in strong terms on 16 December. See also Madison to GW, 24 December.

4. See GW to Madison, 24 Dec., and note 1 of that document.

Letter not found: from Edward Newenham, 9 Dec. 1786. On 25 Dec. 1787 GW wrote Newenham that he had received his letter "of the 9th of Decr 1786."

Letter not found: from John Francis Mercer, 10 Dec. 1786. On 19 Dec. GW wrote Mercer: "I received your favor of the 10th."

Letter not found: from Thomas Seddon & Co., 10 Dec. 1786. GW wrote Seddon & Co. on 9 Jan. 1787: "I have received your letter of the 10th of Decemr."

From George William Fairfax

My Dear Sir,   Bath 12th Decr 1786

Hearing by accident that a Ship will sail in a Day or two from Bristol for Virginia I just Embrace the first opportunity of acknowledging the receipt of your very kind Letter of the 30th of June last, covering your draft on Wakelin Welch Esqr. for 155:14:9 Sterling, which I doubt not will be duly honor'd. And now my good Sir, I am to express my concern, that You should even hint anything about Interest, or paying for the little Furniture I desired you to accept. had it been more than trebble it would be a very poor acknowledgement for the trouble you had previous to the last and you cant think how exceeding[l]y it hurts me to find, that so much of your time has been given up in looking over my Papers and reciting so particularly our Correspondence since I left the Country, for which it will never be in my power to make you suitable returns. all that I can say at present is that every Act of yours meets with my utmost approbation, and that I shall ever gratefully acknowledge them. Yet my good friend I must Confess that many of your refferences are, and will be very satisfactory, as I cannot recur (if there had been occation) but to a very few of the Letters I have received within those periods or during the War, for I was a marked Man and closely watched during the War, and upon a hint from two of my best friends here, I found it necessary to destroy most of them, least they should fall into the Missengers hands that was sent after me, and by comparing them with those that Ld Dunmore stoped and sent to the Secretary of States Office, I might be confined in some loathful Jail or other, if not worse. however to shorten this Subject I was by the interposition of a Friend, who I thought knew not[h]ing of my danger and without sollicitation the Proceedings was stoped and I once again at ease.

Now my Dear Sir I shall proceed with what I intended before I made the above long digression, and that was to say that I should have written to You by our Nephew Mr T. Fairfax had I not just before his leaving Us, wrote to you by one James Bloxham, who I took the liberty to direct his waiting upon you, that you migh[t] Employ him or not as a working husbandman, and should have been doubtful whether the Packet he carried, or indeed himself had arrived safe had not Mr T. Fx mentioned in a Letter to Mr Athawes that he had seen Bloxham.[1] In my Letter by him I said I should be dilligent in my enquiries after a Skilful Farmer or Bailiff, and very truely I have, as well as in engaging many judicious Gent. in the Counties where it's agreed that Agriculture is brought to the greatest perfection to second my enquiries, from some of the Gent. there is a prospect of success, but can come to no determinatn untill they know what Wages you are willing to give and to find such as you describe Bed and Board. I have also the promise of Thomas Gilbert Esq: (who has the direction of all the Duke of Bridgewaters navigations) to look out for a very skilfu⟨l⟩ Person in that way, but such a one holds up their heads and asks high Salaries and wants to be upon a certainty before they Embark, therefore it must rest upon you I find to be Explicit in the Terms, for they all decline naming their own.[2] And then I trust and hope amongst Us you may get proper People to carry on your laudable Plans in such way. I have this instant had notice, that unless my Letters are not in Bristol this night they will loose there conveyance. Therefore have only to add at present, that we both sincerely unite in every sentiment of respect to you and Lady and am Dear Sir your Affect. and obliged humble Servt

G:W: Fairfax

ALS, DLC:GW.

1. See Fairfax to GW, 23 Jan. 1786.

2. Thomas Gilbert (1720–1798), who enjoyed the patronage of the duke of Bridgewater, was a reformist member of Parliament from 1763 to 1795 and was a close associate of James Brindley, Sr. See James Rumsey to GW, 29 Mar. 1786, n.1, and GW to William Moultrie, 25 May 1786.

To Edmund Randolph

Dr Sir,   Mount Vernon 12th Decr 1786

The Gentleman who does me the honor of delivering this letter to you is Mr Anstey. He is introduced to me in a very favorable point of view by our old acquaintance & friend Colol Fairfax of Bath, & by Mr Jay of New York.[1]

Mr Anstey being on a tour to Charleston, & purposeing to take richmond in the route, I use the liberty of introducing him to your civilities—and to assure you of the great regard & respect with which, I have the honor to be &c.

G: Washington

LB, DLC:GW.

1. George William Fairfax's letter introducing John Anstey is dated 25 Jan. 1786; Jay's letter, dated 20 Oct. 1786, is printed in note 1 of Fairfax's letter.

From Charles Little

Sir   Clish Decr 15th 1786

I would have complyed with my promise: given your Execellencey; before this time, but have been from home for several days. I have now colected all the papers; and accounts which relate to Colo. Thos Colvile's; affairs[.] them with a Bond of Sidney Georges, which I found amongst John Colvils, papers, I have Inclosed you.[1] I have The Honour to be with due respect your Excellency's Very Humble Servt

Charles Little

ALS, DLC:GW. An examination of the manuscript reveals that Little probably inserted the punctuation after writing the letter, perhaps explaining the semicolon after "Colvile's."

Charles Little (c.1744–1813), a Scot who came to Virginia in 1768 and married Mary Manley, bought Cleesh, at the head of Hunting Creek, from the estate of Thomas Colvill.

1. Sidney George was the eldest son of Sidney George (d. 1744) of Cecil County, Maryland. According to GW, Little was acting as agent for the Tankervilles in England. For the Tankerville involvement in the Colvill estate, see GW to Tankerville (Charles Bennett, 4th earl of Tankerville), 20 Jan. 1784, n.1; for GW's role in settling the estate, see the references in that note.

To Philip Marsteller

Sir,   M[oun]t Vernon 15th Decr 1786

To the severity of the weather, wch has in a manner shut every thing up, and put a stop to all intercourse; & to some other circumstances unnecessary to mention, is to be ascribed my silence 'till now: and even now, when I recollect how fully I have already explained my ideas to you on what is intended to be the subject of this letter, I find that I have hardly anything to trouble you with by way of illucidation.

I will just observe, however, that having been well informed that seasons & circumstances *have occurred*, and probably *will arive again*, when goods by vendue have sold considerably below the Sterlg cost of them: nay, that they have even been bought for the nominal sum currency, which they cost sterling in the countries from whence they were imported; and having found from experience, that I derive little or no advantage from the ready money payments I make for such articles as are requisite for the use of my Estate, (when I go to the Stores in Alexandria) I had determined to make the proposition to you which was pretty fully explained in the conversation I had with you at our last interview, as has been already mentioned, & which in a word is as follows:[1]

To allow you a Commission of 2½ ⅌ Ct (which you yourself declared was sufficient) upon all purchases you shall make for me at Vendue, of articles which may from time to time be enumerated to you. It is your interest I know to sell high; it is mine to buy low: but there is nothing incompatible that I can conceive, in your agency in both these cases; for when the former is the case, I mean not to become a purchaser—when the latter happens, which no skill or exertion of your's can at all times prevent, is the moment of which I mean, thro' your attention to the business, to avail myself for supplies. To your knowledge of the good[s] which are intended for sale; the circumstances of the sale, & to your honor, of which I entertain a very favourable opinion from the good report made of it by others, I entirely confide for the management. The payments shall always keep pace with the purchases; you have nothing more to do therefore than to give intimation of the latter by a line lodged at the post office, to receive the former: & were you now & then to add a concise list of the principal articles which are for sale, it would be obliging.

To particularize all the articles which are necessary for the use of a large family, would be as tedious as unnecessary. Every Merchant who retails, & every man who provides for one, can be at no loss for them. The heavy articles, & such as at present occur to me are enumerated in the enclosed list:[2] in which you will perceive no mention is made of coarse Woolens; because of these I manufacture a sufficiency to clothe my out-door Negroes— nor have I said anything of Wines, because I import my own; but of the latter, if *good* Claret should at any time go cheap, I would take two or three Boxes. I have been obliged to buy about 200 ells of Ticklenburg for present use; perhaps the 2 or 300 more enumerated in the inclosed, may suffice—possibly more may be wanted. The Blankets will not be wanted before next autumn. Of sugars, my demand (as a private family) is great and constant; but of Coffee & Molasses, I have on hand a large stock.

It is scarcely necessary to impress on you the idea that it is the prospect of *very* cheap buying which has induced me to adopt this mode of obtaining my supplies; and that unless this end is accomplished, my purposes will not be answered, nor my inclination gratified by it; but to prevent mistakes I explicitly declare it. Few of the enumerated articles am I in present want of— those for which I shall soonest have a call, are marked thus (*) in the margin; many of the others I may dispense with a year, or two years.[3] They stand in the List as a memento only, in case *very* favorable moments present, for the purchase of them.

I am told it some times happens that Goods which come under the imputation of being damaged, tho' in fact they have received little or no real injury, are frequently sold uncommonly low indeed—particularly Bale blanketing, & other Bale goods. To embrace such opportunities is recommended, but in this, judgment and a close inspection are necessary; for it is not the lowest priced goods that are always the cheapest—the quality is, or ought to be as much an object with the purchaser, as the price.[4]

I pray you to accept my thanks for the trouble you had with the German redemptioners which were purchased for me: the expense my Nephew, the bearer of this, will pay. I am Sir &c.

G: Washington

LB, DLC:GW.

1. GW's most recent interview with Marsteller may have been on 25 Nov. when GW went up to Alexandria and "Bought the time" of the Overdonck family from Marsteller (*Diaries*, 5:70).

2. The letter-book copy of the "Invoice of Goods wanted by George Washington, on the terms mentioned in his letter to Mr P. Marsteller" lists such cloth and clothing as osnaburg or ticklenburg, linen, Russian sheeting and drillings, cambric, jeans or fustians, striped blanketing, hose "for my Negroes," felt hats for black and white servants, and buttons. He also lists white and red lead, window glass, twine, deep-sea lines, rope, sugar, "letter Paper," porter, Cheshire and Gloucester cheeses, corks, wool cards, nails, locks, steel, files, scythes, hinges, sieves, spades, shovels, salad oil, and mustard.

3. The copyist did not add the asterisk that GW had used to indicate which were priority items.

4. Marsteller replied from Alexandria on 18 Dec.: "I acknowledge the receipt of your favor of the 15th Instant covering a list of Sundry Articles which may from time to time be wanted—I shall use my endeavors to get them at Such time when Sales are lowest in order to Answer your expectations which I hope to be able to do. The Article more particularly wanted now of course will be my first Object, but loaf Sugar seldom comes to Vendue, unless it be much damaged—I am just setting out on Business therefore hope your Excellency will excuse my Short Scetch—as to the redemptioners there is no farther Charge save the Freight to Mr Watson & Co." (DLC:GW).

To Josiah Watson

Sir,   Mount Vernon 15th Decr 1786.

I am exceedingly anxious, to bring the Administration of Colo. Colvill's Estate to a close. To do this, & to discharge some claims on it, (one of which is very pressing) it is become indispensably necessary that the Bond in which you are joined with the late Major Moody, should be paid off. I persuade myself there will be no further delay in doing it when the indulgencies which have already been given, & when the circumstances attending this transaction are, moreover, recurred to. Tho' Majr Moody stands foremost in the Bond, he was not at the time it was taken, nor has he at any period since been considered as the principal. It will be remembered, I am certain, that I was assured on that occasion, (tho' a credit of twelve months was given) the Bond should not remain unpaid so long: five years have since elapsed. More than a year ago when application, thro' Mr Lund Washington, was made for this money, he was referred, as he informed me, to the heir or Executor of the deceased Mr Moody; but under the circumstances of this case, I beg leave to add that I must look to you for payment.[1] I would have waited yet longer in expectation of having this money tendered to me, but for the reasons above; & which I pray you to receive as the apology for my being so urgent & so explicit now. With esteem, I am Sir &c.

G: Washington

P.S. If it is convenient to you, the price of the redemptioners, & the cost of the Osnabrigs may go in payment; if it is not, I will send you the money.[2] In [   ] last the son of Mr Moody paid me £[   ].[3]

LB, DLC:GW.

Josiah Watson, an Englishman, had been a respected merchant in Alexandria since before the Revolution.

1. Benjamin Moody (d. 1784) in 1768 bought about six hundred acres of land on Accotink Creek in Fairfax County from the estate of Thomas Colvill. Moody did not receive title to the land because of a dispute over the survey, but in November 1781 Moody agreed to pay £329 for the land in installments, the first of which his son Thomas paid in May 1786. For a full discussion of GW's dealings as a trustee of the Colvill estate with the Moodys, see GW to John West, Jr., 4 July 1773.

2. Philip Marsteller wrote GW on 18 Dec. that he owed nothing further to Watson except freight for the passage of the redemptioners, the Overdoncks (see GW to Marsteller, 15 Dec., n.4; see also GW to Marsteller, 27 Nov.). In his accounts, GW credits Watson in February 1787 for "two Dutch redemptioners & 1 peice of Oznamburge . . . in part payment of a Bond due from Mr Benjn Moody to the Estate of Colo. Thomas Colvill," valued at £45.15.3, and, on 5 April 1787, with £13.4.9 "on Acct of Colo. Colvill's Estate, in behalf of Mr Thos Moody" (Ledger B, 245).

3. GW gave this receipt dated 18 May 1786 at Mount Vernon to Moody: "Received from Mr Thomas Moody Ninety five pounds thirteen shillings Currt money (Specie) of Virginia; in part payment of a Bond given to me as Execr of the will of Thos Colvil Esqr. deceased, by Mr Benja. Moody his late father, with Messrs Josiah Watson and James Hendricks as Securities thereto, for Three hundred and Twenty nine pounds and dated the 19th of Novr 1781. Go: Washington" (ADS [photocopy], DLC:GW).

To James Madison

My dear Sir,   Mount Vernon Decr 16th 1786.

Your favor of the 7th came to hand the evening before last. The resolutions which you say are inserted in the Papers, I have not yet seen. The latter come irregularly, tho' I am a subscriber to Hays Gazette.[1]

Besides the reasons which are assigned in my circular letter to the several State Societies of the Cincinnati, for my nonattendance at the next General meeting to be holden in Philadelphia the first Monday of May, there exists one of a political nature, which operates more *forceably* on my mind than all the others; and which, in confidence, I will now communicate to you.

When this Society was first formed, I am persuaded not a member of it conceived that it would give birth to those Jealousies, or be chargeable with those dangers (real or imaginary) with which the minds of many, & some of respectable characters, were filled. The motives which induced the Officers to enter into it were, I am confident, truly & frankly recited in the Institution: one of which, indeed the principal, was to establish a charitable fund for the relief of such of their compatriots—the Widows— and dependants of them—as were fit subjects for their support; & for whom no *public* provision had been made. But the trumpet being sounded, the alarm was spreading far & wide; I readily perceived therefore that unless a modification of the plan could be effected (—to anihilate the Society altogether was impracticable, on acct of the foreign Officers who had been admitted)—that irritations wd arise which would soon draw a line betwn the Society, & their fellow Citizens. To prevent this—To conciliate the affections—And to convince the World of the purity of the plan—I exerted myself, and with much difficulty, effected the changes which appeared in the recommendation from the General Meeting to those of the States; the accomplishment of which was not easy; & I have since heard, that whilst some States acceded to the recommendation, others are not disposed thereto, alledging that, unreasonable prejudices and ill founded jealousies ought not to influence a measure laudable in its institution, & salutary in its objects & operation.[2] Under these circumstances, there will be no difficulty in conceiving, that the part I should have had to have acted, would have been delicate. On the one hand, I might be charged with dereliction to the Officers, who had nobly supported, and had treated me with uncommon marks of attention and attachment. On the other, with supporting a measure incompatible (some say) with republican principles. I thought it best therefore without assigning this (the principal reason) to decline the Presidency, and to excuse my attendance at the meeting on the ground, which is firm & just; the necessity of paying attention to my private concerns; the conformity to my determination of passing the remainder of my days in a state of retirement—and to indisposition; occasioned by Rheumatick complaints with which, at times, I am a good deal afflicted. Professing at the same time my entire approbation of the institution as altered, and the pleasure I feel at the subsidence of those Jealousies which yielded to the change. *Presuming*, on the general adoption of them.

I have been thus particular to shew, that under circumstances like these, I should feel myself in an awkward situation to be in Philadelphia on another public occasion during the sitting of this Society. That the pres[en]t æra is pregnant of great, & *strange* events; none who will cast their eyes around them, can deny—what may be brought forth between this and the first of May to remove the difficulties which at present labour in my mind, against the acceptance of the honor, which has lately been conferred on me by the Assembly, is not for me to predict; but I should think it incompatible with that candour which ought to characterize an honest mind, not to declare that under my present view of the matter, I should be too much embarrassed by the meetings of these two bodies in the same place, in the same moment (after what I have written) to be easy in the situation; and consequently, that it wd be improper to let my appointment stand in the way of any other.

Of this, you who have had the whole matter fully before you, will judge; for having received no other than private intimation of my election, and unacquainted with the formalities which are, or ought to be used on these occasions, silence may be deceptious, or considered as disrespectful; The imputation of both, or either, I would wish to avoid. This is the cause of the present disclosure, immediately on the receipt of your letter, which has been locked up by Ice; for I have had no communication with Alexandria for many days, till the day before yesterday.[3]

My Sentiments are decidedly against Commutables; for sure I am it will be found a tax without a revenue. That the people will be burthened—The public expectation deceived—and a few Speculators *only* enriched—Thus the matter will end, after the morals of *some*, are more corrupted than they now are—and the minds of *all*, filled with more leaven, by finding themselves taxed, and the public demands in full force. Tobacco, on acct of the public places of deposit, and from the accustomed mode of negotiating the article, is certainly better fitted for a commutable than any other production of this Country; but if I understand the matter rightly (I have it from report only) will any man pay five pound in specie for five taxables, when the same sum (supposing Tobo not to exceed 20/ pr Ct) will purchase 500 lbs. of Tobo & thus, if at 28/ will discharge the tax on Seven? And will not the man who neither makes, nor can easily procure this commodity, complain of the inequality of such a mode, especially when he finds that the revenue is diminished by the difference be it what it may, between the real & nominal price and that he is again to be taxed to make this good? These, & such like things, in my humble opinion, are extremely hurtful, and are among the principal causes of the present depravity & corruption without accomplishing the object in view for it is not the shadow, but the substance with which Taxes must be paid, if we mean to be honest.[4] With sentiments of sincere esteem & regard—I am—Dear Sir—Yr most Obedt & Affe. Servt

Go: Washington

ALS, PPRF; LB, DLC:GW.

1. The *Virginia Gazette, or, the American Advertiser* (Richmond) was printed by James Hayes.

2. For the record of GW's strenuous and successful efforts in 1784 to persuade the delegates of the Society of the Cincinnati to alter its Institution, or constitution, radically, see General Meeting of the Society of the Cincinnati, 4–18 May 1784 (*Papers, Confederation Series*, 1:328–69).

3. Madison's letter is dated 7 December. Gov. Edmund Randolph's letter officially informing GW of his election as a delegate to the federal convention was dated 6 Dec., but GW did not receive it until 20 Dec. (see GW to Randolph, 21 Dec.).

4. See Madison's letters of 7 and 24 December.

From Henry Knox

My dear Sir   New York 17 December 1786
    I did myself the pleasure of writing to you last month, and
stated generally that certain disturbances existed in Massachusetts. Since that period the legislature have been sitting, and en-
devoring to conciliate the minds of the disafected, and perhaps
in some instances by unjust means. There are people however
who hold that if a measure be right in itself, one Should not be
very delicate respecting the means by which it is to be accomplished. I beleive this doctrine may without much hesitation be
pronound infamous. But such as it is, there have been people in
all ages practising upon it.[1]
    The insurgents of Massachusetts are generally supposed by
the people of the other states to be a class of people who are in
a considerable degree oppressed by that government. It is true
that the legislature have stretched the powers of direct taxation
far, perhaps too much so and that they have expressed their
detestation of paper money.
    But the Source of the evil is in the nature of the government,
which is not constituted for the purposes of man possessing bois-
terous passions, and improper views. This is apparent from the
events which have happened.
    In some of the counties, one fifth part of the people of little
or no property are dissatisfied, more with their pecuniary than
their political circumstances, and appeal to arms. Their first acts
are to annihilate their courts of Justice, that is private debts—
The Second, to abolish the public debt and the third is to have
a division of property by means of the darling object of most
of the States paper money. A Government without any existing
means of coercion, are at a loss how to combat, or avert a danger
so new & so pressing.
    The legislature is convened—They differ in sentiment—They
pass temporizing expedients—The insurgents despise their im-
potency and proceed in the execution of their designs—At last
the goverment begin to think that nothing but force is adequate
to meet usage so blind and so unjust—In this moment they are
beginning to see their true situation.
    The County courts of common pleas which meet four times
in a year, and in which, all actions for debt originate, are the

great greviance of the insurgents—They have therefore in the western counties of Berkshire, Hampshire and Worcester, prevented these courts from proceeding to business for a term or two past. In Bristol the effect has been nearly the same. In middlesex this court was prevented from doing business in Septr last by the insurgents. On the 29h ultimo the same court was by rule to meet at Cambridge—The insurgents determined to prevent, and the government to protect it. The severity of the weather, and the excessive deep snows however prevented the insurgents from meeting at their rendevouz in such numbers As to make the attempt, & the court proceeded to business without molestation.

A Body of horse, which was collected from Boston and its vicinity made a forced march to the extremity of Middlesex and seized three of the principal insurgents of that County, and conveyed them to Boston Goal by virtue of the suspension of the habeus Corpus act.[2]

On the 5th instant the commonpleas were to have met at Worcester, but were prevented by a large body of armed insurgents—These amounted on the 8th instant to about 1500 men, and it is said their object was the liberation of their Associates confined in Boston goal, and that they had for this purpose sent a Messenger to the Governor, and informed him that if he would release the prisoners, they would disband otherwise they would proceed to Boston.[3] This is the last advice the mail not having arrived to day according to custom. I imagine the insurgents will disband without obtaining the release of the prisoners but it is probable they may seize some friends of government as a security of the prisoners in Boston. Things will rankle and fester untill next spring when it is likely they will assume a decided aspect.

How far these commotions may be extended it is not easy to say, because they depend a good deal on the habits of the States, and their compliance with paper money and other measures tending to avert taxation and industry It is probable that about one fifth part of the people of New-England whose habits and manners are similar are liable to be infected by the principles of the Insurgents, and of consequence to act in the same manner.

Were these to be combined into one body they would form a large Army but this is not probable. It is however my opinion that unless matters should be compromised during the Winter, that it is possible that 12, or 15000, men may be embodied next spring or summer, whose veiws may be directed to any object whatever even the establishment of a tyranny, or a return to great Britain.

You are well acquainted with the subtelity of the characters of Sir Guy Carleton now Lord Dorchester, and Mr Wm Smith formerly of New York but now Chief Justice of Canada who have lately arrived at Quebec—At the conclusion of the war, the latter held it up as a maxim, that peace was the only medium of a re-union of America with great Britain—He still persists in that idea.

My apprehension respecting the insurgents are nearly the same as they were respecting a mutiny of the Army—That they must throw themselves into the arms of the british—A rebellion of 10,000 men against our governments would indisputably se-cure encouragement from Canada—Not as a government but in such secret modes, as never could be traced—In the present temper and dispositions of the New England Insurgents 200,000 pounds sterling would I am persuaded, induce 10,000 men to embody next year, and would with what they could ob-tain by their own exertions support them for a campaign—If my conjectures be founded the next year will be an important one indeed.

Mrs Knox joins in presenting our affectionate respects to you and Mrs Washington. I am my dear Sir Your sincere and very humble Servant

H. Knox

ALS, DLC:GW.

1. Knox is undoubtedly referring to measures adopted by the Massachu-setts General Court in its recent session, when it passed a new riot act and authorized the governor to issue a general search warrant and, under certain conditions, to suspend the writ of habeas corpus. See Benjamin Lincoln to GW, 4 Dec. 1786–4 Mar. 1787, editorial note.

2. Armed with a warrant for arrest from Gov. James Bowdoin, a detachment composed of horsemen from the militias of Middlesex and Suffolk counties and a cavalry company formed by young Boston merchants set out for Groton on 29 Nov. and the next day captured the leaders of the Middlesex insurgents, Job Shattuck, Oliver Parker, and Benjamin Paige (Feer, *Shays's Rebellion*, 317–21).

3. For a fuller description of this incident and references to relevant docu-ments, see ibid., 323–25. See also Knox to GW, 21 December.

From Thomas Freeman

Redstone [Pa.]

May it Please your Excellency   Decr the 18th 1786

I had the favour of yours by Mr Lear, and by that I imagine you did not receive mine of the 9th October, in which I gave you an Acct of the Sale of the Negroes &c. therefore I have Inclosed a Copy of the same herewith to you.[1] I have likewise sent the Money in my hands & taken Mr Lears Receipt for the same the sum is Thirty six pounds Fifteen shillings & Sixpence[2] I have not sent any Acct by him as most of the Debt are still unpaid and the Wheat not yet in the Mill, you will see that the Sale of Corn Hay &c. are so verry low that I Determined to keep the wheat in the Mills taking the Millers Receipts untill there may be a Market at present there is none[.] I have Sold only One Hundred Bushell since I came home ⟨asid⟩ that I gave one Years Credit unto Capt. Uriah Springer it being the wheat Paid by Huston & Pounds for your part of the Rattion I sold it at four shillings ℔ Bushl and shall give the Bond into Mr Smiths hand with the rest I have obtained and take his Receipt,[3] I shall endeavour if possible to come down before I set of to Kentucky & make a final settlement with you, that is if any money of Consequence comes into my hands for at present there is a Call for money almost as fast I can Collect it there is a Demand now for somewhere about Fifty Shillings for a Road Tax, Should it prove so that I cannot come down I shall render a true State of all Affairs under my care to Mr Smith who will I make no doubt take care of them, and Deliver them safe to you.

In the Sale of the Negroes there is one Named Dorcas that you Receivd of Mr Simpson as a Slave proves to be free at the Age of Twenty Eight Years the Records from Westmoreland we had & I took the Supreme Judge McKeans Opinion on the matter & he declares her free, so that you must have recourse to Mr Simpson as you Settled with him at the rate of Thirty Pounds and now after keeping her Two Years she Sold at Thirteen Pounds fifteen shillings as ℔ acct.

I should not have Sold the Negroes but they would not be Prevailed with to come down from any Argument I could use.[4]

The Money Paid on Acct of Coll John A. Washington I have sent down the receipts as it may be you will see the Coll before I come down & you can settle with him as you see cause.[5]

The place wher Mr Simpson lived is without any Tenant the Situation &c. Mr Lear will Inform you—as also of all the Tenements in this Quarter, I have had some Applicants in regard to the Sale of the Bottome but I could ⟨*illegible*⟩ not tell what might be the price none would come down to you for fear they should not agree and the Journey being long, and now I have Received your farther Instructions I cannot realy say how they will Sell but Imagine from your giving such Credit there may be some Expectation it will Sell and If any Person or a Number of Persons together would Buy the whole I think it is the likeliest way as it may then be Sold at a Moderate Price and in Selling of Lotts or Parcells it must go high as the best will be first Chosen Small Tracts of about the same Value have been Sold in this Settlement lately at forty Shillings ℔ Acre, tho' Lands as well as other Property at this time is but a Dull Market.

I mentioned before I had not sent down the Accts Nevertheless you may be desirous of knowing Who has paid me since I came from you I have underneath Mentioned the different Names & Sums Received.[6]

The within Memorandum will shew what is & from whom the Sums are Received. I shall Endeavour to State the same Regularly at Settlement till then I hope this will be Satisfactory. I am your Excellencys most Hble Servant

Thomas Freeman

ALS, DLC:GW. "Favoured by Mr Lear" is written on the cover.

1. GW's letter to Freeman is dated 28 Nov.; Freeman's letter to GW of 9 Oct. has not been found. See GW to Tobias Lear, 30 November. Freeman headed his enclosure "Memorandum of the Sale of the Negroes &c. at Washingtons Bottoms Octr 5th 1786." In 1773 GW sent four slaves up to Washington's Bottom on the Youghiogheny where Gilbert Simpson, as GW's partner, was attempting to establish a plantation (GW to Simpson, 23 Feb. 1773, n.1, and Simpson to GW, 1 Oct. 1773, n.2). More than twelve years later, on 16 Oct. 1785, GW instructed his agent in Pennsylvania, Thomas Freeman, to send the slaves at Washington's Bottom down to Mount Vernon "if the measure can be reconciled to them." There were nine slaves on the property, and none of them—including the two surviving of the original four, Simon and Nancy (Nance)—were willing to go to Virginia. Freeman's memorandum shows that Simon was sold to Bazil and Thomas Brown for £100; Joe, Allice, and Dorcas, to Ephraim Douglass for £81, £70.15, and £13.15 respectively; Lydia, to Peter and Thomas Patterson for £45.10; "Nance & Young Child," to James Hammond for £80.5; and "Tom & Charity The Twins to Samuel Burns" for £27.10 (DLC:GW).

2. In his cash accounts GW records receiving by Tobias Lear £29.8.5 Virginia currency (Ledger B, 233).

3. GW in May 1787 received from Freeman £427.3.4½ in Virginia currency for "Bonds & Notes put into the hands of Thomas Smith Esqr. to recover for me, being given for effects sold & rent due from my Estate in Fayette County, Pensylvania" (Ledger B, 233). See also GW to Thomas Smith, 16 Sept. 1787, and Thomas Smith to GW, 5 Feb. 1788.

4. See note 1.

5. GW notes on 28 Dec. 1786 in his account with Freeman the receipt of £9.12.0 in Virginia currency "on Acct of Ejectments brot by Colo. Jno. A. Washingn in Fayette Court" (Ledger B, 233). See also GW to Tobias Lear, 30 Nov. 1786.

6. Inserted here is a partially illegible notation listing collections since 2 Sept. 1786 of money due for rent, or notes, and for sale of corn, totaling £65.1.⟨2⟩, and payments, including £36.15.6 to Tobias Lear for GW and £12 in cash, "pr Receipts," to Thomas Smith.

To John Francis Mercer

Sir,   Mount Vernon 19th Decr 1786.

I received your favor of the 10th, last night.[1] The letter I addressed to you about fourteen days ago I was in hopes would have reached you before your reply to my former, would have been dispatched, & thereby have saved you the trouble of again touching on the subject of negroes.

I can have no idea of giving eighty or ninety pounds a head for slaves when I am well informed that for ready money the best common labouring negroes in this State, may be bought for less than sixty & others in proportion. For this species of property I have no predilection nor any urgent call, being already over stocked with some kind of it; consequently can have no inducement to give 50 pr Ct more than the like property is offered for & doth actually sell at. A payment in negroes, if this was to take place, can be considered in no other light by either of us, than as ready money; it stops the payment of it, & is I presume a convenience. But to supercede the necessity of enforcing these observations, & to remove every suspicion which might have arisen in your mind, of a desire in me to beat you down in the price of your slaves, was the cause of my last address to you.

As the design however has not been accomplished; & it is necessary both for your information, & for my satisfaction & government that something decisive should be resolved on, I will, in one word, fix my ultimatum with respect to the negroes proposed for sale. Which is to allow you three hundred pounds for young Bob (or an other fellow of his age & appearance), Tom the baker—Massey, David, James & Valentine; but this I do on the proviso that they answer your description in their ages, sizes & qualities; for unless the two last named boys are of sufficient size to be put to trades, they would not answer my purpose; because the persons with whom I should place them are Servants in this family whose terms will expire in less than three years. In making you this offer I have exceeded by at least 25 pr Ct the ready money prices which have been reported to me. That you may have given more I by no means question, but possibly your purchases were on credit, or probably the prices have since fallen. My information of the present selling prices is from very well informed characters.

With respect to the corn, it is perfectly agreeable to me, that you should sell it to any person you please, & instead of ten, I wish you may be able to get fifteen shillings pr barl for it. But as Mr Petit is a gentleman with whom I have no acquaintance, I shall not look to him for the purchase money; I do not wish however to deprive you of the price he offers, by making it a ready money sale to him, altho' it would have been so to me. I am also perfectly willing to allow whatever is due on my Bond (with interest thereon) which passed to Messrs Blair & McCoul, provided that Bond is got in; but you would not I am persuaded request me to allow this sum on one accot, & be exposed to the claim of it from another quarter.

When I agreed to take two thousand pounds of Certificates, it was my intention, & still is that it shall comprehend every which relates to this species of property. And you may be assured, Sir, that in whatever light this matter from first to last may have appeared to you, I distress myself exceedingly by these accommodations; because nothing but the money, & that in a lump, would have answered any valuable purposes of mine, for by receiving this debt in driblets, I am actually sinking one sum, without discharging those debts of my own which press upon me & which are accumulating by a heavier interest than I receive. I do not mean however to go over this ground again. I am willing to abide by the propositions now made, & wish to be explicitly resolved on them, because if they are acceded to, I shall endeavour to raise money by the sale of some part of my property, for the purposes alluded to, & do not expect I shall have less difficulty, or sustain less loss in the accomplishment of it than others.[2]

I will enquire of Mr Lund Washington about the Bond you speak of, & am &c.

G: Washington

LB, DLC:GW.

1. Letter not found.
2. For these negotiations, see GW to Mercer, 9 Sept., 6 Nov., and notes in both documents.

From David Stuart

Dear Sir,   19th Decr [17]86

The daily expectation I have been in of meeting with some one bound for Alexa. who could take charge of the nutmegs you requested me to purchase, has been the occasion of my not writing for some time past—To have trusted them to the Stage unprotected, would from my experience have been unsafe. As I have not been so lucky as to meet with such an opportunity, notwithstanding frequent enquiries at the office; I have now concluded it would be best (as I expect the Assembly will rise in a short time) to take them up myself. Inclosed is the almanack for Mrs Washington which would have been sent sooner but for the above reason.

I send you also the warrants for your impressed property[1]— An application to the Clerk for a general Court writ against Williams, he gave me the inclosed proceeding against Cresap—I beg leave to observe on the writ against Williams, that if you should think it necessary to do more than intimidate him, it would be best to sue him in the County Court—If he does not already know it, he soon will, tho. from the number of suits at present in the General Ct the suit against him will not be tried, for at least ten years. In the County Court, judgement would be obtained in the course of the next Summer—The prospect therefore of such speedy justice would probably have a better effect, even towards intimadating.[2]

From the best information I can get, the disappointment in crops of corn is great, and general—the present price of this article in this place, is fifteen shillings. On York river, I am however informed, that large quantities may be purchased for twelve, and even ten shillings—It is generally thought, that it cannot be less than fifteen, at any time in the Spring—Wheat sells currently at a dollar, and flour at six dollars the hundred—Mr Newton informed me, I think, when he was here, that your flour had sustained such damage, as to make it necessary to sell it at vendue—if he comes here again, I shall apply to him for the purpose you mention.

Posey has not run off as you have heard; nor do I believe him to be in such desperate circumstances as are represented—As a proof of it, he is engaged in an expensive repair of his mill. But still it would appear, as if nothing could be got from him: his property being all mortgaged to Coll Clayton: I am well assured, that it is much more than sufficient to satisfy Clayton, and am about bringing suit against Clayton, to campell him to foreclose the mortgage—The issue of this, will disclose the true state of his affairs.[3]

The disturbances to the North-ward give us much uneasiness here, and are truly alarming—The friends to a republican form of government, must feel themselves deeply wounded in the triumph which such disturbances (the sure proof of a want of virtue) afford to the admirers of monarchy.

A report has just arrived here, (too true I fear) that the Governor and principal men in N: Carolina, have been detected in a considerable forgery of some kind of Certificates. This must produce much confusion, and is perhaps the most fatal stab which has been yet given to the dignity of such governments[4]—It is much to be feared, that we shall furnish the same melancholly proofs of unfitness for this species of government which the old world has already done, and that we are preparing apace, for some of those changes, which are there established—The inclosed report will give you some information of the State of our finances[5]—I need not I suppose, inform you, of your being appointed to the Convention to be held at Philadelphia—It appeared to be so much the wish of the House that Mr Maddison concieved, it might probably frustrate the whole scheme, if it was not done—As it was however intimated, that from many circumstances in your situation it might be impossible for you to attend, you will have a fair opening for an excuse, if at the time, you should still think it inconvenient, or incompatible with what has happened, respecting the Society of the Cincinnati—The original imperfection of the fœderal union, and it's present tottering state, may perhaps at that time, present themselves in such a point of view, as to supersede every objection.

The attempt to repeal the Port-bill has failed. It appears from the accounts of the Naval officer from Norfolk, that more revenue has been already collected, from that single port, than what was recieved formerly from the whole State, in the space of a year—It only began to operate in June—Coll Logan who defeated lately the Shawnee Indians and burnt their towns, is here—he seems to think, there can be no lasting peace with those unfortunate people[6]—The report concerning the surrender of the navigation of the Missisppi, gave birth to the instructions you have seen, to the Delegates in Congress from this State—In the consideration of this very serious business, it appeared to me, that the inevitable consequence of such a surrender would be, such a hatred of those people towards us, as might induce them to throw themselves into the arms of the English nation, already perhaps too formidable there for our wellfare—Union and harmony among ourselves are more desireable than any thing else, and of more importance to our existence as a nation.

On saturday our Session will certainly end.[7] You will therefore if you have commands here, be pleased to inform me of them. I am Dr Sir with great respect Your Affecte Hble Servt

Dd Stuart

P:S: I applied to Mrs Randolph on my first arrival in this place, at Mrs Washington's request—She told me 'twas such a trifle she had advanced, as to merit no notice—I shall wait on her again before my departure. D:S:

ALS, DLC:GW.

1. See GW to Stuart, 5 Nov., n.2.

2. For GW's instructions to Stuart regarding his tenant Edward Williams, see GW to Stuart, 6 December. For GW's legal battle with Michael Cresap and

his heirs over the Round Bottom tract in Pennsylvania, see John Harvie to GW, 5 Aug. 1785, and notes, and GW to Edmund Randolph, 12 July 1786.

3. See GW to Stuart, 19 Nov., n.2. William Clayton (d. 1797) of New Kent County was colonel of the county's militia and, since 1756, clerk of its court.

4. In his address at the opening of the session of the North Carolina legislature on 20 Nov. 1786, Gov. Richard Caswell (1729–1789) reported that he had stopped payment on military certificates because of the frequent charges of individuals and "the clamor of the people at large respecting the conduct of the Commissioners for liquidating the army accounts, and their suggestions of many fraudulent accounts being passed." Twenty-three men were arrested, and the legislature launched an investigation that resulted in the expulsion of one member of the lower house and the trial and conviction by a court of oyer and terminer of several prominent men (*N.C. State Records*, 18:iv-vi).

5. Stuart's enclosure has not been found. The report of the committee of the house of delegates appointed "to examine the treasurer's accounts," from 12 Dec. 1785 to 11 Dec. 1786, is printed in the *House of Delegates Journal, 1786–1790*, 6 Jan. 1787.

6. See George McCarmick to GW, 31 Oct., n.1.

7. The session did not end until 11 Jan. 1787.

From Henry Knox

My dear Sir   New York 21st December 1786

The insurgents who were assembled at Worcester in Massachusetts have disbanded. The people at Boston seem to be glad at this event and say it was the effect of fear. But the fact is that the insurgents effected their object, which was to prevent the Court of Common Pleas from proceeding to business. It is probable that the seizing some of the insurgents at Middlesex occasioned a greater number of them to assemble at Worcester than otherwise would have assembled merely on Account of preventing the common Pleas.[1]

By Private Letters of the 13th from Boston it appears that government were determined to try its strength by bringing the insurgents to action but were prevented by the uncommon deep snows, which are four and five feet on a level.

The commotions of Massachusetts have wrought prodigious changes in the minds of men in that State respecting the Powers of Government every body says they must be strengthned, and that unless this shall be effected there is no Security for liberty or Property.

Such is the State of things in the east, that much trouble is to be apprehended in the course of the ensuing year.

I hope you will see Colo. Wadsworth in Philadelphia in a few days. I expect he will be here on Saturday next. I am my dear Sir &.

H.K.

N.B. the last Boston paper.

ADfS, NNGL.
1. See Knox to GW, 17 Dec., and note 3 of that document.

To Leven Powell

Dear Sir, Mount Vernon Decr 21st [17]86

Your favor of the 18th came to hand last night[1]—I by no means wish you to put your self to the smallest inconvenience in hastening the Buck Wheat down—If you have it *secured*, so as that I may rely upon it, in due season, it is all I want. The disappointments I sustained last year, in Seeds that were expected, made me anxious to obtain, long before Seed time, all I should want; because having them in hand I hazarded nothing.[2]

I will thank you for the information promised, respecting this Grain when the other load is sent—which I again desire may not be till it suits your convenience. With great esteem & regard—I am Dear Sir Yr Obedt Hble Ser⟨vt⟩

Go: Washington

ALS (photocopy), DLC:GW.
1. Letter not found.
2. See Powell to GW, 12 Sept., n.3.

To Edmund Randolph

Sir, [21 December 1786]

I had not the honor of receiving your Excellency's favor of the 6th, with its enclosures, till last night.

Sensible as I am of the honor conferred on me by the General Assembly, in appointing me one of the Deputies to a Convention proposed to be held in the City of Philadelphia in May next, for the purpose of revising the Fœderal Constitution; and desirous as I am on all occasions, of testifying a ready obedience to the calls of my Country—yet, Sir, there exists at this moment, circumstances, which I am persuaded will render my acceptance of this fresh mark of confidence incompatible with other measures which I had previously adopted; and from which, seeing little prospect of disengaging myself, it would be disengenuous not to express a wish that some other character, on whom greater reliance can be had, may be substituted in my place; the probability of my non-attendance being too great to continue my appointment.

As no mind can be more deeply impressed than mine is with the awful situation of our Affairs—resulting in a great measure from the want of efficient powers in the fœderal head, and due respect to its Ordinances—so, consequently, those who do engage in the important business of removing these defects, will carry with them every good wish of mine, which the best dispositions towards the attainment, can bestow. I have the honr to be with very grt respect—Your Excellys Most Obedt Hble Servt

Go: Washington

ALS, PHi: Dreer Collection; LB, DLC:GW.

To Gilles de Lavallée

Sir,   Mo[un]t Vernon 23d Decr 1786.

Your letter, Plan & Estimate for establishing a manufacture of Cotton &ca did not reach me 'till within these few days. As the Assembly of this Commonwealth is now sitting, & your proposition would come better before a public body than a private individual, for encouragement, I have transmitted it to the Governor to be laid, if he shall judge it proper, before the assembly. So soon as his answer is received it shall be communicated to you.[1] In the meantime, I am Sir &c.

G: Washington

LB, DLC:GW.

1. Gilles de Lavallée, a French textile manufacturer, came to the United States in late 1785 or early 1786 with recommendations from Benjamin Franklin and Thomas Jefferson. He arrived in Portsmouth, N.H., where in early 1786 he secured the backing of Gen. John Sullivan to set up his looms for the manufacture of cloth. Lavallée's letter and the other papers that he sent to

GW, including a letter of recommendation from Jefferson, have not been found. GW sent to Gov. Edmund Randolph on 25 Dec. Lavallée's letter and its enclosures, with this covering letter: "Sir, To promote industry and œconomy, and to encourage manufactures, is certainly consistent with that sound policy which ought to actuate every State. There are times too, which call loudly for the exercise of these virtues; and the present, in my humble opinion, may be accounted a fit one for the adoption of them in this Commonwealth.

"How far the proposition which I have the honor to enclose merits Legislative encouragement, your Excellency will determine. As it came to me, you will receive it. The writer is unknown to me; of him, or his plan, I had not the smallest intimation till the papers were handed to me from the Post Office. The document in the hand writing of Mr Jefferson (with which it is accompanied) entitles the latter to consideration, but as an individual it is not convenient for me to afford Mr de la Vallée the aids he requires, or to have him upon my hands till he can be properly established; nor indeed is Alexandria, in my opinion, so proper a situation as a more southern one for the manufacture of Cotton. However, if your Excellency should think his plan not worthy of public attention, or judgg otherwise, it should not find encouragement from the Assembly, I would thank you for returning the letter & papers to me, that I may give Mr de la Vallée an answer as soon as possible—his circumstances seeming to require one. With Sentiments of grt esteem & respect I have the honor to be Yr Excellency's Most Obedt Hble Servt Go: Washington" (ALS, PHi: Dreer Collection; LB, DLC:GW). Randolph returned the papers to GW on 4 Jan. 1787, explaining that it was too late in the session for the delegates to consider Lavallée's proposals. There is no record of GW's having written Lavallée after this, and on 13 Mar. 1787 Lavallée wrote that having received no response from GW he was departing that day for Spain, having concluded that "no establishment of European manufacture can succeed" in the United States. See the note in Lavallée to Jefferson, 14 Aug. 1785, in Boyd, *Jefferson Papers*, 8:377–79.

From William Roberts

Sir   Norwick-Mills December 23d—*1786*
     This is to Inform Your Excellency that There has Been Two Millers at My house at Colo. John Pleasents Mills Four Mile Crick Seking Imploy.[1] tha Told me tha Came thru Alaxandria And had Some Talk with Mr Thorn Conserning your Mills & Miller Mr Thorns Answer Was that you had Told Him Youd Better a Givven Me a Hundred & 20£ A Year then the Man you have 60£.[2]—if this Report be True I Shold be Glad to Know the Sertainty of it by a Letter Sent to the Stage offis in Richmond As I Liv but 12 Miles From Richmond on James River 4 mile Crick

if this Report Shold be Groundless Am Sorry To Giv you the Troble of Reding Purhaps What Mite be Desogreeable to you.

However if youd Git a Nother Pare of Burrs And Giv Me My old Lay & Preveleges I woud Drive them On in the Best Maner tha Cold Porsabbly be Drove the Winter Season Which Woud Inable you to Keep up My Wages—And Not Feel it—this year I have but 80£ My Year will be up the 10th of April next the Company Wants Me to Ingage to Lern thare Printeses the Besoness & To Imploy Me a Term of years at 100£ ℔ year & to pay me what Shold be thought Resoneble for Instructing tham in the Besonesss.

I Shold be Vary Happy to Come in to your Imploy Again if it Was Agreable. And am Well Asured youd have No Reson to Complain As My Wife And I have Got to Living in Peic & Quietness Which I hoop May Continue To the Eand of Our Days. From Sir your Most Obedt And Humble Servt

Wm Roberts

ALS, DLC:GW.

1. GW's old miller William Roberts was working at Norwich Mills on Four Mile Creek about a mile from the James River in lower Henrico County. John Pleasants and Thomas Pleasants, Jr., offered the complex of mills for rent or lease in the *Virginia Gazette and Weekly Advertiser* (Richmond) as early as 19 April 1787.

2. Mr. Thorn may be Michael Thorn, a merchant in Alexandria.

From James Madison

Dear Sir   Richmond Decr 24. 1786

Your favour of the 16th inst: came to hand too late on thursday evening to be answered by the last mail. I have considered well the circumstances which it confidentially discloses, as well as those contained in your preceding favor. The difficulties which they oppose to an acceptance of the appointment in which you are included can as little be denied, as they can fail to be regretted. But I still am inclined to think that the posture of our affairs, if it should continue, would prevent every criticism on the situation which the cotemporary meetings would place you in; and wish that at least a door could be kept open for your acceptance hereafter, in case the gathering clouds should become so dark and menacing as to supercede every consideration, but that of our national existence or safety. A suspence of your ultimate determination would be no wise inconvenient in a public view, as the Executive are authorized to fill vacancies and can fill them at any time, and in any event three out of seven deputies are authorized to represent the State. How far it may be admissible in another view, will depend perhaps in some measure on the chance of your finally undertaking the service, but principally on the correspondence which is now passing on the subject between yourself and the Governour.

Your observations on Tobo as a commutable in the taxes are certainly just and unanswerable. My acquiescence in the measure was agst every general principle which I have embraced, and was extorted by a fear that some greater evil under the name of relief to the People would be substituted. I am far from being sure however that I did right. The other evils contended for have indeed been as yet parried, but it is very questionable, whether the concession in the Affair of the Tobo had much hand in it. The original object was paper money. Petitions for graduating certificates succeeded. Next came instalments; and lastly a project for making property a tender for debts at ⅘ of its value. All these have been happily got rid of by very large majorities. But the positive efforts in favor of Justice have been less successful. A plan for reforming the administration in this essential branch, accomodated more to the general opinion than the Assize plan, got as far as the third reading, and was then lost by a single vote. The Senate would have passed it readily and would have even added amendments of the right complexion. I fear it will be some time before this necessary Reform will again have so fair a chance. Besides some other grounds of apprehension, it may well be supposed that the Bill which is to be printed for consideration of the public will instead of calling forth the sanction of the wise & virtuous, be a signal to interested men to redouble their efforts to get into the Legislature.[1] The Revenue business is still unfinished. The present rage seems to be to draw all our income from trade. From the sample given of the temper of the House of Delegates on this subject, it is much to be feared that the duties will be augmented with so daring a hand that we shall drive away our trade instead of making it tributary to our treasury. The only hope that can be indulged is that of moderating the fury. The Port bill was defended against a repeal by about 70 votes agst about 40. The Revised Code is not quite finished, and must receive the last hand from a succeeding Assembly.[2] Several bills of consequence being rendered unfit to be passed in their present form by a change of circumstances since they were prepared, necessarily require revision. Others as the Education bill &c. are thought to be adapted only to a further degree of wealth and population. Others, as the Execution bill which subjects lands to debts, do not yet find an adequate patronage. Several bills also and particularly the bill relating to crimes & punishments, have been rejected and require reconsideration from another Assembly. This last bill after being purged of its objectionable peculiarities was thrown out on the third reading by a single vote. It will little elevate your idea of our Senate to be told that they negatived the bill defining the priviliges of Ambassadours, on the principle as I am told that an Alien ought not to be put on better ground than a Citizen. British debts have not yet been mentioned, and probably will not unless Cong[res]s say something on the matter before the Adjournment. With every sentiment of esteem & affection, I am Dear Sir, Your obedt servt

Js Madison Jr

ALS, PHi: Gratz Collection; signed copy in Madison's hand, DLC: Madison Papers.

1. After the failure of the district court bill in this session, it was not until December 1788 that a court reform bill was enacted.

2. For the legislation that Madison discusses here, see Bill for Completing the Revision of the Laws, c.4 Dec. 1786, in Rutland and Rachal, *Madison Papers*, 9:193–96.

From David Stuart

Dear Sir,   Richmond 25th Decr —86

I acknowledge my omission in not informing you, in my first letters of the passing of an act in conformity to the petition from the Potomac directors. I informed Col. Fitzgerald of it immediately, and supposed I had done the same in my letters to you— It was among the first things done[1]—Since my last, nothing material has happened here, except that the bill establishing district Courts is lost—As the prompt administration of justice, is perhaps the best sumptuary law which can be established in any

Country, and the best means of securing prosperity to the
people, I lament much that it could not take place—I am sorry
to say, that Mr G[eorg]e Nicholas who appears to be aiming at
popularity in all his measures, was the cause of it's miscarriage[2]—I have no doubt but Mr Maddison's virtues and abilities
make it necessary that he should be in Congress; but from what
I already foresee, I shall dread the consequences of another Assembly without him—I flattered myself some time ago, with
great advantages to our part of the world, from the appointment
of Commissioners to meet similar officers from Maryland, for
the purpose of assimilating the duties between the two States—
But, from the present disposition in imposing duties, I don't
concieve it will answer any purpose at all; as I fear no clause will
be agreed to, of their taking place conditionally—Indeed the
interests of the Potomac, seem to be perfectly disregarded in
every instance. The compact law of Coll Masons's, is perhaps the
most fatal stab that was ever given to them. I had never before
occasion to consider it—But, as it is a direct violation of one of
the articles of confederation, it cannot long subsist[3]—I must now
beg my compts to Mrs Washington and to ⟨*mutilated*⟩ at Mt Vernon I am Dr Sir Your affece Hble Servt

Dd Stuart

ALS, DLC:GW.
    1. See GW to Stuart, 5 Nov., n.1.
    2. James Madison does not mention George Nicholas when writing on 7
and 24 Dec. about the defeat of the district court bill.
    3. Stuart seems to be referring to the compact made at the Mount Vernon
conference by George Mason and other commissioners from Virginia and
Maryland relating to the jurisdiction and navigation of the Potomac River. The
compact is printed in Rutland, *Mason Papers*, 2:816–22.

Letter not found: from Daniel Carroll, 26 Dec. 1786. On 9 Jan. 1787 GW
wrote Carroll: "Your letter of the 26th ulto did not reach me 'till within
these few days."

To David Humphreys

My dear Humphreys   Mount Vernon Decr 26th 1786
    I am much indebted to you for your several favors of the 1st
9th & 16th of November. The last came first. Mr Morse keeping

in Mind the old proverb, was determined not to make more haste than good speed in prosecuting his journey to Georgia—so I got the two first but lately.

For your publication respecting the confinement of Captn Asgill, I am exceedingly obliged to you. The manner of making it was as good as could be devised; and the matter, will prove the injustice, as well as illiberality of the reports which have been circulated on that occasion, and which are fathered on that Officer, as the author.

It is with the deepest, and most heart felt concern, I perceive by some late paragraphs extracted from the Boston Gazettes, that the Insurgents of Massachusetts—far from being satisfied with the redress offered by their General Court—are still acting in open violation of Law & Government; & have obliged the Chief Magistrate in a decided tone, to call upon the militia of the State to support the Constitution. What, gracious God, is man! that there should be such inconsistency & perfidiousness in his conduct? It is but the other day we were shedding our blood to obtain the Constitutions under which we now live—Constitutions of our own choice and framing—and now we are unsheathing the Sword to overturn them! The thing is so unaccountable, that I hardly know how to realize it, or to persuade my self that I am not under the vision of a dream.

My mind previous to the receipt of your letter of the first Ulto had often been agitated by thoughts similar to those you have expressed, respecting an old frd of yours; but heaven forbid that a crisis should arrive when he shall be driven to the necessity of making choice of either of the alternatives therementioned. Let me entreat you, my dear Sir, to keep me advised of the situation of Affairs in your quarter. I can depend upon your Accts. Newspaper paragraphs unsupported by other testimony, are often contradictory & bewildering. At one time these insurgents are represented as a mere Mob—At other times as systematic in all their proceedings. If the first, I would fain hope that like other Mobs, it will, however formidable, be of short duration. If the latter, there surely are men of consequence and abilities behind the Curtain, who move the puppits. The designs of whom may be deep & dangerous. They may be instigated by British Councils—actuated by ambitious motives—or being influenced by dishonest principles, had rather see the Country plunged in civil discord than do what Justice would dictate to an honest mind.

Private and Confidential

I had hardly dispatched my circular letters to the several State Societies of the Cincinnati, when I received Letters from some of the principal members of our Assembly, expressing a wish that they might be permitted to name me as one of the Deputies to the Convention proposed to be held at Philadelphia, the first of May next. I immediately wrote to my particular friend Madison (& similarly to the rest) the answer contained in the extract No.1—In reply I got No.2—This obliged me to be *more* explicit & confidential with him, on points which a recurrence to the conversations we have had on this Subject will bring to your mind without my hazarding the recital of them in a letter— Since this interchange, I have received from the Governor the letter No.4 to whom I returned the answer No.5.[1] If this business should be further prest (which I hope it will not, as I have no inclination to go) what had I best do? *You*, as an *indifferent person*—& one who is much better acquainted with the Sentiments, & views of the Cincinnati than I am (for in this State, where the recommendations of the General meeting have been acceded to, hardly any thing is said about it) as also with the temper of the people, and the state of Politics at large, can determine upon fuller evidence, & better ground than myself—especially as you will know in what light the States to the Eastward consider *the Convention* & the measures they are pursuing to contravene, or give efficacy to it. On the last occasion, only five States were represented—none East of New York. Why the New England Governments did not appear I am yet to learn; for of all others the distractions & turbulent temper of their people would, I should have thought, have afforded the strongest evidence of the *necessity* of competent powers somewhere. That the fœderal Government is nearly, if not quite at a stand none will deny: The question then is, can it be propt—or shall it be anihilated? If the former, the proposed Convention is an object of the first magnitude, and should be supported by all the friends of the present Constitution. In the other case, if on a full and dispassionate revision thereof, the continuances shall be adjudged impracticable, or unwise, would it not be better for such a meeting to suggest some other to avoid, if possible, civil discord, or other impending evils. Candour however obliges me to confess that as we could not remain quiet more than three or four years (in time of peace) under the constitutions of our own choice,

which it was believed, in many instances, were formed with deliberation & wisdom, I see little prospect either of our agreeing
upon any other, or that we should remain long satisfied under
it if we could—Yet I would wish to see *any thing* and every thing
essayed to prevent the effusion of blood, and to avert the humili-
ating, & contemptible figure we are about to make, in the Annals
of Mankind.

If this second attempt to convene the States for the purposes
proposed in the report of the partial representation at Annapolis in September last, should also prove abortive it may be considered as an unequivocal proof that the States are not likely to
agree in any general measure which is to pervade the Union, &
consequently, that there is an end put to Fœderal Government.
The States therefore who make this last dying essay to avoid the
misfortune of a dissolution would be mortified at the issue: and
their deputies would return home chagreened at their ill success & disappointment. This would be a disagreeable predicament for any of them to be in, but more particularly so for a
person in my situation. If no further application is made to me,
of course I do not attend. If there is, I am under no obligation
to do it; but as I have had so many proofs of your friendship—
know your abilities to judge—and your opportunities of learning the politicks of the day, on the points I have enumerated,
you would oblige me by a *full* & *confidential* communication of
your sentiments thereon.[2]

Peace & tranquility prevail in this State. The Assembly by a
very great Majority, and in very emp[h]atical terms have rejected an application for paper money; and spurned the idea of
fixing the value of Military certificates by a scale of depreciation.
In some other respects too, the proceedings of the present Session have been marked with Justice, and a strong desire of supporting the fœderal system.

Although I lament the effect, I am pleased at the cause which
has deprived us of your aid in the Attack of Christmas Pyes. We
had one yesterday on which all the company (and pretty numerous it was) were hardly able to make an impression. Mrs Washington, George & his wife (Mr Lear I had occasion to send into
the Western Country) join in affectionate regard for you—
& with sentiments of the warmest friendship I am—sincerely
Yours

Go: Washington

ALS, Uniwersytet Jagielloński, Kracόw, Poland; LB, DLC:GW.

1. The extract (no. 1) is from GW's letter to Madison of 18 Nov.; Madison's reply (no. 2) is dated 7 Dec.; GW wrote his *"more* explicit & confidential" response to Madison on 16 Dec.; Edmund Randolph's letter (no. 4), which GW did not receive until 20 Dec., is dated 6 Dec.; and GW's letter to Randolph (no. 5) is dated 21 December.

2. Humphreys wrote GW on 20 Jan. 1787 urging him not to attend the federal convention.

To Henry Knox

My dear Sir,   Mount Vernon 26th Decr 1786

Nothing but the pleasing hope of seeing you under this roof in the course of last month, and wch I was disposed to extend even to the present moment, has kept me till this time from acknowleging the receipt of your obliging favor of the 23d of October. Despairing now of that pleasure, I shall thank you for the above letter, and the subsequent one of the 17th instt, which came to hand yesterday evening.

Lamentable as the conduct of the Insurgents of Massachusetts is, I am exceedingly obliged to you for the advices respecting them; & pray you, most ardently, to continue the acct of their proceedings; because I can depend upon them from you without having my mind bewildered with those vague & contradictory reports which are handed to us in Newspapers; and which please one hour, only to make the moments of the next more bitter.

I feel, my dear Genl Knox, infinitely more than I can express to you, for the disorders which have arisen in these states. Good God! who besides a tory could have foreseen, or a Briton predicted them! were these people wiser than others, or did they judge of us from the corruption, and depravity of their own hearts? The latter I am persuaded was the case, and that notwithstanding the boasted virtue of America, we are far gone in every thing ignoble & bad. I do assure you, that even at this moment, when I reflect on the present posture of our affairs, it seems to me to be like the vision of a dream. My mind does not know how to realize it, as a thing in actual existence, so strange—so wonderful does it appear to me! In this, as in most other matter[s], we are too slow. When this spirit first dawned, probably it migh[t] easily have been checked; but it is scarcely within the reach of human ken, at this moment, to say when—where—or how it will end. There are combustibles in every State, which a spark may set fire to. In this state, a perfect calm prevails at present, and a prompt disposition to support, and give energy to the fœderal system is discovered, if the unlucky stirring of the dispute respecting the navigation of the Mississipi does not become a leaven that will ferment & sour the mind of it.

The resolutions of the pres[en]t session respecting a paper emission, military certificates—&ca—have stamped justice & liberality on the proceedings of the Assembly, & By a late act, *it* seems very desirous of a General Convention to revise and amend the fœderal Constitution—apropos, what prevented the Eastern states from attending the September meeting at Annapolis? Of all the states in the Union it should have seemed to me, that a measure of this sort (distracted as they were with internal commotions, and experiencing the want of energy in government) would have been most pleasing to them. What are the prevailing sentiments of the one now proposed to be held at Philadelphia, in May next? & how will it be attended? You are at the fountain of intelligence, and where the wisdom of the Nation, it is to be presumed, has concentered; consequently better able (as I have had abundant experience of your intelligence, confidence, & candour) to solve these questions. The Maryland Assembly has been violently agitated by the question for a paper emission. It has been carried in the House of Delegates, but what has, or will be done with the Bill in the Senate I have not yet heard. The partisans in favor of the measure in the lower House, threaten, it is said, a secession if it is rejected by that Branch of the Legislature—Thus are we advancing.

In regretting, which I have often done with the deepest sorrow, the death of our much lamented frd General Greene, I have accompanied it of late with a quaere; whether he would not have preferred such an exit to the scenes which it is more than probable many of his compatriots may live to bemoan.

In both your letters you intimate, that the men of reflection, principle & property in New England feeling the inefficacy of their present government, are contemplating a change; but you are not explicit with respect to the nature of it. It has been supposed, that, the Constitution of the State of Massachusetts was amongst the most energetic in the Union—may not these disorders then be ascribed to an endulgent exercise of the powers of Administration? If your laws authorized, and your powers were adequate to the suppression of these tumults, in the first appearance of them, delay & temporizing expedients were, in my opinion improper, these are rarely well applied, & the same causes would produce similar effects in any form of government, if the powers of it are not enforced. I ask this question for information, I know nothing of the facts.

That G.B. will be an unconcerned spectator of the present insurrections (if they continue) is not to be expected. That she is at this moment sowing the Seeds of jealousy & discontent among the various tribes of Indians on our frontier admits of no doubt, in my mind. And that she will improve every opportunity to foment the spirit of turbulence within the bowels of the United States, with a view of distracting our governments, & promoting divisions, is, with me, not less certain. Her first Manœuvres will, no doubt, be covert, and may remain so till the period shall arrive when a decided line of conduct may avail her. Charges of violating the treaty, & other pretexts, will not then be wanting to colour overt acts, tending to effect the grt objects of which she has long been in labour. A Man is now at the head of their American Affairs well calculated to conduct measures of this kind, & more than probably was selected for the purpose. We ought not therefore to sleep nor to slumber—vigilence in the watching, & vigour in acting, is, in my opinion, become indispensably necessary. If the powers are inadequate amend or alter them, but do not let us sink into the lowest state of humiliation & contempt, & become a byword in all the earth—I think with you that the Spring will unfold important & distressing Scenes, unless much wisdom & good management is displayed in the interim. Adieu—be assured no man has a higher esteem & regard for you than I have—none more sincerely Your friend, and More Affectly yr Hble Servt

Go: Washington

P.S. Mrs Washington joins me in every good wish for you & Mrs Knox, and in congratulatory Compts on the late addition to your family. Will you be so obliging as to give the enclosed a safe conveyance—I have recd one or two very obliging letters from Genl Tupper whilst he was in the Western Country and wish to thank him for them—but know not in what part of Massachusetts he lives.[1]

ALS, NNGL; LB, DLC:GW.
    1. The letter to Benjamin Tupper has not been found. Tupper's letters to GW are dated 26 Oct. 1785 and 23 Nov. 1786.

To Theodorick Bland

Dr Sir,   Mount Vernon 28th Decr 1786.

I am now about to fulfill my promise with respect to the Drill plough and Timothy seed—both accompany this letter to Norfolk, to the care of Mr Newton. The latter I presume is good, as I had it from a Gentleman (Colo. Levin Powell) on whom I can depend. The former, it is scarcely necessary to inform you, will not work to good effect in Land that is very full either of stumps, stones or large clods; but where the ground is tolerably free from these & in good tilth—& particularly in light land, I am certain you will find it equal to your most sanguine expectation for Indian Corn, wheat, Barley, Pease or any other tolerably round grain that you may wish to sow, or plant in this manner. I have sowed Oats very well with it, which is among the most inconvenient & unfit grains for this machine.

To give you a just idea of the use & management of it, I must observe, that the barrel at present has only one set of holes, & these adapted for the planting of Indian Corn only eight inches apart in the row: but by corking these, the same barrel may receive others of a size fitted for any other grain. To make the holes, observe this rule—begin small & encrease the size 'till they emit the number of grains, or thereabouts, you would chuse to deposit in a place. They should be burnt—done by a gage, (that all may be of a size) and made widest on the out side to prevent the seeds choking them.

You may, in a degree, emit more or less through the same holes, by encreasing or lessening the quantity of seed in the barrel. The less there is in it, the faster it issues. The compressure is encreased by the quantity & the discharge is retarded thereby. The use of the band is to prevent the seeds issuing out of more holes than one at a time. It may be slackened or braced according to the influence the atmosphere has on the leather: the tighter it is, provided the wheels revolve easily, the better. By decreasing or multiplying the holes in the barrel, you may plant at any distance you please. The circumference of the wheels being six feet or 72 inches, divide the latter by the number of inches you intend your plants shall be asunder, & it gives the number of holes required in the barrel.

The sparse situation of the teeth in the harrow, is designed that the ground may be raked without the harrow being clogged, if the ground should be clody or grassy. The string, when this happens to be the case, will raise & clear it with great ease, & is of service in turning at the ends of rows; at which time the wheels, by means of the handles, are raised off the ground as well as the harrow to prevent the waste of seed. A small bag, containing about a peck of the seed you are sowing, is hung to the nails on the right handle, & with a small tin cup the barrel is replenished with convenience whenever it is necessary without loss of time, or waiting to come up with the seed bag at the end of the row. I had almost forgot to tell you, that if the hole in the leather band (thro' which the seed is to pass when it comes in contact with the hole in the barrel) should incline to gape, or the lips of it turn out, so as to admit the seed between the band & barrel, it is easily, & must be remedied by rivetting a piece of sheet tin, copper, or brass the width of the band, & about four inches long with a hole through it the size of the one in the leather—I found this effectual. Mrs Washington joins me in presenting the compliments of the season to Mrs Bland & yourself, & with great esteem, I am Dear Sir &c.

G: Washington

LB, DLC:GW.

To George Digges

Dear Sir,   Mount Vernon Decr 28th 1786

Will you permit me, to give you the trouble of enquiring among your friends of the Eastern Shore, now in Annapolis, if I could be furnished with one thousand feet of the best pine plank; precisely 24 feet long (when dressed)—To be without sap, or knots. It is for the floor of my new room.[1]

Many years since, I provided for this, & thought myself secure of that which was perfectly seasoned. It had been dressed & laid by; but when I was about to make use of it, behold! half of it was stolen, and the other half will match no plank I can now get.

I do not expect to get seasoned plank agreeably to this description; but on whom I might depend for the length & quality, I would wish to know; for if I cannot rely with certainty, I shall immediately write to Norfolk[2]—I would thank you for an answer by the Post. I am—Dear Sir Yr Most Obedt Hble Servt

Go: Washington

ALS, ViMtV; LB, DLC:GW.

1. GW first tried to obtain the planking for his New Room, in Alexandria. See GW to Robert Townshend Hooe, 27 November. Digges arranged for GW to get the flooring from Gilliss Polk of Somerset County, Md. (see Digges to GW, 5 Jan. 1787, and note 1 of that document).

2. Digges wrote below GW's signature: "Mr Polk will forward the plank Immediately & if possible to have it Landed at the Generals House or at Alexandria to the Care of Colo. Fitzgerald."

To Thomas Johnson

Dr Sir, Mount Vernon 28th Decr 1786.

It gave me pleasure to find by your letter of the 7th that the Petition of the Directors of the Potomac Company had met so ready & favorable a reception in the assembly of Maryland. I am informed that an act similar to the one you sent me has passed the Legislature of this State, but I have received no official advice of it.[1]

Permit me, my good Sir, to ask if there would be a probability of your Assembly's (if the matter should be laid before it) doing anything to good effect in the case stated in the enclosed letter from Mr Wilson to me. I am one of the Executors, indeed the only surviving one, of Colo. Thomas Colvill; & am exceedingly anxious to have the administration of that Estate closed. I know nothing of the facts mentioned in Mr Wilson's letter respecting the confiscations, sales, & the motives which led to them, in the instance alluded to, but would be thankful for your opinion & advice thereon.[2]

Mr Brindley promised me by letter in Octor that he would call upon me in his way to So. Carolina, but I have not seen or heard from him since the date of his letter.[3] We ought undoubtedly to avail ourselves of all the aids we can derive from experimental knowledge in our reach—I concur readily therefore in sentiment with you & Mr Lee, that it would be proper to see what lights Mr Brindley can afford us in conducting the navigation thro' the little Falls—and the idea of a model for the Locks at the great Falls, I think good for the reasons you offer—the expence will be trifling & the saving may be great.

The lesson you seem fearful of learning will most assuredly be taught us. The strides we have already taken, & are now making, to corruption are inconceivably great; and I shall be exceedingly, but very agreeably disappointed if next Spring does not display scenes which will astonish the world. Nothing, I am certain, but the wisest councils & the most vigorous exertions can avert them. With sentiments of very great esteem & regard I am Dr Sir &c.

G: Washington

LB, DLC:GW.

1. David Stuart wrote GW on 25 Dec. about the passage early in the session of the bill for the Potomac River Company (GW to Stuart, 5 Nov., n.1).

2. Wilson's letter has not been found. William Wilson (d. 1823), a Scot, was a merchant in Alexandria as a partner of the Glasgow firm of James Wilson & Sons. For further information about the letter, see GW to Johnson, 22 Nov. 1787.

3. The only letter from James Brindley that has been found is dated 5 April 1787.

To John Armistead

Sir,   Mount Vernon 29th Decr 1786.

Many months having elapsed since I informed you in explicit terms of my want of the money which is due to me from the Estate of your deceased Father, without having received any acknowledgement of the letter, I presume it has miscarried. To avoid the like accident, I have taken the liberty of putting this letter under cover to Mr Holmes, at the Bowling-green, who I persuade myself, will do me the favor of seeing that it goes safe to your hands.[1]

It will serve to assure you, Sir, that I was disposed to hope,

considering the long standing & nature of the debt, that you
would not have laid me under the necessity of so often re-
minding you of it, & at length to inform you that however disagreeable it will be to me, I must have recourse to a Court of
Justice if the money is not paid me without more delay; for you
may believe me when I assure you I am really in want of it. I
am &c.

G: Washington

LB, DLC:GW.

1. See GW to Armistead, 17 April 1786, and note 1 of that document. John
Hoomes (d. 1805) wrote GW on 16 Jan. 1787 from Bowling Green in Caroline
County, where he owned a tavern frequented before the war by GW on his
trips to and from Williamsburg: "Sir, I this day reced Mr Armsteads letter to
you, which I here inclose. Should you have farther use for my Services, nothing will be more pleasing to me, than to give them" (DLC:GW). Armistead's
letter to GW has not been found.

To William Hull

Dear Sir,   Mount Vernon 29th Decr 1786.
I informed you in my last, that my own knowledge of the
Western Country was rather general than otherwise, but promised to lose no opportunity of collecting every information which
I thought might facilitate your intended settlement.[1] Since
which time I have had occasion to send Mr Lear out as far as
Pittsburg to transact some business for me in that quarter; I directed him to make such enquiries & to gain such information
respecting the points touched upon in your letter as would enable me to answer it with more precision than my own knowledge would permit me to do. He has just returned, & I take the
earliest opportunity of conveying to you such information as I
hope will be satisfactory.[2]
Cattle of every kind may be purchased in the neighbourhood
of Pittsburg very reasonably & in any numbers. Iron castings,
bar iron &c. may be bought there, & perhaps cheaper than they
can be carried out by families that are removing. The prices of
the following articles at & near Pittsburgh, will enable you to
determine whether it wou'd be best to carry them out or purchase them there.

	Pennsa Cury
Cows	£4 d £4:10

The Cows are not so large nor so good as those in Nw England.

Sheep	16/
Hogs	18/ Cwt
Beeves	25/ Cwt
Corn	2/6 d 2/8 pr bushl
Wheat	3/6 d 4/ Do
Flour	15/ Cwt
Salt	20/ & 25/ ℔ bushl
Iron Castings	1/ ℔ lb.
Bar iron	/8d. do
Wrought do	2/ do
Whiskey	3/ ℔ gallon.

Dry goods 40 ℔ Ct from their cost at Philada.

There is no furnace in the Western Country—the nearest to those parts is on the Potomac, sixty miles below Fort Cumberland. Salt may be purchased at Kentucky cheaper than at Pittsburgh, as they have salt Springs in that Country from which they can supply themselves with that article.

You desired my advice respecting the best mode of effecting your plan; but as you did not point out to me the part of the Country where the settlement is intended to be made; I can only give you my opinion as to the best plan of getting over the Alleghany mountains to the western waters.

I should think it would be well (if the settlers intend going out in large bodies) to send some person into that Country to make proper arrangements previous to their going; such as to procure Cattle & provisions, provide boats to go down the river &c. The families could come to Alexandria by water: from thence to Fort Cumberland which is 150 miles there is a good waggon road. From the latter place it would be best to pursue Braddocks road (which is well settled & has good accomodations upon it) to Red Stone 75 miles from Cumberland, where boats are built for the purpose of going down the Ohio, & which is the general rendezvous for people going into the Western Country. These Boats are flat, very large & capable of carrying forty or fifty Tons: they cost from twenty to thirty pounds Pennsylvania currency, according to their size. They generally stop at Pittsburgh in their way down, to procure any Articles they may have occasion for: or boats may be procured at that place which is 50 miles from Red Stone old Fort, & the people can embark there. I am &c.

G: Washington

LB, DLC:GW.

1. GW on 20 Nov. acknowledged Hull's letter of 25 Oct.; it is printed in note 2 of Hull's letter.

2. See GW to Tobias Lear, 30 November.

From Lachlan McIntosh

Sir   Savannah, in Georgia, December 29th 1786

Some time since, I had the honor to receive your letter of the 31st of October last, which I took the earliest opportunity to communicate to the Society of Cincinnati in this State. It is with great, and sincere regret, they received the information you were pleased to communicate, that you should be obliged to decline the acceptance of the Presidency of the Society at the ensuing triennial meeting. Your patronage has been the great, perhaps the only means of composing those jealousies, the Institution had excited in the minds of their fellow citizens; and they cannot for bear to express how much they wish you could reconcile it to your health, your inclination, and pursuits to continue to us the honor of presiding in our general meetings—Besides the lustre it would continue to reflect upon the whole Order of Cincinnati, from the Celebrity of your Character, there are other powerful reasons of policy, that ought to induce them to desire it, which they forbear to mention at present; but they are apprehensive, that should they be deprived of the assistance of your Council and advice, they will with difficulty, if at all, be able to obtain those Charters of incorporation, without which, the beneficent intentions of the founders of the institution can never be brought into effective operation.

From motives easy to be conceived, they feel themselves strongly attached to the institution, rendered illustrious by your patronage, and the principles on which it is founded; and they feel a singular satisfaction from the idea, that the jealousies of their fellow-citizens have subsided: a circumstance to be Attributed to the wisdom of your Counsels.

They lament, 'tho they are compelled to acquiesce, in the justice of those reasons you have been pleased to assign, for declining to accept of the appointment of President-general in future. And they beg leave to return you their warmest acknowledgments for having already devoted so much of that time to the interests of the Society; which you had so many just and powerful motives to induce you to devote to your own repose. They cannot say more to you on this subject—should you decline, they must acknowledge the justice of those motives that induce it—Should you accept it, it will add one more to the numberless instances you have given, how much you wish to honor and improve, this pleasing memento of the toils, and mutual Affections of your late Army.

You are now, Sir, withdrawing from public affairs to spend the remainder of your days in retirement; and the Society of this State embrace this occasion of tendering you there sincerest thanks, for the singular, and repeated instances, of your Affection and zeal for the interest of the Army you commanded with so much glory and Success: And they beg leave to make the only return in their power, which is to pray, as they do most fervently; that you may live many, very many years, and enjoy as much felicity yourself as you have procured for thousands. I have the honor to be very respectfuly Sir Your most obedient & most Humble Servt

Lachn McIntosh
President of the Georgia
Society of the Cincinnati

LS, DLC:GW.

To George Weedon

Dear Sir,   Mount Vernon 29th Decr 1786.
    I have been favored with your official letter of the [   ] ulto in answer to my circular one of the 31st October;[1] but will you permit me, in a private & friendly manner, to ask if my letter or

a copy of it has been sent to the Vice President, General Gates? You would have perceived that that letter was intended to have met him in the double capacity of President of the State Society, & Vice President of the Genl Meeting. In the former case, as he did not attend the State meeting in Richmond, it was unnecessary that he should be furnished with a copy of it; but as Vice President he ought to be made acquainted with my intention of not attending the latter—the reason therefore of this enquiry is, that if it has not been by the State Society; I may do it from hence.[2]

I should be glad to know the names of the Delegates from this State to the general meeting to be held in May next at Philada.

I shall be ready at all times between this and the appointment of my Successor, to sign any Diplomas which may be presented to me; but it will readily occur to you that after this event takes place my powers wou'd cease, & the signature would be invalid. With great esteem &c. I am

G: Washington

LB, DLC:GW.
1. Weedon's letter is dated 17 November.
2. Horatio Gates's draft of a letter dated 19 Jan. 1787, presumably to George Weedon, acknowledges a letter of 5 Jan. enclosing GW's circular letter to the Cincinnati of 31 Oct. (NHi: Gates Papers); but see Gates to GW, 19 Jan. 1787.

From Charles Willson Peale

Dr Sir   Phila[delphi]a Decr 31 1786
I have lately undertaken to form a Museum and have acquired the means of preserving in the natural forms, Birds, Beasts and Fish, my Intention is to collect every thing that is curious of this Country, and to arange them in the best manner I am able, to make the Collection amusing and Intructive, thereby hoping to retain with us many things realy curious which would other wise be sent to Europe.

Having heard that you have been presented with some beautiful Birds of China I take the liberty of requesting in Case of the death of any of them, to have them packed in wool and put in any sort of packing Case, and sent by the Stages to me, and I will preserve them in the best manner I am able, and either send them back to you, or place them in my Museum, as your Excellency may please to direct.

The Object with me is, that such beautiful and rare things should not be wholly lost, and which too often are, even when undertaken to be preserved by Persons not sufficiently skilled in the manner of preserving.[1] Please to present my best respects to your Lady, and believe me with much respect and Esteem Dr Sir your very Hble Servant

C. W. Peale

ALS, DLC:GW; ADfS, PPAmP: Charles Willson Peale Papers.

Charles Willson Peale (1741–1827) in 1782 built a large gallery onto his house in Philadelphia in which to show his paintings. On 7 July 1786 he announced that he was making a "part of his House a Repository for Natural Curiosities" so that he could give the public "the sight of many of the Wonderful Works of Nature which are now closeted and but seldom seen" (Miller, *Peale Papers*, 1:448).

1. Peale himself had not yet perfected his technique for preserving animals (Peale to GW, 31 Dec. 1786, n.2, ibid., 464–65). For future correspondence regarding the carcasses of the birds sent by Lafayette to GW, see GW to Peale, 9 Jan., 16 Feb., 13 Mar. 1787, and Peale to GW, 27 Feb., 31 Mar. 1787.

To Pierre L'Enfant

Sir,   Mount Vernon 1st Jany 1787.

The Letter which you did me the honor of writing to me the 6th ulto together with the Memorial which accompanied it came safe, after some delay.

Without entering into the merits of the latter, which I could only do as an individual, I shall regret that your zeal for the honor, & your wishes to advance what you conceived to be the interests of the Society of the Cincinnati, should have led you into difficulties which are attended with such embarrassing circumstances, & from which none but the general meeting (to be held at Philda in May next) can afford you relief. It shall be my care to hand the Memorial to that body for consideration.

In the mean time, if my resources were adequate, it would afford me much pleasure to advance the sum for which you are engaged; but altho' there is no legal obligation upon me to disclose the state of my own finances, and in prudence it might perhaps be better to avoid it; yet Sir, as a testimony of my disposition to serve you if I had the means, I will assure you that what with the losses I sustained during the war, in having, almost without exception, the monies which were due to me paid in at a depreciated value, (some at less than 6d. in the pound)—my own Debts now to pay at their intrinsic value, with interest thereon—& other circumstances which are unnecessary to enumerate, I find it exceedingly difficult, without the weight of extraneous matters, to make my funds & expenditures accord with each other.

I can only repeat to you the pleasure I should have had, & shall have in seeing you at this seat of my retirement, if circumstances had permitted, or would permit you to visit it—& the assurances of esteem with which, I am &c.

G: Washington

P.S. Not knowing that the picture mentioned in the postscript to your letter had been sent to this Country; I wrote to the Gentn who did me the honor of offering it (as soon as I received his letter) declining the acceptance under conviction that it would not have justice done it in any situation I could place it in my house—Since it is arrived I am at a loss what further to say on the subject, as my letter has long since been dispatched, & if I recollect rightly was addressed to your care. Perhaps it would be best now to await a reply.[1] G: W——n

LB, DLC:GW.

1. See Pierre François Cozette to GW, 15 Feb. 1786, and note 1 of that document.

Mount Vernon Store Book

Editorial Note

The Mount Vernon store book preserved at Mount Vernon lists "Articles recd into the Store" between 6 Jan. and 14 Nov. 1787, and "Articles del[ivere]d out of the Store" from 1 Jan. to 31 Dec. 1787; it also contains the "Rum Acct" from 1 Jan. to 9 Oct. 1787. On the first page of the store book is a listing of the "Skins put into the Vatts Apl 12th 1787" at Mount Vernon farms (House, River, Dogue Run, and Muddy Hole): 32 cowhides, 1 bull hide, 9 calf skins, 6 horsehides, and 7 ass skins. Only the January records for the store are printed here. A transcription of the entire Mount Vernon Store Book is in CD-ROM:GW.

[1–31 January 1787]

Articles recd into the Store

Jany

6   3 Barls Clover seed Contg 10 Bushls @ 54/ pr Bushl each Bushl weighing 68½ lb.

10   6 sides of upper leather from Fairfax

12   30 Sides Sole leather from Do, 9 Sides upper leather from Do, 16 Sides Do from Do & 1 peice

19   4 Balls shoe thread

20   4 lb. of Powder @ 2/6 pr lb.

23   11 Sides upper Leather from Fairfax

26   Recd the following Harness belonging to the Baggage Waggon, viz., 2 breast plates—2 pr traces—2 short swingle trees—1 long Do—4 Collars—2 pr Hames—2 pole chains—

29   11 pr leading lines from the old seine line

Articles del[ivere]d out of the Store.

Jany

1   *200* 10d. & *400* 6d. nails to Mathew for the New Room—*400* old 8d. nails deld to muddy hole will for makg doors

2   *400* 6d. nails to Green for the Bottle rack—A Ditching line to the Ger[ma]n—4 Mattocks & 3 Axes to Sambo to put helves into & to be returned—*Returned*—1 handsaw file to Mahony—4 Mattocks & 3 axes to Frenche's Plantation

4   1 pruning chissel & 2 staves to Muddy hole Will (returned)—*100* 10d. nails to Muddy hole

5   *200* 6d.—*200* 4d. brads to Mathew for the New Room

6   1 Bag timothy seed sent to Col. Bland by the Norfk Packt[1]

8   *50* 3od. nails to Green for a Chaff box

9   *200* 10d. to the Mill

11   1 side sole leather to Shoemakr

12   4 Charges of Powder & Shott to Fairfax

13   1 Ball thread to Shoemaker—1 lb. Powder to Davis to blow Rocks with—*50* tacks to Mathw for listing the dining room door—*50* 2od. nails to Smith the Ship Carpenter

15 1¼ powder to Davis for to blow Rocks
16 60 30d. nails to the Ship Carpenter—2 pr leading lines of the old
    Jack line to Frenche's Qr.—2 pr plow traces to Do—1 Side up-
    per leather to the Shoemaker
18 ½ bagg white lead to Mathew, to put on the mouldings in the
    New Room—1 paper Lampblack to Fairfax to blk Calves Skins
19 25 30d. & 60 8d. nails to Smith Ship Carpenter—½ lb. Powder
    to Overseer—1 lb. Shott to Davis
20 1 side sole leather to Shoemaker—20 bundles Twine to Lawce
    McGinnis for the Seine
22d 1 lb. powder to Cornelius to blow Rocks—50 30d. nails to Tom
    Green to secure rafters in removing Richards House
23 50 20d. nails to Isaac to bond a Cart body—1 Handsaw file to Do
27 1 Frying pan for Dutch woman—2 pr Traces, 2 pr Hames, to
    Frenches Quarter—200 10d. nails to Smith Ship Carpenter
29 1 Pr leadg lines to French's Qr.—1 Spade to the Dutchman
30 1 Spade to Breeche (old one)—1 Side sole leather to Shoemr
31 100 6d. brads to Mathew

1787 Rum Acct Dr
Jany
 1 To 70 Gallons in the Store

Rum—Cr	
Weekly Allowances deld out of the Store	
To the Joiners & Cornelius	10½ pints
To Shoemr & Taylor	3½ Do
To Lawson Ditcher	3 Do
To the German	2 Do
To Davy	2 Do
To Morris	2 Do
To Muddy hole Will	2 Do
To Isaac	2 Do
To Philip ⟨*illegible*⟩ Apl 11th	2 Do
To Thos Green 2 pints	3⅝ Gallons

Jany
12 The white people have one bottle per day from this date on acct
    of the Cyder's being out
 4 Deld Sam 1 bottle for burng the brick kiln
 6 Boatswain 1 pint for the same purpose—2 Bottles for the house
 7 1 quart to Smith the ship Carpenter—1 qt to Sam for burng the
    Kiln
 9 1 qt To Do for Do—1 qt to Smith S. Carpenter—2 qts to Mill

12	2 qts to Do—1 Do to House
15	2 qts to Mill wrights
16	1 Do to Smith Ship Carpr
16	1 Do to Do
17	2 Do to Millwrights
18	1 pint to a sick woman at French's Quarter
19	1 qt to Ship Carpenter—2 qts to the Millwrights
20	1 Do to Smith Ship Carpenter—1 qt to the House
22	2 Gallons to Lawson the Ditcher—2 qts to the Millwrights
24	2 qts to Do
25	1 qt to Smith Ship Carpenter
26	2 qts to the Millwrights
27	1 qt to Smith Ship Carpenter
28	2 qts to the Ho.
29	2 qts to the Mill
31	2 qts to the Mill

D, ViMtV.

1. See GW to Theodorick Bland, 28 Dec. 1786.

To Unknown

Gentn   Mount Vernon Jany 1st 1787

I have no superfine flour in my Mill, at present; nor do I believe I have any Wheat that will make such as I should incline to brand with that mark. This being the case, I have not yet attempted to make any; consequently have fixed no price. I will consult my Miller, and if he thinks the Wheat will yield better flour than I expect I will inform you of it, and the price; but request you would not, by placing the smallest dependence thereon, forbear to purchase elsewhere if it is to be had. I am Gentn Yr Obedt Hble Servt

Go: Washington

ALS, anonymous donor.

From Clement Biddle

Mount Vernon Jany 2d 1787

I have before me your esteemed favour of 5th ultimo—It is necessary that the Certificate remaining here to draw Interest which will be pd every 6 months very near to the day it is due yet the Principal will only sell for 6/ in the Pound—Mr Haines has promised me fifty Bushels of the best Spring Barley for seed without any Engagements on your part for the Produce & I have also bespoke the Red Cloverseed & can have both ready in a few hours warning but our River has been shut up for four Weeks past and tho' there is an appearance of a temporary Opening from the Present Thaw, I cannot find on an inquiry I have just made along the Wharves that there is any Vessel for Potowmack but as there will Certainly be one on the Breaking up of the Ice in February you may depend on the Barley & Seed being Shipped by the first Opportunity—it will [be] time enough to send the money when I shall ascertain the Cost of these Articles. I have made Enquiry of Several for the Jerusalem Artichoke but can find but one person (Jos: James) who knows it he says that he thinks he may find some persons who have Cultivated them & if he can will try to get them—he says they are the same as what we call the Hoppiny which grows in the Woods and are often rooted up by our hogs. &ca

C.B.

ADfS, ViMtV: Clement Biddle Letterbook.

From Henry Emanuel Lutterloh

Sir!   at Wilmington in North Carolina Janry 3d 1787
    Your Excellency will be pleased to excuse the Liberty of addressing myself to You, with a Proposition for a Delivery of Several Hundred German Famelies to settle those large Tracts of Your Own, or any other Virginia Gentlemens Estates, Who may Chuse to be Subscribers, to the Plan—Your Excellys former Publications to encourage Settlers to come, and the late Act passed by Your Assembly, to Stop all future Importations of Negroes, are My Motives, for offering my Service. My being a German, and well-acquainted with all the different Principalities, Their Law's, and the only Way in which a Native is able to get Usefull people out; as also having the Honour to be Known to Your Excell. creates an Earnest Wish to serve the State of Vir-

ginia—It needs no long Explination to Shew, that Such a Rich and large State, Must want an encrease of Settlers and Working hands; That the Germans have Evinced their Superiority in cultivating Tracts, Pensilvania alone proves; and that State, owes its Wealth to them. It is also certain, that white people can Work in hot Climaths, and Their being Settled upon large Tracts will make the Proprietors richer, than by an Equal Numbers of Blacks; and with less expences—By my Plan, at large, I mean to procure Good families, not only for Settling Farms, but also Manufactores, Men who understand Working in the Mines of all Oars [ores], Canall pickers, and able Workmen, &ca. If your Excelly should wish to be acquainted with the Plan, and would honour it with your Protection in Virginia! I will upon the receipt of Your Answer, wait upon you, to convince you more fully, of its Utility,[1] as also to have the great happiness of Assuring you, of my Most profountest Respects, in which I have the Honour to be Yr Excely Most obedt honest Sert

Henry Emanuel Lutterloh

ALS, DLC:GW.

Henry Emanuel Lutterloh, a former member of the duke of Brunswick's guards who served as deputy quartermaster general in the Continental army, bought at the end of the war a plantation near Wilmington, North Carolina.

1. GW expressed his interest in Lutterloh's plan in a letter of 8 April 1787, and Lutterloh wrote GW on 13 June spelling out what he was proposing. For Lutterloh's attempts to secure employment in the new federal government during GW's presidency, see GW to Lutterloh, 1 Jan. 1789, and notes.

To Battaile Muse

Sir,   Alexandria Jany 3d 1787

Having an immediate occasion for a sum of money, it would be very acceptable to me to receive what is in your hands of mine. An order on any person in this place, that would be punctually complied with, will suit me. I am Sir yr Very Hble Servt

Go: Washington

ALS, NcD: Battaile Muse Papers.

From Battaile Muse

Honourable Sir   January 3d 1787

Your Favour dated December the 4th I received a few days ago—which is Very Sattisfactory to me I shall attend Perticularly to Every thing required, and will act as well For your interest In the management of your Business as tho. the leases was my Own always holding in View your Instructions.

I have not received one shillings Since I was at Mount Vernon I have made many application⟨s⟩ In Pressing Terms the Scarcity of money and bad weather prevents a prospect of money before March or april and I Fear May—I shall Take Every Step in my Power To Make the Collecton in due Time and Soon after it Falls into my hands it shall be Conveyed To you—Should you be in want of money Please To inform me by next Post and I will draw on Mr Andrew Wales For one hundred pounds in your Favour—I wish for Timely notice that He Mr Wales may Provide with Certainty. I am Sir your obedient Humble Servant

                                                        Battaile Muse

N.B. Mr Wales I expect Cannot Pay untill the 1st of march—if required sooner I must notify Him of the day therefore Please To write me and oblige. B.M.

ALS, DLC:GW.

From Edmund Randolph

Sir   Richmond Jany 4. 178[7]

Inclosed I return to you the papers which accompanied your favor of the 25th ulto. It did not reach me, until yesterday morning, when I submitted the whole to the assembly. But the approach of the session to an end forbids them to take up new business. The day after tomorrow is fixed for their departure, and much of what is now before them must be left incomplete. I am therefore desired by the speaker of the delegates to send the papers to you; and to assure you, that the assembly are fully sensible of your readiness to embrace every opportunity to improve the manufactures of our country. You know, sir, that the executive cannot give an establishment or even aid to Mr de la Vallée, without the approbation of the legislature.[1]

Altho' I was compelled by duty to lay before the council your answer to my notification of your appointment to Phila., I was happy to find them concurring with me, in the propriety of in-treating you not to decide on a refusal immediately. Perhaps the obstacles, now in view, may be removed, before May; and the nomination of a successor, if necessary at all, will be as effectually made sometime hence, as now. Perhaps too (and indeed I fear the event) every other consideration may seem of little waight, when compared with the crisis, which may then hang over the united states. I hope therefore, that you will excuse me for hold-ing up your letter for the present, and waiting until time shall disclose the result of the commotions now prevailing. I have the honor sir to be with the most perfect exteem and respect yr mo. ob. serv.

Edm: Randolph

ALS, DLC:GW. Randolph dated the letter 1786.

1. There is no reference in the house journals to Lavallée's "letter, Plan & Estimate for establishing a manufacture of Cotton" sent by GW to Randolph (GW to Lavallée, 23 Dec. 1786). The legislature adjourned 11 January.

From George Digges

Dear Sir   Annapolis Jany 5. 1787

Mr Gilliss Polk (who is now here) & lives at Salisbury in Som-erset County will Immediately upon his return home have the plank sawed agreable to your directions & also will forward it by the first Oppertunity[1]—Our Senate have rejected the Money Bill & this day we expect a Message from them given their rea-sons. We have done little or no Public Business nor doe I believe we shall as there seems to be a Party for breaking up at all events next Week with Compts to Mrs Washington & family am Dear Sir with great Respect Yr Most Ob. Sevt

Geo. Digges

N.B. I did not get yr Letter till after the post left Town & Mr Powell the bearer of this has promised to forward it.[2]

ALS, DLC:GW.

1. GW wrote Digges on 28 Dec. 1786 asking him to secure from Maryland's Eastern Shore planking for the flooring of his New Room. Gilliss Polk wrote GW on 14 April 1787 that he had procured "one thousand feet of flooring plank, to be precisely 24 feet long when dressed."

2. GW had requested Digges to answer "by the Post." Mr. Powell may be either Joseph Powell, Jr., of Fairfax County or Leven Powell of Loudoun County.

From John Jay

Dear Sir　　　　　　　　　　　　　　　　New York 7 Jany 1787

They who regard the public good with more Attention & Attachment than they do mere personal concerns, must feel and confess the Force of such Sentiments as are expressed in your Letter to me by Col. Humphreys last Fall. The situation of our Affairs calls not only for Reflection and Prudence but for Exertion. What is to be done? is a common Question, but it is a Question not easy to answer.

Would the giving *any* further Degree of Power to Congress do the Business? I am inclined to think it would not—for among other Reasons[:]

It is natural to suppose there will always be members who will find it convenient to make their *Seats* subservient to partial & personal Purposes; and they who may be *able* and *willing* to concert and promote useful and national measures, will seldom be unembarrassed by the Ignorance, Prejudices, Fears, or interested Views of others.

In so large a Body Secrecy and Dispatch will be too uncommon; and foreign as well as local Influence will frequently oppose and sometimes frustrate the wisest measures.

Large assemblies often misunderstand or neglect the Obligations of Character Honor and Dignity; and will collectively do or omit Things which individual Gentlemen in Private Capacities would not approve. As the many divide Blame and also divide Credit, too little a Portion of either falls to each mans Share, to affect him strongly; even in Cases where the whole Blame or the whole Credit must be national. It is not easy for those to think and feel as Sovereigns, who have always been accustomed to think and feel as Subjects.

The Executive Business of Sovereignty depending on so many wills, and those wills moved by such a Variety of contradictory motives and Inducements will in general be but feebly done.

Such a Sovereign, however *theoretically* responsible, cannot be effectually so in its Departments and Officers, without adequate Judicatories.

I therefore promise myself nothing very desireable from any Change which does not divide the Sovereignty into its proper Departments—Let Congress legislate, let others execute, let others judge.

Shall we have a King? not in my opinion while other Expedients remain untried. might we not have a Governor General limited in his Prerogatives and Duration? might not Congress be divided into an upper and a lower House? the former appointed for Life, the latter annually; and let the Governor General (to preserve the Ballance) with the advice of a Council formed, for that *only* purpose of the great judicial officers, have a negative on their acts. our Government should in some Degree be suited to our manners and Circumstances, and they you know are not strictly Democratical.

What Powers should be granted to the Government so constituted is a Question which deserves much Thought—I think the more the better—the States retaining only so much as may be necessary for domestic Purposes; and all their principal Officers civil and military being commissioned and removeable by the national Governmt.

These are short Hints—Details would exceed the Limits of a Letter, and to you be superfluous.

A convention is in contemplation, and I am glad to find your Name among those of its intended Members.

To me the Policy of such a Convention appears questionable. Their authority is to be derived from acts of the State Legislatures. Are the State Legislatures authorized either by themselves or others, to alter Constitutions? I think not. They who hold Commissions can by virtue of them, neither retrench nor extend the Powers conveyed by them. Perhaps it is intended that this Convention shall not *ordain*, but only *recommend*—if so—there is Danger that their Recommendations will produce endless Discussions, and perhaps Jealousies and Party Heats.

Would it not be better, for Congress plainly and in strong Terms to declare, that the present fœderal Government is inadequate to the Purposes for which it was instituted—That they forbear to point out its *particular* Defects, or to ask for an Extension of any *particular* powers, lest improper Jealousies should thence arise; but that in their opinion it would be expedient for the People of the States without Delay to appoint State Conventions (in the way they chuse their General Assemblies) with the *sole* and express power of appointing Deputies to a general Convention, who or the majority of whom should take into consideration the articles of Confederation, & make such alterations amendments and additions thereto as to them should appear necessary and proper; and which being by them ordained and published should have the same force & obligation which all or any of the present articles now have.

No alterations in the Government should I think be made, nor if attempted will easily take place, unless deduceable from the only Source of just authority—*the People*. accept my dear Sir, my warmest and most cordial wishes for your Health and Happiness, and believe me to be with the greatest Respect and Esteem, Your most obt & hble Servt

John Jay

ALS, DLC:GW.

To Jabez Bowen

Dear Sir,   Mount Vernon Jany 9. 178[7]
    I have received your letter of the 23d of Novr.¹ I should have been happy to have seen you at Mount Vernon agreeable to your intention had you proceeded as far as Annapolis. The Convention at that place would undoubtedly have been productive of some benefit to the Union had it taken place, but the tardiness of the Commissioners from several States rendered abortive every advantage that was expected from it. It is surprising to me that a due punctuality cannot be observed in meetings of this nature, the time is fixed and known, and every Gentleman when he accepts the appointment should consider the business of the meeting as depending upon him, and should determine not to retard its proceedings by a want of punctuality in his Attendance; it is a public duty to which every private consideration should give way.

    I have been long since fully convinced of the necessaty of Granting to Congress more ample and extensive powers than they at present possess; the want of power an[d] energy in that

Body has been severely felt in every part of the United States. The disturbances in new England, The declining state of our Commerce—and the general languor which seems to pervade the Union are in a great measure (if not entirely) owing to the want of proper Authority in the surpreme Council. The extreeme jealousy that is observed in vesting Congress with adequate powers has a tendency rather to distroy than confim our liberty's the wisest resolutions cannot produce any good unless they are supported with energy—they are only applauded, but never followed.

Paper money has had the effect in your State that it ever will have, to ruin commerce—oppress the honest, and open a door to every species of fraud and injustice.

I am entirely in sentiment with you Sir, of the necessity there is to adopt some measures for the support of our national peace & honor; the present situation of our public affairs demands the exertion and influence of every good and honest Citizen in the Union, to tranquilize disturbances, retrieve our Credit and place us upon a respectable footing with other Nations.

The Death of our worthy friend General Greene must be sincerely regreated by every friend to America, and peculiarly by those whose intimacy with him gave them a full knowledge of his Virtues and merits. I am dear Sir Yr most Obedt Hble Servant

Go. Washington

LB, DLC:GW.
    Jabez Bowen (1739–1815), a lawyer in Providence, was deputy governor of Rhode Island from 1778 to 1786.
    1. Letter not found.

To Daniel Carroll

Sir,   Mount Vernon 9th Jany 1787.
    Your letter of the 26th ult. did not reach me till within these 3 days, or it should have received an earlier acknowledgment.[1]
    The Land I advertised for Sale in Fayette County containing 1650 acres or there abouts, by the Patents, may, as a tract, be considered as equal to any in that County, or Country; but as it is my wish that the purchaser should examine it, I will say no

more than that there is an appearance of a rich Iron Ore at the door of the mill, which is now much out of repair.[2]

Small tracts of land in the vicinity of this, of the same quality have sold for three pounds & upwards Pens⟨a⟩ Curry an acre— But if one person will take the whole of mine, I would let it go for Forty shillings that money an acre (payable in specie) one four⟨th⟩ down—the other three fourths in annual payments, with interest [fr]om[3] the date of the Bonds; perhaps a [lo]nger time might be allowed. I am Sir your very Hble Servt

Go: Washington

ALS (facsimile), sold by Superior Auction Galleries, Paul Richards Estate Auction, 2 Feb. 1994; LB, DLC:GW.

1. Letter not found.

2. GW's most recent advertisement of the sale, lease, or rent of Washington's Bottom is printed in GW to Charles Simms, 22 Sept. 1786, n.6.

3. Material in square brackets is taken from the letter-book copy.

Letter not found: from John Nicholson, 9 January. On 23 Jan. GW wrote to Nicholson: "Your letter of the 9th instant . . . came duly to hand."

To Charles Willson Peale

Sir,   Mount Vernon Jany 9th 1787.

Your letter of the 31st of Decemr came duly to hand. I cannot say that I shall be happy to have it in my power to comply with your request by sending you the bodies of my Pheasants; but I am afraid it will not be long before they will compose a part of your Museum, as they all appear to be drooping. One of the Silver Pheasants died sometime before the receipt of your letter, and its body was thrown away—but whenever any of the others make their exit they shall be sent to you agreeable to your request. I am Sir Yr most Obedt Hble Servt

Go: Washington

LS (photocopy), in the hand of Tobias Lear, DLC:GW; LB, DLC:GW. The LS was offered for sale by the American Art Association, 17 Mar. 1931.

To Thomas Seddon & Co.

Gentn   Mo[un]t Vernon 9th Jany 1787.
I have received your letter of the 10th of Decemr together with the several numbers of the Columbian Magazine. I thank you for your attention to me in sending the several numbers which have been published, & wish you to consider me a subscriber; as I conceive a publication of that kind may be the means of conveying much useful knowledge to the community which might otherwise be lost, and when it is properly conducted, it should, in my opinion be properly encouraged.[1] I am Gentn &c.

G: Washington

LB, DLC:GW.
1. Thomas Seddon, who had a book and stationery store in Philadelphia, joined with the editor Mathew Carey, the engraver James Trenchard, and two successful Philadelphia printers, Charles Cist and William Spotswood, to begin publication in 1786 of the *Columbian Magazine: or Monthly Miscellany*. In January and February 1787 the magazine ran David Humphreys' piece relating to GW and the Asgill affair (see Humphreys to GW, 16 Nov. 1786, n.1). On 11 Feb. GW instructed Clement Biddle to pay Seddon & Co. for the *Columbian Magazine*, and Biddle's invoice of 20 Feb. shows his payment of ten shillings. The letter of 10 Dec. 1786 from Thomas Seddon & Co. has not been found.

To Charles Carter

Dear Sir,   Mount Vernon 10th Jany 1787.
I should have presented you with an earlier acknowledgement of your favor of the 4th ulto, but expecting to meet the Directors of the Potomac Company, I delayed writing 'till it was over, that I might give you the trouble of receiving one letter *only*, in answer to the several parts of it.[1]
Having laid before the Directors that part of your letter which respects the opinions of Mr Yates & Captn Harris on inland navigations unincumbered with Locks, I am authorised to say that any information on this head from Captain Harris, containing the principles of the substitutes for Locks, by which so considerable a saving as you speak of can be made, would be most thankfully received; & if upon the investigation or practice on them, they shall be found of such œconomy & utility as is mentioned—

the Board would chearfully give a further proof of their sense of the obligation they would feel themselves under for such important advice.[2]

When you shall have received Mr Yates's observations on the comparison of the Orchard & New river grasses, I shall be obliged to you for a transcript of them; as I am persuaded they have been made with attention, accuracy & judgment. I have never seen, nor do I remember ever to have read or heard of any grass, denominated Egyptian grass. Whence comes it? From the Country of that name? If so, may it not in fact be our Blue grass, not yet perfectly assimilated by the Climate & soil of this meridian?

I am much obliged by the offer of your farm for the accommodation of my lately arrived Jack Ass; (which I think an exceeding fine one) but as he is too young to cover, being only two years old, & females came along with him, the same attendance does for all of them. And besides as they seem (if I was to form an opinion of the two Jacks from present appearances) to be designed for as different purposes as a Courser and Dray, there will be no propriety in separating them hereafter. The one will suit the strong heavy draft, & the other the light & active one for the road.

I pray you to offer my best respects to Mrs Carter, in which Mrs Washington unites. I am Sir, Your Most Obedt hble Servant
                                        G: Washington

LB, DLC:GW.

1. The letter from Charles Carter (1733–1796) of Ludlow has not been found.

2. Charles Yates (1728–1809) came from England in 1752 and became a merchant and planter at Fredericksburg where he took an interest in agricultural experimentation. See *Diaries*, 5:148–49. James Harris was manager of the James River Company.

Letter not found: to William Deakins, Jr., 10 Jan. 1787. Deakins wrote GW on 10 Jan.: "I have your favor of this date."

From William Deakins, Jr.

Sir.   George Town [Md.] 10th Janry 1787
I have your favor of this date.[1] It gives me pain to Inform you I have not yet purchased more than 20 Bushels of Poland Oats

that are in hand. I had Contracted in different Lands for 100 Bushels to be delivered the 1st of this month—but the Farmers from whom I had engaged them, have deceived me, but I have sent out into the Country within these few days past & expect to get you at least 100 Bushels & If possible will make the Quantity 200 Bushels. You may at all Events Calculate to receive at least 100 Bushels by the 15th day of Next month[2]—I am Sir Your Obt Servt

Will. Deakins Junr

ALS, DLC:GW.
   1. Letter not found.
   2. See Deakins to GW, 9 Nov. 1786 and 25, 31 Jan. 1787.

From William Drayton

Sir,   Charleston [S.C.] Jany 10. 1787

I should have done myself the Honour of acknowleging sooner the Receipt of your Letter, dated Novr 12th, but that by some unaccountable Delay it did not reach my Hands, 'till a few Days ago.

The Trouble you have had with my Negro Man demands the most grateful Sentiments, & the warmest Thanks from me; altho' the Event did not answer your kind Intentions on the Occasion.[1]

I beg Leave to offer my most respectful Compliments to Mrs Washington, & to your Nephew and his Lady, & to assure your Excellency, that with the highest Esteem & Regard I am, Sir, your most obedient & obliged humble Servant

Wm Drayton

ALS, DLC:GW.
   1. No letter from GW to Drayton of 12 Nov. has been found, but it seems certain that Drayton is referring to the letter from GW dated 20 November.

To Bushrod Washington

My Dear Bushrod,   Mount Vernon 10th Jany 1787.

I condole most sincerely with you, my Sister & family, on the death of my Brother. I feel most sensibly for this event; but resignation being our duty, to attempt an expression of my sorrow on this occasion would be as feebly described, as it would be unavailing when related.

If there are any occasional services which I can render my Sister or any of you, I shall have great pleasure in the execution. If I could discharge the duties of an Executor, I would undertake the trust most chearfully; but in truth I am not in a situation to do this. Already I am so much involved in, & so perplexed with other peoples affairs, that my own are very much unattended to. Happily, there is not the least occasion of my assistance in the administration of your deceased Father's Estate— Your competency *alone* is sufficient—for this purpose—when joined by that of my Sister & your brother, the task will be easy. It may be an alleviating circumstance of my brother's death, that his affairs fall into such good hands, & that each of you have dispositions & capability to do what is proper.

I hope this letter will find my Sister in a better situation than when your's left her. Every good wish of this family is offered for it, & the sincerest regard for you all. With unfeigned Affection I am &c.

G: Washington

P.S. Mr Lear is returned from the Western Country. In consequence of my request to Majr Freeman, to advance Mr Smith's fees for the Suit depending on accot of your Lands in Fayette Coty, he has sent me the enclosed, which I forward that you may know how that matter stands.[1] G: W——n

LB, DLC:GW.

1. The "enclosed," probably a letter from Freeman to John Augustine Washington, has not been identified.

To James Hill

Sir,   Mo[un]t Vernon 12th Jany 1787.

Your Letter of the 24th of September in answer to mine of the 20th of August was a long time in getting to my hands, & very unsatisfactory when it arrived.[1] If you were ever directed by me to settle your accounts with, & pay the produce of my Estate under your management into the hands of Mr Posey, I should be glad to receive a copy of the order. My memory, nor any paper in my possession does not furnish me with the least trace of my having ever given such an order; yet I will not say the fact is otherwise, because the busy scenes in which I was engaged during my continuance in public life; & the multiplicity of things which were constantly pressing on my mind in those days, may have driven the remembrance of it from me. It is for this reason I ask for a copy of the authority under which that matter was transacted. The last letter I can find any copy of, to you, was written from a place called Fredg in the State of New York and dated the 27th of Octor in answer to one from you of the 5th of September. In this letter I inform you that I had rented my whole Estate, under your care, to Mr Custis, & requested in the most explicit terms, "that all the money you now possess, or may hereafter receive of mine, before you quit Mr Custis's business, may be sent to Mr Lund Washington by him or some other safe hand. And before you remove from your present employment, I must further beg that you will furnish me with an exact accot of every thing sold from, & purchased for my Estate under your care—in short, the exact state of all expenditures & sales for my use since the last account I settled with you myself; & as letters are subject to miscarriage, I shall be obliged to you to leave a copy thereof with a list of the balances due me (if any there should be), with Mr Custis, that I may in case of accidents be provided with another copy from him. When I speak of a list of balances, I hope & trust there will be few or none—first from your care in making your collections, & next from the plenty of money, which leaves every person without even the shadow of excuse to withhold payment of debts, at this time. But if the case should be otherwise, a list of those debts first properly settled & reduced to specialties (to avoid disputes in the collection by a new hand unacquainted with the transactions, & unable to account for things which would not be disputed with you) left with Mr Custis, will enable him, or some other person in my behalf to receive payment of the money, with such interest as may be due on the Bonds or Bills."[2]

In a P.S. to this letter, you are desired to put the Tobacco Notes into Colo. Bassett's hands, to be disposed of for my benefit. If subsequent to these you received orders from me to pay my money, & surrender your accots into the hands of Mr Posey, I should be glad to be informed of it, as it is my desire to act with candour & fairness in this as well as in every other business.[3] To me it seems exceedingly strange, however, that you should have no copies of the accounts you gave up—common prudence I should have thought would have dictated a measure of this kind to any man.

In your letter of the 24th of September last, you say you never received any money from Mr Newton except £180—from one Jacob Williams by his order; but by a letter of your own, in my possession, dated the 10th of May 1777, you not only acknowledge the receipt of the above sum, but of £120 more from Mr Willm Holt in consequence of an order from the same Gentleman; & besides these two sums, I am charged in Mr Newton's account with £100 paid you the 12th of September 1776 at the time you received these orders.[4]

It is indispensably necessary that these matters between you & me shou'd be settled, & it is much my wish that it could be done in an amicable & friendly way. I hope you will therefore pursue the necessary modes to do this & without delay which will be exceedingly pleasing to, Sir, Yr very hble Servt

G: Washington

P.S. I have just written to Mr Posey to surrender your[5] Accots to you or me.

LB, DLC:GW.

1. The letter-book copy of GW's earlier letter to Hill is dated 29, not 20, Aug., and Hill in his letter of 24 Sept. refers to GW's letter of 29 August.

2. Both Hill's letter to GW and GW's reply are in DLC:GW.

3. No letter ordering Hill to surrender his accounts to John Price Posey has been found.

4. Hill's letter of 10 May 1777 has not been found. In Hill's account enclosed in his letter of 1 Feb. 1787 to GW he notes that on 5 May 1777 he received £120 "from Wm Holt for an Order given by T. Newton." In Newton's account with GW in Ledger B (p. 85), a payment of £100 from Newton was recorded on 18 Sept. as having been made to James Hill. For more on GW's settlement of his account with Newton, see GW to Newton, 3 Sept. 1785, n.2.

5. The copyist should have written "his."

To John Price Posey

Sir,   Mount Vernon 12th Jany 1787.

It will not be difficult for you to conceive my surprise when I inform you that after waiting near three years since my return home in expectation that an account would be rendered me of the management of my Estate below; & calling, with some degree of astonishment, on Mr Hill for this neglect, to find by his answer lately received, that the accounts had been settled years ago with you, & not only the produce of that Estate paid into your hands, but that other considerable sums of money which he had collected for me from Mr Newton of Norfolk, for Flour, Fish &c. sent him from my Estate in this County to dispose of on commission had gone this way also.[1]

If it had been inconvenient for you to have delivered me my money, would it not have been right to have given me the accot & to have informed me of the circumstances which had occasioned the detention of it? Strange and unaccountable as this conduct is, I shall for the present (as I am entirely in the dark with respect to this business) content myself with requesting that the accounts & papers which were put into your hands for my use by Mr Hill, may be returned either to him or me, with a statement of any transactions of your own on my account, previously or subsequent thereto, that I may know how to come to a final settlement with Mr Hill.

This request, I expect will meet no denial or delay: reason, Justice & every other consideration call upon you for a compliance therewith.[2] I am Sir Your hble Servt

G: Washington

LB, DLC:GW.

1. See GW to James Hill, 29 Aug. 1786, and Hill to GW, 24 Sept. 1786. For John Price Posey's management of the Custis estate in the York River area, see Bartholomew Dandridge to GW, 13 Mar. 1784, and note 3 of that document.

2. See Posey's answer to this letter, written on 27 January.

From Robinson, Sanderson, & Rumney

Sir   Whitehaven [England] 12th Jany 1787

By the Esther Capt. Ledger we hope you will receive the above safe, & please.[1] We shall always be happy to forward you any thing we can procure in this Part of the Country and are with the greatest Respect Sir Your much Oblig'd & Very Hble Servts

Robinson Sanderson & Rumney

Mr Sanderson presents his Comps. to you & your Lady.
N.B. We shall forward you soon Two Hounds of Slow pace.

LS, DLC:GW.

1. The accompanying invoice from Whitehaven, dated 10 Jan., lists "125 Diamond Flaggs" at a charge of £13.18.1½, which GW had ordered for the floor of his piazza at Mount Vernon. See GW to John Rumney, Jr., 3 July 1784, and citations in that document. They also billed him for "1 pair Best Spectacles, Silver Frames," £1.2, and for "4 pair best Eyes, fitted to the Silver Frames & fixed in Wire @ 2/6," ten shillings. The total charge for the articles and shipping in Virginia currency was £8.6.9.

Letter not found: to William Deakins, Jr., 13 Jan. 1787. Deakins wrote GW on 25 Jan.: "Your favor of the 13th Current did not come to hand till the day before Yesterday."

From Lafayette

My dear General   Paris January the 13th 1787
It is I Hope Easier for You to Conceive than for me to Express the Painful Sensations I feel, when the long Waited for Opportunity of Hearing from You, Happens at last to Arrive without one line of Yours. the Regularity of Packets is now Reestablished, and they will Return to the Havre the Nearest Port to Paris. This will be entrusted to Colonel franks, who is Coming from a Successfull Negociation at Morocco Where Mr Barcklay and Himself Behaved Very Well.[1] I wish our affairs Had taken the Same turn in Algiers, and think the Best Way to Crush those Rascals should Be a Confederation Betwen the Powers at War with them Each Giving a Certain sum, which Would Be Employed By one Man, or Council of Men, in the fitting out, and Constantly Keeping in Cruize a Naval Squadron Adapted to the purpose. the affairs of Holland are not Settled. the State Holder is Stuborn. Some Patriots Carry their Views Very far. prussia wants to keep up the Splendor, if not the Power of A Brother in law—and france, who of all things is Averse to War, Wants to Conciliate, and throws Cold Water on them all. it Seems that the King of Prussia Has not obtained the Wisdom of His Uncle along with His throne. they Say He will go into frivolities. What Great Britain and the United States will do Respecting the forts I do not know, But know Very Well what I wish America to do,

and what part I would like to Act in the Business. the Empress of Russia is Going to Krimée, and Had Been pleased to invite me there. But I Have Been suddenly detained By an Event Which for a long time Had not taken place in france. the King Has Convocated for the End of the Month, an Assembly of Notables, Composed of principal Men in each order of the Kingdom, not Holding offices at Court. it Will Consist of Hundred and forty Members, ArchBishops, Bishops, Nobles, presidents of the Several parliaments, Mayors of towns. Your only Acquaintances in the Assembly are Count d'estaing, duke de laval, and Your Humble Servant, who Are three Among the six and thirty of the order of Noblesse. the King's letter Announces an Examination of the finances to Be adjusted, of the Means to alleviate the taxes of the people, and of Many abuses to Be Redressed. You easely Conceive that there is at Bottom a desire to Make Monney Some How or other, in order to put the Receipt on a level With the Expenses, Which in this Country is Become Enormous on Account of the Sums Squandered on Courtiers and Superfluities. But there Was no Way more patriotic, more Candid, more Noble to Effect those purposes. The King and M. de Calonne His Minister deserve Great Credit for that. and I Hope a tribute of Gratitude and Good Will shall Reward this popular Measure. my Earnest Wish, and fond Hope is that our Meeting will produce popular Assemblies in the provinces, the destruction of Many Schlakles of the trade, and a change in the fate of the protestants, Events Which I will promote By my friends as well as my feeble endeavours with all my Heart. I Had Been on the first lists. on the last one I was not, But Before I Could Enquire Which Was the Motive of Exclusion, the Matter Had Been Set to Rights. I will Give You an account of the Assembly, not only Because What Concerns me Cannot Be Stranger to My dear General, But also Because Every thing is interesting which influences the Happiness of 26 millions of People.[2]

You Have Heard of a Certain Beniousky who Wanted to have a legion in our Army and who Has Since Gone to Madagascar on An Expedition in which some Baltimore Merchants, whom I Had Warned Against it, were interested. Beniousky Has pillaged the french Settlement at Madagascar—a few Men were sent to attak Him from the isle of france, and He Was Killed. I am Going to Versaïlles, and Will Request the Minister to Send Home what Citizens of America may Happen to be there, as I Understand there is one Among the prisoners with the Badge of the Cincinnati. Beniousky's whole forces were Under forty White men.[3]

I Have already wrote to You that the Hams are Arrived in the Best order, and paid my best thanks to Mrs Washington. But I Repeat it in this letter as, from the scarcity of Yours, I Hope Many are lost in the Way. This present Has Been Most Agreable in the family, and it is difficult to Express How wellcomed is a Mount Vernon produce at Such a distance.

There is an Italico American of Your Acquaintance Mr Mazzei Who seems to me a Man very well fitted to Be a Chargé des affaire in italy. à propos of chargé des Affaires, Mr dumas Complains that great deal of Monney is due to Him By Congress, and I think it ought to be paid as soon as possible—as to Mr Mazzey I Have told you, and I think writen my opinion of Him, and it Seems to me that Congress Would Make a good choice.[4]

the late disturbances in the Eastern States Have Given me Great deal of Concern and Uneasiness. Not That I doubt of the disposition of the People to put things to Rights When The Evil is demonstrated to them. But in the Meanwhile they Hurt their Consequence in Europe to a degree which is Very distressing, and what glory they Have Gained By the Revolution, they are in danger of loosing By little and little, at least for a period of time Most Afflicting to their friends. I Hope Congress will not take Such a part in the Business as would destroy the Growing ideas of fœderal measures.

Adieu, My dear General, My Most Affectionate Respects Wait on Mrs Washington, Remember me to the Young family, to George and His lady, to Mrs Stuart dr Stuart, doctor Craig, Coll Humphrey, Harrison, fitzjarald all our friends whom You Happen to meet. Remember me most Respectfully to Your Mother, and the Rest of the family. Mde de lafayette, George Your God Son, My daughters, Beg their Most Respects to You and Mrs Washington. God Bless You, My Beloved General, think often of Your Absent and Most devoted friend, Who With all the Sentiments of Unbounded Gratitude, profound Veneration, and filial love Has the Honour to Be for Ever, My dear General Your Most affectionate, and I Know Your Most Beloved friend

lafayette

Should Some thing turn out that may make it proper for American soldiers to join their Standarts—there is one, Colonel Smith Who Will Be Very fond to Go With me, and I With Him.[5]

ALS, PEL.

1. David Salisbury Franks was secretary to the mission to Morocco and in October 1786 brought to Paris the treaty with Morocco which Thomas Barclay had negotiated. See Thomas Barclay to the American Commissioners, 2 Oct. 1786, in Boyd, *Jefferson Papers*, 10:418–19. Franks did not leave France until mid-February (Franks to Thomas Jefferson, 11 Feb. 1787, ibid., 11:136–38).

2. The "Assembly of Notables" was convened in 1788 to secure support for a general tax, but a deadlock ensued leading to the calling of the Estates General in 1789.

3. Maurice-August de Beniousky (Benyowski, 1744–1786), a Hungarian count who served in the Seven Years War and fought with the Polish Confederation against Russia, had made several attempts to set up a colony in Madagascar before gaining support from Baltimore merchants for his venture. He returned in 1785 to the island and was killed there the next year.

4. Philip Mazzei (1730–1816) came to Virginia in 1773, and in 1774 GW subscribed £50 to a company being organized by Mazzei to produce wine, olive oil, and silk in Virginia. Mazzei visited Mount Vernon on 16 May 1785. For Dumas's complaints, see GW to Gouverneur Morris, 28 Nov. 1788, n.3.

5. Lafayette's former adjutant, William Stephens Smith, at this time was secretary of the United States legation in London.

From Alexander Spotswood

Dear Sir   Nottingham January 13th 1787

I had not lost Sight of the Memorandom given me last fall by Majr Washington, and was about writeing to you when I recd his Favr of decr 30 —86.

The crop before last, I unfortunately had some black oat on my Farm, which Caused a mixture among my white Crop, and in order to get them again pure; I picked a few bushles over, and sowed them in a Corner of my Farm, by which means I have a small Stack of pure Seed, out of this I will Spare some—You no doubt will think them Fine, but I do assure you they are trash to what they were last Year, Occasioned by there being Sewn in very rich ground, which with the quantity of rain run them up into Straw—I have also procured you two bushles of very Fine Poland Oat, Just in From England, this with what I send you of my kind, will, I hope, put you in seed the next Year—what I

shewed you for barley, my old Farmer Says, is what they Call
bear in Scotland, but is Esteemed a Valluable Grain—This also
got much injured by the wet weather—but the crop was good,
Yielding at the rate of 24½ bus. to the acre—one bushle of this
shall be sent—I know not what is Called the bunch pea, Nor
what you can allude to, unless it is the white English Field Pea—
part of what I have, shall be sent with a pint of the Bunch Ho-
mony bean—This last, I am told, is far mor[e] Valluable, than
the runing kind—the Crop much greater—and by Growing in
a bunch, thach[e]s the Roots of the Corn, and does not injure
the Fodder.

Agreable to Your request, in the Majors letter, I have Purchased for you, 150 bushles of Oats of Mr Young, who rents
Colo. Balls place Called Travellers rest[1]—From which place,
they will be delivered, the price is 2s. 6d. pr bus.—and More
may be had shd you want—it wd be well to give about a Weeks
notice to me that they may be in readiness.

Betsy joins me in our most afft. Compts to you Mrs Washington—Not Forgeting the Majr & his lady. I am dr Sr with grt
regard yrs Mt Sinerly

Alexr Spotswood

The Majrs letter never came to hand, until the 11 January this
present Month.

ALS, DLC:GW.

1. Burgess Ball, George Augustine Washington's brother-in-law, owned
Traveller's Rest in King George County. Mr. Young farmed the place (*Diaries*,
5:112, 126). On 8 Mar. GW paid Young £4.16 Virginia currency "for 4 Bushls
Oats @3/ Maryld currency" (Ledger B, 242).

From Henry Knox

New York 14 January 1787.

I thank you my dear Sir for your Kind favor of the 26th ultimo, which I received on the 7th instant.

On the dispersion of the insurgents at Worcester, which was
dictated more by the inclemency of the weather, and the consideration of having effected their object, than by any apprehensions of coercion from Government, many people were of opinion that the disorders were at an end, and that government

would resume its tone. They did not reflect that the court which was the great object of the insurgent's assembly, was adjourned—and that having no further business at that time, they went to their respective homes—But as soon as any object presented, they again reassembled, in suffi[ci]ent numbers to effect it. This was the case at Springfield in the County of Hampshire, the inferior Court of which, was to have met, on the last tuesday of December, but were prevented from doing any business by a party of about 300 armed men.[1]

The Government of Massachusetts are now convinced that all lenient measures instead of correcting, rather enflame the disorders—The executive, therefore, have determined on coercion, and they will soon try this remedy, under the direction of our friend Lincoln—I beleive with you, had this measure been tried in the first instance, the rebellion would not have arisen to its present heigth. But it can scarcly be imagined, that it should now fail, if the arrangement should be well taken on the part of government—If it is not administered now, it may be too late in the Spring or Summer ensuing.[2]

You ask what prevented the eastern states from attending the September meeting at Annapolis?

It is difficult to give a precise answer to this question—perhaps torpidity in New Hampshire, Faction, and heats about their paper money in Rhode Island, & Jealousy in Connecticut—Massachussetts had chosen delegates to attend, who did not decline untill very late, and the finding other persons to supply their places, was attended with delay, so that the convention had broken up, by the time the new chosen delegates reached Philadelphia.

With respect to the convention proposed to meet in May, there are different sentiments—some suppose it an irregular assembly, unauthorized by the Confederation, which points out the mode by which any alterations shall be made. Others suppose, that the proposed convention would be totally inadequate to our situation, unless it Should make an appeal to the people of every State, and a request, to call state conventions of the people, for the sole purpose of choosing delegates to represent them in a general convention of all the United States, to consider, revise, amend, or change the federal system in such a manner, as to them should seem meet, and to publish the same for general observance, without any reference to the parts or states for acceptance or confirmation—were this mode practicable it would certainly be the most summary, and if the choice of delegates was judicious, in proportion to its importance, it might be the most eligible—There are others who are of opinion that Congress ought to take up the defects of the present system, point them out to the respective Legislatures, and recommend certain alterations.

The recommendations of Congress are attended with so little effect, that any alterations by that means seem to be a hopeless business—Indeed every expedient which can be proposed, conditioned on a reference back to the Legislatures, or state conventions seems to be of the same nature.

Some gentlemen are apprehensive that a convention of the nature proposed to meet in May next, might devise some expedients to brace up, the present defective confederation so as just[3] to keep us together, while it would prevent, those exertions for a national character, which is esential to our happiness—that in this point of veiw, it might be attended with the bad effect, of assisting us to creep on in our present miserable condition, without a hope of a generous constitution, that should at once sheild us from the effects of faction, and despotism.

You will see by this sketch my dear sir how various are the opinions of men—and how difficult it will be to bring them to concur in any effective government—I am persuaded, if you were determined to attend the convention, and it should be generally known, it would induce the eastern states to send delegates to it I should therefore be much obliged for information of your decision on this subject—At the same time the principles of the purest and most respectful friendship, induce me to say, that however strongly I wish for measures which would lead to national happiness and glory, yet I do not wish you to be concerned in any political operations, of which, there are such various opinions. There may indeed, arise some solemn occasion, in which you may conceive it to be your duty again to exert your utmost talents for to promote the happiness of your Country. But this occasion might be of an unequivocal nature in which the enlightned and virtuous citizens should generally concur.[4]

Notwithstanding the contra[r]y opinions respecting the proposed convention, were I to presume to give my own judgement, it would be in favor of the convention, and I sincerely hope that it may be generally attended—I do not flatter myself that the public mind is so sufficiently informed and harmonized, as that an effective government would be adopted by the convention, and proposed to the United States, or that if this were practicable, that the people of the several states, are sufficiently prepared to receive it—But it seems to be highly important that some object should be held forth to the people, as a remedy for the disorders of the body politic—were this done by so respectable a set of men as could be sent to the convention, even if it were not so perfect in the first instance, as it might be afterwards, yet it would be a stage in the business, and mens minds would be exercised on the subject, and appreciated towards a good Constitution—were strong events to arise between this and the time of meeting, enforcing the necessity of a vigorous government, it would be a preparation which might be embraced by the convention to propose at once an efficient system.

Although it may be confessed that a convention originating from the respective Legislatures instead of the people themselves, is not the regular mode pointed out by the confederation, yet as our system in the opinion of men of reflection, is so very defective, it may reasonably be doubted, whether the constitutional mode of amendment, would be adequate to our critical situation—if on an examination this should be found to be the case, the proposed convention may be the best expedient that could be devised—unrestrained by forms, it would be able to consider every proposition fully, and decide agreably to the sentiments of the majority—But in a body constituted as congress is, a single Member frequently may frustrate, the Opinions of $^{17}/_{18}$ths of the united States assembled by representation in that body—There are a variety of other reasons which in my mind have the influence to induce a preference for the convention—but the different opinions respecting it, will probably prevent a general attendance.

In my former letters I mentioned that men of reflection and principle were tired of the imbecillities of the present government—but I did not point out any substitute. It would be prudent to form the plan of a new house, before We pull down the old one—The subject has not been sufficiently discused, as yet in publick, to decide precisely, on the form of the edifice. It is out of all question, that the foundation, must be of republican principles; but so modified and wrought together, that whatever shall be erected thereon, should be durable, & efficient—I speak entirely of the federal government, or what would be better *one government* instead of an association of governments—Were it possible to effect, a general government of this kind it might be constituted of an assembly, or lower house, chosen for one two or three years a senate chosen for five six or seven years, and the executive under the title of Governor Generl chosen by the assembly and Senate, for the term of seven years, but liable to an impeachment of the lower house, and triable by the senate— a judicial to be appointed by the Governor General during good behaviour, but impeachable by the lower house and triable by the Senate. The laws passed by the general governmt to be obeyed by the local governments, and if necessary to be enforced by a body of armed men to be kept for the purposes which should be designated—All national objects, to be designed and executed by the general government, without any reference to the local governments. This rude sketch is considered as the government of the least possible powers, to preserve the confederated government—To attempt to establish less, will be to hazard the existence of republicanism, and to subject us, either to a division of the European powers, or to a despotism arising from highhanded commotions.

I have thus my dear sir obeyed what seemed to be your desire, and given you, the ideas which have presented themselves from reflection, and the opinion of others—May heaven direct us to the best means for the dignity, and happiness of the United States.

I hinted in the former part of this letter that the executive, of Massahusetts were determined on coercion under the auspices of Genl Lincoln. He will begin his operations on the 20th instant, with a body of 4000 men, including six companies of artille[r]y with field peices—They will be drafted from the militia for a certain time—If the insurgents decline meeting him in force at Worcester the 23d instant, to which time the court of commonpleas is adjourned, he will proceed to Hampshire County & Berkshire, at which places the Courts will also sit—If the insurgents decline meetg him at those places, he will detach parties to bring him in the most culpable in order for a trial by Law.[5]

The process of this business will be interesting, and its issue important, both of which I shall do myself the pleasure of informing you.

Mrs Knox thanks Mrs Washington and you, with great sincerity for your kind wishes, and prays that you both may enjoy every happiness to which I say amen. I am my dear Sir with the most respectful & unalterable affection Your very humble Sevt

H. Knox

ALS, DLC:GW.

1. For earlier references to the confrontation in Worcester, see Knox to GW, 17 and 21 Dec. 1786. Daniel Shays himself led the party of 300 men into Springfield on 26 Dec. 1786 (see Feer, *Shays's Rebellion*, 331–32).

2. See Benjamin Lincoln to GW, 4 Dec. 1786–4 Mar. 1787, and editorial note.

3. Knox wrote "to some" before "to keep."

4. Knox changed his advice at a crucial point and on 19 Mar. urged GW to attend the convention in Philadelphia.

5. See note 2.

From R.

[c.15 January 1787]

Your Character, Sir, is beyond the reach of applause. Nothing that is mortal can add to it. To engage again would bring you back to a Man. You think as I do as far as your Modesty will permit, I know you do. I love & reverence you, therefore have a Right to your Pardon for this apparently impertinent Card. No Creature living but ourselves shall ever know it was written. I am, without flattery, your adorer.

⟨R.⟩

LS, DLC:GW. The signature begins apparently with the letter R and trails off into an intentionally illegible scrawl. GW docketed it: "anonimous."

From Horatio Gates

Sir   Travellors-Rest 19th January, 1787:—

By the last Alexandria Post I had the Honour to receive Your Excellency's Letter of the 8th of November, Inclosing your Circular Letter of the 31st of October.[1] I am truly Sorry Your Excel-

lency Declines the Presidency of The Cincinnati, as I conceive
your continuing at the Head of the Society, indispensibly necessary to the Support of The Order. The very high consideration
and Respect, in which the whole Continent agree to place Your
Excellency, is absolutely requisite, to defeat the ungenerous Designs of the Enemies of the Order from prevailing against it. I
am happy to find, that in this Critical Hour, The Legislature
have thought proper to call upon Your Excellency, to Step forth
to Rescue Us from Anarchy, by placing you at the Head of that
Committee, which is to meet the 2d of May, in philadelphia; this
is so Important a Station; & the Crisis which calls for it so
alarming; that I will not believe Your Excellencys Patriotism, &
High Regard for Civil Liberty, will permit you to Decline it; you
will there Sir, be upon the Spot, where the Representatives of
the Cincinnati so Ardently desire to see there President. I think
with Your Excellency, that the Malevolence, & Illiberal Jealousy,
which attacked The Order in great measure done away, and
good Men are ashamed it ever was countenanced. Unconnected, & Unsupported, I cannot think of being, even for a day,
placed at the Head of The Institution—For unless your Excellency continues there The Dignity of The Order will be Diminished—Heaven Grant that may not be a prelude to the Greatest
Misfortune that eer befall a Free People. With the Sincerest Sentiments of the Highest Consideration, & Respect, I have the
Honour to be Sir Your most Obedient Humble Servant,

Horatio Gates

ALS, DLC:GW; ADf, NHi: Gates Papers.

Maj. Gen. Horatio Gates lived at Travellers Rest, his house in Frederick
County, Virginia.

1. For GW's letter to Gates of 8 Nov. 1786, see his circular letter to the
Society of the Cincinnati, 31 Oct. 1786, n.4. See also GW to George Weedon,
29 Dec. 1786, and note 2 of that document.

From William Gordon

My dear Sir   London Jany 20. 1787
    I take the opportunity of a vessel for Boston, that so I may
send in the speediest way some seeds which I procured from a
gentlewoman of my acquaintance at Ipswich, where I was first
settled & remained thirteen years. I have likewise added some

seed of the rocket double larkspur, which I saw in blow the last year, & was much pleased with on account of their beauty. I am yet unsettled, which prevents my proceeding in my history with the rapidity intended; but I keep going on, & mean to be at the press the beginning of next winter. Apprehend you have heard from my friend Jonathan Mason Esqr. ⟨Sen⟩ Boston respecting the draft on the party at Warren.[1] Your Excellency must be grieved at the spirit which has discovered itself in the different states. It is to be greatly lamented, that there is no more genuine virtue & patriotism among the inhabitants. A kind Providence, however, I trust will overrule all the commotions & disturbances, which have taken place, for the general good, & make all terminate happily. The enemies of America take occasion, from the confusions in the states, to triumph; that however is but a poor relief for the loss of the colonies & the load of taxes brought upon them by the debt contracted in attempting to deprive the Americans of their liberties. The king I learn feels himself still sore; & it is not to be wondered at. When the parliament meets, there will be as usual great wrangling between the ins & the outs; but the former will most probably carry every important question by dint of power & influence. The character of the prince of Wales is very low in the opinion of many, & that of the duke of York, his brother, as high. I am sorry to observe, that unfriendliness there is in administration with respect to the United States; which will be likely to continue while the late Charles Jenkinson, now lord Hawkesberry, & Dundass are in favour. Some think that a ministerial revolution is not far off, & that a set of men more friendly to the Americans will shortly succeed, but I am fearful of the contrary. The policy of G. Britain appears to me to be still wrong; that it would be for her interest to cultivate a good understanding with the United States I am persuaded: but I leave all to the great Governour of the universe, who will direct the whole wisely & well.

The gentlewoman who has favoured me with the seeds, is fond of the digitalis as a cure for the dropsy, & therefore has sent some of the seed: but from what I have been told, it is so violent & so little to be depended upon in a general way, that I should not choose to make trial of it. Mrs Gordon writes in best regards to your Excellency, your Lady, her posterity, the young George especially, & to Mr & Mrs Lund Washington. I remain most respectfully, my Dear Sir, Your sincere friend & very humble servant

William Gordon

I am obliged to write by candle-light, which does not suit my eyes.

I have no connection with the great, & do not seek it. Visit Mr John Adams once in a while, & am going to him this morning.

ALS, DLC:GW.

1. See Benjamin Lincoln, Jr., to GW, 24 Sept. 1786, and note 1 of that document.

From David Humphreys

My dear General   New Haven [Conn.] Jany 20th 1787

I am indeed much flattered by the private and confidential communications contained in your favor of the 26 of Decr. I trust; on the present critical & momentuous occasion, by disclosing the very sentiments of my soul without reservation; I shall not render myself less deserving of your confidence, or worthy a place in your friendship.

As Colonel Wadsworth will be the bearer of this, I shall not be so minute in detailing the state of affairs in this quarter of the Union, as might otherwise have been requisite. He is so well acquainted with the feelings & politics that I shall principally refer you to him.[1]

So near the scene of tumult as I have been, accounts are different concerning the respectability or contemptability of the persons & numbers who compose the mob. It seems next tuesday (the 23d) is fixed upon to produce some decision respecting the force in favor, or opposition to Government. The Court is then to set at Worcester—The Executive has ordered out 4000 Militia to support the Court & to be embodied thirty days—Liberal private subscriptions have been made to facilitate the expedition—Generals Lincoln & Sheppard are to command. It is said, if the Insurgents should not appear, the force in arms is to progress Westward, apprehend the Leaders, and assist in re-establishing Government. This may bring matters to serious extremities—I think it a good plan, unless by its *secresy* it should too much resemble another Penobscot expedition.[2]

I have lately had an opportunity of conversing with several of the first characters from the neighbouring States. These Gentlemen, viz., Messrs Duane, Chancellor Livingston, Egbert Benson, Judges Yates[,] Haring & Smith—from New York—with Messrs Lowe, King, Parsons & Judge Sullivan from Boston, were Commissioners for settling the boundaries between the two States. They seemed to be all of opinion that something must be done, but what that something was appeared to baffle their deepest penetration.[3] It is however worthy remark that Mr King, Mr Sedgwick & several others (I believe I might say John Jay) who have been mortally opposed to the Cincinnati, now look with considerable confidence to that quarter for our political preservation.[4]

As to a Convention, it has not until lately engrossed but little share in the conversation here. I am induced to expect the only good it can do, will be to demonstrate to the People, that a number of characters in whom they repose confidence, believe seriously we cannot remain as a nation much longer, in the present manner of administering our actual Government. The evil appears to me to consist more in the untowardly dispositions of the States, (who make no hesitation in palpably violating the Confederacy whenever it suits their interest) rather than in the form of our national Compact as it exists on paper. What is to be done to cure these dispositions? We may have what forms we please, but without coertion, they are idle as the wind. Now let us enquire what effect may probably be produced from the Convention. In the first place there is a diversity of sentiment respecting the legality & expediency of such a Meeting. Those who are opposed to the measure say there cannot be a full representation of the People for revising the Confederation, because the freemen at large have not been consulted in any instance; and because the Legislatures who appoint Deputies, are not authorised by their Constituents to make such appointment. Others suppose a Convention to be an interference with, not an usurpation of the functions of Congress, and that, if any recommendations are to go to the People, they should originate with Congress. But neither of these is the reason, why those members of our Assembly, who are perfectly fœderal in their policy, did not urge that the subject should have been taken up & an appointment made. The reason was, a conviction that the persons who would be elected, were some of the most antifœderal men in the State, who believe or act as if they beleived that Congress is already possessed of too unlimited powers, and who would wish, apparently, to see the Union dissolved. These Demagogues really affect to persuade the people (to use their own phraseology) that they are only in danger of having their liberties stolen away, by an artful, designing Aristocracy. This jealousy, I presume, exists in some other Governments. I do not learn that Commissioners have been appointed from any of the New England States. Some of the Assemblies will not convene before May, unless called on an extraordinary emergency. So that it is almost certain that the Convention will be but partial in point of representation. But should it be compleat, and should the members be unanimous in recommending, in the most forcible, the most glowing, the most pathetic terms which language can afford, that it is indispensable to the salvation of the Country, Congress should be cloathed with more ample powers—I am as confident as I am of my own existence, the States will not all comply with the recommendation. They have a mortal reluctance to divest them selves of the smallest attribute of independent, seperate Sovereignty. The personal character of yourself & some other Gentlemen would have a weight on individuals—but on democratic Assemblies & the bulk of the People, your opinions & your eloquence would be "triffles light as air." After the abominable neglects, with which your recommendations of the Army have been treated; he must indeed have faith to remove mountains, who can believe in the good dispositions of the Country. We are already nearly ruined by believing too much—We have believed that the Citizens of the United States were better than the rest of the world; and that they could be managed in Society without compulsion.

In effect, I conceive that, if the Confœderation should not meet with a speedy dissolution, Congress must & will gradually & imperceptably acquire the habits & the means of enforcing their decisions—But if the people have not wisdom or virtue enough to govern themselves, or what is the same thing to suffer themselves to be governed by men of their own election; why then I must think it is in vain to struggle against the torrent, it is in vain to strive to compel mankind to be happy & free contrary to their inclination. The mobility, in that case, or rather their jealous & factious Leaders will produce a crisis of a different nature. All that Patriots & good men can do, will be to wait events, to foresee as far as may be, & make the best of them.

I have dilated thus largely on the general subject, to shew that I concur fully in sentiment with you, concerning the inexpediency of your attending the Convention. This is also the decided opinion of our friend Colo. Trumbull, with whom I have been since the receipt of your letter on purpose to take his advice (he begs his best respects may be presented to you).

As to your particular & private reasons against attending, they are clearly sufficient to convince any reasonable man of the *propriety* & *consistency* of your conduct.

1st You declared, on resigning your Commission that you would not interfere again with public affairs. Should a period ever arrive (& probably it may) when this declaration ought to be dispensed with: the Crisis is certainly not yet come.

2ndly You may urge with peculiar propriety Your private affairs, & a right to enjoy the remainder of life in tranquillity.

3dly You have happily excused yourself, for substantial reasons, from attending the General Meeting of the Cincinnati. This ought to be considered as an addional apology. Your declining to attend that Meeting, will not (under the present circumstances) be considered in an unfavorable light by any description of Men. But should you afterwards attend the Convention, it would more than probably produce uneasiness among the Officers in general, & evidently give an occasion to a certain Class to represent your conduct as influenced by ambition on one hand; & as discovering a derilection of your old friends, on the other.

4thly The result of the Convention may not be perhaps so important as is expected: in which case your character would be materially affected. Other people can work ⟨up⟩ the present scene. I know your personal influence & character, is, justly considered, the last stake which America has to play. Should you not reserve yourself for the united call of a Continent entire?

5thly—If you should attend on this Convention & concur in recommending measures, which should be generally adopted, but opposed in some parts of the Union; it would doubtless be understood that you had, in a degree, pledged yourself for their execution. This would at once sweep you back, irretreivably, into the tide of public affairs.

One feels such a lassitude & inaccuracy in attempting to unbosom himself in writing, as makes him much less explicit & clear than he would be in an oral communication. Was I only at a moderate distance, I should endeavour to communicate verbally many sentiments respecting circumstances & characters, which must now be suppressed.

Mr Trumbull, Mr Barlow & myself have written a good number of peices in prose & verse on political subjects; we have the satisfaction to find that they are reprinted in more papers & read with more avidity than any other performances. I enclose two late papers, which contain specimens of poetry, from which some judgment may be formed of our various exertion & manner of execution. Pointed ridicule is found to be of more efficacy than serious argumentation.[5] Entreating you will be pleased to present my best Compliments & wishes to Mrs Washington & the family I have the honor to be my dear General Your sincere friend & Hble Servant

D. Humphreys

P.S. When I came from York Town with the Standards &c. I recd 100 Dollars, by your Warrant from the Military Chest, to defray my expences. I took vouchers for the expenditure at the time; but on settling my accounts with the Pay Mastr Genl they were not called for—they are now misplaced or lost—As the Public is again indebted to me, I shall have occasion for a Certificate of the ⟨truth⟩ of the enclosed Sketch—& will thank you for it.

ALS, DLC:GW; copy, NN: GW facsimile and transcription box.

1. Jeremiah Wadsworth arrived at Mount Vernon on 17 February.

2. See Benjamin Lincoln to GW, 4 Dec. 1786–4 Mar. 1787.

3. In 1773 New York and Massachusetts agreed to a boundary line about twenty miles east of the Hudson River, but the line was not run. After the Revolution, Massachusetts laid claim to almost six million acres to the west of the 1773 line. After several years of contention, the two states in December 1786 sent commissioners to Hartford to negotiate a settlement. The commissioners agreed, in effect, that New York would have jurisdiction over the disputed area and that Massachusetts would have the right to acquire title to the land from the Indians. The New York commissioners were James Duane, Robert R. Livingston, Egbert Benson, John Haring, Melancton Smith, Robert Yates, and John Lansing; those acting for Massachusetts were John Lowell, James Sullivan, Theophilus Parsons, and Rufus King.

4. Theodore Sedgwick (1746–1813) of Stockbridge in western Massachusetts was a member of the Congress and an ardent opponent of Daniel Shays.

5. See Humphreys to GW, 16 Nov. 1786, n.2.

From Battaile Muse

Honourable Sir   Jany 20th 1787
    your Favour dated the 3d of Instant Came To hand Two days
ago, I have not received One shilling of money From the Tenants Since I was down, altho I have been Very pushing and have
distressed Mr Grantom for the Last years rent and arrears in
order To bring Him to a Sence of his duty, as He is Very able To
Pay So Very Lo a rent on Such Rich Land.[1] I wish to Indulge
the People untill march, if they will not Pay then, I shall distress
them the first week in april, unless they give me Proof that they
will Pay Soon after—I expect To be down in april when you
Shall be Fully informed respecting Every matter, and as often
before as Circumstances will admitt of. I Shall Set out in about
three of Four days To Visit the Tenants in Fauquier Cty—In
order To Spurr them on I shall go To Every Tenament To Examine their Conduct I have heard Frequently From them, that I
am not To Expect more than £20 this Trip & that uncertain—
there are Two Lotts on Cattins run Goose creek—and Two on
the upper Tract unrented, I Fear I must Lower the rents or
Suffer the Tenaments To go To ruin; I will do the best I can
with them.
    With Regard to Tompson—Rector & Kennady I have not yet
determind in What manner I shall Proseed against them—I am
of opinion there is but Little or no hopes of doing any thing
with them.
    Enclosed is and order on Mr Wales, I have written To Him on
the Subject—but I wish you To Notify Him in order that He
may be Punctual Should He Fail I Expect I Shall be able To raise
that Sum by that Time & I have wrote To Mr Wales that in Case
He Should not be able To raise the money To inform me that I
may Endeavour To Accomplish it. Money is hearder To Collect
than I Ever Knew it—I wish To hear From you about the First
of next Month. I am Sir your Obedient Humble Servant.
                                        Battaile Muse

N.B. I have belonging To Colo. Fairfax about 180 lb. of Butter
50 or 60 lbs. is Fresh—if you are in want Please To inform me,
my price is 1s. ℔ lb. for the whole I beleave it's good & reather
than Sell it for a less price I would chews To make use of it on

this Estate It was all made by my House Servt if you require it Please To Inform me by the First Opportunity. I am Sir your Most Obedient. B.M.

ALS, DLC:GW.

1. The first entry in Muse's accounts regarding William Grantom (Granthom) is dated 30 Jan. 1786 and shows that he paid £10 rent on 225½ acres in Berkeley County, above Samuel Washington's Harewood, leased from GW by Alexander Fryer. Muse's account shows Grantom paying the annual rent of £6.15 through 1791.

To Thomas Peters

Sir, Mount Vernon 20th Jan. 1787

It is now more than six weeks since I begged to be informed in decided terms, if you would furnish me with 50 Bushls of Barley, that I might know whether to depend upon that quantity from *you*, or resort to *Philidelphia* for it, where it had been offered to me. I informed you too, that unless the latter was seasonably embraced I might, in case of failure in you, be disappointed altogether. To this momt (when arrangements should not only have been made, but the ground had in full preparation) I am left in uncertainty—a wish to be relieved from it, must be my apology for giving you the trouble of another letter on this subject.[1] I am Sir Yr most Obedt Servt

Go: Washington

ALS (photocopy), DLC:GW; LB, DLC:GW.

1. Peters wrote GW on 3 Feb. and apologized for not having answered GW's letter of 4 Dec. 1786.

From Samuel Blachley Webb

Sir N. York Jany 20th *1787*.

We have been honor'd by the receipt of your Excellency's letter of the 31st of October 1786 directed to the Baron Stuben, our Presdt. So soon as he arrives in Town we presume he will call a meeting of our State Society and communicate to them the Contents.[1]

In the mean time we cannot omit the present opportunity to acquaint your Excellency with the sentiments which the most distinguished characters in this Society entertain with regard to your desire not to be re-elected President of the General Society. Many of them stand high in your good opinion and all of them are warmly attached to you. Their sentiments will pervade this society, and if regret at so unexpected and unfortunate a circumstance can give weight to arguments which added to those of a similar nature in reply to your circular letter from the different States, it is to be hoped you will not decline continuing at the head of a Society brought into existance by a glorious event which crowned you with never fadeing Laurels. A Society, founded on the most noble principles, whose highest Ambition, is to imitate your bright example, should not prematurely be deprived of that ray which for so many years guided our steps in the paths of honor. Should no internal divisions arise on your retireing yet Sir the withdrawing of your patronage will have a most destructive effect on our reputation abroad.

You have exhibited the most noble instance of patriotism that modern history can relate, you glow with affection for your country and must feel interested to promote the honor and dignity of a patriotic band of warriors, who like the arrows in the Eagle's talon will be respected while united to that head who so oft displayed them in the field of Glory; but, seperated, farewell the splendor of Columbia's Eagle in European courts. At home, lukewarmness will take place of the generous zeal which animates every member. Our funds intended for the most laudable purposes may remain unimproved for want of energy or unanimity, while unheeded flow the Widows tears, unheard the Orphan's cry: that source whence gladness should flow to brighten the face of sorrow be choaked up—the noble end of our institution frustrated—Genius of Liberty avert this fate—May that philanthropic spirit which inspires your Excellency to so many acts of public utility induce you to continue the patron of an infant society whose maturer powers shall be one of the many branches, to perpetuate the veneration due to the Savior of his Country.

These Sir are the sentiments of our Society, which we have thought it incumbent on us to apprize you of, I have the honor to be (for & in behalf of the standing Committee) Your Excellys Most Obedt & Affect. Hume Servt

S.B.W.

Copy, in Webb's hand, CtY: Samuel B. Webb Papers.

1. See GW to the Society of the Cincinnati, 31 Oct., 1786. The copy sent to Steuben has not been found, but Steuben wrote GW on 26 Jan. from New York: "I have had the honor to receive your Excellencys Circular Letter of the 31 Octr to the Society of the Cincinnati of this State & perceive with great regret your intention of declining to be President of the Society after May next. I shall communicate the contents of your Letter to the Society at their first meeting and to the Delegates to the general Meeting indeed, individually, they have almost all been made acquainted with your intention and express much concern at it—nor can we yet help flattering ourselves that with the assistance of the Vice President matters may be so arranged that the society may still have the honor of retaining you without interrupting the tranquillity of your retirement" (DLC:GW).

From Henry Knox

New York 21st January 1787.

I wrote you my dear Sir last week and then mentioned to you the operations against the insurgents were to commence the 19th or 20th since then I have received in confidence the enclosed orders of the governor.[1] You will be able having this for the explanation to judge more clearly of the progress of the business. You will please to retain these papers in your hands for although, no object will be frustrated by a publication in Virginia yet my friend who communicated them would not like to have it known that he did so.

I have no clear information of the determination of the insurgents whether they will meet general Lincoln or not—Some verbal information of a gentleman who came through the Country from Boston informs that the insurgents are in high spirits, and declare, that they wish for nothing more than to meet the governmental forces in the field. The great danger to the government appears to me to consist in the circumstance of the insurgents eluding General Lincolns troops, who are drafted for *thirty days*. The insurgents will know this and if they act accordingly and wait untill the Militia are disbanded, the exertions of government will be rendered abortive. But if they can be brought to face General Lincolns whole force I am persuaded they will be ruined.

After a period of upward of two months when Congress should have met agreably to the confederation, a sufficient number of members from seven states met one day last week. But not agreeing in the choice of a President they adjourned from day to day. It is expected they will be organized in the course of the present week so far as to proceed to business, that is such business as can be done by seven states. It is probable however that nine states will be represented in two or three weeks. I am my dear Sir with respectful compliments to Mrs Washington Your respectfully Affectionate

H. Knox

LS, DLC:GW.

1. These probably were the series of orders that Gov. James Bowdoin issued on 4 January. They included one order placing Gen. Benjamin Lincoln in command of 4,400 troops to be raised which were to meet on 19 Jan. wherever Lincoln should designate. Another order instructed Gen. William Shepard to march with 1,200 Hampshire County militiamen to Springfield on 18 Jan. to guard the federal arsenal there. See Feer, *Shays's Rebellion*, 348, n.1.

Letter not found: from John Cannon, 22 Jan. 1787. On 13 April GW wrote Cannon: "I have recd your letter of 22d of Jany."

To David Humphreys

My dear Humphreys   Mount Vernon 23d Jan. 1787.

Since I have heard of the robbery of the Mail at New Ark, on the 4th instt, I have been under great apprehension that a long & confidential letter which I wrote to you on the 26th Ulto was in it—My only hope is, a strange one you will say, that the inattention to, and practice of *bringing back*, instead of *exchanging Mails*, which frequently happens, and did actually happen about that time may have been the means of its preservation—without this interposition it most assuredly would have been in that mail—To relieve me from this state of disagreeable suspence, I pray you to write me by the first Post after you receive this letter.[1]

All here join me in offering every good wish for you—and with sentiments of the greatest friendship & regard I am—Yr most Affecte Hble Servt

Go: Washington

ALS, NNPM.

1. Humphreys duly received GW's letter of 26 Dec. (Humphreys to GW, 11 Feb. 1787).

To John Nicholson

Sir,   Mount Vernon 23d Jany 1787.
Your letter of the 9th instant, together with a statement of the Finances of the State of Pennsylvania, came duly to hand.[1] You will accept of my best thanks for your attention & politeness in transmitting to me the above Statement.

The prosperity of any part of the Union gives me a singular pleasure, & I cannot but express the satisfaction I feel at the happy situation of your Finances. I am Sir Your Most Obedt hble Servant

G: Washington

LB, DLC:GW.
    John Nicholson (c.1757–1800) was comptroller general of Pennsylvania.
    1. Letter not found.

To Alexander Spotswood

Dear Sir,   Mount Vernon 23d Jany 1787.
Your favor of the 13th came to my hands a few days after my Nephew G: Washington left this for New-Kent, which, & his not seeing you on his way down, were unlucky circumstances as he could, & no doubt would have arranged matters so as that a Vessel which is sent from Colchester to York river for Negroes which Colonl Bassett has given him, might have stopped at the mouth of Potomac creek for the Oats & other articles you have been so obliging as to provide for me.

Immediately upon the receipt of your letter, I wrote to George informing him of the Contents of it, requesting him to order the Vessel to stop at the above place for the purpose mentioned; but the chances, I fear, are against the letter's getting to his hands. Nevertheless, I pray you to desire Mr Young to get his Oats ready without delay as the Vessel will not, indeed ought not to be detained a moment longer on her passage, than is indispensably necessary to transport the Oats & other things across, which will be done at one trip if waggons can be hired. To this end my nephew (if the letter reaches him) is instructed. If this Vessel should not stop, another shall be sent to Potomac creek—it will be proper therefore that no time should be lost in preparing the Oats.[1]

For the different kinds of seeds, you have promised me of your own growth, I pray you to accept my thanks. I shall be attentive to make the most of them—& shall be obliged to you for letting me know whether the Barley, or bear (as your farmer calls it) is a Spring or Winter grain; & at what time it ought to be sown. Your bunch-bean accounts for the mistake of asking for bunch peas. George led me into it, for I had never heard of them before. The Beans must be valuable, & I shall esteem them an acquisition. When ought they to be planted? Is your field pea subject to the bug, as the garden peas are? How did your field beans turn out? If you have any of these to spare I would thank you for some. They are (if of the proper sort) highly esteemed in the present husbandry of England as a preparatory crop for wheat.

Mrs Washington & Fanny join me in offering every good wish for you, my niece[2] & the family; & with sentiments of great regard & affection, I am Dear Sir, &c.

G: Washington

LB, DLC:GW.

1. GW's letter to George Augustine Washington, who left Mount Vernon on 12 Jan. and was back by 2 Feb., has not been found. GW in March planted oats sent by Spotswood. See *Diaries*, 5:93, 101, and 123.

2. Spotswood's wife was Elizabeth Washington Spotswood (1750–1814), eldest daughter of GW's half brother Augustine.

To George Gilpin

Dear Sir,   Mount Vernon Jany 24th 1787.

As (if I understood you rightly the other day at Lomax's) you are high Sheriff of this County, I shall be obliged to you for the Public accts against me for Taxes, Levies, &ca, that I may make provision, without delay, for payment.[1]

Can you tell me whether the writ against Edward Williams (given to you at the above time & place) has been served?[2]

Mr Brindley & his Son-in-law called here about ten days ago on their way to South Carolina, but appeared so anxious to get on that I did not press the former to attend to the Service pointed at in Mr Johnson's letter.[3] I am—Dear Sir Yr obedt

Go: Washington

P.S. If you have not the acct ready please to lodge it at the Post Office where I commonly send twice or thrice a week.

ALS, MHi: H.H. Edes Papers.

1. On 3 Jan. GW "Rid to Alexandria to a meeting of the board of Directors of the Potomack Co. Did the business which occasioned the Meeting. Dined at Lomax's & returned home in the evening" (*Diaries*, 5:89). Gilpin took his oath as sheriff of Fairfax County on 21 Nov. 1786.

2. For GW's problems with Edward Williams, his tenant at Mount Vernon, see GW to David Stuart, 6 Dec. 1786.

3. James Brindley and his son-in-law came to Mount Vernon on 10 January.

From Benjamin Lincoln, Jr.

Sir   Boston Jany 24 1787

I have the honour to enclose your Excellency the receipt for the bill on Mr Gray from the Agent of Dr Gordon. His detention of it needs an apology but I can only plead in excuse that I was absent from this place the greater part of the last month & had no opportunity of calling for it untill a few weeks since when the present public commotions and the preparations to oppose them really occasioned my forgetting the business.[1]

Your Excellency I hope will excuse me if I should take the liberty of communicating to you a sketch of our present political situation. The General Court at their last Sessions requested the Governor to make use of every necessary and constitutional exertion for suppressing every insurrection & outrage against the Government & pledged themselves to refund the expence. The Governour finding that all the measures which the Legislature had adopted to remove burthens and give relief were Spurned at and that the insurgents were encreasing in inveteracy and in numbers orders were issued about three weeks since to detach a body of militia consisting of 4000 rank & file to take the field under the command of General Lincoln & to remain in service a month from Yesterday. That Gentleman is now at Worcester with 2000. General Shepherd is at the magazine at Springfield with 1000 & General Warner in the neighbourhood of Worcester with another thousand. The object this force is to embrace is to support the Judicial Courts in the Counties of Worcester Hampshire & Berkshire—aid the civil magistrate—repel all insurgents against the government and to apprehend all disturbers of the public peace. The Insurgents are assembling Four hundred at West Springfield under the command of Luke Day—A larger body at Pelham under the command of Shaize. It seems the general sentiments that about 2000 will take the field. But from the disposition of the Governments troops they probably will not collect into one body. Two of General Shepherds men without arms falling in with a party of Insurgents have been dangerously wounded. Every thing wears the appearance of hostility. It is a happy circumstance that men of principle & property are taking their stands on the side of government and seem universally determined at all hazards to put an end to the present insurrections The General Court will meet the next week and if the western counties continue obstinate a rebellion will probably be declared & martial law put in force Should this take place insurrection I think will soon hide her head: God grant that the period may be speedy or the goodly fabric of freedom will soon be pulled down & thrown into ruins.[2] I must once more beg your Excellency to excuse this freedom I have taken with you in writing this lengthy letter. Knowing that your Excellency must be exceedingly anxious I could not refrain from doing myself the honour of making every communication within my knowledge. I have the honour to be with the highest respect Your Excellency's humble servant

Benj. Lincoln Junr

ALS, DLC:GW.

1. GW sent the bill to Lincoln on 8 Nov. 1786. See also GW to Lincoln, Jr., 24 February.

2. See Benjamin Lincoln to GW, 4 Dec. 1786–4 Mar. 1787.

From Mandrillon

Sir,   [Amsterdam, 24 January 1787]

The 24th of last October I had the honor of sending to your Excellency a memorial containing my submission to the resolution of the approaching General Meeting of the Cincinnati. I am impressed with the most sanguine hopes, that, as it is under the Auspices of your Excellency that the proposition will be made, I shall be admitted. The Marquis de la Fayette wrote to me that I could not have a more powerful advocate than you, Sir, as you are the President. Be that as it may, if the Statutes of the Society absolutely oppose my election as an honorary member, I beg your Excellency to be persuaded that I shall have no less zeal & desire to inform myself of the interest of the 13 united States, & no less assiduous, on that account, to publish the triumph, the Glory & the examples of wisdom which America offers to Europe.[1]

Your Excellency knows that a writer is always unsatisfied when he wants information respecting any subject upon which he wishes to treat. This, without doubt, will plead a pardon for the request which I make of an exact list of the Members of the Society, and all which relates to its constitution & Laws. I have already many interesting objects, but they will not suffice, and I only wait for this suppliment to compleat a new work which I am about to publish.

Europe is actually engaged in errecting new monuments of Glory, in justice, to you, by adorning your happy Country with the Statue of your Excellency: permit me to give you a Copy of an interesting letter inserted lately in the Parisian Journal; I am employed in answering it, to pay publickly to your Excellency a new tribute of my respect & admiration.[2]

When the subject is well understood, I will venture to say that no one is more capable of writing a good inscription than I am; but the subject here requires superior talents, & I, unfortunatly possess but too much Zeal, receive therefore, Sir, this peice of verse & this inscription, with candour & indulgence.

I would remind your Excellency that I have the image of my Hero continually impressed upon me, & that I should be happy to have it in my power to be interesting to him for a moment. I have the Honor to be, with the most perfect admiration of your Excellency, Sir Yr very Hble & Obedt Servt

Jh de Mandrillon

fellow of the Academies of Science at Holland, Bresse & Philadelphia

Translation, DLC:GW; ALS, DSoCi. For the transcriptions of the letter and enclosure in the original French, see CD-ROM:GW.

1. See Mandrillon to GW, 24 Oct. 1786.

2. A contemporary translation of the enclosed "Extract of a Letter inserted in the Journal of Paris[,] 1786. No. 350" of Mandrillon's response and comments, addressed "To the Authors of the Journal," reads: "I have been, Gentlemen, to see the Bust of General Washington, made by Mr Houdon. I viewed it with all that interesting attention which the figure of a great man, executed by the hand of an eminent Artist, naturally inspires. It is a fine employment of the talents to transmit to posterity the portraits of those who have honored humanity by their Genius & Virtue. And who better deserves this homage than the man, who, patriotic without fanaticism, humane in the field of battle, calm in the bosom of faction, modest in the career of victory, mantained the liberty of his Country with unlooked-for success, and resigned, after his triumph, without ostentation or regreat, that authority which he received from the confidence of the publick, unblemished with any deed which even envy itself can darken, & who voluntarily mixed with the body of his Citizens with the same dignified simplicity which he carried with him in the command of their Armies.

"But, Gentlemen, this bust is about to be sent to America. Shall it return without an inscription which may immortalize the Object? What man of letters is there in France who would not wish to partake of the honor which a french Artist has acquired by executing so celebrated a w⟨ork⟩ A Frenchman, whose virtues, eminence, & administration render ⟨him⟩ immortal⟨,⟩ has composed, for the portrait of Doctr Franklin, a latin inscription of such precission, elegance & energy that all Europe seems to have adopted it. The Portrait of General Washington is no less worthy of ⟨ex⟩ercising the talents of our Poets. America finally owes to the A⟨rms⟩ of France* that liberty which she had so nobly defended by her courage. She would, without doubt, be likewise willing to owe to the abilities of our Artists & Writers those monuments which will ⟨per⟩petuate the memory of this great revolution. I have the Honor to be &c.

"In answer to those Gentlemen⟨,⟩ I sent the following

> *Respectable aux héros & cher aux immortels*
> *Washington ent tous lieux, mérite des autels.*
> To him whom Heaven approves, & men revere,
> To Washington, let all their Alters rear.

But as it is the taste of the day to have a short, expressive latin inscript⟨ion⟩ I have offered this

WASHINGTON.
Supremis illius resonat virtutibus orbis.
The World resounds with his exalted Virtues.

I wish for some one better performed, & more adapted to the publick idea & the Grandeur of the subject.

Your Excellency reminds me of this latin passage upon Cincinnatus.

Et gaudebat tellus vomere laureato.

And the Earth will smile under the *laureled* plowshire. *Altho this assertion may be general in France; I would never adopt it; it suffices th⟨at it is⟩ true &

well known that the advantages were reciprocal—& the Americans think differe⟨ntly⟩."

To Battaile Muse

Sir,   Mount Vernon 24th Jan: 1787
   It would seem by your letter of the 3d instt that you had not received my last; in which I desired that whatever money you had, or could command of mine, might be sent to me; or an order drawn on some responsible person in Alexandria; as I was much in want of it. This request I now repeat, as I have, since that time been disappointed of other sums wch I thought myself sure of receiving. & shall be a good deal distressed if I can receive none from you till the late periods mentioned in your letter. I am Sir yr Very Hble Servt

                                                  Go: Washington

ALS, CSmH.

From William Deakins, Jr.

Sir.   George Town [Md.] Janry 25th 1787
   Your favor of the 13th Current did not come to hand till the day before Yesterday, I fear I shall fail in geting you the Poland Oat[1]—some have been Offered, but they were so much degenerated that they Appeared no better than the Common Oat, & the price 25 ℔ Ct higher I have procured 200 Bushels of the Common Oat of the best Quality & well Cleaned & You may send for them or any part you Want, on Tuesday Next—& Very possible by that time I may get in some Poland Oats, as I have sent one of my Young Men into the Country & If they are to be had he will get them, tho most of our Farmers who have growed them, think them a Very uncertain Crop, & now give the preference to the Country Oat. there are two or three Craft here & I expect I can get them to take down the Oats at 4d. ℔ Bushel If you want 200 Bushels or Upwards and I can now send You any Quantity you want the price 3/ for the Comn & 3/9 for the Poland this Currency.
   Mr Benjamin Reader who goes to Mrs Slauters tomorrow promises to sent his Boy to your House with this, otherwise I

would have sent a Servant on purpose fearing my letter would be Neglected or omitted to be forwarded by the Post master[2]— I am with the Most perfect Respect Sir Your Obt Servt

Will. Deakins Jur

ALS, DLC:GW.

1. Letter not found, but see Deakins to GW, 10 January.

2. Mrs. Slauter was Ann Clifton Slaughter (d. 1798). Benjamin Reeder (Reader) was married to Mrs. Slaughter's daughter Eleanor.

From Robert Townsend Hooe

Dr Sir,   Alexandria Jany 25th, 1787.

I some time last Year mention'd to Major Washington a small Acct which Mr Harrison wrote me he had paid to Mr Carmichael for expences of your Jack Asses in Spain, and as the Major afterwards informed me Mr Carmichael had not given you any Acct of such Payment I wrote to Mr Harrison for the particulars which I now have the Honor to enclose. the Amt is 71¼ Dollars equal to £21.7.6 Va Currency.[1] I am Dr Sir, Yr Excellency's most Obt servt

R. Td Hooe

ALS, DLC:GW.

1. The contemporary translation of the enclosure, dated 9 Aug. 1785, is headed "An acct of Provisions & other Charges attending the Embarkment of 2 Jack-Asses & of what was supplied to Peter Thellez conductor of one of them that was Ship'd on Bd of Capt. Knights." A transcription of the document is in CD-ROM:GW. William Carmichael signed the account certifying that he had been paid the amount by Richard Harrison. The ship captain Giles Sullivan (Sulivan) confirmed that it was "a true Translation from the Spanish &c." For the role of William Carmichael and Richard Harrison in securing a Spanish jackass for GW, see Carmichael to GW, 3 Dec. 1784, n.1.

Letter not found: to Henry Knox, 25 Jan. 1787. On 8 Feb. Knox wrote GW: "I have received your favor of the 25 Jany."

From Henry Knox

New York 25, Jany 1787

I wrote you my dear Sir on the 21st instant and then enclosed you the General orders of Governor Bowdoin—By the post last evening I have received information from Genl Sheppard, that he took post at the Magazine of the United States at Springfield on the 18th. That the insurgents were collecting in his neighbouhood, and he expected to be attacked by them as the public Stores seemed to be their object—and from a variety of other information I am of opinion that his conjecture will be found to be true, and that they will attack him.

Genl Lincoln's force was collecting at Weston about 14 miles from Boston on the 19th & he was to be at Worcester on the 23d—The insurgents boast that they will have 5000 strong, but they probably overate their strength in this instance—Should they defeat or disgrace the governmental troops it is probable they then may muster the above number and more—Matters are critically disposed[1]—By the post, which will arrive on the 27th, or by an express sooner, we shall be more fully informed of events which I shall communicate to you by the post on the 29th—In the mean time with respects to Mrs Washington I am my dear Sir Your respectfully affectionate

H. Knox

ALS, DLC:GW.
    1. See Benjamin Lincoln to GW, 4 Dec. 1786–4 Mar. 1787.

Letter not found: from Jaques Campion, 26 Jan. 1787. On 24 Feb. GW wrote Campion: "Your letter of the 26th of Jany came duly to hand."

From Samuel Hanson

Sir   Alexa[ndria] 27th Jany 1787
    Your instructions of this date, respecting your Nephews, I shall punctually follow.[1] I have taken an Acct of the cloathes they brought with them, and shall take care that they are neither lost or abused. I had advised them to send their Shoes to be mended at Mount-Vernon, as the Tradesmen charge nearly the first cost of the shoes for the slightest repairs. If my proposal meet with your approbation, I shall see that they are sent; as also any of their cloth cloathes that require the Tailor—I think it my duty to promote your views relative to their frugality, and shall endeavour to check any inclinations they may discover of a con-

trary tendency. With perfect respect I remain, Sir your most obedt Servt

S. Hanson of Saml

ALS, DLC:GW.

1. GW's nephews, the brothers George Steptoe and Lawrence Augustine Washington, had begun boarding at Samuel Hanson of Samuel's house while attending Alexandria Academy. It would appear that GW either wrote to Hanson or sent verbal instructions to him on this date. No letter has been found. On 18 Dec. Hanson wrote George Augustine Washington setting out the terms on which he had agreed to take in the two boys: "According to my promise of this Morning, I take this Method to inform you of the terms upon which I propose taking Young Gentlemen as Boarders.

"1st The Expence of Board & Washing & mending 35£.

"2d One fourth of the above sum to be advanced at the beginning of Each Quarter.

"3d The Boys to find their own Beds.

"4th The Boys to be informed by their Parents or Guardians that they are to be accountable to me for their Conduct *out of School*, and to be impressed with a conviction that in Case of Misbehaviour & Complaint made in Consequence thereof, to the Teacher at the Academy, reproof or Chastisement will ensue.

"This regulation I hope will be thought necessary not only with respect to the preservation of Decorum in my family, but with regard to the morals of the Boys themselves, who, without such a restriction, would, I apprehend, be apt to keep bad hours, & get in to improper Company especially on the Sabbath, when I should think it incumbent on me to see that they attended some place of publick religious Worship.

"The price of Board I have set down as low as possible, following the only guide I could on this Subject (never having had Boarders) viz. the price paid in this place by Grown Gentlemen, which is 45£, exclusive of Lodging & Wash-⟨ing⟩" (DLC:GW). From Hanson's correspondence with GW, it would appear that his pay was well earned. See Hanson's letters of 23 Sept., 18 Nov. 1787, 16, 23 Mar., 4 May, 7 Aug., and 2 Oct. 1788.

From John Price Posey

New Kent

Worthy & Most respectfull Sir. 27th Januy 1787

This will Acknowledge the receipt of your Letter Dated 12th Inst.—the Contents of which Woud have been hurtfull to the Feelings of allmost any Man that Cou'd not have Justified his Conduct but I am happy in this Instance & doubt not I can Satisfie you that I have not Acte'd with that unjustice to you as you So pointedly have Charg'd me with.

The Answer of Mr Hill to you be not a Little Supriseing to me informing that he had Years agoe Settled the Management of you[r] Estate & the Accounts with me had Allso charg'd me with other Moneys pd by Newton of Norfolk &c.[1] I Shall sir assert Nothing but what I Shall support & Conceale Nothing that may now Support the State of the Management of your Business in *1779* Transacted by Jams Hill & Devenport—prior to that date I had nothing to do with Hill.[2]

I do Assert that I never Settled an Accot with Mr Jams Hill on your Accot (*neither did I ever Settle any Accot with him on Acct of the late Mr Custis.*) the inclosd state of the Money receivd On your Accot Will fully explain—from the hands of Jams Hill only £130 in July 79. the other Money receivd as the Accot Explains[3]—As for Money from Mr *Newton* I never receivd a Shilling on your accot or did I know that Newton paid Hill—Mr Hill Soon after He had receivd your letter Chargeing him with Neglect, & unjustice,[4] He made application to me I gave him as a Justification for my Conduct in receivg the Money as a copy of your Letter Stated—Hill than Compaird his Accot & never mentioned that He had made a Settlement with me & the Accot of Cash Agreed—as Allso the Date—Majr D. Ragsdale applyd to Colo. Bassett on Accot Mr Hill (Lately) in Conversation the Colo. informed him I had paid him On your Accot the Certificate of 100⟨o⟩ As *Stated*—Your Letter of 1779 Desirg my Assistance to Colo. Bassett in bringing a Close of your Business in the hads of Jams Hill was What Authoris'd me to receive the Money as ℔ Stated, (in that Letter,) a Copy of which Hill promisd to in close you & the Originals Majr Ragsdale has got otherwise I woud inclose it *you*—You Directed me to be governd intitely by Colo. Bassett[5] He directed me to fund the Money & deliver him the Certificate, untill now I had not the least doubt but Colo. Bassett had given you a full State of the Business—It was not my Business to Close a Final Settlement with Hill Haveing no directions so to do—The Books of Mr Custis's Estate He deliverd me but I never made a Settlement With him on Accot of that Gentleman—Mr Hill Certainly had given you a Very unperfect Accot & done me much wrong.

I am just return from the Mountains & am this Eve[n]ing informd that Mr Washington is on his return up[6]—therefor have hurried this Letter & Wish much I coud have Waited on Mr Washington to Mr Hill's for I will not Suffer Mr Hill or any other man to injure my reputation & More particular to you *sir* that I ever Wishd to please & the Most ungratefull (that has receivd the favors I have done from you) Cou'd not have thought of Deceiveing.[7]

I Shall be ready when Call'd on to support More fully (*by my Vouchers*) the Justice of my *Conduct* & will attend you in Fairfax when you may please to Call on me—in hart I am Sir With every sentiment of respect, Yrs

John P. Posey

ALS, DLC:GW.

1. James Hill's letter to GW was dated 24 Sept. 1786.

2. On 23 April 1779 GW wrote to Posey, John Parke Custis's manager: "Sir you will oblige me by lending your aid to bring my business under the care of Mr Hill & Mr Davenport to a close. In doing this I wish you to be governed entirely by the advice & direction of Colo. Bassett. I would have every thing belonging to me (& not taken by Mr [John Parke] Custis) deposed of and the money remitted to Mr Lund Washington for my use. I am Yr sincere friend & obt Servt G. Washington" (DLC:GW). Joseph Davenport was for a number of years the overseer of Claiborne's plantation, which was a part of Martha Washington's dower land.

3. The account has not been found, but this payment agrees with Hill's account enclosed in his letter of 1 Feb. to GW.

4. GW's letter to Hill was dated 29 Aug. 1786.

5. For GW's letter requesting his aid, see note 2 above. For Hill's accounts, see Hill to GW, 1 Feb. 1787, n.1. Major Ragsdale was Drury Ragsdale (d. 1804) of King William County who served in the 1st Continental Artillery during the Revolution.

6. George Augustine Washington had gone to New Kent County in the middle of January. See GW to Alexander Spotswood, 23 Jan. 1787.

7. Posey's "reputation," including two previous brushes with the law, must have been well known to GW at this time. In 1784 Posey and another man were tried and convicted in the General Court of having on 4 Jan. 1783 "with force and arms unlawfully entered into the Close of George Washington Parke Custis" in New Kent County where they "took and drove away one Cow" and did "other enormities" to young Custis (*Calendar of Virginia State Papers*, 3:616). In March 1786 Posey was convicted of defrauding Bartholomew Dandridge and others and destroying "in a passion" an arbitration bond given Posey by Dandridge and others in Northampton County on the Eastern Shore of Virginia (ibid., 4:95). For GW's earlier references to Posey's behavior, see his letters to Bartholomew Dandridge, 25 June, 18 Dec. 1782, to Posey, 7 Aug. 1782, and to David Stuart, 19 Nov. 1786.

In the summer of 1787 Posey was jailed for attacking the sheriff of New Kent County, but he escaped and returned on the night of 15 July to burn down the county jail and the clerk's office. He was found guilty of arson by the General Court and hanged in Richmond on 25 Jan. 1788 (see Harris, *Old New Kent*, 1:97–99).

From James Swan

Alexandria Saturday Morng 27 Jany [1787]
Major Swan's most respectfull Compliments to Genl Washington: And intending to set off to morrow on his journey to Boston, has sent his servant with this Card of leave, and to request the honor of the General & his Lady's Commands. Would have waited upon them in person, but some business & urgent causes of departure to morrow, prevents him.[1]

Requests the favor of the General's accepting a Copy of a Pamphlet lately published at Boston on the resources of Massachusetts. There are some observations in it, which will apply to all the States, and if useful notwithstanding their incorrectness, will be regarded with approbation by every friend to œconomy & agriculture. The preface was struck off in the author's absence, & is very incorrect and if the Dedication & heads of the Chapters coud be preserved, would be well to be destroyed.[2]

If there is any thing which the Genl or Mrs Washington or any of their friends might want from Boston, Mr Swan shall esteem it the most fortunate circumstance, to be the executor of their wishes.

Begs his best respects may be offered to the Generals Lady & to Mrs Washington—and to be remembred to young Mr George & Miss Custus.

AL, DLC:GW.

1. James Swan, for whom GW wrote letters of recommendation in 1785 to Chastellux and Rochambeau, spent the nights of 17 and 21 Jan. at Mount Vernon. See GW to Henry Knox, 28 Feb. 1785, n.1, and *Diaries*, 5:95, 97, 98.

2. Swan's pamphlet, a copy of which Swan also sent to Thomas Jefferson (Boyd, *Jefferson Papers*, 12:541–42), is entitled *National Arithmetick: or, Observations on the Finances of the Commonwealth of Massachusetts: with Some Hints respecting Financiering and Future Taxation in This State* (Boston, 1786).

From Henry Knox

My dear Sir   New York 29 January 1787.

By an express received by me Yesterday affairs at Springfield were most critically circumstanced. At 4 oClock last Thursday afternoon Genl Sheppard and the insurgents were drawn up in battle array and Shepperd expecting to be momently attacked. Capt. Cushing an officer in the troops now raising was dispatched as an express to Hartford for asistance to Shepperd says that he was confident an action commenced in half an hour after his departure. Sheppard had 1200 rank and file, well armed, and 4 peices of Cannon—Shays had the same number on the ground, and six hundred within half an hours march, part of which were in motion.

Genl Lincoln, who had a large force of 3000 and upwards was probably on the march from Worcester, to join Shepperd, he probably marched from Worcester on Wednesday, but I am apprehensive not in time to save Shepperd—Not having received any subsequent intelligence to the one received yesterday induces rather an unfavorable opinion of the issue, or that no action happened.[1] The post will regularly set out from hence for the four days ensuing. I will inform you of any thing I may receive. I am Dear Sir Your respectfully affectionate humble Servant

H. Knox

ALS, DLC:GW.

1. See Benjamin Lincoln to GW, 4 Dec. 1786–4 Mar. 1787.

From Henry Knox

New York 30 January 1787

I wrote you my dear Sir by the post of yesterday and stated the high probability of an action between Genl Shepperd, on the part of government, and the insurgents at Springfield on Thursday the 25th instant, but since then I have received no further information. This is a cruel suspense and difficult to account for, but on the principle of the expected action being avoided by some circumstances not known, perhaps by the arrival of Lincoln or some of his force.

I have omitted writing this letter untill the last moment of the mail, in hopes of being able to give you further information. Even if I should receive nothing by the arrival of the post tomorrow I will write you a line. With most respectful compliments to Mrs Washington I am my dear Sir your respectfull affectionate

H. Knox

ALS, DLC:GW.

From Thomas Stone

Dr Sir   Annapolis 30 Jan. 1787.

The Senate and House of Delegates of Maryland having differed upon the Subject of issuing Paper Money on Loan and the latter having appealed to the People I take the Liberty of inclosing You the Papers of each house and if not disagreable I shall be much obliged by a communication of your Sentiments upon a Subject which is likely to create great & perhaps dangerous divisions in this State.[1] and am with perfect Esteem Sir yr most Obt Sert

T. Stone

ALS, PHi: Sprague Collection; LS, DLC:GW.

1. Thomas Stone, who had been a member of the Maryland senate since 1781, worked closely with GW in early 1785 to secure the passage of the Potomac River Company bill. See Stone to GW, 28 Jan. 1785, and notes. The enclosed broadside (DLC:GW), dated 20 Jan. 1787, includes the Maryland senate's message to the house of 5 Jan. rejecting the house's paper money bill as well as subsequent exchanges between the two houses. Stone died not long after writing this letter but lived long enough to see the ensuing public debate over Samuel Chase's paper money bill end in the collapse of the paper money movement, which had been the focus of political strife in Maryland since 1785.

From William Deakins, Jr.

Sir   Geo[rge] Town [Md.] Janry 31. 1787

Altho I have made the most Anxious enquiry for Poland Oats could not till to day get a Single Bushel, have now sent 7 Bushels by your Boat & I am promisd 30 Bushels more by the end of the Week but such is the want of punctuality amongst Men, that I cannot promise with Certainty that this man will comply with

his promise. When I last Wrote You[1] that 200 Bushels would be
ready by Monday last, I had then engaged the Quantity from
two of our Most respectable Farmers to be delivered on Saturday last & I at the time Informed them I had appointed that day
for You to send for them & that they must not disappoint me
but altho I was so pointed they have not yet brought them in, &
they live too distant to detain Your Boat till they can be sent
for—have therefore engaged of Mr Notley Young (now in town)
about 100 Bushels of his Oats which he says are Very good &
your Boat will receive them at his Landing,[2] I was promised
Early in the Fall a Quantity of Poland Oats in two hands but in
them I was also deceived—I am with the greatest Respect—Sir
Your Obt Servt

Will. Deakins Jur

ALS, DLC:GW.
   1. On 25 January.
   2. For the shipment of oats by Deakins, see his letter of 9 Mar. 1787.

From Henry Knox

New York, 31 January 1787
No distinct accounts have arrived but by the post this evening
we shall expect some particulars, which I will communicate tomorrow. Thus much is certain that no action has happened. I
am my dear Sir Respectfully Your humble Servt

H. Knox

ALS, DLC:GW.

Index

NOTE: Identifications of persons, places, and things in previous volumes of the *Confederation Series* are noted within parentheses.

Abingdon (house): id., 363
Adam, Robert: GW's land purchases from, 249
Adam & Campbell (firm): and the bloomery, 138
Adams, John, 224; demands western posts, 82, 83, 132, 170; and Barbary pirates, 312; and William Gordon, 526; *letters to:* from John Jay, 132
Agriculture: corn, 18, 396; buckwheat, 21, 246, 277, 471; flax, 21; planting instructions, 28–29; lambs, 52, 77, 94, 112, 142; seed and supplies for, 53; barley, 77, 142–43, 146, 329, 372, 383, 438, 441–42, 498, 518, 532, 537; Bloxham hired, 86–88; grass seed, 90, 134, 195, 197, 372; crops ruined by rain, 117; clover seed, 156, 188, 329, 438, 440–41, 498; wheat seed, 167–68, 179, 372, 396; English equipment, 195; English vegetable and grass seed, 195, 197, 370, 372; English tools, 196; GW's views on, 196; English plowman sought, 197; timothy, 246, 277, 379; pumpkin, 279, 280; sweet potato, 279, 280; peas, 333–34, 518, 537; seed from Arthur Young, 370, 372; beans, 372, 518, 537; oats, 372, 508–9, 517–18, 536–37, 542, 550–51; drill plow, 378, 484–85; Jerusalem artichoke, 498; and Alexander Spotswood, 517
Alcorn, Captain (shipmaster), 208
Alexander, Colonel ——: and Samuel Washington's estate, 234
Alexander, Robert: id., 363; indebtedness to GW, 363; *letters to:* from GW, 363
Alexander, William (*see* 1:247), 292

Alexandria (Va.): as a port, 364
Alexandria Academy (*see* 3:383): admission of girls, 135; and GW's gift, 135; and GW's nephews, 545; *letters from:* to GW, 135
Alice (slave): sold at Washington's Bottom, 463, 464
Amesbury, Charles Dundass, baron, 525
Anderson, Mr. ——: legacy of, 150–51
Anderson, Harriot Rebecca: her parent's legacy to, 150–51; and Colvill legacy, 150–52, 166, 190, 262, 263, 440
Anderson, Rebecca: legacy of, 150–51
Anderson, Robert: and Harriot Rebecca Anderson's legacy, 151
André, John: capture of, 176
Andrews, Captain (shipmaster), 144
Ann (ship), 93
Annapolis Convention, 231, 241–42, 294, 369, 479, 480, 482, 504, 519; GW's queries about, 241–42; and report of, 326; and Virginia house of delegates, 344, 347
Annemours (Anmour), Charles-François-Adrien le Paulinier, chevalier d': id., 161
Anstey, John (*see* 3:524), 128; introduction of, 452
Anterroche, Jeanne-Françoise Teyssier (Tessier) de Chaunay, comtesse d': *letters from:* to GW, 249–52, 252
Anterroche, Jean-Pierre, comte d', 251; id., 252
Anterroche, Joseph-Louis, chevalier d': GW's patronage of sought, 249–50; id., 252
Anterroche, Mary Vanderpoel: id., 252

Argyle, duke of. *See* Campbell, John
Ariss, John (*see* 2:24): as GW's tenant, 205; *letters from:* to GW, 205
Armand (Charles Armand-Tuffin, marquis de La Rouërie; *see* 1:103; 3:3): congratulations on his marriage, 203–4; *letters to:* from GW, 203–4
Armistead, John: and estate of William Armistead, 19–20; id., 20; indebtedness to GW, 487–88; *letters to:* from GW, 19–20, 487–88
Armistead, William: estate of, 19–20, 487–88; id., 20
Armistead, Mrs. William: indebtedness of, 20
Arnold, Benedict: GW's account of the treachery of, 174–77
Asbury, Francis: *An Address . . . to the Members of the Methodist Society,* 27; id., 27; *letters from:* to GW, 27
Asgill, Charles (*see* 2:407): as a hostage, 79, 80, 97–99
Asgill affair, 262, 296; GW's recollections of, 80, 97–99; and James Tilghman's inquiries about, 150, 165–66, 190, 237–38, 440; GW's records of, 236–37; Humphreys' publication regarding, 351, 358, 373, 374, 478, 507
Ashley, John: and militia defeat of Shaysites, 433, 436
Ashton, John (shipmaster): and Spanish jack, 2
Assembly of Notables: Lafayette's description of, 515; id., 517
Athawes, Samuel: and Arthur Young, 117; and GW's correspondence with Fairfax, 126, 129; forwards letters, 145, 147; and George William Fairfax, 451; *letters from:* to GW, 139, 141; *letters to:* from GW, 129
Atkinson (Aitkinson), Captain (shipmaster), 96
Austin, Benjamin: id., 227
Austin, Jonathan Loring: id., 227; *Oration . . .,* 227; *letters to:* from GW, 227
Austin, Samuel, 325, 351; id., 326
Austin (slave; *see* 1:442): rides a horse, 88, 89

Ayen, Jean-Paul-François de Noailles, duc d': and Lafayette, 72

Bailey, Samuel: as GW's tenant, 155, 156
Bailey, William: as GW's tenant, 187
Baker, Philip: deals with Mount Vernon storehouse, 496
Balch, Stephen Bloomer (*see* 3:84): and Georgetown (Md.) Presbyterian Church, 10–11
Balfour & Barraud (firm), 83; indebtedness to GW, 66–67, 145
Ball, Burgess (*see* 1:164; 2:155): id., 518
Ballendine, John: and navigation of Potomac, 3
Bank of England stock: payment of interest on, 144–46; drawn on, 191
Banks, John: dealings with Nathanael Greene, 283–85
Banks & Co., John (firm): and Nathanael Greene, 283–85, 298
Barbary pirates, 188–89, 514; negotiations with, 26; policy towards, 312
Barclay, Thomas (*see* 1:30; 3:334): conducts Morocco negotiations, 4, 67, 514, 517
Barlow, Joel: and George Washington Greene, 299; as Connecticut Wit, 373, 530; id., 374
Barnes (Barns), Joseph: and Rumsey's boat, 253–54; id., 254
Barrauds (firm): and Lafayette's gifts, 409
Barrett, Nathaniel (*see* 3:546): conveys letter, 41
Bartlett, William: as GW's tenant, 155
Bartlett, William (shipmaster), 388
Bassett, Burwell (*see* 1:57): servant of, 18; and gift of slaves, 308, 310, 536; and GW's Custis property, 511–12, 546, 547; and James Hill, 546; and John Price Posey, 546
Bath (Va.): GW's buildings at described, 228–29
Baylor, John (*see* 2:518): and John Parke Custis estate, 347

Baynham, William (*see* 3:78): conveys letter, 126
Beard, Thomas: as carpenter at Bath, 240
Bedwell, Thomas: id., 103; *letters from:* to GW, 80; *letters to:* from GW, 102–3
Belle Air (house), 127
Belt, ——, Dr.: of Leesburg, 17
Belvale (house), 116
Belvoir (house; *see* 1:435): sale in 1774 at, 137–38, 140; furnishings of, 139, 450
Beniousky, Maurice-Auguste de: in Madagascar, 515–16; id., 517
Benson, Egbert (*see* 1:53): as Mass.-N.Y. boundary commissioner, 527, 530
Berard frères & Co. (firm), 381
Biddle, Clement (*see* 1:20), 57; and GW's Pennsylvania certificates, 121, 294–95; makes payment for GW, 507; *letters from:* to GW, 125–26, 208–9, 294–95, 329–30, 497–98; *letters to:* from GW, 53–55, 121, 177–78, 218, 262, 313, 440–42
Biddle, John: acts for GW, 53; id., 55
Biddle, Rebekah Cornell (*see* 1:20): greetings to, 55, 178, 442; greetings from, 126, 209, 295
Blair, Alexander: as attorney for Mercer creditors, 385, 386, 466
Bland, Martha Dangerfield: id., 211; greetings to, 379, 485
Bland, Theodorick: nocturnal journey of, 210; id., 211; as candidate for governor, 345, 346; and legislative session, 377–78; given drill plow, 484–85; timothy seed for, 484–85, 495; *letters from:* to GW, 327; *letters to:* from GW, 210, 377–79, 484–85
Blodget, Nathan, 211
Bloomery: and Adam & Campbell, 138; and George William Fairfax, 138; and John Carlyle, 139; attempted sale of, 140–41
Bloxham, James: instructions to, 29; GW's agreement with, 86–88, 127–28; id., 88; conveys letter, 126; letter for, 141; as farmer at

Mount Vernon, 157, 198; and passage of his wife, 192, 370–71, 375–76; wife of, 193–95; and George William Fairfax, 451; *letters from:* to William Peacey, 193–95
Bloxham, Thomas, 194
Boatswain (slave): deals with Mount Vernon storehouse, 496
Bob (slave): property of John Francis Mercer, 394, 466
Bomford, Sarah: and Margaret Savage, 15
Bordley, John Beale (*see* 3:106), 383, 384
Bourdon des Planches: *letters from:* to GW, 443
Bowdoin, James: and Shays' Rebellion, 418, 462, 534–35, 543; *letters from:* to Benjamin Lincoln, 422–23; *letters to:* from Benjamin Lincoln, 426–27
Bowe, Caven: as GW's indentured tailor, 93
Bowen, Jabez: id., 505; *letters to:* from GW, 504–5
Bowen, Penuel: id., 38
Bower Hill (house), 405
Bowie, F. John: id., 90; *letters from:* to GW, 134
Bowler, Metcalf: *A Treatise on Agriculture*, 220, 221; id., 221; *letters from:* to GW, 167; *letters to:* from GW, 220–21
Bowling Green: GW lodges at, 50, 51
Braddock's Road, 412, 489
Bradley, Philip Burr: elected to Connecticut legislature, 265; id., 267
Branden (Brandon), Samuel: and ass from Surinam, 388–89; *letters from:* to GW, 171; *letters to:* from GW, 388–89
Brant, Joseph: and the Iroquois, 321
Brent, George: and GW's land purchase, 308, 309
Brereton, Thomas: and Margaret Savage's estate, 14–15, 22–23, 348–50; *letters from:* to GW, 14–15; *letters to:* from GW, 22–23
Bridgewater, Francis Egerton, duke of (*see* 3:613), 6, 73, 451, 452

Brindley, James (*see* 3:613): and Potomac River Company, 3, 447, 486–87; and Santee Canal, 6, 7, 111; and Robert Neilson, 49; and Susquehanna canal, 73; letters to and from, 321; at Mount Vernon, 537, 538; *letters to:* from GW, 202; from William Moultrie, 202

Brindley, James (1716–1772; *see* 3:613), 73, 452

Bristow, Mary (*see* 1:448): and Robert Bristow's estate, 91; *letters to:* from GW, 91

Bristow, Robert: Virginia estate of, 91

Britain: anti-Americanism of, 275

Bronaugh, Jeremiah, 32

Brown, Bazil: buys GW's slave, 464

Brown, David: and Alexander Steel, 58; id., 60

Brown, Jabez: *letters from:* to GW, 391

Brown, John (*see* 2:162): recommends Joseph Jenckes, 323–24; and proposed city on Potomac, 324; *letters from:* to GW, 323–24

Brown, John, 31; id., 32

Brown, Joseph: makes prints of GW's and Greene's portraits, 84–86; *letters from:* to GW, 84, 85; to Charles Thomson, 85, 85–86, 86; to Nathanael Greene, 85; *letters to:* from GW, 84–86

Brown, Thomas: buys GW's slave, 464

Brown, William (*see* 3:383): and Alexandria Academy, 135; *letters from:* to GW, 130; *letters to:* from GW, 135

Bruin, Peter Bryan: at Bath, 410; id., 412

Bryan, George: and runaway slave, 17

Buchanan, James (*see* 2:4–5): as treasurer of James River Company, 31

Bullskin land. *See* Landholdings of GW

Burbidge, Mrs. Julius King, 48

Burbidge, Julius King: id., 48

Burgoyne, John, 59

Burnham, John: accused of rioting, 115

Burns, Samuel: buys GW's slaves, 464

Bushfield (house; *see* 1:262), 279

Butler, Richard: and Indian vocabulary, 398–400; id., 400; and letter to, 410; *letters to:* from GW, 398–400

Byrd, Mary Willing: id., 76

Calonne, Charles Alexandre de (*see* 1:30; 3:547): and Assembly of Notables, 515; *letters from:* to Thomas Jefferson, 311, 313

Campbell, John, marquis of Lorne: id., 304

Campion, Jaques: and Lafayette's jackasses, 359, 360, 361, 380–81, 385; at Mount Vernon, 381, 408–9; *letters from:* to GW, 544

Cannon, John: and Millers Run ejectment suits, 256, 257, 260; as GW's land agent, 342, 401, 405–6, 408, 411, 413; id., 406; *letters from:* to GW, 535; *letters to:* from GW, 405–6

Carey, Mathew (*see* 2:228): and *Columbian Magazine*, 507

Carleton, Guy, 462; as governor general of Canada, 357, 373

Carlyle, John: and the bloomery, 138, 139, 140, 141

Carmarthen, Francis Osborne, marquess of: reply of to John Adams, 82, 83, 132, 170

Carmichael, William (*see* 2:164), 439; id., 154; and Toledo swords, 391; and Royal Gift (jackass), 543

Carns, Peter: and Charles MacIver, 95

Carrington, Edward (*see* 1:222): as member of Congress, 51, 346

Carroll, Charles (of Carrollton; *see* 2:179): *letters to:* from GW, 5

Carroll, Daniel (*see* 2:563): and GW's Washington's Bottom, 505–6; *letters from:* to GW, 477; *letters to:* from GW, 505–6

Carroll, John (*see* 2:563): as Roman Catholic bishop, 11

Carter, Charles (of Ludlow): and locks for Potomac River Company, 507–8; id., 45, 508; *letters*

Carter, Charles (of Ludlow) (*cont.*)
from: to GW, 415; *letters to:* from
GW, 507–8
Carter, Charles, Jr.: seeks wolf-
hound, 44
Carter, Robert (of Nomini Hall; *see*
3:136), 218; id., 238
Cary & Co., Robert (firm): payment
from, 100
Cary, Sarah Blair: id., 141
Cary, Wilson: id., 141
Cary, Wilson Miles: id., 141
Castiglioni, Count Luigi: movements
of, 6
Castries, Armand-Charles-Augustin
de La Croix, duc de (*see* 1:499),
72; id., 73
Castries, Charles-Eugène-Gabriel de
La Croix, marquis and marechal
de (*see* 1:149), 72
Caswell, Richard: and corruption in
North Carolina, 468, 470; id.,
470
Catherine II of Russia: and Indian
vocabulary, 44, 398–99; and La-
fayette, 311–12, 515; and the
Ottoman Empire, 71; and uni-
versal dictionary, 222
Cazenove, John Henry: and George
Mercer, 386
Cedar Grove (house), 116
Certificates (Pennsylvania). *See* Penn-
sylvania certificates
Chapman, George (*see* 2:184): *letters
to:* from GW, 127, 129
Charity (slave): sold at Washington's
Bottom, 463, 464
Charles (slave; *see* 3:408): id., 217
Charles Theodore (Elector of Ba-
varia), 134, 180
Charlotte (slave): dispute of with
Mrs. MacIver, 113–15; id., 115
Charming Polly (ship): id., 238
Charton, Henry L.: and GW's west-
ern lands, 63–66, 167; id., 66; *let-
ters from:* to GW, 33; *letters to:*
from GW, 63–66, 167
Chase, Samuel (*see* 2:179): and Mary-
land politics, 70; and Maryland
paper money debate, 550
Chastellux, François-Jean de Beau-
voir, chevalier de (*see* 1:86): and
David Humphreys, 210, 211,

219; *Travels in America*, 218–19,
294, 395; *Voyages de M. le
Marquis de Chastellux dans l'Amérique . . .*, 220; and Virginia hams,
313; *letters from:* to GW, 68; *letters
to:* from GW, 218–20
Chatham (house), 28, 227
Chatsworth (house), 227
Chew, Samuel: id., 153
Chew, Samuel Lloyd: id., 153
Child, Cromel & Caleb (firm), 24,
268
Cincinnati, Society of: and L'Enfant's
purchase of insignia, 89, 108–
11, 184, 443–45; certificates of,
182, 217–18, 238, 335–36; and
GW's nonattendance at General
Meeting, 264–65, 266, 378,
382–83, 387–88, 529; reform of
rejected, 265, 266; and GW's circular letter, 296, 297, 316–18,
321–22, 324, 326, 330, 335,
339, 350, 376–77, 388, 418,
490–91, 491–92, 523–24,
532–34; Mandrillon's address to,
302–3; article on in *Encyclopédie
Méthodique*, 364–66; and GW's
role in, 457–58; GW's description of, 457–58; and GW's attendance at Federal Convention,
469; GW seeks report on, 479;
writings on, 539–40
Cincinnati china. *See* Mount Vernon
Cipher: of William Gordon, 24
Cist, Charles: and *Columbian Magazine*, 507
Clagett, Horatio: conveys letter, 68;
id., 69; *letters from:* to GW, 218
Clagett, John: id., 69
Clam Town (N.J.), 58; id., 60
Clapham, John: and Balfour & Bar-
raud, 83
Clark, Abraham: and Mississippi
River navigation, 449–50
Clark, George Rogers, 402; and at-
tack on Shawnee, 320–21, 362;
id., 321
Clayton, William: as John Price Po-
sey's creditor, 468; id., 470
Cleesh (house), 271; id., 452
Cleveland, James: id., 36
Clifton, William: and GW's land pur-
chase, 308, 309

Clinton, Cornelia Tappen: greetings to, 330

Clinton, George: GW's indebtedness to, 243–44; and GW's Cincinnati circular letter, 330; and GW's joint land purchase, 330; *letters to:* from GW, 330

Clinton, Henry: at New York, 175–76

Clinton, James: id., 60

Cloth: manufacture of, 102–3

Clymer, Elizabeth Meredith, 190

Cobb, David: and Massachusetts rioters, 265; id., 266; speech of, 297

Cockburn, Ann Bronaugh: greetings to, 32

Cockburn, Martin: id., 32; *letters to:* from GW, 32

Cocks, Samuel: and William Hansborough, 391

Coke, Thomas: *An Address . . . to the Members of the Methodist Society*, 27

Colfax, William (*see* 1:132), 124; id., 125

Colston, Elizabeth, 354

Colston (Coulston), Rawleigh: conveys seed, 62; and William Hickman, 286–88, 353–54; and sale of George Mercer's Shenandoah lands, 335, 353–54; and John Francis Mercer, 337, 353, 393, 442–43; id., 354; *letters from:* to GW, 286, 353–54; *letters to:* from GW, 415–16

Columbian Magazine or Monthly Miscellany, 507

Colvill, Frances: and Thomas Colvill's estate, 151

Colvill, John: and Thomas Colvill's estate, 166, 452

Colvill, Thomas: estate of, 132–33, 150–52, 166, 190, 338–39, 440, 452, 486

Combs, John J., 338

Combs, Joseph: and John Francis Mercer, 337, 338, 393

Congress: and the impost, 26, 50–51; and cession of land to Connecticut, 81, 82; delayed meeting, 534–35

Connecticut: land cession to, 81, 82, 169

Connecticut Wits, 373, 374

Constable & Co., Rucker (firm): and Cincinnati china, 148, 201

Cooke, Jacob, 130

Cooper, Captain (shipmaster), 84, 85

Corbin, Richard (*see* 2:442): dispute with brother, 128

Corbin, Thomas (*see* 2:442): dispute with brother, 128

Couteulx, I. L. & C. Le (firm): id., 289

Couteulx, Louis Le, 366; id., 288–89; and the fur trade, 363–64

Cozette, Pierre François: offers picture of Louis XV, 494

Craik, James (*see* 1:178), 160, 312, 516; attends GW, 234, 235, 237

Crane, James (*see* 2:45): as Berkeley County sheriff, 155, 156, 188

Craven, Peyton: as Fairfax's land agent, 140; death of, 140

Crawford, Hannah (*see* 1:423): indebtedness of, 36; slaves of, 36; and Millers Run ejectment suits, 256–57

Crawford, Valentine: indebtedness of, 36–37, 257, 258, 261; and Millers Run tract, 256; *letters from:* to GW, 37

Crawford, William, 63; death of, 36; as surveyor of Millers Run tract, 172, 173, 255–57, 260

Cresap, Elizabeth: as heir of Michael Cresap, 157

Cresap, Michael (*see* 3:173): and claims to Round Bottom tract, 157, 467

Cresap, Sarah: as heir of Michael Cresap, 157

Cresap, Thomas: id., 36; *letters from:* to GW, 7; *letters to:* from GW, 35–36

Cromwell, Oliver: saltcellar of, 304–5

Cunningham, Captain (shipmaster), 68

Cunningham, William: and Alexander Steel, 59; id., 61

Cushing, Capt. ——: and Shays' Rebellion, 549

Cushing, Deborah Fletcher (*see* 3:298): greetings to, 2

Cushing, Thomas (*see* 3:297–98):
and Spanish jackass, 2–3; *letters
to:* from GW, 2–3
Custis, Daniel Parke: estate of, 20
Custis, Eleanor Parke, 127, 548
Custis, George Washington Parke,
127, 312, 548; greetings to,
525
Custis, John Parke: estate of, 11, 18,
100, 232, 546; and Bank of England stock, 145–46; annual payment of estate to GW, 334, 335,
362; and debt to Robert Alexander, 363; and James Hill,
510–12; and John Price Posey,
511–12
Custis, Martha Parke: and Bank of
England stock, 145–46

Dalby, Philip: and runaway slave,
15–17, 29–30
Dandridge, Bartholomew (*see* 1:209):
death of, 48; and GW's Custis
lands, 263; and John Price Posey, 547
Dandridge, Frances Jones: id., 48
Dandridge, John: *letters from:* to GW,
47–48
Dandridge, Mary Burbidge, 48
Darrell, Sarah McCarty Johnston,
123; and Hite-Fairfax suit, 102;
id., 116; *letters to:* from GW,
115–16
Dashiell, Joseph (*see* 2:386): id., 122;
letters from: to GW, 162–63; *letters
to:* from GW, 122
Davenport, Joseph (*see* 2:480–81): as
Mount Vernon miller, 57, 78,
497
David (slave): property of John Fran-
cis Mercer, 394, 466
Davy (slave; *see* 3:407): deals with
Mount Vernon storehouse, 496
Day, Daniel: defeat of near Spring-
field, 423–25; arrest ordered,
436
Day, Luke: and Shays' Rebellion, 539
Dayton, Elias: and Charles Asgill, 99,
236; and workmen for Potomac
River Company, 99; and GW's
Cincinnati circular letter, 335;
letters to: from GW, 335–36
Deakins, William, Jr. (*see* 3:243): and

indentured servants, 93; and
Potomac River Company, 99;
acts for GW, 350, 508–9, 542,
550–51; *letters from:* to GW, 350,
508–9, 542–43, 550–51; *letters to:*
from GW, 508, 514
Deer. *See* Mount Vernon
Démeunier, Jean Nicholas: and
Encyclopédie Méthodique, 366
Dermont, Mrs. James: as GW's ten-
ant, 398
Desdevens, Maurice: Knox's opinion
of, 225, 302; id., 225–26; *letters
from:* to GW, 152, 225; *letters to:*
from GW, 226
d'Estaing. *See* Estaing
Dickinson, Philemon: and Alexander
Steel, 58; id., 60
Digby, Robert: and Alexander Steel,
59; id., 60–61
Digges, George, 134; conveys seed,
90; id., 91; seeks flooring for
New Room, 501; *letters from:* to
GW, 501–2; *letters to:* from GW,
485–86
Dillon, ——: and workmen for Poto-
mac River Company, 99
Dinwiddie, Robert: proclamation of,
255
District Court bill: defeat of, 476,
476–77
Doilliamson. *See* Oilliamson
Dolphin (ship), 125
Dorcas (slave): sold at Washington's
Bottom, 463, 464; freed, 464
Dorsey, Richard, 355; id., 356
Douglass, Ephraim: buys GW's
slaves, 464
Dow, Peter: rents Hunting Creek
tract, 118–19; GW's land pur-
chases from, 249; *letters from:* to
GW, 118–19
Doyle, Alexander: and Trinity
Church (Georgetown, Md.), 10;
letters from: to GW, 10–11
Drayton, William (*see* 3:381): at
Mount Vernon, 174, 177, 359;
introduction of, 177; and run-
away slave, 358–59, 389–90; *let-
ters from:* to GW, 509; *letters to:*
from GW, 389–90
Drusina Ridder & Clark (firm): acts
for GW, 370

Duane, James: as Mass.-N.Y. boundary commissioner, 527, 530

Dublin Packet (ship), 208

Dulany, Benjamin Tasker (*see* 3:381): and French-Dulany tract, 249, 270

Dulany, Elizabeth French (*see* 3:381): and French-Dulany tract, 249

Dumas, Charles-Guillaume-Frédéric (*see* 3:23): as U.S. chargé d'affaires in Holland, 516

Dunlap & Claypool (printers): GW's account with, 54; and *Pennsylvania Advertiser,* 65; receipt of, 125; and GW's advertisement, 295

Dunmore, John Murray, fourth earl of, 333; and George William Fairfax's letters, 451

Duplessis. *See* Mauduit du Plessis

Dwight, Timothy (*see* 1:157): *Conquest of Canaan,* 149–50; *letters from:* to GW, 149–50; *letters to:* from GW, 12–13, 150

Earle, John (shipmaster), 9

Eckley, Joseph: and newspapers for GW, 8; id., 23; and William Gordon, 39; *letters from:* to GW, 23; *letters to:* from GW, 39

Edinburgh, University of: study of medicine at, 314

Edward (ship), 85, 86

Elector of Bavaria. *See* Charles Theodore

Elizabeth River Canal (*see* 1:247–48): GW's support for sought, 245

Ellwood (Elwood), John, Jr. (shipmaster), 294; id., 238

Ellzey, William: as Loudoun County justice, 337; id., 338

Ennis, Ann, 22; and Margaret Savage's estate, 14–15, 348–50, 366–68; letter to forwarded, 371; *letters to:* from GW, 366–68

Ennis, Richard: and Margaret Savage's estate, 14–15

Estaing, Charles-Hector, comte d' (*see* 1:21), 160–61, 163, 165; and Mauduit du Plessis, 71, 217; appointed to Assembly of Notables, 515; *letters from:* to GW, 164; *letters to:* from GW, 164–65

Esther (ship), 513

Exeter (N.H.): riot at, 281, 282

Fairfax, Bryan: as Margaret Savage's trustee, 14, 22, 349, 367

Fairfax, George William, 141; and engineer for Potomac River Company, 74; and James Bloxham, 88, 127–28, 198, 370; GW's correspondence with, 126, 129, 135–41, 450–51; and Robert Edge Pine, 126–27, 129; and Thomas and Richard Corbin, 128; GW's handling of affairs of, 135–41; GW's indebtedness to, 136–37; and the bloomery, 138; will of, 139; death of, 142; and Hite-Fairfax suit, 155; and Battaile Muse, 155–56, 531–32; Berkeley County land of, 155–56, 187–88, 234; GW's payment to, 191; and Belvoir furniture, 450; and John Anstey, 452; *letters from:* to GW, 450–52; *letters to:* from GW, 126–29, 135–41

Fairfax, John (*see* 2:403): and Spanish jack, 2, 3; sent for Lafayette's presents, 358, 359, 360; conducts Drayton's runaway slave, 389; deals with Mount Vernon storehouse, 495, 496

Fairfax, Sarah Cary, 141; and seed for GW, 127; complimented, 127, 128

Fairfax, Thomas (*see* 3:521): returns from abroad, 141; and George William Fairfax, 451; *letters from:* to GW, 141–42

Fairfax, Thomas, Lord: and Hite suit, 101

Fanny (ship), 105, 106, 108; id., 68

Farmers-general (*see* 3:547): and Lafayette's opposition to, 72

Field, John, Jr.: apprenticeship of, 276; id., 277

Field, Thomas, 160; and William Gordon, 276

Fisher, George: id., 125; *letters from:* to GW, 124–25

Fithian, Philip, 218

Fitzgerald, Jane Digges: illness of, 242

Fitzgerald, John (*see* 1:301, 530), 114, 516; acts for GW, 68, 486; and Potomac River Company, 93, 99, 234–36, 476; at Mount Vernon, 217; *letters from:* to GW, 99, 108; *letters to:* from GW, 93, 107, 234–36, 241–42; from George Mason, 320

Fitzhugh, Ann Frisby Rousby (*see* 1:243): greetings to, 52, 146–47; greetings from, 112, 143

Fitzhugh, Ann Randolph: *letters from:* to Elizabeth Willing Powel, 227

Fitzhugh, Elizabeth Chew: greetings from, 153; id., 153

Fitzhugh, Peregrine (*see* 1:243): expresses appreciation, 112; and lambs for GW, 142, 146, 152–53; *letters from:* to GW, 152–53

Fitzhugh, William (1725–1791; of Marmion), 82; id., 83

Fitzhugh, William (of Chatham; *see* 1:398; 3:336), 227; at Mount Vernon, 210, 211

Fitzhugh, William, Jr. (of Md.; *see* 1:243), 70, 77; mares of at Mount Vernon, 52; and lambs for GW, 112, 142, 152–53; *letters from:* to GW, 50, 77, 112–13; *letters to:* from GW, 52–53, 94

Fitzhugh, William, Sr. (of Md.; *see* 1:243), 70, 77; accident of, 52, 142; id., 52; mares of, 94; and Charles MacIver, 95; and lambs for GW, 142, 152–53; blindness of, 143; *letters from:* to GW, 142–43; *letters to:* from GW, 146–47

Flood, Henry: praises GW, 60; id., 61

Floridablanca, José Monino y Redondonde, conde de (*see* 2:165): thanks to, 107; and Spanish jacks, 233; *letters from:* to GW, 379, 380

Forrest, Uriah (*see* 3:68): id., 193

Forrest & Stoddert (firm): acts for GW, 192, 193, 370, 371, 375

Foster, William (shipmaster): id., 124; *letters from:* to GW, 124

Fountain Inn (tavern): id., 61

Four Mile Run tract. *See* Lands of GW

Francastle, Mr. ——: as designer of Society of Cincinnati emblem, 109, 110, 111

Frank (slave): escape of, 15–17, 29–30; owned by Philip Dalby, 15–17, 29–30

Franklin, Benjamin, 541; and Edward Newenham, 207; and d'Anterroche, 252; and Gilles de Lavallée, 472; *letters to:* from Edward Newenham, 208; from GW, 327

Franklin, Samuel: and Balfour & Barraud, 83

Franklin, Walter: and Balfour & Barraud, 83

Franks, David Salisbury: and Arnold's treachery, 176; and Morocco negotiations, 514; id., 517

Frederica Sophia Wilhelmina of Prussia: id., 313

Frederick II of Prussia, 41, 180, 514; illness of, 71, 134

Fredericksburg: horse races at, 279

Frederick William II of Prussia (*see* 3:546), 311, 514

Freeman, Thomas: as GW's land agent, 258, 259, 342, 407–8, 412, 463–65; and John Augustine Washington, 510; *letters from:* to GW, 289, 463–65; *letters to:* from GW, 36, 407–8

French, Penelope Manley, 271; and French-Dulany tract, 119, 248–49, 268–74, 274–75; as Harrison Manley's heir, 248, 249

French-Dulany tract. *See* French, Penelope Manley

Fryer, Alexander: as GW's tenant, 532

Gallatin, Albert: and western settlement, 66

Gálvez, Bernardo de: and Gardoqui, 379

Gardoqui, Diego Maria de (*see* 2:362; 3:490): and vicuña cloth, 200, 201, 205–6, 232–33, 240; and negotiations with Jay, 224, 225; *letters from:* to GW, 106–7, 107,

Gardoqui, Diego Maria de (*cont.*) 379; *letters to:* from GW, 232–33, 413–14

Gates, Horatio (*see* 1:354): and GW's Cincinnati circular letter, 317, 326, 491–92, 523–24; urges GW's attendance at Federal Convention, 523–24; *letters from:* to GW, 523–24; *letters to:* from GW, 318

General Court (Va.): delays in, 467

George, Sidney (d. 1744): id., 453

George, Sidney, Jr.: and John Colvill's papers, 452; id., 453

George III of England, 525

Gibbs, Caleb (*see* 3:317), 374; conveys letter, 125, 177; at Mount Vernon, 126; id., 375

Gibson, James (shipmaster), 67, 188

Gilbert, Thomas: and George William Fairfax, 451; id., 452

Gildart, James: bill drawn on, 22

Giles (slave): as GW's groom, 146; as messenger, 279; id., 280

Gilpin, George (*see* 2:563), 242; and Potomac River Company, 99, 108, 152, 234–36, 447; acts for GW, 155, 179, 187; as Fairfax County sheriff, 537–38; *letters to:* from GW, 234–36, 537–38

Girty, Simon: and the Iroquois, 321

Gladowe & Co. (bankers), 59

Glass, Michael: accused of rioting, 115

Glisson (Gleason), Capt. ——: death of, 58

Gordon, Elizabeth Field: greetings from, 8, 160, 277, 525

Gordon, James: and Charles Asgill, 97, 236; id., 237

Gordon, William (*see* 1:177–78): returns to England, 7–8, 159; criticism of, 8, 159–60; and Joseph Eckley, 23; and subscriptions to his *History*, 23–24, 24–25, 103, 104, 158, 267–68, 275–76, 352, 525, 538; and publication of his *History*, 159–60; *letters from:* to GW, 7–8, 8, 157–60, 275–77, 524–26; *letters to:* from GW, 23–24

Gore, Amos: accused of rioting, 115

Graham, Catharine Sawbridge Macaulay (*see* 2:65): letter to forwarded, 132; and GW's Pine portrait, 289; *letters from:* to GW, 289–90; *letters to:* from GW, 56

Grant, Daniel, 60; id., 61

Grantom (Granthom), William: as GW's tenant, 531–32; id., 532

Gray, ——: and William Gordon, 538

Grayson, William, 107; as member of Congress, 51, 346, 347; as GW's attorney, 102, 123, 124; conveys letter, 106; and Mississippi River navigation, 224, 225, 448–49, 450; *letters from:* to GW, 81–83; *letters to:* from GW, 169–70

Greaves (Graves), John: and military certificates, 243

Green, Charles, 349; estate of, 367

Green, Frederick (printer), 70

Green, John: and Hite-Fairfax suit, 155, 205

Green, Thomas: and Mount Vernon storehouse, 495, 496

Green, Thomas & Samuel (printers), 353

Green, Valentine: as an engraver, 84, 85

Greene, Catharine Littlefield: rumors about, 282–83, 284; as Nathanael Greene's executor, 283; remarriage of, 285; and Nathanael Greene's death, 298; and George Washington Greene, 299

Greene, George Washington: id., 298–99

Greene, Nathanael (*see* 1:125), 71; and print of Peale portrait of, 84–86; death of referred to, 154, 171, 180–81, 184–85, 216, 282–83, 285, 298, 302, 312, 482, 505; conflict with James Gunn, 283, 284, 298; dealings with John Banks, 283–85, 298; *letters to:* from Charles Thomson, 85; from Joseph Brown, 85

Griffin, Samuel: and Battaile Muse, 33

Griffith, David (*see* 1:70), 312; busi-

Griffith, David (*cont.*)
  ness affairs of, 5; id., 5; conveys
  books, 147, 170; conveys letter,
  226
Grymes, Benjamin: sends does, 28;
  letters from: to GW, 28
Gunn, James (*see* 2:522): and Nathanael Greene, 298
Gunning, Elizabeth: id., 304
Gunston Hall (house), 388

Haigh, ——: as Baltimore jeweler, 60
Haines, Reuben: as a brewer, 329,
  438, 498; id., 330
Haines & Co., Twelff (firm), 330
Hall, Caleb: as English wheelwright,
  376
Hamilton, Alexander: and Arnold's
  treachery, 176
Hamilton, James, sixth duke of: id.,
  304
Hamilton, Milady. *See* Gunning, Eliz-
  abeth
Hamlin, Perez: and Stockbridge
  raid, 433–34, 436
Hammond, James: buys GW's slaves,
  464
Hammond, William: *letters from:* to
  GW, 13
Hanburys (firm): and Balfour & Bar-
  raud, 67, 83, 145; payment
  from, 100
Hancock, John: as governor of Mas-
  sachusetts, 418
Hand, Edward (*see* 1:40): and Alexander Steel, 58; id., 60
Hansbrough, William: as GW's
  tenant, 390–91; testimonials for,
  390–91; *letters from:* to GW,
  390–91
Hanson (of Samuel), Samuel: and
  GW's nephews, 544–45; sets
  terms for boarders, 545; *letters
  from:* to GW, 544–45; to George
  Augustine Washington, 545
Harewood (house; *see* 1:70, 164;
  2:21), 532
Haring, John: as Mass.-N.Y. boundary commissioner, 527, 530
Harris, Hannah Stewart, 76
Harris, James: conveys letter, 49; as
  manager of James River Company, 507–8

Harris, John, 76
Harrison, Richard (*see* 2:2): and Toledo swords, 154, 391; id., 154;
  and Royal Gift, 543; *letters from:*
  to GW, 154; *letters to:* from GW,
  391
Harrison, Robert Hanson (*see* 1:291),
  516
Hartshorne, William (*see* 2:226): and
  Spanish jack, 2–3; and seed for
  GW, 21; house of, 95; GW's pay-
  ment to, 191; acts for GW, 350;
  letters from: to GW, 236; *letters to:*
  from GW, 21, 236
Hatfield (Mass.) Resolutions: and
  Shays' Rebellion, 241
Haven, Samuel: *letters from:* to GW,
  34–35
Hayes, James (printer): *Virginia
  Gazette* (Richmond), 459
Haynes, —— (lawyer), 168
Haywood (house), 36
Hazard, Ebenezer (*see* 1:378): and
  William Gordon's *History,*
  159
Hazen, Moses: and Charles Asgill,
  236–37
Hendricks, James, 456
Henley, Leonard (*see* 3:466): and
  corn for GW, 18; *letters from:* to
  GW, 18–19; *letters to:* from GW,
  1, 11
Henry, John: presents saltcellar, 304;
  letters from: to GW, 304–5; *letters
  to:* from GW, 305
Henry, John (of Md.): id., 305
Henry, John (son of Patrick), 305
Henry, Patrick, 305, 345; as gover-
  nor, 91; rejects reelection, 326;
  opposes Jay-Gardoqui treaty,
  362; views on Mississippi River
  navigation, 448; *letters to:* from
  Virginia congressional delega-
  tion, 50–51
Henry, prince of Prussia (*see* 3:546),
  41, 71
Herbert, Francis: and James Rum-
  sey, 239
Herbert, Sarah Carlyle: and Mrs.
  MacIver, 114–15; id., 115
Herbert, William, 115
Heth, William (*see* 1:351): and GW's
  Cincinnati circular letter,

Heth, William (*cont.*)
317–18; *letters to:* from GW,
317–18
Hickman, Jane, 288
Hickman, William: and George Mercer's Shenandoah River tract,
286–88, 353, 416; and John
Francis Mercer, 393; *letters from:*
to GW, 286–88
Hill, Ann Meredith: id., 190
Hill, Henry (*see* 2:55): payment to,
191; and Madeira wine, 242–43;
letters from: to GW, 242–43; *letters
to:* from GW, 190
Hill, Mrs. Henry: illness of, 242–43
Hill, Henry, Jr., 328, 329; as member
of Pennsylvania Council, 281;
letters from: to GW, 280–81
Hill, James: accounts of with GW, 9,
231–32, 510–12, 513, 546; as
manager of Custis lands,
231–32; and his accounts of
Custis estate, 232, 263–64; id.,
232; and John Price Posey, 388,
510–12, 546–47; and Thomas
Newton, Jr., 512; *letters from:* to
GW, 263–64; *letters to:* from GW,
231–32, 510–12
Hite, ——: and GW's land on Little
Miami, 61
Hite, Isaac: and Hite-Fairfax suit,
205; and GW's land on Bullskin
Run, 234
Hite, Jost: landholdings of, 101, 102;
and GW's Bullskin lands, 115,
116, 122, 123, 187, 230
Hite, Thomas: and Hite-Fairfax suit,
100–102, 115–16, 122–24, 155,
156, 187, 205, 229–30, 233–34,
285; and Edmund Randolph,
395
Holland: political situation in, 133–
34, 276, 311, 514
Hollyday (Holliday), Henry (*see*
3:306): and Thomas Colvill estate, 262, 263
Holt, William: sends beans, 47–48;
id., 48; and Thomas Newton,
512
Hooe, Robert Townsend (Townshend; *see* 1:66, 469), 393, 403,
442; acts for GW, 126, 543; *let-*

ters from: to GW, 543; *letters to:*
from GW, 400
Hoomes, John: and John Armistead,
487; id., 488; *letters from:* to GW,
488
Hopkins, John: and James River
Company: id., 31; as Virginia
commissioner of loans, 446;
letters from: to GW, 31–32
Horticulture: seeds and plants for
Versailles listed, 120; larkspur
seed, 524–25; digitalis, 525. *See
also* Mount Vernon
Houdon, Jean-Antoine (*see* 2:178):
statue of GW, 183–84, 313; bust
of Lafayette, 313; and inscription for GW's bust, 541–42
House, Mrs. ——: and George
Fisher, 125
Howe, Bezaleel (*see* 1:132), 124; id.,
125
Howe, William, 59
Howell, Arthur: as a tanner, 209,
218
Huddy, Joseph: and Alexander
Steel, 59; id., 61
Huddy, Josiah: and the Asgill affair,
79
Hughes, Samuel: as manager of Susquehanna Canal Company, 49;
id., 111–12; letters to and from,
111–12, 201, 202, 321
Hull, William (*see* 1:350), 413; and
Ohio Company (1786), 305–7;
id., 306–7; GW's advice to about
western settlement, 488–90; *letters from:* to GW, 305–7; *letters to:*
from GW, 307, 488–90
Humphreys, Daniel (printer), 125;
GW's account with, 54
Humphreys, David (*see* 1:15), 183,
283, 392, 516; at Mount
Vernon, 68–69, 217, 219; movements of, 68–69, 119, 241; and
Asgill affair, 80, 98, 99, 236–37,
296, 351, 352, 373, 374, 507;
and Cincinnati china, 148; conveys letters and books, 148, 150,
240; poems of, 210, 211, 220,
296; and Chastellux, 219; and
Society of Cincinnati, 264–65,
266; elected to Connecticut legis-

Humphreys, David (*cont.*)
lature, 265; "Mount Vernon: an
Ode," 267; and GW's Cincinnati
circular letter, 296, 297, 324,
326, 350; Connecticut regiment
of, 325, 374; and Cincinnati entry in *Encyclopédie*, 365; as Connecticut Wit, 373, 374, 530;
"The Conduct of General Washington Respecting the Confinement of Captain Asgill,"
374; his account of Shays' Rebellion, 417, 526; his opinion of
Federal Convention, 527–29; opposes GW's attendance at Federal Convention, 529–30; Revolutionary accounts of, 530; *letters
from:* to GW, 68–69, 264–67,
350–52, 373–75, 526–30; to *New
Haven Gazette*, 374; *letters to:*
from GW, 119, 236–37, 296–97,
477–81, 535–36
Hunter, Andrew: and Society of Cincinnati, 218
Hunter, William, Jr. (*see* 1:479), 10,
442; conveys horse, 88; at
Mount Vernon, 89; and Matthew Whiting, 205; forwards letters, 221; *letters to:* from GW,
221–22
Huntington, Jedediah: elected to
Conn. legislature, 265; id., 266
Huston, ——, 463
Hutchins, Thomas (*see* 1:200; 3:324):
and Indian vocabulary, 222,
343–44, 398–400; id., 344; *letters
from:* to GW, 343–44; *letters to:*
from GW, 222

Independent Chronicle (Boston): sent
by Gordon, 39
Indian vocabulary, 222, 343–44,
398–400
Industry (ship), 67, 188
Innes, James: elected attorney gen-
eral, 326, 327
Ireland, William, Jr.: and William
Hickman, 286–87, 416; and
Rawleigh Colston, 353; conveys
letter, 415
Iris (ship), 330; to Baltimore, 410
Isaac (slave): deals with Mount Ver-
non storehouse, 496

Izard, Ralph: at Mount Vernon, 359
Izard, Walter: id., 174

Jack (slave; of William Drayton):
runs away, 389–90, 509
Jackasses (from Surinam), 388–89,
413–14
Jackasses (Maltese): from Lafayette,
43, 312, 385, 408–10, 413–14;
description of, 508
Jackasses (Spanish), 233, 380;
charges for, 2, 3; as a stud, 18,
43, 52, 90, 94, 112, 134, 146; description of, 508; cost of transport of, 543
Jackson, Mr. ——, 142
Jackson, Harry: as commander of
Connecticut regiment, 373; id.,
375
Jackson, J.: id., 160
Jackson, James: acts for William Gordon, 158; id., 160
Jackson, William: *An Oration . . .*,
223; *letters from:* to GW, 223 *letters to:* from GW, 223
Jacobs, John Jeremiah (*see* 3:173):
and Michael Cresap, 157
Jacobs, Mary Whitehead Cresap:
and claims to Round Bottom
tract, 157
James, Joseph: and Jerusalem artichoke, 498
James (slave): carries letters for Fitzhugh, 142, 143, 146
James (slave; John Francis Mercer's),
394, 466
Jameson, John: and Arnold's treachery, 176
James River Company: GW's shares
in, 31
Jamieson, Neil: and Balfour & Barraud, 83; *letters to:* from GW,
66–67
Jay, John: and dispute with Littlepage, 4, 26, 43, 55; instructs
John Adams, 83; attends convention of Episcopal church, 130,
132; his report on the conduct
of the states, 130–31, 132; views
on condition of the country,
130–32; and Edward Newen-
ham, 207, 208; Monroe's views

Jay, John (*cont.*)
of, 224; and John Anstey, 452;
and separation of powers,
502–4; his plan for new government, 502–4; and Society of Cincinnati, 527; *letters from:* to GW,
130–32, 502–4; *letters to:* from
GW, 55–56, 212–13
Jay, John (1817–1894): and GW's letter, 213
Jay, Sarah Livingston: greetings to,
56
Jay-Gardoqui treaty: Henry Lee's
opinion of, 290–92; terms of,
291–92; opposition to, 362
Jefferson, Thomas, 74, 108, 201,
224; GW's opinion of, 44; and
L'Enfant, 89, 90; his views of Society of Cincinnati, 89, 364–66;
and d'Anterroche, 252; and William Hull, 306; Lafayette's
praise of, 311; and Barbary pirates, 312; recommends Couteulx, 363–64; and Gilles de Lavallée, 472–73; and James Swan,
548; *letters from:* to GW, 363–66;
letters to: from GW, 183–85; from
Colonne, 311, 313; from James
Madison, 345, 347, 362
Jemmison. *See* Jameson, John
Jenckes, Crawford, 293
Jenckes, John, 293
Jenckes, Joseph: introduced to GW,
293
Jenckes, Winsor & Co. (firm), 324;
id., 293
Jenifer, Daniel of St. Thomas (*see*
2:4), 70; *Report of the Committee to
Inspect into the Books, Papers, and
Accounts of the Intendant*, 70; as
Maryland intendant, 70–71; *let-
ters from:* to GW, 70–71; *letters to:*
from GW, 71
Jenkinson, Charles, 525
Jenny (ship), 124
Joe (slave): as postilion, 28, 29
Joe (slave): sold at Washington's
Bottom, 463, 464
Johns, Captain (shipmaster), 370
Johnson, Thomas (*see* 2:51, 297):
and Potomac River Company,
152, 235, 238–39, 359, 360,

447, 486–87; as governor of
Md., 355; letter of, 538; *letters
from:* to GW, 447; *letters to:* from
GW, 152, 359–60, 486–87
Johnston, George: and GW's Bull-
skin lands, 100–101, 101–2,
115–16, 122, 123, 187, 230; id.,
116
Johnston, Samuel: and Clifton's
Neck, 308, 309
Johnston, W. & N. (firm): and
Thomas Ridout, 246
Jones, Joseph (*see* 2:156): id., 51;
elected to Congress, 345, 346,
347; *letters from:* to GW, 50–51;
letters to: from GW, 51
Joseph II of Austria, 311; policies of,
71
Judd, William: elected to Connecti-
cut legislature, 265; id., 267

Kanawha lands. *See* Lands of GW
Keith, James: and Potomac River
Company, 235; and William
Hickman, 287
Kennedy, David (*see* 3:591): as
debtor to GW, 1–2, 398, 531; as
GW's tenant, 437
Kerwin, Peter (shipmaster), 77, 78
Key, Philip: id., 70–71
Keyes (Keas), David: as GW's tenant,
92, 93
Keyes (Keas), Margaret: as GW's tenant, 398
King, Rufus (*see* 2:539), 357; appears
before Pennsylvania legislature,
280–81; and Shays' Rebellion,
351–52; and Society of Cincinnati, 527; as Mass.-N.Y. boundary commissioner, 527, 530
Kirwins, Peter: to convey GW's flour,
221
Knight, John (shipmaster), 543
Knox, Henry (*see* 1:7), 344, 357,
375; *A Plan for the General Arrangement of the Militia*, 26; as
secretary-general of the Cincinnati, 46; and L'Enfant, 108–11,
184; and Society of Cincinnati,
264; as army secretary, 281; his
accounts of Shays' Rebellion,
295, 331, 417, 460–62, 470–71,

Knox, Henry (*cont.*)
518–19, 522–23, 534, 543–44, 549; and his analysis of Shays' Rebellion, 299–301; and U.S. military establishment, 301; views on the condition of the country, 301–2; and *Encyclopédie* article on Society of Cincinnati, 366; forwards letter, 435; views on proposed Federal Convention, 519–21; proposals for new government, 521–22; *letters from:* to GW, 108–11, 299–302, 460–62, 470–71, 518–23, 534–35, 543–44, 549, 549–50, 551; *letters to:* from GW, 89–90, 225–26, 481–82, 543
Knox, Lucy Flucker: greetings to, 89–90; greetings from, 110, 462, 523; gives birth, 302; congratulations to, 483

Lafayette, George Washington, 516
Lafayette, Marie-Adrienne-Françoise de Noailles, marquise de (*see* 1:30), 516; invitation to, 40; hams for, 68, 104–5; greetings from, 73, 313; greetings to, 216; *letters to:* from GW, 39–40
Lafayette, Marie-Joseph-Paul-Yves-Roch-Gilbert du Motier, marquis de, 66, 163, 165; and Doilliamson, 30; travels of, 41, 72; his gift of asses and birds, 43, 330–31, 381, 385, 408–10, 413–14; his letters sent to, 44, 68; and Saint-Simon-Montbléru, 46; and plants for Louis XVI, 62; packages from, 68, 312, 358, 359, 360–61; and engineer for Potomac River Company, 74; and L'Enfant, 108, 109, 110, 184; introduces Michaux, 120; and William Gordon, 160; and Benedict Arnold, 175; and Edward Newenham, 207; and Mauduit du Plessis, 217; packages for, 245–46; and d'Anterroche, 252; and Couteulx, 288, 366; as George Washington Greene's guardian, 299; and Mandrillon, 303, 540; opinion of Jefferson, 311, 540; and Barbary pirates, 312;

and French Protestants, 312, 313; and his Houdon bust, 313; and Indian vocabulary, 343, 398–99; and Cincinnati entry in *Encyclopédie*, 365; and Assembly of Notables, 515; and Catherine of Russia, 515; hams for, 516; his views of Shays' Rebellion, 516; *letters from:* to GW, 71–73, 164, 288–89, 311–13, 514–17; to Knox, 110–11; *letters to:* from GW, 41–45, 104–5, 214–16, 385
La Luzerne, Anne-César de La Luzerne, chevalier de (*see* 1:128), 66, 179; *letters to:* from GW, 185–87
Lamar, Hill, Bisset & Co. (firm), 190; and cost of Madeira wine, 328–29; *letters from:* to GW, 328–29; *letters to:* from GW, 191
Lamb, John (*see* 1:255): as agent in Algiers, 4, 67
Land Ordinance of 1785: changes in, 81–82, 83; GW's view of, 169; and survey of Northwest territory, 344, 391–92
Lands of GW:
Four Mile Run tract: GW's purchase of confirmed, 385–86
Great Meadows tract: and purchase of, 256; and Thomas Freeman, 342; examination of, 412
in Fauquier County: and Fielding Lewis, Jr., 416–17
in Frederick County: purchased from George Mercer, 32
in Hampshire County: inspection of, 410, 412
in York and New Kent counties: James Hill's management of, 510–12
and John Price Posey, 545–48
Millers Run tract: proposed sale of, 63–66, 172–74, 411–12; and ejectment suits, 172–74, 254–59, 259–61, 314–15, 339–43; advertised, 258–59, 295, 315; offer to evictees, 401, 402, 404, 405–6; and John Cannon, 413
on Bullskin Run: and Hite-Fairfax suit, 115–16, 155, 205, 229–30, 285

Lands of GW (*cont.*)
 on Great Kanawha: attempted sale
  of, 63–66, 167; GW's praise of,
  63–66; prewar settlers on, 333,
  335
 on Little Miami: and surveys of,
  61–62
 on Ohio: attempted sale of, 63–66,
  167
 Round Bottom tract: Cresap
  claims to, 157
 Washington's Bottom tract: proposed sale of, 172–74, 257–58,
  258–59, 295, 405, 407, 411–12,
  464, 505–6; and purchase of,
  256; and Thomas Freeman,
  342; condition of mill, 407;
  slaves at, 463–64
Langdon, John: id., 34: *letters from:*
 to GW, 34
Lansing, John: as Mass.-N.Y. boundary commissioner, 527, 530
La Rouërie. *See* Armand
La Rouërie, marquise de, 203, 204
La Touche, William-George-Digges:
 and Alexander Steel, 59; id., 61
Lauzun, Armand-Louis de Gortaut,
 duc de (*see* 1:91): and Michaux,
 120, 178; *letters to:* from GW,
 178–79
Laval, Anne-Alexandre-Marie-
 Sulpice-Joseph Montmorency
 duc de: appointed to Assembly
 of Notables, 515
Lavallée, Gilles de, 472; as cotton
 manufacturer, 472–73; id.,
 472–73; departure of, 473; and
 Edmund Randolph, 500, 501;
 letters to: from GW, 472–73
Lawson, James: as a ditcher, 394;
 deals with Mount Vernon storehouse, 496, 497
Lear, Tobias (*see* 3:493): salary of, 12;
 recommended, 21, 32, 34–35; as
 GW's agent, 31; arrival of at
 Mount Vernon, 34, 103; as
 GW's secretary, 34, 80, 127, 162,
 183, 236, 258; describes duties
 at Mount Vernon, 38; and GW's
 account of Arnold's treachery,
 174–77; diary of, 177; and trip
 west, 399–400, 402, 404, 406,

 407, 408, 410–13, 463–65, 480,
 488, 510; *letters from:* to GW,
 34–35; to John Langdon, 38; *letters to:* from GW, 410–13
Ledger, Captain (shipmaster), 513
Lee, Arthur: at Mount Vernon, 20,
 21
Lee, Charles (*see* 2:374): lends law-
 books, 38; id., 104; acts for GW,
 205–6, 240; and GW's purchase
 of French-Dulany tracts,
 247–49; *letters from:* to GW,
 247–49
Lee, Gen. Charles: estate of, 31, 412,
 413
Lee, Henry, Jr. (*see* 1:351; 2:140):
 and navigation of Mississippi,
 25–26; as member of Congress,
 51; and Charles Lee, 103, 104;
 forwards vicuña cloth, 107; forwards letter, 119; and Cincinnati
 china, 147, 148–49, 170–71,
 200, 240; and death of Nathanael Greene, 154; cites critical state of Union, 240–41; his
 reports on Shays' Rebellion,
 266, 295–96, 417; and Jay-
 Gardoqui treaty, 290–92; fails to
 be reelected, 345, 346, 383; reelected to Congress, 345, 347;
 letters from: to GW, 25–26,
 147–49, 154, 200–201, 205–6,
 240–41, 281–82, 290–92,
 295–96, 357–58; *letters to:* from
 GW, 3–5, 116–18, 170–71,
 318–20; from James Madison,
 345
Lee, Matilda Lee (*see* 2:140): greetings from, 148, 241; greetings
 to, 320
Lee, Mr. ——: lot of, 155
Lee, Richard Henry (*see* 2:7), 200;
 Jay's criticism of, 131, 132; as
 candidate for governor, 326,
 345, 346; elected to Congress,
 346
Lee, Sidney: and Charles Lee's
 estate, 413
Lee, Thomas Sim: and Potomac
 River Company, 152, 235, 239,
 447, 487
Lee (ship), 124

Leet, David: and Millers Run ejectment suits, 256, 257; id., 258

Le Fendant (ship), 161

Leigh, John: *An Experimental Inquiry into the Properties of Opium*, 314; id., 314; *letters from:* to GW, 313–14; *letters to:* from GW, 314

Leinster, William Robert Fitzgerald, 2d duke of, 57; id., 60

Lemart, Ann: as GW's tenant, 398

Le Mayeur, Jean: and his horses, 11; at Mount Vernon, 11; and GW's house at Bath, 228, 229, 231; *letters from:* to GW, 11, 231

L'Enfant, Pierre (*see* 1:29): and purchase of Cincinnati emblems, 89, 108–11, 184, 443–45, 493–94; memorial of, 445; *letters from:* to GW, 443–45; *letters to:* from GW, 493–94

Lewis, Betty Washington (*see* 1:146), 312

Lewis, Catherine Daingerfield: id., 229

Lewis, Fielding (*see* 1:146): and GW's accounts with, 9, 10; and George William Fairfax, 138

Lewis, Fielding, Jr. (*see* 1:146): id., 293; given timber, 416–17, 437; GW's disapproval of, 416–17; *letters from:* to GW, 293; *letters to:* from GW, 416–17

Lewis, George: and GW's house at Bath, 228–29, 231; id., 229; *letters from:* to GW, 228–29

Lewis, John: and lots in Fredericksburg, 162

Lewis & Sons, Robert (firm): GW's account with, 54, 56–57, 125; *letters to:* from GW, 56–57

Lewis, Thomas (*see* 1:97; 3:588): as surveyor, 255

Lincoln, Benjamin (*see* 1:167; 3:588): and Tobias Lear, 12, 21, 32, 127; and William Gordon, 24–25; recommends Tobias Lear, 37–38; and Maine property of, 38, 418–19, 435; recommends Penuel Bowen, 38; and Shays' Rebellion, 266, 417–36, 519, 522, 526, 534–35, 544,

549; and subscription to Gordon's *History*, 268; and GW's Cincinnati circular letter, 339; his analysis of Shays' Rebellion causes, 419–22; pleads for leniency on defeated Shaysites, 430–33; *letters from:* to GW, 32–33, 37–38, 38, 417–36; to Daniel Shays, 425; to Bowdoin, 426–27; to Selectmen of Worcester and Hampshire, 427; to Daniel Shays and others, 428; *letters to:* from GW, 12, 24–25, 103–104, 339; from Bowdoin, 422–23; from Daniel Shays, 426; from Daniel Shays and others, 427

Lincoln, Benjamin, Jr.: news of Shays' Rebellion from, 266; id., 267; and subscription to Gordon's *History*, 267–68, 352; his account of Shays' Rebellion, 538–39; *letters from:* to GW, 267–68, 538–39; *letters to:* from GW, 352

Lincoln, Theodore: as manager of Maine property, 435

Lindo, Elias: and George Mercer, 386

Lite. *See* Leet

Little, Charles (*see* 1:66): and Thomas Colvill's estate, 166, 440, 452; and French-Dulany tract, 269–71; id., 271, 452; *letters from:* to GW, 452–53

Little, Mary Manley, 452; id., 271

Little Egg Harbor (N.J.), 58, 60

Littlepage, Lewis (*see* 3:306): and dispute with John Jay, 4, 26, 43, 55

Livingston, Robert R.: as Mass.-N.Y. boundary commissioner, 527, 530

Lloyd, Edward (*see* 2:567), 383; id., 384

Lloyd, John (*see* 1:112): and Balfour & Barraud, 83

Logan, John: and attack on Shawnee, 320–21, 362; id., 321; in Richmond, 469

Lomax's Tavern (*see* 2:563), 537–38

Louisville (Ky.): route to, 49

Louis XVI of France: at Cherbourg, 134; and David Humphreys' poem, 219–20; and Assembly of Notables, 515

Low, Henry: accused of rioting, 115

Lowell, John: and Maine property of, 419, 435; as Mass.-N.Y. boundary commissioner, 527, 530

Lowry (Lowrie), Stephen: and Alexander Steel, 58; id., 60

Lucky Hit (house): id., 227

Ludlow (house), 45

Lutterloh, Henry Emanuel: and German settlers, 498–99; id., 499; *letters from:* to GW, 498–99

Lydia (slave): sold at Washington's Bottom, 463, 464

Lyle (Lyles), William: at Mount Vernon, 217; and Robert Alexander, 363

Lynch, Thomas: id., 7

Lyons, Peter (*see* 3:419), 141; id., 142

Macarty de Marteigne (Marteigue): id., 161; *letters from:* to GW, 160–61

McCabe, Alexander: *letters from:* to GW, 129–30

McCarmack (McCarmick), John: at Detroit, 321

McCarmack (McCarmick), George: and Millers Run ejectment suits, 172, 256, 257; as GW's land agent, 259, 314–15, 342, 406, 408, 411; *letters from:* to GW, 314–15, 320–21; *letters to:* from GW, 401–2

McCarmack (McCormick), James: and Millers Run ejectment suits, 256, 257

McCarty, Denis: id., 116

McCoull, Neil: as attorney for Mercer creditors, 385, 386, 466

McCracken, Ovid, 410, 412

McCracken, Virgil, 410, 412

McDermott Roe, Cornelius: GW's agreement with, 183; deals with Mount Vernon storehouse, 496

McDonald, Angus: bond of, 138; id., 140

McDougall, Alexander (*see* 1:354): id., 185; death of, 216

McGinnis, Lawrence: deals with Mount Vernon storehouse, 496

MacGregor, Colt: and Neil Jamieson, 67; *letters from:* to GW, 83–84

McHenry, James (*see* 2:418; 3:168): and Lafayette's presents to GW, 330–31, 358, 359, 385, 408–9; urges GW to write memoirs, 361; and Drayton's runaway slave, 389, 390; *letters from:* to GW, 330–31, 356, 380–81, 381; *letters to:* from GW, 358–59, 375, 408–10

McIntosh, Lachlan (*see* 1:293): and GW's Cincinnati circular letter, 322, 490–91; *letters from:* to GW, 490–91

MacIver, Charles: lectures of, 104; and theft of a dress, 113–15; *letters from:* to GW, 94–95, 113–15; *letters to:* from GW, 104

MacIver, Mrs. Charles: and quarrel with slave woman, 113–15

McIver, Colin: and Thomas Newton, 78; GW's land purchases from, 249

McKean, Thomas: as Pennsylvania judge, 463

McMahan, William: id., 392

McQueen, John: and Mauduit du Plessis, 163; id., 165

Madagascar: Beniousky's raid on, 515–16, 517

Madison, Dolley: at Mount Vernon, 292

Madison, James: at Mount Vernon, 292; and William Hull, 306–7; elected to Congress, 346; and GW's election to federal convention, 347, 448, 468–69, 475, 477; and district court bill, 449; value of to Virginia legislature, 477; *letters from:* to GW, 326–27, 344–45, 448–50, 474–76; to Henry Lee, Jr., 345; to Thomas Jefferson, 345, 347, 362; *letters to:* from Edmund Randolph, 157; from GW, 331–32, 382–83, 457–59

Magnifique (ship), 161

Magnolio (horse; *see* 3:408): id., 11; as stud, 94, 112, 142, 146; received from Custis estate, 100

Mahoney, Thomas: GW's agreement with, 182–83

Mahony, Timothy, 189

Mandrillon, Joseph (*see* 1:441): *Fragmens de politique et de litterature*, 304; and Society of Cincinnati, 539–40; and inscription for GW's Houdon bust, 540–42; *letters from:* to GW, 302–3, 539–42; to editors of *Journal of Paris*, 541–42

Manley, Harrison, 271; estate of, 248–49

Manley, John: and William Foster, 124; as Harrison Manley's heir, 248, 249; and GW's Dogue Run land, 268, 271

Manley, Margaret Barry. *See* Sanford, Margaret Barry Manley

Manley, Mary: as Harrison Manley's heir, 248, 249

Manley, Sarah: as Harrison Manley's heir, 248, 249

Manley, Sarah Harrison Triplett: id., 271

Manning, James: id., 293; introduces Joseph Jenckes, 293; *letters from:* to GW, 293

Mannsfield (house): id., 162

Marie Antoinette, queen of France: pregnancy of, 72; and David Humphreys' poem, 219–20

Marion, Francis: and Santee Canal, 7

Marlborough (house), 90, 134

Marmion (house): id., 83

Marshall, John: as GW's attorney, 20; as candidate for Virginia attorney general, 326; as delegate to Virginia house, 327

Marshall, Thomas (*see* 2:554): as a surveyor, 205; *letters from:* to GW, 61–62

Marsteller, Philip: as GW's commission agent, 403, 453–55; secures indentured servants, 403; and Overdonck family, 456; *letters from:* to GW, 403–4, 455; *letters to:* from GW, 402–3, 453–55

Martin, Luther (*see* 3:173): and Cresap's claims to Round Bottom tract, 157

Mason, George: and Ohio Company, 35; and Daniel Jenifer, 70; and navigation of Mississippi, 292; and Virginia assembly, 319–20; absence of from legislature, 347, 388; and Mount Vernon Conference, 477; *letters from:* to John Fitzgerald, 320

Mason, Jonathan, Jr.: id., 160

Mason, Jonathan, Sr.: and William Gordon, 158, 267, 268, 525; id., 160

Mason, Miriam Clark, 160

Mason, Thomson: and Margaret Savage, 14

Massachusetts: General Court of, 417, 429, 435–36; and settlement of boundary dispute with New York, 530

Massey, Lee (*see* 1:476): id., 228

Massey (slave; John Francis Mercer's), 466

Mathew (slave): deals with Mount Vernon storehouse, 495, 496

Mauduit du Plessis, Thomas-Antoine (*see* 1:183): and Lafayette, 71; id., 164; at Mount Vernon, 211, 216, 217; *letters from:* to GW, 163–65; *letters to:* from GW, 165

Mauduit, Israel: and the Asgill affair, 79

Maury, James: id., 415; *letters to,* 415; *letters from:* to GW, 415

Mazzei, Philip: Lafayette's opinion of, 516; id., 517

Meade, Ann Randolph: id., 227

Meade, Richard Kidder, 227

Ménonville, Louis-Antoine Thibaut de: letter for, 44; greetings to, 46–47

Mercer, George: sale of estate of, 29, 32; and bonds from sale of his property, 206, 207; and sale of his Shenandoah lands, 286–88, 337, 353–54, 415–16; and Four Mile Run tract, 385–86

Mercer, James: subscribes to Gordon's *History*, 24, 158, 160; and purchase of George Mercer's land, 32, 337; and John Mercer estate, 207; and Four Mile Run tract, 385–86; *letters to:* from GW, 385–86

Mercer, John, 90; and his estate debt, 207, 243, 244

Mercer, John Francis (*see* 1:489), 396; id., 90; jackasses of, 134; arrangements for payment on estate debt, 206, 207, 243, 244, 393–95, 442, 465–67; and debt of John Mercer estate, 207, 336–37; and slaves of, 336, 466; at Mount Vernon, 338, 394–95; and Rawleigh Colston, 353, 393; and Four Mile Run tract, 386; and Charles Simms, 393; and Joseph Combs, 393; and William Hickman, 393, 416; GW's criticism of, 393; ten-day loan to, 394; and George Mercer's affairs, 415–16; *letters from:* to GW, 223, 286, 296, 391, 450; *letters to:* from GW, 206, 243–44, 336–38, 393–95, 442–43, 465–67

Mercer, Richard: id., 338

Mercer, Sophia Sprigg: at Mount Vernon, 338, 394–95

Meredith, Samuel, 190

Meyler, James: *letters from:* to GW, 207

Michaux, André (*see* 3:225): and his botanical mission, 120, 178–79; at Mount Vernon, 120; *letters from:* to GW, 120

Miles, John: and Ohio Company, 307

Miller, Phineas: id., 285; as George Washington Greene's tutor, 298–99

Millers Run tract. *See* Lands of GW

Mississippi, navigation of, 25–26, 117–18, 241, 414; Henry Lee's views on, 148, 200–201; GW's views on, 171; James Monroe's views on, 223–24; and Jay-Gardoqui negotiations, 224,

225, 290–92; and Virginia legislature, 326, 362, 448–49, 469

Mitchell, Henry, 9

Monroe, James: as member of Congress, 51; views on navigation of Mississippi, 223–24; id., 225; appears before Pennsylvania legislature, 280–81; at Mount Vernon, 292; *letters from:* to GW, 223–25

Montgomery, Richard: as a general, 225

Moody, Benjamin: and Thomas Colvill estate, 455–56; id., 456

Moody, Thomas: and Thomas Colvill estate, 456; payments by, 456

Moore, Francis: and Margaret Savage's estate, 14

Moore, Hannah: and Margaret Savage's estate, 14

Moore, William: and Margaret Savage's will, 367–68

Morgan, Charles: and Millers Run ejectment suits, 256, 257, 314–15

Morgan, Daniel (*see* 1:305): and Potomac River Company, 1; and David Kennedy's debt, 1–2; *letters from:* to GW, 1–2

Morgan, George: "Essay on a Farm-Yard System," 45–46, 226; and Philadelphia Agriculture Society, 75; *letters to:* from GW, 222

Morris, Mary White (*see* 1:11): greetings to, 16; greetings from, 30

Morris, Robert, 78 (*see* 1:11); and Philip Dalby, 29–30; and farmers-general, 72; bills on, 205; *letters from:* to GW, 29–30; *letters to:* from GW, 5, 15–17

Morris, Samuel: and hunting horn, 53–54; id., 55

Morris (slave): as overseer, 28; deals with Mount Vernon storehouse, 496

Morse, Jedediah: conveys letters, 325, 351, 477–78; id., 326; conveys pamphlet, 352

Mortimer, Captain (shipmaster), 360, 381

Morton, Andrew: as tenant at Belvoir, 139, 141
Motte, Jacob: id., 7
Moultrie, Hannah Motte Lynch: greetings from, 7, 174; id., 7; greetings to, 74–75
Moultrie, William (*see* 1:270): and Santee Canal, 6, 7, 201–2; and GW's Cincinnati circular letter, 321–22; *letters from:* to GW, 6–7, 174–77, 201–2; to James Brindley, 202; *letters to:* from GW, 73–75, 111–12, 321–22
Mount Vernon, 13; flagstones for, 19, 53, 62, 96, 514; deer for, 28, 127, 156; flour from its mill, 33, 48, 77–78, 144, 187, 221, 497; glass and cloth for, 54–55; wine for, 67, 68, 188, 190, 191, 242–43, 246, 328–29; dogs for, 90, 134, 514; grass seed for, 90; and millrace, 93; hams cured at, 104–5; peach brandy made at, 105; and work on New Room, 106; posts and rails for, 122, 162; window glass for, 125; deer paddock at, 127; paper hangings for, 144; china (Cincinnati) for, 147, 148–49, 170–71, 200, 201, 206, 240, 244, 320; household items for, 178; leather for, 178, 209; fig trees and grape vines for, 188; window curtains for, 218, 262, 294, 440–41; and French-Dulany tracts, 247–49; material for to cover chairs, 262; early remodeling of, 271; iron for, 288; GW's description of soil of, 372; plans for barn of, 372; plans for farm yard of, 372; vases and pictures for, 384; flooring for New Room of, 400, 485–86, 501; nails for, 440–41; supplies for from commission agent, 453–55; nutmeg for, 467; storehouse of, 494–97; supplies of listed, 494–97; English larkspur for, 524–25; and digitalis, 525; butter for, 531–32
Mount Vernon Conference (*see* 2:297), 477

Moyston, Edward: and Drayton's runaway slave, 359
Mulberry Grove (Ga.; house), 154, 299
Muse, Battaile: and David Kennedy's debt, 1; and his wheat, 33, 48, 92, 144, 167–68, 179, 436–37; as GW's land agent, 92–93, 155–56, 206, 233–34, 390, 391, 397–98, 437, 500, 531–32; and Hite-Fairfax suit, 102; as Fairfax's land agent, 138, 140, 155–56, 531–32; forwards letter, 315; and his flour, 397; *letters from:* to GW, 33, 92–93, 102, 154–56, 179, 233–34, 397–98, 500, 531–32; *letters to:* from GW, 33, 48, 102, 144, 167–68, 187–88, 436–37, 499, 542

Nancy (Nance) and child (slaves; *see* 3:409): sold at Washington's Bottom, 463, 464
Neilson, Robert (*see* 3:588): conveys letter, 49
Nessey (slave): property of John Francis Mercer, 394
Neville, John: id., 405
Neville, Presley (*see* 1:305; 3:278): id., 342–43; advice sought, 410–11; *letters from:* to GW, 307; *letters to:* from GW, 404–5
Newenham, Edward (*see* 1:440): seeks consulship for son, 207–8, 327; *letters from:* to GW, 207–8, 361, 397, 450; to Benjamin Franklin, 208; *letters to:* from GW, 62, 84, 105–6
Newenham, Robert O'Callahan: and Marseilles consulship, 208
New Hampshire: disturbances in, 265, 281, 282
New Post (house): id., 88
Newton, Thomas, Jr. (*see* 1:80; 2:260), 378; and GW's accounts with, 9–10, 231, 232, 446, 512–13; and GW's flour, 9–10, 77–78, 221, 468; and Balfour & Barraud's debt, 66; and James Hill, 263, 264; and Custis crops, 362; acts for GW, 484; and John

Newton, Thomas, Jr. (*cont.*)
    Price Posey, 546; *letters to:* from
    GW, 9–10, 77–78, 221
New York: and settlement of Massa-
    chusetts boundary, 530
Nicholas, George (*see* 2:55): and
    George William Fairfax, 138,
    140, 155, 188; criticism of, 477
Nicholas, Robert Carter: and George
    William Fairfax, 138, 140
Nichols, Henry: and Asgill affair, 78–
    79, 80, 190; *letters from:* to Tench
    Tilghman, 78–79
Nichols, Solomon: and William Hans-
    brough, 391
Nicholson, Captain (shipmaster), 69
Nicholson, John: id., 536; *letters from:*
    to GW, 506; *letters to:* from GW,
    536
Nomini Hall (house), 218, 238
Norfolk Packet (ship), 495
Norwich Mill, 474

O'Bannon, John: as a surveyor,
    61–62; id., 62
Ogle, Benjamin: and deer for GW,
    127, 156; *letters from:* to GW, 156
Ohio Company: and Thomas
    Cresap, 35–36
Ohio Company (1786): establish-
    ment of, 305, 307
Ohio lands. *See* Lands of GW
Oilliamson, comtesse d': and French
    hounds, 30–31
Oilliamson, Marie-Gabriel-Eléanor,
    comte d': *letters from:* to GW,
    30–31
Osbrey, William: and Alexander
    Steel, 57, 60; id., 60
Oswald, Eleazer (printer): GW's ac-
    count with, 54; receipt of, 125
Otto, Louis-Guillaume, comte de
    Mosloy (*see* 3:230): and L'Enfant,
    111; and d'Anterroche, 250
Overdonck, Daniel, 455, 456; as
    ditcher, 404; deals with Mount
    Vernon storehouse, 495, 496
Overdonck family: and terms of in-
    denture, 402–3

Page, ——: and John Parke Custis's
    estate, 347

Page, Mann, Jr. (*see* 1:80), 161; id.,
    162
Paige, Benjamin: capture of, 462
Pamocra (house), 48
Paper currency: in South Carolina,
    143; rejected in Virginia, 326
Parker, Josiah (*see* 2:259): id., 70;
    and Cincinnati china, 148, 200,
    240, 244; and Elizabeth River
    Canal, 244–45; *letters from:* to
    GW, 69–70, 244–45; *letters to:*
    from GW, 220
Parker, Oliver: capture of, 462
Parsons, Eli: arrest ordered, 436
Parsons, Samuel Holden (*see* 3:332):
    and Society of Cincinnati, 265;
    id., 266
Parsons, Theophilus: as Mass.-N.Y.
    boundary commissioner, 527,
    530
Patriotic Society, 368–70; purposes
    of, 274–75, 322–23
Patterson, Peter: buys GW's slave,
    464
Patterson, Thomas: buys GW's slave,
    464
Payne's church: id., 228
Peacey, William: and James Blox-
    ham, 88, 128, 198, 371, 375–76;
    id., 88; *letters to:* from GW, 192–
    93, 375–76
Peale, Charles Willson: and portraits
    of GW and Greene, 84, 85; and
    GW's birds, 492–93, 506; mu-
    seum of, 492–93, 506; id., 493;
    letters from: to GW, 492–93; *letters
    to:* from GW, 506
Pearce, David: and passage of Span-
    ish jack, 2
Peck, John: and Society of Cincinnati
    diplomas, 217–18, 335–36; id.,
    218; *letters from:* to GW, 217–18,
    238, 336
Peggy (ship), 68
Pendleton, John: as state auditor,
    361, 362
Pennock & Skipworth (firm): and
    Thomas Newton, 9
Pennsylvania certificates of GW: dis-
    position of, 126; interest on,
    177–78, 208–9, 440–41; value
    of, 295

Perrin, Joseph-Marie (*see* 1:327): id.,
 217
Persse, William: and Edward Newenham, 130; id., 130; *letters from:* to
 Alexander McCabe, 129, 130
Peters, Thomas (*see* 1:530): and barley for GW, 383, 438, 532; id.,
 384; *letters from:* to GW, 383–84;
 letters to: from GW, 296, 438,
 532
Peters & Co., Thomas (firm): as brewers, 384
Peterson & Taylor (firm): lumber
 bought from, 400
Petit, Mr. ——: and John Francis
 Mercer, 466
Peyton, Craven: and sale at Belvoir,
 137–38; as Fairfax's land agent,
 137–38
Peyton, Edward: *letters from:* to GW,
 161–62
Philadelphia Agriculture Society:
 awards prizes, 45, 46, 75
Pike, Nicholas (*see* 3:608): *letters from:*
 to GW, 49; *letters to:* from GW,
 120–21
Pine, Robert Edge (*see* 1:435): and
 George William Fairfax, 126–27,
 129; and his Mount Vernon portraits, 289, 290; and his Revolutionary War paintings, 289, 290
Pintard, John Marsden (*see* 3:190):
 and plants for GW, 67, 188; *letters to:* from GW, 67, 188–89
Pitt, William (the younger; *see* 1:29):
 Rochambeau's opinion of, 134
Pittsburgh: as hub for emigrants,
 404; Lear's route to, 410; prices
 of goods at, 488–89
Plater, Elizabeth Rousby (*see* 2:103):
 greetings to, 52; id., 53
Plater, George (*see* 2:103, 179), 53;
 greetings to, 52
Pleasants, John (*see* 3:451): and Wil-
 liam Roberts, 473–74
Pleasants, Thomas, Jr., 474
Plumer, William: and Exeter riot,
 282
Pohick Church, 209, 227; id., 228
Poirey, Joseph-Leonard, 381
Polk, Gilliss: supplies New Room
 planking, 486, 501

Polly (ship), 294
Pomeroy, Ralph: and Society of Cincinnati, 265; id., 266
Pool, Peter: as GW's tenant, 274
Pope, ——: and John Parke Custis
 estate, 347
Port Act (Va.): amended, 347–48;
 support for, 469, 475–76
Porter, Thomas (*see* 2:324): conveys
 letter, 262
Porter & Ingraham (firm), 262
Posey, John: land warrant of, 173;
 bond of, 255
Posey, John Price (*see* 1:208, 210):
 and John Parke Custis's estate,
 263, 264, 546, 547; criminal conduct of, 388, 547–48; financial
 circumstances of, 468; and GW's
 Custis property, 510–11, 513;
 dealings with James Hill, 510–
 12, 513, 546–48; and GW's accounts with Thomas Newton,
 513; rejects GW's charges,
 545–47; id., 547–48; death of,
 548; *letters from:* to GW, 545–48;
 letters to: from GW, 512–13, 547
Potomac (ship), 84
Potomac Planter (ship), 370
Potomac River Company, 278; progress of, 1, 3–4, 117, 203; and engineer for, 43, 74; workmen for,
 93, 99; meeting of directors of,
 152, 234–36, 242, 285, 286,
 334–35, 538; GW's payment to,
 191; finances of, 202, 203; annual report of, 202–3; its address to its directors, 235–36; its
 petition to legislatures, 235–36,
 286, 333, 334–35, 359–60, 447,
 476, 486–87
Pounds, ——, 463
Powel, Elizabeth Willing (*see* 1:398):
 greetings from, 45–46; message
 to, 75; postscript from: to GW,
 226–27
Powel, Samuel (*see* 1:398): *letters from:*
 to GW, 45–46, 226; *letters to:*
 from GW, 5, 75–76
Powell, Joseph, Jr., 501–2
Powell, Leven, 501–2; and seed for
 GW, 246–47; and buckwheat,
 471; and drill plow, 484; *letters*

Powell, Leven (*cont.*)
    from: to GW, 246–47, 465; *letters to:* from GW, 165, 277, 471
Powell, William H.: and Leven Powell, 246; id., 247
Presel, William: estate of, 207
Provost Prison (N.Y.), 59; id., 61
Purviance, Samuel: and western land, 49; *letters from:* to GW, 49–50, 356; *letters to:* from GW, 356
Purviance, Henry (*see* 3:588): travels of, 49
Putnam, Rufus (*see* 1:264–65): and Ohio Company, 307; delivers letter, 426; parlays with Adam Wheeler, 428; relationship of with Daniel Shays, 435

Quakers: aid to slaves by, 15–18, 29–30
Quarles, James: as a witness, 263; id., 264

Rack, Edmund (*see* 3:520): and James Bloxham, 198
Ragsdale, Drury: and John Price Posey, 546; id., 547
Ramsay, David: and his history of the Revolution in South Carolina, 5–6; *letters to:* from GW, 5–6
Randall, Thomas (*see* 3:302): and news from Algiers, 201
Randolph, Anne Harrison: at Mount Vernon, 294
Randolph, Edmund (*see* 1:110): illness of, 157; at Mount Vernon, 231, 294, 395, 396; and rebuke to George Rogers Clark, 321; elected governor, 326, 327, 345, 346; congratulated by GW, 387; hates law practice, 395; and GW's election to Federal Convention, 445, 475, 479, 501; and Gilles de Lavallée, 472; *letters from:* to GW, 150, 395–96, 445–46, 459, 500–501; to James Madison, 157; *letters to:* from GW, 157, 294, 387, 452, 471–72, 473
Randolph, Elizabeth Nicholas (*see* 1:110): gives birth, 157; does fa-
vor for Martha Washington, 396, 469
Randolph, John Jennings: birth and death of, 157
Rawlins, John (*see* 3:208): and Mount Vernon New Room, 106
Rector, Charles: as GW's tenant, 397, 398, 437, 531
Rector, Jacob: as GW's tenant, 92, 93, 155, 390, 397, 398
Rector Town, 416–17; and Fielding Lewis, Jr., 293
Reed, Joseph (*see* 2:498): sells Peale's portraits of GW and Greene, 85
Reeder (Reader), Benjamin: conveys letter, 542; id., 543
Rendón, Francisco (*see* 3:474): departure of, 439; *letters from:* to GW, 439
Revenue Act of 1785 (Virginia), 348
Revision of Virginia laws: Madison's report on, 476
Reynolds, Edward: and lambs for GW, 77, 94, 112, 142, 146, 153; id., 77
Rhinoceros (ship), 59
Richards, ———: house of, 496
Richards, Edmund, 168
Ridout, Thomas (*see* 2:524): and packages for Lafayette, 68, 105, 106; and wine shipment, 68; sets sail, 108; *letters from:* to GW, 245–46; *letters to:* from GW, 68
Rising Sun Hotel (Trenton, N.J.): and Stephen Lowry, 60
Roach, William: and Alexander Steel, 58, 59, 60
Roberts, William (*see* 2:152–53): as Mount Vernon miller, 57; id., 474; *letters from:* to GW, 473–74
Roberts, Mrs. William, 474
Robertson, James: id., 249
Robertson, John: as Penelope Manley French's tenant, 248, 249, 268–71, 273–74; id., 249
Robinson, Sanderson, & Rumney (firm): and flagstones, 53, 96, 514; *letters from:* to GW, 513–14
Rochambeau, Jean-Baptiste-Donatien de Vimeur, comte de (*see* 1:29): and the Asgill affair, 79, 98, 99; and L'Enfant, 111; and

Rochambeau, comte de (*cont.*)
GW's shares in James and Potomac river companies, 133; GW's meeting with at Hartford, 176; *letters from:* to GW, 133–34; *letters to:* from GW, 179–81
Rootes, John (*see* 1:99): GW's land warrant of, 62
Ross, James: and Millers Run ejectment suits, 260–61, 341; fee of, 261; id., 342
Rotherham plow: praised by GW, 197
Round Bottom tract. *See* Lands of GW
Round Hill (house), 271
Royal Gift. *See* Jackasses (Spanish)
Rumney, John, Jr. (*see* 1:484): and flagstones, 19, 53, 62; *letters from:* to GW, 19; *letters to:* from GW, 53, 96
Rumsey, James: and GW's buildings at Bath, 229, 231, 239–40; and Potomac River Company, 238–39, 242, 286; and his mechanical boat, 239, 240, 253–54; *letters from:* to GW, 238–40, 253–54
Russell, Thomas: Maine property of, 419, 435
Rust, Benjamin: and William Hansborough, 391
Rust, Samuel: and William Hansborough, 391
Rutherford, Robert (*see* 3:611): debt of, 233, 234
Rutledge, Edward (*see* 1:112): and Santee Canal, 7; as Nathanael Greene's executor, 283, 298; id., 285
Rutledge, John (*see* 1:112, 427): and Santee Canal, 7; id., 177; and the Greenes, 285; *letters from:* to GW, 177
Ryan, Thomas: as GW's indentured shoemaker, 93

Saint-Simon-Montbléru, Claude-Anne de Rouvroy, marquis de (see 1:187): letter for, 44; and Society of Cincinnati, 46; *letters to:* from GW, 46–47
Sam (slave): deals with Mount Vernon storehouse, 496

Sanderson, Robert, 514; goes to England, 19, 53; and flagstones, 62, 96; *letters from:* to GW, 62
Sanford, Edward: id., 249
Sanford, Margaret Barry Manley: and Harrison Manley's will, 248–49
Santee Canal, 111; proposal for, 6–7; id., 7; and James Brindley, 73, 202
Sargent, Winthrop (*see* 1:140): and Ohio Company, 307
Savage, Mr. ——: as planter on Eastern Shore, 334, 347
Savage, Margaret (*see* 1:135): estate of, 14–15, 348–50, 367; will of, 22, 23, 367–68; and GW's dealings with, 22–23; and Ann Ennis, 348–54
Savage, William (*see* 2:276): and Margaret Savage, 14–15, 348–50; misconduct of, 367
Schaak, John: and Charles Asgill, 237
Schaw (Shaw), John: and Balfour & Barraud, 66, 83
Scott, James, Jr. (*see* 2:196): and Millers Run ejectment suits, 339, 340, 342
Searle & Co., John (firm): as wine merchant, 67; wine from, 188
Seddon, Thomas: id., 507
Seddon & Co., Thomas (firm): and *Columbian Magazine*, 507; *letters from:* to GW, 450; *letters to:* from GW, 507
Sedgwick, Theodore: and Society of Cincinnati, 527; id., 530
Sedwick, John: and Snickers' suit, 14; *letters from:* to GW, 14
Selden, Wilson (*see* 3:359): and Battaile Muse, 33, 92, 155, 197
Senf, Christian (*see* 1:284): and Santee Canal, 7; inspects Great Falls, 108; and L'Enfant, 444–45
Shattuck, Job: capture of, 462
Shaw, Samuel: and Cincinnati china, 148
Shaw, William (*see* 3:67): as GW's secretary, 90, 120, 140, 155, 162, 233; conveys letters, 99, 118;

Shaw, William (*cont.*)
    acts for GW, 118; movements of,
    241
Shawnee: attack on, 320–21
Shays, Daniel: movement of forces
    by, 418; defeat of near Spring-
    field, 423–25; rout of at Peter-
    sham, 428–29; arrest ordered,
    436; at Springfield, 523, 549; at
    Pelham, 539; *letters from:* to Ben-
    jamin Lincoln, 426, 427; *letters
    to:* from Benjamin Lincoln, 425,
    428
Shays' Rebellion: Benjamin Lincoln,
    Jr.'s account of, 538–39; causes
    of, 297, 299–301, 331, 351,
    419–22, 460–62; and reports of,
    265, 266, 295–96; outbreak of,
    281–82; beginnings of, 295,
    325; GW's inquiries about, 339;
    rumors about, 357; course of,
    422–36; Henry Knox's reports
    on, 460–62, 470–71, 518–19,
    522–23, 543–44; GW's com-
    ments on, 478, 481–82, 482–83
Shepard, William: at Springfield,
    281, 423–25, 535, 549; id., 282;
    and Shays' Rebellion, 418, 526,
    538–39; and U.S. magazine at
    Springfield, 544
Sherman, Isaac (*see* 3:324): as Con-
    necticut surveyor, 392
Shiell, Ann Harris: id., 76
Shiell, Hugh: and Alexander Steel,
    57, 76; id., 60
Shoemaker: deals with Mount Ver-
    non storehouse, 495, 496
Simms, Charles: and GW's Millers
    Run ejectment suits, 37, 254–59,
    261; and Potomac River Com-
    pany, 235; id., 258; and Valen-
    tine Crawford's debt, 261; and
    John Francis Mercer, 337, 338,
    393; conveys letter, 341; *letters to:*
    from GW, 254–59
Simon (slave): sold at Washington's
    Bottom, 463, 464
Simpson, Gilbert, Jr. (*see* 1:118): and
    GW's Pennsylvania certificates,
    54, 55, 125; and Washington's
    Bottom, 172, 174, 407, 463; and
    freed slave, 463; and GW's
    slaves, 463

Slaughter, Ann Clifton, 542; id., 543
Slaughter, Eleanor, 543
Slaves: runaways, 15–18, 29–30,
    358–59, 389–90, 509; Lafa-
    yette's emancipation of, 43; ac-
    cused of thefts, 113–15; dispute
    of with white woman, 114; as
    payment for debts, 243, 244,
    336, 394, 442, 465–66; esti-
    mated cost of their needs,
    271–72; given to George Au-
    gustine Washington, 308, 310,
    536; offered in payment of rent,
    390; sale of, 407, 463, 464; at
    Washington's Bottom, 463, 464;
    manumission of, 463, 464; re-
    fusal of to return to Virginia,
    463, 464; price of, 465–66; com-
    pared to free laborers, 499
Smallwood, William (*see* 1:110): and
    Alexander Steel, 58; id., 60; and
    sheep for GW, 146; lands of,
    147; receives teeth implants,
    231
Smith, ——: as Philadelphia jeweler,
    60
Smith, —— (ship carpenter): deals
    with Mount Vernon storehouse,
    495, 496, 497
Smith, Isaac & William (firm), 2
Smith, James: as manager of Poto-
    mac River Company, 447
Smith, John: and Hite-Fairfax suit,
    100, 122
Smith, Melancton (*see* 2:112): as
    Mass.-N.Y. boundary commis-
    sioner, 527, 530
Smith, Nathaniel: account with Mary-
    land, 354–56; Revolutionary ca-
    reer of, 354–56; *letters from:* to
    GW, 354–56; *letters to:* from GW,
    356
Smith, Thomas: and Valentine Craw-
    ford's debt, 36–37; and Millers
    Run ejectment suits, 172–73,
    178, 255–58, 259–61, 315, 339–
    43, 401, 402, 404–5; letter for-
    warded to, 209; fee of, 258, 261,
    341, 342, 412; and appreciation
    of GW, 340; and John Stephen-
    son's account, 408; payments
    made by, 463; and John Au-
    gustine Washington, 510; *letters*

Smith, Thomas (*cont.*)
  from: to GW, 203, 339–43; *letters to:* from GW, 36–37, 172–74, 259–61
Smith, W. B. (shipmaster): id., 68
Smith, William: as chief justice of Canada, 373, 462; id., 375
Smith, William Stephens (*see* 1:53; 2:418): and Lafayette, 517; id., 517
Snickers, Edward (*see* 1:393): and John Sedwick, 14; and sale of Mercer's Shenandoah lands, 288
Snowden, Thomas: id., 288; iron sought from, 288; *letters to:* from GW, 288
Sotterly (house): id., 53
Spencer, Nicholas: and French-Dulany tract, 248
Spencer, Oliver: and Alexander Steel, 58; id., 60
Spotswood, Alexander (*see* 3:337): lends horse to GW, 88–89; and seed for GW, 518, 536–37; *letters from:* to GW, 517–18; *letters to:* from GW, 88–89, 536–37
Spotswood, Elizabeth Washington: greetings to, 88; greetings from, 518; id., 537
Spotswood, William: and *Columbian Magazine*, 507
Sprigg, Margaret Caile: greetings to, 134
Sprigg, Richard: jennies of, 90, 134; *letters from:* to GW, 90–91; *letters to:* from GW, 134–35
Springer, Uriah, 463
Sproat (Sprout), Ebenezer: id., 392
Stanard, Beverley, 162
Stanard, William: id., 162
Steel, Alexander: Revolutionary career of, 57–61; *letters from:* to GW, 57–61; *letters to:* from GW, 76
Steel, William: and Alexander Steel, 60
Stelle, Benjamin, 55; and GW's Pennsylvania certificates, 125, 177–78
Stephen, Adam: bond of, 138; id., 140
Stephens, William: and William Hansbrough, 391
Stephenson, Hugh, 408; and Valentine Crawford, 37

Stephenson, John (*see* 1:119): and Millers Run ejectment suits, 256; debt of, 408; *letters to:* from GW, 408, 410
Stephenson, Marcus: and Millers Run ejectment suits, 256, 257
Sterling, Lord. *See* William Alexander
Steuben, Friedrich Wilhelm Ludolph Gerhard Augustin, Baron von (*see* 1:85): writes as *Bellisaurius,* 357, 358; and GW's Cincinnati circular letter, 532–34; *letters from:* to GW, 534
Stewart, Captain (shipmaster), 125
Stewart, Charles: and Alexander Steel, 58; id., 60
Stewart (Stuart), Richardson: as Potomac River Company manager, 242, 286, 447; charges against, 242
Stiles, Ezra: and Society of Cincinnati, 265; and Phineas Miller, 285; and election sermon, 352–53; views of Shays' Rebellion, 352–53; id., 353; *United States Elevated to Glory and Honor,* 353; *letters from:* to GW, 352–53
Stobagh, John Martin, 355; id., 356
Stoddert, Benjamin (*see* 3:68): id., 193
Stone, ——: and George Mercer's Shenandoah lands, 353, 416
Stone, Francis: *letters from:* to Benjamin Lincoln, 427
Stone, John Hoskins: id., 354
Stone, Michael Jenifer (*see* 2:464; 3:34): id., 354
Stone, Thomas (*see* 2:297; 3:429): id., 354, 550; and Maryland paper money debate, 550; *letters from:* to GW, 550
Stothard, Thomas: makes drawings for Joseph Brown, 84, 85
Strother, James: and William Hansborough, 391
Stuart, David (*see* 1:210), 9, 277, 312, 487, 516; slaves of, 113; as translator, 164; invited to dinner, 217; and Potomac River Company, 235; conveys books, 294; conveys saltcellar, 304; as delegate to Virginia Assembly, 305;

Stuart, David (*cont.*)
and John Parke Custis's estate,
335; *letters from:* to GW, 100,
361–62, 467–70, 476–77; *letters
to:* from GW, 217, 333–35,
387–88, 396–97, 446
Stuart, Eleanor Calvert Custis, 277,
312, 516; invited to dinner, 217;
at Mount Vernon, 334
Suffren-Saint-Tropez, Pierre-André,
bailli de (*see* 1:21): and Lafayette, 409
Sugar House (N.Y.), 59; id., 61
Sullivan, Mr. —— (of Mass.), 189
Sullivan, Giles (shipmaster), 391,
543; at Mount Vernon, 154
Sullivan, James: as Mass.-N.Y. boundary commissioner, 527, 530
Sullivan, John: and Alexander Steel,
58; id., 60; as governor of New
Hampshire, 265; stops New
Hampshire disturbances, 281,
282; and Exeter mob, 297; and
Gilles de Lavallée, 472; *letters
from:* to GW, 189; *letters to:* from
GW, 189
Sumter, Thomas: and Santee Canal,
7
Susquehanna Canal Company, 202;
and Samuel Hughes, 49; and
James Brindley, 73
Swan, James (*see* 2:401): at Mount
Vernon, 548; *National Arithmetick
. . .*, 548; *letters from:* to GW, 548
Swearingen, Van: and Millers Run
ejectment suit, 257
Swift, Ann Roberdeau: marriage of,
400
Swift, Jonathan: id., 400

Tankerville, Charles Bennett, fourth
earl of (*see* 1:65): and Colvill estate, 452–453
Taylor, George, Jr.: sends apples and
oysters, 61; *letters to:* from GW,
61
Taylor, Robert: and Alexander Steel,
58, 59; id., 60
Tellez, Pedro: and Spanish jack, 2, 3,
543
Templeman, James, 15

Tharpe (Thorpe), Richard: as plas-
terer of New Room, 106
Thomas, Isaiah (printer), 353
Thomas, Lewis: and GW's Bullskin
lands, 100, 102, 115, 116, 122,
123, 187, 230
Thomas, Richard: *letters from:* to GW,
168–69
Thompson, John: as GW's tenant,
397, 398
Thompson, William: as GW's tenant,
437, 531
Thomson, Charles: *letters from:* to Nathanael Greene, 85–86; *letters to:*
from Joseph Brown, 84–85, 85,
85–86, 86
Thomson, James: id., 228
Thorn, Michael: and William Roberts, 473, 474
Throckmorton, Albion (*see* 1:114,
305): conveys letter, 122; at
Mount Vernon, 123–24
Throckmorton, Mildred Washington
(*see* 1:114, 305): at Mount Vernon, 123–24
Tilghman, Ann Francis, 27
Tilghman, James, 27; id., 80; and
death of Tench Tilghman, 150;
and Harriot Anderson's legacy,
150–52, 262, 263, 440; and Asgill controversy, 236, 237, 237–
38, 262, 296, 374; and inscription on Tench Tilghman's tomb,
366; *letters from:* to GW, 78–80,
150–52, 190, 262–63, 366; *letters
to:* from GW, 96–99, 165–67,
237–38, 440
Tilghman, Richard: id., 190; reported death of, 190
Tilghman, Tench (*see* 1:232), 190;
death of, 27, 30, 96, 150, 185,
216; and GW's appreciation of,
47; Revolutionary papers of, 78,
80, 97; and Richard Sprigg, 90;
Revolutionary correspondence
of, 97; and Benedict Arnold,
175; inscription on tomb of,
366; and Asgill affair, 374; and
GW's approval of his tomb, 440;
letters to: from Henry Nichols,
78–79

Tilghman, Thomas Ringgold: id., 27; and Tench Tilghman's accounts, 47; and Robert Morris, 78; *letters from:* to GW, 27, 80; *letters to:* from GW, 47, 80

Tilton, James (*see* 1:67): *letters to:* from GW, 343

Tobacco: as specie for taxes, 449–50, 459, 475

Tom (slave): sold at Washington's Bottom, 463, 464

Tom (slave; baker): property of John Francis Mercer, 394, 466

Tom Davis (slave): deals with Mount Vernon storehouse, 495, 496

Toms River (N.J.), 59, 61

Traveller's Rest (house; King George County, Va.): id., 518

Traveller's Rest (house; Frederick County, Va.), 524

Trenchard, James: and *Columbian Magazine*, 507

Trenor, Peter: and the Savage affair, 348; and Ann Ennis, 366; *letters from:* to GW, 348–50; *letters to:* from GW, 376

Trenton (N.J.): magazine at, 58

Trinity Church (Georgetown, Md.): building of, 10

Triplett, Thomas: as Harrison Manley's executor, 249; id., 271

Triplett, William: as Harrison Manley's executor, 248, 249; and French-Dulany land, 268–71; id., 271; *letters to:* from GW, 268–74

Trumbull, Benjamin: and Society of Cincinnati, 264

Trumbull, Eunice Bachus: greetings to, 13

Trumbull, John, 529; as Connecticut Wit, 373, 530; id., 374

Trumbull, Jonathan (*see* 1:12): as governor of Connecticut, 353

Trumbull, Jonathan, Jr. (*see* 1:13; 3:220): and Society of Cincinnati, 264; *letters to:* from GW, 12–13

Tryal (ship), 78

Tupper, Anselm, 392

Tupper, Benjamin (*see* 1:265;

3:323–24): and Ohio Company, 307; as surveyor, 391–92; *letters from:* to GW, 391–92; *letters to:* from GW, 483–84

Turenne, Henri de La Tour d'Auvergne, vicomte and marechal de, 72

Turner, Thompkins Hilgrove: and Charles Asgill, 237

Union (ship), 154

Valcoulon, Savary de: and western settlement, 66

Valentine, Joseph: as manager of Custis lands, 232, 263, 546, 547

Valentine (slave; John Francis Mercer's), 394, 466

Van Berchem, Mr. —— (of Nantes): and d'Anterroche, 251

Vanderpoel, David, 252

Vaudreuil, Louis-Philippe de Rigaud, marquis de (*see* 1:182), 161

Vaughan, Samuel (*see* 1:46): greetings to, 247; *letters to:* from GW, 247, 384

Vaughan, Sarah Hallowell: goes to England, 247

Vernon, Colonel ——: as a traveler, 303–4

Vicuña cloth. *See* Washington, George

Virgin, Brice: and John Logan, 320; id., 321

Virginia Gazette, or the American Advertiser (Richmond): GW's subscription to, 459

Vulture (ship): and Benedict Arnold, 176

Wading (Weaden) River (N.J.), 48; bridge over, 58; id., 60

Wadsworth, Jeremiah (*see* 1:30; 2:498): and Society of Cincinnati, 264, 265, 266; elected to Connecticut legislature, 265; defense of Mrs. Greene, 282–83, 284; his account of Nathanael Greene's death, 282–83, 285; as Greene's executor, 283, 298;

Wadsworth, Jeremiah (*cont.*)
and Catharine Littlefield
Greene, 298; and Nathanael
Greene, 298; in Philadelphia,
471; conveys letter, 526; at
Mount Vernon, 530; *letters from:*
to GW, 282–85; *letters to:* from
GW, 298–99
Wakefield (house), 36
Wales, Andrew Watts (*see* 3:359): as
brewer, 438; and Battaile Muse,
500, 531
Wallace, Mr. —— (Irishman): conveys letter, 105; at Mount Vernon, 106
Wallace, John: at Mount Vernon,
106, 130; introduction of, 129
Walters, John: id., 103
Warburton Manor (house), 91
Warner, Jonathan: and Shays' Rebellion, 538–39
Washington, Augustine (*see* 1:262),
36, 537; and Ohio Company, 35
Washington, Bushrod (*see* 1:49, 262),
341; and Royal Gift, 18; and Patriotic Society, 274–75, 322–23,
368–70; and death of John Augustine Washington, 509–10;
letters from: to GW, 274–75,
322–23; *letters to:* from GW, 18,
278–79, 368–70, 509–10
Washington, Charles (*see* 1:164), 312;
land of, 285
Washington, Corbin (*see* 1:262, 504):
and death of John Augustine
Washington, 510
Washington, Elizabeth Foote (*see*
2:197), 277, 525; greetings to,
160
Washington, Frances Bassett (*see*
1:251), 13, 118, 119, 160, 211,
279, 312, 480, 509, 516, 518,
537, 548; marriage of, 12; trip
of, 280; Pine portrait of, 290;
Mount Vernon as home of, 307–
8, 309, 310
Washington, George: his trip to Richmond, 28, 29, 32, 88–89; and
James River Company, 31; and
Hannah Crawford's slaves, 36;
and his Pennsylvania certificates,
54, 55, 121, 125, 126, 177–78,
208–9, 440–41; print of Peale's
portrait of, 84–86; and tenants
of, 92–93; and Potomac River
Company, 93, 152, 191; settlement with John Parke Custis estate, 100; and girls at Alexandria Academy, 135; and his
papers, 135–36, 140; and affairs
of George William Fairfax,
135–41; correspondence with
George William Fairfax, 135–41,
450–51; debts of, 136–37,
243–44; estimate of his financial
losses, 137; and his need for
money, 144, 206, 207, 363, 493–
94, 499, 542; his account of Arnold's treachery, 174–77; praises
Arthur Young's *Annals*, 196; and
his mode of composition, 198;
and his buildings at Bath, 228–
29, 239–40; illnesses of, 234,
235, 237, 241, 414; faulty memory of regarding Asgill, 236–37;
and military certificates, 243,
244, 336–37, 346–47; his estimate of cost of plantation operation, 271–73; offers to rear
George Washington Greene,
298; advice sought by Ohio
Company, 305–6; and Dunmore
War certificates, 333, 335, 361–
62, 388, 396, 467; uncertainty
of his attendance at Federal Convention, 345, 378, 382–83,
387–88, 445, 449, 457–59,
471–72, 479–80, 482, 501,
529–30; urged to write memoirs, 361; refusal of to separate
slave families, 394; seeks information about the West, 399; criti-
cizes publicity regarding Lafayette's presents, 409–10; advice
of about western settlement,
488–90; eyeglasses for, 514
gifts to: hunting horn, 53–54;
apples and pickled oysters, 61;
vicuña cloth, 107, 200, 201,
205–6, 232–33, 379; Toledo
swords, 154, 391; Chastellux's
Travels, 218–19, 220; gold fish,
244–45; Cromwell's saltcellar,
304–5; asses and birds from La-

Washington, George (*cont.*)
fayette, 312, 330–31, 358, 359, 360–61, 381, 385, 408–10; cutting box, 378; vases and pictures from Vaughan, 384
views on: condition of the country, 4, 42, 55–56, 169, 213, 220, 318–19, 331–32, 359–60, 369–70; rule of law, 15–16; abolition of slavery, 16, 43–44, 243; lawyers, 22; horrors of war, 41; newspapers, 41, 54, 478; a general convention, 42, 55–56, 479–80; Annapolis convention, 42; occupation of western posts, 42–43, 184; Thomas Jefferson, 44; Tench Tilghman, 47, 96; inland waterways, 74; navigation of Mississippi, 117–18, 171, 319–20; British debts, 144–45; Land Ordinance of 1785, 169; Kentucky settlers, 171; human progress, 180, 215–16; his dress for Houdon statue, 183–84; paper money, 184, 331; British policy, 186, 214–16; science of agriculture, 196, 210–11, 370; marital bliss, 203–4; humor, 210; paper currency, 211; schools, 211; strengthening the federal government, 212–13, 331–32, 387–88, 504–5; Franco-American trade, 214–16; Barbary pirates, 216; praise of himself, 219; instructing political representatives, 278–79; private political organizations, 278–79; Shays' Rebellion, 278–79, 319, 332, 360, 481–82, 482–83; his possible widowerhood, 308; purchase of slaves, 336; representation, 368–69; taxes paid in commodities, 369; treatment of tenants, 437; Massachusetts constitution, 482–83. *See also* Slaves; Lands of GW; Mount Vernon; Society of Cincinnati; Agriculture
Washington, George Augustine (*see* 1:30, 164), 73, 118, 119, 160, 211, 231, 312, 439, 480, 509, 516; marriage of, 12; and William Washington, 13; servant of,

18; as farm manager, 28–29; and Lafayette's letters, 44; as witness, 87; letter from forwarded, 126; and his phaeton, 217; at horse races, 279; trip of, 280; as GW's heir, 307–9, 310; slaves given to, 308, 310, 536; and letter for, 358; and William Drayton, 389; letters of, 517, 537; and Alexander Spotswood, 536–37; and Robert Townsend Hooe, 543; in New Kent County, 547; *letters from:* to GW, 310; *letters to:* from GW, 28–29, 279–80, 307–10; from Samuel Hanson, 545
Washington, George Steptoe (*see* 1:70): as Hanson's boarder, 544–45
Washington, Hannah Bushrod: and death of John Augustine Washington, 509–10
Washington, John Augustine (*see* 1:262): at Mount Vernon, 18, 286; and GW's house at Bath, 229, 231; and Thornton Washington, 230; death of, 286, 509–10; ejectment suit of, 412, 465; payments to, 463, 465; Fayette County (Pa.) lands of, 510; *letters from:* to GW, 229; *letters to:* from GW, 285–86
Washington, Lawrence: and GW's Bullskin lands, 100–101
Washington, Lawrence Augustine (*see* 1:70): as Hanson's boarder, 544–45
Washington, Lund (*see* 1:30), 114–15, 277, 525; retirement of, 23, 157; seeks to collect rent for GW, 118; and Belvoir sale, 138, 140; greetings to, 160; and Custis lands, 232; as Harrison Manley's executor, 247–48, 249; and James Hill, 263; accounts of, 264; and William Triplett, 268–71; and his frontier lands, 315; and John Francis Mercer, 467; as GW's estate manager, 511, 547
Washington, Martha, 40, 71, 308; greetings from, 2, 13, 16, 24,

Washington, Martha (*cont.*)
32, 44, 52, 55, 74–75, 88, 89–90,
118, 119, 128, 204, 211, 216,
320, 330, 480, 483, 485, 537;
compliments to, 7, 8, 11, 26, 28,
30, 34–35, 45–46, 62, 69, 73, 77,
78, 82, 90, 110, 112, 126, 132,
142, 143, 148, 153, 160, 174,
204, 209, 231, 243, 277, 280,
289, 295, 302, 306, 312, 313,
314, 325, 347, 357–58, 361,
392, 439, 462, 477, 493, 501,
509, 514, 516, 518, 523, 525,
544, 548, 550; and Armistead estate, 20; news sent to, 48; expresses appreciation, 61; and
hams for Madame Lafayette, 68,
104–5, 313, 516; invitation
from, 75; English watch for,
144; and Bank of England
stock, 145–46; nostrums for,
158–59; and loan to John Mercer, 207; declines invitation,
217; thanked for invitation, 226;
as witness in a wedding, 285;
portrait of, 290; and childbear-
ing, 310; request of, 362; alma-
nac for, 396, 467; buys books for
grandchildren, 396; seeks nutmeg, 396; debt of, 469; *letters
from:* to the marquise de Lafayette, 44
Washington, Mary: compliments to,
40, 73, 312, 516
Washington, Samuel (*see* 1:70), 532;
and GW's Bullskin land, 101; estate of, 234; land of, 285
Washington, Thornton (*see* 2:21):
and Hite-Fairfax suit, 100–102,
156, 229–30, 285; and Bullskin
landholdings of, 101; and GW's
land on Bullskin Run, 187,
229–30; *letters from:* to GW, 100–
102; *letters to:* from GW, 122–24,
229–30
Washington, William (*see* 1:271;
2:153): and seeds and plants,
13; *letters to:* from GW, 13
Washington, William Augustine (*see*
1:262): and Ohio Company, 35;
id., 36
Watson, Elkanah (*see* 2:162): and
John Brown, 324

Watson, Jonah: id., 456
Watson, Josiah (*see* 1:485), 47; and
payments to William Gordon,
268, 352; and Thomas Colvill estate, 455–56; *letters to:* from GW,
455–56
Watson & Co., Josiah (firm), 24, 27;
and payment to William Gordon, 268
Watts, John: and William Hansborough, 391
Weatherby, Benjamin: and Alexander Steel, 58; id., 60
Webb, Samuel Blachley: and GW's
Cincinnati circular letter,
532–34; *letters from:* to GW,
532–34
Webster, Noah (*see* 3:138): and instructor for GW's wards, 20–21;
letters to: from GW, 20–21
Weedon, George (*see* 1:351): and
GW's goldfish, 69; and GW's
Cincinnati circular letter,
376–77, 491–92; *letters from:* to
GW, 376–77; *letters to:* from GW,
491–92
Welch, Wakelin (*see* 2:13): orders on,
19, 53, 137, 190, 191, 197, 328;
and GW's indebtedness to,
144–45; and GW's Bank of Eng-
land stock, 144–46; and Arthur
Young, 196; acts for GW, 370–
71, 372, 375; *letters to:* from
GW, 144–46, 191, 195, 199,
370–71
West, Benjamin: and GW's dress for
Houdon statue, 183–84
West, John, Jr.: and Thomas Colvill's
estate, 133, 151, 166, 262, 263
West, Thomas: and Thomas Colvill's
estate, 132–33, 166, 167, 338–
39, 440; id., 133; *letters from:* to
GW, 132–33, 133; *letters to:* from
GW, 133, 338–39
West, William (*see* 2:528; 3:13): as
executor of Colvill estate, 151
Western Reserve: id., 82
West Point: and Benedict Arnold's
command of, 175–77
Whaley, Benjamin: and Valentine
Crawford, 37
Wheeler, Adam: parlays with Rufus
Putnam, 428; arrest of ordered,

Wheeler, Adam (*cont.*)
    436; *letters from:* to Benjamin Lincoln, 427
White, Alexander (*see* 1:401): and Charles Lee's estate, 31, 412, 413; *letters from:* to GW, 31
Whiting, Matthew: id., 205; payments of, 205; *letters from:* to GW, 204–5
Will (slave; Muddy Hole): deals with Mount Vernon storehouse, 495, 496
Willard, Joseph: id., 34; *letters from:* to GW, 35
William (slave; Billy, Will): as hairdresser, 119
William V, prince of Orange, 276; Lafayette's opinion of, 311; as stadtholder, 313
Williams, Edward: as GW's tenant, 446, 467–68; misconduct of, 446, 467; id., 447; writ against, 537
Williams, Jacob: and Thomas Newton, 263, 512; id., 264
Williams, Otho Holland (*see* 1:24): and Society of Cincinnati, 108
Williams, Peter: accused of rioting, 115
Willis, Francis, Jr. (*see* 1:305, 531): as Fairfax's collector, 139, 141; leaves Virginia, 140
Wilson, Mr. —— (of Petersburg): transmits package, 205–6
Wilson, James: as Presbyterian minister, 209, 228
Wilson & Sons, James (firm), 487
Wilson, William: id., 487; *letters from:* to GW, 486

Wine. *See* Mount Vernon
Witherspoon, John (*see* 1:200; 2:497): recommends minister, 209; as George Washington Greene's tutor, 298–99; *letters from:* to GW, 209–10; *letters to:* from GW, 227–28
Woodbury (house): id., 264
Woodville (house), 342–43
Woolsey, Benjamin: and John Stephenson's account, 408
Wright, —— (of Alexandria), 415
Wright, Matthew: and Rawleigh Colston, 353; id., 354
Wuibert, Antoine-Felix (*see* 3:362); *letters to:* from GW, 181–82
Wye (house), 384
Wyllys, Samuel: elected to Connecticut legislature, 265; id., 266–67

Yates, Charles: and inland navigation, 507–8; and experimental agriculture, 508; id., 508
Yates, Robert: as Mass.-N.Y. boundary commissioner, 527, 530
Young, Mr. ——: and Alexander Spotswood, 518, 536
Young, Arthur, 26; *Tour through the North of England,* 54, 125; works of, 116–17, 118, 148; and his *Annals,* 141, 197, 371; letter from forwarded, 147; *Tour through Ireland,* 170; seeds and supplies from sought, 195, 370, 371, 372; *letters to:* from GW, 196–200, 371–72
Young, Notley: and oats, 551